CLASSICAL ETHIOPIC

LANGUAGES OF
THE ANCIENT NEAR EAST

Editor-in-Chief

GONZALO RUBIO, *Pennsylvania State University*

Classical Ethiopic

A Grammar of Gəʿəz

JOSEF TROPPER AND
REBECCA HASSELBACH-ANDEE

UNIVERSITY PARK, PA | EISENBRAUNS

Library of Congress Cataloging-in-Publication Data

Names: Tropper, Josef, author. | Hasselbach, Rebecca, author.
Title: Classical Ethiopic : a grammar of Ge'ez, including sample texts and a glossary / by Josef
　　Tropper, Rebecca Hasselbach-Andee.
Other titles: Altäthiopisch. English | Languages of the ancient Near East.
Description: University Park, Pennsylvania : Eisenbrauns, 2021. | Series: Languages of the
　　ancient Near East | Includes bibliographical references and index.
Summary: "A translation and revision of Josef Tropper's Altäthiopisch: Grammatik des
　　Ge'ez mit Übungstexten und Glossar, providing a comprehensive grammar of Classical
　　Ethiopic, the historical language of Ethiopian Christianity. Uses both the Ethiopian script and
　　transliterations to aid the reader's understanding of the language"—Provided by publisher.
Identifiers: LCCN 2020043401 | ISBN 9781575068411 (hardback)
Subjects: LCSH: Ethiopic language—Grammar.
Classification: LCC PJ9021 .T76 2021 | DDC 492/.8182—dc23
LC record available at https://lccn.loc.gov/2020043401

Eisenbrauns is an imprint of The Pennsylvania State University Press.

The Pennsylvania State University Press is a member of the
Association of University Presses.

It is the policy of The Pennsylvania State University Press to use acid-free paper. Publications
on uncoated stock satisfy the minimum requirements of the National Standard for Information
Sciences—Permanence of Paper for Printed Library Material, ANSI Z39.48—1992.

For Lucas, my constant inspiration (RHA)

Contents

Preface

The present grammar of Classical Ethiopic (Gəʿəz) serves two purposes: it is designed, first, as a tool for introductory classes and, second, as a basic reference work. As such it contains brief descriptions of the phonology and morphology of the language, in addition to a detailed discussion of its syntax. The grammar thus provides a tool for acquiring the basic grammatical concepts and forms of Classical Ethiopic (CE) in a concise manner. At the same time, it is designed to deepen the understanding and knowledge of those grammatical concepts with the help of a detailed treatment of Gəʿəz syntax. It further includes numerous text samples that can be used as exercises.

The book can consequently be of use for scholars who have previous knowledge of other Semitic languages, as well as for students who study Gəʿəz as their first Semitic language, be it in an academic class setting or on their own.

The grammar is structured in a systematic way and contains cross-references that provide links between the individual sections and discussions. Numerous paradigms and tables within the grammatical sections and a collection of basic central paradigms in appendix C summarize the most important morphological features. An index of Gəʿəz words that lists basic word formations and meanings (appendix D) can be used as a glossary for words occurring in the main text and text samples. Although the volume can be used as a reference work, it is not intended as a substitute for August Dillmann's *Grammatik der äthiopischen Sprache* (Leipzig, 1857/1899), which, despite its age, still constitutes the most comprehensive reference grammar of Classical Ethiopic available.

Contrary to other introductory works of Classical Ethiopic, Gəʿəz words and forms are presented in both the original Ethiopic script and in transliteration in the grammatical sections and glossary. Presenting the grammar and examples in Ethiopic script has long been a desideratum for the more recently published grammatical treatments of Classical Ethiopic. The presentation in transliteration in addition to the original script has two main advantages: First, Ethiopic writing, consisting of a syllabic system, is significantly more complex and more difficult to learn than other West Semitic scripts. Experience has shown that it takes intensive training and exposure to the script before students are able to read the Ethiopic script fluently. During this period, students can benefit from a grammatical representation in transliteration. In particular, providing paradigms in transliteration makes sense from a didactical perspective. Second, despite its complexity, the Ethiopic writing system has deficiencies that make understanding the structure of the language difficult for the beginner. For example, the orthography does not indicate consonantal gemination or the distinction between a vowelless consonant /CØ/ and a consonant followed by the central vowel *schwa* /Cə/. Furthermore, in many cases, the writing system does not differentiate individual elements of words that are composed of more than one grammatical element, such as nouns with proclitic prepositions or other clitic particles. Only a transliteration based on a detailed linguistic analysis of the language can provide the necessary clarity that is important at the beginner's level of acquiring the language.

Learning the Ethiopic script is nevertheless of crucial importance for all those who wish to work with Classical Ethiopic in more detail. Fluency in reading the Ethiopic script can only be attained by an early handling of original Ethiopic literature. The use of the Ethiopic script throughout the grammar and the sample texts provided (appendix A) can serve as an introduction.

Despite the fact that the present volume contains a comprehensive list of words cited, it does not include an all-encompassing glossary. Students should consequently use the existing dictionaries for Gəʿəz from the very beginning (see §1.6.).

This volume is a translation of Josef Tropper's 2002 grammar *Altäthiopisch: Grammatik des Geʿez mit Übungstexten und Glossar* (Ugarit-Verlag). The translation closely follows the original text in both outline and content. Some changes have been made by the translator, however. These changes include the use of the Ethiopic script, but also certain changes in the content. Wherever deemed necessary, the content has been updated to reflect more current views on Ethiopian and Semitic grammar. In some cases, for example, in the discussion of tense and aspect, the system used was adjusted to reflect linguistic concepts and terminology more commonly found in anglophone literature. The introduction has been expanded to provide more historical background to the language than found in the original edition. The reader should be aware that these changes somewhat alter the content compared to the original German version. In general, the changes made reflect the opinions of the translator and not necessarily those of the original author.

1. Introduction

1.1. General Remarks

Classical Ethiopic is an ancient Semitic language that was spoken in northern Ethiopia in the area around the ancient city of Aksum. Aksum is located near the northern edge of the great Ethiopian plateau that rises west of the Red Sea coast. Today, its location is close to the border of Eritrea.[1] Classical Ethiopic is also called Gəˁəz, which is the native designation for the language (ልሳነ ግዕዝ *ləssāna gəˁz*). The native term is derived from the noun ግዕዝ *gəˁz* 'nature, manner, custom, conduct'.[2]

The city of Aksum constituted the center of Ethiopian culture. It was the capital of the Aksumite Empire, a nation that was one of the major players in the trade network between India and the Mediterranean from ca. 100 (all dates given are Common Era unless otherwise specified). At its height, the Aksumite Empire stretched from what today is northern Ethiopia to Eritrea, Sudan, Egypt, and Yemen. Around 340, the kingdom of Aksum converted to Christianity under the reign of king ˁEzānā (ca. 330–365).[3] In time, the Ethiopian church became associated with the Oriental Orthodox Churches. The spread of Christianity in Ethiopia is commonly attributed to foreign missionaries, specifically Syriac missionaries, who were active in the late fifth/early sixth century. This theory, however, has been challenged in more recent years.[4] Syriac influence on Ethiopia can be established for a later period, the so-called Solomonic period (1270–1770), but at this time, this influence was most commonly mediated by Arabic-speaking Christianity.[5] Nevertheless, the Christianization of Ethiopia triggered the rise of a productive period of translation of (mostly) Christian literature from Greek, and

---

[1] The spelling of the name Aksum and the corresponding adjective, as in "Aksumite Empire," differs in various publications. It is also written as Axum/Axumite. The transliteration "Aksum" has been chosen throughout this grammar because it more faithfully reflects the Ethiopic spelling of the name አክሱም. The etymology of the name Aksum is unclear.

[2] Also compare the verbal root ግዕዘ *gəˁza* (II) 'to become free, be set free' and its derivates አግዓዝ *ʔagˁāz* and አግዓዚ *ʔagˁāzi*, 'free man, Ethiopian'.

[3] For a general description of Aksum and the Aksumite Empire, see Phillipson 2012.

[4] See specifically Marrassini 1990, who argues that loanwords that had been considered to be from Syriac can mostly only be proven to be from Aramaic in general, and that the personal names of certain personalities associated with the Christianization of Ethiopia cannot be shown to be Syriac.

[5] For Syriac influence on Ethiopia see, for example, Butts 2011.

after the rise of Islam, from Arabic, into Classical Ethiopic. With the rise of Islam, the Aksumite kingdom began to decline. The ultimate end of the Aksumite kingdom is commonly thought to have occurred around 960. In accordance with the aforementioned three major historical periods, scholars distinguish a pre-Aksumite, Aksumite (pre-Christian and Christian), and a post-Aksumite period.

The origin of groups of Semitic-speaking people in Ethiopia is still a matter of debate. The most common theory is that Semitic groups migrated in various waves from southern Arabia, although the linguistic evidence for such a theory is unconvincing since Ethiopian Semitic is not a descendant of any of the known Old South Arabian languages as far as it is possible to tell. However, if this theory is indeed correct, at least one migration wave, possibly the first, must have taken place as early as the first half of the first millennium BCE (probably during the eighth or seventh century BCE), since evidence for a South Arabian presence in the area around Aksum is attested in the form of Sabaic inscriptions from this time on. Cultural and economic contacts between South Arabia and Ethiopia continued until the fall of the Aksumite kingdom.

1.2. Literature

The oldest written material for Ethiopian is attested in the form of stone inscriptions. Twelve such inscriptions were found in Aksum, which are in part written in the unvocalized script of South Arabia, partly in a non-vocalized or partially vocalized version of the Ethiopic script, and partly in a fully vocalized variant of the Ethiopic script (cf. §2.3.1.). The oldest inscriptions of the fully vocalized type are inscriptions from the king ʿEzānā (ca. 330–365). These inscriptions do not provide much data for the understanding of Ethiopian grammar, but they are nevertheless of significance since they reflect the only evidence for literature written in Gəʿəz during the Aksumite period that is not based on translations.

The majority of Classical Ethiopic literature is transmitted in manuscript-form.[6] We can distinguish two main periods: the first period constitutes the height of the Aksumite kingdom in the time between the fourth and seventh centuries, while the second period begins, after a longer period of non-productivity that followed the collapse of the Aksumite kingdom, at around 1270 with the takeover of the Solomonic dynasty. This period lasted until the nineteenth century (with its peak in the fourteenth-sixteenth centuries). Despite the fact that Gəʿəz ceased

---

[6] See also Littmann 1954 and Weninger 2001, 8–12.

to be a spoken language around 1000, the composition of literary works in Gəʿəz continued uninterrupted during the fourteenth through nineteenth centuries. The majority of manuscripts preserved and known today date to the post-Aksumite period (after the fourteenth century). Notable exceptions include the Abba Garima gospels, dated to Late Antiquity, and a manuscript fragment that is datable to prior to the 1230s.[7] Contrary to Gəʿəz, Amharic was only rarely used as a literary language up to the nineteenth century.

Classical Ethiopic literature from the Aksumite period almost exclusively consists of translations of Greek originals. Among the oldest texts are the translations of the Gospels and Psalter. A complete translation of the Bible, except for Maccabees and a few other apocryphal books (such as the two additional books of Ezra, the Paralipomena of Jeremiah, the Ascension of Isaiah, Jubilees, and Enoch) was completed by the seventh century. Besides the biblical and apocryphal books, there are also several works composed by early church fathers that were translated from Greek.

Ethiopic literature dating to the post-Aksumite period contains many translations from Arabic, including numerous literary works of the Coptic church of Egypt (e.g., the Calendar of Saints "Synaxar" = Sənkəsār). These translations are often very literal. The post-Aksumite period further saw the composition of independent literary works such as homilies, lives of saints, liturgical works, and theological treatises (including works against Islam and the Roman-Catholic Church), magical literature, secular literature (philosophy, philology, and legal literature), and the Chronicles of Kings. The latter differs from other literary works from a linguistic point of view.

Contrary to the translations from Greek dating to the Aksumite period, translations into Gəʿəz from Arabic in the post-Aksumite period attest to a strong influence of Arabic on the syntactic structures (especially on the use of verbal categories) and the lexicon of Gəʿəz. These influences from Arabic that originated in translations also had a significant impact on the language of the independent literary works dating to the post-Aksumite period.

Classical Ethiopic still serves as the liturgical language in the Ethiopic and Eritrean church today and is taught in Christian schools.

---

[7] For the Abba Garima gospels, see Mercier 2000 and McKenzie and Watson 2016; for the Ethiopic manuscript fragment, see el-Antony, Blid, and Butts 2016.

1.3. Linguistic Classification

Classical Ethiopic is a Semitic language and belongs to the West Semitic branch of the language family. Within this branch, it shares certain archaic characteristics with Modern South Arabian languages, such as the prefix conjugation base *yVqattVl*. These archaisms are not sufficient, however, to group Ethiopian Semitic and Modern South Arabian together into one branch. Ethiopian Semitic is thus best considered an independent sub-branch of West Semitic – with the note that its relationship to Modern South Arabian still requires further study.[8] Close contact also existed between Ethiopian Semitic and the Ancient South Arabian languages (Sabaic, Minaic, Qatabanic, and Ḥaḍramitic), as exhibited by the Ethiopian writing system, which is derived from the Old South Arabian alphabet. It is further noteworthy that there seem to be significant morphological and lexical correspondences between Classical Ethiopic and Akkadian, that is, East Semitic, which is both geographically and chronologically quite distant from the Ethiopian branch of Semitic.[9]

The Ethiopian languages, including Classical Ethiopic, were from the very beginning subject to influence from the surrounding Cushitic languages. Obvious influences from Cushitic are found in the Ethiopian lexicon and syntax, while other basic categories of the language, such as morphology and phonology, were mostly unaffected by language contact and remained surprisingly archaic. Classical Ethiopic thus cannot be considered a mixed language.

1.4. Other Ethiopian Languages

Classical Ethiopic ceased to be spoken shortly after the demise of the Aksumite kingdom in 960. Today, a large number of Ethiopian languages and dialects are spoken in Ethiopia and beyond, in addition to Cushitic and other languages.[10]

In the northern region we find (a) Tigre with ca. 800,000 mostly Muslim speakers (in the lowland of Eritrea and in the neighboring regions of Sudan), and (b)

---

[8] For the yet unresolved issue of the relationship between Ethiopian Semitic and Modern South Arabian, see Porkhomovsky 1997. More recently, for the dismissal of such a relationship, see Kogan 2015, 124.

[9] For the presumed connection between Akkadian and Classical Ethiopic, see especially von Soden 1987. Von Soden, for example, assumes that the element ʔan- attested in ʔənbala 'without' is connected to the Akkadian preposition *ina* (1987, 560). For the assumption that there are lexical cognates between Akkadian and Classical Ethiopic, see Kogan 2006.

[10] See also Ullendorff 1973 and Hetzron 1972.

Tigrinya (*Tǝgrǝñña*) with about 8.8 million mostly Christian speakers (in the Eritrean highlands and in the northern Ethiopian province of Tigray). Both languages are closely related to Gǝʿǝz.[11]

Amharic is spoken in the southern region by ca. 15 million speakers and represents the most widely spoken and one of the typologically most innovative Ethiopian languages. Smaller linguistic units are represented by (a) Gurage, a dialect cluster spoken by ca. 1.8 million people southwest of Addis Ababa, (b) Harari (the language of the city Harar in eastern Ethiopia and of diaspora communities with about 26,000 speakers), and (c) Argobba, (spoken northwest of Addis Ababa, close to Ankober), which is close to extinction (the 1994 census listed about 100 monolingual speakers, while the 2007 census counted as many as 43,000 speakers, although most of these speak Amharic as their main language). Southern Ethiopian further includes (d) Gafat, which used to be spoken in western Ethiopia in the province of Goǧǧam but has now ceased to exist as a spoken language. Amharic and Tigrinya represent the second- and third-largest living Semitic languages today (after Arabic and before Modern Hebrew).

1.5. Grammars

The first linguistic description of Classical Ethiopic was made by August Dillmann: *Grammatik der äthiopischen Sprache* (1st ed. Leipzig, 1857). The second revised edition of Dillmann's grammar by Carl Bezold (Leipzig, 1899) and its English translation by James A. Crichton (London, 1907), which contains additions to the German edition and several indexes, represents the most important reference work for Classical Ethiopic. Dillmann and Bezold's grammar still reflects the state of the art of grammatical treatments of Classical Ethiopic, mostly because no comprehensive grammar of Gǝʿǝz has been published in the twentieth century. Unfortunately, Dillmann's grammar is difficult to use because it follows an order in the presentation of grammatical features that differs from more common and contemporary approaches.

---

[11] Traditionally, Ethiopian languages are divided into a northern and southern branch (see Cohen 1931 and Hetzron 1972). The northern branch includes Classical Ethiopic, Tigre, and Tigrinya, while the southern branch contains the remaining Ethiopian languages. It has further been assumed that Tigre is particularly close to Classical Ethiopic and might represent a direct descendant of Classical Ethiopic. The idea that Ethiopian Semitic consists of two main branches, a northern and a southern branch, has recently been challenged, however, and requires further study (see Voigt 2009 and especially Bulakh and Kogan 2010 and 2013).

Other descriptions of Classical Ethiopic that are designed as introductory
textbooks include:

- Franz Praetorius, *Aethiopische Grammatik mit Paradigmen, Litteratur,
  Chrestomathie und Glossar* (= Praetorius 1886a)
- Franz Praetorius, *Grammatica aethiopica* (= Praetorius 1886b)
- Marius Chaîne, *Grammaire éthiopienne* (1938)
- Carlo Conti Rossini, *Grammatica elementare della lingua etiopica* (1941)
- Thomas O. Lambdin, *Introduction to Classical Ethiopic (Geʿez)* (1978)

Two works by Stefan Weninger should likewise be mentioned:

- *Gəʿəz* (1993), a brief grammatical description (50 pages) primarily
  designed for general linguists
- *Das Verbalsystem des Altäthiopischen* (2001)

1.6. Dictionaries

The only scholarly dictionary of Classical Ethiopic that contains references to
textual evidence is August Dillmann's *Lexicon Linguae Aethiopicae* (DL), which
follows the order of the Ethiopic syllabary (Dillmann 1865).[12] Although not
strictly a dictionary, see also Grébaut (1952) for textual references. For beginners,
the easiest dictionary to use is W. Leslau's *Comparative Dictionary of Geʿez* (CDG),
which makes use of transliterations and is ordered according to the (modified)
Latin alphabet. The CDG also includes numerous etymological references. A
briefer version of the *Comparative Dictionary* intended for students that is
arranged according to the Ethiopic syllabary was published by the same author
under the title *Concise Dictionary of Geʿez* (Leslau 1989).

1.7. General Studies

For a general reference work on Ethiopian and Eritrean Studies, the reader can
refer to the *Encyclopedia Aethiopica* I: *A-C*; II: *D-Ha*; III *He-N*; IV: *O-X*; V: *Y-Z*, which
was published between 2003–2014 by S. Uhlig et al., with cooperation by A. Bausi
on volumes IV-V.

---

[12] Dillmann's dictionary has been digitized and is available online as part of *TraCES – From
Translation to Creation: changes in Ethiopic Style and Lexicon from Late Antiquity to the Middle Ages.*

2. Writing and Orthography

2.1. General Introduction

The Ethiopic script developed out of the Old South Arabian (OSA) alphabet, sometimes involving a 90 or 180 degree rotation of the original letters (as in OSA Ɓ /m/ versus Classical Ethiopic መ /ma/ and OSA Ψ /ḥ/ versus Classical Ethiopic ሐ /ḥa/). The script represents a syllabary with a basic inventory of 182 signs, which consists of 26 consonants that each have seven variations or "orders."

The first order reflects the basic form of the letter derived from the Old South Arabian alphabet and stands for consonant plus /a/. The six other orders are combinations of the respective basic consonant with the vowels /u/, /i/, /ā/, /e/, /ə/ or Ø-vowel, and /o/ (second-seventh orders). In addition to this basic inventory, the Ethiopic syllabary has 20 signs that represent four labialized velars (/qʷ, ḫʷ, kʷ, gʷ/) with five vowels each (/a/, /i/, /ā/, /e/, and /ə/ or Ø-vowel). This means that labialized consonants do not occur with vowels that share articulatory features with /w/, in particular back articulation and roundness (vowels /u/ and /o/). Together with the signs indicating labiovelars, the Ethiopic syllabary has an inventory of 202 signs. The order of the 26 consonants of the Ethiopic "alphabet" is fixed and parallels the order of the Old South Arabian alphabet from which it is derived.[13]

The Ethiopic syllabary has the advantage of indicating vowels, contrary to the consonantal alphabetic writing systems used for other West Semitic languages, although the addition of vowels makes it significantly more complex than the latter. Despite its relative complexity, the writing system still has deficiencies. It cannot distinguish between single and doubled (geminated) consonants or between vowelless consonants and those that are followed by the ultra-short vowel /ə/. Stress is equally not indicated in the writing system. The exact phonological structure of a word can thus often only be determined through a morphological analysis. This means that the reader has to know the structure of a word in order to be able to pronounce it correctly.

---

[13] The order of the Old South Arabian alphabet is: *h, l, ḥ, m, q, w, s₂, r, b, t, s₁, k, n, ḫ, ṣ, s₃, f, ʾ, ʿ, ḍ, g, d, ġ, ṭ, z, d, y, t, ẓ*. A similar letter order has been discovered on tablets in Ugarit, besides the more common Northwest-Semitic order starting with *ʾ, b, g*, etc., showing that the letter orders attested in OSA and Ethiopic were also known further north.

2.2. List of Signs

2.2.1. Introduction

The following pages contain two tables: the first (§2.2.2.) represents the consonants according to the traditional Ethiopic order. The second (§2.2.3.) follows the Latin alphabet and the transliteration values used in the present volume. Another table that represents the vowel transliterations provided by Leslau (1995) is given in appendix B. It should be noted that the sixth order, which is transliterated as consonant plus /ə/ also stands for vowelless consonants.

Students who wish to familiarize themselves more thoroughly with Classical Ethiopic should memorize the first table and may ignore the second since knowledge of the Ethiopic consonantal order is necessary for the use of the standard dictionaries. An exception is W. Leslau's *Comparative Dictionary of Geʿez* (= CDG), which is arranged according to the modified Latin alphabet as represented in table §2.2.3.

2.2.2. The Classical Ethiopic Order

The 26 consonants (not including labiovelars):

Name of sign	1st	2nd	3rd	4th	5th	6th	7th	translit-	OSA[14]
	a	*u*	*i*	*ā*	*e*	*ə*	*o*	eration[15]	
1 ሀይ:	ሀ	ሁ	ሂ	ሃ	ሄ	ህ	ሆ	*h*	𐩠
2 ላዊ:	ለ	ሉ	ሊ	ላ	ሌ	ል	ሎ	*l*	𐩡
3 ሐውት:	ሐ	ሑ	ሒ	ሓ	ሔ	ሕ	ሖ	*ḥ*	𐩢
4 ማይ:	መ	ሙ	ሚ	ማ	ሜ	ም	ሞ	*m*	𐩣
5 ሣውት:	ሠ	ሡ	ሢ	ሣ	ሤ	ሥ	ሦ	*ś* (*š*)	𐩦
6 ርእስ:	ረ	ሩ	ሪ	ራ	ሬ	ር	ሮ	*r*	𐩧
7 ሳት:	ሰ	ሱ	ሲ	ሳ	ሴ	ስ	ሶ	*s*	𐩪

---

[14] The Old South Arabian signs presented in this column reflect a stylized version of the Old Sabaic script (ca. eighth — third century BCE). Hyphens indicate that the respective letter does not exist in Old South Arabian.

[15] The varying transliterations found in the scholarly literature are indicated in parentheses in this table and are discussed in §3.1.6. and §3.2.4. below.

8 ቃፍ:	ቀ	ቁ	ቂ	ቃ	ቄ	ቅ	ቆ	q (ḳ)	៛
9 ቤት:	በ	ቡ	ቢ	ባ	ቤ	ብ	ቦ	b	∏
10 ታዊ:	ተ	ቱ	ቲ	ታ	ቴ	ት	ቶ	t	Χ
11 ኀርም:	ኀ	ኁ	ኂ	ኃ	ኄ	ኅ	ኆ	ḫ	५
12 ነሃስ:	ነ	ኑ	ኒ	ና	ኔ	ን	ኖ	n	ᒵ
13 አልፍ:	አ	ኡ	ኢ	አ	ኤ	እ	ኦ	ʾ ᖷ	
14 ካፍ:	ከ	ኩ	ኪ	ካ	ኬ	ክ	ኮ	k	ᔿ
15 ዋዊ:	ወ	ዉ	ዊ	ዋ	ዌ	ው	ዎ	w	Ф
16 ዓይን:	ዐ	ዑ	ዒ	ዓ	ዔ	ዕ	ዖ	ʿ	ο
17 ዘይ:	ዘ	ዙ	ዚ	ዛ	ዜ	ዝ	ዞ	z	🞪
18 የመን:	የ	ዩ	ዪ	ያ	ዬ	ይ	ዮ	y	۴
19 ደንት:	ደ	ዱ	ዲ	ዳ	ዴ	ድ	ዶ	d	ᖷ
20 ገምል:	ገ	ጉ	ጊ	ጋ	ጌ	ግ	ጎ	g	˥
21 ጣይት:	ጠ	ጡ	ጢ	ጣ	ጤ	ጥ	ጦ	ṭ	▥
22 ጸይት:	ጰ	ጱ	ጲ	ጳ	ጴ	ጵ	ጶ	ṗ	-
23 ጸዳይ:	ጸ	ጹ	ጺ	ጻ	ጼ	ጽ	ጾ	ṣ	♣
24 θኣ:	θ	ፁ	ፂ	ፃ	ፄ	ፅ	ፆ	ḍ (ṣ́)	🗔
25 አፍ:	ፈ	ፉ	ፊ	ፋ	ፌ	ፍ	ፎ	f	◇
26 ፐ:	ፐ	ፑ	ፒ	ፓ	ፔ	ፕ	ፖ	p	-

The labiovelars (qʷ, ḫʷ, kʷ, gʷ):

ቀ	ቈ	-	ቊ	ቋ	ቌ	ቍ	-	qʷ
ኀ	ኈ	-	ኊ	ኋ	ኌ	ኍ	-	ḫʷ
ከ	ኰ	-	ኲ	ኳ	ኴ	ኵ	-	kʷ
ገ	ጐ	-	ጒ	ጓ	ጔ	ጕ	-	gʷ

2.2.3. Consonantal Order According to the Modified Latin Alphabet[16]

	1st	2nd	3rd	4th	5th	6th	7th
	Ca	Cu	Ci	Cā	Ce	Cə	Co
ʾ	አ	ኡ	ኢ	አ	ኤ	እ	ኦ
ʿ	ዐ	ዑ	ዒ	ዓ	ዔ	ዕ	ዖ
b	በ	ቡ	ቢ	ባ	ቤ	ብ	ቦ

---

[16] Emphatics and labiovelars follow the respective plain consonants.

d	ደ	ዱ	ዲ	ዳ	ዴ	ድ	ዶ
ḍ	ጸ	ጹ	ጺ	ጻ	ጼ	ጽ	ጾ
f	ፈ	ፉ	ፊ	ፋ	ፌ	ፍ	ፎ
g	ገ	ጉ	ጊ	ጋ	ጌ	ግ	ጎ
gʷ	ጐ	-	ጒ	ጓ	ጔ	ጕ	-
h	ሀ	ሁ	ሂ	ሃ	ሄ	ህ	ሆ
ḥ	ሐ	ሑ	ሒ	ሓ	ሔ	ሕ	ሖ
ḫ	ኀ	ኁ	ኂ	ኃ	ኄ	ኅ	ኆ
ḫʷ	ኈ	-	ኊ	ኋ	ኌ	ኍ	-
k	ከ	ኩ	ኪ	ካ	ኬ	ክ	ኮ
kʷ	ኰ	-	ኲ	ኳ	ኴ	ኵ	-
l	ለ	ሉ	ሊ	ላ	ሌ	ል	ሎ
m	መ	ሙ	ሚ	ማ	ሜ	ም	ሞ
n	ነ	ኑ	ኒ	ና	ኔ	ን	ኖ
p	ፐ	ፑ	ፒ	ፓ	ፔ	ፕ	ፖ
ṗ	ጰ	ጱ	ጲ	ጳ	ጴ	ጵ	ጶ
q	ቀ	ቁ	ቂ	ቃ	ቄ	ቅ	ቆ
qʷ	ቈ	-	ቊ	ቋ	ቌ	ቍ	-
r	ረ	ሩ	ሪ	ራ	ሬ	ር	ሮ
s	ሰ	ሱ	ሲ	ሳ	ሴ	ስ	ሶ
ś (š)	ሠ	ሡ	ሢ	ሣ	ሤ	ሥ	ሦ
ṣ	ጸ	ጹ	ጺ	ጻ	ጼ	ጽ	ጾ
t	ተ	ቱ	ቲ	ታ	ቴ	ት	ቶ
ṭ	ጠ	ጡ	ጢ	ጣ	ጤ	ጥ	ጦ
w	ወ	ዉ	ዊ	ዋ	ዌ	ው	ዎ
y	የ	ዩ	ዪ	ያ	ዬ	ይ	ዮ
z	ዘ	ዙ	ዚ	ዛ	ዜ	ዝ	ዞ

2.3. Comments on the Writing System

2.3.1. The earliest known writing from Ethiopia is attested in the form of Sabaic inscriptions dating to the pre-Aksumite period (ca. 500 BCE). These inscriptions in the Sabaic language and script were not found in Aksum itself but in Yeha, about 30 kilometers east of Aksum, and come from a time when Yeha was a South Arabian trade colony. 179 inscriptions of this type are known so far (RIÉ 1–179).

The first longer inscriptions in the Ethiopic language itself originate in Aksum and date to ca. the mid-fourth to late fifth centuries. Six of these inscriptions, which can all be characterized as "royal inscriptions," are written in the Old South Arabian alphabet (RIÉ 185 I, 185 bis I, 186, 190–92), three are written in an unvocalized version of the Ethiopic script (RIÉ 180–84), while another four are written in an early form of vocalized Ethiopic. The inscriptions written in Old South Arabian script are commonly referred to as "pseudo-Sabaic," since they are written in the Sabaic alphabet but can clearly be classified as Ethiopic from a linguistic point of view – although they also contain a few Sabaic forms. Furthermore, there are about 230 other short inscriptions from the same period originating in Aksum that are written in both unvocalized and vocalized Ethiopic.[17]

The transition from unvocalized to vocalized script started in the first half of the fourth century, approximately at the beginning of the Christian era in Ethiopia during the reign of king ꜤEzānā (ca. 340). The indication of vowels is still irregular in the earliest material and some inscriptions are only partially vocalized. In these cases, letters of the first order, that is, the basic form of the letters, are also used for other vowel orders. On coins, the vowelless script remained in use for a longer period.

2.3.2. The typical characteristics of the graphemes of the various vowel orders can be described as follows:

Letters containing the vowel /a/ (first order) are represented by the inherited basic form of the (originally consonantal) letter. The shape of all other orders is characterized by certain modifications of the basic letter. These modifications are primarily made through small strokes or circles that are added to the letter in specific places. In handwritten material, these "strokes" resemble a (horizontal) line, whereas in print they tend to look like dots. The placement of these lines and circles are applied systematically in the individual orders according to the following principles.

Letters with a /u/-vowel (second order) are commonly marked by a horizontal line that is added at the middle of the right side of the letter (e.g., ለ <la> basic shape and ሉ <lu> with modification; ሐ <ḥa> basic form, ሑ <ḥu> with modification). Letters to be especially noted are ሩ <ru> and ፉ <fu>, where the

---

[17] See Gragg 2004, 430.

basic shape of the letter is altered by a downward elongation in the middle of the letter. The sign *ጠ* <wu> is equally unexpected since its horizontal stroke is placed at the bottom of the right side, not in the middle of the letter.

Letters with an /i/-vowel (third order) generally have a stroke at the bottom of the right side of the letter (as in *ሊ* <li> and *ኺ* <ḫi>). When letters have a round shape at the bottom, the stroke is attached to a downward line that is added to the letter (due to this additional line, *ዊ* <wi> closely resembles *ቂ* <qi>). The letters *ሪ* <ri>, *ፊ* <fi>, and *ዪ* <yi> behave differently: the lower line is bent upwards in <ri> and <fi>, while in the grapheme <yi>, the stroke is attached at the middle of the letter with the help of an additional line, probably to avoid confusion with the letter *ዲ* <di>.

Letters expressing consonant plus /ā/ (fourth order) are characterized by a downward elongation of the right line or foot of the basic letter (as in *ላ* <lā> and *ባ* <bā>). If a letter has only one foot, this line is both elongated and curved to the left (as in *ታ* <tā> and *ፓ* <pā>). Letters that are rounded at the bottom acquire an additional downward line at the bottom of the right side of the letter (e.g., *ማ* <mā>). The letter *ዋ* <wā> receives this additional line in the middle, not on the right side, while *ራ* <rā>, *ፋ* <fā> and *ና* <nā> have unusual forms that have to be memorized separately.

Letters with an /e/-vowel (fifth order) are closely connected to the letters with /i/. The line that is added at the bottom right to express /i/, however, is bent upwards and closed to form a small circle (as in *ሌ* <le> and *ኼ* <ḫe>).

Letters with /ə/- or Ø–vowel (sixth order) have a wide variety of forms. In some of the letters, a vertical straight stroke is bent to the side (*ስ* <sə>). In others, a line is curved into a small circle (*ል* <lə> and *ግ* <gə>). Several letters have an additional small stroke bent to the left side, either at the top (*ሕ* <ḥə>, *ቅ* <qə>, *ት* <tə>, *እ* <ʔə>, *ዝ* <zə>), or in the middle (*ብ* <bə>). Others have a stroke on the right side (*ው* <wə>, *ድ* <də>, *ጵ* <ṗə>, *ጽ* <ṣə>), while yet others have an additional vertical stroke, either at the top (*ዕ* <ʕə>, *ዥ* <ḍə>) or in the lower half (*ሥ* <śə>, *ም* <mə>, *ይ* <yə>, *ፍ* <fə>).

Letters with an /o/-vowel (seventh order) exhibit two main modifications:

- A few letters have an elongated left line or foot while the corresponding variants with /ā/ have an elongated right foot (as in በ <bo> versus ባ <bā>). The letters ሞ <mo> and ሦ <śo> have an elongated line in the middle, whereas ፖ <po> is marked by slanting the foot to the left (similar to ፓ <pā>).

- Several other letters have a small circle at the upper right side of the letter (a simplified form of ወ <wa>), as in ሆ <ho>. The letter ሎ <lo> has the circle attached at the middle of the right side.

ዮ <yo> only has a stroke instead of a circle, probably in order to avoid two consecutive circles. The letter ጎ <go> has a vertical line at the upper end instead of a circle.

2.3.3. The letters of the Ethiopic alphabet traditionally have the following names (cf. §2.2.2. and DG, plate 1 [1st and 2nd column]):

ሆይ *hoy*, ላዊ *lāwi*, ሐውት *ḥāwt*, ማይ *māy*, ሣውት *śāwt* (n° 5), ርእስ *rəʾəs*, ሳት *sāt*, ቃፍ *qāf*, ቤት *bēt*, ታዊ *tāwi* (n° 10);

ጎርም *ḫarm*, ነሃስ *nahās*, አልፍ *ʾalf*, ካፍ *kāf*, ዋዊ *wāwi* (n° 15), ዓይን *ʿāyn*, ዘይ *zay*, የመን *yaman*, ደንት *dant*, ገምል *gaml* (n° 20);

ጣይት *ṭāyt*, ጰይት *p̣āyt*, ጸዳይ *ṣadāy*, ө̣ዳ *ḍap̣p̣ā*, አፍ *ʾaf* (n° 25), and ፐ *pa* besidesፕሳ/ፕሳ *psa/ā* (n° 26).

Eighteen of these names correspond to their counterparts in the Northwest Semitic alphabet containing 22 letters, with slight adjustments to Classical Ethiopic phonology. This means that they approximately correspond to the names of the Hebrew letters. Four letter names, however, diverge from the Northwest Semitic ones (ሣውት *śāwt*, ሳት *sāt*, ነሃስ *nahās*, የመን *yaman* [n° 5, 7, 12, and 18]). These divergences can in part be explained by inner Ethiopic adjustments. The meaning of the NWS letter *yod* 'hand', for example, was not available in Classical Ethiopic since the word for 'hand' is እድ *ʾəd*. Instead, the name was adjusted to a word used in Classical Ethiopic, namely የመን *yaman* 'right hand'. Not included in the Northwest Semitic alphabet are the letters ጎርም *ḫarm*, ጰይት *p̣āyt*, ө̣ዳ *ḍap̣p̣ā*, and ፐ/ፕሳ/ፕሳ *p(s)a/(ā)*. It is disputed when the names of the letters developed. Some names were probably coined as late as the sixteenth century (see Daniels 1991).

2.4. Basic Principles of Handwriting

2.4.1. The handwritten rendering of the Ethiopic letters does not differ significantly from the printed versions since the printed form (which was only established late in Ethiopia – the first printing press was brought to Ethiopia by European Christian missionaries in 1863) is based on the handwritten form. The most important principles and differences of handwriting compared to the printed form of the letters are as follows:

- Almost all handwritten letter shapes consist of several independent lines.
- Letters are generally written starting at the upper left going to the lower right.
- Letter elements that have a circular shape in print (as in ቀ <qa>) consist of two half circles in handwriting or a loop and a straight line.
- Elements that have the shape of a semicircle in print (such as the base form of *b* ብ) consist of a straight vertical line (left) and an added loop (right) in handwriting.
- The handwritten signs መ *ma*, ወ *wa*, የ *ya*, ዳ *da*, and ጠ *ṭa* require special attention since they consist of several separate lines that are combined into a single letter.
- Vowel orders are primarily differentiated by short strokes that have a thicker, dot-like end or a small hook. The corresponding printed forms have the shape of a simple dot.

2.4.2. The following pages contain a table of handwritten letter shapes based on the handwritten rendering of the text ሥነ፡ ፍጥረት *Śǝna fǝṭrat* that was compiled by Getatchew Haile and Misrak Amare (*Beauty of Creation*, Manchester, 1991). The beginning of this handwritten text is shown in appendix A. The table contains gaps since some letters are not attested in the text.

Ethiopic handwriting has only changed slightly during its history in terms of the relative size of signs, orientation of signs, shape of hooks and lines, and how these are attached.[18]

---

[18] Uhlig (1988) distinguishes eight stylistic periods.

	a	u	i	ā	e	ə/∅	o
h	ሀ	ሁ	ሂ	ሃ		ህ	ሆ
l	ለ	ሉ	ሊ	ላ	ሌ	ል	ሎ
ḥ	ሐ	ሑ	ሒ		ሔ	ሕ	ሖ
m	መ	ሙ	ሚ	ማ	ሜ	ም	ሞ
ś	ሠ	ሡ	ሢ	ሣ		ሥ	
r	ረ	ሩ	ሪ	ራ	ሬ	ር	ሮ
s	ሰ	ሱ	ሲ	ሳ	ሴ	ስ	ሶ
q	ቀ	ቁ	ቂ	ቃ	ቄ	ቅ	ቆ
b	በ	ቡ	ቢ	ባ	ቤ	ብ	ቦ
t	ተ	ቱ	ቲ	ታ	ቴ	ት	ቶ
ḫ	ኀ		ኂ	ኃ	ኄ		

n	ነ	ኑ	ኒ	ና	ኔ	ን	ኖ
ʾ	አ	ኡ	ኢ	ኣ	ኤ	እ	ኦ
k	ከ	ኩ	ኪ	ካ		ክ	ኮ
w	ወ	ዉ	ዊ	ዋ	ዌ	ው	ዎ
ʿ	ዐ	ዑ		ዓ		ዕ	ዖ
z	ዘ	ዙ	ዚ	ዛ	ዜ	ዝ	ዞ
y	የ			ያ		ይ	ዮ
d	ደ	ዱ	ዲ	ዳ	ዴ	ድ	ዶ
g	ገ	ጉ	ጊ	ጋ	ጌ	ግ	ጎ
ṭ	ጠ	ጡ	ጢ	ጣ	ጤ	ጥ	ጦ
ṗ				ጳ			
ṣ	ጸ	ጹ		ጻ		ጽ	

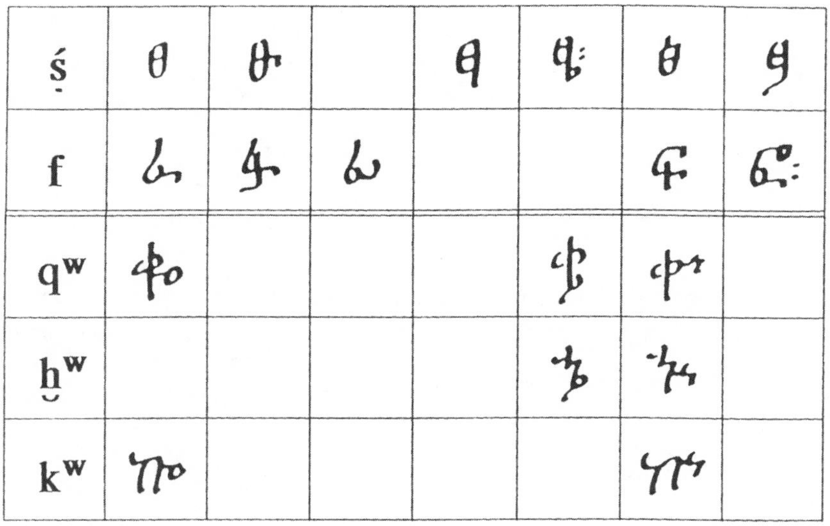

ś	θ	θ̣			q	q̣	θ	g
f	�						f̣	f̣:
qʷ						q̣	q̣ʷ	
ḥʷ						ḥ̣	ḥ̣ʷ	
kʷ							kʷ	

2.5. Numerical Signs

2.5.1. In addition to signs indicating consonants plus vowels, the Ethiopic writing system contains the following numerical signs. These signs consist of modified capital letters of the Greek alphabet and their numerical values. In some cases, the original Greek letter has been modified to look more like an Ethiopic letter, as is, for example, the case with the numbers *ḡ* '40' and *ŷ* '50', which look like the signs *śā* and *hā*. In order to avoid confusion with the syllabic signs, all numerical signs are marked by a horizontal line above and below the sign and are thus clearly distinguishable. Whether Ethiopic ever used Ethiopic letters to indicate numbers is unknown – already the earliest inscriptions use the Greek-based system.

Ethiopic	Greek	Ethiopic			Ethiopic	Greek
1 δ̣	A	11 ī δ̣	and	ī ⱺ δ̣	20 ǩ	K
2 ḝ	B	12 ī ḝ		ī ⱺ ḝ	30 ɡ̄	Λ
3 ṟ	Γ	13 ī ṟ		ī ⱺ ṟ	40 ḡ	M
4 ȯ	Δ	14 ī ȯ		ī ⱺ ȯ	50 ŷ	N
5 ẕ	E	15 ī ẕ		ī ⱺ ẕ	60 x̱	Ξ
6 ẕ̇	Ϛ	16 ī ẕ̇		ī ⱺ ẕ̇	70 ḉ	O
7 ẕ̣	Z	17 ī ẕ̣		ī ⱺ ẕ̣	80 ṯ	Π

8 ፰	H	18 ፲፰	፲ወ፰	90 ፺	ρ
9 ፱	Θ	19 ፲፱	፲ወ፱	100 ፻	P
10 ፲	I			200 ፪፻	
				1000 ፲፻	
				10,000 ፻፻	
				100,000 ፲፻፻	

2.5.2. Only the Greek alphabetic signs *alpha* to *rho* and their corresponding values 1–200 are used. Higher numbers are rendered by combinations of two or more elements:

1–10	alpha–iota
20–100 (full tens)	kappa–rho
200	2–100 (= 2 and 100)
1000	10–100 (= 10 and 100)
10,000	100–100 (= 100 and 100)
100,000	10–100–100 (= 10 and 10,000)

2.5.3. The compound numbers 11–99 are often joined by ወ– *wa–* 'and' (see §4.3.1.7.); for example ፲ወ፩ '10-*wa*-1' = 11; ፵ወ፭ '40-*wa*-5' = 45. The individual digits can also stand right next to each other without an intervening ወ– *wa–*.

2.5.4. Year dates, for example on title pages of books, are introduced by ዓመተ፡ ምሕረት *ʿāmata məḥrat* 'in the year of grace …' or construed according to the following model:

| እምልደተ፡ እግዚአብሔር፡ ኢየሱስ፡ ክርስቶስ | Since/after the birth of the |
| *ʾəm-lədata ʾəgziʾab(ə)ḥer ʾiyasus krəstos* | Lord Jesus Christ |

| በ፲ወ፱፻፺ ወ፮ ዓም | In the year 1996 … |
| *ba 10-wa-9-100-90 wa 6 ʿām* | |

2.6. Word Dividers, Punctuation, and Text-Arrangement

2.6.1. In almost every handwritten and printed text words are divided by means of word dividers, which have the form of a colon (፡). Documents that do not use word dividers exist but are rare. In the latter case, word boundaries are indicated by increased spacing between individual words. Very early Ethiopic inscriptions use word dividers in the form of a vertical line, based on Old South Arabian usage.

Numerals and the counted item are not commonly divided by word dividers, as in ርእየ፡ ፫ሰብእ *rəʾya 3 sabʾa* 'he saw three men'. Proclitic and enclitic particles are likewise written without a divider and joined to the word to which they are attached, as in እምቤት *ʾəm-bet* 'from the house'. If, however, two or more proclitic particles are used at the same time, they are often, but not always, orthographically treated as separate words (as in ለዘ፡ አዘዘ *la-za ʾazzaza* 'for the one who commanded' [two separate words], but also ለዘይፈርሆ *la-za-yəfarrəho* 'for the one he fears' [one word]).

2.6.2. Larger syntactic units such as verses are separated by a double colon (፨). The Amharic name of this sign is *mulu näṭəb*, meaning 'drop' or 'point'.

For marking smaller syntactic units, Ethiopic further uses a colon with a horizontal line above and below the sign (፤; Amharic name *dərrəb säräz*). This sign is used for the approximate function of a full stop or semicolon, e.g., as a sentence divider within a verse and in enumerations separating the individual words. Even smaller semantic units, meaning units below the sentence level, are marked by a colon with a horizontal line between the two dots (፥; Amharic name *säräz*). None of these signs, however, are used regularly. In general, they occur more often in later rather than in earlier manuscripts.

As a marker of a section or paragraph, Ethiopic either uses two verse dividers (፨=፨) or a symmetrical, diamond shaped formation that is composed of various dots (※, ❊).

2.6.3. In order to highlight certain words (e.g., the word for 'God'), handwritten and printed texts use red instead of black ink. In later prints, a horizontal line above the respective word serves the same highlighting function.

3. Phonology

3.1. Consonants

3.1.1. Classical Ethiopic distinguishes 26 consonantal phonemes in the writing system. 24 of these phonemes are clearly inherited from Common Semitic, while the other two, the bilabial stops **𐓀** /p/ and **ጰ** /ṗ/, seem to have been added secondarily to the basic consonantal inventory through borrowing, since they are almost exclusively used in loanwords of non-Semitic origin.[19]

3.1.2. The 26 consonantal phonemes of Classical Ethiopic consist of stops and fricatives (/t/, /f/, etc.), nasals (/m/ and /n/), and approximants. The latter include liquids (/l/ and /r/) and semivowels (/w/ and /y/). Consonantal phonemes further distinguish three articulations: voiced, voiceless, and emphatic.

The consonantal phonemes of Classical Ethiopic can be summarized as follows:[20]

	voiceless	voiced	emphatic	nasal
Bilabial	p	b	ṗ	m
Labiodental	f			
Dental	t	d	ṭ	n
Dental Sibilants	s	z	ṣ	
Lateral	ś (> s)		ḍ (> ṣ)	
Velar	g	k	q (=kʾ)	
Uvular	ḫ			
Pharyngeal	ʿ	ḥ		
Glottal	ʾ	h		
Approximants	Alveolar	Lateral	Palatal	Labiovelar
	r	l	y	w

---

[19] Some authors consider /ṗ/, a voiceless bilabial emphatic, Proto-Semitic. The reconstruction of such a phoneme for Proto-Semitic is based on Ethio-Semitic (see, e.g., Militarev and Kogan 2000, CV–CXVI). Since, however, the phoneme is primarily attested in loanwords, it is unlikely that it constitutes an inherited phoneme.

[20] For a study of the Classical Ethiopic sound system in general, see Weninger 2010.

3.1.3. Compared to common Semitic, which has an inventory of 29 consonants, Classical Ethiopic lacks the interdentals /θ = t/ (voiceless), /ð = d/ (voiced), and /θˀ = z̤/ (emphatic), as well as the phoneme /ġ/.

In Classical Ethiopic, the interdentals have merged with sibilant phonemes, specifically *θ + *s > s, *ð + *dz > z, and *θˀ + *sˀ > ṣ. It further seems that common Semitic /θ/ might have merged with Ethiopic /ś/ in a few cases and common Semitic /θˀ/ with Classical Ethiopic /ḍ/.[21]

Semitic /ġ/ commonly corresponds to Ethiopic /ʿ/, in fewer cases to /ḫ/.[22]

Examples of the correspondence of Ethiopic /ʿ/ and Classical Arabic /ġ/ include:

Classical Ethiopic	Classical Arabic
ʿbr 'be dry'	ġabara, ġubār 'dust'
ʿlw 'to break the law'	ġlw 'to cross the line, border'
sʿr 'to remove, destroy'	tġr 'to break, destroy'
ʿrb 'to go down (sun)'	ġrb 'to leave, go down (sun)'[23]

Examples of the correspondence of Ethiopic /ḫ/ with Classical Arabic /ġ/ include:

Classical Ethiopic	Classical Arabic
rḫb 'to be hungry'	rġb 'to wish, desire'
ṣbḫ 'to dip into'	ṣbġ 'to dye, dip into'
ድማኅ/ኻ dəmāḫ/ḫ 'skull'	dimāġ 'brain'[24]

3.1.4. As in Classical Arabic but contrary to many other Semitic languages, such as Hebrew, the Common Semitic phonemes /ᵗs/ (Hebrew /ṣ/) and /s/ (Hebrew /š/) merged to /s/ in Ethiopic; that is, Classical Ethiopic /s/ reflects three original phonemes, *ᵗs, *s, and *θ.

---

[21] For this assumption, see Voigt 1994.

[22] Cf. Voigt 1989, 640, Dolgopolsky 1999, 19, and especially Kogan 2005 and Weninger 2002.

[23] The origin of /ġ/ in this word in Arabic is still difficult to determine. It seems to be secondary based on cognates such as Sabaic mʿrb 'West' and Ugaritic ʿrb 'to enter'.

[24] Ethiopic ድማኅ/ኻ dəmāḫ/ḫ could also be an Arabic loanword. Regarding Arabic loanwords in Ethiopic in general, see Leslau 1990, 58–99.

3.1.4.1. The correspondences of the Classical Ethiopic consonants with their Proto-Semitic (PS), OSA, Classical Arabic (CA), Ugaritic (Ug.), Hebrew (Heb.), Aramaic (Aram.), and Akkadian (Old Babylonian = OB) equivalents are listed in the following table. It has to be stressed that the table only includes regular correspondences.

CE	PS	OSA	CA	Ug.	Heb.	Aram.	OB
ʔ	*ʔ	ʔ	ʔ	ʔ	ʔ	ʔ	ʔ ($ʔ_1$)
ʕ	*ʕ	ʕ	ʕ	ʕ	ʕ	ʕ	ʔ/Ø ($ʔ_4$)
ʕ	*γ	ġ	ġ	ġ	ʕ	ʕ	ʔ/Ø ($ʔ_5$)
b	*b	b	b	b	b	b	b
d	*d	d	d	d	d	d	d
ḍ	*ṭʔ	ḍ	ḍ	ṣ	ṣ	ʕ	ṣ
f	*p	f	f	p	p	p	p
g	*g	g	j	g	g	g	g
h	*h	h	h	h	h	h	ʔ/Ø ($ʔ_2$)
ḥ	*ħ	ḥ	ḥ	ḥ	ḥ	ḥ	ʔ/Ø ($ʔ_3$)
ḫ	*χ	ḫ	ḫ	ḫ	ḥ	ḥ	ḫ
k	*k	k	k	k	k	k	k
l	*l	l	l	l	l	l	l
m	*m	m	m	m	m	m	m
n	*n	n	n	n	n	n	n
q	*kʔ	q	q	q	q	q	q
r	*r	r	r	r	r	r	r
s	*s	s_1	s	š	š	š	š
s	*ṣ	s_3	s	s	s	s	s
ś	*ṭ	s_2	š	š	ś	s	š
ṣ	*ṣʔ	ṣ	ṣ	ṣ	ṣ	ṣ	ṣ
ṣ	*θʔ	ẓ	ẓ	ẓ/ġ	ṣ	ṭ	ṣ
t	*t	t	t	t	t	t	t
ṭ	*tʔ	ṭ	ṭ	ṭ	ṭ	ṭ	ṭ
w	*w	w	w	w/#y	w/#y	w/#y	w
y	*y	y	y	y	y	y	y
z	*ᵈz	z	z	z	z	z	z
z	*ẟ	d	d	d/ḏ	z	d	z

3.1.5. Labiovelars

Classical Ethiopic is unique in that it has labialized variants of the four postpalatal, that is velar and uvular consonants /q, ḫ, k, g/, namely /qʷ, ḫʷ, kʷ, gʷ/. These labialized consonants are listed under the corresponding non-labialized variants in the common dictionaries, despite the fact that they are phonemic, as can be seen in the minimal pairs ከረበ *karaba* 'to hang up, gather' vs. ኰረበ *kʷaraba* 'to hew, carve' and ገደለ *gadala* 'to strive' vs. ጐደለ *gʷadala* 'to be missing, lack'. The development of these four consonants in Ethiopic probably occurred under Cushitic influence, since sounds of this type are attested in neighboring Cushitic languages.[25]

The letters /q, ḫ, k, g/ are commonly labialized (with following /ə/-vowel that is closely pronounced to /u/)[27] when they were originally followed by short /u/ or, in fewer cases, when they were preceded by /u/, as in ኲሕል *kʷəḥl* < **kuḥl*, Arabic *kuḥl* 'antimony' and *kʷəll* < **kull* 'all'. The resulting labialized consonants were subsequently extended to derivatives of the same root in which they were not followed by original /u/. This means that labiovelars also appear in combination with four other vowels, /a, i, ā, e/.[28]

In some cases, labialization secondarily spread to other velar or uvular radicals of a root, as in ኍልቍ *ḫʷəlqʷ* (< **ḫulq*) 'number' and ኍለቈ *ḫʷallaqʷa* 'to count'. In other instances, Classical Ethiopic has biforms with simple velars besides labialized variants, as in ኆልቅ *ḫolq* besides ኍልቍ *ḫʷəlqʷ* 'number' and ቀሩጽ *qəruṣ* besides ቈሩጽ *qʷəruṣ* 'engraved'.

---

[25] Some scholars consider these labialized consonants an inherited feature from Proto-Semitic (see, e.g., Militarev and Kogan 2000, CXVI–CXXIV). Since it is possible to explain the origin of the labiovelars based on inner Ethiopic developments it is unlikely that they were inherited from Proto-Semitic.

[27] The vowel /ə/ is pronounced with different colorations depending on its phonological environment (see §3.2.3.).

[28] When labiovelars precede original long **/ū/ and **/ō/, which are transliterated as /u/ and /o/ in this grammar (see §3.2.4.), they are not pronounced as labialized consonants, as in ርኩስ *rəkus* 'dirty, impure' from the root *rkʷs* and ለሐኮሙ *laḥakomu* 'he created them' from **laḥakʷa* + **–homu*. Besides ርኩስ *rəkus* we also find the graphic variant ርኵስ *rəkʷ(ə)s* (/ku/ = /kʷ(ə)/).

3.1.6. Other Transliteration Traditions

Several consonants of Classical Ethiopic are transcribed in certain grammars and publications on the lexicon of the language with symbols distinct from those used in this grammar:

- The letter *ś* is, based on Arabic and the assumption that it used to be pronounced similar to [ʃ], transliterated as *š* in older publications.[29]
- In a few cases, *ḫ* is transcribed as *x*.
- The letter transcribed as *q* is sometimes, although rarely, transcribed as *ḳ*. This transliteration is more accurate than the symbol *q*, which reflects Arabic transliteration conventions, since the Classical Ethiopic phoneme is realized as the emphatic (glottalized) variant of /k/ and not as a uvular as in Classical Arabic (see §3.1.7.1.).
- The phoneme /y/ is often, particularly in German publications, transliterated as *j*.
- The letter *ḍ* is, in some publications, transliterated as /ṣ́/. The transliteration /ḍ/, which is based on Arabic transliteration conventions and has nothing to do with the actual pronunciation of the phoneme, has nevertheless been chosen in this grammar because it is the most common transliteration used and is also found in the common dictionaries.

3.1.7. Phonological Realization of the Consonants According to the Traditional Pronunciation

The pronunciation of the Classical Ethiopic consonants at early periods of the language can only be inferred indirectly. The primary source is the so-called traditional pronunciation of Classical Ethiopic, that is, the form of recitation of Classical Ethiopic texts by native scholars.[30] This tradition was established by speakers of Amharic and is thus influenced by the modern pronunciation of Amharic. The most important features of the traditional pronunciation are briefly described in the following.

3.1.7.1. All emphatic consonants are glottalized, that is, they are articulated with a following glottal stop: /ṭ/ = [tˀ], /ṣ/ and /ḍ/ = [ˈsˀ], /q/ = [kˀ], /ṗ/ = /pˀ/ (the

---

[29] This transliteration is not used any longer in order to avoid a confusion with Amharic /š/.
[30] One of the most important studies of the traditional pronunciation is Mittwoch 1926.

latter is a secondarily derived emphatic consonant). This articulation is in contrast to the Arabic velarization of emphatic consonants.

3.1.7.2. The phonemes /p, d, t, k/ are articulated with aspiration, that is [p^h, d^h, t^h, k^h]. The bilabial /b/ is pronounced as simple [b] except when it occurs in post-vocalic position. In this case, it is articulated as a bilabial with spirantization [b], as in ገብረ [gäbrä] 'he did'. When /b/ is geminated, no spirantization occurs, even in post-vocalic position.[31]

3.1.7.3. The four labiovelars /q^w, ḫ^w, k^w, g^w/ are pronounced like their non-labialized counterparts with following /w/ (=/u̯/).

3.1.7.4. As in Amharic, some consonants are no longer distinguished in the pronunciation. Consonants of this type are post-velar /ʿ, ʾ/ and /ḫ, ḥ, h/, which can be subsumed as "gutturals," as well as the original laterals /ḍ/ and /ś/.

- /ʿ/ is generally pronounced like /ʾ/, namely as a simple glottal stop.
- After /ā/ in syllable-closing and word-internal position, /ʾ/ and /ʿ/ can be pronounced as the glide /y/, as in [sämaᵞku] 'I heard' for ሰማዕኩ samāʿku (§3.7.1:1).
- Word-finally, /ʾ/ and /ʿ/ are often not pronounced, e.g., in nominal forms of the pattern qVtl when either of them is the third radical, as in ሰብእ sabʾ 'men' = [säb] or ዘርእ zarʾ 'seed' = [zär].
- /h/, /ḥ/, and /ḫ/ are generally pronounced as [h].
- The original lateral articulation of /ḍ/ and /ś/ was lost during the course of Classical Ethiopic. Today, /ḍ/ is pronounced like /ṣ/ = [ᵗsʾ] and /ś/ like /s/ = [s].

3.1.7.5. The sonorants /l/, /r/, and /n/ are pronounced syllabically as [ḷ], [r̩], and [n̩] respectively in post-consonantal word-final position, as in ይብል [yəbḷ] 'he speaks', ምድር [mədr̩] 'earth, land', and ስምን [səmn̩] 'eight(fold)'. The phoneme /r/ is pronounced in the front of the mouth with a dental, and not a velar or uvular articulation.

---

[31] The spirantization of /b/ can, according to the traditional pronunciation, also occur after certain consonants, in particular after the sonorants /l/, /n/, and /r/.

3.1.7.6. Word-initial /yə/ is pronounced as [(ʔ)i] and word-initial /wə/ as [(ʔ)u], as in [(ʔ)ulud] for **ው·ሱ·ድ** *wəlud* 'sons, children'.

3.1.8. Recommended Pronunciation for Students

The pronunciation of Classical Ethiopic used in the classroom can either strictly follow the traditional pronunciation just outlined, or it can be archaizing in certain aspects.

3.1.8.1. This grammar recommends a more historical articulation of the Classical Ethiopic gutturals, according to which /ʕ/ is pronounced as a voiced pharyngeal fricative as in Classical Arabic, /ḥ/ as a voiceless pharyngeal fricative, likewise as in Classical Arabic, and /ḫ/ as a voiceless fricative uvular as in German "Bach" and its Arabic equivalent.

The phonological differentiation of the gutturals is recommended for two reasons: First, the respective consonants are distinguished in the Classical Ethiopic writing system (only late manuscripts tend to confuse them). Second, the differentiation of gutturals, except /ḫ/ and /ḥ/, is attested in Tigre and Tigrinya, which represent the most closely related descendant languages of Classical Ethiopic.

3.1.8.2. The remaining consonants should be pronounced as in the traditional pronunciation, except /yə/ and /wə/ in word-initial position, which should be articulated as semi-vowels, not as glottal stop plus vowel (cf. §3.1.7.6.).

- The phoneme /ś/ was most likely pronounced like a voiceless fricative lateral at an early period of Classical Ethiopic, as is still the case in Modern South Arabian languages. Since a lateral pronunciation is difficult to produce, the phoneme can, like /s/, be pronounced as simple [s]. The phoneme should not be pronounced as [ʃ] = /š/, meaning like the letters *sh* in the English word "fish." The latter pronunciation is problematic because Amharic secondarily developed a phoneme /š/ that is not derived from the original lateral /ś/.
- Classical Ethiopic /ḍ/ is not to be pronounced as its Classical Arabic counterpart. Historically, it most likely never resembled /ḍ/ but represented an emphatic lateral [ɬˀ].[32] Since such a sound is difficult to

---

[32] According to Mittwoch (1926, 11, note 3), /ḍ/ was pronounced like [θˀ], that is, close to a voiceless glottalized interdental, at early stages of Classical Ethiopic. An important

produce, it can be pronounced like /ṣ/, following the traditional pronunciation (see below). A pronunciation [ᵗšʔ] is not recommended since Amharic has a secondarily derived phoneme /čʔ/ that is articulated in this way but that is not derived from /ḍ/.

- The remaining emphatic consonants /ṭ/, /q/, /ṣ/, and /ṗ/ should be articulated according to the traditional pronunciation as glottalized consonants, not like Arabic velarized emphatics.

- The base consonants of the emphatic consonants /ṭ/, /q/, and /ṗ/ are /t/, /k/, and /p/ respectively. The emphatic and non-emphatic variants differ in their type of coarticulation. Emphatics have a coarticulation in the form of a glottal stop, while their non-emphatic counterparts are aspirated, that is /t/ = [tʰ] and /ṭ/ = [tʔ]. The phoneme /ṣ/ has an affricated base [ᵗs] to which a glottal stop is added [ᵗsʔ].

3.1.8.3. The following table provides a summary of the pronunciation of Classical Ethiopic consonants recommended for use in the classroom:

Phoneme	Recommended articulation
f ፈ	[f] (as in English 'fish')
p ፐ	[pʰ] (voiceless aspirated)
ṗ ጰ	[pʔ] (glottalized [p])
b በ	[b] (with optional spirantization after vowels)
t ተ	[tʰ] (voiceless aspirated)
ṭ ጠ	[tʔ] (glottalized [t])
d ደ	[dʰ] (voiced aspirated)

---

indication for the original pronunciation of Classical Ethiopic /ḍ/ is attested in a transliteration of the Classical Ethiopic place name *mḍ* into Greek, where it is spelled as ματλια (inscriptions RIÉ 185 [bis] and 270 [bis]; see also Weninger 1998). Based on this transliteration, early Ethiopic /ḍ/ was pronounced like the Greek sequence τλι. The phoneme was thus affricated (because of τ) and lateral (because of λ[ι]); Greek ι (after τλ) might be evidence for the glottal stop that is coarticulated together with emphatic consonants. The α at the end of the word reflects the accusative case.

s ሰ	[s] (voiceless; as in English 'sun')
ṣ ጸ	[ˈsˀ] (glottalized affricated voiceless [s])
z ዘ	[z] (voiced; as in 'zone')

ś ሠ	[s] (same as *s*)
ḍ θ	[ˈsˀ] (same as *ṣ*)

k ከ	[kʰ] (voiceless aspirated)
q ቀ	[kˀ] (glottalized [k])
g ገ	[g] (voiced)

ḫ ኀ	[χ] (like Classical Arabic *ḫ* and German *ch* in 'Bach')
ḥ ሐ	[ħ] (like Classical Arabic *ḥ*)
h ሀ	[h]
ʿ ዐ	[ʕ] (like Classical Arabic ʿ)
ʾ አ	[ʔ] (glottal stop)

m መ, n ነ	[m], [n]
l ለ, r ረ	[l], [r] (rolled [r] as in Spanish)
w ወ	[w] (as in English 'water')
y የ	[y] (as in English 'yellow')

3.1.9. It should be noted that most of the features of the traditional pronunciation are based on older traditions. Based on these traditions, frequently found "mistakes" or the confusion of certain consonants in manuscripts, such as the use of ኀ *ḫ* for etymological ሐ *ḥ* and sometimes for ሀ h, ሠ *ś* for ሰ s, θ *ḍ* for ጸ *ṣ* and vice versa, and the use of አ ʾ for ዐ ʿ and vice versa in later manuscripts, can be explained. Knowledge of the traditional pronunciation is thus important for understanding Classical Ethiopic orthography and phonology.

3.2. Vowels

3.2.1. The Classical Ethiopic writing system distinguishes seven vowels that are transcribed as /a, u, i, ā, e, ə, o/ in this grammar. In order to understand this transliteration and the underlying vowel system, it is necessary to briefly discuss the historical background of these vowels.

3.2.2. Early Ethiopic had five long vowels, /*ā, *ī, *ū, *ē, *ō/, one short vowel /*a/, and an ultra-short vowel /*ə/ (also referred to as *schwa* based on Hebrew). These vowels are derived from the following Proto-Semitic vowels and diphthongs:

Long vowel (type A)	/ā/ < *ā ; /*ī/ < *ī; /*ū/ < *ū
Long vowel (type B)	/*ē/ < *ay; /*ō/ < *aw[33]
Short vowel	/a/ < *a
Ultra short vowel	/ə/ < *i, *u[34]

The following rules can be deduced from the preceding table:

(a) Proto-Semitic long vowels were preserved in early Ethiopic.
(b) The inherited diphthongs were usually contracted: *aw became /*ō/ (= /o/; for the transliteration as /o/ see [§3.2.4.]) and *ay was contracted to /*ē/ (= /e/), although the latter diphthong was preserved in certain lexemes.

   Examples of *aw > /o/ include ዮም *yom* < *yawm 'today' and ቆም *qom* < *qawm 'height'.
   Examples of *ay > /e/ include ቤት *bet* < *bayt 'house'; ብሔር *bəher* < *buḥayr 'region, land'; ሴሰየ *sesaya* < *saysaya 'he nourished' (root *sysy*).
   Examples of preserved *ay include ዐይን *ʿayn* 'eye, spring' and በይን *bayna* 'between'.

(c) Only /*a/ was preserved of the three Proto-Semitic short vowels. Inherited /*i/ and /*u/ were reduced to /ə/.

---

[33] In some cases it seems that /*ō/ is derived from /u/, as in the Classical Ethiopic third person plural pronominal suffixes -ሆሙ *-homu* (masc.) and -ሆን *-hon* (fem.), which go back to the Common Semitic forms *–humu and *–hun(nV). The vowel /o/ in these forms, however, is an analogical extension of the /*ō/ in the 3ms, where it is derived from *-ahu > *-aw > *-ō.

[34] In rare cases, Classical Ethiopic /ə/ can be derived from /a/, as in ርእስ *rəʾ(ə)s* < *raʾas (?) < *raʾs 'head', and in the nominal pattern *qətul* < *qutūl used for adjectives, which is derived from *qatūl via vowel harmony.

3.2.3. In a later period of the language, vowel quantity was lost as a distinctive feature. The opposition /a/: /ā/ was replaced by the qualitative distinction /ä/: /a/.[35]

It has been suggested that the development of short vowels in later Classical Ethiopic be interpreted as "centralization" (cf. Voigt 1983; Tropper 2002): *a* > *ä*, *i* > *ə*, *u* > *ə*. This analysis is certainly true for /i/ and /u/, which merged into a central vowel. It is, however, difficult in the case of /a/, which is fronted from central /a/ to /ä/, and thus loses its original central articulation.

The traditional pronunciation thus distinguishes the following seven vowel qualities (in the order of the seven vowel orders of the CE writing system):

   1. /ä/   2. /u/   3. /i/   4. /a/   5. /e/   6. /ə/[36] 7. /o/

The first vowel /ä/ and the sixth vowel /ə/ are realized differently in certain phonological environments according to the traditional pronunciation:

- /ä/ is usually realized as open [æ] (as in English "man"). In proximity to the gutturals /ʾ, ʿ, h, ḥ, ḫ/, however, this vowel is pronounced as [a] and is consequently realized in the same way as /a/. Following the velar consonants /k, g, q/, the vowel is likewise pronounced closer to [a] than [æ]. After /w/ and generally after labiovelars, the vowel of the first order acquires a deeper color and is pronounced as [ɔ], as in ወፅአ [wɔˈsʾä] 'he left'.
- The ultra-short vowel /ə/ is pronounced as [u] in proximity to /w/ and labiovelars and as [i] in the vicinity of /y/, as in ውስተ wəsta = [wustä] 'in'; ኵሉ kʷəllu = [kʷul(l)u] or [kul(l)u] 'each, all'; and ርእስየ rəʾ(ə)səya = [rəʾəsiyä] 'my head'. /ə/ is further frequently pronounced as [u] when it precedes /m/, as in the 2mp pronominal suffix -ክሙ -kəmu = [-(k)kumu].

Furthermore, according to the traditional pronunciation, the phoneme /e/ is articulated with a preceding semivowel /y/ (except when it follows a laryngeal), and the phoneme /o/ with preceding /w/ (in all environments), that is they are

---

[35] In the traditional pronunciation, /i/, /u/, /e/, and /o/ are still pronounced relatively long whereas /ā/ is realized as a short vowel. The transliteration symbols used in this grammar (§3.2.4.) are thus not directly reflecting the traditional realization of these vocalic phonemes.
[36] The Ethiopic writing system does not distinguish between /ə/– and Ø–vowel (see §2.1. above).

pronounced as [ʸe] and [ʷo] respectively, as in ቤት *bet* = [bʸet] 'house' and ሖረ *ḥora* = [ḥʷorä] 'he went'. This articulatory phenomenon is not reflected in the orthography.

3.2.4. Classical Ethiopic vowels are not transliterated uniformly in the scholarly literature. The following presents the most important transliteration systems used. The first three reflect a historical interpretation of the vowels whereas the last one is based on the traditional pronunciation.

1. a, u, i, ā, e, ə, o   (Leslau [CDG])
2. a, u, i, ā, ē, e, o   (e.g., Lambdin 1978)
3. ă, ū, ī, ā, ē, ĕ, ō   (Dillmann [DG]; Praetorius 1886a–b)
4. ä, u, i, a, e, ə, o   (Ullendorff 1955; Diem 1988 etc.)

This grammar uses the first transliteration type.

Some grammars indicate two types of *schwas* or /ə/. Besides normative *schwa*, there can be another *schwa*-vowel that is not phonologically relevant and primarily occurs after gutturals. This /ə/-vowel is either presented in the same way as normative *schwa*, or as /ᵊ/, as in ርእስ *rəᵊs* 'head' and ክህለ *kəhᵊla* < *kahila 'to be able'. In many cases, this secondary /ᵊ/ is justified from a historical perspective, as in ምሕረ *məḥᵊra* < *maḥira 'to show mercy'. In other cases, there is no historical reason for the presence of this vowel, as in aforementioned *rəᵊs* < *raʔasʔ < *raʔs. This secondary /ᵊ/-vowel is audible in a careful pronunciation of the preceding guttural according to the traditional pronunciation. The vowel is not, however, relevant for word stress, that is, /ᵊ/ is not commonly stressed, as in *rə́ᵊs*, where the first /ə/ bears the accent.[37] Most reference grammars and dictionaries do not indicate this vowel – the words cited are transcribed as *rəʔs*, *kəhla*, and *məḥra* respectively. This grammar will follow the convention found in most grammars and dictionaries and omit this secondary vowel in the transliterations given.

3.2.5. In the classroom, vowels should be pronounced based on the traditional pronunciation (independent of the transliteration system used), although the

---

[37] It should be noted, however, that a form like *məḥᵊra* (3ms G-perfect, II-guttural root) is pronounced with an accent on the second *schwa* by some speakers (see Mittwoch 1926, 58). Verbs II-guttural that are also III-y are, according to Mittwoch (1926, 73) regularly stressed on the penultima, as in *rəʔʔəya* 'he saw', which has a variant *rəʔya*.

palatalized and labialized articulation of /e/ (= [ʸe]) and /o/ (= [ʷo]) can be neglected so that these vocalic phonemes are pronounced as simple [e] and [o] respectively.

If students choose a pronunciation based on a historical approach, /a/ should always be pronounced as open short [a] and all other vowels except /ə/, meaning /ā, i, u, e, o/, with a clearly articulated distinction in length (according to the transliteration system presented as n° 3 above).

Knowledge of the traditional pronunciation is important since it explains the frequently attested confusion of /a/ and /ā/ after gutturals in manuscripts (both vowels are pronounced in the same manner according to the traditional pronunciation). It is also a prerequisite for understanding the rules involving gutturals (§3.7.1.).

3.3. Lengthening (Gemination) of Phonemes

3.3.1. Most likely all consonants and the three basic vowels (a, i, u) could be articulated as simple or lengthened in an early form of Ethiopic. According to the traditional pronunciation, lengthening is only preserved as a distinctive feature in consonants, while vowels are not distinguished for vowel quantity. The only exceptions are the Classical Ethiopic gutturals /ʔ, ʕ, h, ḥ, ḫ/, which are, except in very few cases (§3.7.1.), not commonly articulated as geminated.

Gemination of consonants is realized in word-final position, as in ልብ *ləbb* 'heart', ሕግ *ḥəgg* 'law', and ወለት *walatt* 'daughter' (< **waladt*).[38] The only environment in which consonantal gemination cannot occur is, as is common across Semitic, in word-initial position.

3.3.2. Consonantal gemination is usually either morphologically motivated, as in *yənaggər* 'he says' (3ms impf.) and *ləbb* 'heart' from the nominal pattern **qill*, or the result of consonantal assimilation, as in *walatt* < **waladt* 'daughter'.

Classical Ethiopic further has many examples of consonantal gemination that are secondary, meaning unexpected from a morphological or regular phonological point of view. In many of these cases, word stress seems to be the motivation for the unexpected gemination, which especially occurs preceding a stressed syllable ("pre-tonic gemination" [§3.3.2.1.]). Cases of gemination that are clearly

---

[38] See Mittwoch 1926, 20.

motivated by this type of secondary gemination are, contrary to, e.g., CDG, not considered in the transliterations provided in this grammar.

3.3.2.1. Secondary gemination in pre-tonic position is most likely responsible for the following word forms, which are cited according to their traditional pronunciation:

- The 2nd person plural independent personal pronouns አንትሙ *ʾanttə́mu* (masc.) and አንትን *ʾanttə́n* (fem.) as well as their equivalent pronominal suffixes –ክሙ –*kkə́mu* and –ክን –*kkə́n*; see also the 2mp perfect suffix ነገርክሙ *nagarkkə́mu* 'you (mp) spoke' compared to the 2ms ነገርክ *nagárka*.
- The demonstrative pronouns ዝኩ *zəkkú* 'that', እንትኩ *ʾəntəkkú*, እልኩ *ʾəlləkkú* 'those'.
- The geminated final consonant of certain perfect forms before pronominal suffixes might likewise be caused by pre-tonic gemination, as in ነገረትኒ *nagarattə́nni* 'she spoke to me', ነገርክኒ *nagarkkə́nni* 'you (ms) spoke to me', and ነገርክኒ *nagark(k)ə́nni* 'you (fs) spoke to me'.[39]

These forms will be transcribed without pre-tonic gemination in this grammar, that is, as *ʾantəmu*, *ʾantən*, *zəku*, *ʾəntəku*, *ʾəlləku*, *nagaratanni*, *nagarkanni*, and *nagarkənni*.

In cases in which it is uncertain whether or not we are dealing with pre-tonic gemination, gemination is indicated in the transcription. Cases of this type include:

- ቦቱ *bottú*, ባቲ *bāttí*, ቦንቱ/ቦቶን *bonttú/bottón* 'in/with him, her, them';
- ሎቱ *lottú*, ላቲ *lāttí*, ሎንቱ/ሎቶን *lonttú/lottón* 'for him, her, them';
- the feminine *qattāl* of adjectives of the pattern *qatil* (for expected *qatāl);*
- the frequently attested plural *qattalt* (besides the plural *qatalt*) of adjectives of the pattern *qatil* and the perfective-participle *qatāli* (for expected *qatalt*);

---

[39] The same gemination is attested in certain forms even when the phoneme in question does not occur in pre-tonic position, as in ነገርኩ *nagarkkāhú* 'you (ms) spoke to him' and ነገረትክሙ *nagarattakkə́mu* 'she spoke to you (mp)'. These occurrences are caused by analogy with the just mentioned geminated pre-tonic forms.

- The nominal suffix -ánnā, which probably goes back to original -(ə)nā (§4.2.1.5.8.).[40]

3.3.2.2. Secondary gemination can also occur after a stressed vowel. This phenomenon occurs, for example, in the forms of the imperfect, jussive, and imperative when they have a vocalic ending, as in ይነግሩ yənaggárru 'they speak' (3mp impf.), ይንግሩ yəngárru 'let them speak' (3mp juss.), and ንግሩ nəgárru 'speak!' (mp imp.).[41]

This grammar does not indicate this type of gemination in the transcription. The forms in question are transcribed as yənaggəru, yəngəru, and nəgəru respectively.[42]

3.3.2.3. Secondary gemination can also occur without being motivated by stress. Forms that exhibit secondary gemination of this type include the distributive forms ለለ lalla (< *la–la), በበ babba (< *ba–ba), and ዘዘ zazza (< *za–za); cf. also ዘለለ zallalla (< *za–la–la) (§5.6.). These particles are transcribed with gemination in this grammar.

3.4. Syllable Structure

3.4.1. Classical Ethiopic has four types of syllables. The two most frequently occurring syllable types are CV and CVC (C = consonant; V = vowel), while the two less frequently occurring types are CVCC and CV:C. Syllables ending in a vowel are commonly referred to as "open" and those ending in a consonant as "closed." As this overview of possible syllable types shows, every syllable in Classical Ethiopic has to begin with a consonant and can only contain one vowel, which is typical for many classical Semitic languages.

CVC-syllables always contain a short vowel from a historical point of view, as in ነጸረ naṣṣara = naṣ–ṣa–ra 'he looked' (syllable structure CVC–CV–CV). Syllables of

---

[40] Transcriptions provided in this grammar generally follow Mittwoch 1926 in doubtful or ambiguous cases. Leslau (CDG) transcribes numerous words with gemination, contrary to Mittwoch, such as ክልኤቱ kəl'ettu, ክልኤቲ kəl'etti 'two', which Mittwoch transcribes as kələ'etu.
[41] Mittwoch considers this gemination a secondary phenomenon as well (1926, 31). He refers to these occurrences as "Konsonantenlänge" and "Lautverlängung" as opposed to "Lautverdoppelung."
[42] A form that is not caused by post-tonic gemination is ነገረኒ nagaránni 'he spoke to me' (perfect with pronominal suffix [§4.4.2.1.1.]).

the type CəC go back to original CVC (either CiC or CuC), as in ልብየ *ləbbəya* = *ləb–ba–ya* 'my heart' < **lib–bV–ya*.

CV syllables can contain a historically short (V) or historically long (V:) vowel:

CV:	e.g., ተናገረ *tanāgara* (L) = *ta–nā–ga–ra* (CV–CV: –CV–CV)
CV, V=a	e.g., ነገረ *nagara* = *na–ga–ra* (CV–CV–CV)
CV, V=ə	e.g., ክቡር *kəbur* = *kə–bur* (CV–CVC)[43]

Syllables of the types CVC and CV: are considered long syllables, those of the type CV are referred to as short, and those with *schwa* (Cə) as ultra-short.

Ultra-long syllables (CV:C) and doubly closed syllables (CVCC) represent secondary developments. They are commonly derived from bisyllabic forms, as in ነፍሳት *nafsāt* 'souls' < **nafsā–tə* and ነፍስ *nafs* 'soul' < **naf–sə*, where the final case vowels **-i* (gen.) and **-u* (nom.) merged to /ə/. /ə/ was subsequently lost in word-final position, resulting in the closing of the originally open syllable. This led to the attested ultra-long syllable. Words of the type ባሕር *bāḥr* 'sea, ocean' go back to original **baḥ–rə*, where original short /a/ was lengthened because of the following guttural (§3.7.1:1). The ultra-long syllables of the D and L stems, e.g., ይኔግር *yəneggər* (D) and ይናግር *yənāggər* (L) are due to paradigmatic leveling – imperfects of all verbal stems exhibit gemination of the second radical.

3.4.2. Whether a syllable of a word containing a sixth order letter is to be pronounced as /ə/ or without a vowel – the two options are not distinguished in the orthography – is based on rules that depend on the permissible syllable structures discussed in the previous paragraph. The four most important rules for the pronunciation of the sixth order are:[44]

1. /ə/ has to be pronounced after a word-initial consonant since two consonants at the beginning of a word are impermissible, as in ክሳድ *kəsād* 'neck' (NOT **ksād).
2. Word-finally, the sixth order is always to be read as vowelless, as in ይንግር *yəngər* 'let him speak' and ነፍስ *nafs* 'soul'. An exception is the demonstrative pronoun ዝ- *zə-* 'this', where the *schwa* is usually stressed and proclitic.

---

[43] Historically, the vowel /ə/ derives from either short /*i/ or short /*u/.
[44] See also Bulakh 2016.

3. /ə/ has to be pronounced preceding or following two consecutive consonants, including geminated consonants, in order to avoid three consecutive consonants, as in **ይነግር** *yənaggər* 'he speaks' (NOT **yənaggr) and **እምነ** *ʾəmənna* 'from' (NOT **ʾəmnna). Two consecutive consonants without following /ə/ can only appear in word-final position, as in **ልብ** *ləbb* 'heart' (§3.3.1.).

4. A consonant following a short or ultra-short open syllable and preceding a sequence CV (that is, a sequence CV-CØ-CV) is to be pronounced as vowelless, even if historically there used to be a vowel in this position, as in **ለብሰ** *labsa* < *labəsa < *labisa 'he dressed himself'. In other words, an original sequence *CV–CV–CV is always syncopated to CVC–CV.

3.5. Word Stress

3.5.1. Since there is no evidence for word stress in early Classical Ethiopic, the traditional pronunciation is of special importance in this matter. The standard grammars, however, offer different and opposing descriptions regarding certain details. The following rules are taken from Mittwoch (1926). They differ in several points from the accent rules given by Trumpp (1874) and Dillmann (DG 110–13) but correspond to those given in Lambdin (1978).

3.5.2. According to Mittwoch (1926), stress falls on either the last (ultimate) or second-to-last (penultimate) syllable in Classical Ethiopic. Which syllable is stressed depends on the following rules:

1. Finite verbal forms without pronominal suffixes are stressed on the penultima. The only exception is the 2fp perfect **ነገርክን** *nagarkán* 'you (fp) spoke', which is stressed on the ultima.[45] According to Mittwoch (1926, 52), the imperative of the masc. sing. is likewise stressed on the penultima, **ንግር** *nágər* 'speak!', **ልበስ** *lábas* 'dress yourself!'.[46] Word accent never goes back to the third syllable from the back.[47]

---

[45] The reason why this form is stressed on the ultima could be its possible origin in either *-*kənā* or *–*kəna*, that is an original form with a final vowel. The form –*kənā*– is attested before object suffixes, as in **ነገርክናሁ** *nagarkənāhu* 'you (fp) spoke to him'.

[46] Other authors assume that this form is accented on the ultima, as in *nəgár* and *ləbás*.

[47] The description given by Dillmann (DG) differs in this regard. According to Dillmann, perfects of the C-stems, *asta*- stems (CGt, CDt, and CLt), and quadriliteral verbs (Q) are stressed on the ante-penultima, that is **ተቃተለ** *taqˈātala* (Lt), **አስተንገረ** *ʾastángara* (CGt), and

2. Pronouns ending in a vowel – which include most pronouns – are either stressed on the ultima or penultima, depending on the quality of the final vowel. Original long final /u/ and /i/ are stressed in most cases; short /a/ (= marker of the accusative) remains unstressed. The following more detailed rules apply:

    Demonstrative and interrogative pronouns, except those ending in *-a* (e.g., ዘንተ *zánta* 'this' [acc.], መኒ *mánna* 'who' [acc.], ምንተ *mánta* 'what' [acc.]) are accented on the ultima, as in ዝንቱ *zəntú* 'this' (masc. sing. nom./gen.) and ዛቲ *zāttí* 'this' (fem. sing. nom./gen.), versus acc. ዛተ *z'átta*.

    Most independent personal pronouns are accented on the penultima. A few forms, however, take their stress on the ultima, such as አንትን *'antán* (2fp) and እሙንቱ *'əmuntú* (3mp).

3. Nominal forms of the nominative and genitive in the unbound state are stressed on the ultima. When the ending *-a* is suffixed to the form, the accent remains on the original syllable, that is, the word form is stressed on the penultima, as in ንጉሥ *nəgúś* 'king' (nom./gen.) and ንጉሠ *nəgúśa* 'king' (acc.). This rule also applies to nouns that have become frozen adverbial forms, such as ጥቀ *ṭáqqa* 'exactly, very'.[48]

4. All cardinal numbers, including their acc. forms, are stressed on the ultima, as in አሐዱ *'aḥadú* 'one' (masc. nom./gen.) and አሐደ *'aḥadá* 'one' (masc. acc.); አሐቲ *'aḥattí* 'one' (fem. nom/gen.) and አሐተ *'aḥattá* 'one' (fem. acc.).

5. Most adverbs are accented on the last syllable, in particular adverbs that end in /-u/, /-e/, and /-ā/, such as ታሕቱ *tāḥtú* 'below' and ላዕሉ *lā'lú* 'above'. Penultimate stress is, for example, attested in ዝየ *záya* 'here', as opposed to ህየ *həyyá* 'there', and ከሐ/ካሐ *káha/káhā* 'yonder, down there'.

6. Suffixed enclitic particles such as -ሁ *-hu*, -ኑ *-nu*, -መ *-mma*, -አ *-'ā*, -ዪ *-hi*, -ኒ *-ni*, -ስ *-ssa*, and -ኬ *-ke* are stressed. Words with these enclitic particles are thus accented on the ultima, as in ንጉሠስ *nəguśə-ssá* 'the king, however …'.

መንደበ *mándaba* (Q). In the *asta*-stems, verbs II-gutt., however, have penultima stress according to Dillmann. Main stress can even fall on the fourth- or fifth-to-last syllable according to Dillmann (DG: 110), as in the perfect forms በረከተ *bárakata* and በረከተከ *bárakàtaka*.

[48] According to Dillmann, certain nouns are stressed on the penultima even in the nom./gen., such as ሀገር *hágar* 'city' and መሳፍንት *mas'áfənt* 'judges, governors' (DG: 111).

7. Several words do not bear stress. These include short nouns in the construct state, short prepositions, such as እስከ *ʾəska* 'until' and ቀድመ *qədma* 'before', short conjunctions, such as እመ *ʾəmma* 'if', እስመ *ʾəsma* 'because, since', እንዘ *ʾənza* 'while', and ሶበ *soba* 'when', and the negative particle ኢ- *ʾi-*. These forms are considered proclitic.

8. Certain words can bear secondary stress. Secondary stress occurs in particular when the syllable bearing primary stress is directly or indirectly preceded by a closed syllable of the type CVC, as in ዛቲ *zāˋttí* 'this (fs)', እሙንቱ *ʾəmùntú* 'those (mp)', አስተናፈሰ *ʾàstanāfása* 'he made breath' (CLt 3ms pf.).

3.6. Consonantal Sound Changes

3.6.1. Confusion of Guttural Consonants

The consonants /ʾ/ and /ʿ/ on the one hand and /ḫ/, /ḥ/, and /h/ on the other are not distinguished in the traditional pronunciation (§3.1.7.4.). The at least partial merger of the two groups of consonants can be traced to early periods of Classical Ethiopic. Because of these mergers, manuscripts often exhibit a mix up of the respective guttural signs. The confusion of the signs for /ḥ/ and /ḫ/ occurs very frequently, as well as the interchangeability of /ʾ/ and /ʿ/ – although the latter only occurs in later manuscripts. Signs for the phonemes /h/ and /ḥ/ are confused significantly less often, as in ህ/ሐጕለ *h/ḥagʷla* 'to perish' and ህ/ሐው *h/ḥaw* 'fire'. Equally less frequent is the confusion of /ḫ/ and /h/ as in ኄ/ጼጠ *ḫ/heṭa* 'to deceive, seduce'.

Besides these orthographic confusions, Classical Ethiopic has lexemes that generally exhibit the wrong guttural from a comparative perspective, such as እጕል *ʾəgʷl*, እጓል *ʾəgʷāl* 'the young of any animal, child' for which Central Semitic has **ʿigl*. A form ***ʿəgʷl* that would be expected according to §3.1.4. is not attested in Classical Ethiopic.

3.6.2. Loss of Guttural Consonants

3.6.2.1. Since gutturals are generally weakened in Classical Ethiopic, they can be lost in certain frequently used word formations. This type of loss is attested in all positions and particularly affects the phonemes /h/ and /ʾ/. Examples include:

(a) In syllable-initial position:	ይበል *yəbal* < *yəbhal 'let him speak' (G 3ms juss. of root *bhl*)
	አበለ *ʾabala* < *ʾabhala 'he caused to speak' (C 3ms perf.)
(b) Between vowels:	ሊቅ *liq* < *ləhiq 'old man' (root *lhq*); ንስቲት *nəstit* < *nəʾəstit 'small' (root *nʾs*)
(c) In syllable-final position:	ሞዳ *moḍā* < *mawḍāʾ < *mawḍaʾ 'offering, gift' (root *wḍʾ*)

3.6.2.2. A special case of "loss" of /ʾ/ occurs when the proclitic negative particle **ኢ–** *ʾi–* is prefixed to a verbal form that begins with /ʾ/. *ʾi–* + /ʾ/ does not result in /ʾiʾ–/, but in /ʾiy–/, as in **ኢያፍቀረ** *ʾiyafqara* < *ʾi-ʾafqara 'he did not love' (C perf.) and **ኢይነግር** *ʾiyənaggər* < *ʾi-ʾənaggər 'I will not speak' (G 1cs impf.).[49] In this case, the /ʾ/ of the verbal form is assimilated to the preceding /i/-vowel, that is, it is palatalized under the influence of the preceding vowel.

In manuscripts, we often find the orthographic variant **ኢያፍቀረ** *ʾiyāfqara* for **ኢያፍቀረ** *ʾiyafqara* (C 3ms pf.). Such orthographic variants are not "wrong" since the vowels in /ʾa/ and /yā/ are both pronounced as [a] according to the traditional pronunciation, whereas the vowel in /ya/ is pronounced as [æ].

For further phonological changes in connection with gutturals, see §3.7.1., in particular §3.7.1:6.

3.6.3. Loss of Word-Final /l/

The loss of word-final /l/ is attested in the frequently used verbal form **ይቤ** *yəbe* < *yəbel 'he spoke' (root *bhl* [§4.4.6.5.2.]). When the verb has a vocalic ending, however, /l/ is preserved, as in **ይቤሉ** *yəbelu* 'they (mp) spoke'. The loss of /l/ in these forms is not so much caused by phonological changes, but by reanalysis. The verb *bəhla* 'to speak' is often used with the preposition **ለ–** *la–* 'to, for' plus pronominal suffix. In the form under discussion, this would result in **yəbel+lo* 'he spoke to him', which was reanalyzed as *yəbe + lo*. This type of reanalysis was not

---

[49] Forms such as **ኢይነግር** *ʾiyənaggər* are thus ambiguous. They can stand for the 3ms, that is, *ʾi–yənaggər*, or for the 1cs, **ʾi–ʾənaggər*. According to some traditions, which Leslau follows (CDG), /y/ is doubled in the 3ms, that is, *ʾiyyənaggər*.

possible in forms ending in a final vowel, such as ይቤሉ *yəbelu* 'they spoke', so that the original form is preserved.

3.6.4. Metatheses

3.6.4.1. Metatheses of consonants that occur to ease pronunciation are not common in Classical Ethiopic.[50] The only exceptions are a few attestations of metatheses involving a semivowel or liquid in the vicinity of a guttural:

- አስተኈልሐወ *ʾastagʷālḥawa* besides አስተኈሕለወ *ʾastagʷāḥlawa* 'to cause to deceive' (CLt of ጐሕለወ *gʷaḥlawa* 'to be crafty, deceive').

3.6.4.2. There are, however, a number of Classical Ethiopic lexemes that exhibit a different consonantal order than in other Semitic languages. This phenomenon is particularly frequent when the lexeme contains a liquid, especially /r/, nasals, and gutturals. Examples include:

- በርሀ *barha* 'to shine' as opposed to Central Semitic **bhr* 'to be pure, white, to shine'.
- ረምሰሰ *ramsasa* and አረምሰሰ *ʾaramsasa* (CG) 'to grope, feel the way' besides መርሰሰ *marsasa* and አመርሰሰ *ʾamarsasa* (CG); cf. Central Semitic **mss* 'to grope'.
- ሐቀፈ *ḥaqafa* 'to hug, embrace' as opposed to Semitic **ḥb/pq*.
- ፈኀረ *faḥara* 'to engage' as opposed to West Semitic **ḥrp* (N) 'to be engaged'.
- ፈለጸ *falaṣa* 'to split, divide' as opposed to West Semitic **pṣl*.
- ምሕረ *məḥra* 'to show mercy' as opposed to Semitic **rḥm* (metathesis of all root radicals).
- መትከፍ(ት) *matkaf(t)* 'shoulder' as opposed to Central Semitic **katip*.[51]

---

[50] The consonant order /ts/, for example, is not changed to /st/ as in many other Semitic languages; /ts/ assimilates to /ss/ instead (§3.6.5.1.).

[51] It has been suggested that እግር *ʾagr* 'foot' is likewise the result of metathesis and that it is related to Central Semitic **rigl*, possibly through the development **rigl* > **ligr* > **ləgr* > **ʾəgr*. Voigt (1998) considers the development **ligr* > **ʾəgr* the result of metanalysis: **ligr* presumably was analyzed as *li-gr* (preposition **li–* + **gr*) and the metanalyzed element **gr* subsequently developed a prothetic syllable **ʾə–*. For a different etymology that derives the form from Afroasiatic **ʾi(n)gi/ur* 'foot', see SED I: 9 (Nr.7).

3.6.5. Total Regressive Assimilation

3.6.5.1. The vowelless derivational morpheme /t/ that is added to *t*-verbal stems (Gt, Dt, Lt) regularly assimilates to a following dental, sibilant, or lateral in the imperfect and jussive (meaning to /t/, /ṭ/, /d/, /s/, /ṣ/, /z/, /ś/, and /ḍ/). The root consonant is thus dominant over the derivational morpheme. Examples include ይጠመቅ *yəṭṭammaq* < **yəttammaq* 'he will be baptized'; ይሰሞይ *yəssammay* < **yətsammay* 'he will be named'; ይጽዐን *yəṣṣəʕan* < **yətṣəʕan* 'he will ride'; ይዘከር *yəzzakkar* < **yətzakkar* 'he will be mentioned'; ይሠጠቅ *yəśśaṭṭaq* < **yətśaṭṭaq* 'he will be split' (all impf. Gt).

3.6.5.2. In a few cases, vowelless /d/ assimilates to the (nominal) feminine ending -*t*, as in ወለት *walatt* < **waladt* 'daughter' and አሐቲ *ʾaḥatti* < **ʾaḥadti* 'one' (fem.), although in general the sequence /*dt/ more frequently assimilates progressively to /dd/ [§3.6.6.1.].

3.6.5.3. In rare cases, and only in late texts, /n/ assimilates to certain stops, specifically to /g/, /k/, and /t/, as in አዕይቲ- *ʾaʕyə(t)ti-* instead of አዕይንቲ- *ʾaʕyənti-* 'eyes' (with pronominal suffix); እምድግል *ʾəm-də(g)gəl* instead of እምድንግል *ʾəm-dəngəl* 'from a virgin' (cf. DL: 99).

3.6.6. Total Progressive Assimilation

3.6.6.1. The feminine ending -*t* often assimilates to a preceding dental (/t/, /ṭ/, /d/). In these cases, the root consonant remains dominant (but cf. also §3.6.5.2.):

- /dd/ < /*dt/: ክብድ *kəbədd* < *kəbədt* (masc. ክቡድ *kəbud*) 'heavy, honored'; ባዕድ *bāʕadd* < **bāʕadt* 'other, different'; ትውልድ *təwlədd* < **təwlədt* 'generation';
- /ṭṭ/ < /*ṭt/: ስጥጥ *śəṭəṭṭ* < **śəṭəṭt* (masc. ስጡጥ *śəṭuṭ*) 'torn'.

3.6.6.2. Perfect suffixes containing /k/ assimilate their initial consonant to the last radical of a verbal root when the latter is a velar (/q/, /g/). Again, the root consonant dominates:

- /qq/ < /*qk/: ወደቁ *wadaqqu* < **wadaqku* 'I fell'
- /gg/ < /*gk/: ኀደግሙ *ḫadaggəmu* < **ḫadagkəmu* 'you (mp) abandoned, left'

3.6.7. Partial Assimilation

If a voiced consonant immediately precedes a voiceless consonant, it assimilates in voice in certain lexemes, that is, it becomes voiceless. This phenomenon is, for example, attested in the lexeme ኅብስት ḫəbəst < *ḫəbəzt 'bread' (pl. ኅባውዝ ḫabāwəz; cf. also ኀ/ኅብዝ ḫa/əbz 'bread').

3.7. Vocalic Sound Changes

3.7.1. Rules Concerning Gutturals

Vowels are subject to certain changes when they occur in proximity to gutturals. These changes can be described by the following six rules (cf. particularly Voigt 1983 and Diem 1988). The phenomena described under 1–4 are already attested in inscriptional material and require the early Ethiopic vowel system that distinguished between long and short vowels (§3.2.2.).

The most prevalent rules affecting vowels in the proximity of gutturals are the following (rules 1–3):

1. /a/ > /ā/ when it immediately precedes a syllable-closing guttural. Examples include: ሰማዕኩ samāʿku < *samaʿku 'I heard'; ባሕር bāḥr < *baḥr 'sea, ocean'; ማእመን māʾman < *maʾman 'faithful, believing' (besides ምእመን məʾəman); ማእከል māʾkal < *maʾkal 'middle'; ማእከለ māʾkala 'between'. An exception to this rule is /a/ after word-initial /ʾ/, as in አዕበየ ʾaʿbaya 'he made big', not **ʾāʿbaya (CG 3ms perf.). In the traditional pronunciation, /āʾ/ and /āʿ/ are articulated as /āʸ⁽ᵊ⁾/, as in māʾkala = [maʸkælæ]; /āh/, /āḥ/, and /āḫ/ are pronounced [āh(ᵊ)].[52]
2. /a/ > /ə/ before a guttural that is followed by a vowel other than /a/ or /ā/, meaning /a/ regressively assimilates in height to a following vowel. Examples include: ልሒቅ ləhiq < *lahiq 'old'; ልህቀ ləhqa < *lahəqa 'he grew old'; ተብህለ tabəhla < *tabahəla 'it was said'; ይምጽኡ yəmṣəʾu < *yəmṣaʾu 'let them come' (G 3mp juss.), as opposed to ይምጻእ yəmṣāʾ < *yəmṣaʾ 'let him come'. This rule does not operate across morpheme boundaries such as

---

[52] Leslau (CDG) and other authors therefore mostly transcribe syllable-closing gutturals with a following /ə/-vowel, as in ማእከለ māʾəkala 'between'. The transcriptions used in this grammar do not include this vowel and transcribe māʾkala instead.

those that separate prefixes from word bases, as in **ተእኅዘ** *taʾəḥza* 'he was taken' (not ****təʾəḥza*). /a/ in proclitic particles is equally not affected by this rule, as in **በእግር** *ba-ʾəgr* 'on foot' (not ****ba-ʾəgr*).

3. /ə/ > /a/ before a guttural followed by /a/ or /ā/ (= regressive vowel assimilation), as in **የዐርግ** *yaʿarrəg* < **yəʿarrəg* 'he ascends'. This rule does not operate across morpheme boundaries such as those that separate word bases from suffixes, as in **አባጎ** *ʾabāgə-a* 'sheep' (with suffixed acc.-marker), not ****ʾabāgaʿa*. However, the rule operates in prefixes of verbal forms, as shown in the first example.[53]

Besides these three basic rules, the following phenomena can be observed in connection with gutturals (rules 4–6):

4. /*a/ is generally reduced to /ə/ in open syllables when it precedes a guttural plus vowel, even if the vowel following the guttural is /a/ or /ā/ (cf. rule 2), as in **ነስሐ** *nassəḥa* < **nassaḥa* 'he repented' (but **ነሳሕነ** *nassāḥna* < **nassaḥna* 'we repented' according to §3.7.1:1); **አግብአ** *ʾagbəʾa* < **ʾagbaʾa* 'he brought back'; **አምጎ** *ʾamməḥā* < **ʾammaḥā* 'greeting'; cf. also **አንብዕ** *ʾanbəʿ* < **ʾanbaʿV* (form with case ending) 'tear' (§4.2.1.6.3:2).

5. Orthographically, /a/ can interchange with /ā/ after a guttural. This phenomenon is caused by the fact that /a/ and /ā/ are pronounced the same in the traditional pronunciation when they follow a guttural. This feature is not attested in early Classical Ethiopic inscriptions and is more frequent in later manuscripts than in earlier ones.

6. Because of the tendency not to pronounce /ʾ/ and /ʿ/, it is possible for the phoneme sequences /C–G*–a/ and /C–G*–ā/, where C = any consonant and G = /ʾ/ or /ʿ/, to orthographically interchange with the sequence /C–ā–G*/, that is, a guttural in original syllable-initial position can orthographically occur in syllable-closing position, as in **አሣእን** *ʾaśāʾn* 'shoes' for (correct) **አሥአን** *ʾaśʾān*. Both variants are pronounced [ʾasan]. Another example is **ሰባዕቱ** *sabāʿtu* 'seven' besides (correct) **ሰብዐቱ** *sabʿatu*, which are both pronounced [säbatu].

---

[53] Rules 2 and 3 could also be formulated as a single rule: vowels followed by a guttural assimilate in height to the vowel following the guttural. In the case of rule 2, the vowel /a/ is raised, while it is lowered in rule 3. The underlying process of vowel height assimilation is the same in both cases.

The guttural rules 1–3 assume that guttural consonants were not pronounced as geminated at an early period of Ethiopic (§3.3.1.).[54] If a guttural is indeed pronounced as geminated in rare cases, another rule applies, as in ይዋዕል yəwāʿʿəl < *yəwaʿʿəl 'he passes the day' (G impf.), or the vowels remain unchanged, as in ይመህር yəmahhər besides ይምህር yəməhər < *yəmahər 'let him teach' (juss. D).[55]

3.7.2. Vowel Changes in the Proximity of /w/ and /y/

Since /ə/ is pronounced [i] in the vicinity of /y/ (§3.2.3.), /i/ and /ə/ can be interchanged in this environment. The change /i/ > /ə/ before /y/ is particularly frequent in later texts, commonly in the following environments:

- Nominal forms with the derivational affix -ⴀዊ -āwi in combination with the plural endings -ān and -āt exhibit the forms -ⴀዊያን -āwiyān/ -ⴀዊያት -āwiyāt besides -ⴀዉያን -āwəyān/-ⴀዉያት -āwəyāt.

- Before the pronominal suffix of the 1cs -ይ -ya, nouns in the nom./gen. sporadically have /i/ instead of expected /ə/, as in አምላኪየ ʾamlākiya 'o my Lord' (Jub. 1:19).

- Similarly, the ending –i– used before pronominal suffixes on nouns in the pl. often occurs as /ə/ before the suffix -ይ -ya, as in አበዉየ ʾabawəya (besides አበዊየ ʾabawiya) 'my forefathers' (§4.2.4.5.2.).

- The adverb ዝየ zəya 'here' also occurs as ዚየ ziya. The same occurs with ህየ həyya, which also occurs as ሂየ hiyya 'there'.

- Infinitives of III-y roots in the G-stem have a form ብኪይ bakiy besides ብከይ bakəy.

- Infinitives of II-y roots in the G-stem exhibit the same phenomenon as roots III-y, as in ሠዪጥ śayiṭ besides ሠይጥ śayəṭ. By analogy, roots II-w sometimes exhibit the same vowel alternation, as in ቀዊም qawim besides ቀዉም qawəm (root qwm).

---

[54] A number of scholars (e.g., Lambdin 1978) differ in this point and transcribe ይልህቅ yələhhəq instead of yələhəq. If this is correct, rules 2 and 3 should also be valid for geminated gutturals.

[55] The lenition and loss of gutturals occurred to different degrees in different areas. Tigre and Tigrinya, for example, preserve the pharyngeals /ʿ/ and /ḥ/, whereas other Ethiopian languages such as Amharic lost these phonemes.

For vowel changes that are caused by the vocalic realization of the semivowels /w/ and /y/ see §3.8.2. below. For the interchangeability of /wə/ and /u/ see §3.8.2.3.

3.7.3. Shortening of Vowels in Closed Syllables

In closed syllables (synchronically mostly doubly-closed syllables involving the fem. ending -t) original long vowels are commonly shortened. Concerning individual vowels we can notice the following developments:

- /u/ is commonly shortened to /ə/, as in ክብርት kəbərt (< *kəbur-tV) 'honored' (fem. sing.), with the masc. form ክቡር kəbur;
- /i/ is often, but less frequently than /u/, reduced to /ə/, as in ልህቅት ləhaqt < *ləhiq-tV) 'old' (fem. sing.); እግዝእት ʾəgzəʾt 'lady' with the masc. እግዚእ ʾəgziʾ 'lord';
- /ā/ either does not undergo any changes or it becomes /a/, as in ሠነይት śannayt (besides ሠናይት śannāyt) 'beautiful' (fem. sing.); ሰማንቱ samāntu and ሰመንቱ samantu 'eight'.[56]

In the corresponding masculine forms of the patterns *qət(t)ul and *qat(t)il, which are singly closed, /u/ and /i/ are not shortened. The second syllable in these forms was historically open since nouns originally ended in a case vowel in the nom./gen., that is *qət(t)ul-u/i. Note the acc. kəbura that still preserves the case vowel.

The original vowels /u/ and /i/ do not reappear in forms of words in which they have been shortened when the syllable structure is changed by adding a vocalic inflectional ending or suffix, as in ልህቅት ləhaqta 'the old woman' (acc.), from ልህቅት ləhaqt (nom./gen.).[57]

---

[56] /ā/ is also preserved in forms such as ዛቲ zātti 'this' (fem. sing.), ባቲ bātti 'in her', and ላቲ lātti 'for her' (although the gemination of /t/ in these forms is most likely secondary).

[57] There are a few lexemes in which /a/ in synchronically doubly-closed syllables alternates with /ə/, as in ኀ/ኅብዝ ḫa/əbz 'bread', ማኅለ/ልቅት māḫla/əqt 'end', and እጕ/ጕልት ʾagʷa/əlt 'calf'. These variations primarily reflect morphological, not phonological variants, that is, they are based on different nominal patterns, namely *qitl versus *qatl and *maqtal versus *maqtil respectively.

3.7.4. Vowel Shortening Motivated by Dissimilatory Tendencies

Expected /i/ is commonly reduced to /ə/ before another syllable containing /i/, that is, two /i/-vowels in consecutive syllables are dissimilated:

- **መዛርዕኪ** *mazārəʿəki* 'your (fem. sing.) arms' < **mazārəʿi-ki*[58]
- **ትነግረኒ** *tənaggərənni* 'you (fem. sing.) speak to me' < **tənaggəri–nni* (G 2fs impf.)
- **ሀበኒ** *habənni* 'give (fem. sing) to me' < **habi–nni* (G fem. sing. impv. **whb*)

3.7.5. Change of /*ia/ > /e/

The vowel sequence /*ia/ has regularly been monophthongized to /e/ in Classical Ethiopic. This phenomenon is primarily noticeable in nouns ending in –*i* that have an acc. and construct state in –*e*, as in **bəʾəsi-a* 'man' (acc.) > **ብእሰ** *bəʾese* and **ṣaḥāfi-a* 'scribe' (acc.) > **ጸሐፈ** *ṣaḥāfe*.

3.8. Sound Changes Involving Semivowels

As mentioned in §3.2.2., the Proto-Semitic diphthong /*aw/ was regularly contracted to /o/ in nouns in Classical Ethiopic, as in **ዮም** *yom* 'today' < **yawm* and **ሞት** *mot* < **mawt* 'death', whereas Proto-Semitic /*ay/ was often, but not always, contracted to /e/, as in **ቤት** *bet* 'house' < **bayt* versus **ዐይን** *ʿayn* 'eye'. As these examples show, contraction and preservation occur in the same phonological environments. For the behavior of these diphthongs in verbs, see §3.8.2.4.

3.8.1. Loss of Word-Initial /y/ and /w/

Since /yə/ and /wə/ in word-initial position are pronounced as [(ʾ)i] and [(ʾ)u] respectively (§3.1.7.6.), initial /y/ and /w/ have been lost in some words. A development of this type underlies the lexeme **እድ** *ʾəd* 'hand', which is derived from a basic form **yad* through the process **yad* > **yid* > **(i)id* > **ʾid* (where /ʾ/ is a prothetic consonant) > *ʾəd*.

---

[58] /ə/ instead of /i/ also regularly occurs before the 1cs suffix –**ይ** –*ya*, as in **መዛርዕይ** *mazārəʿəya* 'my arms' (§4.2.4.5.2.).

3.8.2. Vocalic Realizations of Semivowels

3.8.2.1. The semivowels /w/ and /y/ can be realized as vowels in certain environments. In these cases, /w/ alternates with /u/ and /o/-vowels and /y/ with /i/ and /e/. The various changes can be described as follows:

/w/ in proximity to /ə/ alternates with /u/	/wə/, /əw/ = /u/
/w/ in proximity to /a/ alternates with /o/	/aw(a)/, /wa/ = /o/
/y/ in proximity to /ə/ alternates with /i/	/yə/, /əy/ = /i/
/y/ in proximity to /a/ alternates with /e/	/ay(a)/, /ya/ = /e/

The following paragraphs treat these changes in more detail and provide examples.

3.8.2.2. /i/ and /əy/ on the one hand and /u/ and /əw/ on the other are phonologically equivalent and can alternate with each other. The respective differentiations are purely of an orthographic nature, since /ə/ is (generally) pronounced [i] before /y/ and as [u] before /w/ (§3.2.3.).[59] This phenomenon is primarily attested in roots III-w/y (§4.4.5.8.; §4.4.5.9.).

- Verbal forms without suffixes primarily exhibit the vocalic variants, as in ይተሉ yətallu 'he will follow' and ይሰቲ yəsatti 'he will drink'. Before vocalic suffixes, Classical Ethiopic only exhibits the variants with consonantal /w/ and /y/, as in ይተልዉ yətalləwu 'they (masc. pl.) will drink' (pronounced [yətälluwu]) and ይሰትዮ yəsattəyyo 'he will drink it (masc. sing.)' (pronounced [yəsättiyyo]). Also note ርእኩ rəʾiku < *rəʾəyku 'I saw' where the suffix has an initial consonant.
- When nominal forms are voweless, they tend to have the variant with a preserved semivowel; as in ለያልይ layāləy 'nights' (and many other broken plural formations of this type) and ዐለዉ ʿələw 'evil, bad'. When

---

[59] In the traditional pronunciation, /əy/ is pronounced as [iy] and /əw/ as [uw]. In general, /i/ stands for [ii] and /u/ for [uu]. Furthermore, [ii] and [iy] on the one hand and [uu] and [uw] on the other are phonologically equivalent.

the feminine ending is attached, these forms primarily exhibit the vocalic variant, as in ዕሉት ʿəlut < *ʿəlawt 'evil, bad' (fem. sing.) and ብሊት bəlit < *bələyt < *bəluyt 'old'. The phoneme sequence /əyt/ can also be preserved, as in ላሕይት lāḥəyt (besides ላሒት lāḥit) 'beautiful' (masc. ላሕይ lāḥəy) and ድዉይት dəwwəyt 'sick, weak' (masc. ድዉይ/ድዉይ dəwwəy/dəwuy).

- The same phenomenon can be observed in certain word formations of roots I-w/y, as in ሙላድ mulād < *məwlād 'place of birth' (root *wld).

3.8.2.3. /wə/ and /u/ as well as /yə/ and /i/ are phonologically equivalent and can alternate.

The developments /wə/ > /u/ and /yə/ > /i/ are attested in jussive forms of roots II-w/y, as in ይቁም yəqum < *yəqwəm 'let him stand' and ይኪድ yəkid < *yəkyəd 'let him tread (down)'.

The development /u/ > /wə/ is attested in several *qətul-formations of roots II-w, such as ሞውት məwwət besides ሞዉት məwut 'dead' (pl. ሞውታን/ሙታን məwwətān/mutān); ድዉይ dəwwəy besides ድዉይ dəwuy 'sick'.[60] Cf. also ሀጕል/ሀጉል həgʷəl/həgul 'destroyed'.

The independent personal pronouns ውእቱ wəʾətu (masc. sing) and ይእቲ ʾyəʾəti (fem. sing.) probably go back to *(h)uʾatu and *(h)iʾati respectively.

3.8.2.4. Furthermore, /aw/ and /o/ as well as /ay/ and /e/ can alternate (note that the vowels /o/ and /e/ are always derived from /aw/ and /ay/ respectively [§3.2.2.]).

In verbal forms of roots III-w/y that do not have a suffix, /o/ can occur for word-final /aw/, as in ይትረኈው/ይትረኆ yətraḫ(ḫ)aw/yətraḫ(ḫ)o 'it will open'; ይሕየው/ይሕዮ yəḥyaw/yəḥyo 'let him live' (§4.4.5.8.1b), while /ay/ is usually preserved in this environment. Verbal forms with suffixes that have an initial consonant behave in a similar manner in that /o/ frequently occurs instead of /aw/, as in ተለውኩ/ተሎኩ talawku/taloku 'I followed', while /e/ only rarely appears instead of /ay/ (e.g., most often በከይከ bakayka 'you [masc. sing.] wept').

---

[60] CDG assumes a base with geminated /w/ for all of these forms, that is, məwwut and dəwwut.

Nouns prefer the vocalic variant, as in ፍሬ *fəre* < *fəray 'fruit'.

3.8.2.5. The syllable /wa/ can contract to /o/ and /ya/ to /e/, as in ፍቶት *fətot* (besides ፍትወት *fətwat*) 'desire', ይሐር *yəḥor* < *yəḥwar 'let him go' (G juss.), አቆመ *ʔaqoma* < *ʔaqwama 'he caused to rise' (CG perf.), አሤመ *ʔaśema* (besides አሥየመ *ʔaśyama* [§4.4.5.7.]) 'to cause to set, set in order' (CG perf.), ምስየት/ምሴት *məsyat/məset* 'evening' (§4.2.1.2:2).

This phenomenon particularly occurs in connection with labiovelars, which often have forms alternating between /ʷa/ and /o/, as in ኈልቆቶሙ *ḫʷalləqotomu*, which has a variant ኆልቆቶሙ *ḫolləqotomu* 'to count them', and ሰኵት *sakʷat* with the biform ሰኮት *sakot* 'street'.

3.8.2.6. The change of /awa/ to /o/ is attested in the verb ሀለወ/ሀሎ *hallawa/hallo* 'to be' (§4.4.5.8.3.), and perhaps in the perfect of roots II-w, such as ቆመ *qoma* < *qawama 'he rose'. A change of /aya/ to /e/ might underlie the perfect of II-y roots, as in ሤመ *śema* < *śayama 'he put'. Alternatively, the long vowel in these II-w/y roots might come from *qoma* < *qawma < *qawama and *śema* < *śayma < *śayama.

3.8.2.7. /ay/ can sometimes alternate with /əy/ = /i/ and even with /ey/. The jussive of ሰረየ *saraya* 'to forgive', for example, has the biforms ይስረይ *yəsray* and ይስሪ *yəsri* (< *yəsrəy). The plural of ፍሬ *fəre* 'fruit' has the variant forms ፍሬያት *fəreyāt* and ፍርያት *fərəyāt* (but not **farayāt).

3.8.2.8. Word-final /āy/ is sometimes reduced to /ā/ in words III-y, as in ዕዳ *ʕədā* < *ʕədāy 'debt'.[61]

---

[61] For the derivation of this noun from the verbal root *ʕdy, see Leslau (CGD).

4. Morphology

4.1. Pronouns

4.1.1. Independent Personal Pronouns

	Singular			Plural		
1c	አነ	ʾana	'I'	ንሕነ	nəḥna	'we'
2m	አንተ	ʾanta	'you'	አንትሙ	ʾantámu	(trad. ʾanttəmu[62]) 'you'
2f	አንቲ	ʾanti	'you'	አንትን	ʾantán	(trad. ʾanttən) 'you'
3m	ውእቱ	wəʾətu	'he'	እሙንቱ	ʾəmuntú[63],	
				ውእቶሙ	wəʾətomu 'they'	
3f	ይእቲ	yəʾəti	'she'	እማንቱ	ʾəmāntú, ውእቶን	
				wəʾətón 'they'		

These pronouns are stressed on the penultima unless indicated otherwise. The 1cs pronoun has the form ʾanə- before enclitic –ሰ –ssa (§4.5.8.7.), that is, አንሰ ʾanəssa 'but I'.[64] The 3ms and 3fs pronouns have different forms in the accusative, namely ውእተ wəʾəta and ይእተ yəʾəta respectively.

4.1.2. Pronominal Suffixes

4.1.2.1. The following introduces the full or long form of the pronominal suffixes. If not otherwise indicated, these suffixes are not accented.

---

[62] Cf. §3.3.2.1. The form of the 2mp is transcribed as ʾantəmmu in the older secondary literature (and in Weninger 1993, 13). This transcription does not conform to the traditional pronunciation.

[63] Leslau (CDG) transcribes the forms of the 3p as ʾəmmuntu and ʾəmmāntu, contrary to Mittwoch (1926, 47).

[64] Leslau (CDG 26a) provides the transcription ʾan-sa.

	Singular	Plural
1c	–የ –ya, –ኒ –ni (on verb only)	–ነ –na
2m	–ከ –ka	–ከሙ –kə́mu (trad. –kkə́mu[65])
2f	–ኪ –ki	–ክን –kə́n (trad. –k(k)ə́n)
3m	–ሁ –hú	–ሆሙ –hómu
3f	–ሃ –h'ā	–ሆን –hón

These full or long forms of the pronominal suffixes are attached to nouns that end in a historical long vowel, that is, after /–ā–/, /–e–/, /–o–/, and /–i–/, as in ሥጋሁ śəgāhu 'his flesh', እምኔሁ ʔəmənnehu 'from him', ዲቤሃ dibehā 'on her', ታሕቴሆሙ tāḥtehomu 'below them', and ጸሓፊሁ ṣaḥāfehu 'his scribe (acc.)' (for prepositions with pronominal suffixes, see §4.5.2.4.1.).

They are further attached to plural nouns when their stem ends in a consonant. In this case, the vowel /i/ is attached between the nominal stem and the suffix (§4.2.4.5.1.), as in ነገሥቲሆሙ nagaśtihomu 'their kings' (from ነገሥት nagaśt 'kings') and እዘኒሃ ʔəzanihā 'her ears' (from እዘን ʔəzan 'ears'). The connecting vowel is usually /ə/ instead of /i/ before a 1cs suffix, as in እዘንየ ʔəzanəya 'my ears'.[66] Before the suffix of the 2fs, both /i/ and /ə/ occur, as in እዘኒ/ንኪ ʔəzani/əki 'your (fs) ears'.

4.1.2.2. Nouns in the singular that end in a consonant take a different set of pronominal suffixes that distinguishes an accusative and non-accusative form:[67]

Singular	Nom./Gen.	Accusative
1c	–ብየ –əya[68]	–ብየ –əya
2m	–ብከ –əka	–ብከ –aka

---

[65] Cf. §3.3.2.1.

[66] Especially older manuscripts exhibit forms with /i/ as a linking vowel, as in አበዊየ ʔabawiya 'my forefathers'.

[67] The form of the pronouns written in Ethiopian script assume a noun ending in the letter /b/.

[68] In rare cases the 1cs appears as –iya (§3.7.2.).

2f	–ስኪ. –əki	–ስኪ. –aki
3m	–ሁ –ú (< *-əhu)	–ሶ –ó (< *-ahu)
3f	–ሃ –'ā (< *-əhā)	–ሃ –'ā (< *-ahā)
Plural		
1c	–ሰን –əna	–ሰን –ana
2m	–ስከሙ –əkə́mu	–ስከሙ –akə́mu
2f	–ስክን –əkə́n	–ስክን –akə́n
3m	–ሶሙ –ómu (< *-əhomu)	–ሶሙ –ómu (< *-ahomu)
3f	–ሶን –ón (< *-əhon)	–ሶን –ón (< *-ahon)

These suffixes have a linking vowel /ə/ or /a/ before the actual suffixes. The two vowels go back to the original case vowels – the nom./gen. in the case of /ə/ (< /*u/ and /*i/ respectively), which were lost, and the preserved acc. vowel /a/ – and are distributed according to their case-marking properties. The 1cs is an exception since it has the linking vowel /ə/ in both the acc. and non-acc. The linking vowels bear the stress, as in **ሀገርየ** *hagarə́ya* 'my city' etc., except when otherwise indicated.

The third person forms have lost the original /h/ of the suffix, which resulted in various vowel contractions, as in **ንጉሡ** *naguśu* '(of) his king' (nom./gen.) versus **ንጉሦ** *naguśo* 'his king' (acc.). For further remarks concerning the form of the noun before pronominal suffixes, see §4.2.4.5. below.

4.1.2.3. Finite verbal forms take the following object suffixes:

	Singular	Plural
1c	–(ን)ኒ –(an)ni	–(ን)ን –(an)na
2m	–(ን)ከ –(ak)ka	–(ን)ከሙ –(ak)kəmu
2f	–(ን)ኪ. –(ak)ki	–(ን)ክን –(ak)kən
3m	–ሁ -hu, –ሶ -o,	–ሆሙ –homu,
	–(ን)ዎ –(əw)wo,	–(ን)ዎሙ –(əw)womu,
	–(ን)ዮ –(əy)yo	–(ን)ዮሙ –əy)yomu
3f	–ሃ -hā, ሃ -ā,	–ሆን –hon,
	–(ን)ዋ –(əw)wā,	–(ን)ዎን –(əw)won,
	–(ን)ያ –(əy)yā	–(ን)ዮን –(əy)yon

A few forms have to be pointed out: (a) the form -(ብ)ኒ -(an)ni for the 1cs on verbs, as opposed to -ya used with nouns; (b) the variety of forms in the third persons, which is dependent on whether the finite verbal form ends in a consonant, original short, or long vowel, and (c) the gemination of the initial consonant of the suffix in the first and second person forms after the connecting vowel /a/. For a more detailed discussion of the forms and their use, see §4.4.2. below.

When an object suffix of the third person is attached to the suffix of the 1cs, the resulting forms are -ኒዮ -niyo, -ኒያ -niyā, -ኒዮሙ -niyomu, -ኒዮን -niyon, as in ሀበኒያ habanniyā 'give it (f.) to me'. The /h/ of the original third person suffix thus palatalizes into the glide /y/.

4.1.3. Forms of the Emphasized Personal Pronoun

The independent forms ለሊ- lalli- and ኪያ- kiyā-, in combination with a pronominal suffix, serve to express an emphasized personal or suffixed pronoun. The form ለሊ- lalli- + pronominal suffix is either used to express the subject or stands in apposition to the subject (§5.1.3.1.), while ኪያ- kiyā- + pronominal suffix most commonly expresses the direct object (§5.1.3.2.).

4.1.3.1. The subject pronoun ለሊ- lalli- (ለለ lallə- before the suffix of the 1cs) is formed through the repetition of the preposition ለ- la- 'to, for' (the basic form is *lalla, see §5.6.). The following forms with pronominal suffixes are attested:

	Singular	Plural
1c	ለለየ lalləya	ለሊነ lallina
2m	ለሊከ lallika	ለሊከሙ lallikəmu
2f	ለሊኪ lalliki	ለሊክን lallikən
3m	ለሊሁ lallihu	ለሊሆሙ lallihomu
3f	ለሊሃ lallihā	ለሊሆን lallihon

According to the traditional pronunciation, the initial /l/ is geminated after the conjunction ወ- wa- and after ዘ- za-, as in ወለሊሁ wallallihu (this grammar, however, transcribes wa-lallihu). The basic translation value for ለሊሁ lallihu is 'he himself, he alone'.

4.1.3.2. The lexeme ኪያ– *kiyā*– has the following forms with pronominal suffixes:[69]

	Singular	Plural
1c	ኪያየ *kiyāya*	ኪያን *kiyāna*
2m	ኪያከ *kiyāka*	ኪያክሙ *kiyākəmu*
2f	ኪያኪ *kiyāki*	ኪያክን *kiyākən*
3m	ኪያሁ *kiyāhu*	ኪያሆሙ *kiyāhomu*
3f	ኪያሃ *kiyāhā*	ኪያሆን *kiyāhon*

The basic translation value of ኪያሁ *kiyāhu* is 'him, the very same'.

4.1.4. Demonstrative Pronouns and Related Expressions

Classical Ethiopic has several paradigms of demonstrative pronouns. Semantically, these paradigms distinguish between demonstrative pronouns expressing near deixis ('this') and those expressing remote deixis ('that', 'that... yonder').

4.1.4.1. The paradigm expressing 'this' (paradigm I) has the following forms, all of which are stressed on the ultima:

Near deixis Paradigm I

Masc. sing	Fem. sing.	Masc. pl.	Fem. pl.
ዝ– *zə*– (acc. ዘ– *za*–)	ዛ– *zā*– (= acc.)	እሉ *ʾəllu*	እላ *ʾəllā*

The forms of the singular are used proclitically, in fewer cases enclitically, and form an orthographic unit with the following or preceding word (§2.6.1.), as in ዝብእሲ *zə-bəʾsi* 'this man', ዝኮነ *zə-kona* 'this happened', and ለዝ፡ መጽሐፍ *la-zə mashaf* 'this writing (acc.)' (Dan 5:16), በዝ፡ ቤት *ba-zə bet* 'in this house',

---

[69] The lexeme ኪያ– *kiyā*– is possibly a combination of *ka*– (as preposition, cf. Gəʿəz ከመ *kama* 'as, like' and Central Semitic *ka/ki* with the same meaning) and the *nota accusativi* *ʾiyā* (cf. Arabic *ʾiyyā* and Hebrew *ʾet*).

ውስተዝ፡ ዓለም wəsta-zə ʿālam 'in this world', ገበርከዝ gabarka-zə 'you did this', and
ወእምድኅረዝ፡ ሕግ wa-ʾəm-dəḫra-zə ḥəgg 'according to this law' (Jub 50:1).

4.1.4.2. Classical Ethiopic has a second paradigm that expresses near deixis
(paradigm II), which consists of longer, independent forms. In the accusative,
these forms are stressed on the penultima, while in all other forms they are
stressed on the ultima:

Near deixis Paradigm II

Masc. sing.	Fem. sing.	Masc. pl.	Fem. pl.
ዝንቱ zəntú	ዛቲ zāttí	እሎንቱ ʾəllontú	እላንቱ ʾəllāntú
(acc. ዘንተ zánta)	(acc. ዛተ z′ātta)	(acc. እሎንተ ʾəllónta)	(acc. እላንተ ʾəll′ānta)

4.1.4.3. Remote deixis ('that', 'that ... yonder', 'that ... there') is likewise expressed
by more than one paradigm. The first paradigm has the following forms, which
are stressed on the ultima unless they appear in the accusative, in which case
they are stressed on the penultima.

Remote deixis paradigm I

Masc. sing.	Fem. sing.	Com. pl.
ዝኩ zə(k)kú	እንትኩ ʾənta(k)kú	እልኩ ʾəllə(k)kú
(acc. ዝኰ zá(k)kʷa)[70]	(acc. እንትኰ ʾəntá(k)kʷa), እንትኩ ʾənta(k)kú	

4.1.4.4. The same semantic range of remote deixis is further expressed by the
following forms (paradigm II), which represent morphologically expanded forms.
As in the other paradigm, stress is on the ultima except in the accusative, where
it is on the penultima.

---

[70] According to the traditional pronunciation, the /k/ is geminated in all forms (ዝኩ zəkku,
ዝኰ zəkkʷa etc.); see Mittwoch 1926, 45. The gemination in the form of the masc. sing. might
be original from a historical perspective since it is likely derived from *zənku (cf. ዝንቱ zəntu).

Remote deixis paradigm II

Masc. sing.	Fem. sing.	Masc. pl.	Fem. pl.
ዝክቱ zəktú (acc. ዝክተ zə́kta)	እንታክቲ ʾəntāktí (acc. እንታክተ ʾəntākta)	እልክቱ ʾəlləktú (acc. እልክተ ʾəllə́kta)	እላክቱ ʾəllāktú (acc. እላክተ ʾəllˈākta)
ዝኵቱ zəkʷtú (acc. ዝኵተ zə́kʷta)		እልኵቱ ʾəlləkʷtú (acc. እልኵተ ʾəllə́kʷta)	

4.1.4.5. The (anaphoric) personal pronouns of the third persons, 3ms ውእቱ wəʾatu (acc. ውእተ wəʾata), 3fs ይእቲ yəʾati (acc. ይእተ yəʾata), 3mp እሙንቱ ʾəmuntu, and 3fp እማንቱ ʾəmāntu are also frequently used as demonstratives. In most cases, they connote remote deixis 'that', as in በውእቱ፡ መዋዕል ba-wəʾatu mawāʿəl 'in those days', ውእተ/ይእተ፡ ጊዜ wəʾata/yəʾata gize 'at that time' (with adverbial accusative).

4.1.4.6. The connotation 'such, such as, like this' is expressed periphrastically by the relative phrase ዘከመዝ za-kama-zə; as in ወትቤ፡ እፎኑ፡ ዘከመዝ፡ አምኃ wa-təbe ʾəffo-nu za-kama-zə ʾamməḫā 'and she pondered what sort of greeting this might be' (Lk 1:29). The feminine equivalent is እንተ፡ ከመ፡ ዛቲ ʾənta kama zātti, the plural has the form እለ፡ ከመዝ ʾəlla kama-zə or ዘከመ፡ እለ za-kama ʾəlla.

4.1.4.7. Classical Ethiopic does not have a definite article, unlike Central Semitic languages such as Arabic, Aramaic, and Canaanite. In order to mark a noun as definite, Classical Ethiopic uses certain periphrastic constructions (§5.2.2.).

4.1.5. Determinative and Relative Pronouns

Classical Ethiopic uses the following morphemes in the function of determinative ('the one of') and relative pronouns:

Masc. sing.	Fem. sing.	Com. pl.
ዘ– za–	እንተ ʾənta (also ዘ– za–)	እለ ʾəlla

These pronouns do not bear stress. The masc. sing. form ዘ– za– is always written together with the following word.

The lexeme ዘ- za- (masc. sing.) is, from both a formal and etymological perspective, the accusative of the demonstrative pronoun ዝ- zə- 'this' (§4.1.4.1.). It can be used for all genders and numbers, that is, the masc. sing., fem. sing., masc. pl. and fem. pl. This use of ዘ- za- as a form neutral with respect to gender and number is relatively frequent.

When ዘ- za- is emphasized, it has the form ዘውእቱ za-wə'ətu 'that is to say, namely'. The word ዘዘ- zazza-, formed through the repetition of the relative pronoun ዘ- za-, has a distributive function (for examples, see §5.6.5.).

4.1.6. Independent Possessive Pronouns

The relative pronoun with pronominal suffixes functions as an independent possessive pronoun with the meaning 'his, her, its, of his/hers' etc. In this use, the base of the relative pronoun is followed by the linking morpheme –$i'a$– and the construction as a whole has to follow a noun in the construct state (see §5.1.2. for examples). In cases in which the possessive pronoun does not follow a noun in the construct state, the relative pronoun ዘ- za- has to be prefixed, that is ዘዚአሁ za-zi'ahu etc.

The base forms of the independent possessive pronouns are:

Masc. sing.	Fem. sing.	Com. pl.
ዚአ- zi'a-	እንቲአ- 'anti'a-	እሊአ- 'alli'a-

The attachment of pronominal suffixes results in the following forms:

	ዚአ- zi'a-	እንቲአ- 'anti'a-	እሊአ- 'alli'a-
1cs	ዚአየ zi'aya	እንቲአየ 'anti'aya	እሊአየ 'alli'aya
2ms	ዚአከ zi'aka	እንቲአከ 'anti'aka	እሊአከ 'alli'aka
2fs	ዚአኪ zi'aki	እንቲአኪ 'anti'aki	እሊአኪ 'alli'aki
3ms	ዚአሁ zi'ahu	እንቲአሁ 'anti'ahu	እሊአሁ 'alli'ahu
3fs	ዚአሃ zi'ahā	እንቲአሃ 'anti'ahā	እሊአሃ 'alli'ahā
Etc.			

4.1.7. Interrogative Pronouns

4.1.7.1. The common substantivally used interrogative pronouns are:

'who?'	'what?'
መኑ *mannú*	ምንት *mánt*
Pl. also እለ ፡ መኑ *ʾəlla mannu*	
acc. መነ *mánna* 'whom?'	acc. ምንተ *mánta*

The interrogative pronoun መኑ *mannu* is neutral with respect to gender and number and can consequently be used for more than one person, as in መኑ ፡ አንትሙ *mannu ʾantəmu* 'who are you (pl.)?'. In some cases, the plural can be expressed by a periphrastic construction involving the relative pronoun እለ ፡ መኑ *ʾəlla mannu*.

The interrogative ምንት *mənt* can also refer to classes of people, as in ምንትኑ ፡ ውእቱ ፡ ዝንቱ *məntə-nu wəʾətu zəntu* 'who (lit. 'what') is this?' (Lk 5:21), or, in the accusative, for 'why', as in ምንትኑ ፡ ወፃእክሙ ፡ ገዳም ፡ ትርኣዩ *məntə-nu waḍāʾkəmu gadāma tərʾayu* 'why did you (mp) go out into the wilderness?' (Lk 7:24) (lit. 'what did you go out into the wilderness to see?').

The interrogative pronouns መኑ *mannu* and ምንት *mənt* can also be used in combination with prepositions. In the case of ምንት *mənt*, this combination results in specific adverbial expressions (§4.5.1.7b). Examples include:

- ለመኑ *la-mannu* 'for whom?'; ኀበ ፡ መኑ *ḫaba mannu* 'to whom?'; እምኀበ ፡ መኑ *ʾəm-ḫaba mannu* 'from whom?'; በእንተ ፡ መኑ *ba-ʾənta mannu* 'because of whom?, for whose sake?'.
- በምንት *ba-mənt* 'in what way, why?'; ለምንት *la-mənt* 'why?'; በእንተ ፡ ምንት *ba-ʾənta-mənt* 'why?'; እስከ ፡ ምንት *ʾəska mənt* 'how long?'; ከመ ፡ ምንትኑ *kama məntə-nu* 'how much?'.

4.1.7.2. Besides ምንት *mənt*, the proclitic lexeme ሚ– *mi–* functions as an interrogative pronoun for inanimate and abstract references ('what?'). This particle is only rarely used and primarily occurs in specific semantic contexts, as in:

- ሚሊተ ፡ ወለከ *mi-lita wa-laka* 'what have I to do with you?'

- **ሚላዕሌነ** *mi-lāʿlena* 'what is that to us?' (Mt 27:4)
- **ሚሀለወክሙ፡ትግበሩ** *mi-hallawakkəmu təgbaru* 'what will you do (then)?' (En 101:2)

The particle **ሚ**- *mi*- is further used as an interjection with the meaning 'how (much)!', as in **ሚአዳም** *mi-ʾaddām* 'how pleasant!' (§4.5.7.3.) and is used to form interrogative adverbs (§4.5.1.7a) and the conjunction **ሚመ** *mimma* 'or' (§4.5.3.1c).

4.1.7.3. The adjectival interrogative pronoun 'which?, what?, what kind?' is **አይ** *ʾay* (acc. **አየ** *ʾaya*; pl. **አያት** *ʾayāt*; acc. pl. **አያተ** *ʾayāta*).[71]

4.1.7.4. The interrogative pronoun **ምንት** *mənt* and other interrogative words are often extended by the enclitic question particle **-ኑ** *-nu* or, less often, **-ሁ** *-hu* (§4.5.9.1.), as in **ምንተኑ፡ርእየ** *mənta-nu rəʾya* 'what did he see?'.[72] The interrogative pronoun **መኑ** *mannu* is not extended in this way since it already contains the particle **-ኑ** *-nu* in its basic form.

4.1.8. Indefinite Pronouns and Related Forms

4.1.8.1. Classical Ethiopic primarily uses the aforementioned interrogative pronouns extended by the enclitics **-ሂ** *-hi*, **-ኒ** *-ni* (§4.5.8.4.) or, in negated form, by the negative particle **ኢ**- *ʾi*-, as indefinite pronouns. The following forms should be noted:

Not negated	**መኑሂ** *mannu-hi*, **መኑኒ** *mannu-ni*	'anyone'
	ምንትሂ *mənta-hi*, **ምንትኒ** *mənta-ni*	'any, anything, whatever'
	አይሂ *ʾay-hi*, **አይኒ** *ʾay-ni*	'whichever, whoever, whatever'
Negated	**ኢመኑሂ/ኒ** *ʾi-mannu-hi/-ni*	'no one'
	ኢምንትሂ/ኒ *ʾi-mənta-hi/-ni*	'nothing, not any'

---

[71] This form is stressed on the ultima *ʾayātá* according to Mittwoch (1926, 46).

[72] The form of **ምንት** *mənt* before enclitics is pronounced *mənta*-, as in **ምንተኑ** *mənta-nu* and **ምንትሂ** *mənta-hi*.

4.1.8.2. In order to express an indefinite pronoun referring to human beings, Classical Ethiopic also uses the lexeme እገሌ *ʾəgale* (fem. እገሊት *ʾəgalit*) 'so-and-so, such-and-such, a certain (person)', and, with the adjectival Nisbe-ending, እገሌያዊ *ʾəgaleyāwi* 'so-and-so, a certain (place)'.

4.1.8.3. Lastly, the lexeme ኵል- *kʷəll-* with the (substantival) basic meaning 'totality, entirety' can be used as an indefinite pronoun referring to inanimate entities.[73] In combination with pronominal suffixes, ኵል- *kʷəll-* can express 'each, every, all' (§5.1.9.1.). It either occurs independently, as in ኵልን *kʷəlləna* 'all of us', ኵሎሙ *kʷəllomu* 'all of them', ኵሎ *kʷəllo* 'all (acc.)', or, with a third person suffix, before (less often after) another noun, as in ኵሉ፡ ብእሲ *kʷəllu baʾəsi* or ብእሲ፡ ኵሉ *baʾəsi kʷəllu* 'every man, each man' and ኵሎሙ፡ ኃጥኣን *kʷəllomu ḫāṭəʾān* 'all sinners'.

The noun ኵለንታ *kʷəllantā* 'totality, entirety' is used similarly to ኵል- *kʷəll-* (§5.1.9.2.).

4.2. The Noun

The following description includes both substantives and adjectives since adjectives behave in the same manner as substantives from a morphological point of view. Numerals, which are also nouns, will be discussed separately (§4.3.). The various nominal patterns attested in Classical Ethiopic are listed in §4.2.1. Nominal inflection in Classical Ethiopic exhibits four categories: gender, number, case, and state (§§4.2.2.–4.2.5.).

4.2.1. Nominal Patterns

Nouns and adjectives do not differ significantly with regard to the way they are formed. There are, however, quite a few patterns that are primarily or exclusively used for adjectives. These patterns include *qətul (= verbal adjective to G), *qəttul (= verbal adjective to D), *qutul (= verbal adjective to L), *qatil and *qattil, *qātəl, *qattāl, as well as formations with the suffixes –āwi and –āy – the so-called Nisbe-endings.

---

[73] According to the traditional pronunciation, the lexeme is pronounced with simple /l/, that is, *kʷəl–*; see Mittwoch 1926, 18.

The following overview categorizes and exemplifies the most important nominal formations of Classical Ethiopic. Patterns with a triradical base are illustrated with the paradigmatic root q-t-l (*qatala* 'he killed'), as in **qətl*, **qatl* etc. For biradical roots, the list employs the root letters q-t and q-t-q-t for reduplicated roots. Patterns that are formally feminine are marked by "f." and are discussed together with their corresponding masculine forms. Occasionally, related plural formations are mentioned as well. A formation is considered "strong" when it does not contain any phonological peculiarities or irregularities.

4.2.1.1. Patterns of Roots with Less Than Three Radicals

4.2.1.1.1. Formally biradical formations:

*qət   እድ *ʾəd* hand'; ስም *səm* 'name'; cf. also እኁ *ʾəḫʷ*, እኃው *ʾəḫaw* (pl. አኀው *ʾaḫaw*) 'brother'.
         f. እኅት *ʾəḫt* (pl. አኃት *ʾaḫāt*) 'sister'.

*qat   አብ *ʾab* (pl. አበው *ʾabaw*) 'father'; ሐም *ḥam* (pl. አሕማው *ʾaḥmāw*) 'father-in-law, son-in-law' (√ḥmw); አፍ *ʾaf* (pl. አፈው *ʾafaw*) 'mouth'; ደም *dam* 'blood'.
         f. ሐማት *ḥamāt* 'mother-in-law, daughter-in-law' (√ḥmw).

Most of these nouns exhibit irregularities in their inflection in that they tend to be treated like roots III-*w*.

4.2.1.1.2. Formally identical with the patterns **qət* and **qat* are certain nominal forms derived from roots I-*w* that do not have any reflex of the first radical. Feminine nouns of this type end in either -*t* or -*at*:

*qət   ለድ *ləd* 'son, child' (√wld).
         f. ለደት *lədat* 'birth' (√wld); ዕለት *ʿəlat* 'day, time' (√wʿl); ድቀት *daqat* 'fall, ruin, downfall' (√wdq); ርስት *rəst* 'inheritance' (√wrs); ጥንት *ṭənt* 'beginning' (√wṭn).

*qat f.   ፀአት *ḍaʾat* 'exit, going out, departure' (√wḍʾ); ሀብት *habt* 'gift' (√whb).

4.2.1.1.3. Nouns with two radicals and a long /ā/-vowel formally look like the lengthened variant of nouns of the pattern **qat*. They are, however, contracted forms of triradical roots II-*w/y* and are derived from the triradical pattern **qatal*.

*qāl (from original *qawal or *qayal)

ዓም ʿām 'year' (√ʿwm); ቃል qāl 'voice' (√qwl).

f. ዓመት ʿāmat 'year, epoch' (√ʿwm).

4.2.1.2. Triradical Patterns Consisting of One Syllable

1 *qatl   Nouns of this pattern are commonly isolated or primary nouns or verbal nouns related to the G-stem. For the feminine, this pattern has the forms *qatəlt, *qatalt, and *qətəlt.

strong   አብድ ʾabd 'fool'; አድግ ʾadg 'donkey'; በድን badn 'corpse'; ገብር gabr 'slave, servant'; ከልብ kalb 'dog'; ከርሥ karś 'belly, stomach'; መርሕ marḥ 'leader'; ነፍስ nafs 'soul'; ቀትል qatl 'killing, slaughter'; ረድእ radʾ 'helper, assistant'; ጸብእ ṣabʾ 'battle, war'; ተክል takl 'plant'; ተምር tamr 'date, date palm'; ወልድ wald 'son'; ወርኅ warḫ 'moon'; ወርቅ warq 'gold'.

f. *qatəlt: አብድ ʾabədd 'fool' (fem. of አብድ ʾabd; see §3.6.6.1.); አንስት ʾanəst 'woman, wife', አድግት/እድግት ʾadəgt/ʾədəgt 'she-ass'.

f. *qatalt: አረፍት ʾaraft 'wall'; ዐዘቅት ʿazaqt 'cistern, well'; ወለት walatt 'daughter' (see §3.6.5.2.); ተመርት tamart 'date(palm)'.

gem.   ገጽ gaṣṣ 'face'; ነድ nadd 'flame'.

f. ገነት gannat 'garden, paradise'.

II-gutt.   ባሕር bāḥr 'sea'; ካሕድ kāḥd 'lack of faith, heresy'; ላህብ lāhb 'flame'; ላህም lāhm 'ox, bull'; ማእስ/ዐስ māʾs/ʿs 'skin, leather'; ሥህል śāhl 'grace, compassion'; ሥእን śāʾn 'shoe, sandal'; ሥዕር śāʿr[74] 'herb, grass'; ራእይ rāʾ(ə)y 'vision'; ወዕይ wāʿ(ə)y 'heat'.

f. ሥዕርት śəʿərt < *śaʿərt (§3.7.1:2) 'hair'.

III-gutt.   f. *qatalt: ገራህት garāht (§3.7.1:1) 'field'.

II-w   ሞት mot 'death'; ዮም yom 'today'; ቆም qom 'stature, height'; ዖፍ ʿof 'bird'; ሶር sor 'ox, bull'. With preserved diphthong: ዘውግ zawg 'pair' (Arabic or Aramaic loanword).

f. ኆኅት ḫoḫət 'door, gate'.

---

[74] According to the tradition also śāʿr.

II-y   ቤት *bet* 'house'; ሤጥ *śeṭ* 'price, value'; ኄር *ḫer* 'good' (adj.). With preserved diphthong: ዐይን *ʿayn* 'eye'; ገይስ *gays* 'journey'; ሐይቅ *ḥayq* 'shore'; ኃይል *ḫayl* 'strength, might'; ሰይፍ *sayf* 'sword' (Arabic loanword); ወይን *wayn* 'wine, vine' (loanword).

III-w   በድው *badw* 'desert, wasteland'; ላሕ *lāḥ* (shortened from **lāḥw < *laḥw*) 'mourning, grief'.

        f. ሰኰት/ሰኮት *sakʷat/sakot* 'street' (cf. §3.8.2.5.).

III-y   ራእይ *rāʔ(ə)y* 'vision'; ዋዕይ *wāʿ(ə)y* 'heat'.

2 *qətl*   This category consists of primary nouns and verbal nouns of the G-stem. The feminine of this pattern primarily has the form *qətlat* and serves as a verbal noun of the G-stem. The plural is always formed by *–āt*. Classical Ethiopic *qətl* is most frequently derived from common Semitic **qitl* or **qutl*, less frequently from **qatl* (e.g., እብን *ʔəbn* 'stone'; እልፍ *ʔəlf* '1000, 10,000'; ርእስ *rəʔ(ə)s* 'head').[75]

strong   እብን *ʔəbn* 'stone'; እጐል *ʔəgʷl* 'the young of any animal or fowl'; እግር *ʔəgr* 'foot' (§3.6.4.2.); ክብር *kəbr* 'glory'; ምስል *məsl* 'likeness, image'; ንስር *nəsr* 'eagle'; ርእስ *rəʔs* 'head'.

        Verbal nouns (always with the plural *-āt*): ፍቅር *fəqr* 'love'; ንግሥ *nəgś* 'rule, reign'; ዝክር *zəkr* 'record, memory', ግብር *gəbr* 'affair, matter, thing'.

        f. Verbal nouns: ብትከት *bətkat* 'fracture, breaking'; ግብረት *gəbrat* 'work, working'; ፍልሰት *fəlsat* 'exile'; ፍጥረት *fəṭrat* 'act of creation, creation'; ግዝአት *gəzʔat* 'dominion, ownership'; ንብረት *nəbrat* 'sitting down, dwelling'; ርክበት *rəkbat* 'discovery, finding'; ስብከት *səbkat* 'preaching, sermon'; ስግደት *səgdat* 'worship'; ጥምቀት *ṭəmqat* 'baptism'.

gem.   ሕግ *ḥəgg* 'law'; ልብ *ləbb* 'heart'; ስን *sənn* 'tooth'.

        f. ንደት *nəddat* 'flame, fever'; ሥጠት *śəṭṭat* 'tearing, tear'.

II-w   ኑኅ *nuḫ* 'length'.

        f. ዑደት *ʿudat* 'circle, turn'; ሑረት *ḥurat* 'course, walking'; ኑኀት *nuḫat* 'length'; ቈመት *qumat* 'standing, size, condition'; ሩጸት *ruṣat* 'running, run'; ሡዐት *śuʿat* 'act of sacrificing'.

II-y   ቢጽ *biṣ* 'individual, fellow, friend'.

---

[75] Dolgopolsky (1999, 95) considers these lexemes to be derived from the Proto Semitic forms **ʔabun*, **ʔalup*, and **raʔiš* because of the irregular corresponding forms in Classical Ethiopic.

f. ሚጠት *miṭat* 'turning, return'; ቂሕት *qiḥat* 'redness'.

III-w   f. ፍትወት/ፍቶት *fǝtwat/fǝtot* 'desire, wish' (cf. §3.8.2.5.); ፍኖት *fǝnot* 'way, path'.

III-y   ሥን *śǝn* (< *śǝny) 'beauty, charm'.

f. ምስየት/ምሴት *mǝsyat/mǝset* 'evening, twilight' (cf. §3.8.2.5.); ንድየት/ ንዴት *nǝdyat/nǝdet* 'poverty, want'; ቅንየት/ቅኔት *qǝnyat/qǝnet* 'domination, servitude'; ርእየት *rǝ'yat* 'appearance, vision'; ውዕየት *wǝ'yat* 'burning, burn'.

II+III-w/-y f. ሕይወት *ḥǝywat* 'life, lifetime'.

Note: Nouns I-w do not exhibit the pattern *qǝtl* but a form *qǝt, that is, the first root letter /w/ is not reflected in this nominal form (cf. §4.2.1.1.2.).
The pattern *qǝtl frequently appears in free variation with *qatl, as in ረምሕ/ርምሕ *ramḥ/rǝmḥ* 'spear' and ኈልቍ/ኈልቍ *ḫʷǝlqʷ/ḫʷalqʷ* 'number'.

4.2.1.3. Triradical Patterns Consisting of Two Syllables

1 *qǝtal   This pattern serves as a verbal noun of the G-stem and is especially frequent for abstract nouns denoting quantities.[76] It is derived from both original *qital and *qutal.

strong   እከይ *'ǝkay* 'evil thing, malice'; ዐበይ *'ǝbay* 'greatness'; ጠበብ *ṭǝbab* 'wisdom'; ይበስ *yǝbas* 'dryness', ግዘፍ *gǝzaf* 'thickness', ዐመቅ *'ǝmaq* 'depth'.
f. ዐረፍት *'ǝraft* 'rest, peace'; ገረምት *gǝramt* 'terror, dread'.

II-gutt.   ከሓድ *kaḥad* 'lack of faith, heresy' (cf. §3.7.1:3); ሠሐቅ *śaḥaq* 'laughter'.

III-y   ፍሬ *fǝre* 'fruit'; ርሔ *rǝḥe* 'perfume, odor'; ስቴ *sǝte* 'drink, beverage'; but also compare verbal nouns III-y that are treated as strong, such as *'ǝkay* 'evil thing, malice'; ዐበይ *'ǝbay* 'greatness'.

2 *qǝtāl   This pattern is primarily used for nouns, including verbal nouns of the G-stem, and is rare for adjectives. In some cases, the pattern reflects a diminutive connotation. The plural is formed with –āt. Classical Ethiopic *qǝtāl is derived from Semitic *qitāl and *qutāl.

strong   ዐራቅ *'ǝrāq* 'emptiness, nakedness'; ብካይ *bǝkāy* 'weeping, lamentation'; ድካም *dǝkām* 'weakness, exhaustion'; ሐዳጥ *ḥǝdāṭ* 'a small amount'; ክሳድ

---

[76] Fox 2003, 214.

ከሳድ *kəsād* 'neck'; ክታብ *kətāb* 'writing, book'; ንባብ *nəbāb* 'speech'; ንዳድ *nədād* 'fever'; ንዋይ *nəwāy* 'vessel'; ሥራይ *śarāy* 'incantation, medicine'; ትካት *təkāt* 'antiquity, ancient times'; ዝናም *zənām* 'rain'.

Diminutive: ሕፃን *ḥəḍān* 'child', እጓል *ʾəgʷāl* 'the young of any animal, child'; ጎዳጥ *ḫədāṭ* 'small amount'.

Adjectives: ሕያው *ḥəyāw* 'living, alive'; ጥራይ *ṭarāy* 'raw, crude'.

f. እጐ/ጐልት *ʾəgʷa/əlt* 'calf, heifer'.

II-gutt.   ረዓም/ርዓም *raʿām/rəʿām* 'shouting, thunder clap'.

Adjective: ረኃጽ *raḫāṣ* 'tender, delicate'.

III-y   ዕዳ *ʿədā* (< *ʿədāy) 'debt, compensation'. Compare also the strong formation ብካይ *bəkāy* 'weeping, lamentation'.

3 *qətul This pattern is primarily used for adjectives, specifically verbal adjectives of the G-stem, and, less often, for nouns. As a verbal adjective, it has the semantic range expected for verbal adjectives based on the basic meaning of the root, that is, primarily passive for transitive verbs, descriptive for stative verbs, and resultative for intransitive verbs. The feminine has the form qətəlt (§3.7.3.). The fem. pl. is *qətulāt or, less often, *qətəltāt.

strong   ሕዙን *ḥəzun* 'sad'; ክቡር *kəbur* 'honored'; ንኡስ *nəʾus* 'small'; ንቡር *nəbur* 'sitting, seated'; ርቡብ *rəbub* 'stretched out, expanded'; ስቁል *səqul* 'hung up, crucified'; ስሩር *sərur* 'flying'; ጽዱቅ *ṣəduq* 'true, sincere, honest'; ጽኑዕ *ṣənuʿ* 'strong, mighty'; ትሑት *təḥut* 'low, lowered, humble'; ጥሙቅ *ṭəmuq* 'baptized' (from C); see also ሀጉል *həgul* and (more frequently) ህጒል *həgʷəl* 'lost, destroyed'.

Nouns: ብሩር *bərur* 'silver, money' (cf. በረ *barra* 'to purify, make white'); ንጉሥ *nəguś* 'king'.

f. ንግሥት *nəgəst* 'queen'.

III-dental: ከቡድ *kəbud* (f. ክብድ *kəbədd* [§3.6.6.1.]) 'heavy'; ሥጡጥ *śaṭuṭ* (f. ሥጥጥ *śaṭaṭṭ*) 'torn'.

II-w   ድዊይ/ድውይ *dawuy/dəwwəy* (f. ድውይት *dəwwəyt*) 'sick'; ምዊት/ምውት *məwut/məwwət* (f. ምውት *məwwətt*, masc. pl. ምውታን *məwwətān* and ሙታን *mutān* < *məwutān) 'dead' (cf. §3.8.2.3.).

III-w   ዕለው *ʿələw* (f. ዕሉት *ʿəlut*) 'crooked, perverse, evil'. Noun: ዕድው *ʿədəw* 'enemy, adversary'.

III-*y*   ብሉይ *bəluy* (f. ብሊት *bəlit*) 'old'; ኅሩይ *ḫəruy* (f. ኅሪት *ḫərit*) 'chosen'; ውዑይ *wəʿuy* (f. ውዒት *wəʿit*) 'hot, burning'.

4 *qatal* This pattern is used for primary nouns and verbal nouns of the G-stem.

strong   በረድ *barad* 'hail, ice'; ፈረስ *faras* 'horse' (loanword); ገመል *gamal* 'camel'; ሀገር *hagar* 'city'; ሐመር *ḥamar* 'ship'; ዘነብ *zanab* 'tail'; ሐዘን *ḥazan* 'sadness, grief'; ቀበር *qabar* 'burial'; ሰገል *sagal* 'divination, magic'; ዘመድ *zamad* 'family, tribe'; ነገር *nagar* 'speech'.
          f. በረከት *barakat* 'blessing'.
Note: Roots II-*w/y* have contracted forms of the type *qāl*; see §4.2.1.1.3.

5 *qatāl* This pattern is used for primary nouns and verbal nouns of the G-stem. It also underlies the fem. of the adjectival pattern *qatil* (see no. 6 below), although in the traditional pronunciation, the fem. form is pronounced with geminated C_2, that is *qattāl*.

strong   በዓል *baʿāl* 'festival, feast'; ፈቃድ *faqād* 'wish, desire'; ነፋስ *nafās* 'wind'; ቀላይ *qalāy* 'ocean, abyss'; ረዓም *raʿām* 'shouting, thunderclap'; ሰላም *salām* 'peace'; ሰማይ *samāy* 'heaven' (often in pl. ሰማያት *samāyāt*); ፀሐይ *ḍaḥāy* 'sun'; ፀጋም *ḍagām* 'left hand, left'; የማን *yamān* 'right hand, right side'.

6 *qatil* This pattern has a variety of usages. It is common for verbal adjectives of the G-stem and their substantivized use, the perfective participle, the infinitive of the G-stem, and a few nouns.

(a)   Adjectives: In some cases, the distinction between *qatil* and *qattil* is difficult or debated. The feminine of *qatil* is, according to the traditional pronunciation, formed by the pattern *qattāl*, which also serves as the feminine of the pattern *qattil*. Originally, the feminine of *qatil* had the form *qatāl*, that is, the gemination of the second radical is secondary. The masc. pl. is most frequently expressed by *qattalt*,[77] less often by *qatalt* (broken plural formations), as in ዐበይት *ʿabbayt* 'big'; በላኅት *ballāḫt* 'sharp, quick'; ጠበብት *ṭabbabt* 'wise'. The regular plural formation *qatilān* sporadically occurs besides the broken plural pattern, as in ጠቢባን *ṭabibān* (besides ጠበብት *ṭabbabt*) 'wise ones', and ረሲዓን *rasiʿān* 'impious

---

[77] The gemination of the second radical is also likely to be a secondary development.

ones'. The fem. pl. is either *qatilāt*, based on the masc. sing., *qattālāt*, based on the fem. sing., or *qattalt* like the masc. pl.

strong   ዐቢይ *ʿabiy* (f. ዐባይ *ʿabbāy*) 'big'; ባሊኅ *baliḫ* (f. ባላኅ *ballāḫ*) 'sharp, quick'; ደቂቅ *daqiq* (f. ደቃቅ *daqqāq*) 'small, young, child'; መሪር *marir* (f. መራር *marrār*) 'bitter'; ነኪር *nakir* (f. ነካር *nakkār*) 'strange, foreign'; ነዊኅ *nawiḫ* (f. ነዋኅ *nawwāḫ*) 'long'; ረሲዕ *rasiʿ* (f. ረሳዕ *rassāʿ*) 'godless'; ጠቢብ *ṭabib* (f. ጠባብ *ṭabbāb*) 'wise'.[78]

II-gutt.   ልሒቅ *ləhiq* (cf. §3.7.1:2) (f. ልሒ/ህቅት *ləhi/əqt*) 'old' (cf. also ሊቅ *liq* < *ləhiq* 'elder, chief' [§3.6.2.1b]); ርሒብ *rəhib* (f. ረሐብ *raḥab*) 'broad, wide'; ስሒት *səhit* 'error, deceit'.

(b)   The perfective participle of the G-stem only occurs in combination with pronominal suffixes (§4.4.3.2.2.), as in the following example with 3ms suffixes:

ነጊሮ *nagiro* 'he, having said'; ቀቲሎ *qatilo* 'he, having killed'.

Note: The perfective participles of the derived stems have the forms *qattil-* (D); *qātil-* (L); *taqatil-* (Gt); *taqattil-* (Dt); *taqātil-* (Lt); *ʾaqtil-* (CG); *ʾaqattil-* (CD); *ʾaqātil-* (CL) and are discussed in §4.4.3.2.

(c)   Infinitive of the G-stem: *qatil(ot)* (§4.4.3.3.).

Note: The infinitives of the derived stems have the forms: *qattəlo(t)* (D); *qātəlo(t)* (L); *taqatəlo(t)* (Gt); *taqattəlo(t)* (Dt); *taqātəlo(t)* (Lt); *ʾaqtəlo(t)* (CG); *ʾaqattəlo(t)* (CD); *ʾaqātəlo(t)* (CL) and are discussed in §4.4.3.3.

(d)   Nouns (rare), as in አሚን *ʾamin* 'belief, faith'.

7 *qatul This pattern is used for ordinal numbers [§4.3.2.3.] and a few nouns.

እሑድ *ʾəhud* 'first, first day (of the week)'; ሠሉስ *śalus* 'third (day of the week)'.
Nouns: ሐጹር *ḥaṣur* 'fence, wall'.

8 *qātəl This pattern is used for verbal adjectives, substantivized verbal adjectives, ordinal numbers (§4.3.2.1.), and less often for nouns.

---

[78] Leslau (CDG) transliterates *ʿabiyy* (sic!), *balliḫ*, and *nawwiḫ*.

strong Adjectives: በዐድ *bāʿəd* (f. በዐድ *bāʿədd*) 'different, foreign'; በዐል *bāʿəl* 'rich';
ዳኅን *dāḫən* 'safe, sound, well'; ራትዕ *rātəʿ* 'straight, just'; ጻድቅ *ṣādəq* 'just,
righteous'; ዋሕድ *wāḥəd* 'unique, only'.
Substantivized adjectives: በዐል *bāʿəl*[79] 'lord, owner'; ኃጥእ *ḫāṭəʾ* 'sinner';
ራድእ *rādəʾ* 'helper'; ወርስ *wārəs* 'heir'.
Ordinals: ካልእ *kāləʾ* 'second, other, another'; ሣልስ *śāləs* 'third'; ራብዕ *rābəʿ*
'fourth'.
Nouns: ጋንን *gānən* 'demon, evil spirit'.
f. በዐልት *bāʿəlt* 'lady, mistress'.

9 **qātāl* This pattern serves as a verbal noun of the L-stem.

ጸማ *ṣāmā* (< **ṣāmāw*) 'toil, labor'.

10 **qutāl* This pattern likewise serves as a verbal noun of the L-stem, although it
occurs only rarely.

ሱታፍ *sutāf* 'companion, associate'.

11 **qutul* This pattern is the most frequent form of the verbal adjective associated
with the L-stem.

ቡሩክ *buruk* (f. ቡርክት *burəkt*) 'blessed'; ሙሱን *musun* (f. ሙስንት *musənt*)
'corrupt, spoilt'; ሱቱፍ *sutuf* 'companion, partner'.

4.2.1.4. Triradical Patterns with Gemination of the Second Radical

1 **qəttul* This pattern serves as a verbal adjective of the D-stem, less often of the
Dt. Multiplicative numbers are likewise formed with this pattern
(§4.3.5.). The feminine regularly has the form **qəttəlt*, as in ቅድስት *qəddəst*
'holy' (§3.7.3.). The distinction between **qəttul* and **qətul* can be difficult
in some cases.

---

[79] Because of the feminine form በዐልት *bāʿəlt*, it is unlikely that this noun has an underlying
pattern **qatl* (**bāʿl*) as commonly assumed.

strong   Verbal adjectives: እዙዝ ʾəzzuz 'commanded, ordered'; ፍሡሕ fəśśuḥ 'glad, joyful'; ፍጹም fəṣṣum 'accomplished, completed'; ቅዱስ qəddus 'holy'; ስቡሕ səbbuḥ 'praised, glorified'; ጥዩቅ ṭəyyuq 'certain, sure'.

   Multiplicative numbers: ሥሉስ śəllus 'threefold, triple'; ስቡዕ səbbuʿ 'sevenfold'.

II-w   ፍውስ fəwwəs (< *fəwwwus) 'healed, cured'.

III-w   ድልው dəlləw (f. ድሉት dəllut) 'fit, proper, ready'; ፍኑው fənnəw (f. ፍኑት fənnut) 'sent'; ምጡው məṭṭəw 'handed over, surrendered'.

III-y   እኩይ ʾəkkuy (f. እኪት ʾəkkit) 'evil' (related to G); ዕቡይ ʿəbbuy (f. ዕቢት ʿəbbit) 'proud, arrogant'; ሥኑይ śənnuy (f. ሥኒት śənnit) 'adorned'.

2 *qattəl Used for nouns and, rarely, adjectives; cf. also the D-infinitive **qattəlo(t).*

   ፈውስ fawwəs[80] 'healing, cure'; ሐድስ ḥaddəs 'excellent'.

3 *qattāl Used for adjectives, frequently including the verbal adjective of the D-stem, substantivized adjectives, and terms for professions. The feminine of this pattern either has the form **qatta/ālt* or is formally identical to the masculine.

strong   Adjectives: አዳም ʾaddām 'pleasant, pleasing'; በሃም bahām[81] 'mute, dumb'; ፈራህ farrāh 'fearful, coward'; ኃያል ḫayyāl 'strong, powerful'; ለሓይ laḥāy 'beautiful'; ነዳይ naddāy 'poor'; ነቋር naqqʷār 'one-eyed, cross-eyed'; ነዋኅ nawwāḫ 'long, high'; ቀዋም qawwām 'tall, high, erect'; ረዓድ raʿād 'trembling'; ሠናይ śannāy (f. ሠናይት śannāyt) 'beautiful'; ጸጓር ṣaggʷār 'hairy, shaggy'; ጸሃቅ ṣahāq 'longing'; የዋህ yawwāh 'gentle, innocent', ከዋው kawwāw 'energetic'.

   Nouns denoting professions and habitual actions: አጋር ʾaggār 'pedestrian'; በዓል baʿāl 'owner'; ገባር gabbār 'worker', መራሕ marrāḥ 'guide, leader'; ሰታይ sattāy 'drinker'.

   Other nouns: ዐራዝ ʿarrāz 'clothing, garment'.

Note: This pattern also serves to form the feminine of adjectives of the patterns **qatil* and **qattil* (§4.2.1.3:6; §4.2.1.4:4).

---

[80] Leslau (CDG) transcribes *faws.*

[81] The gemination of the second radical is absent in roots II-guttural (§3.3.1.).

4 *qattil This pattern is used for adjectives, most frequently related to the D-stem, and adjectives denoting colors. The feminine is most frequently irregularly formed as *qattāl, as in ሐዳስ ḥaddās f. of ሐዲስ ḥaddis 'new'. The normative masc. plural is *qattalt. The pattern *qattil is also used to express the perfective participle of the D-stem (§4.4.3.2.1.).

strong   ሐዲስ ḥaddis 'new'; ቀጢን qaṭṭin 'fine, thin'; ቀይሕ/ቀዪሕ qayyəḥ/qayyiḥ (f. ቀያሕ/ቀይሕት qayyāḥ/qayyəht) 'red'; ጸሊም ṣallim 'black, dark'.
Perfective participle of D: ሐዲሶ ḥaddiso 'he, having restored'.

4.2.1.5. Triradical Patterns with Suffixes

4.2.1.5.1. Patterns with suffixed -i (fem. -it; masc. pl. most often with the ending -əyān; fem. pl. -əyāt). The pattern *qatāli also has a broken plural *qatalt [§4.2.3.5:3]).

1 *qatāli This pattern serves to form agent nouns, most commonly of the G-stem. The agent noun denotes the one who performs the action of the verb, commonly habitually or professionally. The feminine has the form qatālit and can have an abstract or collective meaning. A number of lexemes form a broken plural *qatalt and/or *qattalt. [82]

strong   ፈታሒ fatāḥi 'judge'; ፈጣሪ faṭāri 'creator'; ገባኢ gabā'i 'hireling'; ሐላዪ ḥalāyi 'singer'; ሐዋሪ ḥawāri 'traveler'; መሐሪ maḥāri 'merciful, compassionate'; መዋኢ mawā'i 'victor, conqueror'; መዋቲ mawāti 'mortal, dead'; ቀዳሚ qadāmi 'first, previous, ancient' (§4.3.2.1.) (pl. ቀደምት qaddamt 'forefathers, ancients'); ረዳኢ radā'i 'helper'; ሠዋዒ śawā'i 'sacrificer, priest'; ሠያጢ śayāṭi 'merchant, seller'; ጸሐፊ ṣaḥāfi 'scribe'; ወዓሊ wa'āli 'guard, attendant'; ወላዲ walādi 'father'.
III-y   በካዪ bakāyi (with alternate form በካይ bakāy [§4.4.5.9.1.]) 'one who weeps'.
f. ወላዲት walādit 'mother'; ሐላይት ḥalāyt (< *ḥalāyit) 'singer (f.)'.
Collectives: በዋኢት bawā'it 'crowd of people entering'; ኃላፊት ḥalāfit 'people traveling or passing by, crowd'.

---

[82] For the side-by-side existence of both *qatalt and qattalt, see Mittwoch 1926, 29.

2 *qattāli Used for agent nouns of the D-stem (besides *maqattəl).

strong   አባሲ *ʾabbāsi* (pl. አባስያን *ʾabbāsəyān*) 'wicked, criminal'; ሐዋጺ *ḥawwāṣi*
'overseer, watchman'; ኰናኒ *kʷannāni* 'ruler, governor'; ነሳሒ *nassāḥi*
'penitent'; ዘማሪ *zammāri* 'musician, psalmist'.

3 *qātāli Used for agent nouns of the L-stem, sometimes also of the CL or Lt.

strong   ባላሒ *bālāḥi* 'liberator'; ናዛዚ *nāzāzi* 'consoler, comforter'; ሣራሪ *śārāri*
'founder'.

4 Other formations with suffixed *-i* (often comparable in meaning to the Nisbe
endings *-āwi* and *-āy* [§4.2.1.5.5.–6.].):

strong   ዐረቢ *ʿarabi* 'Arabian, Arabic' (cf. ዐረባዊ *ʿarabāwi*); ዐረቢ *ʿarabi* 'western' (cf.
ዐረባዊ *ʿarabāwi*); ብእሲ *bəʾəsi* 'man'; ተባዒ *tabāʿi* 'male, strong'; ተፍጻሚ
tafṣāmi 'last' (with prefix).
f. ባሕቲት *bāḥ(ə)tit* 'solitude'; ብእሲት *bəʾəsit* 'woman'; ትእልፊት *təʾəlfit* 'a
vast number, ten thousand' (with prefix).

4.2.1.5.2. Patterns with Suffixed *-e* (f. *-et*)

1 *qutāle Serves as a verbal noun of the L-stem and is also used to form collective
numbers (§4.3.6.1.).

strong   ቡራኬ *burāke* 'blessing'; ኩፋሌ *kufāle* 'partition, division' (መጽሐፈ ፡ ኩፋሌ
maṣḥafa kufāle 'Book of Jubilees'); ኑፋቄ *nufāqe* 'division, separation'; ኑዛዜ
nuzāze 'consolation, comfort'; ሱታፍ(ሬ *sutāf(e)* 'companion, partner';
ሡራሬ *śurāre* 'foundation, founding'.
f. ኑፋቄያት *nufāqeyāt* 'heresy' (formally pl.).

2 *qattāle with the variant *qəttale serves as a verbal noun, most frequently of the
D-stem and often has an abstract meaning. This pattern is also used to
form collective numbers (§4.3.6.1.).

strong   እኳቴ *ʾəkkʷāte* 'glorification' (related to CG); እማኄ *ʾəmmāḫe* 'greeting,
salutation'; እማሬ *ʾəmmāre* 'sign, indication'; ድማኔ *dəmmāne* 'darkness,
cloudy sky'; ፍካሬ *fəkkāre* 'interpretation, commentary'; ፍጻሜ *fəṣṣāme*

'completion'; **ፍዋሴ** *fawwāse* 'healing'; **ግማኔ** *gəmmāne* 'profanation, pollution'; **ህላዌ** *həllāwe* 'substance, essence, nature'; **ሕዳሴ** *həddāse* 'renewal, restoration'; **ሕዋጼ** *ḥəwwāṣe* 'watching, contemplation'; **ክዋኔ** *kəwwāne* 'being, existence, nature'; **ልባዌ** *ləbbāwe* 'intelligence, mind' (cf. **ልብ** *ləbb* 'heart' and **ለበወ** *labbawa* 'to understand'); **ንጻሬ** *nəṣṣāre* 'view, vision'; **ቅዳሴ** *qəddāse* 'sanctification, consecration'; **ይዋሄ** *yəwwāhe* 'gentleness, mildness'.

Variant **qəttale*: **ኵነኔ** *kʷənnane*[83] 'rule, domain, judgement'.

3 *qattale Used for abstracts. The pattern is generally rare.

  f. **አኰቴት** *ʾakkʷatet* 'praise, glorification' (cf. **አኳቴ** *ʾakkʷāte* 'glorification').

4 Other formations with –e and –et Used for abstracts.

strong **ትንሣኤ** *tənśāʾe* 'ascent, resurrection'.

  f. **ዐብሬት** *ʿəbret* 'sterility'; **ረድኤት** *radʾet* 'help, assistance'.

4.2.1.5.3. Formations with the Suffix -ā (f. -āt):

1 *qətlā and *qatlā These patterns are often used as verbal nouns of the G-stem, commonly with an abstract meaning. In the feminine, formations with -āt alternate with those in -at.

strong **ንፍቃ** *nəfqā* 'half, middle' (cf. **ንፍቅ** *nəfq* 'half').
II-gutt. **ዳኅና/ድኅና** *dāḫnā/dəḫnā* 'health, safety'.

  f. **ሐብላት** *ḥablāt* 'plaited work' (besides **ሐብለት** *ḥablat*); **ልህቃት** *ləhqāt* 'old age, mature age'; **ቅንያት** *qənyāt* 'servitude, slavery'.

2 *qatalā Most often used as a verbal noun of the G-stem with an abstract meaning. The distinction between **qatalā* and **qattalā* can be difficult.

strong **ሐተታ** *ḥatatā* 'searching, inquiry'; **ኀሠሣ** *ḫaśaśā* 'inquiry, request'. Other nouns: **ሐመዳ** *ḥamadā* 'snow, frost'; **ሰቀላ** *saqalā* 'tent, oblong house'.

---

[83] Leslau (CDG 287b) incorrectly gives the transliteration *kʷənnāne*.

3 *qattalā Used as a verbal noun of the D-stem with an abstract meaning. The distinction between *qatalā and *qattalā can be difficult.

strong አበሳ *ʾabbasā* 'sin, transgression'; ዐመፃ *ʿammaḍā* 'injustice, violence'; ደመና *dammanā* 'cloud'; መከራ *makkarā* 'trial, testing'; ቀበላ *qabbalā* 'meeting, encounter'.[84]

III-gutt. አምኃ *ʾamməḫā* (§3.7.1:4) 'salutation, greetings'.

III-w ጸጋ *ṣaggā* (< *ṣaggawā) 'grace, favor'.

4 *qattəlā Used as a verbal noun of the D-stem.

strong ፍሥሓ *fəśśəḥā* 'joy'; ምምዓ *məmmə'ā* 'anxiety, fear'; ንስሓ *nəssəḥā* 'penitence, repentance'; ጸውዓ *ṣəwwə'ā* 'call, invitation, summons'.

f. ቅድሳት *qəddəsāt* 'holiness, sanctuary'.

5 Other formations with suffixed –ā Used for abstracts.

strong አንስት/ቲያ *ʾanəstə/iyā* (from አንስት *ʾanəst* 'woman, wife') 'womenfolk, women'; ሳኒታ *sānitā* 'the next day' (cf. ሳንይ/ሳኒት *sānəy/sānit* 'the next day').

4.2.1.5.4. Formations with Suffixed –o (f. –ot)

1 *qətlo, *qatlo, and *qatalo These patterns are used as verbal nouns, primarily expressing products of crafts and similar connotations.

strong እንሞ *ʾənmo* 'texture, web'; ብስሎ *bəslo* 'cooked food'; ግልፎ *gəlfo* 'carved work, statue'; ከበሮ *kabaro* 'drum, timbrel'; ከረቦ *karabo* 'woven basket, pouch'; ስ/ሥብኮ *s/śəbko* 'casting, smelting'; ጸልቦ *ṣalbo* 'cross, gallows'.

2 *qatil(ot) (G), **qattəlo(t)* (D), **qātəlo(t)* (L), **ʾaqtəlo(t)* (CG), **ʾaqattəlo(t)* (CD); **ʾaqātəlo(t)* (CL); **taqatəlo(t)* (Gt), **taqattəlo(t)* (Dt), **taqātəlo(t)* (Lt), **ʾastaqatəlo(t)* (CGt), **ʾastaqattəlo(t)* (CDt), **ʾastaqātəlo(t)* (CLt). These forms reflect the infinitives of the indicated verbal stems [§4.4.3.3.1.]. Before pronominal suffixes, the form is –ot, without pronominal

---

[84] Leslau (CDG) transcribes *ʾabasā*, *ʿamaḍā*, and *makarā*, but *dammanā* and *qabbalā*.

suffixes it is –o. In the G-stem, the ending when no pronominal suffixes are attached is –∅.

strong አምልኮ(ት) *ʾaml⸱ko(t) 'cult, godliness' (of CG አምለከ *ʾamlaka); ናፍቆ(ት) nāfaqo(t) 'heresy' (of L ናፈቀ nāfaqa); ተበቅሎ(ት) tabaqq⸱lo(t) 'punishment, vengeance' (of Dt ተበቀለ tabaqqala).

3 Other formations with –o(t) often have abstract meanings. They can also include loanwords from Aramaic (Aramaic nouns ending in -ūt).

strong አሶት *ʾasot 'healing, gift' (loanword); ሃይማኖት hāymānot 'faith' (loanword); መለኮት malakot 'godhead, divinity'; መለኮት malakot 'lordship, kingdom' (loanword); ምልኮት m⸱lkot 'property, possession'.

4.2.1.5.5. (Nisbe-)Formations with Suffixed –āwi (f. –āwit)

The suffix –āwi indicates the state of "pertaining to" the base lexeme (Arabic: Nisba) and corresponds to English adjectives in –ly. It can theoretically be attached to any noun and creates adjectives out of base nouns. Formations with –āwi are also known from ordinal numbers (§4.3.2.2.). The suffix is declined as follows: fem. sing. –āwit; masc. pl. -āwiyān and –āw⸱yān; fem. pl. –āwiyāt and –āw⸱yāt (§3.7.2.).

strong አረጋዊ *ʾaragāwi 'old, old person'; ብርሃናዊ b⸱rhānāwi 'luminous, radiant'; ገባራዊ gabbārāwi 'workman, laborer'; ሀላዊ hallāwi (< *hallaw-āwi) 'essential, substantial' (cf. ሀሎ/ሀሉ hallawa/hallo 'he was'); ክብርታዊ k⸱b⸱rtāwi 'revered' (based on fem. adjective ክብርት k⸱b⸱rt); ምድራዊ m⸱drāwi 'earthly, worldly'; ሰማያዊ samāyāwi 'heavenly, divine'; ጻዱቃዊ ṣ⸱duqāwi 'who likes truth'; ወንጌላዊ wangelāwi 'evangelist'.
Numbers: ሣልሳዊ śāl⸱sāwi 'third'; ራብዓዊ rāb⸱ʿāwi 'fourth' (§4.3.2.2.).

4.2.1.5.6. (Nisbe-)Formation with Suffix –āy (f. –āyt, also –it)

The suffix –āy, just as the suffix –āwi, expresses (adjectival) belonging to a certain base lexeme. Forms with –āy, however, occur significantly less frequently than those with –āwi. Formations with –āy are also attested for ordinal numbers (§4.3.2.2.) and occur as free variants of formations with –āwi. The declination of –āy is as follows: fem. sing.

-āyt; masc. pl. -āyān; fem. pl. -āyāt. Ordinal numbers of the pattern *qātəlāy, however, take the ending –it, as in ⵘⵍⵙⵉⵜ śāləsit 'third'.

strong   ባዕላይ bāʿəlāy 'rich, wealthy'; ላዕላይ lāʿlāy 'upper'; ተባዕታይ tabāʿtāy 'male, masculine'; ታሕታይ tāḥtāy 'lower, inferior'. Numbers: ⵘⵍⵙⵉⵌ śāləsāy 'third'; ራብዓይ rābəʿāy 'fourth' (§4.3.2.2.).

4.2.1.5.7. Formations with Suffixed –ān

Used for abstracts, mostly of the pattern *qətlān.

strong   ዕርቃን ʿərqān 'nakedness'; ብርሃን bərhān 'light'; ፍልጣን fəlṭān 'separation, divorce'; ኪዳን kidān (< *kəydān) 'pact, covenant'; ልህቃን ləhqān 'seniority, old age'; ርሥአን rəśʾān 'old age'; ሥልጣን śəlṭān 'dominion, authority'.

4.2.1.5.8. Formations with Suffixed –(ən)nā (f. –(ən)nāt, rare)

This morpheme is an abstract marker for nouns of all types of patterns, although it is commonly found with patterns exhibited by the verbal adjectives *qətul, *qəttul, and *qutul. The second vowel in these patterns is typically reduced to /ə/ when the suffix is attached. Other base patterns can equally exhibit vowel reduction, as in ምስፍና məsfənnā < *masfənnā 'leadership, governance'. The gemination of /n/ in –ənnā might be secondary (§3.3.2.1.). When the ending is suffixed to verbal adjectives of III-w/y roots, the /n/ is not geminated, as in ጥዒና ṭəʿinā < *ṭəʿəy-nā 'health'.

(a)   Formations based on verbal adjectives
strong   ፍጽምና fəṣṣəmənnā 'perfection, integrity'; ቅድስና qəddəsənnā 'holiness, sanctity'; ጥይቅና ṭəyyəqənnā 'exactness, thoroughness'.
III-w   ህሉና həllunā 'essence' (ህሎው həlləw 'existing').
III-y   ዕሪና ʿərinā 'equality, agreement' (ዕሩይ ʿəruy 'equal'); ጥዒና ṭəʿinā 'health' (ጥዑይ ṭəʿuy 'healthy').
III-n   ሙስና/ሙሱና musənnā/musunnā 'spoiling, corruption' (ሙሱን musun 'corrupt, decayed').

(b)   Other formations

አብና ʾabənnā, አበውና ʾabawənnā 'paternity, fatherhood'; አምላክና ʾamlākənnā 'divinity, worship of God'; ግብርና gəbrənnā 'service, action'; ኅሊና ḫəllinā 'thinking, mind' (of ኅለየ ḫallaya 'to consider, think'); ክርስትና kərəstənnā 'Christianity'; ልህቅና ləhqənnā 'old age'; ምስፍና məsfənnā 'leadership, governance' (መስፍን masfən 'judge, governor'); ርሥእና rəśʾənnā 'old age'; ወልድና waldənnā 'sonship, filiation'; የውህና yawwəhənnā 'gentleness' (የዋህ yawwāh 'gentle, meek'); ዘለዓለምና za-la-ʿālamənnā 'eternal'.

f. ግብርናት gəbrənnāt 'service, servitude'; ርስዕናት rəśʿənnāt 'negligence, impiety'.[85]

4.2.1.5.9. Formations with Two or More Suffixes

Classical Ethiopic has word formations that exhibit two or more suffixes, e.g., ሐዋርያ ḥawārəyā 'traveler, messenger' (cf. ሐዋሪ ḥawāri 'traveler'); ኵለንታ kʷəllantā 'totality, entirety'; ኵለንታዊ kʷəllantāwi 'total' (cf. ኵል- kʷəll- 'all, every, each').

4.2.1.6. Triradical Patterns with Prefixes

4.2.1.6.1. Formations with Prefixed m–

1 *maqtal This pattern is used for nouns of place, nouns of instrument, and nouns of action (nomina actionis, with a wide range of meanings). Adjectives are not formed through this pattern.

strong መንበር manbar (pl. መናብርት manābərt) 'throne, seat'; (ቤተ፡)መንደድ (beta) mandad 'kitchen'; መንፈቅ manfaq 'half, faction'; መንፈስ manfas 'spirit'; መቅደስ maqdas 'temple, sanctuary'; መጽሐፍ maṣḥaf (pl. መጻሕፍት maṣāḥəft) 'book, writing'; መትከፍ(ት) matkaf(t) 'shoulder'; መትከል matkal 'peg, nail'.
f. መግረምት magramt 'terror'; መንበርት manbart 'state, condition'; መቅበርት maqbart 'grave, tomb'; መቅሠፍት maqśaft 'punishment, beating'; መሥገርት maśgart (pl. መሣግር maśāgər) 'snare, trap, net', መልአክ malʾak 'messenger, angel'.

---

[85] Leslau (CDG) transcribes gəbrənāt and rəśʿənnat.

I-gutt.   ማዕበል *māʿbal* 'wave, flood' (besides ማዕብል *māʿbəl*); ማኅለቅት *māḥlaqt* 'end, conclusion' (besides ማኅልቅት *māḥləqt*).

III-gutt. f. መጽያሕት *maṣyāḥt* 'beaten path, paved road'.

I-w   f. ሞዐልት *moʿalt* (< *mawʿalt*) 'day' (also መዓልት *maʿālt*).

II-w   መካን *makān* 'place'.

III-w   መርኆ *marḫo* (< *marḫaw*) (pl. መራኁት *marāḫut*) 'key'.

III-y   f. ማሕሌት *māḥlet* (< *maḥlayt*) 'song, hymn' (also I-gutt.).

2 *maqtəl (f. *maqtəlt*) This pattern is used to form agent nouns and nouns with meanings similar to *maqtal*.

(a)   Agent nouns of CG and G
       ማእምር *māʾmər* 'learned, wise man' (I-gutt.); መብከይ *mabkəy* 'mourner'; መፍርህ *mafrəh* 'fearful, frightening'; መምህር *mamhər* 'teacher'; መምክር *mamkər* (pl. መማክርት *mamākərt*) 'counselor'; መንክር *mankər* 'miracle, wonder'; መጥምቅ *maṭməq* 'who baptizes'.

(b)   Nouns with meanings similar to *maqtal*
       መትከል *matkəl* 'peg, nail'; መሥዕርት *maśʿərt* 'comb'.
       f. መንግሥት *mangəst* 'kingdom'; መልእክት *mal(ə)ʾəkt* 'letter, message'; መልዕልት *malʿəlt* 'upper part, height'; መልህቅት *malhəqt* 'eldest, senior, chief'; መንሱት *mansut* (< *mansəwt*) 'temptation, test' (cf. ነሰወ *nasawa* 'to try, tempt', denominative መንሰወ *mansawa* [quadriliteral]); መስኀንት *masḫənt* 'pot, oven'; መሥልስት *maśləst* 'triple, third rank'.

Note: The form of feminine nouns of this pattern can sporadically alternate between *maqtalt and *maqtəlt, as in ማኅለቅት *māḥlaqt* besides ማኅልቅት *māḥləqt* 'ceasing, end'.

3 *məqtāl (f. *məqtālt* [rare]; pl. most commonly *məqtālāt*.) This pattern is used for nouns of place, often with a semantic relation to the G-stem. Other usages are specialized and not easily derived from the basic verbal meaning.

strong   ምንባብ *mənbāb* 'place of reading, reading'; ምንባር *mənbār* 'seat, throne, abode'; ምንዳድ *məndād* 'fireplace, furnace'; ምስካብ *məskāb* 'couch, bed'; ምግባር *məgbār* 'action, deed'; ምርካብ *mərkāb* 'acquisition, pay'.

I-w   መ፡ላድ *mulād* (< *mawlād) 'birthplace, native land'.

4 *maqattāl Used for nouns of place and nouns of instrument, semantically related to the D-stem.

> ምእላድ *ma'allād* 'gathering place'; ምህላው *mahallāw* 'dwelling place'; ምኵናን *mak*ʷ*annān* 'court, judgement'; ምስዋር *masawwār* 'hiding place, hidden place'; ምጽላይ *maṣallāy* 'place of prayer, chapel'.

5 *maqattal Used for agent nouns, most frequently of D or CD-verbs. The pattern has a function similar to that of *qattāli.

> መፈውስ *mafawwas* 'physician, healer'; መገሥጽ *magaśśaṣ* 'teacher'; መሰግል *masaggal* 'magician, diviner'; መሠግር *maśaggar* 'fisherman'; መሠንይ *maśannay* 'beautiful, who does good'.

II-gutt.   መምህር *mam(a)har* 'teacher, instructor'.

6 *maqātal Often used for agent nouns of L-verbs and similar in function to *qātāli.

> መናፍቅ *manāfaq* 'heretic, hypocrite'; መናዘዝ *manāzaz* 'consoling, comforting'.

4.2.1.6.2. Formations with Prefixed *t-*

1 *taqtalt For verbal nouns, most often relating to the Dt or D.

> ትእምርት *ta'(a)mart* 'sign, signal'; ትዕቢት *ta'(a)bit* 'haughtiness, pride' (III-y); ትፍሥሕት *tafśaḥt* 'joy'; ትግብርት *tagbart* 'production, yield'; ትምህርት *tam(a)hart* 'teaching, study'; ትንቢት *tanbit* 'prophecy, oracle'; ትርሲት *tarsit* 'ornament, adornment'; ትስብእት *tasba't* 'assumption of human nature, human nature'; ትውልድ *tawladd* (< *tawladt) 'generation' (no relation to either Dt or D); ትዝምድ *tazmadd* (< *tazmadt) 'race, family, tribe'.

2 *taqtāl For verbal nouns, mostly relating to the Dt or D.

ተፍጻም *tafṣām* 'completion, ending'; ተግባር *tagbār* 'work, workmanship'; ተምሃር *tamhār* 'teaching, study'; ተምያን *tamyān* 'fraud, deceit'; ተስፋ *tasfā* (< *tasfāw) 'hope'; ተውዳስ *tawdās* 'praising'; ተውሳክ *tawsāk* 'addition, increase, supplement'.

I-gutt. ትእዛዝ *taʾazāz* (< *taʾzāz [§3.7.1:2]) 'commandment, decree'.

3 *taqattal Used for verbal nouns of the D or Dt (rare).

II-gutt. ተመሃር *tamahar* 'instruction, teaching'.

4.2.1.6.3. Formations with Prefixed ʾ– (rare in general)

1 *ʾaqtVl This pattern is not productive. The syllable ʾa– is primarily a prothetic syllable.

> እግዚእ *ʾagziʾ* 'master, lord' (ገዝአ *gazʾa* 'to dominate, master').
> f. እግዝእት *ʾagzaʾt* 'lady, mistress'.

2 *ʾaqtal This pattern is likewise not productive. It should not be interpreted as elative and is borrowed in some cases.

strong አንቀጽ *ʾanqaṣ* 'door, gate'; አዜብ *ʾazeb* 'south, south wind' (cf. Arabic *ʾazyab*); አዝማር *ʾazmar* 'purple, scarlet' (cf. Arabic *ʾasmar*).
III-gutt. አንብዕ *ʾanbaʿ* 'tear' (§3.7.1:4); አንጕዕ *ʾangʷaʿ* 'marrow'.
> f. አጽባዕት *ʾaṣbāʿt* 'finger' (√ṣbʿ).

4.2.1.6.4. Formations with the Prefix *masta*–

The prefix *masta*– consists of *ma*– plus the marker of the derivational stem *-st*– and is always related to *"asta"*-verbal stems.

1 *mastaq(a)tal Agent noun of CGt.

> መስተኃሥሥ *mastaḫaśaś* 'inventor, discoverer'; መስተስርይ/መስተስሪ *mastasray/mastasri* 'forgiving, asking for forgiveness'.

2 *mastaqātəl Agent noun of CLt.

መስተሣህል mastaśāhəl 'compassionate, merciful'.

3 *mastaqattəl Agent noun of CDt.

መስተዐግሥ mastaʿaggəś 'patient, ascetic'.

4.7.1.7. Triradical Formations with Prefixes and Suffixes

1 *ʾaqtalā Verbal noun of CG (rare).

አርአያ ʾarʾayā 'likeness, appearance'.

2 *ʾaqtāli Agent noun of CG (not very productive).

አግባሪ ʾagbāri 'causing to be done/performed'; አንባቢ ʾanbābi 'reader'.

3 *ʾaqātāli Agent noun of CL.

አማሳኒ ʾamāsāni 'destroyer'.

4 *ʾaqattāli Agent noun of CD.

አገባሪ ʾagabbāri 'cultivating land'.

5 *maqtali Agent noun of CG, same function as maqtəl.

strong   መድኃኒ madḫani 'redeemer, savior'; መፍቀሪ mafqari 'lover, friend'
          (መፍቃሬ፡ እግዚአብሔር mafqare ʾəgziʾab(ə)ḥer 'loving god').
I-gutt.   ማእመሪ māʾmari 'knower of, who possesses knowledge'; ማሕየዊ māḥyawi
          'life-giving, savior'; ማሕዘኒ māḥzani 'saddening, sorrowful'.

6 *maqtalit Verbal noun of CG and abstract of *maqtali.

መድኃኒት madḫanit 'salvation, deliverance' (cf. መድኃኒ madḫani 'savior').

7 *təqtāle Verbal noun of Gt.

ትንሣኤ *tənśāʾe* 'ascent, resurrection'.

8 *taqtālet Expansion of *taqtāl related to Dt or D.

ተፍጻሜት *tafṣāmet* 'completion, fulfillment' (cf. ተፍጻም *tafṣām*).

9 *taqātāli With nouns I-gutt. mostly *taqatāli. Agent noun of Lt.

ተሳላቂ *tasālāqi* 'making fun of, mocker'; ተአማሪ *taʾamāri* (I-gutt.) 'interpreter, soothsayer'; ተሐታቲ *taḥatāti* (I-gutt.) 'investigator, examiner'.

10 *taqattāli Agent noun of Dt and some abstract nouns.

ተገባሪ *tagabbāri* 'workman, farmer'; ተመሃሪ *tamahāri* 'disciple, student' (II-gutt.); ተነባዪ *tanabbāyi* 'who acts as prophet'. Abstract: ተሠዋዒ *taśawwāʿi* 'sacrifice, offering'.

11 *taqtəlot Verbal noun, same functions as taqtāl.

ተግብሮት *tagbərot* 'labor'.

12 *ʾastaqātāli Agent noun of CLt.

አስተጋባኢ *ʾastagābāʾi* 'who gathers, magician'; አስተላጸቂ *ʾastalāṣāqi* 'who unites'.

4.2.1.8. Quadriliteral Formations

Note: Quadriliteral roots can be categorized into four groups according to the following formal criteria:

1. Reduplicated roots of the type *q-t-q-t* (1–2–1–2) (= red. [reduplicated]);
2. Roots with /n/ or /r/ as the second radical (= II-*n/r*);
3. Roots with /y/ or /w/ as the second radical (= II-*y/w*);
4. Other roots (also including the reduplicated type *qtll* [1–2–3–3]).

1 *1ə23ə4 Primary nouns.

red.   ብድብድ *bədbəd* 'plague, pestilence'.

II-*n*   ድንግል *dəngəl* (pl. ደናግል *danāgəl*) 'virgin'; ቀንፍዝ *qʷənfəz* 'hedgehog';
         ቀንጽል *qʷənṣəl* 'fox, jackal'.

2 *1a23a4 Primary nouns.

red.   ሐዝሐዝ *ḥazḥaz* 'flint, swamp, pool'; ኮከብ *kokab* (< **kawkab* < **kab-kab*; pl.
         ከዋክብ *kawākəb*) 'star'; ቈልቈል *qʷalqʷal* 'slope'.

II-*n*   ሐንዘር *ḥanzar* 'pig'; ከንፈር *kanfar* 'lip, language'; ሰንሰል *sansal* 'chain'.

II-*r*   ሐርገጽ *ḥargaṣ* 'crocodile'.

IV-*y*   አርዌ *ʾarwe* (pl. አራ/ረዊት *ʾarā/awit*) 'wild animal, beast'; ሰርዌ *sarwe*
         'army, troops' (pl. ሰራዊት *sarāwit*, ስረ/ራው *səra/āw*).[86]

3 *1ə23ā4 Primary and verbal nouns.

II-*n*   ድንጋግ *dəngāg* 'edge, border, rim'; ግንፋል *gənfāl* 'brick'.

II-*y*, red. ሊላይ *lilāy* 'separation, distinction'; ሲሳይ *sisāy* 'food, nourishment'.

4 *1a23ā4 Verbal nouns.

red.   ከብካብ *kabkāb* 'wedding'.

II-*y*, red. ጌጋይ *gegāy* 'iniquity, sin'; ዜና *zenā* (< **zenāw*) 'report, narrative'.

others   ዐውያት *ʿawyāt* (from ዐውየወ *ʿawyawa* 'to moan, lament') 'wailing,
         lamentation'.

5 *1a23i4 Primary nouns.

red.   ሌሊት *lelit* (< **laylit*; pl. ለያልይ *layāləy*) 'night'; ለጽሊጽ *laṣliṣ* 'tongue of a
         scale'.

others   ከንፊፍ *kanfif* 'border, limit' (cf. ከንፍ *kənf* 'wing, border').

6 *1ə23u4 Verbal adjectives, also substantivized.

red.   ድግዱግ *dəgdug* 'meager, thin'; ለምሉም *ləmlum* 'soft, tender'.

---

[86] Alternatively, these could be triradical **qatle*– formations.

II-n   ድንጉፅ *dəngud* 'frightened, dismayed'; ምንዱብ *məndub* 'tormented, afflicted'; ምንሰው *mənsəw* 'tempted, tried'.

II-y   *1ə/i3ə4*: ጊጉይ *giguy* 'faulty, guilty'; ፅውው/ፂውው *ḍəwəw/ḍiwəw* 'captive, prisoner'.

II-w   *1u3u4*: ሙቁሕ *muquḥ* 'captive, prisoner'.

7 *1ə23ā4i* Agent nouns.

II-y   *1e3ā4i*: ዴጋኒ *degāni* 'pursuer'; ጌጋዪ *gegāyi* 'sinner'; ዜናዊ *zenāwi* 'one who brings news, announcer'.

II-w   *1o3ā4i*: ኖላዊ *nolāwi* 'shepherd'.

8 *1ə23ā4e* Verbal nouns.

red.   ድግዳጌ *dəgdāge* 'leanness, meagerness'; ውልዋሌ *wəlwāle* (and ውላውሌ *wəlāwle*) 'perturbation, confusion'.

II-n   ድንጋሌ *dəngāle* 'virginity'; ምንሳዌ *mənsāwe* 'temptation, peril'.

II-y   *1e/i3ā4e*: ዴ/ዲዋዌ *ḍe/iwāwe* 'captivity, imprisonment'.

II-w   *1u3ā4e*: ሙቃሔ *muqāḥe* 'imprisonment, punishment by chaining'.

9 *1ə23ə4ənnā* Abstracts in general.

II-n   ድንግልና *dəngələnnā* 'virginity, chastity'.

10 *ma1a23ə4* Agent nouns.

II-y   *ma1e3ə4*: መዜነው *mazenəw* 'announcer, messenger'.

11 *ma1a23a4*

መስንቆ *masanqo* (< *masanqaw*) 'one-stringed fiddle' (loanword; cf. ሰንቀወ *sanqawa* 'play a musical instrument').

12 *ma1a23ā4i* Agent nouns.

II-y   መዜናዊ *mazenāwi* 'announcer, messenger'.

4.2.1.9. Quinquiliteral Formations

Note: quninquiliteral patterns can be divided into three groups based on formal criteria:

1. (Usually) reduplicated roots of the type *1-2-3-2-3*, often with /n/ as the first radical (= red.).
2. Other roots with /n/ as the first radical, including those with /y/ or /w/ as the third radical (= I-*n*).
3. Roots with /s/ as the first radical, including those with /y/ or /w/ as the third radical (= I-*s*).

The verbal paradigm of quinquiliteral roots solely consists of forms of the CG and Gt-stems. Because of this, quinquiliteral root types also exhibit nominal derivates with prefixed *ʾ–*.

1 **1a2a34i5* Adjectives, sometimes with intensified meanings (only with reduplicated roots).

red.   **1a2a32i3:* አበድቢድ *ʾabadbid* 'foolish, inept' (cf. አብድ *ʾabd* 'fool'); ደመንሚን *damanmin* 'rather cloudy, very gloomy' (cf. ደመነ *dammana* 'to be clouded'); ሐመልሚል *hamalmil* 'green'; መዐርዒር *maʿarʿir* 'sweet'; ጸዐድዒድ *ṣaʿadʿid* 'whitish' (cf. ጸዐዳ *ṣāʿdā* 'white').
          f. በራህርህት *barāhrəht* 'glittering, sparkling' (cf. በርሀ *barha* 'to shine').

2 **1a2a34ā5* Verbal nouns; only reduplicated roots.

red.   **1a2a32ā3:* ሐመልማል *hamalmāl* 'green color'.
I-*n*, red. **na1a21ā2:* ነበልባል *nabalbāl* 'flame'; ነጕድጓድ *nagʷadgʷād* 'thunder'; ነጎጋው *nagogāw* (< **nagawgāw*) 'hesitation, erring'; ነጸፍጻፍ *naṣafṣāf* 'drops' (cf. ጸፍጸፍ *ṣafṣāf* 'drops').
I-*s*, red. **sa1a21ā2:* ሰቆቃው *saqoqāw* (< **saqawqāw*) 'lamentation, grief'.

3 **1ə2ə34ə5* Verbal nouns; primarily of reduplicated roots.

ድልቅልቅ *dələqləq* 'shaking, quaking'; ድቍንድቍ *dəqʷəndəqʷ* 'axe, crowbar'; cf. also ድ/ደብዕኵል *də/abəʿkʷəl* and ድብዕንኵል *dəbʿənkʷəl* 'snare, trap'.

4 *1ə2ə34u5 Verbal adjectives.

I-n   ንዘሀሉል *nəzəhlul* 'languid, sluggish' (4=5).

5 *ma12a34ə5 Agent nouns; reduplicated roots.

I-n   መንጐርጕር *mangʷargʷər* 'who murmurs, mutters'; መንጎገው *mangogəw* (<
           *mangawgəw) 'vagabond' (cf. እንጎጋዊ *ʾəngogāwi* 'vagabond').
I-s   መስቆቀው *masqoqəw* (< *masqawqəw) 'one who chants a dirge, mourner'.

6 *ma12a3ā4ə5 Agent nouns; same function as *ma12a34ə5; reduplicated roots.

           መንጐራጕር *mangʷarāgʷər* 'who murmurs, mutters'.

7 *ə12a34ə5 Agent nouns; reduplicated roots.

I-n   እንጐገው *ʾəngugəw* 'erring, wandering'.

8 *ə12a34ā5 Verbal nouns; same function as *1a2a34ā5; reduplicated roots.

I-n   እንጌጋይ *ʾəngegāy* 'aberration, going astray'; እንጐጋው *ʾəngugāw*
           'aberration, wandering'.

9 *ʾa12a34ā5i and *ʾə12a34ā5i Agent nouns; reduplicated roots.

I-n   አንገርጋሪ *ʾangargāri* 'rolling, spinning'; አንጐርጓሪ *ʾangʷargʷāri*
           'murmuring, muttering'; እንጎጋዊ *ʾəngogāwi* 'vagabond' (cf. መንጎገው
           mangogəw).

10 *ʾa12a34ā5e and *ʾə12a34ā5e Verbal nouns; reduplicated roots.

I-n   አንጐጋዌ *ʾangugāwe* 'aberration'.

4.2.2. Gender

4.2.2.1. Classical Ethiopic has two genders, masculine and feminine. From a
formal perspective, the masculine is usually unmarked while nouns that are
grammatically feminine exhibit the ending *-at* or *-t*, as in ከብርት *kəbərt*

'honored (f.)', ብእሲት *baʾasit* 'woman' (cf. ብእሲ *baʾasi* 'man', ክቡር *kabur* 'honored' [m.]), and ወለት *walatt* 'daughter' (< *waladt*). The ending –*at* is used after nominal bases ending in two consonants, as in እምነት *ʾamnat* 'faith' and ነደት *naddat* 'flame', while the ending -*t* is used otherwise (as in the examples given above). Exceptions to this distribution occur but are rare.

4.2.2.2. A few nouns that are naturally feminine do not exhibit the feminine marker, such as እም *ʾam(m)*[87] 'mother' and ድንግል *dangal* 'virgin'. In the plural, these nouns are most commonly construed with the feminine plural marker -*āt*, as in እማት *ʾammāt* 'mothers'.

4.2.2.3. Despite the rules give above, it has to be noted that gender is only fixed for nouns denoting human beings. All other nouns have variable gender, that is, they can be construed as either masc. or fem. A specific gender can be preferred for certain inanimate nouns, although there is still sufficient variability to make the attribution of a specific gender impossible. Some examples, for which the more frequently occurring gender is listed first, include: አሚር *ʾamir* (m., f.)[88] 'day, sun'; ቤት *bet* (m., f.) 'house'; ፀሐይ *ḍaḥāy* (f., m.) 'sun'; ፍኖት *fanot* (f., m.) 'way, path'; ሀገር *hagar* (f., m.) 'city'; ሐመር *ḥamar* (f., m.) 'boat'; ሌሊት *lelit* (m., f.) 'night'; ምድር *madr* (m., f.)[89] 'land, earth'; ሰማይ *samāy* (m., f.) 'heaven, sky'; ዝናም *zanām* (m., f.) 'rain'.

Dillmann always notes the gender of a given noun in DL. Leslau, on the other hand, does not indicate gender in CDG or Leslau (1989).

4.2.2.4. Adjectives of the types **qatil* (§4.2.1.3:6) and **qattil* (§4.2.1.4.) form the feminine by changing the pattern to **qattāl* and not by adding the feminine marker -(a)t (this is also called "broken feminine formation"); as in ጠቢብ *ṭabib* (masc.), fem. ጠባብ *ṭabbāb* 'wise'. The feminine plural is either ጠቢባት *ṭabibāt* or ጠባባት *ṭabbābāt*.

---

[87] According to the traditional pronunciation, the gemination at the end of the lexeme is not pronounced in forms without suffixes (Mittwoch 1926, 18).

[88] E.g., ውእተ/ይእተ፡ አሚረ *waʾata/yaʾata ʾamira* 'on that day'.

[89] E.g., ምድር፡ ሠናይ *madr śannāy* and ምድር፡ ሠናይት *madr śannāyt* 'a beautiful land'.

4.2.3. Number

4.2.3.1. Classical Ethiopic has two productive categories of number: singular and plural. It does not have a productive dual like other Semitic languages (cf. Classical Arabic). The plural is used in instances in which languages with a productive dual would use this morpheme, as for example for paired body parts (እዘኒሃ *ʾəzanihā* 'her ears').

Vestiges of the old dual-marker are most likely found in the ending *-e* (< *-ay) attested in the lexemes ክልኤ *kəlʾe* 'two, both' and ሐቍ *ḥaqʷe* 'hip'. The construct of the noun እድ *ʾəd* 'hand', እዴ *ʾəde* might also go back to the old dual-ending.[90]

The formation of the plural distinguishes two types: a "regular" or "external" (§4.2.3.2.–3.5.) and a "broken" or "internal" (§4.2.3.6.) plural formation.

4.2.3.2. The *external plural* exhibits the endings *-ān* (m.) and *-āt* (f.).

The feminine ending *-āt* conforms to the widely attested feminine plural marker *-āt* used across Semitic. The masculine plural ending *-ān*, however, differs from the commonly used masculine plural markers *-ūm(a)/-ūn(a)* and *-īm(a)/-īn(a)* attested in Central and East Semitic (the latter without nunation). The morpheme *-ān* in the Classical Ethiopic masculine plural is probably related to the plural-marking morpheme *-ān* that is known from other Semitic languages, such as the (particularizing) plural *-ān* in Akkadian (*ilū* 'gods' versus *ilānū* 'a certain group of gods').

Most adjectives exhibit external plural markers. Exceptions are adjectives of the pattern **qatil* (§4.2.1.3:6a), **qattil* (§4.2.1.4.), and, in some cases, the pattern **qatāli*, which have an irregular (masculine) plural **qatalt* and **qattalt* (e.g., ጠቢብ *ṭabib* 'wise', pl. ጠበብት *ṭabbabt*; ቀዳሚ *qadāmi* 'first, previous', pl. ቀደምት *qaddamt*). Nouns on the other hand, more frequently exhibit broken plural formations than external plural markers.

---

[90] Alternatively, the form እዴ- *ʾəde*– might be the result of an analogy with the forms of prepositions before pronominal suffixes, which regularly end in *-e* (§4.5.2.4.), especially since the word እድ *ʾəd* 'hand' can be used in compound prepositions, as in በእድ *ba-ʾəda* 'by, through', which takes the form በእዴ– *ba-ʾəde*– before pronominal suffixes (§4.5.2.3.1.). For a study on traces of the dual in Classical Ethiopic, see also Heide 2006.

4.2.3.3. In addition to the external plural markers *-ān* and *-āt*, Classical Ethiopic has a third external plural marker *-aw*. This marker, however, is only used for six nouns that all have a two-consonantal base: እድ *ʾəd*, pl. እደው *ʾədaw* 'hands'; ዕፅ *ʿəḍ*, pl. ዕፀው *ʿəḍaw* 'trees'; ዕድ *ʿəd*, pl. ዕደው *ʿədaw* 'males'; አፍ *ʾaf*, pl. አፈው *ʾafaw* 'mouths'; አብ *ʾab*, pl. አበው *ʾabaw* 'fathers'; እኁ *ʾəḫʷ*, pl. አኀው *ʾaḫaw* 'brothers'.

4.2.3.4. The following table shows the endings that mark gender and number in Classical Ethiopic based on the verbal adjective ክቡር *kəbur* 'honored, glorious'.

	Singular Nom./Gen.	Plural Nom./Gen.
Masc.	ክቡር *kəbur*	ክቡራን *kəburān*
Fem.	ክብርት *kəbərt*	ክብርታት *kəbərtāt*

4.2.3.5. The following points still have to be noted with regard to the use of the external plural markers:

1. The plural ending *-āt* usually replaces the singular ending *-(a)t*. In some cases, however, it is suffixed after the feminine singular ending so that the noun in question is doubly marked for feminine gender, as in ንግሥት *nəgəśt* 'queen', pl. ንግሥታት *nəgəśtāt*; ሕልቀት *ḥəlqat* 'ring', pl. ሕልቀታት *ḥəlqatāt* (besides ሕልቃት *ḥəlaqāt*).
2. The combination of masc. and fem. plural endings is equally attested, as in ሊቅ *liq* 'elder', pl. ሊቃናት *liqānāt* (besides regular masc. pl. ሊቃን *liqān* and broken plural ሊቃውንት *liqāwənt*). In this case, the marker *-āt* usually follows the marker *-ān*.
3. The plural ending *-āt* can be suffixed to broken plurals without any apparent change in meaning, as in ሀገር *hagar* 'city', broken pl. አህጉር *ʾahgur* and አህጉራት *ʾahgurāt*; ፍኖት *fənot* 'way, path', broken pl. ፍነው *fənnaw* and ፍነዋት *fənawwāt*.
4. The plural ending *-ān* is usually only used with nouns denoting male human beings. The ending *-āt* has no gender restrictions and can be used to mark the plural of both male and female human beings. The use for male human plurals is particularly frequent with nouns denoting professions, such as ነቢያት *nabiyāt* 'prophets' (singular ነቢይ *nabiy*); ካህናት *kāhənāt* 'priests' (sing. ካህን *kāhən*); ጳጳሳት *pāppāsāt*

'patriarchs, bishops' (sing. ጳጳስ *ṗāṗṗās*). The marker *-āt* can nevertheless be considered a "feminine" plural marker in the sense that it regularly occurs with attributive adjectives modifying feminine nouns denoting human beings in the plural. It is not used for adjectives modifying male human nouns, for which *-ān* is used.

5. The plural endings are in some cases attached to an extended bisyllabic form of the patterns *qatl* and *qətl*, as in sing. ከልብ *kalb* 'dog', pl. ከለባት *kalabāt* (cf. the plural formation of *qa/i/utl* nouns in Hebrew, as in *kɛlɛb* [< *kalb*] 'dog', pl. *kəlābīm* [< *kalabīm*]).

4.2.3.6. *Broken* or *internal plural formations* are more frequent with nouns than the external plural markers just discussed. In this type of formation, the pattern of the noun in the singular is changed in the plural. The plural is thus expressed by pattern replacement.

In the following table, the most frequent broken plural patterns are introduced and illustrated by examples. Only one plural pattern is given for each lexeme even if the noun in question exhibits more than one broken plural formation. The order of the patterns follows formal criteria and does not reflect their relative frequency. Frequently used patterns are **ʾaqtāl*, **qətal*, **ʾaqtəlt*, **qat(t)alt*, and **1a2ā3ə4(t)*.

Singular	Plural	Translation
1 *qətal (often for singular nouns of the pattern **qətl*)		
እግር *ʾəgr*	እገር *ʾəgar*	'foot'
እዝን *ʾəzn*	እዘን *ʾəzan*	'ear'
ሕዝብ *ḥəzb*	ሕዘብ *ḥəzab*	'tribe, people'[91]
2 *qətul (very rare)		
ወልድ *wald*	ውሉድ *wəlud*	'son'
3 *qatalt (often of **qatāli*)[92]		
መሣጢ *maśāṭi*	መሠጥ *maśaṭṭ*	'robber'
ነጋሢ *nagāśi*	ነገሥት *nagaśt*	'king, ruler'
ንጉሥ *nəguś*	ነገሥት *nagaśt*	'king'

---

[91] The plural ሕዘብ *ḥəzab* has the meaning 'tribes', while the plural አሕዛብ *ʾaḥzāb* has the meaning 'nations, people'.

[92] Concerning the difficulty of distinguishing between **qattalt* and **qatalt*, see Mittwoch 1926, 29.

ጸሓፊ ṣaḥāfi	ጸሓፍት ṣaḥaft	'scribe'
ጸላኢ/ጸላእ ṣalā'i/ṣal(l)ā'	ጸላእት ṣalā't	'enemy'

4 *qattalt (often of *qatil, *qattil, and *qatāli)

ዐቢይ ʿabiy	ዐበይት ʿabbayt	'big'
ሓዲስ ḥaddis	ሓደስት ḥaddast	'new'
ጠቢብ ṭabib	ጠበብት ṭabbabt	'wise'

5 *qəttal (relatively rare)

ፍኖት fənot	ፍነው fənnaw	'way, road'

6 *'aqtəl

በትር batr	አብትር 'abtər	'stick, scepter'
ቄጽል qʷaṣl	አቍጽል 'aqʷṣəl	'leaf, foliage'

7 *'aqtəlt (frequent, in particular of *qatl)

ገብር gabr	አግብርት 'agbərt	'servant'
ባሕር bāḥr	አብሕርት 'abḥərt	'sea, ocean'
መርሕ marḥ	አምርሕት 'amrəḥt[93]	'leader'
ቀርን qarn	አቅርንት 'aqrənt	'horn'
ርእስ rə's	አርእስት 'ar(ə)'əst	'head'
ረድእ rad'	አርድእት 'ardə't	'helper'

8 *'aqtāl (very frequent, especially of *qətl, *qatl, and *qatal)

ሕዝብ ḥəzb	አሕዛብ 'aḥzāb	'people, nation'
ክንፍ kənf	አክናፍ 'aknāf	'wing'
ምት mət	አምታት 'amtāt	'husband'
ቤት bet (< *bayt)	አብያት 'abyāt	'house'
ደብር dabr	አድባር 'adbār	'mountain'
ሣእን śā'n	አሥአን 'aś'ān[94]	'shoe, sandal'
ወርኅ warḥ	አውራኅ 'awrāḥ	'month'
ሓመር ḥamar	አሕማር 'aḥmār	'boat, ship'

9 *'aqtul (relatively rare)

አድግ 'adg	አእዱግ 'a'dug	'donkey'
አንስት 'anəst	አእኑስ 'a'nus	'woman, wife'
ዐጽቅ ʿaṣq	አዕጹቅ 'a'ṣuq	'branch'

---

[93] Also አምሕርት 'amḥərt.

[94] Also አሣእን 'aśā'ən (see §3.7.1:6).

	ሀገር *hagar*	አህጉር *ʾahgur*	'city'
10 **ʾaqātəl (formally corresponding to **1a2ā3ə4*)			
	አጽባዕት *ʾaṣbāʿt*	ዐጽብዕ *ʾaṣābəʿ*	'finger, toe'
	በግዕ *baggəʿ*	አባግዕ *ʾabāgəʿ*	'sheep, ram'
	ወለት *walatt*	አዋልድ *ʾawāləd*	'daughter, girl'
11 **qatāw/yəl (formally corresponding to **1a2ā3ə4*)			
	ደቂቅ *daqiq*	ደቃው/ይቅ *daqāw/yəq*	'child, offspring'
	ኅብስት *ḫəbəst*[95]	ኅባውዝ *ḫabāwəz*	'bread'
	ኃጢአት *ḫaṭiʾat*	ኃጣውእ *ḫaṭāwəʾ*	'sin'
12 **qatāw/yəlt (formally corresponding to **1a2ā3ə4t*)			
	ደቂቅ *daqiq*	ደቃውቅት *daqāwəqt*	'small, child'

13 **1a2ā3ə4* (for formally quadriliteral patterns consisting of either triradical nouns with the prefixes *m–* and *t–*, triradical nouns with suffixes, or of quadriliteral nouns)

*maqātəl	ማዕቀብ *māʿqab*	መዓቅብ(ት) *maʿāqəb(t)*	'guard'
	ማሕሌት *māḥlet*	መሓልይ *maḥāləy*	'song, hymn'
	ማኅደር *māḫdar*	መኃድር *maḫādər*	'dwelling, abode'
	ሞዐልት *moʿalt*	መዋዕል *mawāʿəl*	'day'
	መዓልት *maʿālt*	መዋዕል *mawāʿəl*	'day'
*taqātəl	ትእምርት *təʾəmərt*	ተአምር *taʾāmər*[96]	'sign, miracle'
others	አንቀጽ *ʾanqaṣ*	አናቅጽ *ʾanāqəṣ*	'door, gate'
	ድንግል(ት) *dəngəl(t)*	ደናግል *danāgəl*	'virgin'
	ሌሊት *lelit*	ለያልይ *layāləy*	'night'
	ወሬዛ *warezā*	ወራዝው *warāzəw*	'young man'

14 **1a2ā3ə4t* (for formally quadriliteral patterns consisting of either triradical nouns with the prefixes *m–* and *t–*, triradical nouns with suffixes, or of quadriliteral nouns)

*maqātəlt	መንበር *manbar*	መናብርት *manābərt*	'throne, seat'
	መንፈስ *manfas*	መናፍስት *manāfəst*	'spirit'

---

[95] Derived from **ḫəbəzt* (§3.6.7.).

[96] For ተአምር *taʾāmər*, see Mittwoch 1926, 82. CDG only lists ተአምር *taʾammər*.

	መጽሐፍ *maṣḥaf*	መጻሕፍት *maṣāḥəft*	'book'
others	ኦርዌ *ʔarwe*	ኦራ/ረዊት *ʔarā/awit*	'animal, beast'
	ኮከብ *kokab*	ከዋክብት *kawākəbt*	'star'
	ሰርዌ *sarwe*	ሰራዊት *sarāwit*	'army, troops'
	ወሬዛ *warezā*	ወራዙት *warāzut*	'young man'
15 *1a2a3ā4ə5 (of quinquiliteral nouns)			
	መሰንቆ *masanqo*	መሰናቅው *masanāqəw*	'one-stringed fiddle'

4.2.3.7. Many nouns can have more than one plural formation, including broken and external plurals. In some cases, but not in all, different plural formations denote different meanings. Examples include:

- ሕዝብ *ḥəzb* 'people' with the plurals ሕዘብ *ḥəzab* 'tribes' and አሕዛብ *ʔaḥzāb* 'nations'.
- ከልብ *kalb* 'dog' with the plurals ከለባት *kalabāt*, አክላብ *ʔaklāb*, አክልብት *ʔakləbt*, and አካልብት *ʔakāləbt*.
- ሊቅ *liq* 'elder' with the plurals ሊቃን *liqān*, ሊቃናት *liqānāt*, and ሊቃውንት *liqāwənt*.

4.2.3.8. A few singular nominal bases do not form plurals. In such cases, other lexemes are used to indicate plurality, as in:

- ብእሲ *bəʔəsi* 'man', for which the lexeme ሰብእ *sabʔ* 'men, people' is used for the plural.[97]
- ብእሲት *bəʔəsit* 'woman', for which the lexemes አንስት *ʔanəst* and አእኑስ *ʔaʔnus* are used as plurals.

4.2.3.9. Broken and external plurals exhibit the same agreement patterns. They are both construed with a plural attributive adjective when the noun refers to a human being, but with a singular or plural adjective when it refers to an inanimate entity. This means that strict adjectival number agreement only exists for nouns denoting human beings. The phrase 'the just kings' can thus

---

[97] The lexeme ሰብእ *sabʔ* can also be used for the singular with the meaning 'man'.

only be expressed by ንጉሥት፡ጻድቃን *nagaśt ṣādəqān*, while the phrase 'the glorious cities' can be expressed by አህጉር፡ክቡር *ʾahgur kəbur*, አህጉር፡ክብርት *ʾahgur kəbərt*, አህጉር፡ክቡራን *ʾahgur kəburān*, and አህጉር፡ክብርታት *ʾahgur kəbərtāt* – note also the lack of gender agreement with inanimate nouns. Verbal forms, on the other hand, commonly appear in the plural even with inanimate subjects, although the singular can occur as well (§6.2.2.).

4.2.4. Case

4.2.4.1. Classical Ethiopic has two cases, an accusative and a non-accusative. The latter represents the merger of the common Semitic nominative and genitive in the singular. These two cases had fallen together already before the earliest written attestations of Classical Ethiopic.[98] The non-accusative, or historical nominative and genitive, is unmarked in both the singular and plural. The accusative on the other hand is marked by a final *a*-vowel in both the singular and plural (external and broken plurals); as in ዓመታት *ʿāmatāt* 'years' (non-acc.) versus ዓመታተ *ʿāmatāta* (acc.), and ንጉሥት *nagaśt* 'kings' (non-acc.) versus ንጉሥተ *nagaśta* (acc.).[99]

4.2.4.2. Classical Ethiopic thus exhibits the following diptotic case inflection (using the words ንጉሥ *nəguś* 'king' as the masc. and ንጉሥት *nəgəśt* 'queen' as the fem. paradigmatic forms):

	Sing.	Pl.
Non-acc. (= nom./gen.)	ንጉሥ *nəguś*	ንጉሥት *nagaśt*
Acc.	ንጉሠ *nəguśa*	ንጉሥተ *nagaśta*

Non-acc. (= nom./gen.)	ንጉሥት *nəgəśt*	ንጉሥታት *nəgəśtāt*
Acc.	ንጉሥተ *nəgəśta*	ንጉሥታተ *nəgəśtāta*

---

[98] The merger of the original nom. and gen. was motivated by phonological changes. Classical Ethiopic lost the Proto Semitic short vowels */i/ and */u/, which were both reduced to /ə/. At the end of a word, this /ə/ was then lost. For the original nom. and gen. the development was thus as follows: *$nVguśu$ (nom.) > *$nVgusə$ > *nəguś* and *$nVguśi$ (gen.) > *$nVguśə$ > *nəguś*.

[99] In other Semitic languages, the oblique (= gen. and acc.) of the external plural has the form -*ī* or -*i*. In Classical Ethiopic, the plural has been analogically modified based on the -∅/-*a* distinction of the singular.

4.2.4.3. Nouns ending in a vowel exhibit the following peculiarities:

- Nouns ending in -ā, -e, or -o do not change their form in the acc., as in መርኆ *marḫo* 'key' (non-acc. and acc.) and ጸማ *ṣamā* 'labor, toil' (non-acc. and acc.).

- Nouns ending in -i have an acc. in -e (contraction of *ia > e [§3.7.5.]), e.g., ጸሐፊ *ṣaḥāfi* 'scribe', acc. ጸሐፌ *ṣaḥāfe* and ብእሲ *bəʾəsi* 'man', acc. ብእሴ *bəʾəse*.

- The few nouns ending in -u have an acc. in -o, as in ከንቱ *kantu* 'nothingness, emptiness', acc. ከንቶ *kanto*. Cardinal numbers ending in -u, on the other hand, have an acc. in -a (§4.3.1.1.).

4.2.4.4. Further Remarks on the Basic Paradigm

Personal names are either not inflected for case or take a special accusative-marker -ሃ *-hā*, as in ወጸወዖ፡ ስሞ፡ ኢየሱስሃ *wa-ṣawwəʿa səmo ʾiyasus-hā* 'and he named him Jesus' lit. 'and he named his name Jesus' (Mt. 1:25). The morpheme -ሃ *-hā* always bears the primary stress of the word.

When nouns appear in the construct state, they have the same form in the non-accusative as in the accusative since all nouns in the construct are marked by final -a, as in ረከበ፡ ቤተ፡ መቅደስ *rakaba beta maqdas* 'he found the temple', where the -a on *beta* can be interpreted as either the accusative or construct marker.

4.2.4.5. The Noun with Pronominal Suffixes

From a historical perspective, pronominal suffixes in Semitic are attached to the noun in the construct state. Due to phonological and analogical developments, the construct has developed allomorphs before pronominal suffixes in some Semitic languages, e.g., Hebrew, Aramaic, and Classical Ethiopic. Despite the fact that nouns with pronominal suffixes formally differ from nouns in the construct state in Classical Ethiopic, this grammar does not treat nouns with pronominal suffixes as reflecting a separate state.

4.2.4.5.1. In the singular, the noun exhibits a linking vowel /ə/ in the non-accusative. This /ə/ is a reflex of the original case vowels /u/ and /i/ that merged to /ə/. Unlike in nouns without pronominal suffixes, this /ə/ was not lost since it was not word-final. In the acc., Classical Ethiopic has the expected case vowel /a/. The forms of the non-acc. and acc. are therefore **ንጉሥከ** *nəguśə-ka* 'your (ms) king' (non-acc.) (< *nVguśuka* [nom.] and *nVguśika* [gen.]), and **ንግሥተከ** *nəgəśta-ka* 'your (ms) queen' (acc.).

Nouns in the plural have a linking vowel /i/, independent of case, reflecting the common Semitic oblique masculine plural ending *-ī, as in **ነቢያቲሁ** *nabiyāti-hu* 'his prophets' and **ነገሥቲሆሙ** *nagaśti-homu* 'their (mp) kings'.

Formally singular nouns with plural or collective meanings sporadically exhibit the linking vowel /i/ before pronominal suffixes as well, as in **ምግባሪክሙ ፡ ሠናየ** *magbāri-kamu śannāya* 'your (mp) good works (acc.)' (Mt 5:16); **ማኅደሪሆሙ** *māḫdari-homu* 'their (mp) dwelling(s)' (En 46:6); **ምስካቢሆሙ** *maskābi-homu* (variant **ምስካቦሙ** *maskābomu*) 'their resting-place' (En 46:6); **ስብሐቲሁ** *sabḥati-hu* 'his glory' (En 47:3); **ገጸ ፡ ዐረቢሁ** *gaṣṣa ʿarabi-hu* 'towards the west' (lit. 'facing its west') (Jub 50:4); **ፍትሐተ ፡ ሕጋጊሁ** *fathata ḥagagi-hu* (variant **ሕጊሁ** *ḥaggi-hu*) 'the statutes of its law(s)' (Jub 50:6).

4.2.4.5.2. Before the 1cs pronominal suffix –*ya*, the acc. usually ends in –*a*–, as in **ብርሃንየ** *bərhān-ə-ya* 'my light' (acc.), not **bərhān-a-ya. The linking vowel /i/ of the plural likewise appears as /ə/ before this suffix in most cases (§3.7.2.). The same dissimilatory tendency can also often be observed before the 2fs suffix –**ኪ** –*ki* (§3.7.4.), that is, **ነገሥትየ** *nagaśtəya* (besides rare **ነገሥቲየ** *nagaśtiya*) 'my kings' and **ነገሥትኪ** *nagaśtəki* (besides **ነገሥቲኪ** *nagaśtiki*) 'your (fs) kings'.

4.2.4.5.3. The nouns **አብ** *ʾab* 'father', **እኍ/እኈው** *ʾəḫʷ/ʾəḫəw* 'brother', **ሐም** *ham* 'father-in-law', and **አፍ** *ʾaf* 'mouth' differ from the normal patterns in that they have the vowel /u/ as linking vowel before pronominal suffixes in the non-acc. and the vowel /ā/ in the acc., as in **አቡከ** *ʾabu-ka* (non-acc.) and **አባከ** *ʾabā-ka* (acc.) 'your (ms) father'; **አፉከ** *ʾafu-ka* (non-acc.) and **አፋከ** *ʾafā-ka* (acc.) 'your (ms) mouth'.[100]

---

[100] The idiosyncratic behavior of these nouns is attested across Semitic. In Akkadian and Classical Arabic, these nouns exhibit a triptotic inflection with a long vowel before the pronominal suffix. In Hebrew and Aramaic, they have a frozen form with only one vowel quality that equally reflects a historically long vowel.

The noun እኀው/እኁ ʾəḫaw/ʾəḫw has the form እኁ- ʾəḫu- before pronominal suffixes in the non-acc. and the form እኃ- ʾəḫʷā- or እኍ- ʾəḫʷa- in the acc.: እኁከ ʾəḫu-ka (non-acc.) and እኃከ ʾəḫʷā-ka (acc.) 'your (ms) brother'.

The noun ሐም ḥam has the form ሐሙ- ḥamu- before pronominal suffixes, independent of case: ሐሙከ ḥamu-ka 'your (ms) father-in-law' (non-acc. and acc.).

4.2.4.5.4. Nouns ending in –i like ጸሐፊ ṣaḥāfi 'scribe' commonly only distinguish between non-acc. and acc. before suffixes of the second persons, as in acc. ጸሐፈከ/-ኪ/-ክሙ/-ክን ṣaḥāfe-ka/-ki/-kəmu/-kən as opposed to non-acc. ጸሐፊከ ṣaḥāfi-ka (etc.). Before all other suffixes, these nouns usually have /i/ for all cases, as in ጸሐፊየ/-ሁ/-ሃ/-ሆሙ/-ሆን ṣaḥāfi-ya/-hu/-hā/-homu/-hon. Before the 1cs suffix -የ –ya, the final vowel of the noun sometimes appears as /ə/ instead of /i/ (according to §3.7.2.), as in መድኀንየ madḫanəya 'my savior' (besides regular መድኀኒየ madḫaniya).

4.2.4.5.5. The noun እድ ʾəd 'hand' has the irregular form እዴ- ʾəde- before pronominal suffixes in the singular, as in እዴሁ ʾəde-hu 'his hand' (§4.2.3.1.).

4.2.4.5.6. Most prepositions likewise have a linking vowel /e/ before pronominal suffixes, as in ምስሌየ məsle-ya 'with me'; ድኅሬየ dəḫre-ya 'behind me' (§4.5.2.4.).

4.2.4.6. Nouns ending in a consonant exhibit a linking vowel /ə/ before suffixed enclitic particles, as in ዓለመኒ ʿāləma-ni 'even the world'. According to the traditional pronunciation, this /ə/ can be dropped, as in ʿālam-ni (besides ʿāləma-ní). Nouns ending in a vowel do not change before enclitic particles.

4.2.4.7. Besides the two main cases, the acc. and non-acc., Classical Ethiopic exhibits an ending –u that is used to form certain adverbs, such as ላዕሉ lāʿlu 'above, upward' and ታሕቱ tāḫtu 'below, under' (§4.5.1.1.). This morpheme corresponds to the so-called locative in other Semitic languages.[101]

---

[101] This morpheme is still productive in the oldest periods of Akkadian, although with limitations, and perhaps in Ugaritic poetry. Vestiges of this morpheme are attested in Classical Arabic and in Biblical Hebrew, where it is solely used to form adverbs. Although the morpheme has often been described as a "case," it is in essence an adverbial marker that

4.2.4.8. The Vocative

Classical Ethiopic has no specific morpheme to mark the vocative and uses the unmarked base form of the noun instead, as in **ገብር፡እኩይ** *gabr ʾəkkuy* 'o you evil servant!'; **ሐር፡እምድኅሬየ፡ሰይጣን** *ḥur ʾəm-dəḥreya sayṭān* 'go away from me, Satan!' (Mt 4:10).

The unmarked noun in vocative function is frequently emphasized by the particle **አ** *ʾo* (§4.5.7.2.). This particle can precede or follow the noun. When it precedes the noun it constitutes a proclitic, **አ–** *ʾo–*. When it is suffixed, it has the form –*o*, as in **አገብር፡ኄር** *ʾo-gabr ḥer* 'o (you) good servant!'; **እግዚአ** *ʾəgziʾ-o* 'o lord!' (Jub 1:19); **ብእሲቶ** *bəʾasit-o* 'o woman!'; **እም** *ʾəmm-o*[102] 'o mother!'. In certain cases, the particle can be both prefixed and suffixed, as in **አብእሲቶ** *ʾo-bəʾasit-o* 'o woman!'. When the particle is suffixed, it is always stressed, as in **እም** *ʾəmm-ó*.

The noun **አብ** *ʾab* 'father' exhibits a special form of the vocative, **አባ** *ʾabbā* 'o father!'.

4.2.5. State

4.2.5.1. Classical Ethiopic has two states that are dependent on the syntactic context of the noun: 1. the absolute or unbound state, and 2. the construct or bound state.

4.2.5.2. The *absolute* or *unbound* state is the independent basic form of the noun that is also used as citation form (e.g., in dictionaries, lists, etc.). For the inflection of nouns in the absolute state, see §4.2.4.2.

4.2.5.3. The *construct* or *bound* state marks the noun as having a dependent, specifically a dependent in the genitive, which can be another noun, adjective, or a pronoun in the form of a pronominal suffix.

Formally, the construct looks like the accusative: the majority of nouns, that is, nouns ending in a consonant, exhibit suffixed –*a* in the construct in both the singular and plural. Nouns that end in final –*i* have a construct in –*e*, while nouns ending in the vowels –*ā*, –*e*, or –*o* do not change in the construct.

---

expresses the adverbial notion of place.

[102] Also with the phonetic variant **እሙ** *ʾəmm-u*.

Examples include: **ንጉሠ፡ሀገር** *nəguśa hagar* 'the king of the city'; **ወልደ፡ንጉሥ** *walda nəguś* 'the son of the king'; **ጸሓፌ፡ሕዝብ** *ṣaḥāfe ḥəzb* 'the scribe of the people'; **ውሉደ፡ንጉሥ** *wəluda nəguś* 'the sons of the king'.[103]

4.2.6. Adverbs Ending in –*m*

A few adverbs based on nominal forms end in -*m* in Classical Ethiopic:[104]

* **ጌሰም/ጌሠም** *gesam/geśam* 'tomorrow, the morrow'.[105]
* **ትማልም** *təmāləm* 'yesterday'.

4.2.7. Summary Chart of the Regular Nominal Inflection

The following chart provides an overview of the regular nominal inflection with regard to the categories of gender, number, case, and state. The paradigmatic words used are **ሊቅ** *liq* 'elder' for the masculine and **ዐዘቅት** *ʿazaqt* 'cistern, well' for the feminine.

	Singular		Plural	
	Non-acc.	Acc.	Non-acc.	Acc.
Masc. noun				
Abs. state	**ሊቅ** *liq*	**ሊቀ** *liqa*	**ሊቃን** *liqān*	**ሊቃነ** *liqāna*
Cstr. state	**ሊቀ** *liqa*	**ሊቀ** *liqa*	**ሊቃነ** *liqāna*	**ሊቃነ** *liqāna*
+ pron. suffix	**ሊቀ–** *liqə–*	**ሊቀ–** *liqa–*	**ሊቃኒ–** *liqāni–*	**ሊቃኒ–** *liqāni–*

---

[103] For a comparative study of the construct state in Ethiopic, see Tropper 2000.

[104] It has been suggested that this final –*m* is a vestige of mimation in Classical Ethiopic (e.g., Tropper 2002, 79). This derivation, however, does not explain the adverbial use of the supposed mimated form in **ትማልም** *təmāləm*, where it would have to be formally derived from either an original nom. or gen., both of which are not commonly used to form adverbs. It is more likely that the final –*m* is a vestige of the original Semitic adverbial marker –*um*, also referred to as "locative," which has reflexes in Akkadian and also in Hebrew forms such as *piṯʾōm* 'suddenly'. In Classical Ethiopic, the final -*m* would then have been reinterpreted as a general adverbial ending and been extended to forms of the noun not ending in –*um*.

[105] This word is also attested as **ጌስ/ሠመ** *ges/śama*, with an additional acc.-ending to mark adverbial function.

Fem. noun				
Abs. state	**ዐዘቅት** ʿazaqt	**ዐዘቅተ** ʿazaqta	**ዐዛቃት** ʿazaqāt[106]	**ዐዛቃተ** ʿazaqāta
Cstr. state	**ዐዘቅተ** ʿazaqta	**ዐዘቅተ** ʿazaqta	**ዐዛቃተ** ʿazaqāta	**ዐዛቃተ** ʿazaqāta
+ pron. suffix	**ዐዘቅት–** ʿazaqtə–	**ዐዘቅተ–** ʿazaqta–	**ዐዛቃቲ–** ʿazaqāti–	**ዐዛቃቲ–** ʿazaqāti–

4.3. Numerals

4.3.1. Cardinal Numbers

4.3.1.1. The cardinal numbers 1–10 are listed in the following table (forms listed below each other are variants of the same numeral):

	Form with masc. counted noun		Form with fem. counted noun	
	Non-acc.	Acc.	Non-acc.	Acc.
1	**አሐዱ** ʾaḥadú	**አሐደ** ʾaḥadá	**አሐቲ** ʾaḥattí	**አሐተ** ʾaḥattá[107]
2	**ክልኤቱ** kəlʾetú **ክልኤ** kəlʾe	**ክልኤተ** kəlʾetá	**ክልኤቲ** kəlʾetí **ክልኤቱ** kəlʾetú **ክልኤ** kəlʾe	**ክልኤተ** kəlʾetá **ክልኤተ** kəlʾetá
3	**ሠለስቱ** śalastú	**ሠለስተ** śalastá	**ሠላስ** śalās	**ሠላሰ** śalāsá
4	**አርባዕቱ** ʾarbāʿtú	**አርባዕተ** ʾarbāʿtá	**አርባዕ** ʾarbāʿ	**አርባዐ** ʾarbāʿá
5	**ኀምስቱ** ḫaməstú	**ኀምስተ** ḫaməstá	**ኀምስ** ḫams	**ኀምሰ** ḫamsá
6	**ስድስቱ** sədəstú	**ስድስተ** sədəstá	**ስሱ** səssú	**ስሱ** səssú[108]
7	**ሰብዐቱ** sabʿatú **ሰባዕቱ** sabāʿtú[109]	**ሰብዐተ** sabʿatá **ሰባዕተ** sabāʿtá	**ሰብዑ** sabʿú **ሰብዕ,** **ሰብዕ** sabʿ, səbʿ	**ሰብዑ** sabʿú

---

[106] Also **ዐዘቅታት/ተ** ʿazaqtāt(a) with double feminine-marking.

[107] **አሐቲ/አሐተ** ʾaḥatti/a < *ʾaḥadti/a.

[108] **ስሱ** səssu < *sədsu.

[109] **ሰባዕቱ** sabāʿtu < *sabaʿtu < *sabʿatu (§3.7.1:6).

8	ሰመንቱ samantú ሰማኒቱ samānitú	ሰመንተ samantá ሰማኒተ samānitá	ሰማኒ samāni	ሰማኒ samāni
9	ት/ተስዐቱ tə/asʿatú ተሳዕቱ tasāʿtú	ት/ተስዐተ tə/asʿatá ተሳዕተ tasāʿtá	ት/ተስዑ tə/asʿú	ት/ተስዑ tə/asʿú
10	ዐሠርቱ ʿaśartú	ዐሠርተ ʿaśartá	ዐሥሩ ʿaśrú	ዐሥሩ ʿaśrú

Notes on the listed forms (for their syntactic use, see §5.3.1.):

- According to Mittwoch (1926, 43) all cardinal numbers, including their form in the acc., are stressed on the last syllable as indicated in the transcriptions in the table above (§3.5.2:4).[110]

- The widespread ending –u among the cardinal numbers has been analyzed as either a vestige of the original nominative marker *-u, which is usually lost at the end of a word, or as a reflex of the common abstract marker –ū attested throughout Semitic. The latter analysis would better explain the otherwise unusual preservation of final /u/,[111] but requires that the ending would have secondarily been reanalyzed as a non-acc. marker.

- The forms of the cardinal numbers are given as "form with masc. counted noun" and "form with fem. counted noun" above. This functional distribution can be observed to a certain degree, but it is more common for gender agreement to be absent and for numerals ending in -tu to be generalized.

- In order to stress the notion of "one," Classical Ethiopic uses the lexeme ዋሕድ wāḥəd (f. ዋሕድ wāḥədd) instead of አሐዱ ʾaḥadu and አሐቲ ʾaḥatti; which has the basic meaning 'unique, only, one'.

- The root of the number 'two' √klʾ differs from the commonly attested root for the same lexeme *√tny used in most other Semitic languages. The root found in Classical Ethiopic is only known as a collective

---

[110] According to other sources, at least the acc. forms are stressed on the penultima, that is, śalʾāsa, ʾarbʾāʿa, ḥámsa etc.

[111] An exception to the proposed analysis of –u in cardinal numbers as a reflex of the original nom. marker might be ክንቱ kantu 'nothingness', where the acc. in –o indicates that the final -u might be the original vocalic ending of the noun.

number in other Semitic languages, as in Classical Arabic *kilā-* 'the two, both of them' and Hebrew *kilʾayim*. The common Semitic root *√tny* is attested in Classical Ethiopic (as *sny*) but does not occur for cardinal numbers (cf. the forms ሰኑይ *sanuy* 'second [day]' and ሳንይ/ሳኒት *sānəy/sānit* 'the next day').

- The form ክልኤቱ *kəlʾetu* 'two' is used for masc. and fem. counted nouns.
- The forms of the cardinal numbers 6–10 used with fem. counted entities have no separate form for the acc.
- Leslau (CDG) transcribes *kəlʾettu*, *ḥamməstu*, *səddəstu* and *ʿaśśartu*. According to Mittwoch (1926), however, the respective consonants do not exhibit gemination.

4.3.1.2. In some cases, the pattern *qətl* (that is ሥልስ *śəls*, ርብዕ *rəbʿ*, ኀምስ *ḫəms*, and ስድስ *səds*; acc. ሥልሰ *śəlsa*, ርብዐ *rəbʿa*, ኀምሰ *ḫəmsa*, ስድስ *sədsa*) is employed for cardinal numbers with counted entities that are construed as feminine.

4.3.1.3. The cardinal numbers 11–19 are composites based on the pattern "ten + ወ- *wa-* + ones." The conjunction ወ- *wa-* can be missing but occurs in most cases. It is noteworthy that the cardinal numbers 13–19 do not exhibit chiastic concord in Classical Ethiopic, that is, the ones and tens have the same gender and base form, unlike in other Semitic languages, where the ones exhibit chiastic concord with the gender of the counted entity:

	Form with masc. counted noun	Form with fem. counted noun
11	ዐሠርቱ፡ወአሐዱ *ʿaśartu wa-ʾaḥadu*	ዐሥሩ፡ወአሐቲ *ʿaśru wa-ʾaḥatti*
12	ዐሠርቱ፡ወክልኤቱ *ʿaśartu wa-kəlʾetu*	ዐሥሩ፡ወክልኤ *ʿaśru wa-kəlʾe*
13	ዐሠርቱ፡ወሠለስቱ *ʿaśartu wa-śalastu*	ዐሥሩ፡ወሠላስ *ʿaśru wa-śalās*
14	ዐሠርቱ፡ወአርባዕቱ *ʿaśartu wa-ʾarbāʿtu*	ዐሥሩ፡ወአርባዕ *ʿaśru wa-ʾarbāʿ*
Etc.		

When enumerating days and months (in both cardinal and ordinal function), Classical Ethiopic uses the pattern *qatul* instead (§4.3.2.3.).

4.3.1.4. Tens (20–90) have the following forms:

20	ዕሥራ ʿəśrā	60	ስሳ səssā
30	ሠላሳ śalāsā	70	ሰብዓ sabʿā
40	አርብዓ ʾarbəʿā	80	ሰማንያ samānyā
50	ኃምሳ ḫamsā	90	ት/ተስዓ tə/asʿā[112]

4.3.1.5. In the compounded numbers 11–99, the tens precede the ones and are commonly connected by ወ– wa–:

	Form with masc. counted noun	Form with fem. counted noun
21	ዕሥራ፡ ወአሐዱ ʿəśrā wa-ʾaḥadu	ዕሥራ፡ ወአሐቲ ʿəśrā wa-ʾaḥatti
22	ዕሥራ፡ ወክልኤቱ ʿəśrā wa-kəlʾetu	ዕሥራ፡ ወክልኤ ʿəśrā wa-kəlʾe
23	ዕሥራ፡ ወሠለስቱ ʿəśrā wa-śalastu	ዕሥራ፡ ወሠላስ ʿəśrā wa-śalās

4.3.1.6. The numeral 100 and higher units have the following forms. (When the underlying relationship of the numbers is that of multiplication, the smaller number precedes the higher one.)

100	ምእት məʾət[113], acc. ምእት məʾəta (pl. አምእት ʾamʾāt)
200	ክልኤቱ፡ ምእት kəlʾetu məʾət and ክልኤ፡ ምእት kəlʾe məʾət ('2x100')
1000	ዐሠርቱ፡ ምእት ʿaśartu məʾət ('10x100'); also እልፍ ʾalf
2000 etc.	ዕሥራ፡ ምእት ʿəśrā məʾət ('20x100'); ሠላሳ፡ ምእት śalāsā məʾət; አርብዓ፡ ምእት ʾarbəʿā məʾət etc.
10,000	እልፍ ʾalf
100,000	ዐሠርቱ፡ እልፍ ʿaśartu ʾalf

In compounded numbers, the individual units are connected by ወ– wa– and higher units precede lower ones, as in ምእት፡ ወዕሥራ፡ መሳፍንት məʾata wa-ʿəśrā

---

[112] For the ending –ā on cardinal numbers, see also the Akkadian tens (ešrā, šalāšā, erbā, ḫamšā). This ending is a reflex of the original plural function of -ā that was relegated to dual function after the introduction of the newly created fem. pl. morpheme *–āt (< *–ā + –t).

[113] According to Mittwoch (1926, 50), the lexeme is stressed on the second syllable məʾə́t.

masāfənta '120 satraps' (acc.) (Dan 6:1); **ዐሠርቱ፡ወአሐዱ፡ምእት** *ʿaśartu wa-ʾaḥadu məʾət* and **ዐሥሩ፡ወአሐቲ፡ምእት** *ʿaśru wa-ʾaḥatti məʾət* '1100'.

Indiscriminately high numeric values (ten thousands, myriads) are expressed by the plural of **እልፍ** *ʾəlf*, **አእላፍ** *ʾaʾlāf* and **አእላፋት** *ʾaʾlāfāt*, in addition to other derivatives of the same root such as **ኡላፌ** *ʾulāfe*, **ምእልፊት** *məʾəlfit*, and **ተእልፊት** *təʾəlfit*. Compounded expressions such as **አእላፈ፡አእላፍ** *ʾaʾlāfa ʾaʾlāf* and **ምእልፊት/ተ፡አእላፍ** *məʾəlfit(a) ʾaʾlāf* ('myriads over myriads') are common as well (e.g., Dan 7:10, which exhibits both variants just mentioned).

4.3.1.7. Cardinal and ordinal numbers are frequently written logographically by using special numeric signs (see §2.5.). When units are connected by **ወ-** *wa-*, this **ወ-** *wa-* is commonly written between the two numerals, as in **፲ወ፪** 10-wa-2 = 12 (**ወልደ፡፲ወ፪፡ዓመት** *walda 10-wa-2 ʿāmat* 'a 12 year old boy'). The conjunction **ወ-** *wa-* can also be missing in logographically written numbers, so that the signs for tens and ones are written next to each other without any formal connection. All logographic number signs should be read as the respective cardinal or, depending on context, ordinal numbers, as in **ወልደ፡፲ወ፪፡ዓመት** *walda 10-wa-2 ʿāmat* = *walda ʿaśru wa-kəlʾe ʿāmat* 'a 12 year old boy'.

Spellings that exhibit logographic numerals with syllabically written phonetic complements are common as well, as in **ወኮነ፡መዋዕል** ... **፯ታ፡ዓመተ፡ወ፮ታ፡አውራኀ** *wa-kona mawāʿəl ... 7-ta ʿāmata wa-6-ta ʾawrāḫa* 'and the time was ... seven years and six months' (7-ta = *sabʿata*; 6-ta = *sədəsta*).

4.3.2. Ordinal Numbers

4.3.2.1. Ordinal numbers from 'two' onward follow the pattern **qātəl* (f. **qātəlt*):

2.	**ካልእ** *kāləʾ* (acc. **ካልአ** *kāləʾa*); fem. **ካልእት** *kāləʾt* (acc. **ካልእተ** *kāləʾta*)
3.	**ሣልስ** *śāləs* (acc. **ሣልሰ** *śāləsa*); fem. **ሣልስት** *śāləst* (acc. **ሣልስተ** *śāləsta*)
4.–10.	**ራብዕ(ት)** *rābəʿ(t)*; **ኃምስ(ት)** *ḫāməs(t)*; **ሳድስ(ት)** *sādəs(t)*; **ሳብዕ(ት)** *sābəʿ(t)*; **ሳምን(ት)** *sāmən(t)*; **ታስዕ(ት)** *tāsəʿ(t)*; **ዓሥር(ት)** *ʿāśər(t)*

Classical Ethiopic uses the lexeme **ቀዳሚ** *qadāmi* (f. **ቀዳሚት** *qadāmit*; m.pl. **ቀደምት** *qaddamt*; f.pl. **ቀዳምያት** *qadāməyāt*) for 'first'. The lexeme **ዋሕድ** *wāḥəd* is not used for 'first' but means 'unique, only, one'.

For 'second' (and 'other'), Classical Ethiopic further uses certain lexemes of the same pattern but different roots, specifically ዳግም *dāgəm* (f. ዳግምት *dāgəmt*), ካዕብ *kāʿəb* (f. ካዕብት *kāʿəbt*), and ባዕድ *bāʿəd* (f. ባዕድ *bāʿədd*).

4.3.2.2. The aforementioned ordinal numbers, except ካልእ *kāləʾ*, can also be extended by the Nisbe-endings –*āwi* and –*āy* (§4.2.1.5.5.–1.5.6.): ቀዳማዊ *qadāmāwi* (f. ቀዳማዊት *qadāmāwit*), ቀዳማይ *qadāmāy* (f. ቀዳማይት/ቀዳሚት *qadāmāyt/qadāmit*); ሣልሳዊ *śāləsāwi* (f. ሣልሳዊት *śāləsāwit*), ሣልሳይ *śāləsāy* (f. ሣልሲት *śāləsit* [§4.2.1.5.6.]); etc.

Ordinary ordinal numbers can thus be formed in three ways (the following table only lists masc. forms):

1.	ቀዳሚ *qadāmi*	ቀዳማዊ *qadāmāwi*	ቀዳማይ *qadāmāy*
2.	ካልእ *kāləʾ*		
	ዳግም *dāgəm*	ዳግማዊ *dāgəmāwi*	ዳግማይ *dāgəmāy*
3.	ሣልስ *śāləs*	ሣልሳዊ *śāləsāwi*	ሣልሳይ *śāləsāy*
4.	ራብዕ *rābəʿ*	ራብዓዊ *rābəʿāwi*	ራብዓይ *rābəʿāy*
5.	ኃምስ *ḥāməs*	ኃምሳዊ *ḥāməsāwi*	ኃምሳይ *ḥāməsāy*
6.	ሳድስ *sādəs*	ሳድሳዊ *sādəsāwi*	ሳድሳይ *sādəsāy*
7.	ሳብዕ *sābəʿ*	ሳብዓዊ *sābəʿāwi*	ሳብዓይ *sābəʿāy*
8.	ሳምን *sāmən*	ሳምናዊ *sāmənāwi*	ሳምናይ *sāmənāy*
9.	ታስዕ *tāsəʿ*	ታስዓዊ *tāsəʿāwi*	ታስዓይ *tāsəʿāy*
10.	ዓሥር *ʿāśər*	ዓሥራዊ *ʿāśərāwi*	ዓሥራይ *ʿāśərāy*

4.3.2.3. Classical Ethiopic further has specific lexemes that are formed with the pattern **qatul* (note particularly ሰኑይ *sanuy* 'second'). These forms are primarily used to indicate dates and times, that is, days of the week or month and hours of the day:

- እሑድ *ʾəḥud*   'first day of the week, Sunday'
- ሰኑይ(፡ ዕለት) *sanuy* (*ʿəlat*)   'the second day (of week or month)'
- ሠሉስ፡ ሌሊት *śalus lelit*   'the third night'

- በሥሉስ *ba-śalus*   'on the third (day)/the third hour'[114]
- ረቡዕ፡ ለወርኅ *rabuʿ la-warḫ*   'the fourth (day) of the month'
- በዐሡር(፡ ዕለት) *ba-ʿaśur (ʿəlat)* 'on the tenth (day of the month)'
- ዐሡር፡ ወስኑይ *ʿaśur wa-sanuy* 'the twelfth (day)'
- ዐሡር፡ ወሥሉስ *ʿaśur wa-śalus* 'the thirteenth (day)' etc.

These lexemes can also be used as cardinals, as in ስኑይ፡ መዋዕል *sanuy mawāʿəl* 'two days'; ኀሙስ፡ መዋዕል *ḫamus mawāʿəl* 'five days'; ሥሉስ፡ ዕለት፡ ወሥሉስ፡ ሌሊተ *śalus ʿəlata wa-śalus lelita* '(during) three days and three nights'; ሰዱስ፡ ዕለተ *sadusa ʿəlata* '(during) six days'; በዐሡር፡ ወረቡዕ *ba-ʿaśur wa-rabuʿ* 'in 14 days'.

4.3.2.4. The days of the week are primarily formed with the pattern **qatul* used for ordinal numbers. They are: (ዕለተ፡)እሑድ (*ʿəlata*) *ʾəhud* 'Sunday' (also እሑድ፡ ዕለት *ʾəhud ʿəlat* and እሑድ፡ ሰንበት *ʾəhud sanbat*); ስኑይ *sanuy* 'Monday'; ሥሉስ *śalus* 'Tuesday'; ረቡዕ *rabuʿ* 'Wednesday'; ኀሙስ *ḫamus* 'Thursday'; ዐርብ *ʿarb* 'Friday' (lit. 'evening' [before Saturday]); ሰንበት *sanbat* 'Saturday' (= Sabbath).

4.3.2.5. Ordinal numbers are not formed for numbers higher than 10 – except for full tens such as 20, 30 etc. An ordinal connotation is expressed by cardinal numbers in these cases.

Ordinal numbers of full tens are expressed by the ending –*āwi* (f. –*āwit*): ዕሥራዊ *ʿəśrāwi* 'twentieth'; ሠላሳዊ *śalāsāwi* 'thirtieth' etc.

The numbers 100 (ምእት *məʾət*) and 1000/10,000 (እልፍ *ʾəlf*) likewise do not form ordinals.

'Last' is expressed by the lexemes ዳኅ/ኃራዊ *dāḫ(ā)rāwi*, ዳኅ/ኃራይ *dāḫ(ā)rāy*, ደኃሪ *dahāri*, and ተፍጻሚ *tafṣāmi*.

4.3.2.6. Ordinal adverbs with the connotation 'secondly', 'thirdly', etc. are expressed by numbers plus the suffixed enclitic particle –መ –*mma* (§4.5.8.6.). As a base, Classical Ethiopic either uses the lexemes used for fractions or ordinals, as in ሥልሰመ *śəlsa-mma* 'thirdly' (cf. ሥልስ *śəls* 'third'); ራብዕመ *rābəʿə-mma* 'fourthly'.

---

[114] The counted object is often left out.

4.3.3. Fractions

4.3.3.1. Classical Ethiopic commonly uses periphrastic constructions of the type "ordinal number + እድ *ʾəd* 'hand'" or – less often – of the type "ordinal number + ክፍል *kəfl* 'part'" instead of fractions.

If እድ *ʾəd* is used, the ordinal number can be either masc. or fem., as in ራብዕት፡እዴሃ፡ለምድር *rābəʿt ʾədehā la-mədr* 'a quarter of the land'. The ordinal number can also appear in the construct state, as in ሣልስት፡እድ *śāləsta ʾəd* 'a third'; ራብዕት፡እድ *rābəʿta ʾəd* 'a fourth'.

4.3.3.2. Certain lexemes that are derived from roots expressing numeric values can likewise be used as fractions, such as ሥልስ *śəls* 'a third' and ዐሥራት *ʿaśrāt* (also ዐሥራት፡እድ *ʿaśrāta ʾəd*) 'a tenth, tithe'.

Fem. ordinals and – less often – masc. ordinals can be used in the same way, as in ሣልስት/ሣልሲት *śāləst/śāləsit* or ሣልስ *śāləs* 'a third, the third part of the day': እምሣልስታ፡ለዕለት፡እስከ፡ሣልስታ፡ለሌሊት *ʾəm-śāləstā* (variant ሣልሲታ *śāləsitā*) *la-ʿəlat ʾəska śāləstā* (same variant) *la-lelit* 'from the third part of the day until the third part of the night' (Jub 49:10).

4.3.3.3. The construction "cardinal number + መክፈልት *makfalt* 'part'" is likewise used to express fractions, as in ክልኤ፡መክፈልታ፡ለዕለት፡ተውህበ፡ለብርሃን *kəlʾe makfaltā la-ʿəlat tawəhba la-bərhān* 'two parts of the day have been given for light' (Jub 49:10).

4.3.3.4. 'Half' and 'middle' are expressed by derivatives of the root √*nfq* 'to tear off, divide': ንፍቅ *nəfq* 'half, middle', ንፍቀት *nəfqat* 'half, section', ንፍቃ *nəfqā* 'half, middle', and መንፈቅ *manfaq* 'half, part'.

4.3.4. Cardinal Adverbs

4.3.4.1. The notion of iterativity or doing actions repeatedly ('twice', 'three times' etc.) is commonly expressed by a numeral in the adverbial accusative. From the number 'three' onward, these numbers exhibit the pattern **qətl*:

'once'	አሐተ *'aḥatta*, ምዕረ *mə'ra* (from ምዕር *mə'r* 'moment, time')
'twice'	ካዕበ *kā'əba*, ዳግመ *dāgəma* (both lexemes mean 'secondly, again, furthermore')
'three times' etc.	ሠልሰ *śalsa*, ርዕበ *rə'ba*, ኀምስ *ḫamsa*, ስድስ *sədsa*, ስብዐ *səb'a*, ስምነ *səmna*, ትስዐ *təs'a*, ዕሥረ *'əśra*

4.3.4.2. Iterative connotation of the type 'for the first/second/third etc. time' is expressed by ordinal numbers, either in the masc. and preceded by the preposition በ- *ba-*, as in በሣልስ *ba-śāləs* 'for the third time', or in the fem. in the accusative, as in ራብዕተ *rābə'ta* 'for the fourth time'.

4.3.5. Multiplicatives

Classical Ethiopic primarily uses the pattern *qəttul to indicate the notion 'twofold, threefold' etc., as in the following examples:

- ከዑብ *kə'ub* 'double'; ካዕበት *kā'əbat* 'double' (noun); forms in the acc. serve as adverbs: ከዑበ *kə'uba* 'doubly'; ካዕበተ *kā'əbata* 'doubly, twofold'
- ሠሉስ *śəllus* 'threefold, triple'
- ርቡዕ *rəbbu'* 'fourfold'
- ስቡዕ *səbbu'* 'sevenfold'

For other lexemes with a multiplicative connotation, see §4.3.6.2.

4.3.6. Collective Numbers and Related Lexemes

4.3.6.1. Classical Ethiopic uses the patterns *qutāle and *qəttāle for collective numbers of the type 'triad' etc. Examples include:

ሠላሴ *śəllāse* 'triad, trinity'; ኅማሴ *ḫumāse* 'the five'; ሱባዔ *subā'e* 'seven-year cycle, year'; ቱሳዔ *tusā'e* 'the union of nine'.

4.3.6.2. Further to be noted are lexemes derived from roots designating numeric values that have either prefixed *m-* or *t-*, including the patterns *maqtəlt and *təqtəlt, and that have various meanings, as in:

ትሥልስት *təśləst* 'trinity, threefold'; ምሥልስት *məśləst*, መሥልስት *maśləst*, መሥለስት *maśləst* 'triple, threefold, third order'; ትርብዕት *tərbəʿt* 'fourfold, quadruple'; መራብዕት *marābəʿt* 'square, fourth part'; ምስምኒት *məsmənit* 'eightfold'; ትምእት *təmʾət* 'hundredfold'.

A 'pair' of something is expressed by ዘውግ *zawg*.

4.3.7. Numeric Expressions with Distributive Meaning

Classical Ethiopic does not have specific lexemes that express distributive numbers. Instead, distributive connotations are related through periphrastic constructions (cf. §5.6.) such as:

1. Repetition of the uninflected cardinal number, as in ክልኤ፡ክልኤ *kəlʾe kəlʾe* 'two each'; ሰባዕት፡ሰባዕት *sabāʿt sabāʿt* 'seven each';

2. Constructions with በበ *babba*, ለለ *lalla*, and ዘዘ *zazza* (§5.6.), as in ወወሀቦሙ፡ዐራዘ፡በበ፡ክልኤቱ *wa-wahabomu ʿarrāza babba kəlʾetu* 'he gave them garments, two each', that is, 'he gave each of them two garments' (Gen 45:22); በበ፡ክልኤቱ *babba kəlʾetu* '(he sent them) two each', that is, '(he sent them) in pairs of two' (Lk 10:1);

3. Combinations of (1.) and (2.), as in ወለለ፡ጀምግባሮሙ *wa-lalla ʾaḥadu məgbāromu* '(I wrote down ... regarding) ... the deeds of each one of them' (En 13:6).

4.4. The Verb

Most of the verbs in Classical Ethiopic have three root letters or radicals. The following description relates to such triradical verbs (§4.4.1.–6.). The inflection of verbs with more than three radicals will be discussed in §4.4.7.–9. The citation form of the Classical Ethiopic verb is the 3ms perfect, commonly of the basic or G-stem, which is rendered as an infinitive in the English glosses.

4.4.1. The Finite Verbal Forms of the Basic (G)-Stem

4.4.1.1. Introduction

Classical Ethiopic has four finite forms or conjugational paradigms of the verb: (1) the perfect, (2) the imperfect (also called "present tense"), (3) the jussive (also called "subjunctive"), and (4) the imperative. These four forms are cited according to the following abbreviations and with the paradigmatic verb ቀተለ qatala ('to kill'):

Perfect　　　= pf.　　　= ቀተለ qatala
Imperfect　= impf.　　= ይቀትል yəqattəl
Jussive　　　= juss.　　= ይቅትል yəqtəl
Imperative　= imp.　　= ቅትል qətəl

The following sections introduce the finite forms of the G-stem. The forms of the respective paradigms of the other verbal stems is represented in the table of verbal paradigms in §4.4.4.4. The inflectional prefixes and suffixes are the same in all verbal stems.

4.4.1.2. The Perfect

4.4.1.2.1. The perfect of the G-stem distinguishes two main paradigms:

(a) The "nagara"-type consisting of three syllables (ነገረ nagara 'to speak');
(b) The "gabra"-type (< *gabəra) consisting of two syllables (ገብረ gabra 'to do, make').

The nagara-type with three syllables primarily occurs with transitive verbs while the gabra-type with two syllables primarily occurs with intransitive verbs, although this basic distributional pattern simply represents a tendency and has exceptions (see, e.g., ገብረ gabra 'to do, make'). The formal distinction of the two types is only evident in third person forms, that is, in forms that end in a vowel or have suffixes beginning with a vowel.

This means that when a vowel (the "theme vowel") is present between the second and third radical, it always has the quality /a/. There are no forms with the theme vowels /i/ and /u/ since original *qatila and *qatula were reduced to *qatla < *qatəla through regular sound changes (see §3.2.2.).
A few verbs, especially verbs denoting states and verbs with either /r/ or /l/ as second radical, exhibit both perfect types, such as ቀርበ/ቀረበ qarba/qaraba 'to draw near'; ጸልመ/ጸለመ ṣalma/ṣalama 'to grow dark, be black'; ተርፈ/ተረፈ tarfa/tarafa 'to be left (behind)'; ዐጽበ/ዐጸበ ʿaṣba/ʿaṣaba 'to be difficult, hard'.

4.4.1.2.2. The following introduces the inflectional paradigm of the perfect (the forms of the perfect are stressed on the penultima, except in the 2fp).[115] Two characteristics have to be noted in comparison with the paradigm of Central Semitic languages: 1. The forms of the second persons and the 1cs have a suffix starting with the consonant /k/ as opposed to Central Semitic /t/; 2. The form of the 3fp has the ending -ā (as in Akkadian).

	Singular		Plural	
3 masc.	ነገረ *nagára*	ገብረ *gábra*	ነገሩ *nagáru*	ገብሩ *gábru*
3 fem.	ነገረት *nagárat*	ገብረት *gábrat*	ነገራ *nagárā*	ገብራ *gábrā*
2 masc.	ነገርከ *nagárka*	ገብርከ *gabárka*[116]	ነገርከሙ *nagarkə́mu*	ገብርከሙ *gabarkə́mu*[117]
2 fem.	ነገርኪ *nagárki*	ገብርኪ *gabárki*	ነገርክን *nagarkə́n*	ገብርክን *gabarkə́n*
1 c.	ነገርኩ *nagárku*	ገብርኩ *gabárku*	ነገርነ *nagárna*	ገብርነ *gabárna*

4.4.1.2.3. For the phenomenon of progressive assimilation in verbs ending in a velar, as in **ወደቁ** *wadaqqu* < *wadaqku* 'I fell', see §3.6.6.2. For verbs of the *nagara*-type, such an assimilated form of the 1cs cannot be distinguished from the form of the 3mp in the orthography, as in the case of **ኀደጉ** *ḫa-da-gu*, which can be read as *ḫadagu* 'they left' and *ḫadaggu* 'I left'.

The same orthographic ambiguity is found in verbs with final /n/ between forms of the 1cp and 3ms, as in **ከደነ** *ka-da-na*, which can be read as *kadanna* 'we covered' and *kadana* 'he covered'.

When the final root consonant is a labiovelar, it often becomes a simple velar before person suffixes starting with a /k/, as in **ለሐከ** *laḥakka* 'you formed' (besides regular **ለሐኵከ** *laḥakʷka*).

---

[115] In Ethiopia, finite verbal forms are presented in a different order: 3ms, 2ms, 3mp, 2mp, 3fs, 2fs, 3fp, 2fp, 1cp, 1cs (that is, masc. before fem., sing. before pl, and third and second person before first person).

[116] Theoretically, we would expect forms such as **gabərka, gabərki*, etc. The forms of the type *gabarka* are probably the result of analogy with the transitive type.

[117] According to the traditional pronunciation, the form of the 2mp is pronounced with a geminated /kk/ (§3.3.2.1.), as in **ነገርከሙ** *nagarkkəmu* (2fp, however, **ነገርክን** *nagarkən*) (Mittwoch 1926, 52).

The perfect primarily serves to denote the (perfective) expression of past actions, although it has a variety of other functions (§5.4.1.).

4.4.1.3. The Imperfect

4.4.1.3.1. The imperfect (*yəqattəl*), which is also called "present," is, from a formal point of view, the long form of the prefix conjugation. Its form is characterized by two features: 1. the vowel /a/ between the first and second root radicals; and 2. the gemination of the second root radical.

The form of the Classical Ethiopic imperfect thus corresponds exactly to that of Akkadian (*iparras* < **yVparrVs*). At the same time, it differs significantly from the form of the imperfect (indicative) of Central Semitic languages (*yaqtulu*). This fact is important for comparative purposes and for the classification of Classical Ethiopic within the Semitic language family.[118]

4.4.1.3.2. The forms of the imperfect are always stressed on the penultima (that is, *yənággər*, *yənaggóru* etc.). Prefixes and suffixes mostly correspond to those known from other Semitic languages. Notable is the ending *-ā* in the 3fp and 2fp, which corresponds to Akkadian as opposed to Hebrew an Arabic *-na*.

	Singular	Plural
3 masc.	ይነግር *yənággər*	ይነግሩ *yənaggóru*
3 fem.	ትነግር *tənággər*	ይነግራ *yənaggórā*
2 masc.	ትነግር *tənággər*	ትነግሩ *tənaggóru*
2 fem.	ትነግሪ *tənaggóri*	ትነግራ *tənaggórā*
1 c.	እነግር *ʾənággər*	ንነግር *nənággər*

---

[118] The middle radical of the imperfect is articulated as a geminate in all verbal stems according to the traditional pronunciation (see Mittwoch 1926, 20). Contrary to the traditional pronunciation, the middle radical is commonly written as non-geminated in older grammars of Classical Ethiopic (e.g., DG); that is, G *yəqatəl*; D *yəqetəl*; L *yəqātəl*; the form of the L-impf. would thus be the same as that of the jussive. There has been a long debate whether the gemination in the imperfect is original or not – in particular regarding the L and its derived stems. If the gemination is secondary, the formal correspondence with Akkadian would be coincidental. Voigt (1990) has brought forth convincing arguments in favor of the original character of the gemination in the imperfect. This assumption is further strengthened by the fact that secondary gemination in Classical Ethiopic is most commonly attested before a stressed syllable and only rarely after a stress-bearing syllable (§3.3.2.).

4.4.1.3.3. The imperfect primarily serves to express verbal actions relating to the present and future but can also express imperfective connotations relating to actions in the past (§5.4.2.3.).

4.4.1.4. The Jussive

4.4.1.4.1. The jussive (*yəqtəl*) – traditionally called the "subjunctive" – is the short form of the prefix conjugation from a formal point of view. It corresponds to the jussive of Central Semitic languages (**yaqtul*) and the precative of Akkadian (*l-iprus*).

The Classical Ethiopic jussive of the G-stem has a bisyllabic base with the vowel /ə/ in the prefix and /ə/ or /a/ as theme vowel (in the second syllable, between the second and third root radicals).

The vowel of the second syllable is connected to the vowel of the perfect. Verbs of the *nagara*-type commonly have /ə/ as theme vowel in the jussive, that is, **ይንግር** *yəngər* (corresponding to common Semitic **yaqtu/il*), while verbs of the *gabra*-type tend to have /a/ as theme vowel in the jussive, that is, **ይግብር** *yəgbar*. There are, however, quite a few exceptions to this rule, as well as verbs that can have both /ə/ and /a/ as jussive theme vowel, such as **ተርፈ/ተረፈ** *tarfa/tarafa* 'to be left' with the jussives **ይትርፍ** *yətrəf* and **ይትረፍ** *yətraf*. Verbs with two theme vowels commonly also exhibit both perfect types, as in the example of **ተርፈ/ተረፈ** *tarfa/tarafa* just mentioned.

4.4.1.4.2. The prefixes and suffixes added to the jussive base are the same as in the imperfect. The paradigm thus has the following form (with penultimate stress in all forms):

	Singular		Plural	
3 masc.	ይንግር *yə́ngər*	ይግብር *yə́gbar*	ይንግሩ *yəngə́ru*	ይግብሩ *yəgbáru*
3 fem.	ትንግር *tə́ngər*	ትግብር *tə́gbar*	ይንግራ *yəngə́rā*	ይግብራ *yəgbárā*
2 masc.	ትንግር *tə́ngər*	ትግብር *tə́gbar*	ትንግሩ *təngə́ru*	ትግብሩ *təgbáru*
2 fem.	ትንግሪ *təngə́ri*	ትግብሪ *təgbári*	ትንግራ *təngə́rā*	ትግብራ *təgbárā*
1 c.	እንግር *ʾə́ngər*	እግብር *ʾə́gbar*	ንንግር *nə́ngər*	ንግብር *nə́gbar*

4.4.1.4.3. The jussive functions as a volitive form in main clauses and is further used for consecutive clauses and clauses expressing purpose or result (§5.4.3.2.).

4.4.1.5. The Imperative

4.4.1.5.1. The imperative (*qatəl*) formally corresponds to the base of the jussive in terms of theme vowel but has /ə/ between the first and second root letters, as in ንግር *nəgər* 'speak!' (masc. sing.) compared to jussive ይንግር *yəngər*, and ግበር *gəbar* 'make!' compared to the jussive ይግበር *yəgbar*.

4.4.1.5.2. The inflectional endings of the imperative correspond to those of the second persons of the jussive and imperfect. All forms are, according to Mittwoch (1926, 52), stressed on the penultima:[119]

masc. sing.	fem. sing.	masc. pl.	fem. pl.
ንግር *nə́gər*	ንግሪ *nəgə́ri*	ንግሩ *nəgə́ru*	ንግራ *nəgə́rā*
ግበር *gə́bar*	ግበሪ *gəbári*	ግበሩ *gəbáru*	ግበራ *gəbárā*

4.4.1.5.3. The imperative cannot be negated. Classical Ethiopic uses a negated form of the second person jussive instead, as in ኢትንግር *ʾi-təngər* 'do not speak!'.

4.4.2. Finite Verbs with Object-Suffixes

4.4.2.1. The Perfect with Object-Suffixes

4.4.2.1.1. The pronominal object-suffixes are directly attached to the respective perfect forms. For the forms of the pronominal suffixes, see §4.1.2. In the perfect, some forms of the verb remain unchanged (3ms/3mp; 2ms/2mp), while others change slightly before suffixes. The latter include the 3fs -*at*, which becomes -*ata*-, the 2fs -*ki*, which becomes -*kə*-, and the 1cp -*na*, which becomes -*nā*-. The 2fp -*kən* has two forms before pronominal suffixes, -*kənā*- and -*kā*-.

After verbal forms of the 3s and 2s (that is, verbal forms ending in /a/ or /ə/), the initial consonant of the pronominal suffixes is pronounced as geminated, as in ነገረከ *nagarákka* 'he said to you'. In other forms, the initial suffix consonant is not geminated, as in ነገሩከ *nagarúka* 'they (m) said to you (ms)' (see Mittwoch 1926, 74–77).

Combinations of perfect and object forms of the same person (in reflexive function) are not used. Such reflexive meanings are commonly circumscribed.

---

[119] Other authors assume stress on the ultima in the masc. sing., that is, *nəgár* and *ləbás*.

The paradigm of verbal forms with pronominal suffixes of the first and second persons has the following form (with penultima stress, except in the case of forms with the 2fp the suffix –ክን –kə́n):

	Suffix	1cs	2ms	2fs	1cp	2mp	2fp
Verbal form							
3ms	ነገረ- nagara-	–ኒ –nni	–ህ –kka	–ኪ –kki	–ን –nna	–ሆሙ –kkəmu	–ክን –(k)kən
3fs	ነገረተ- nagarata-	–ኒ –nni	–ህ –kka	–ኪ –kki	–ን –nna	–ሆሙ –kkəmu	–ክን – (k)kən
2ms	ነገርከ- nagarka-	–ኒ –nni	--	--	–ን –nna	--	--
2fs	ነገርከ- nagarkə-	–ኒ –nni	--	--	–ን –nna	--	--
1cs	ነገርኩ- nagarku-	--	–ህ –ka	–ኪ –ki	–ሆሙ –kkəmu	--	–ክን – (k)kən
3mp	ነገሩ- nagaru-	–ኒ –ni	–ህ –ka	–ኪ –ki	–ን –na	–ሆሙ –kkəmu	–ክን – (k)kən
3fp	ነገራ- nagarā-	–ኒ –ni	–ህ –ka	–ኪ –ki	–ን –na	–ሆሙ –kkəmu	–ክን – (k)kən
2mp	ነገርክሙ- nagarkəmu-	–ኒ –ni	--	--	–ን –na	--	--
2fp	ነገርክና- nagarkənā-	–ኒ –ni	--	--	–ን –na	--	--
	ነገርካ- nagarkā-	–ኒ –ni	--	--	–ን –na	--	--
1cp	ነገርና- nagarnā-	--	–ህ –ka	–ኪ –ki[120]	--	–ሆሙ –kkəmu	–ክን –(k)kən

4.4.2.1.2. The forms of the third person suffixes are attached with various changes to the basic form of the perfect verb. Only verbs ending in /ā/ do not change their form before these suffixes (as in ነገራሁ nagarāhu 'they [fp] told him'). All other forms undergo changes.

---

[120] According to the traditional pronunciation, the /k/ is also sometimes pronounced as geminated in this form (see Mittwoch 1926, 77, note 1).

The rules for the attachment of object-suffixes to third person perfect forms are as follows:

- The suffixes are attached to the same modified bases as the suffixes of the first and second persons.
- After perfect forms ending in /a/, the initial /h/ of the third person suffixes disappears and the resulting diphthong is contracted, as in ነገሮ *nagaro* < *nagaraw < *nagarahu 'he told him' and ነገራ *nagarā* < *nagaraa < *nagaraha 'he told her'.
- Final /i/ in the perfect of the 2fs is reduced to /ə/ with a following geminated glide /əyy/, while final /u/ becomes /əww/ (§3.8.2.2.). The same suffixes that are attached to perfects ending in -a are then added to this base, that is -əyyo, -əyyā, -əwwo, -əwwā etc. The gemination of /y/ and /w/ in these forms is the result of the progressive assimilation of the original /h/ of the suffix (cf. §3.6.6), that is *nagarkəyyo* < *nagarkəyhu and *nagarkəwwo* < *nagarkəw-hu.[121] The /o/-vowel in these forms is most likely the result of a secondary analogy with forms such as ነገሮ *nagaro* and ነገርኮ *nagarko*.
- The perfect forms of the 2ms and 2fp have two different forms with pronominal suffixes of the third person singular. In the 2ms, the /a/ vowel of the person marker -ka can appear lengthened as -kā- before suffixes, as in ነገርኩሁ *nagarkāhu* and ነገርካሃ *nagarkāhā* (2ms), although this form occurs less frequently than the regularly formed ነገርኮ *nagarko*. The 2ms with -kā- is formally identical to the second, shortened, form of the 2fp with the same suffixes (ነገርኩሁ-*nagarkāhu* and ነገርካሃ *nagarkāhā*).
- Verbal forms with third person suffixes are frequent because of their use in the common *qatalo la-nəguś* construction (§5.2.3.2.).

The paradigm of third person perfects with object-suffixes is as follows (stress is on the penultima in -(h)ómu, -ə́yyo/-ə́yyā, -ə́wwo/-ə́wwā, -ə́wwon, and -ə́yyon, otherwise stress is on the ultima):

Verbal form	3ms suffix	3fs suffix
3ms	ነገሮ *nagaró*	ነገራ *nagar'ā*
3fs	ነገረቶ *nagarató*	ነገርታ *nagarat'ā*

---

[121] The gemination of /y/ and /w/ is confirmed by Mittwoch (1926, 75, notes 5 and 6).

2ms	ነገርኮ nagarkó	ነገርካ nagarkʾā
	ነገርካሁ nagarkāhú	ነገርካሃ nagarkāhʾā
2fs	ነገርኪ nagarkə́yyo	ነገርኪያ nagarkə́yyā
1cs	ነገርኮዎ nagarkə́wwo	ነገርኮዋ nagarkə́wwā
3mp	ነገሮዎ nagarə́wwo	ነገሮዋ nagarə́wwā
3fp	ነገራሁ nagarāhú	ነገራሃ nagarāhʾā
2mp	ነገርክሞዎ nagarkəmə́wwo	ነገርክሞዋ nagarkəmə́wwā
2fp	ነገርክናሁ nagarkənāhú	ነገርክናሃ nagarkənāhʾā
	ነገርካሁ nagarkāhú	ነገርካሃ nagarkāhʾā
1cp	ነገርናሁ nagarnāhú	ነገርናሃ nagarnāhʾā

Verbal form	3mp suffix	3fp suffix
3ms	ነገሮሙ nagarómu	ነገሮን nagarón
3fs	ነገረቶሙ nagaratómu	ነገረቶን nagaratón[122]
2ms	ነገርኮሙ nagarkómu	ነገርኮን nagarkón
2fs	ነገርኪሙ nagarkəyyómu	ነገርኪን nagarkə́yyon[123]
1cs	ነገርኮሙ nagarkəwwómu	ነገርኮን nagarkə́wwon[124]
3mp	ነገሮሙ nagarəwwómu	ነገሮን nagarə́wwon
3fp	ነገራሆሙ nagarāhómu	ነገራሆን nagarāhón
2mp	ነገርክሞሙ nagarkəməwwómu	ነገርክሞን nagarkəmə́wwon
2fp	ነገርክናሆሙ nagarkənāhómu	ነገርክናሆን nagarkənāhón
1cp	ነገርናሆሙ nagarnāhómu	ነገርናሆን nagarnāhón

4.4.2.1.3. According to the traditional pronunciation, the consonant of various perfect forms with pronominal suffixes is geminated before a stressed syllable (§3.3.2.1.), as in ነገረተኒ nagarattánni (3fs + 1cs suffix); ነገረቶ nagaratto (3fs + 3ms suffix); ነገረታ nagarattā (3fs + 3fs suffix); ነገርከኒ nagarkkánni (2ms + 1cs suffix);

---

[122] For the fact that these forms (except ነገረቶሙ nagaratómu) are stressed on the last syllable, see Mittwoch (1926, 75). Older grammars claim penultima stress for all of these forms, such as ነገረቶ nagaráto, ነገረቶን nagaráton etc.

[123] According to Mittwoch (1926, 75) this form is pronounced as nagarkiyyon.

[124] According to Mittwoch (1926, 75) this form is pronounced as nagarkuwwon.

ነገርኮ *nagarkko* (2ms + 3ms suffix); ነገርካ *nagarkkā* (2ms + 3fs suffix).[125] This gemination is most likely secondary and is not reflected in the transliterations used in this grammar.

4.4.2.2. The Imperfect with Object Suffixes

4.4.2.2.1. When the imperfect ends in a vowel (/–i/, /–u/, or /–ā/), pronominal suffixes are attached directly to the base (with the typical change of *–i* > *–əyy* and *–u* > *–əww* before third person suffixes).

When the imperfect ends in a consonant, the suffixes are attached to a linking vowel /a/, as in ይነግርክ *yənaggər-a-ka* 'he tells you (ms)', which is traditionally pronounced with a geminated /k/, that is *yənaggərakka*.

The pronominal suffixes of the third persons have the forms *-o* (3ms), *-ā* (3fs), *-omu* (3mp), and *-on* (3fp) after imperfects ending in a consonant. These forms are the result of the loss of the /h/ of the original suffix and the subsequent contraction of the original linking and suffix vowels, as in *yənaggəro* < **yənaggəraw* < **yənaggərahu*.

The following table provides an overview of the various forms of the imperfect with a representative choice of pronominal suffixes (stress is on the penultima if not otherwise indicated):

Verbal form	1cs suffix	2ms suffix
3ms	ይነግረኒ *yənaggəránni*	ይነግርክ *yənaggərákka*
3fs	ትነግረኒ *tənaggəránni*	ትነግርክ *tənaggərákka*
2ms	ትነግረኒ *tənaggəránni*	--
2fs	ትነግርኒ *tənaggərənni*	--
1cs	--	እነግርክ *'ənaggərákka*
3mp	ይነግሩኒ *yənaggərúni*	ይነግሩከ *yənaggərúka*
3fp	ይነግራኒ *yənaggər'āni*	ይነግራከ *yənaggər'āka*
2mp	ትነግሩኒ *tənaggərúni*	--
2fp	ትነግራኒ *tənaggər'āni*	--
1cs	--	ንነግርክ *nənaggərákka*

[125] No gemination occurs in forms such as ነገርኩ *nagarkāhu* (2ms + 3ms suffix) and ነገርካ *nagarkāhā* (2ms + 3fs suffix).

Verbal form	3ms suffix	3fs suffix
3ms	ይነግሮ *yənaggəró*	ይነግራ *yənaggərˊā*
3fs	ትነግሮ *tənaggəró*	ትነግራ *tənaggərˊā*
2ms	ትነግሮ *tənaggəró*	ትነግራ *tənaggərˊā*
2fs	ትነግርዮ *tənaggəróyyo*	ትነግርያ *tənaggəróyyā*
1cs	እነግሮ *ʾənaggəró*	እነግራ *ʾənaggərˊā*
3mp	ይነግርዎ *yənaggəráwwo*	ይነግርዋ *yənaggəráwwā*
3fp	ይነግራሁ *yənaggərāhú*	ይነግራየ *yənaggərāhˊā*
2mp	ትነግርዎ *tənaggəráwwo*	ትነግርዋ *tənaggəráwwā*
2fp	ትነግራሁ *tənaggərāhú*	ትነግራየ *tənaggərāhˊā*
1cs	ንነግሮ *nənaggəró*	ንነግራ *nənaggərˊā*

4.4.2.3. The Jussive with Object Suffixes

4.4.2.3.1. Jussive forms ending in a vowel and the jussive of the first persons (sing. and pl.) behave in the same manner as those of the imperfect when pronominal suffixes are attached. Other forms differ from the imperfect:

- The suffixes of the second persons are directly attached to the base of the jussive without a linking vowel, as in ይንግርk *yəngərka* 'let him tell you'.
- When third person suffixes are attached to a jussive ending in a consonant, the final consonant is geminated, as in ይንግሮ *yəngárro*, ይንግራ *yəngárrā*, ይንግሮሙ *yəngərrómu*, ይንግርን *yəngárron* (consistently with stress on the penultima).[126] This gemination most likely goes back to the assimilation of the initial /h/ of the respective suffixes, that is *yəngərro* < **yəngərhu*.

The following paradigm provides representative forms of the jussive with pronominal object-suffixes:

---

[126] See Mittwoch 1926, 79. Verbs with a guttural as third root radical do not exhibit this type of gemination.

Person	1cs suffix	2ms suffix
3ms	ይንግረኒ *yəngəránni*	ይንግርክ *yəngárka*
3fs	ትንግረኒ *təngəránni*	ትንግርክ *təngárka*
2fs	ትንግርኒ *təngəránni*	--
3mp	ይንgrሩኒ *yəngərúni*	ይንግሩክ *yəngərúka*
3fp	ይንግራኒ *yəngərˀāni*	ይንግራክ *yəngərˀāka*

Person	3ms suffix	3fs suffix
3ms	ይንግሮ *yəngórro*	ይንግራ *yəngórrā*
3fs	ትንግሮ *təngórro*	ትንግራ *təngórrā*
2fs	ትንግርዮ *təngəráyyo*	ትንግርያ *təngəráyyā*
3mp	ይንግርዎ *yəngəráwwo*	ይንግርዋ *yəngəráwwā*
3fp	ይንግራሁ *yəngərˀāhu*	ይንግራሃ *yəngərˀāhā*

4.4.2.4. The Imperative with Object Suffixes

The imperative can only be connected with pronominal suffixes of the first and third persons. The suffixal paradigm operates according to the same principles as in the case of the jussive. According to the traditional pronunciation, however, the vowel between the second and third root radicals is syncopated unless it is stressed, as in ንግረኒ *nəgránni* instead of expected **nəgəránni*, but ንግሮ *nəgórro*. The paradigm is thus:

Person	1cs suffix	1cp suffix	3ms suffix	3fs suffix
ms	ንግረኒ *nəgránni*	ንግረነ *nəgránna*	ንግሮ *nəgórro*	ንግራ *nəgárrā*
fs	ንግርኒ *nəgránni*	ንግር/ረነ *nəgró/ínna*	ንግርዮ *nəgráyyo*	ንግርያ *nəgráyyā*
mp	ንግሩኒ *nəgrúni*	ንግሩነ *nəgrúna*	ንግርዎ *nəgráwwo*	ንግርዋ *nəgráwwā*

4.4.3. Verbal Nouns

4.4.3.1. Introduction

Nominal derivatives of the verb include the following categories (citation forms
of the G-stem are given on the right side):

1. the perfective participle   = ቀቲሎ *qatilo*
2. the infinitive   = ቀቲል/ቀቲሎት *qatil(ot)*
3. the common verbal adjective   = ቅቱል *qətul*
4. the agent noun   = ቀታሊ *qatāli*
5. other verbal nouns

The following sections introduce the basic formations of these categories for all
stem types.

4.4.3.2. The Perfective Participle

The basic morphological form of the perfective participle (§5.5.2.) in the G-stem
is *qatil–* and thus reflects the common Semitic pattern **qatīl*. This form is
identical with the G-stem infinitive without suffixed *–ot*. The perfective
participles of the other verbal stems have the same vocalic pattern but also
exhibit the morphological characteristics of each stem. The basic forms of the
perfective participle are listed in the following table:

G	ቀቲል– *qatil–*	D	ቀቲል– *qattil–*
CG	አቅቲል– *ʾaqtil–*	CD	አቀቲል– *ʾaqattil–*
Gt	ተቀቲል– *taqatil–*	Dt	ተቀቲል– *taqattil–*
CGt	አስተቅቲል– *ʾastaqtil–*	CDt	አስተቀቲል– *ʾastaqattil–*

L	ቃቲል– *qātil–*
CL	አቃቲል– *ʾaqātil–*
Lt	ተቃቲል– *taqātil–*
CLt	አስተቃቲል– *ʾastaqātil–*

4.4.3.2.2. Perfective participles are always construed in combination with pronominal suffixes and always occur in the adverbial accusative – the suffixes thus have the form of those attached to nouns in the accusative (§4.1.2.2.). Stress lies on the penultima in most cases, although forms with the suffixes of the 3ms (–*o*), 3fs (–*ā*), 3fp (–*on*), and 2fp (–*akən*) are stressed on the last syllable (as in **ቀቲሎ** *qatiló*, **ቀቲላ** *qatil'ā*, **ቀቲሎን** *qatilón*, and **ቀቲለክን** *qatilakə́n*). The forms of the G perfective participle with pronominal suffixes are the following:

With sing. suffix	**ቀቲሎ** *qatilo*, **ቀቲላ** *qatilā*, **ቀቲለከ** *qatilaka*, **ቀቲለኪ** *qatilaki*, **ቀቲልየ** *qatiləya*
With pl. suffix	**ቀቲሎሙ** *qatilomu*, **ቀቲሎን** *qatilon*, **ቀቲለከሙ** *qatilakəmu*, **ቀቲለክን** *qatilakən*, **ቀቲለነ** *qatilana*

4.4.3.2.3. In most cases, the perfective participle denotes an action that has been completed prior to that of the main verb. Perfective participles can only be rendered periphrastically in English in the form of a temporal clause 'when, after' or participial phrases 'having killed, he ...'. Whether a perfective participle is active or passive depends on the verbal stem in which it is used. It is not naturally connected to either active or passive meaning. Examples include:

ቀቲሎ *qatilo*	'having killed, he ...; after he killed'
ቀቲሎሙ *qatilomu*	'having killed, they ...; after they killed'
ሰሚዖሙ *samiʿomu*	'having heard, they ...; after they heard'
ተቀቲሎ *taqatilo*	'having been killed, he/it ...'

For the syntactic functions of the perfective participle, see §5.5.2.

4.4.3.3. The Infinitive

4.4.3.3.1. The basic form of the infinitive in the various verbal stems is similar to that of the perfective participle. Infinitives, however, have a final vowel –*o* in all stems except the G-stem, which has no vocalic ending, and exhibit an ending –*ot* before pronominal suffixes and (often) before the ending -*a* of the construct state (§4.2.1.5.4.). Furthermore, infinitives of derived stems have the stem vowel /ə/ between the second and third root letter, not /i/ as seen in the perfective participle.

The paradigm of the infinitive is as follows (endings in parentheses are those that occur before pronominal suffixes):

G	ቀቲል/ቀቲሎት qatil(ot)	D	ቀትሎ(ት) qattəlo(t)
CG	አቅትሎ(ት) ʾaqtəlo(t)	CD	አቀትሎ(ት) ʾaqattəlo(t)
Gt	ተቀትሎ(ት) taqatəlo(t)	Dt	ተቀትሎ(ት) taqattəlo(t)
CGt	አስተቅትሎ(ት) ʾastaqtəlo(t)	CDt	አስተቀትሎ(ት) ʾastaqattəlo(t)

L	ቃትሎ(ት) qātəlo(t)
CL	አቃትሎ(ት) ʾaqātəlo(t)
Lt	ተቃትሎ(ት) taqātəlo(t)
CLt	አስተቃትሎ(ት) ʾastaqātəlo(t)

4.4.3.3.2. The form of the suffixes attached to the infinitive with final -ot depends on the function of the suffixes (§5.5.1.8.):

- If the suffixes function as objects, which is the most frequently occurring function, they are attached as and have the form of suffixes on a noun in the accusative, as in ቀቲሎትየ qatilotəya, ቀቲሎተከ qatilotaka, ቀቲሎቶ qatiloto 'to kill me/you (ms)/him'.
- If the suffixes function as subjects, they are attached like suffixes to a noun in the nominative, as in ቀቲሎትየ qatilotəya, ቀቲሎትከ qatilotəka, ቀቲሎቱ qatilotu 'my/your (ms)/his killing'. If, however, the infinitive appears in the accusative syntactically, even suffixes expressing the subject have the form of accusative suffixes, that is, ቀቲሎተከ qatilotaka etc.

4.4.3.3.3. In the construct state, the G-infinitive ends, as expected, in final -a. This -a is usually suffixed directly to the base, ቀቲለ qatila, and only rarely to the pre-suffixal form of the infinitive ቀቲሎት *qatilota*. Infinitives of derived stems have the same form in the bound as in the unbound state with final –o.

A few examples include: ነዲፈ፡ቀስት *nadifa qast* 'shooting a bow' (G); ንዒወ፡ኦራዊት *nəʿiwa ʾarāwit* 'hunting animals' (G); ሰሚዖተ፡ቃሎ *samiʿota qālo* 'to hear his voice' (G); ተጸዕኖ፡ፈረስ *taṣaʿəno faras* 'to ride a horse' (Gt).

4.4.3.4. The Verbal Adjective

4.4.3.4.1. Every verbal stem, in principle, has a specific verbal adjective. Frequently attested, however, are only those of the G, D, and L-stems.

The most important verbal adjective of the G-stem has the pattern ቅቱል *qətul*, which is derived from the pattern **qutūl*,[127] as in ክቡር *kəbur* 'glorious' (§4.2.1.3:3). The most important verbal adjectives of the D and L stems exhibit a similar formation:

- The most frequent verbal adjective of the D-stem is *qəttul* < **quttūl* (§4.2.1.4:1), as in እዙዝ *ʾəzzuz* 'commanded, ordered'; ፍውስ *fəwwəs* (< **fəwwus*) 'healed, cured'; ሥኑይ *śənnuy* (f. ሥኒት *śənnit*) 'adorned'. Furthermore, the patterns ቀቲል *qəttil* and ቀታል *qəttāl* serve as verbal adjectives of the D-stem (§4.2.1.4:3–4).
- The verbal adjective of the L-stem has the pattern *qutul* < **qūtūl* (§4.2.1.3:11), as in ቡሩክ *buruk* (f. ቡርክት *burəkt*) 'blessed'; ሙሱን *musun* (f. ሙስንት *musənt*) 'corrupt, destroyed'.

4.4.3.4.2. The G-verbal adjective *qətul* commonly has a passive meaning when derived from transitive fientive verbs, as in ብዱዕ *bəduʿ* 'dedicated'; ብቱክ *bətuk* 'broken'; ፍቁር *fəqur* 'beloved'; ቅቡር *qəbur* 'buried'; ቅቱል *qətul* 'killed'; ጥሙቅ *ṭəmuq* 'baptized'. An exception is እኁዝ *ʾəḫuz*, which can also have the transitive meaning 'holding' besides passive 'taken', as in እኁዛነ፡ወልታ፡ወኵናት *ʾəḫuzāna waltā wa-kʷināt* 'carriers of shield and spear'.

The verbal adjective *qətul* of intransitive fientive verbs usually has a resultative meaning (that is, it expresses the state that results from the underlying verbal

---

[127] Classical Ethiopic ቅቱል *qətul*, however, functionally corresponds to the common Semitic pattern **qatūl*.

action), as in **ንቡር** *nəbur* 'sitting, seated'; **ስኩብ** *səkub* 'lying'; **ፅንስት** *ḍənəst* 'pregnant'.

Verbal adjectives of stative roots have a descriptive meaning, that is, they express the basic adjectival notion of the verbal root, as in **ሕዙን** *ḥəzun* 'sad'; **ንኡስ** *nə'us* 'small'.

4.4.3.5. The Agent Noun

4.4.3.5.1. Classical Ethiopic does not have an active participle of the pattern **qātil* as attested in most other Semitic languages. The corresponding functions and meanings are expressed by other nominal formations (in relation to the individual verbal stems) or, more frequently, through periphrastic constructions involving the relative pronoun **ዘ–** *za–* + imperfect (§5.1.5d).

4.4.3.5.2. Agent nouns in Classical Ethiopic are commonly marked by the ending *-āCi* (where C= third root letter). In substantivized function, they are often used to express professions. This use is found for the following formations (AN = agent noun):

qatāli (§4.2.1.5.1:1)	AN of G; as in **ፈጣሪ** *faṭāri* 'creator' (construct **ፈጣሬ** *faṭāre*; as in **ፈጣሬ፡ ምድር** *faṭāre mədr* 'creator of the earth')
qattāli (§4.2.1.5.1:2)	AN of D; as in **አባሲ** *'abbāsi* 'sinner'
qātāli (§4.2.1.5.1:3)	AN of L; as in **ባላሒ** *bālāḥi* 'liberator'
'aqtāli (§4.2.1.7:2)	AN of CG; as in **አንባቢ** *'anbābi* 'reader'
'aqattāli (§4.2.1.7:4)	AN of CD; as in **አገባሪ** *'agabbāri* 'forcing'
'aqātāli (§4.2.1.7:3)	AN of CL; as in **አማሳኒ** *'amāsāni* 'destroyer'
maqtali (§4.2.1.7:5)	AN of CG, as in **መድኅኒ** *madḫani* 'redeemer, savior'
taqatāli (§4.2.1.7:9)	AN of Gt, as in **ተአማሪ** *ta'amāri* 'interpreter, soothsayer'
taqattāli (§4.2:1.7:10)	AN of Dt, as in **ተነባዪ** *tanabbāyi* 'who predicts, who acts as a prophet'
'astaqātāli (§4.2.1.7:12)	AN of CLt; as in **አስተጋባኢ** *'astagābā'i* 'who gathers'

4.4.3.5.3. The following formations with *ma-* and *masta-* likewise frequently function as agent nouns:

maqtəl (§4.2.1.6.1:2)	AN of CG and G; as in መምህር mamhər 'teacher'
maqattəl (§4.2.1.6.1:5)	AN of D and CD; as in መሠግር maśaggər 'fisherman'
maqātəl (§4.2.1.6.1:6)	AN of L, as in መናዘዝ manāzəz 'consoling'
mastaq(a)təl, mastaqattəl, mastaqātəl (§4.2.1.6.4.1.-3.)	AN of CGt, CDt, CLt; as in መስተሣህል mastaśāhəl 'compassionate, merciful'

4.4.3.6. Other Verbal Nouns

4.4.3.6.1. Classical Ethiopic has a few other formations of deverbal nouns (so-called "verbal nouns"), which are semantically related to the G-stem. The most important patterns are *qətlat* (most frequent pattern), *qətl*, *qətal*, *qətāl*, *qatal*, *qatāl*, and *qatl* (cf. §4.2.1.2.–1.3.).

4.4.3.6.2. Patterns of verbal nouns of stems other than the G-stem include:

Related to D	qəttəl, qəttəlā, qəttəlāt, qəttələnnā, qəttāl, qəttāle, qattālā, qattəl[128]
Related to L	qutāle, qutəlā, qātāl
Related to CG	ʔaqatalā (rare)
Related to Dt	təqtəlt, taqtāl, taqtālet

4.4.3.6.3. Almost all verbal nouns take the external fem. pl. *-āt*, although their grammatical gender is not uniform (they occur as both masc. and fem. nouns).

4.4.4. The Verbal Stems

4.4.4.1. Introduction

Even before the classical period, Classical Ethiopic developed a system of twelve verbal stems for triradical verbs.[129] The stems express notions of verbal "Aktionsart" and mood.

The morphological markers used to differentiate the individual verbal stems consist of (a) consonantal prefixes (ʔ and *t*), (b) lengthening of one consonantal

---

[128] These forms are often difficult to differentiate from forms without gemination since both have the same orthographic reflex in Classical Ethiopic.

[129] For stems used for quadri- and quinquiliteral verbal roots, see §4.4.7.–8.

root morpheme, (c) lengthening of a vocalic root morpheme, and (d) combinations of (a) and (b) or (a) and (c).

Both finite and non-finite forms occur in these stems.

4.4.4.2. Terminology

The twelve stems of Classical Ethiopic have been designated with different terms and sigla throughout the history of scholarship. The following table provides a summary of the different systems.

This grammar uses the sigla indicated in the first column, which is the system commonly used in comparative studies of Semitic languages.

	DG, Chaîne	Praetorius	Conti Rossini	Lambdin	Tropper[130]
G	I, 1	I 1	I 1	G	0_1
D	I, 2	I 2	II 1	D	0_2
L	I, 3	I 4	III 1	L	0_3
CG	II, 1	II 1	I 2	CG	A_1
CD	II, 2	II 2	II 2	CD	A_2
CL	II, 3	II 4	III 2	CL	A_3
Gt	III, 1	IV 1	I 3	Gt	T_1
Dt	III, 2	IV 2	II 3	Dt	T_2
Lt	III, 3	IV 4	III 3	Lt/Glt	T_3
CGt	IV, 1	VII 1	I 4	CGt	Ast_1
CDt	IV, 2	VII 2	II 4	CDt	Ast_2
CLt	IV, 3	VII 4	III 4	CLt/CGLt	Ast_3

4.4.4.3. Comparative Notes

The majority of the Classical Ethiopic verbal stems have equivalents in other Semitic languages:

---

[130] Chaîne 1938; Praetorius 1886; Conti Rossini 1941; Lambdin 1978; Tropper 2002.

CE	G	D	L
Hebrew	Qal	Piˤˤel	(Poˤel, very rare)
Aramaic	Peˤal	Paˤˤel	--
Arabic	I (faˤala)	II (faˤˤala)	III (fāˤala)
Akkadian	G	D	--

CE	CG	CD	CL
Hebrew	Hifˤil	--	--
Aramaic	ʾAfˤel	--	--
Arabic	IV (ʾafˤala)	--	--
Akkadian	Š	ŠD	--

CE	Gt	Dt	Lt
Hebrew	--	Hitpaˤˤel	--
Aramaic	Etpeˤel	Etpaˤˤal	--
Arabic	VIII (ʾiftaˤala)	V (tafaˤˤala)	VI (tafāˤala)
Akkadian	Gt	Dt	--

CE	CGt	CDt	CLt
Hebrew	Hištafˤel	--	--
Aramaic	Eštafˤal	--	--
Arabic	X (ʾistafˤala)	--	--
Akkadian	Št	--	--

The table shows that eight of the twelve stems of Classical Ethiopic are clearly inherited (G, D, L, t-stems, CG, and CGt). Three stems have no correspondence in other Semitic languages (CL, CDt, and CLt). The CD only has a corresponding form in Akkadian, where it is exclusively used in poetic texts and seems to be a secondary development.[131]

Among the inherited stems, the L and Lt only have a direct correspondence in Arabic, although vestiges of at least the L might be present in Hebrew in the rare forms of strong triradical verbs that reflect the pattern *$q\bar{o}t\bar{e}l$.

The marker of the causative C-stems is /ʾ/ in Classical Ethiopic. This /ʾ/ is historically derived from /h/, which in turn goes back to /s/. The morpheme

---

[131] See Kouwenberg 2010, 334.

/s/ as marker of the causative is only attested in lexicalized vestiges in Classical Ethiopic (§4.4.8.) and indirectly in the CGt, CDt, and CLt, the so-called "asta"-stems.

It is further important to note that the N-stem (Arabic VII; Hebrew Nifꜥal), which is well attested throughout Semitic except in Aramaic, is not productive in Classical Ethiopic. A morpheme /n/ is attested as a stem-morpheme in a few lexicalized vestiges, although in these cases the verbs in question have a different function than those attested in the N-stem in other Semitic languages (§4.4.8.).

4.4.4.4. Paradigm

The following paradigm introduces the verbal stems of Classical Ethiopic including their finite and most important non-finite forms (perfect, imperfect, jussive, imperative, perfective participle [=PP], infinitive). ነገረ *nagara* 'to speak, say' (transitive type) and ለብሰ *labsa* 'to put on clothes' (intransitive type of G [cf. §4.4.1.2.1.]) are used as paradigmatic verbs, although it has to be noted that not all forms of the paradigm given for ነገረ *nagara* are actually attested in Classical Ethiopic. The verbal stems are presented in their traditional order.

The jussive and imperative of the CD, Dt, and CDt are given with a geminated second radical. According to the traditional pronunciation, these are articulated without gemination (§4.4.4.4.4.).

Furthermore, according to the traditional pronunciation, all finite verbal forms are stressed on the penultima (§3.5.2:1).[132] For the articulation of the perfective participle and infinitive, see §4.4.3.2.–3.3.

	Primary stems			
	G		D	L
Perf.	ነገረ *nagara*	ለብሰ *labsa*	ነገረ *naggara*	ናገረ *nāgara*
Impf.	ይነግር *yənaggər*	ይለብስ *yəlabbəs*	ይኔግር *yəneggər*	ይናግር *yənāggər*
Juss.	ይንግር *yəngər*	ይልብስ *yəlbas*	ይነግር *yənaggər*	ይናግር *yənāgər*

---

[132] See Mittwoch 1926, 52. According to Dillmann (DG), stress is on the ante-penultima in the CGt, CDt, and CLt.

Imp.	ንግር nəgər	ልበስ ləbas	ነግር naggər	ናግር nāgər
PP	ነጊር- nagir-	ለቢስ- labis-	ነጊር- naggir-	ናጊር- nāgir-
Inf.	ነጊር/ሮ(ት) nagir(ot)	ለቢስ/ሶ(ት) labis(ot)	ነግሮ(ት) naggəro(t)	ናግሮ(ት) nāgəro(t)

Causative stems		
CG	**CD**	**CL**
Perf. አንገረ ʾangara[133]	አነገረ ʾanaggara	አናገረ ʾanāgara
Impf. ያነግር yānaggər	ያኔግር yāneggər	ያናግር yānāggər
Juss. ያንግር yāngər	ያነግር yānaggər	ያናግር yānāgər
Imp. አንግር ʾangər	አነግር ʾanaggər	አናግር ʾanāgər
PP አንጊር- ʾangir-	አነጊር- ʾanaggir-	አናጊር- ʾanāgir-
Inf. አንግሮ(ት) ʾangəro(t)	አነግሮ(ት) ʾanaggəro(t)	አናግሮ(ት) ʾanāgəro(t)

t-stems		
Gt	**Dt**	**Lt**
Perf. ተነገ/ግረ tanag(a)ra	ተነገረ tanaggara	ተናገረ tanāgara
Impf. ይትነገር yətnaggar	ይትኔገር yətneggar	ይትናገር yətnāggar
Juss. ይትነገር yətnagar	ይትነገር yətnaggar	ይትናገር yətnāgar
Imp. ተነገር tanagar	ተነገር tanaggar	ተናገር tanāgar
PP ተነጊር- tanagir-	ተነጊር- tanaggir-	ተናጊር- tanāgir-
Inf. ተነግሮ(ት) tanagəro(t)	ተነግሮ(ት) tanaggəro(t)	ተናግሮ(ት) tanāgəro(t)

Ct-stems		
CGt	**CDt**	**CLt**
Perf. አስተንገረ ʾastangara	አስተነገረ ʾastanaggara	አስተናገረ ʾastanāgara
Impf. ያስተነግር yāstanaggər	ያስተኔግር yāstaneggər	ያስተናግር yāstanāggər
Juss. ያስተንግር yāstangər	ያስተነግር yāstanaggər	ያስተናግር yāstanāgər
Imp. አስተንግር ʾastangər	አስተነግር ʾastanaggər	አስተናግር ʾastanāgər
PP አስተንጊር- ʾastangir-	አስተነጊር- ʾastanaggir-	አስተናጊር- ʾastanāgir-

---

[133] After the negative particle ኢ– ʾi–, the form is ኢየንገረ ʾiyangara (§3.6.2.2.).

Inf.	አስተንግሮ(ት)	አስተነግሮ(ት)	አስተናግሮ(ት)
	ʾastangəro(t)	ʾastanaggəro(t)	ʾastanāgəro(t)

4.4.4.4.1. The Causative Stems

- C-stems in the perfect often occur with /ā/ instead of /a/ in the first syllable (as in አንገረ ʾāngara [§3.2.5.; §3.7.1:5]).
- The imperfect and jussive of the C-stems differ from the corresponding primary stems (G, D, L) in that the quality of the prefix vowel is /ā/ as opposed to /ə/. The /ā/ of the C-stem prefixes is the result of vowel contractions: impf. yānaggər (< *ya-ʾanaggər) < *yə-ʾanagger; juss. yāngər (< *ya-ʾangər) < *yə-ʾangər.
- Impf. and juss. of the 1cs often orthographically appear with /a/ in the C-stems instead of /ā/ in the first syllable (አነግር ʾanaggər; አንግር ʾangər [§3.7.1:5]). In later texts, other persons sometimes have the prefix vowel /a/ instead of /ā/ as well, as in የአምሩ yaʾamməru 'they know' (for ያአምሩ yāʾamməru).

4.4.4.4.2. The t-Stems

- The perfect of the Gt commonly has the pattern *taqatla. Some verbs, primarily verbs I-guttural and/or III-w/y, have forms with an /a/-vowel between the second and third root radicals (type *taqatala), as in ተዐቀበ taʿaqaba 'to be watched', ተዐደወ taʿadawa 'to go beyond, step over'. The base is always *taqatal before consonantal suffixes, as in ተወለድኩ tawaladku 'I was born'.
- The imperfect, jussive, and imperative always have /a/ as a theme vowel between the second and third root letters. All other stems, except the G juss./imp. of the type ለብስ labsa (ይልበስ yəlbas, ልበስ ləbas) have the theme vowel /ə/ instead.
- Verbal roots that have a dental, sibilant or (original) lateral (/t, ṭ, d, s, ṣ, z, ś, ḍ/) as their first radical assimilate the stem morpheme /t/ to the following consonant, that is to the first root radical, e.g., ይሰመይ yəssammay < *yətsammay 'he is/will be named' (§3.6.5.1.). Such impf. and juss. forms differ from their respective primary stems through the theme vowel /a/ that appears between the second and third root letter.

4.4.4.4.3. Ct-Stems

- The perfect of the CGt commonly has the form *ʾastaqtala*. Some verbs, especially those I-guttural or II-guttural, have the form *ʾastaqatala* with /a/ between the first and second radical.

- The perfect of these stems is also attested with the vowel /ā/ instead of /a/ in the first syllable, that is አስተንገረ *ʾāstangara*, አስተነገረ *ʾāstanaggara*, አስተናገረ *ʾāstanāgara*.

4.4.4.4.4. The D-Stems

- The imperfect of the D-stem and its derived stems exhibit an /e/-vowel between the first and second root radical (as opposed to /a/ in the G and its derived stems and /ā/ in the L and its derivatives). It is a matter of debate where this /e/-vowel comes from. One explanation is to consider /e/ the lengthened variant of /a/.[134] The long vowel occurs as compensation for the fact that the following already geminated consonant of the imperfect cannot be lengthened further (that is, *yəneggər* is the compensation for impossible **yənagggər*; the same is true for the imperfect of the stems that are derived from the D).[135] The same phenomenon can be observed in some G-verbs of the type II-guttural + III-y (§4.4.6.3.1.). These verbs have /e/ before the second radical since the guttural cannot be geminated, as in ይሬኢ *yəreʾi* 'he sees' (instead of **yəraʾʾi*).

- According to Mittwoch (1926, 21), the juss. and imp. of the CD, Dt, and CDt – except for a few exceptions of the Dt[136] – are pronounced without gemination of the second radical (ያነግር *yānagər* instead of *yānaggər*; አነግር *ʾanagər* instead of *ʾanaggər* [CD]; ይትነገር *yətnagar* instead of *yətnaggar*; ተነገር *tanagar* instead of *tanaggar* [Dt]; ያስተነግር *yāstanagər* instead of *yāstanaggər*; አስተነግር *ʾastanagər* instead of *ʾastanaggər* [CDt]).

---

[134] A lengthened variant /ā/, according to this approach, would not have been possible because /ā/ is the marker of the L-stems (furthermore, /ā/ is traditionally most often pronounced as a short vowel, while /e/ is considered a long vowel [§3.2.3.]).

[135] Voigt (1997, 587) on the other hand assumes the following development (paradigm verb ፈጸመ *faṣṣama* 'to complete'): **yəfaṣṣṣəm* (with triple consonant) > **yəfayaṣṣəm* (formation based on analogy with II-y quadriliteral verbs) > **yəfeṣṣəm* (contraction of **aya > e*).

[136] Mittwoch mentions ይትነበይ *yətnabbay*, ይትገበር *yətgabbar*, and ይትፈሳሕ *yətfassāḥ*, as well as the corresponding imperatives.

It is uncertain whether this type of articulation goes back to an older tradition or not. This grammar – contrary to Mittwoch – transcribes the respective forms with a geminated middle radical since gemination is considered the characteristic marker of all forms of the D-stems.[137]

4.4.4.4.5. The Morphological Distinction between Imperfect and Jussive

- In the G and CG, the imperfect has three syllables while the jussive has two syllables in its basic form.
- In all D-stems, the imperfect and jussive are distinguished by the vowel between the first and second root letter, which is /e/ in the impf. and /a/ in the juss.
- In several stems, specifically in the L-stems and the Gt, the impf. and juss. are solely distinguished by the gemination or non-gemination of the second radical. They are thus indistinguishable in the orthography. A distinction can only be made based on a syntactic and semantic analysis in these cases.

4.4.4.5. The Function of the Verbal Stems

In Classical Ethiopic, the derived stems stand in different semantic relationships than in most other Semitic languages. In most Semitic languages, there exists a basic stem from which the other stems of the verbal system, such as the D and L-stem, are derived. In Classical Ethiopic, the derivational relationship between the G, D, and L has been lost and the stems have been lexicalized.[138] As a consequence, all three serve as "basic" or "primary" stems for derivational forms, namely the C and *t*-stems, as will be illustrated below.

G   "Basic stem" ("G" from German "Grundstamm"). This stem originally denoted the basic underived meaning of the verb, as in ነገረ *nagara* 'to speak', ነበረ *nabara* 'to sit, dwell'.

D   From German "Dopplungsstamm," which refers to the gemination of the second radical. This stem originally functioned as factitive, for certain aspects of verbal plurality, and as a denominative verbal stem. These functions are only attested in vestiges in Classical Ethiopic since the D, as well as the L-stem, as mentioned above, have lost their derivative functions and have become lexicalized in most instances.

---

[137] For arguments in favor of a geminated articulation, see especially Voigt 1990, 3.
[138] See, for example, Zaborski 2005.

This means that they commonly no longer have a corresponding form in the G. Some vestiges of the original functions include ጠየቀ *ṭayyaqa* with the meaning 'to observe closely' (verbal plurality); ቀደሰ *qaddasa* 'to sanctify, make holy' (factitive); ወሰነ *wassana* 'to delimit' (denominative from ወሰን *wasan* 'boundary, limit'), and ሠለሰ *śallasa* 'to triple, act thrice' (cf. ሠላስ/ሠለስቱ *śalās/śalastu* 'three'). Many D-verbs have no such semantic connotations, however, and simply reflect the lexicalized character of the stem, as in ነጸረ *naṣṣara* 'to look'; ረሰየ *rassaya* 'to put, place'; ሠነየ *śannaya* 'to be beautiful'.

L From German "Längungsstamm," which refers to the lengthening of the first root vowel. This stem is not particularly frequent in Classical Ethiopic. Like the D, this stem has been lexicalized so that L-stem verbs usually do not have a corresponding form in the G. Unlike in the case of the D, it is not possible to trace the original function of the stem from the attested verbs with certainty. Frequently occurring verbs in the L include ባልሐ *bāləḥa* 'to rescue, save'; ባረከ *bāraka* 'to bless'; ዳደቀ *dādaqa* 'to knock down, strike'; ላሐወ *lāḥawa* 'to mourn for, lament'; ማሰነ *māsana* 'to decay, be spoiled'; ናፈቀ *nāfaqa* 'to divide'; ናሥአ *nāśəʾa* 'to take away, carry off'; ናዘዘ *nāzaza* 'to console'; ሳ/ሰኰየ *sā/akʷaya* 'to go astray'; ሣቀየ *śāqaya* 'to vex, torment'; ሣረረ *śārara* 'to lay a foundation, establish'; ጣግዐ *ṭāgəʿa* 'to adhere tightly'; ዋሐየ *wāḥaya* 'to walk around, visit'; ዛወገ *zāwaga* 'to be equal'.

These three stems form the basis of the derived stems, namely the C and *t*-stems.

C "Causative-stems." These stems express a causative function and, since there is no productive factitive stem, they also partially express factitive function of the G, D, and L-stems. This means that the C-stems have partly taken over the original functions of the no-longer productive D-stem. In general, the CG occurs significantly more often than the CD and CL.[139]

CG The CG usually functions as the causative or factitive of the G, as in causative አብአ/አቦአ *ʾabəʾa/ʾaboʾa* 'to bring (in)' (G ቦአ *boʾa* 'to enter');

---

[139] Causativity can also be expressed by periphrastic constructions, such as constructions involving the verb ገብረ *gabra* 'to do, make', as in ወከመ፡ ኢይግብርዎሙ፡ከመ፡ይኅጥኡ፡ለከ *wa-kama ʾi-yəgbarəwwomu kama yəḫṭəʾu laka* 'lest they make them sin against you' (Jub 1:19).

አሕየወ *ʾaḥyawa* 'to keep alive, let live' (G ሐይወ *ḥaywa* 'to live'); አቅተለ *ʾaqtala* 'to cause somebody to kill somebody' (G ቀተለ *qatala* 'to kill'); አርአየ *ʾarʾaya* 'to show' (G ርእየ *rəʾya* 'to see'); አርጸ *ʾaroṣa* 'to cause to run' (G ሮጸ *roṣa* 'to run'); አስከበ *ʾaskaba* 'to lay, lay down' (G ሰከበ *sakaba* 'to lie, lie down'); factitive አእከየ *ʾaʾkaya* 'to make bad' (G አከየ *ʾakya* 'to be bad'); አድከመ *ʾadkama* 'to weaken, make weak' (G ደክመ *dakma* 'to become weak, be tired'); አቅረበ *ʾaqraba* 'to bring near' (G ቀርበ/ቀረበ *qarba/qaraba* 'to draw near, be near'); አጽንዐ *ʾaṣnəʿa* 'to strengthen, fortify' (G ጸንዐ *ṣanʿa* 'to be strong'); አርኩስ *ʾarkʷasa* 'to declare/hold clean' (G ረኩስ *rakʷsa* 'to be clean').

The CG can also function as a denominative, as in አስመየ *ʾasmaya* 'to become renowned/famous' (ስሙይ *səmuy* 'named, one of renown'); አስገለ *ʾasgala* 'to practice magic' (ሰገል *sagal* 'divination, magic'); አዸረረ *ʾadrara* 'to become an enemy' (ዐር *ḍar* 'enemy').

In some cases, the CG has acquired special meanings, as in አንበበ *ʾanbaba* 'to read' (G ነበበ *nababa* 'to speak'); አንፍኀ *ʾanfəḫa* 'to sound a wind instrument' (G ነፍኀ *nafḫa* 'to blow').

CD   The CD is the causative or factitive of the D, as in አነስሐ *ʾanassəḥa* 'to cause to repent' (D ነስሐ *nassəḥa* 'to repent'); አሠነየ *ʾaśannaya* 'to beautify, adorn' (D ሠነየ *śannaya* 'to be beautiful').

CL   The CL is the causative or factitive of the L-stem, as in አማሰነ *ʾamāsana* 'to spoil, destroy' (L ማሰነ *māsana* 'to decay, be spoiled'). The CL is a very rare stem since its primary stem, the L, does not occur very often itself.

t   So-called "passive-stems" mostly function as passives of the G, D, and L.

Gt   The Gt most often functions as the passive of the G, sometimes also of the CG, as in ተቀትለ *taqatla* 'to be killed' (G 'to kill'); ተሐንጸ *taḥanṣa* 'to be built' (G 'to build'). There are further some reflexive Gts, such as ተዐቀበ *taʿaqaba* 'to watch oneself' (besides its passive meaning 'to be watched'); ተመይጠ *tamayṭa* 'to turn (oneself)' (besides passive 'to be turned'); ተለብሰ *talabsa* 'to clothe oneself'. A few Gt verbs have active meanings and have no relation to the G (in some cases, no corresponding G is attested), as in ተልእከ *taləʾka* 'to assist, serve'; ተምዐ0/ተምዐ *taməʿəʿa/tamməʿa* 'to be angry'; ተሐሠየ *taḥaśya* 'to rejoice';

ተዐድ/ደወ *taʿad(a)wa* 'to transgress'. The Gt can further reflect denominatives, as in ተክህነ *takəhna* 'to perform priestly duties' (cf. ካህን *kāhən* 'priest').

Dt   Most commonly the Dt is the passive of the D, as in ተፈነወ *tafannawa* 'to be sent' (D 'to send'); ተጸውዐ *taṣawwəʿa* 'to be called, summoned' (D 'to call, summon'). Reflexive meanings occur as well, but not frequently, as in ተአመረ *taʾammara* 'to show oneself' (D 'to show'). Some Dt verbs have active meanings, e.g., ተነስሐ *tanassəḥa* 'to repent' (similar meaning to D); ተመጠወ *tamaṭṭawa* 'to receive, accept' (also passive 'to be handed over'); ተመህረ *tamahara* 'to learn' (ultimately from original passive 'to be instructed'). Among the Dts, in part with active meanings, are also verbs of denominative origin, such as ተነበየ *tanabbaya* 'to act as a prophet' (ነቢይ *nabiy* 'prophet'); ተአመረ *taʾammara* 'to be signaled, be made as a sign' (ትእምርት *təʾəmərt* 'sign'). Some Dt verbs express the notion of 'pretending to be/do something', as in ተደወየ *tadawwaya* 'to feign illness'; ተጸደቀ *taṣaddaqa* 'to give the appearance of being righteous'. The latter type is usually derived from G stative verbs.

Lt   The Lt has various functions: it serves as a passive of the L, as in ተጋብአ *tagābaʾa* 'to be collected, gathered' (passive of ጋብአ *gābəʾa* 'to gather, collect'), but can also be related to the G or Gt and have a reciprocal or iterative function.[140] Examples of reciprocal function include: ተቃረበ *taqāraba* 'to approach one another, have sexual intercourse'; ተቃተለ *taqātala* 'to kill one another'; ተጸብአ *taṣābəʾa* 'to fight with one another'; ተናጸረ, ተራእየ *tanāṣara, tarāʾaya* 'to see one another, look at one another'. Examples of the iterative function of the Lt include ተኃለፈ *taḫālafa* 'to wander to and fro'; ተዋለደ *tawālada* 'to procreate, increase by procreation' (cf. ወለደ *walada* 'to give birth, beget').

     In quite a few cases the meaning of the Lt cannot be derived from its basic L equivalent but has to be taken from the dictionaries. Examples of this type include: ተጋብአ *tagābəʾa* 'to gather, assemble'; ተካየደ *takāyada* 'to make a treaty, promise' (cf. ኪዳን *kidān* 'covenant, pact'); ተሣየጠ *taśāyaṭa* 'to buy (back)' (cf. G ሤጠ *śeṭa* ሤጠ 'to sell').[141]

---

[140] Dillmann thus calls the Lt also "Gegenseitigkeitsstamm" or "reciprocal stem" (DG 175).
[141] Lambdin considers these verbs as a separate stem since they are commonly derived from G, not from L verbs, and designates this stem as Glt (Lambdin 1978, 101).

asta   Waltisberg has undertaken a detailed investigation about the function of the Classical Ethiopic stems with an *asta*-prefix (Waltisberg 2000). According to his study, about 65% of the verbs occurrung with this prefix, have a causative-factitive function related to the Gt, Dt, Lt, or G respectively, and only rarely have a reflexive connotation (relating to the CG, CD, and CL). They never have passive meanings. Other functions include: estimative (7%), declarative (2.5%), desiderative, simulative, indicator of verbal plurality, and denominal (5%). Furthermore, the stems marked by prefixed *asta*– are commonly semantically related to other stems derived of the same primary stem, that is the CGt is related to G-stem derivatives, the CDt to those of the D-stem, and the CLt mostly to those of the L – although the CLt is an exception since about a third of its attestations are in fact unrelated to L derivatives, and are instead related primarily to the G, CG, and Gt. Of the approximately 5800 verbs of Classical Ethiopic, 403 have a derived *asta*-stem (= 7%). Among these stems, the CLt is the most frequently occurring one (58%), followed by the CGt (31%), and the CDt (11%).

CGt   The CGt is mostly the causative or factitive of the Gt or of the G, as in አስተመልኅ *ʾastamalḫa* 'to cause to draw a sword' (causative of G 'to draw [a sword]'); አስተል/ለሐፈ *ʾastal(a)ḥafa* 'to cause concern, give worries' (causative of Gt 'to be troubled, worry'). Reflexive meanings are rare, as in አስተርአየ *ʾastarʾaya* 'to show oneself, appear' (cf. አርአየ *ʾarʾaya* 'to show' CG). The CGt can also have estimative, declarative, and desiderative functions, as in አስተበቍዐ *ʾastabqʷəʿa* 'to ask for a favor, beseech' (desiderative of G 'to be useful, worthy'); አስተምሐረ *ʾastamhara* 'to seek mercy, have pity' (desiderative of G 'to have mercy').

CDt   The CDt most commonly functions as the causative or factitive of the Dt or, less often, the D, as in አስተነስሐ *ʾastanassəḥa* 'to make do penance' (of D 'to do penance'); አስተመክሐ *ʾastamakkəḥa* 'to cause to boast, praise oneself' (of Dt 'to praise oneself, boast'); አስተቀደስ *ʾastaqaddasa* 'to make to be consecrated' (of Dt 'to be sanctified, consecrated'). The CDt can also have an estimative function, as in አስተኅየስ *ʾastaḫayyasa* 'to regard as preferable' (of D 'to be better').

CLt   The CLt mostly functions as the causative or factitive of the Lt, less often of the G or L, as in አስተጸደለ *ʾastaṣādala* 'to cause to shine, illuminate' (of G 'to shine'); አስተላጸየ *ʾastalāṣaya* 'to cause to shave' (of L 'to shave'); አስተማልኅ *ʾastamāləḫa* 'to cause to draw swords on one

another' (of Lt 'to draw swords on one another'); አስተማወጸ *ʾastamāwaṣa*
'to reconcile' (Lt 'to be reconciled with one another'); አስተጋብአ
ʾastagābəʾa 'to gather' (Lt 'to be collected, gathered'). The CLt can
further have an estimative or declarative function (mostly in relation
to the G-stem), as in አስተአከየ *ʾastaʾākaya* 'to despise' (G 'to be evil,
bad'); አስተናጸሐ *ʾastanāṣəḥa* 'to purify, declare pure' (G 'to be pure').
Reflexive meanings are rare, as in አስተሐመመ *ʾastaḥāmama* 'to trouble
oneself, be anxious' (CG 'to harm, torment').

4.4.5. The Inflection of "Weak" Verbs

4.4.5.1. Geminated Verbs

Verbs with a doubled second radical (i.e., $C_2 = C_3$) generally inflect like strong
roots, as in *nababa* 'to speak' pf., *yənabbəb* impf., *yənbəb* juss. A few
particularities should nevertheless be noted:

- Forms of the imperfect of the G-stem that have a vocalic suffix can
  optionally lose a syllable, as in ይነቡ *yənabbu* (besides strong ይነብቡ
  yənabbəbu) 'they speak'; ትነቡ *tənabbu* (besides ትነብቡ *tənabbəbu*) 'you
  (mp) speak'.
- A relatively large group of verbs II-gem. form their G-perfect both
  according to the *nagara-* and *labsa*-type (the latter form can be
  explained by vowel syncope), as, e.g., ጐየየ/ጐየ *gʷayaya/gʷayya* 'to flee';
  ሐጸጸ/ሐጸ *ḥaṣaṣa/ḥaṣṣa* 'to be little, deficient'; ነደደ/ነደ *nadada/nadda* 'to
  burn'.

Inflectional irregularities are exhibited by the root √*mʿʿ* (Gt 'to be angry'),
which is II-gem. and II/III-guttural (§4.4.6.1.).

4.4.5.2. Verbs I-Guttural

4.4.5.2.1. Verbs I-guttural only exhibit few variations compared to the paradigm
of strong verbs. These variations are usually the result of regular guttural rules
(§3.7.1., especially §3.7.1:3).

- The imperfect of the G and the jussive of the D have the prefix vowel
  /a/ instead of /ə/, as in G impf. የአስር *yaʾassər* < **yəʾassər* 'he ties', and

የአኪ *ya'akki* < *ya'akki* 'he is evil' (also III-*y*), and juss. D የአዝዝ *ya'azzəz* < *yə'azzəz* 'let him command' (according to guttural rule §3.7.1:3).

- The perfect of some Gt I-guttural verbs follows the type *taqatala* (with /a/ between the second and third radicals) instead of *taqatla* (§4.4.4.4.2.), as in ተዐቀበ *ta'aqaba* 'to be watched, guard oneself' (besides ተዐቅበ *ta'aqba*), and ተሐበየ *taḥabaya* 'to take care of, oversee'.

- The imperfect of the CG is usually formed regularly (e.g., የአስር *yā'assər* 'he causes to bind'). In later texts, the prefix vowel often appears as /a/, which makes the form look like the imperfect of the G, as in የአምር *ya'ammər* instead of የአምር *yā'ammər* 'he knows' and የዓርፍ/ተዓርፍ *ya'ārrəf/ta'ārrəf*[142] instead of የዐርፍ/ታዐርፍ *yā'arrəf/tā'arrəf* 'he/she will find rest' (En 62:12, 14 etc.).

- All other forms of the CG and other derived stems follow the paradigm of the strong verb.

4.4.5.2.2. This and the following sections concerning the inflection of weak verbs do not provide full verbal paradigms. Forms given primarily reflect those that exhibit morphological deviations from strong verbs. The conjugations of the individual verbal stems are presented in the following order: perfect, imperfect, jussive, imperative, (perfective participle, infinitive).[143]

The paradigm of I-guttural verbs is given in the following table (አስረ *'asara* 'to bind' [G, *nagara*-type]; አምነ *'amna* 'to believe' [G, *labsa*-type]; አዘዘ *'azzaza* 'to command' [D]):

	G		D
Perf.	አስረ *'asara*	አምነ *'amna*	አዘዘ *'azzaza*
Impf.	የአስር *ya'assər*	የአምን *ya'ammən*	ይኤዝዝ *ya'ezzəz*
Juss.	ይእስር *yə'sər*	ይእመን *yə'man*	የአዝዝ *ya'azzəz*
Imp.	እስር *'əsər*	እመን *'əman*	አዝዝ *'azzəz*

---

[142] Note also the /ā/ instead of /a/ after the guttural /ʿ/ (§3.2.5.; 3.7.1:5).
[143] The perfective participle and infinitive are only listed when the forms exhibit morphological peculiarities.

	CG
Perf.	አእሰረ *ʾaʾsara*[144]
Impf.	ያአስር *yāʾassər*[145]
Juss.	ያእስር *yāʾsər*
Imp.	አእስር *ʾaʾsər*

	t-stems		
Perf.		ተአም/መን *taʾam(a)na*	ተአዘዘ *taʾazzaza*
Impf.		ይትአመን *yətʾamman*	ይትኤዘዝ *yətʾezzaz*
Juss.		ይትአመን *yətʾaman*	ይትአዘዝ *yətʾazzaz*
Imp.		ተአመን *taʾaman*	ተአዘዝ *taʾazzaz*

4.4.5.3. Verbs II-Guttural

4.4.5.3.1. Since gutturals cannot be geminated in Classical Ethiopic (§3.3.1.), this type of verb exhibits quite a few deviations from the strong paradigm. The most important of these deviations are:

- Several forms of the G formally merge with those of the D. In some forms of the paradigm, the differentiation between these stems has disappeared, either completely or in part. The consequence of this development is that certain II-gutt. verbs exhibit forms in both the G and its derivatives as well as in the D and its derivatives without any difference in meaning, such as መሀረ *mahara* (D) and ምህረ *məhra* (G) 'to teach'.

- The G-perfect primarily follows the (intransitive) *labsa*-type (< *labəsa*), which, according to guttural rule §3.7.1:2 has the phonological reflex ክሕደ *kəḥda* < *kahəda* 'to deny, repudiate' with stress on the first syllable.[146] Perfect-forms of the type *nagara* are less frequent, such as ከዐወ *kaʿawa* 'to pour (out)' (these are formally identical with the D-perfect in this verb type). Many II-gutt. verbs exhibit both types, including መሐረ/ምሕረ *mahara/ məhra* 'to have mercy'; ሰአለ/ስእለ

---

[144] The first /a/ is not lengthened to /ā/ before the syllable-closing guttural because of the initial /ʾ/ (§3.7.1:1).

[145] Also ያስር *yaʾassər* (with /a/ in the prefix).

[146] Mittwoch (1926, 58) also gives a form *kəḥáda* with a stressed vowel between the second and third radical.

saʔala/səʔla 'to ask'; ሰሐጠ/ስሕጠ *saḥaṭa/səḥṭa* 'to wound, hurt'; ሰኅነ/ስኅነ *saḥana/ səḥna* 'to warm oneself, become warm'; ጠዐመ/ጥዐመ *ṭaʕama/ṭəʕma* 'to taste'.

- The G-imperfect usually has the form ይከሕድ *yəkəḥəd* (< *yakaḥəd*) (cf. guttural rule §3.7.1:2). Sporadically, it is possible to observe the following deviations:

- The verb ውዕለ/ወዐለ *wəʕla/waʕala* 'to pass the day' has two forms of the imperfect, the expected form ይውዕል *yəwəʕəl* and another form ይዋዕል *yəwāʕəl* (< *yəwaʕʕəl*). The /ā/-vowel of the second syllable can be explained by guttural rule §3.7.1:1 (/*a/ > /ā/ before a syllable-closing guttural).[147] A few verbs, especially those that are also III-y, form their G-impf. by analogy with the D-stem (with /e/ as the second vowel), as in ይሬኢ *yəreʔi* 'he sees' (for more detail, see §4.4.6.3.1.).

- The G-juss. always has /a/ as a theme vowel, corresponding to the type *yəlbas*, as in ይክሐድ *yəkḥad*.

- The G-imp. has an /a/-vowel in the first syllable according to guttural rule §3.7.1:3, as in ከሐድ *kaḥad* (< *kəḥad*).

- The G-perfective participle and infinitive have the basic form ከሒድ *kaḥid* because of guttural rule §3.7.1:2.

- The D-juss. and imp. attest to both the vowel sequences /ə-ə/ and /a-ə/, as in ይምህር/ይመህር *yəməhər/yəmahər* (< *yəmahhər*) and ምህር/መህር *məhər/mahər* (< *mahhər*). The latter forms require at least a virtual doubling of /h/. The first forms are the result of guttural rule §3.7.1:2.

- The CG-impf. usually has the form ያድኅን *yādəḥən* < *yādaḥən* (from the verb አድኅነ *ʔadḥana* 'to save').

- In the L- and t-stems, the impf. and juss. are formally identical, as in juss. Gt ይሰአል *yəssaʔal* = impf. Gt *yəssaʔal* (< *yətsaʔʔal*).

4.4.5.3.2. The paradigms of II-guttural roots are listed in the following table (roots used are √*kḥd* G 'to deny', Lt 'to dispute'; √*kʕw* G 'to pour (out)'; √*rʔy* 'to see'[148]; √*mhr* D 'to teach'; √*dḥn* CG 'to save'; √*lʕl* CD 'to lift up'; √*wḥd* CL 'to unite'; √*rḥq* CGt 'to remove'; √*dḥr* CLt 'to preserve to the last'.

---

[147] The development *yəwaʕʕəl > yəwāʕəl requires an exceptional gemination of /ʕ/.

[148] For additional forms of ርአየ *raʔya*, see §4.4.6.3.2.

	G			D
Perf.	ከሐደ kəhda	ከዐወ kaʿawa	ርእየ rəʾya	መሀረ mahara
Impf.	ይከሕድ yəkəhəd	ይከዑ yəkəʿu	ይሬኢ yəreʾi	ይሜህር yəmehər
Juss.	ይክሐድ yəkhad	ይከዐው yəkʿaw		ይምህር yəməhər[149]
Imp.	ክሐድ kahad	ከዐው kaʿaw		
PP	ክሒድ- kəhid-			
Inf.	ክሒድ/ዶት kəhid(ot)			

C-stems	CG		CD	CL
Perf.	አድኀነ ʾadhana	አከዐወ ʾakʿawa	አለዐለ/አልዐለ ʾalaʿala/ʾalʿala	አዋሐደ ʾawāhada
Impf.	ያድኅን yādəhən		ያሌዐል yāleʿal	ያዋሕድ yāwāhəd
Juss.	ያድኅን yādhən		ያልዐል yāləʿal	ያዋሕድ yāwāhəd
Imp.	አድኅን ʾadhən		አልዐል ʾaləʿal	አዋሕድ ʾawāhəd

t-stems	Gt	Dt	Lt
Perf.	ተከሕደ takəhda[150]	ተመሀረ tamahara[151]	ተካሐደ takāhada
Impf.	ይትከሐድ yətkahad	ይትሜህር yətmehar	ይትካሐድ yətkāhad
Juss.	ይትከሐድ yətkahad	ይትመህር yətmahar	ይትካሐድ yətkāhad
Imp.	ተከሐድ takahad	ተመሀር tamahar	ተካሐድ takāhad
PP	ተከሒድ- takəhid-		
Inf.	ተከሕዶ(ት) takəhədo(t)		

asta-stems	CGt	CLt
Perf.	አስተረ/ርሐቀ ʾastar(a)haqa	አስተዳኀረ ʾastadāhara
Impf.	ያስተርሕቅ yāstar(ə)həq	ያስተዳኅር yāstadāhər

[149] For the normalization *yəməhər*, see Mittwoch 1926, 59; Leslau (CDG, 334a) lists this form as *yəmhər*, that is, as G-stem, not as D.

[150] Some verbs, such as ተገዕዘ *tagəʿza* 'to become free' have a biform ተገዐዘ *tagaʿaza* formed by analogy with the Dt.

[151] This verb also has a biform ተምህረ *taməhra* formed in accordance with Gt verbs.

Juss.	ያስተርሕቅ *yāstarḥəq*	ያስተዳግር *yāstadāḥər*
Imp.	አስተርሕቅ *ʾastarḥəq*	አስተዳግር *ʾastadāḥər*

4.4.5.4. Verbs III-Guttural

4.4.5.4.1. The paradigm of III-guttural verbs is determined by two guttural rules:

- (a) Guttural rule §3.7.1:1 (**a > ā /_G$*; that is before a syllable-closing guttural).
- (b) Guttural rule §3.7.1:4 (**a > ə /_GV*; that is before a guttural in an open syllable).

Rule (a) is reflected in forms such as መጻእኩ *maṣāʾku* (< **maṣaʾku*) 'I came' (G perf.) and ይፍታሕ *yəftāḥ* (< **yəftaḥ*) 'let him open' (G juss.). Rule (b) underlies forms such as ይምጽኡ *yəmṣəʾu* 'let them come' (G juss. 3mp), ነስሐ *nassəḥa* 'he repented' (D perf.), and ጋብአ *gābəʾa* 'he gathered' (L perf.).

Further characteristics of III-guttural verbs include:

- The G-perfect always follows the *labsa*-type, that is, it is formed without a vowel between the second and third radicals, as in ፈትሐ *fatḥa* (< **fatəḥa* [§3.7.1:4]) 'he opened'. The forms of the G-perfect are (√*mṣʾ* 'to come'): sing. መጽአ *maṣʾa*, መጽአት *maṣʾat*, መጻእከ *maṣāʾka*, መጻእኪ *maṣāʾki*, መጻእኩ *maṣāʾku*; pl. መጽኡ *maṣʾu*, መጽአ *maṣʾā*, መጻእክሙ *maṣāʾkəmu*, መጻእክን *maṣāʾkən*, መጻእነ *maṣāʾna* (cf. §3.7.1:1). The CG-perfect is formed in the same manner (√*mṣʾ* 'to bring'): አምጽአ *ʾamṣəʾa*, አምጽአት *ʾamṣəʾat*, አምጻእከ *ʾamṣāʾka* etc.
- The juss. and imp. of the G-stem are formed according to the type *yəlbas* and *ləbas* respectively. The underlying /a/-vowel of the second syllable, however, is changed to either /ā/, when syllable-closing, or to /ə/, when followed by a vowel, according to rules §3.7.1:1 and §3.7.1:4, as in ይምጻእ *yəmṣāʾ* (< **yəmṣaʾ*) 'let him come', ይምጽኡ *yəmṣəʾu* (< **yəmṣaʾu*) 'let them come'. Sporadically, a form ይምጻኡ *yəmṣāʾu* with

/ā/ instead of expected /ə/ as second vowel appears as well. This /ā/ is an analogical extension of the /ā/ in ይምጻእ *yəmṣā*ʾ.[152]

- Verbs III-gutt. that are also II-w exhibit either a strong form (with second radical) and/or a weak form (without second radical), as in ቦሐ *boḥa* 'to receive authority' (√bwḥ) with the CG-perfects አብሐ *ʾabəḥa* and አበውሐ *ʾabawḥa* 'to permit, allow', and the CGt perfects አስተብሐ *ʾastabəḥa* and አስተበውሐ *ʾastabawəḥa* 'to give permission'. D and L-stem forms and their derivatives are formed like strong verbs (as in Lt ተባውሐ *tabāwəḥa* 'to give one another permission').

4.4.5.4.2. The following table lists the basic forms of III-guttural verbs (roots used are √ftḥ G 'to open'; √nsḥ D 'to repent'; √gbʾ L 'to gather', Lt 'to be collected'; √bqʷʿ CGt 'to ask for a favor'):[153]

	G	D	L
Perf.	ፈትሐ *fatḥa*	ነስሐ *nassəḥa*	ጋብአ *gābəʾa*
Impf.	ይፈትሕ *yəfattəḥ*	ይኔስሕ *yənessəḥ*	ይጋብእ *yəgābbəʾ*
Juss.	ይፍታሕ *yəftāḥ* ይፍትሑ *yəftəḥu*	ይነስሕ *yənassəḥ*	ይጋብእ *yəgābəʾ*
Imp.	ፍታሕ *fətāḥ* ፍትሑ *fətəḥu*	ነስሕ *nassəḥ*	ጋብእ *gābəʾ*

D-stems	CG	CD	
Perf.	አፍትሐ *ʾaftəḥa*	አነስሐ *ʾanassəḥa*	
Impf.	ያፈትሕ *yāfattəḥ*	ያኔስሕ *yānessəḥ*	

---

[152] This type of form is particularly frequent with verbs that are also II-w in addition to III-gutt., such as ቦአ *boʾa* 'to enter', with the juss. ይባእ *yəbāʾ*, and ሞአ *moʾa* 'to conquer' with the juss. ይማእ *yəmāʾ* (besides ይሙእ *yəmuʾ*) (§4.4.5.6.1.).

[153] Other frequently occurring roots III-gutt. include: በጽሐ *baṣḥa* 'to arrive'; ፈርሀ *farha* 'to fear'; መልአ *malʾa* 'to fill'; መርሐ *marha* 'to guide, lead'; መጽአ *maṣʾa* 'to come'; ነሥአ *naśʾa* 'to take, receive'; ረድአ *radʾa* 'to help'; ሰምዐ *samʿa* 'to hear'; ጸብአ *ṣabʾa* 'to fight'; ጠብሐ *ṭabḥa* 'to slaughter'; ወፅአ *waḍʾa* 'to go out'; ባልሐ *bāləḥa* 'to rescue' (L). The root √nśʾ has a regular Gt ተነሥአ *tanaśʾa* 'to be taken' (passive of G) and a seemingly irregular formation ተንሥአ *tanśəʾa* 'to arise', which most likely is a denominative form derived from ትንሣኤ *tənśāʾe* 'ascent, rising' and thus formally quadriliteral. The quadriliteral forms that are in part irregular are discussed in §4.4.7.3.–7.4.

| Juss. | ያፍትሕ yāftəḥ | ያነስሕ yānassəḥ | |
| Imp. | አፍትሕ ʾaftəḥ | አነስሕ ʾanassəḥ | |

t-stems	Gt	Dt	CLt
Perf.	ተፈትሐ tafatḥa	ተነስሐ tanassəḥa	ተጋብአ tagābəʾa
Impf.	ይትፈታሕ yətfattāḥ ይትፈትሑ yətfattəhu	ይትኔሳሕ yətnessāḥ	ይትጋብእ yətgābbaʾ
Juss.	ይትፈታሕ yətfatāḥ ይትፈትሑ yətfatəhu	ይትነሳሕ yətnassāḥ	ይትጋብእ yətgābaʾ
Imp.	ተፈታሕ tafatāḥ ተፈትሑ tafatəhu	ተነሳሕ tanassāḥ	ተጋብእ tagābaʾ

asta-stems	CGt	CDt	CLt
Perf.	አስተብ/በቈዐ ʾastab(a)qʷaʿa	አስተነስሐ ʾastanassəḥa	አስተጋብአ ʾastagābəʾa
Impf.	ያስተበቍዕ yāstabaqqʷaʿ	ያስተኔሳሕ yāstanessəḥ	ያስተጋብእ yāstagābbaʾ
Juss.	ያስተብቍዕ yāstabqʷaʿ	ያስተነስሕ yāstanassəḥ	ያስተጋብእ yāstagābaʿ
Imp.	አስተብቍዕ ʾastabqʷaʿ	አስተነስሕ ʾastanassəḥ	አስተጋብእ ʾastagābaʾ

4.4.5.5. Verbs I-w and I-y

4.4.5.5.1. The formation of I-w verbs only exhibits a few peculiarities in the G-stem. All other verbal stems behave regularly:

- The juss. often has /a/ as the second or the theme vowel (type yəlbas) and less frequently /ə/ (type yəngər), although quite a few verbs have jussives of both types. Forms with the theme vowel /a/ are commonly weak (formed without /w/), as in ይረድ yərad 'let him descend', ይደይ yəday 'let him put' (√wdy, also III-y). Jussives with /ə/ on the other hand most often exhibit a strong form (with /w/), as in ወሰደ wasada 'to lead' with the juss. ይውስድ yəwsəd (and the biforms ይስድ yəsəd and ይሰድ yəsad); ወገረ wagara 'to throw (stones)' with the juss. ይውግር

yəwgər; **ወጠነ** *waṭana* 'to begin' with the jussives **ይጠን** *yəṭan* and **ይውጥን** *yəwṭan*; **ውሕዘ** *wəḥza* 'to flow' (also II-gutt. [§4.4.6.6.1.]) with the juss. **የሐዝ** *yaḥaz* and also **ይውሕዝ** *yəwḥaz* (strong form with /a/-vowel).

- The G-imperative is formed in analogy with the G-juss. Verbs that have a weak form in the juss., usually have a monosyllabic imp. with an /a/-theme vowel, such as **ረድ** *rad* from **ወረደ** *warada* 'to descend' (corresponding to the juss. **ይረድ** *yərad*). Imperatives with an /ə/-vowel most commonly have a strong form, such as **ውጥን** *wəṭən* from **ወጠነ** *waṭana* 'to begin' (cf. juss. **ይውጥን** *yəwṭən*). In a few cases, weak formations with /ə/ appear as well. Some verbs attest to all three forms of the imperative, such as **ወገረ** *wagara* 'to throw' with the imps. **ውግር** *wəgər*, **ገር** *gar*, and **ግር** *gər*.

- Verbal nouns of the G-stem most often do not have a reflex of /w/ (§4.2.1.1.2.), as in **ልደት** *lədat* 'birth' (from **ወለደ** *walada*); **ፀአት** *ḍaʾat* 'exit' (from **ወፅአ** *waḍʾa*); **ጥንት** *ṭənt* 'beginning' (from **ወጠነ** *waṭana*); **ህብት** *habt* 'gift' (from **ወሀበ** *wahaba*).

4.4.5.5.2. The basic forms of I-w verbs are given in the following table (roots used are √wrd 'to descend'; √wgr 'to throw (stones)'; √wdq 'to fall' [G intransitive]; √wsk 'to add' [D]; √wld 'to be born' [Gt]):

G		
Perf.	**ወረደ** *warada*	**ወገረ** *wagara*	**ወድ/ደቀ** *wad(a)qa*
Impf.	**ይወርድ** *yəwarrəd*	**ይወግር** *yəwaggər*	**ይወድቅ** *yəwaddəq*
Juss.	**ይረድ** *yərad*	**ይውግር/ይገር** *yəwgər/yəgar*	**ይደቅ** *yədaq*
Imp.	**ረድ** *rad*	**ውግር/ገር/ግር** *wəgər/gar/gər*	**ደቅ** *daq*
D		
Perf.	**ወሰከ** *wassaka*		
Impf.	**ይዌስክ** *yəwessək*		
Juss.	**ይወስክ** *yəwassək*		
Imp.	**ወስክ** *wassək*		

C-stems	CG		
Perf.	አውረደ ʾawrada		
Impf.	ያወርድ yāwarrəd		
Juss.	ያውርድ yāwrəd		
Imp.	አውርድ ʾawrəd		

t-stems	Gt	Dt	
Perf.	ተወልደ tawalda	ተወሰከ tawassaka	
Impf.	ይትወለድ yətwallad	ይትዌሰክ yətwessak	
Juss.	ይትወለድ yətwalad	ይትወሰክ yətwassak	
Imp.	ተወለድ tawalad	ተወሰክ tawassak	

4.4.5.5.3. Verbs I-y are rare in Classical Ethiopic. Only the following verbs of this type occur with relative regularity: የብሰ yabsa 'to be dry' (G); የበበ yabbaba 'to jubilate' (D); የውሀ yawwəha 'to be gentle, mild' (D, also የሀወ yahwa); አይድዐ ʾaydəʿa 'to inform, tell' (CG). These verbs are conjugated like strong roots, preserving the initial /y/ throughout their paradigms. The finite forms of የብሰ yabsa are: perf. የብሰ yabsa; impf. ይየብስ yəyabbəs; juss. ይይብስ yəybas; imp. ይብስ yəbas.

4.4.5.6. Verbs II-w

4.4.5.6.1. The inflection of verbs II-w exhibits a few peculiarities in the G, CG, and, in the perfect, the Gt. The forms of all other stems are regular (e.g., Lt ተቃወመ taqāwama 'to oppose, withstand' √qwm and CGt አስተሐውረ ʾastaḥawra 'to bring back, report to' √ḥwr).

The following characteristics should be noted:

- G-perfect: The majority of II-w verbs do not exhibit a consonantal /w/ in the perf. Instead, these verbs have the vowel /o/ (< *awa) between the first and third root letters. The forms of *qwm 'to stand' are thus: sing. ቆመ qoma, ቆመት qomat, ቆምከ qomka, ቆምኪ qomki, ቆምኩ qomku; pl. ቆሙ qomu, ቆማ qomā, ቆምክሙ qomkəmu, ቆምክን qomkən, ቆምነ qomna.

- A few II-*w* verbs that are also III-gutt. or III-*w/y*, such as ሠውዐ *śawᶜa* 'to sacrifice',[154] preserve the second radical in consonantal form. Some of these verbs also exhibit vocalic, that is, contracted forms besides their "strong" variants. The forms of ሠውዐ *śawᶜa* 'to sacrifice' are: sing. ሠውዐ *śawᶜa*, ሠውዐት *śawᶜat*, ሠዋዕከ *śawāᶜka*, ሠዋዕኪ *śawāᶜki*, ሠዋዕኩ *śawāᶜku* (also ሦዐ *śoᶜa*, ሦዐት *śoᶜat*, ሦዕከ *śoᶜka* etc.); pl. ሠውዑ *śawᶜu*, ሠውዓ *śawᶜā*, ሠዋዕከሙ *śawāᶜkəmu*, ሠዋዕክን *śawāᶜkən*, ሠዋዕን *śawāᶜna*.

- In the juss. and imp. of the G, most verbs II-*w* have a form with a /u/-vowel between the first and third radicals, as in juss. ይቁም *yəqum*, imp. ቁም *qum* from ቆመ *qoma* 'to stand', and juss. ይሩጽ *yəruṣ*, imp. ሩጽ *ruṣ* from ሮጸ *roṣa* 'to run'. This type includes verbs like ሠውዐ *śawᶜa*, which has the juss. ይሡዕ *yəśuᶜ*. A few verbs have /o/ or /u/, such as ይጾር/ይጹር *yəṣor/yəṣur* 'let him carry'; ይሖር/ይሑር *yəhor/yəhur* 'let him go'; imp. ጾር/ጹር *ṣor/ṣur* and ሖር/ሑር *hor/hur* (in earlier manuscripts most commonly with /o/, in later manuscripts with /u/). Forms with /u/ correspond to the transitive *nagara - yəngər* type of the strong paradigm (ይቁም *yəqum* < **yəqwəm*), while forms with /o/ correspond to the intransitive *labsa - yəlbas* type (ይጾር *yəṣor* < **yəṣwar*). Verbs II-*w* that are also III-ʔ, such as ቦአ *boʔa* 'to enter' and ሞአ *moʔa* 'to conquer', have /ā/ in the juss. and imp. (corresponding to *labsa - yəlbas*), such as ይባእ *yəbāʔ* < **yəbaʔ* (§4.4.5.4.1.). This /ā/ is preserved before forms with vocalic suffixes, as in ይባኡ *yəbāʔu* (3mp). The verb ሞአ *moʔa*, on the other hand, also attests to forms with /u/, as in juss. ይማእ/ይሙእ *yəmāʔ/yəmuʔ*; imp. ማእ/ሙእ *māʔ/muʔ*.

- CG perfect: The CG has the forms አቆመ *ʔaqoma* (< **ʔaqwama*) and, less often, አቀመ *ʔaqama* (by analogy with the strong verb). Very rarely, the CG reflects the strong form, e.g., አጥወቀ *ʔaṭwaqa*, besides አጠቀ *ʔaṭaqa* 'to oppress' √*ṭwq*. The inflection of አቆመ *ʔaqoma* corresponds to that of ቆመ *qoma*, that is, አቆምኩ *ʔaqomku* (1cs) etc. The verbs ቦአ *boʔa* and ሞአ *moʔa* (II-*w* and III-ʔ) have the forms አሞአ *ʔamoʔa* (2ms አሞእከ *ʔamoʔka*) besides አማእ *ʔamaʔa* (2ms አማእከ *ʔamāʔka*). The CG perf. of ሠውዐ *śawᶜa* is አሦዐ *ʔaśoᶜa*.

---

[154] Also ሠውዐ *śawwəᶜa* (D) with the same meaning.

- CG juss. and imp.: II-*w* verbs have forms with /u/ and forms with /ə/ between the first and third radicals, that is, juss. ይቁም *yāqum* (< *yāqwəm*) and ይቅም *yāqəm*; imp. አቁም *ʾaqum* and አቅም *ʾaqəm*. The forms with /ə/ are most likely secondary and the result of an analogy with strong verbs (cf. *yāngər, ʾangər*).
- Gt perf.: The Gt is most commonly formed like strong verbs (ተቀውመ *taqawma*). There are, however, a few verbs that exhibit contracted forms, such as ተሞአ *tamoʾa* 'to be conquered'.[155] Furthermore, there are verbs, primarily those that are also I-gutt., that have four syllables in the perf., such as ተሀወከ *tahawaka* 'to be disturbed, agitated' (besides more common ተሀውከ *tahawka*). Some verbs exhibit all the aforementioned types, such as ተሀወከ *tahawaka*, ተሀውከ *tahawka*, ተሆከ *tahoka* (of ሆከ *hoka* 'to disturb') and ተሐወሰ *tahawasa*, ተሐውሰ *tahawsa*, ተሐሰ *tahosa* (passive of ሐሰ *hosa* 'to move, shake').

4.4.5.6.2. The basic forms of II-*w* verbs are as follows (roots used are √*qwm* 'to stand'; √*ṣwr* 'to carry'; √*mwʾ* 'to conquer' [also III-gutt.; cf. §4.4.5.4.]; √*fws* D 'to cure, heal'):[156]

	G		
Perf.	ቆመ *qoma*	ጾረ *ṣora*	ሞአ *moʾa*
Impf.	ይቀውም *yəqawwəm*	ይጸውር *yəṣawwər*	ይመውዕ *yəmawwəʾ*
Juss.	ይቁም *yəqum*	ይጾር/ይጹር *yəṣor/yəṣur*	ይማእ/ይሙእ *yəmāʾ/yəmuʾ*
Imp.	ቁም *qum*[157]	ጾር/ጹር *ṣor/ṣur*	ማእ/ሙእ *māʾ/muʾ*
PP	ቀዊ/ውም- *qawi/əm-*		
Inf.	ቀዊ/ውም(ሞት) *qawi/əm(ot)*		

---

[155] Contracted forms primarily occur with verbs that are also III-gutt.

[156] Other commonly used verbs II-*w* include: ዖደ *ʿoda* 'to go around'; ዖቀ *ʿoqa* 'to know, take heed'; ሖረ *hora* 'to go'; ሖሰ *hosa* 'to move, shake'; ኮነ *kona* 'to be(come)'; ሞቀ *moqa* 'to grow hot, be warm'; ሞተ *mota* 'to die'; ኖኀ *noha* 'to be high'; ኖመ *noma* 'to sleep'; ሮጸ *roṣa* 'to run'.

[157] Besides juss. ይቁም *yəqum* and imp. ቁም *qum*, this verb has the variant forms ይቍም *yəqʷəm* and ቍም *qʷəm* in a few isolated cases.

D		
Perf.	ፈወስ *fawwasa*	
Impf.	ይፈውስ *yəfewwəs*	
Juss.	ይፈውስ *yəfawwəs*	
Imp.	ፈውስ *fawwəs*	

CG		
Perf.	አቆመ/አቀመ *ʾaqoma/ʾaqama*[158]	አሞአ/አምአ *ʾamoʾa/ʾaməʾa*
Impf.	ያቀውም *yāqawwəm*	
Juss.	ያቁም/ያቅም *yāqum/yāqəm*	
Imp.	አቁም/አቅም *ʾaqum/ʾaqəm*	

Gt		
Perf.	ተቀውመ *taqawma*	ተሀወ/ውከ *tahaw(a)ka*	ተሞአ/ተመውአ *tamoʾa/tamawʾa*
Impf.	ይትቀወም *yətqawwam*		
Juss.	ይትቀወም *yətqawam*		
Imp.	ተቀወም *taqawam*		

Dt		
Perf.	ተፈወስ *tafawwasa*	
Impf.	ይትፈወስ *yətfewwas*	
Juss.	ይትፈወስ *yətfawwas*	
Imp.	ተፈወስ *tafawwas*	

4.4.5.7. Verbs II-y

4.4.5.7.1. The paradigm of verbs II-y is formed in the same way as that of verbs II-w. Particularities appear in the G and CG, all other stems are regular:

---

[158] Also *ʾaqwama* in rare instances (e.g., አጥወቀ *ʾaṭwaqa* √ṭwq).

- G perf.: Most verbs II-*y* have G-perfects of the type **ሤመ** *śema* (√*śym* 'to set, put') with an /e/-vowel between first and third radical: Sing. **ሤመ** *śema*, **ሤመት** *śemat*, **ሤምከ** *śemka*, **ሤምኪ** *śemki*, **ሤምኩ** *śemku*; pl. **ሤሙ** *śemu*, **ሤማ** *śemā*, **ሤምክሙ** *śemkəmu*, **ሤምክን** *śemkən*, **ሤምነ** *śemna* (**ሤመ** *śema* 'to put, place, appoint'). Strong forms are, on the other hand, found for doubly weak verbs such as **ሐይወ** *ḥaywa* (< *ḥayawa) 'to live' (also I-gutt. and III-*w* [§4.4.6.8.]) and the less common verb **ረየመ** *rayama* 'to be high, long' (juss. **ይርም** *yərim*).
- The G juss. and imp. exhibit an /i/-vowel, as in juss. **ይሢም** *yaśim* 'let him put' and imp. **ሢም** *śim* 'put!'.
- CG perf.: Classical Ethiopic exhibits both strong and weak formations, that is, it has the types **አሤመ** *ʾaśema* and **አሥየመ** *ʾaśyama* (√*śym* 'to put, place, appoint'). Several verbs exhibit both perfect types.
- CG juss. and imp.: These forms most commonly have /i/ between the first and third root letters. Forms with /ə/ in this position occur but are rare. The forms of the juss. are thus **ያሢም** *yāśim* (< *yāśyəm) and **ያሥም** *yāśəm*; imp. **አሢም** *ʾaśim* and **አሥም** *ʾaśəm*. The forms with /ə/ are most likely secondary and formed by analogy with strong roots.
- Gt perf.: The Gt perfect most commonly follows the paradigm of strong verbs, that is **ተሠይመ** *taśayma* (besides rare **ተሠየመ** *taśayama*). A few verbs also attest to contracted forms, such as **ተሜጠ** *tameṭa* (besides **ተመይጠ** *tamayṭa*) 'to be turned'.

4.4.5.7.2. The paradigm of II-*y* verbs is provided in the following table (roots presented include √*śym* 'to put, place, appoint'; √*ḥyw* 'to live, be alive';[159] √*tyq* D 'to observe, look'; √*myṭ* 'to turn', Gt 'to be turned'):[160]

	G		D
Perf.	**ሤመ** *śema*	**ሐይወ** *ḥaywa*	**ጠየቀ** *ṭayyaqa*
Impf.	**ይሠይም** *yaśayyəm*		**ይጤይቅ** *yəṭeyyəq*
Juss.	**ይሢም** *yaśim*		**ይጠይቅ** *yəṭayyəq*

---

[159] The root is also I-gutt. and III-*w*. For other peculiarities of its inflection, see §4.4.6.8.

[160] Other II-*y* verbs that commonly occur are: **ጌሰ** *ʿela* 'to go astray, roam about'; **ሐሰ** *ḥesa* 'to blame, rebuke'; **ጌለ** *ḫela* 'to become strong'; **ኬደ** *keda* 'to tread (down)'; **ሤጠ** *śeṭa* 'to sell'; **ጼሐ** *ṣeḥa* 'to make level, even'; **በየነ** *bayyana* 'to discern' (D); **ደየነ** *dayyana* 'to judge' (D denominative).

Imp.	ሢም śim		ጠይቅ ṭayyəq
PP	ሠዪ/ይም- śayi/əm-		
Inf.	ሠዪ/ይም(ሞት) śayi/əm(ot)		

	CG		
Perf.	አሤመ/አሥየመ ʾaśema/ʾaśyama	አሕየወ ʾaḥyawa	
Impf.	ያሠይም yāśayyəm		
Juss.	ያሢም/ያሥም yāśim/yāśəm		
Imp.	አሢም/አሥም ʾaśim/ʾaśəm		

	Gt		Dt
Perf.	ተሠይ/የመ taśay(a)ma ተመይጠ/ተሜጠ tamayṭa/tameṭa		ተጠየቀ taṭayyaqa
Impf.	ይሠየም yəśśayyam		ይጤየቅ yəṭṭeyyaq
Juss.	ይሠየም yəśśayam		ይጠየቅ yəṭṭayyaq
Imp.	ተሠየም taśayam		ተጠየቅ taṭayyaq

4.4.5.8. Verbs III-w

4.4.5.8.1. The paradigm of III-w verbs is characterized by three sound changes:

(a) Word-final /-əw/ is regularly contracted to /u/, as in ይፈቱ yəfattu < *yəfattəw 'he desires' (§3.8.2.2.). When these forms have a vocalic suffix, no contraction occurs, as in ይፈትዉ yəfattəwu 'they desire'; ይፈትዎ yəfattəwwo 'he desires it'.

(b) Word-final /aw/ can contract to /o/ (§3.8.2.4.), although the diphthong is preserved in the majority of cases, as in ይትፈተው yətfattaw 'he is desired'. When a vocalic suffix is attached, no contraction occurs, as in ይትፈተዉ yətfattawu 'they are desired, loved' (Gt impf.).

(c) In the middle of the word, /aw/ alternates with /o/ (§3.8.2.4.), as in
ፈነውኩ *fannawka* and ፈኖኩ *fannoka* 'you (ms) sent', which appear in free
variation.

Other peculiarities are:

- G-perf.: The G-perf. exhibits forms of the type *nagara* (e.g., ዐደወ *ʿadawa*
  'to cross'; አተወ *ʾatawa* 'to come home') and forms of the type *labsa* (e.g.,
  በድወ *badwa* 'to be a desert, wasteland'). Some verbs exhibit both types,
  such as ፈት/ተወ *fat(a)wa* 'to desire'. The perf. of the *nagara*-type has the
  following forms (√ʿdw): sing. ዐደወ *ʿadawa*, ዐደወት *ʿadawat*, ዐደውኩ/ዐዶኩ
  ʿadawka/ʿadoka; ዐደውኪ/ዐዶኪ *ʿadawki/ʿadoki*; ዐደውኩ/ዐዶኩ *ʿadawku/*
  ʿadoku; pl. ዐደዉ *ʿadawu*; ዐደዋ *ʿadawā*; ዐደውከሙ/ዐዶከሙ *ʿadawkəmu/*
  ʿadokəmu; ዐደውክን/ዐዶክን *ʿadawkən/ʿadokən*; ዐደውነ/ዐዶነ *ʿadawna/ʿadona*.
- Perfect forms of other stems are formed based on the same basic rules,
  as in ፈነወ *fannawa*, ፈነውኩ/ፈኖኩ *fannawka/fannoka* (√fnw D 'to send').
- G juss. and imp.: The majority of verbs, including those with a perfect
  of the type *labsa*, have a final vowel /u/ (< *-əw), as in ዐደወ *ʿadawa* 'to
  cross' with the juss. ይዕዱ *yəʿdu* and imp. ዕዱ *ʿdu*, or በድወ *badwa* 'to be
  a desert' with the juss. ይብዱ *yəbdu* and imp. ብዱ *bədu*. Forms with
  /-aw/ or /-o/ occur less often, e.g., ፈትወ *fatwa* (besides ፈተወ *fatawa*)
  'to desire' with the jussives ይፍተው/ይፍቶ *yəftaw/yəfto* and imp.
  ፍተው/ፍቶ *fətaw/fəto*, besides ይፍቱ *yəftu*, ፍቱ *fətu*. The latter formation
  corresponds to the transitive type *yəngər*, the former to the
  intransitive type *yəlbas*.
- Gt impf., juss., imp.: In the Gt, Classical Ethiopic frequently exhibits the
  vowel /-o/ instead or besides /-aw/, as in ይትዐዶ *yətʿaddo* besides
  ይትዐደው *yətʿaddaw* 'to go beyond, pass'.

4.4.5.8.2. The paradigm of III-w verbs is listed in the following table (√ʿdw 'to
cross' [also I-gutt.]; √fnw D 'to send', Dt passive; √sfw CD 'to give hope'):

G		
Perf.	ፈተወ *fatawa*	ፈትወ *fatwa*	ዐደወ *ʿadawa*
Impf.	ይፈቱ *yəfattu*	ይፈቱ *yəfattu*	የዐዱ *yaʿaddu*
	ይፈትዉ *yəfattəwu*	ይፈትዉ *yəfattəwu*	የዐደዉ *yaʿaddəwu*

Juss.	ይፍቱ yəftu	ይፍተዉ/ይፍቶ yəftaw/yəfto	ይዕዱ yəˁdu
	ይፍትዉ yəftəwu		ይዕድዉ yəˁdəwu
Imp.	ፍቱ fətu	ፍተዉ/ፍቶ fətaw/ fəto	ዕዱ ˁədu
	ፍትዉ fətəwu		ዕድዉ ˁədəwu

	D	
Perf.	ፈነወ fannawa	
Impf.	ይፈኑ yəfennu	
	ይፈንዉ yəfennəwu	
Juss.	ይፈኑ yəfannu	
	ይፈንዉ yəfannəwu	
Imp.	ፈኑ fannu	
	ፈንዉ fannəwu	

	CG	CD	
Perf.	አፍተወ ʾaftawa	አሰፈወ ʾasaffawa	
Impf.	ያፈቱ yāfattu	ያሴፉ yāseffu	
	ያፈትዉ yāfattəwu	ያሴፍዉ yāseffəwu	
Juss.	ያፍቱ yāftu	ያሰፉ yāsaffu	
	ያፍትዉ yāftəwu	ያሰፍዉ yāsaffəwu	
Imp.	አፍቱ ʾaftu	አሰፉ ʾasaffu	
	አፍትዉ ʾaftəwu	አሰፍዉ ʾasaffəwu	

	Gt		Dt
Perf.	ተፈትወ tafatwa	ተዐደ/ድወ taˁad(a)wa	ተፈነወ tafannawa
Impf.	ይትፈተዉ/ይትፈቶ yətfattaw/yətfatto		ይትፈነዉ yətfennaw
Juss.	ይትፈተዉ/ይትፈቶ yətfataw/yətfato		ይትፈነዉ yətfannaw
Imp.	ተፈተዉ/ተፈቶ tafataw/tafato		ተፈነዉ tafannaw

4.4.5.8.3. The verb ሀለወ/ሀሎ hallawa/hallo 'to be, exist' (D, also I-gutt.) requires special treatment. Besides the regularly formed perf. ሀለወ hallawa, there exists

a frequently occurring biform with a contracted diphthong **ሀሎ** *hallo* (§3.8.2.6.).
The juss. has the form **የሀሉ** *yahallu* < *yəhalləw (pl. **የሀልዉ** *yahalləwu*); the rarely
attested impf. is **ይሄሉ** *yəhellu* (pl. **ይሄልዉ** *yəhelləwu*).

The perf. of **ሀለወ/ሀሎ** *hallawa/hallo* is also idiosyncratic from a semantic
perspective since it expresses both past and present/future meaning, that is, it
expresses 'he was' as well as 'he is/will be', as in **አነ፡ ዉእቱ፡ ዘሀሎ** *ʾana wəʾətu za-
hallo* 'I am the one who is' (Ex 3:14). For the use of **ሀለወ/ሀሎ** *hallawa/hallo* as
copula, see §5.4.5.

4.4.5.9. Verbs III-*y*

4.4.5.9.1. The paradigm of verbs III-*y* is characterized by two sound changes:

(a) Word-final /–əy/ is regularly contracted to /–i/, as in **ይሰቲ** *yəsatti* <
*yəsattəy 'he drinks.' When a vocalic ending is suffixed, no contraction
occurs, as in **ይሰትዩ** *yəsattəyu* 'they (mp) drink'; **ይሰትዮ** *yəsattəyyo* 'he
drinks it'.

(b) The diphthong /ay/ can contract to /e/ in word-middle and word-final
position (§3.8.2.4.), as in **ሰተይከ** *satayka* and **ሰቴከ** *sateka* 'you (ms) drank'.
In most cases, however, the diphthong is preserved (the contraction of
/ay/ > /e/ is in general much less common than the contraction /aw/ >
/o/).

Further characteristics of III-*y* verbs include:

- G-perf.: The G-perfect exhibits forms of both the *nagara*-type (e.g., **በከየ**
bakaya 'to weep') and *labsa*-type (e.g., **ሰትየ** *satya* 'to drink'). Some verbs
have both forms, such as **አከየ/አክየ** *ʾakaya/ʾakya* 'to be evil'. The perfect
forms of the type *labsa* are the following:[161] Sing.: **ሰትየ** *satya*; **ሰትየት**
satyat; **ሰተይከ** *satayka* (**ሰቴከ** *sateka*); **ሰተይኪ** *satayki* (**ሰቴኪ** *sateki*); **ሰተይኩ**
satayku (**ሰቴኩ** *sateku*). Pl.: **ሰትዩ** *satyu*; **ሰትያ** *satyā*; **ሰተይክሙ** *sataykəmu*
(**ሰቴክሙ** *satekəmu*); **ሰተይክን** *sataykən* (**ሰቴክን** *satekən*); **ሰተይነ** *satayna* (**ሰቴነ**
satena). Perfect-forms of other stems are formed in the same manner,
as in **ጸለየ** *ṣallaya*; **ጸለይከ** *ṣallayka* (**ጸሌከ** *ṣalleka*); etc. (√*ṣly* D 'to pray').

---

[161] For III-*y* verbs that are also II-gutt., see §4.4.6.3.2.

- G-juss. and imp.: Verbs of the *nagara*-type commonly form their juss. with final /–i/ (< *–əy), such as በከየ *bakaya* 'to weep, mourn' with the juss. ይብኪ *yəbki* and imp. በኪ *bəki*. Verbs of the *labsa*-type most commonly have forms with final /–ay/, such as ሰትየ *satya* 'to drink' with the juss. ይስተይ *yəstay* and imp. ስተይ *sətay*.

- Agent nouns of the type *qatāli*, *qattāli*, *qātāli* etc. are most often formed regularly, as in በካዪ *bakāyi* 'one who weeps'. Besides the regular formation, Classical Ethiopic also has forms without final /i/, as in በካይ *bakāy*.

4.4.5.9.2. Paradigm of III-y verbs (√*bky* 'to weep'; √*sty* 'to drink'; √*ʾky* 'to be evil' [also I-gutt.]; √*rsy* D 'to put, place', CD causative, Dt 'to adorn oneself'; √*kry* Gt 'to be dug'):[162]

G		
Perf.	በከየ *bakaya*	ሰትየ *satya*	አከ/ከየ *ʾak(a)ya*
Impf.	ይበኪ *yəbakki*	ይሰቲ *yəsatti*	የአኪ *yaʾakki*
	ይበከዩ *yəbakkəyu*	ይሰትዩ *yəsattəyu*	የአከዩ *yaʾakkəyu*
Juss.	ይብኪ *yəbki*	ይስተይ *yəstay*	ይአከይ *yəʾkay*
	ይብከዩ *yəbkəyu*		
Imp.	በኪ *bəki*	ስተይ *sətay*	አከይ *ʾəkay*
	በከዩ *bəkəyu*		
PP	ከ.ኪ/ከይ– *baki/əy–*		
Inf.	በኪ/ከይ(ዮት) *baki/əy(ot)*		

D		
Perf.	ረሰየ *rassaya*		
Impf.	ይሬሲ *yəressi*		
	ይሬሰዩ *yəressəyu*		
Juss.	ይረሲ *yərassi*		
	ይረሰዩ *yərassəyu*		

---

[162] Frequently occurring verbs III-y include: ሐለየ *ḥalaya* 'to sing'; ሰፈየ *safaya* 'to sew'; ጸለየ *ṣallaya* 'to pray'; ጠዐየ *ṭəʿya* 'to be healthy'; ወዐየ *wəʿya* 'to burn' (also I-w and II-gutt.).

Imp.	ረሲ rassi		
	ረስዩ rassəyu		

	CG	CD	
Perf.	አብከየ ʾabkaya	አረሰየ ʾarassaya	
Impf.	ያበኪ yābakki	ያሬሲ yāressi	
	ያበክዩ yābakkəyu	ያሬስዩ yāressəyu	
Juss.	ያብኪ yābki	ያረሲ yārassi	
	ያብክዩ yābkəyu	ያረስዩ yārassəyu	
Imp.	አብኪ ʾabki	አረሲ ʾarassi	
	አብክዩ ʾabkəyu	አረስዩ ʾarassəyu	

	Gt	Dt	
Perf.	ተከርየ takarya	ተረሰየ tarassaya	
Impf.	ይትከራይ yətkarray	ይትሬሰይ yətressay	
Juss.	ይትከራይ yətkaray	ይትረሰይ yətrassay	
Imp.	ተከረይ takaray	ተረሰይ tarassay	

4.4.6. Doubly-Weak Verbs and Irregular Verbs

The following discusses verbs that exhibit irregular paradigms and certain doubly-weak verbs that have special characteristics in their morphology. Less problematic types of doubly-weak verbs are included in §4.4.5.

4.4.6.1. Verbs II-Geminated and II-Guttural

The root √mʿr (Gt 'to be angry') has three different perfect-formations:

- ተምዕዐ taməʿəʿa, ተምዕዐት taməʿəʿat, ተምዓዕከ taməʿāʿka etc.
- ተምዐ tamməʿa, ተምዐት tamməʿat, ተማዕከ tammāʿka etc.
- ተመዐዐ tamaʿaʿa, ተመዐዐት tamaʿaʿat, ተመዓዕከ tamaʿāʿka etc. (rare variant)

The other conjugations of the Gt and stems that are attested for this root follow the expected forms of III-gutt. roots (§4.4.5.4.):

- CG perf.: **አምዐዐ** *ʔamʕəʕa* (< **ʔamʕaʕa*); also **አምዐ** *ʔaməʕa*.
- Lt perf.: **ተማዐዐ** *tamāʕəʕa* (< **tamāʕaʕa*);
- CLt **አስተማዐዐ** *ʔastamāʕəʕa*.

4.4.6.2. Verbs I-Guttural and II-Guttural

The verb **አኀዘ** *ʔaḫaza* 'to take, catch' has special forms in the G-impf., juss., and imp. because of the guttural rules:

Impf.	Juss.	Imp.
ይአኀዝ *yəʔaḫəz* (< **yəʔaḫəz* [§3.7.1:2])	**ይእኀዝ** *yəʔḫaz* (regular) and **የአኀዝ** *yaʔaḫaz*[163]	**አኀዝ** *ʔaḫaz* (< **ʔəḫaz* [§3.7.1:3])

4.4.6.3. Verbs II-Guttural and III-y

4.4.6.3.1. As mentioned in §4.4.5.3.1., several verbs that are II-gutt., especially those that are also III-y, have a G-imperfect with /e/ instead of expected /ə/ as their second vowel, which resembles the formation of the impf. of the D-stem. Similar formations also occur in the CG, Gt, and CGt.

Verbs II-gutt. and III-y with this type of G-impf. include:

- **ርእየ** *rəʔya*: **ይሬኢ** *yəreʔi* 'he sees' (also rarely **ይርኢ** *yərəʔi*).[164]
- **ርዕየ** *rəʕya*: **ይሬዒ** *yəreʕi* 'he herds' (besides more frequent **ይርዒ** *yərəʕi*). The form **ይሬዒ** *yəreʕi* could also be interpreted as D-impf. since the G-perf. has a biform **ረዐየ** *raʕaya*, which is formally identical to the D-perf. The Gt **ተርዕየ** *tarəʕya* likewise has a biform **ተረዐየ** *taraʕaya*, which could also be interpreted as a Dt. The biforms have the same meaning as the basic forms.
- **ጥዕየ** *ṭəʕya*: **ይጤዒ** *yəṭeʕi* 'he is healthy' (besides **ይጥዒ** *yəṭəʕi*).

Other verbs II-gutt. with the same type of imperfect according to Praetorius (1886a: 74) and Dillmann (DG: 161) are:

---

[163] Most likely by analogy with the imp. **አኀዝ** *ʔaḫaz*.

[164] The CG and CGt impf. on the other hand most commonly have the forms **ያርኢ** *yārəʔi* (much less often **ያሬኢ** *yāreʔi*) and **ያስተርኢ** *yāstarəʔi*.

- √s²n: ይሴእን *yase²ən* 'he is unable', besides more common ይስእን *yasə²ən*
- √l⁰l: ያሌዕል *yāleʿəl* 'he lifts up' (CG)
- √tḥt: ያቴሕት *yātehət* 'he humiliates, casts down' (CG)
- √s⁰n: ያጼእን *yāseʿən* 'he loads an animal' (CG); ይጼእን *yəssˤeʿən* 'he mounts an animal, rides' (Gt)
- √s²l: ይሴአል *yəsseʾal* 'he enquires' (Gt)
- √m⁰z: ይትሜዐዝ *yətmeʿaz* 'it is scented' (Gt)
- √bhl: ይቤ *yəbe*, ይቤሉ *yəbelu* 'they spoke' (past meaning).

Most of the imperfects with /e/ can be interpreted as D-stem forms since the verbs in question either exhibit a perfect that corresponds to the D as well, as in ተሰአለ *tasaʾala* 'to be asked, inquire' besides ተስአለ *tasəʾla*, or because the semantics of the verb rather correspond to those of the D than the G-stem, as in ያቴሕት *yātehət*, which is denominative and has the perfects ትሕት *təhta* and ተሐተ *tahata*. The irregular form ይቤ *yəbe* (√bhl) 'he spoke' could likewise reflect a D-stem (§4.4.6.5.2.).

4.4.6.3.2. *G-perfect.* G-perfs. of verbs that are II-gutt. and III-y, such as ርእየ *rəʾya* 'to see', ጥዕየ *tˤəʿya* 'to be healthy', and ውዕየ *wəʿya* 'to burn' have an /i/-vowel between the second and third root letter before consonantal suffixes, as in ርኢከ *rəʾika* < *rəʾəyka* 'you (ms) saw'.[165] The perfect-paradigm is thus:

Sing.	Pl.
ርእየ *rəʾya*, ርእየት *rəʾyat*, ርኢከ *rəʾika*, ርኢኪ *rəʾiki*, ርኢኩ *rəʾiku*	ርእዩ *rəʾyu*, ርእያ *rəʾyā*, ርኢከሙ *rəʾikəmu*, ርኢክን *rəʾikən*, ርኢነ *rəʾina*

4.4.6.3.3. The remaining basic forms of these types of verbs are illustrated in the following table based on the verbs ርእየ *rəʾya* 'to see' and ውዕየ *wəʿya* 'to burn' (cf. §4.4.5.9.2.):

---

[165] Mittwoch assumes a *schwa*-vowel after the guttural, that is, *rəʾəya* instead of *rəʾya*. According to him, this second /ə/ bears the stress of the word (Mittwoch 1926, 73).

	G	
Perf.	ርእየ *rəʾya*	ውዕየ *wəʿya*
Impf.	ይሬኢ/ይርኢ *yəreʾi/yərəʾi* ይሬእዩ/ይርእዩ *yəreʾəyu/yərəʾəyu*	ይውዒ *yəwəʿi*[166] ይውዕዩ *yəwəʿəyu*
Juss.	ይርአይ *yərʾay*	የዐይ *yaʿay* (< *yəʿay)
Imp.	ርኢ/ርአይ *rəʾi/raʾay* ርእዩ *rəʾəyu*	

	CG	
Perf.	አርአየ *ʾarʾaya*	አውዐየ *ʾawʿaya*
Impf.	ያርኢ/ያሬኢ *yārəʾi/yāreʾi* ያርእዩ/ያሬእዩ *yārəʾəyu/yāreʾəyu*	
Juss.	ያርኢ *yārʾi* ያርእዩ *yārʾəyu*	
Imp.	አርኢ *ʾarʾi* አርእዩ *ʾarʾəyu*	

	Gt	CGt
Perf.	ተርእየ *tarəʾya*	አስተርአየ *ʾastarʾaya*
Impf.	ይትረአይ *yətraʾay*	ያስተርኢ *yāstarəʾi*[167]
Juss.	ይትረአይ *yətraʾay*	ያስተርኢ *yāstarʾi*
Imp.	ተረአይ *taraʾay*	አስተርኢ *ʾastarʾi*

The perfective participle has the forms ርኢይ– *rəʾiy*– and ርእይ– *rəʾəy*–, and the infinitive is ርኢይ(ዮት) *rəʾiy(ot)* and ርእይ(ዮት) *rəʾəy(ot)*.

The agent noun of the G-stem has the forms ረአዪ *raʾāyi* and ረአይ *raʾāy* (with loss of final /i/ [§4.4.5.9.1.]); the plural is ረአያን/ረእያን *raʾāyān/raʾəyān* and ረአይት *raʾayt*.

---

[166] Leslau transcribes *yəʿwi* (CDG: 603b).

[167] Leslau transcribes *yāstarʾi* (CGD: 459a); see also, however, Mittwoch 1926, 80, for the transcription *ʾi-tāstarəʾi* of Gen 1:2 ኢታስተርኢ.

4.4.6.4. Verbs II-Guttural and III-w

The imp. **ና** *naʿā* (also **ንዓ** *nəʿā* and **ነዐ** *naʿa*), which is used like an interjection 'come!, come now!' and followed by another imp. or juss., might be derived from a verbal root **nʿw*. This imp. is conjugated as follows:

	Masc.	Fem.
Sing.	**ና** *naʿā* (< **naʿaw?*)	**ንዒ** *nəʿi* (< **naʿi*; §3.7.1:2)
Pl.	**ንዑ** *nəʿu* (< **naʿu*)	**ና** *naʿā*

4.4.6.5. Irregular Verbs II-h and III-l (**ክህለ** *kəhla* and **ብህለ** *bəhla*)

The paradigms of the verbs **ክህለ** *kəhla* 'to be able' and **ብህለ** *bəhla*[168] 'to say' exhibit several irregular and phonetically reduced forms because of the frequent use of these verbs.

4.4.6.5.1. **ክህለ** *kəhla* 'to be able' typically has a G-impf. without /h/: **ይክል** *yəkəl*[169] < **yəkahəl* (§3.6.2.1.). A form **ይክህል** *yəkəhəl* is also attested but only rarely. The remaining forms correspond to those typical for verbs II-gutt.:

	G	CG	Gt
Perf.	**ክህለ** *kəhla* (before consonantal suffixes **ክህልከ** *kəhəlka*, **ክህልኪ** *kəhəlki* etc.)	**አክህለ** *ʾakhala*	**ተክህለ** *takəhla*
Impf.	**ይክል** *yəkəl* (and **ይክህል** *yəkəhəl*)	**ያክህል** *yākəhəl*	**ይትክህል** *yətkahal*
Juss.	**ይክህል** *yəkhal*	**ያክህል** *yākhəl*	**ይትክህል** *yətkahal*
Imp.	**ክህል** *kahal*	**አክህል** *ʾakhəl*	**ተክህል** *takahal*

---

[168] Mittwoch gives the pronunciations *kəhála* and *bəhála* (1926, 58).

[169] The traditional transcription of this form is *yəkl* (see, e.g., Leslau CDG: 277b). According to the traditional pronunciation, the /l/ is pronounced as syllabified sonorant, that is, *yəkl̩*.

4.4.6.5.2. The paradigm of ብህለ *bəhla* 'to say' contains several irregular forms:

- The impf., juss., and imp. are formed without /h/ (§3.6.2.1.): impf. ይብል *yəbəl*[170] < *yəbəhəl*; juss. ይበል *yəbal* < *yəbhal*; imp. በል *bal* < *bəhal*.
- The verb has a past-tense prefix conjugation ይቤ *yəbe* 'he said' (pl. ይቤሉ *yəbelu*), which is formed without /h/ and, in word-final position, without /l/. The interpretation of this form and its place in the stem-system of Classical Ethiopic is a matter of debate.
- The CG-perfect is likewise formed without /h/: አበለ *ʾabala* < *ʾabhala*.

The most important forms of the paradigm of ብህለ *bəhla* are given below (the infinitive and the perfective participle are regularly formed with the base ብሂል- *bəhil-*; the forms of the Lt and CLt are formed regularly as well):

	G	CG	Gt
Perf.	ብህለ *bəhla*	አበለ *ʾabala*	ተብህለ *tabəhla*
Impf.	ይብል *yəbəl*	ያብህል *yābəhəl*	ይትበሀል *yətbahal*
Juss.	ይበል *yəbal*	ያብህል *yābhəl*	ይትበሀል *yətbahal*
Imp.	በል *bal*	አብህል *ʾabhəl*	ተበሀል *tabahal*

The very frequently employed form ይቤ *yəbe* (< *yəbel*; with stress on the ultima) that functions like a perfect and is most commonly found introducing direct speech is conjugated as follows (note that the root letter /l/ is preserved before vocalic suffixes):

Sing.	Pl.
ይቤ *yəbe*, ትቤ *təbe*, ትቤ *təbe*, ትቤሊ *təbeli*, እቤ *ʾəbe*	ይቤሉ *yəbelu*, ይቤላ *yəbelā*, ትቤሉ *təbelu*, ትቤላ *təbelā*, ንቤ *nəbe*

The origin of the form ይቤ *yəbe* is debated.[171] There are two competing approaches concerning the issue.

---

[170] The traditional transcription is *yəbl*, again with the traditional pronunciation of /l/ as syllabified sonorant *yəbl̥*.

[171] See, e.g., Voigt 1997 and 2000.

The first approach considers ይቤ(ል) *yəbe(l)* a short form of the prefix conjugation of the G-stem with perfect(ive) meaning, corresponding to forms such as Akkadian *iprus* and Hebrew *way-yiqtol*, which is possible from a comparative point of view. The base form of *yəbe(l)* would then have been **yəbhal*, since the juss. and original preterite have the same form. Starting with a form **yəbhal*, however, causes problems since its phonological development would be rather complex and irregular. The development would have been approximately **yəbhal* > **yəbal* (loss of /h/) > **yəbay* (otherwise unattested change from /*al/ > /ay/) > **yəbe*. Proponents of this approach assume that the forms containing /l/ are the result of paradigmatic leveling. The obvious weaknesses of this derivation are the otherwise unparalleled change from *al* > *ay* and the rather weak explanation for the reintroduction of /l/ in forms that end in a vowel.

The second approach assumes that ይቤ(ል) *yəbe(l)* goes back to an imperfect form **yəbehəl*.[172] The loss of final /l/ is assumed to be due to a reanalysis of the frequently occurring form with a dative suffix ይቤሎ *yəbelo* 'he said to him' as *yəbe-lo*, where *–lo* is reinterpreted as the preposition *l–* + 3ms suffix. This reanalysis did not take place in forms with vocalic suffixes because the conditions for its application were not met. The perfect-function of the form can presumably be explained as a historical present or the reflex of a similar function, since other Semitic languages often use a verbal conjugation with a present/future connotation for introducing direct speech in narratives.

The majority of proponents of the latter approach consider the reconstructed underlying form of ይቤ *yəbe* < **yəbehəl* as an irregular G-imperfect with the vowel /e/, as it is attested in a few other verbs II-gutt. (§4.4.6.3.1.).[173] Tropper, who follows this analysis in general, on the other hand, prefers the interpretation of the underlying form as a D-imperfect because of (a) the typical D-stem imperfect vowel /e/, (b) the fact that ብህለ *bəhla* has a G-impf. ይብል *yəbal*, (c) the particular use of the form for introducing direct speech (§5.4.2.4.), and (d) comparative material that shows that other Semitic languages tend to often use the D, Dt, or Gt instead of or in addition to the G,

---

[172] For this interpretation see, e.g., Lambdin 1978, 182. The same analysis is found in Voigt 1997, 585.

[173] As shown in §4.4.6.3.1., G-imperfects with an /e/-vowel are exceptional. This phenomenon cannot be confirmed with certainty outside verbs of the type II-gutt. that are also III-y, since all other respective imperfects with /e/ can also be interpreted as D-stems.

especially for introducing direct speech, in order to stress the pluralic-iterative connotation of the verbal action.[174]

4.4.6.6. Verbs I-w and II-Guttural

4.4.6.6.1. Verbs that are both I-w and II-gutt. exhibit forms that follow the characteristics of both root types. The forms of the verb ውሕዘ wəḥza 'to flow' are representative for this type (cf. §4.4.5.5.1.):

	G	CG
Perf.	ውሕዘ wəḥza	አውሐዘ ʾawḥaza
Impf.	ይወሕዝ yəwəḥəz	ያወሕዝ yāwəḥəz
Juss.	የሐዝ yaḥaz	ያወሕዝ yāwḥəz
	(also ይወሕዝ yəwḥaz)	
Imp.	ሐዝ ḥaz	አውሕዝ ʾawḥəz

The only noteworthy form is the juss. የሐዝ yaḥaz. It requires the following development: (*yəwḥaz >) *yəḥaz > yaḥaz (§3.7.1:3).

4.4.6.6.2. An exception is the verb ወሀበ wahaba 'to give'. This verb has an irregular G-impf. ይሁብ yəhub < *yəhwəb (§3.6.4.) < *yəwhəb < *yəwəhəb. The finite forms of this verb are: perf. ወሀበ wahaba; impf. ይሁብ yəhub; juss. የሀብ yahab; imp. ሀብ hab.[175]

4.4.6.7. Verbs I-w and III-Guttural

Verbs that are I-w and III-gutt. exhibit the forms that are expected based on the characteristics of both root types. The forms of the verb ወፅአ waḍʾa 'to go out, leave' are representative for this root type:

---

[174] Cf. the situation in Akkadian, Hebrew, and Arabic: Akkadian √zkr Gt 'to speak' (durative izzakkar) before direct speech in epics (the root √zkr is used in the G-stem otherwise); Hebrew √dbr D 'to speak' (the G is not productive for this verbal root, although note the active participle dober); Arabic √klm D and √ḥdt D and Dt 'to speak, tell', etc.

[175] This imp. is also used as an interjection 'come on!, now then!' (ms ሀብ hab; fs ሀቢ habi; mp ሀቡ habu; fp ሀባ habā).

	G	CG	CGt
Perf.	ወፅአ waḍʾa	አውፅአ ʾawḍəʾa	አስተውፅአ/አስተወፅአ ʾastawḍəʾa/ʾastawaḍ(ə)ʾa
Impf.	ይወፅእ yəwaddəʾ	ያወፅእ yāwaddəʾ	
Juss.	ይፃእ yəḍāʾ (< *yəḍaʾ)	ያውፅእ yāwḍəʾ	
Imp.	ፃእ ḍāʾ	አውፅእ ʾawḍəʾ	

Forms of the G-jussive and imperative with vocalic suffixes preserve /ā/ (it is not reduced to /ə/ [§4.4.5.4.1.]), as in ይፃኡ yəḍāʾu, ይፃአ yəḍāʾā, ትፃኢ təḍāʾi, etc.

4.4.6.8. Verbs II-w/y and III-w/y

Verbs that are both II-w/y and III-w/y usually treat the second root letter like a strong consonant, that is the /w/ or /y/ is preserved. Special attention has to be given to the verb ሐይወ ḥaywa 'to be alive' since it is also I-gutt. The most important forms of this verb are given in the following list:

	G	CG
Perf.	ሐይወ ḥaywa	አሕየወ ʾaḥyawa (§4.4.5.7.)
Impf.	የሐዩ yaḥayyu < *yəḥayyəw (§3.7.1:3)	ያሕዩ yāḥayyu
Juss.	ይሕየው yəḥyaw and ይሕዩ yəḥyu < *yəḥyəw	ያሕዩ yāḥyu
Imp.	ሕየው ḥəyaw	አሕዩ ʾaḥyu

The G-perf. of ሐይወ ḥaywa is conjugated according to the paradigm of III-w roots (§4.4.5.8.1.):

Sing.	Pl.
ሐይወ ḥaywa	ሐይዉ ḥaywu
ሐይወት ḥaywat	ሐይዋ ḥaywā
ሐየውከ/ሐዮከ ḥayawka/ḥayoka	ሐየውክሙ/ሐዮክሙ ḥayawkəmu/ḥayokəmu
ሐየውኪ/ሐዮኪ ḥayawki/ḥayoki	
ሐየውኩ/ሐዮኩ ḥayawku/ḥayoku	ሐየውክን/ሐዮክን ḥayawkən/ḥayokən
	ሐየውነ/ሐዮነ ḥayawna/ḥayona

The CG perf. is conjugated in the same way.

4.4.6.9. Verbs I-*w* and III-*w/y*

Verbs that are both I-*w* and III-*w/y* follow the expected paradigms of both root types. The G-stem forms of **ወረወ** *warawa* 'to throw, cast off' (juss. of type *yəngər*) and **ወደየ** *wadaya* 'to put' (juss. of type *yəlbas*) are:

	√*wrw*	√*wdy*
Perf.	**ወረወ** *warawa*	**ወደየ** *wadaya*
Impf.	**ይወሩ** *yəwarru* < *yəwarrəw	**ይወዲ** *yəwaddi* < *yəwaddəy
Juss.	**ይውሩ** *yəwru* < *yəwrəw	**ይደይ** *yəday*
Imp.	**ውሩ** *wəru*	**ደይ** *day*

Note: For verbs that are both II-*w* and III-guttural, such as **ቦሐ** *boḥa* 'to receive authority/permission'; see §4.4.5.4., especially §4.4.5.4.1.

4.4.7. Quadriliteral Verbs

4.4.7.1. Compared to other Semitic languages, Classical Ethiopic has a rather large amount of verbs that contain more than three root radicals, that is, verbs with four or five radicals.[176]

Quadriliteral verbs distinguish three formally determined categories in Classical Ethiopic:

1. Normal quadriliteral verbs of various sub-types:
   (a) Genuine quadriliteral roots, such as **ደንገጸ** *dangaḍa* 'to be terrified, shocked'; **ጐንደየ** *gʷandaya* 'to delay, tarry'; **ሰንደደ** *sandada* 'to throw, forget'; **ጠንቀቀ** *ṭanqaqa* 'to be exact, accurate'; **ተአንተለ** *taʾantala* 'to be impatient, resent' (Gt);[177] **ተመርጐዘ** *tamargʷaza* 'to lean upon a staff, rely' (Gt); **ተቄናደየ** *taqʷanādaya* 'to be proud, haughty' (Lt); **አሰርገወ** *ʾasargawa* 'to adorn, decorate'; **ሐብለከ** *ḥablaka* 'to go away for good, vanish from sight'; **ጐ/ኈሕለወ** *gʷa/āḥlawa* 'to be crafty,

---

[176] On this topic, see Gensler 1997; especially pp. 235, 252.

[177] Cf. the reduplicated formation **ተአንተልተለ** *taʾantaltala* 'to be impatient, unwilling' (§4.4.9.).

cheat'; ተጓህነወ tagʷāhnawa 'to shout to one another' (√gʷḥn; besides triradical ተጓሀነ tagʷāhana with the same meaning).

(b) Verbs with /m/ as their first radical, which are almost all denominative from a nominal form maqta/əl or məqtāl, including መድበለ madbala 'to come together' (from መድበል madbal 'assembly, gathering' √dbl); አማኅበረ ʾamāḫbara (CG) 'to assemble together, join' (ማኅበር māḫbar 'association, community' √ḫbr).

(c) Other denominative verbs (often in the Gt-stem), such as ተአምለከ taʾamlaka 'to become God, be worshipped' (አምላክ ʾamlāk 'God'); ተአንገደ taʾangada 'to travel about, become a stranger' (እንግዳ ʾəngədā 'foreigner, stranger'); ተአርወየ taʾarwaya 'to be brutal, become wild' (አርዌ ʾarwe '[wild] animal'); ተደንገለ tadangala 'to be a virgin' (ድንግል dəngəl 'virgin'); ተጓህነወ tagʷāhnawa 'to be interpreted, be revealed' (ጒሃን gʷəhān 'sacred secret, mystery'); ተመትሀተ tamathata 'to appear as a specter, appear in disguise' (ምትሀት məthat 'specter, ghost'); መንሰወ mansawa 'to be in danger, be led to temptation' (መንሱት mansut 'temptation'); ባሕተወ bāḥtawa 'to be alone' (ባሕታዊ bāḥtāwi 'hermit'); ጸዐደወ ṣāʿdawa 'to be white' (ጸዐ/ዕዳ ṣāʿ(a)dā 'white').

(d) Verbs based on a borrowed root, such as መንኮሰ mankʷasa 'to become a monk'; መጽወተ maṣwata 'to give alms'; ተርጐመ targʷama 'to translate'; አመስጠረ ʾamasṭara 'to write in mysteries, hide as a secret'; አሰንበተ ʾasanbata 'to keep the Sabbath'; አሠልጠነ ʾaśalṭana 'to give authority/dominion'.

2. Reduplicated verbs:

(a) Verbs of the type 1-2-1-2, such as በድበደ badbada 'to perish, disappear'; ፈድፈደ fadfada 'to increase, become numerous'; ጐድጐደ gʷadgʷada 'to knock'; ለምለመ lamlama 'to be verdant'; ለጽለጸ laṣlaṣa 'to weigh, measure'; ቀጥቀጠ qaṭqaṭa 'to smash, crush'; ጣእጥአ ṭāʾṭəʾa 'to be properly arranged, settled'; ወልወለ walwala 'to doubt, hesitate'.[178]

---

[178] Cf. also the verb ሰሰለ sassala 'to withdraw', which is derived from original *salsala (regressive assimilation of /l/). This verb is conjugated in analogy with the D-stem and its derivatives, that is ሰሰለ sassala (D); አሰሰለ ʾasassala (CD); ተሰሰለ tasassala (Dt).

This type also contains reduplicated verbs with /y/ or /w/ as the second root letter. These verbs formally correspond to category (3) below (type ደገነ *degana* and ሞቀሐ *moqǝḥa* respectively): ጌጋየ *gegaya* < *gaygaya* 'to err, go astray'; ሌለየ *lelaya* < *laylaya* 'to separate, divide'; አሌለየ *ʾalelaya* 'to spend the night'; ሴሰየ *sesaya* 'to feed, nourish'; ጎገወ *gogawa* < *gawgawa* 'to err'.

(b) Verbs of the type *1-2-3-3* (many of these have a sonorant as the second root letter): ደምሰሰ *damsasa* 'to abolish, obliterate'; ሐብቄቄ/ሐብቀቀ *ḥabq^(w)aq^(w)a* 'to bedaub oneself, stain'; ሰክተተ *saktata* 'to cook on a griddle'; ዘንጎጎ *zang^wag^wa* 'to mock, deride'. This type also contains reduplicated verbs with /y/ or /w/ as the second root letter, which are formally equivalent to category (3) below: ዼወወ *ḍewawa* 'to take prisoner, capture'.

3. Verbs with /y/ or /w/ as the second radical, usually in the G-stem with the forms *1e3a4a* (< *1ay3a4a*) and *1o3a4a* (< *1aw3a4a*), that is, the second radical is reflected only vocalically, as in ደገነ *degana* 'to pursue' and ቤዘወ *bezawa* 'to redeem' on the one hand, and ሞቀሐ *moqǝḥa* 'to put in chains, cast into prison' and ኖለወ *nolawa* 'to be a shepherd' on the other.

4.4.7.2. General characteristics of the inflection of quadriliteral verbs:

- The system of stems employed for quadriliteral verbs corresponds to that of triradical verbs. However, only the G and its derivatives (the CGt occurs but is rare) as well as the Lt (and CLt, although again this stem is rare) are common. Many of these verbs do not have a G-stem since they are often of denominative origin. In these cases, it is the CG or Gt that expresses the basic meaning of the verb.

- The imperfect generally exhibits a geminated third radical, not second radical, as in ይለመልም *yǝlamallǝm* (√lmlm G 'to be verdant, mild').

- The L-stem and its derivatives have the characteristic /ā/-vowel between the second and third root letters, as in ተሰናሰለ *tasanāsala* (√snsl Lt 'to be linked together, chained together').

- Quadriliteral verbs with weak radicals undergo the same phonological changes as the corresponding triradical verbs.

- The G-infinitive has a form with final –o when no pronominal suffixes are attached, as in ተርጕሞ(ት) *targʷəmo(t)*, as opposed to the form ነጊር *nagir* without final –o of triradical verbs.

4.4.7.3. The following represents the paradigm of genuine and reduplicated quadriliteral verbs (√*trgʷm* 'to translate'; √*fdfd* 'to increase'; √*mndb* CG 'to torment'; √*snbt* CGt 'to keep the Sabbath'; √*snsl* Lt 'to be chained together'; √*gʷndy* CLt 'to cause to delay' (also IV-*y*]):

G		
Perf.	ተርጐመ *targʷama*	ፈድፈደ *fadfada*
Impf.	ይተረጕም *yətaraggʷəm*	ይፈደፍድ *yəfadaffəd*
Juss.	ይተርጕም *yətargʷəm*	ይፈድፍድ *yəfadfəd*
Imp.	ተርጕም *targʷəm*	ፈድፍድ *fadfəd*
PP	ተርጕም– *targʷim–*	ፈድፊድ– *fadfid–*
Inf.	ተርጕሞ(ት) *targʷəmo(t)*	ፈድፍዶ(ት) *fadfədo(t)*

CG		
Perf.	አመንደበ *ʾamandaba*	አፈድፈደ *ʾafadfada*
Impf.	ያመነድብ *yāmanaddəb*	ያፈደፍድ *yāfadaffəd*
Juss.	ያመንድብ *yāmandəb*	ያፈድፍድ *yāfadfəd*
Imp.	አመንድብ *ʾamandəb*	አፈድፍድ *ʾafadfəd*
PP	አመንዲብ– *ʾamandib–*	አፈድፊድ– *ʾafadfid–*
Inf.	አመንድቦ(ት) *ʾamandəbo(t)*	አፈድፍዶ(ት) *ʾafadfədo(t)*

Gt		
Perf.	ተመንደበ *tamandaba*	ተፈድፈደ *tafadfada*
Impf.	ይትመነደብ *yətmanaddab*	ይትፈደፈድ *yətfadaffad*
Juss.	ይትመንደብ *yətmandab*	ይትፈድፈድ *yətfadfad*
Imp.	ተመንደብ *tamandab*	ተፈድፈድ *tafadfad*
PP	ተተርጕም– *tatargʷim–*	ተፈድፊድ– *tafadfid–*
Inf.	ተተርጕሞ(ት) *tatargʷəmo(t)*	ተፈድፍዶ(ት) *tafadfədo(t)*

	Lt	
Perf.	ተሰናሰለ *tasanāsala*	
Impf.	ይሰናሰል *yəssanāssal*	
Juss.	ይሰናሰል *yəssanāsal*	
Imp.	ተሰናሰል *tasanāsal*	
PP	ተሰናሲል- *tasanāsil-*	
Inf.	ተሰናስሎ(ት) *tasanāsəlo(t)*	

	CGt	CLt
Perf.	አስተሰንበተ *ʾastasanbata*	አስተጐናደየ *ʾastagʷanādaya*
Impf.	ያስተሰነብት *yāstasanabbət*	ያስተጐናዲ *yāstagʷanāddi* ያስተጐናድዩ *yāstagʷanāddəyu*
Juss.	ያስተሰንብት *yāstasanbət*	ያስተጐናዲ *yāstagʷanādi* ያስተጐናድዩ *yāstagʷanādəyu*
Imp.	አስተሰንብት *ʾastasanbət*	አስተጐናዲ *ʾastagʷanādi* አስተጐናድዩ *ʾastagʷanādəyu*
PP	አስተሰንቢት- *ʾastasanbit-*	አስተጐናድ/ዲይ- *ʾastagʷanādə/iy-*
Inf.	አስተሰንብቶ(ት) *ʾastasanbəto(t)*	አስተጐናድ/ዲዮ(ት) *ʾastagʷanādə/iyo(t)*

4.4.7.4. Weak roots exhibit the following peculiarities and irregular formations:

- Verbs that are III-guttural cannot geminate their third root letter in the impf., as in ያስተሰነአል *yāstasanaʾal* instead of **yāstasanaʾʾal (√*snʾl* 'to grant leave, dismiss'); ይሰናአው *yəssanāʾaw* impf. and juss. (√*snʾw* Lt 'to live in peace'); ያስተሰናኡ *yāstasanāʾu* impf. and juss. (√*snʾw* CLt 'to let live in peace').

- The paradigm of verbs IV-guttural exhibits forms that correspond to those of verbs III-guttural of triradical roots, that is, they have /ə/ instead of /a/ between the last and second to last radicals. The root √*šḥšḥ* 'to move backward and forward, agitate' (also II-gutt.), for example, has the following perfect forms: ሳሕስሐ *sāḥsəḥa* (G) and ተሳሕስሐ *tasāḥsəḥa* (Gt, passive of G).

- The root √rmss forms the CG perfects አረምሰሰ ʾaramsasa and አርመሰሰ ʾarmasasa 'to grope, trample'.[179]
- The verb ተንሥአ tanśaʾa 'to rise up', which is a denominative derived from ትንሣኤ tanśāʾe 'ascent, rising' (verbal noun of ነሥአ naśʾa 'to raise, lift') is formally treated like a quadriliteral root √tnśʾ and thus forms its perfect and imperative according to the paradigm of quadriliteral verbs. The imperfect and jussive, however, follow the paradigm of the Gt of triradical III-gutt. roots (§4.4.5.4.2.; also compare the forms of ተነሥአ tanaśʾa, the Gt and passive of ነሥአ naśʾa): Perf. ተንሥአ tanśaʾa < *tanśaʾa; impf. ይትነሣእ yatnaśśāʾ (like Gt ተነሥአ tanaśʾa); juss. ይትነሣእ yatnaśāʾ (like Gt ተነሥአ tanaśʾa); imp. ተንሥእ tanśaʾ. Based on the meaning of ተንሥአ tanśaʾa, the root also forms a CLt with a causative meaning: አስተናሥአ ʾastanāśaʾa 'to make rise, elevate'.

4.4.7.5. Quadriliteral verbs that have a semivowel (/y/ or /w/) as their second radical commonly contract the original diphthongs /ay/ and /aw/ to /e/ and /o/ respectively in forms of the G-stem and its derivatives, as in ዴገነ degana (< *daygana) 'he pursued', ሞቀሐ moqaḥa (< *mawqaḥa) 'he took prisoner', and ቶስሐ tosḥa (< *tawsaḥa) 'he mixed, mingled'.

These forms formally correspond to those of triradical verbs in the L-stem and are conjugated respectively. Many grammars consequently describe this type of verb as triradical and note that such verbs constitute a variant of the L-stem (with /e/ or /o/ after the first radical instead of /ā/). CDG lists these verbs as triradical as well; the verb ዴገነ degana, for example, is listed under the root √dgn (DL, on the other hand, has d-y-g-n).

The verb ጠውቀየ ṭawqaya 'to be narrow, painful'[180] and the verb ዐውየወ ʿawyawa 'to howl, groan', which contains several weak radicals, differ from verbs like ሞቀሐ moqaḥa in that they form perfects with consonantal /w/ in the G-stem:

---

[179] The root √rmss is the result of a metathesis (§3.6.4.2.) of the root √mrss, which has the forms መርሰሰ marsasa 'to grope for' (G), አመርሰሰ ʾamarsasa (CG, causative), and ተመርሰሰ tamarsasa (Gt, passive).

[180] The strong formation of this verb in the G could be motivated by the fact that this verb only forms L-stems with consonantal /w/ besides the G: Lt ተጠዋቀየ taṭawāqaya; CLt አስተጠዋቀየ ʾastaṭawāqaya. The verb ጠውቀየ ṭawqaya is etymologically connected to ጠቀ ṭoqa 'to be oppressed, compress'.

Perf. 0ው·የመ ʿawyawa; impf. የ0ወዩ yaʿawayyu, የ0ወይዉ -əwu; juss. የ0ዉ·ዩ yaʿawyu, የ0ዉ·ይዉ -əwu. These verbs are listed as quadriliteral in CDG.

In the L-stem and its derivatives, the second radical always appears in consonantal form for verbs II-w/y. Verbs II-y either have an /a/-vowel or an /e/-vowel (probably in analogy to G-stem forms) between the first and second radicals, or no vowel, as in the Lt perf. ተዘያነወ/ተዜያነወ/ተዝያነወ tazayānawa/tazeyānawa (most common form)/tazyānawa 'to announce to one another'; and the CLt perf. አስተዜያነወ/አስተዝያነወ ʾastazeyānawa/ʾastazyānawa (causative of Lt). Verbs II-w have an /a/-vowel or no vowel in the perfect, as in the Lt ተተዋስሐ tatawāsəḥa 'to be mingled with each other'; ተምዋቅሐ tamwāqəḥa (< *tam(a)wāqaḥa) 'to take each other captive', and the CLt perf. አስተጠዋቀየ ʾastaṭawāqaya 'to cause to oppress one another', አስተምዋቅሐ ʾastamwāqəḥa (causative of Lt).

The following paradigm contains the verbal roots: √dygn 'to pursue'; √mwqḥ (also IV-gutt.) G 'to take captive', Lt 'to take each other captive' (not productive), CLt 'to cause to take each other captive' (not productive); √twsḥ (also IV-gutt.) G 'to mix, mingle', Lt 'to be mingled with one another'; √zynw (also IV-w) G 'to report, inform' (2ms ዜነዉ·ክ/ዜነዓክ zenawka/zenoka), Lt 'to announce to one another', CLt 'to cause to announce to one another':

G		
Perf.	ዶገነ degana	ሞቅሐ moqəḥa[181]	ቶስሐ tosḥa
Impf.	ይዶግን yədeggən	ይሞቅሕ yəmoqqəḥ	ይቶስሕ yətossəḥ
Juss.	ይዶግን yədegən	ይሞቅሕ yəmoqəḥ	ይቶስሕ yətosəḥ
Imp.	ዶግን degən	ሞቅሕ moqəḥ	ቶስሐ tosəḥ

CG		
Perf.	አዶገነ ʾadegana	አሞቅሐ ʾamoqəḥa	
Impf.	ያዶግን yādeggən	ያሞቅሕ yāmoqqəḥ	
Juss.	ያዶግን yādegən	ያሞቅሕ yāmoqəḥ	
Imp.	አዶግን ʾadegən	አሞቅሕ ʾamoqəḥ	

---

[181] 3fs ሞቅሐት moqəḥat; 2ms ሞቃሕከ moqāḥka, etc.

Gt			
Perf.	ተዴገነ *tadegana*	ተሞቅሐ *tamoqəha*	ተቶስሐ *tatosha*
Impf.	ይዴገን *yəddeggan*	ይትሞቃሕ *yətmoqqāḥ*	ይቶሳሕ *yəttossāḥ*
Juss.	ይዴገን *yəddegan*	ይትሞቃሕ *yətmoqāḥ*	ይቶሳሕ *yəttosāḥ*
Imp.	ተዴገን *tadegan*	ተሞቃሕ *tamoqāḥ*	ተቶሳሕ *tatosāḥ*

Lt			
Perf.	ተዘያነወ *tazayānawa* ተዜያነወ *tazeyānawa* ተዝያነወ *tazyānawa*[182]	ተምዋቅሐ *tamwāqəha*	ተተዋስሐ *tatawāsəha*
Impf.	ይትዘያነው *yətzayānnaw* ይትዜያነው *yətzeyānnaw*	ይትመዋቃሕ *yətmawāqqāḥ*	ይተዋሳሕ *yəttawāssāḥ*
Juss.	ይትዘያነው *yətzayānaw* ይትዜያነው *yətzeyānaw*	ይትመዋቃሕ *yətmawāqāḥ*	ይተዋሳሕ *yəttawāsāḥ*
Imp.	ተዘያነው *tazayānaw* ተዜያነው *tazeyānaw*	ተምዋቃሕ *tamwāqāḥ*	ተተዋሳሕ *tatawāsāḥ*

CLt		
Perf.	አስተዝያነወ *ʾastazyānawa*[183] አስተዜያነወ *ʾastazeyānawa*	አስተምዋቅሐ *ʾastamwāqəha*
Impf.	ያስተዝያኑ *yāstazyānnu* ያስተዜያኑ *yāstazeyānnu* ያስተዜያንነዉ *yāstazeyānnəwu*	ያስተምዋቅሕ *yāstamwāqqəḥ* ያስተመዋቅሕ *yāstamawāqqəḥ*
Juss.	ያስተዝያኑ *yāstazyānu* ያስተዜያኑ *yāstazeyānu* ያስተዜያንዉ *yāstazeyānəwu*	ያስተምዋቅሕ *yāstamwāqəḥ* ያስተመዋቅሕ *yāstamawāqəḥ*
Imp.	አስተዝያኑ *ʾastazyānu* አስተዜያኑ *ʾastazeyānu* አስተዜያንዉ *ʾastazeyānəwu*	አስተምዋቅሕ *ʾastamwāqəḥ* አስተመዋቅሕ *ʾastamawāqəḥ*

[182] Other verbs most commonly have /a/ after the first radical, such as ተጠዋቀየ *taṭawāqaya* 'to oppress one another'.

[183] Other verbs most commonly have /a/ after the first radical, such as አስተጠዋቀየ *ʾastaṭawāqaya* (causative of Lt).

4.4.8. Quinquiliteral Verbs

4.4.8.1. Almost all verbs in Classical Ethiopic that have five root radicals have an underlying reduplicated root structure. These verbs can be derived from bases that are bi-, tri-, or quadriliteral, some of which are attested in the shorter base in Classical Ethiopic. The most important formal sub-groups are (the citation form of these verbs is usually the CG [§4.4.8.2.]):

1. Verbs of the reduplicated type *1-2-3-2-3*, such as አድለቅለቀ *ʾadlaqlaqa* 'to shake, tremble' (based on triradical *d-l-q*); አሕመልመለ *ʾaḥmalmala* 'to grow green' (cf. ሐምል *ḥaml* 'vegetation, herbs'); አቅያሕየሐ *ʾaqyāḥyəḥa* 'to gleam red, become reddish' (cf. ቀይሕ *qayyəḥ* 'red'); አርሳሕስሐ *ʾarsāḥsəḥa* 'to render impure'; ኀሰርሰረ *ḫasarsara* 'to be reviled, humiliated' (G-stem).

2. Very common are verbs with /n/ as the first radical. These verbs commonly describe repeated actions, that is, they have iterative connotation. The majority of these verbs also have the reduplicated root structure *1-2-3-2-3*, such as አንቀልቀለ *ʾanqalqala* 'to move, shake' (basic root *q-l-q-l*); አንቀጥቀጠ *ʾanqaṭqaṭa* 'to shake, quiver'; አንጐድጐደ *ʾangʷadgʷada* 'to thunder' (cf. ጐድጐደ *gʷadgʷada* 'to knock'); አንጸፍጸፈ *ʾanṣafṣafa* 'to ooze, drip'; አንገርገረ *ʾangargara* 'to revolve, roll'; አንጐርጐረ *ʾangʷargʷara* 'to murmur, grumble'; አንበልበለ *ʾanbalbala* 'to blaze, emit flames'; cf. also አንዛህለለ *ʾanzāhlala* 'to grow weak, be indolent' (type *1-2-3-4-4*); አንሶሰወ *ʾansosawa* 'to move, walk' (III-w); አንፈርዐጸ *ʾanfarʿaṣa* 'to exult, leap, spring'.

    Several of these verbs have corresponding quadriliteral roots without /n/, such as አንሳሕስሐ *ʾansāḥsəḥa* < **ʾansaḥsaḥa* and አንስሐስሐ *ʾansəḥasḥa* < **ʾansaḥasḥa* 'to be in motion, stir' (cf. ሳሕስሐ *sāḥsəḥa* 'to move backward and forward'); አንገጋየ *ʾangegaya* 'to lead to sin' (cf. ጌጋየ *gegaya* 'to err, go astray'; አንጎጎወ *ʾangogawa* 'to wander (about restlessly)' (cf. ጎጎወ *gogawa* 'to err').

    These verbs are generally considered as quadriliteral by the common dictionaries (DL and CDG). The verb አንቀልቀለ *ʾanqalqala*, for example, is listed under *q-l-q-l*.[184]

---

[184] From a comparative point of view, these forms should not be compared to the common Semitic N-stem, but, because of their iterative function, to other iterative stems such as the

3. Verbs that correspond to category (2) but that have /s/ as their first
    radical, such as አስቆቀወ ʾasqoqawa (< *ʾasqawqawa) 'to howl, lament'
    (also III-w); አስቆረረ ʾasqorara 'to feel horror, loathe'.

    These verbs are often described as so-called "as"-stems of tri- or
    quadriliteral roots in the grammars. CDG lists these verbs under
    triradical roots. The verb አስቆቀወ ʾasqoqawa, for example, is listed
    under q-q-w. DL, on the other hand, lists them as quinquiliteral, e.g., s-
    q-w-q-w.

    The first radical /s/ of this type of verb is historically derived from
    a no longer productive and lexicalized marker of a stem marked by
    initial /s/ (§4.4.4.3.).[185]

4.4.8.2. Quinquiliteral verbs are commonly only attested in the CG and Gt. The
CG has an active meaning and the Gt is most often the passive of the CG.

Only few verbs have a G-stem, such as ጸምሀየየ/ጸማሀየየ ṣamhayaya/ṣamāhyaya 'to
fade away, wither' (cf. ጸምሀየ ṣamhaya, same meaning) and ኀሰርሰረ ḫasarsara 'to
be reviled, humiliated' (cf. ኀርሰ ḫarsa 'to be disgraced').

The verb አስቆረረ ʾasqorara 'to feel horror, loathe' has a CGt አስተቈረረ
ʾastaqʷarara (< *ʾastaqwarara) 'to hold in abomination', which is based on the
quadriliteral root √qwrr. This form is not included in the paradigm given in
§4.4.8.4.

4.4.8.3. The imperfect of this verb type is characterized by the gemination of
the fourth radical, as in ያድለቀልቅ yādlaqalləq (√dlqlq CG impf.).

To be noted in particular are the impf. and juss. of the Gt. In these forms, the
stem-marking /t/ is commonly dropped completely, as in impf. ይንቀለቀል
yənqalaqqal < *yəntalaqqal and juss. ይንቀልቀል yənqalqal < *yəntqalqal.[186]

Akkadian *tan-/tn*-stems.

[185] Compare the /s/ attested as a stem-marker in the CGt, CDt, and CLt and the causative
morpheme *s in other Semitic languages such as Akkadian.

[186] In the reconstruction provided here, the /t/ is assumed to be in the second position, after
/n/, which itself originally represented a stem-marker.

4.4.8.4. The paradigm of quinquiliteral verbs presented below uses the following roots: √ḥsrsr G 'to be reviled, humiliated'; √dlqlq CG 'to shake'; √nqlql CG 'to move, shake', Gt 'to totter'; √sqwqw CG and Gt 'to howl, lament':

G			
Perf.	ኀሰርሰረ ḫasarsara		
Impf.	ይኀስረስር yəḫasrassər		
Juss.	ይኀስርስር yəḫsarsər		

CG			
Perf.	አድለቅለቀ ʾadlaqlaqa	አንቀልቀለ ʾanqalqala	አስቆቀወ ʾasqoqawa
Impf.	ያድለቀልቅ yādlaqalləq	ያንቀለቅል yānqalaqqəl	ያስቆቁ yāsqoqqu ያስቆቅዉ yāsqoqqəwu
Juss.	ያድለቅልቅ yādlaqləq	ያንቀልቅል yānqalqəl	ያስቆቁ yāsqoqu ያስቆቅዉ yāsqoqəwu
Imp.	አድለቅልቅ ʾadlaqləq	አንቀልቅል ʾanqalqəl	አስቆቁ ʾasqoqu አስቆቅዉ ʾasqoqəwu
PP	አድለቅሊቅ- ʾadlaqliq-	አንቀልቄል- ʾanqalqil-	
Inf.			
	አድለቅልቆ(ት) ʾadlaqləqo(t)	አንቀልቅሎ(ት) ʾanqalqəlo(t)	

Gt			
Perf.	ተንቀልቀለ tanqalqala		ተስቆቀወ tasqoqawa
Impf.	ይንቀለቀል yənqalaqqal (!)		ይስቆቀዉ yəsqoqqaw (!)
Juss.	ይንቀልቀል yənqalqal (!)		ይስቆቀዉ yəsqoqaw (!)
Imp.	ተንቀልቀል tanqalqal		ተስቆቀዉ tasqoqaw

4.4.9. Six-Radical Verbs

The only formally six-radical verbal form is ተአንተልተለ taʾantaltala 'to be impatient, unwilling' (formal G-perf.). This verb is a reduplicated formation of

ተአንተለ *taʾantala* with the same meaning, which might go back to triradical *ʾ-t-l*. This verb is only attested in the perfect.

4.5. Particles

4.5.1. Adverbs

4.5.1.1. Adverbs in Classical Ethiopic are most commonly based on nouns. They usually reflect indeclinable nominal forms in an adverbial case. From a formal perspective, the following particularities can be noted:

- Many adverbs have the ending *–a*, which is the marker of the accusative, as in ቅድመ *qədma* 'before'; ሌሊት *lelita* 'at night'; ሕቀ *ḥəqqa* 'a little'; ብዙኀ *bəzuḫa* 'much'; ፍጡነ *fəṭuna* 'quickly'; መሪረ *marira* 'bitterly' (the latter three adverbs have adjectives as their base).
- Besides adverbs ending in *–a*, Classical Ethiopic also has adverbs ending in *–u*. This *–u* reflects the common Semitic locative-adverbial *-u(m)* that is particularly prominent in Akkadian and Arabic, although this morpheme is not productive in Classical Ethiopic any longer. Adverbs of this type include lexemes such as ላዕሉ *lāʿlu* 'above, upward' and ታሕቱ *tāḥtu* 'below, under'. In other cases it is difficult to ascertain whether or not the final *–u* of an adverb reflects the locative-adverbial marker or a 3ms pronominal suffix, as in ዳእሙ *dāʾmu* 'verily, really'; ለዝሉፉ *la-zəlufu* 'forever'; ባሕቱ *bāḥəttu* 'only, but'; ቀዲሙ *qadimu* 'first, at the beginning'.
- Several adverbs are based on nouns without case or adverbial endings, such as ዮም *yom* 'today' and አማን *ʾamān* 'verily'.
- There are further nouns ending in *–ā* that are used adverbially, such as ከዋላ *kawālā* 'behind' and ግሙራ *gəmurā* 'completely'.
- Numerous adverbs contain a third person pronominal suffix (masc. and fem.), such as አሜሃ/አሜሁ *ʾamehā/ʾamehu* 'at the time, next'; ሶቤሃ *sobehā* 'at that time, immediately'; በጊዜሁ *ba-gizehu* 'at its proper time'; በጊዜሃ *ba-gizehā* 'right away, at once'; እምኔሁ *ʾəmənnehu* 'thereafter'; ከማሁ *kamāhu* 'similarly, so'.

4.5.1.2. Most adverbs are stressed on the last syllable, specifically those ending in the vowels *–u, –i, –ā*, and *–e*, as in ላዕሉ *lāʿlú* 'above'.

Adverbs ending in –a, on the other hand, are stressed on the penultima, as in ዝየ *záya* 'here'; ጥቀ *ṭáqqa* 'very'; ብዙኀ *bəzúḫa* 'much'.

4.5.1.3. The following sections are ordered according to semantic principles. They only include adverbs in the strict sense of the term, excluding certain logical sentence and enclitic particles. The latter are treated in §4.5.8.–9.

4.5.1.4. Local Adverbs

'here'	ዝየ *zəya*, ዚየ *ziya*, በዝየ *ba-zəya* (penultimate stress)
'there'	ህየ *həyya*, ሂየ *hiyya*, በህየ *ba-həyya* 'there'; ከሐ *kaha*, ከሓ *kahā*, በከሐ *ba-kaha*, ከሐክ/ከ *kahak(a)* 'yonder, thither, there'; (lexeme **fe*) ለፈ *lafe*, እምለፈ *'əm-lafe* 'to this side, that way' (ለፈ ... ወለፈ *lafe ... wa-lafe* 'this way ... and that way')[187]
'above'	ላዕሉ *lāˁlu*, በላዕሉ *ba-lāˁlu*, ላዕለ *lāˁla* 'above, upward' (also እምላዕሉ *'əm-lāˁlu* 'from above')
'below'	ታሕቱ *tāḥtu*, ታሕተ *tāḥta*
'before'	ቀድም *qədma*
'behind'	ከወላ *kawalā*, ከዋላ *kawālā*, ኳላ *kʷālā* 'behind, hind part'
others	አፍአ/አ *'afʾa/ā* 'out, outside'; ኩልዬ/ኩለዬ *kʷəllə-he/kʷəlla-he* 'everywhere, wherever' (cf. §4.5.9.3.).

4.5.1.5. Temporal Adverbs

'now'	ይእዜ *yəʾəze* 'now'
'then, afterwards'	አሜሃ *'amehā*, less often አሜሁ *'amehu*, 'then, at that time'; ሶቤሃ *sobehā* 'then, at that time, thereupon'; እምነሁ *'əmənnehu* (preposition *'əmənna*+hu) 'thereafter'; ድኅረ *dəḫra*, ድኅሩ *dəḫrehu*, ዳኅረ *dāḫra* 'then, afterwards'; እምዝ *'əm-zə* 'thereafter, after this'; እምድኅረ፡ዝንቱ *'əm-dəḫra zəntu* 'after this' = 'afterwards'; እምህየ *'əm-həyya* 'from there, thence'

---

[187] For the etymology of this lexeme compare Hebrew *peʾāh* 'edge, side' and Akkadian *pātu* 'edge' (see CDG 154a).

'before, first'	**ቅድም** *qədma* 'formerly'; **ቀዲሙ** *qadimu* 'first, at the beginning'; **ቀዲማ** *qadima* 'at the first time, earlier, before'; **ቀዳሚ** *qadāmi* 'first, former, earlier'; **ትካተ** *təkāta* 'before, once'
'always, forever'	**ለዝሉፉ** *la-zəlufu*, **ዝሉፉ** *zəlufa*, **ለዘላፉ** *la-zallāfu*, **ለዝላፉ** *la-zəlāfu*, **ለዘልፍ** *la-zalf*, **ዘልፋ** *zalfa* 'continually, always, forever'; **ወትረ** *watra*, **ውቱረ** *wətura* 'continuously, always'
'immediately, suddenly'	**በጊዜሃ** *ba-gizehā* 'straightaway, immediately'; **ግብተ** *gəbta* (√wgb) 'suddenly, instantly'
'once'	**ምዕረ** *mə'ra* 'once, at one time',[188] **ለምዕር** *la-mə'r* 'for a moment'
'still, again'	**ዓዲ** *'ādi* 'still, again' (often with a pronominal suffix, as in **ዓዲነ፡ ሕያዋን** *'ādi-na ḥəyāwān* 'we are still alive'; **ዓዲ ... ኢ-** *'ādi ... 'i-* 'not yet')[189]
'again'	**ካዕበ** *kā'əba* 'a second time, again'
'today'	**ዮም** *yom* 'today'; **ዛቲ፡ ዕለት** *zātti 'əlat* 'today'
'tomorrow'	**ጌሰም** *gesam*, **ጌሠም** *geśam* 'tomorrow, the morrow' (√gys [§4.2.6.])
'yesterday'	**ትማልም** *təmāləm* 'yesterday' (√tml [§4.2.6.])
'at night'	**ሌሊተ** *lelita* 'at night'

4.5.1.6. Modal Adverbs

'likewise, so'	**ከመዝ** *kama-zə* 'such, like this'; **ከማሁ** *kamāhu* 'likewise, so'; **በከመ** *ba-kama* 'according to, likewise, how'; **በከመ ... ከማሁ** *ba-kama ... kamāhu* 'like ... so (as well)'
'verily'	**(በ)አማን** *(ba-)'amān*, **አማነ** *'amāna* 'truly, verily'[190]
'almost'	**ከመ** *kəmma* 'almost, nearly, thus'

---

[188] E.g., **ምዕረ፡ ለዓመት** *mə'ra la-'āmat* 'once a year' (Jub 49:7, 15).

[189] As in **ወዓዲሆሙ፡ እልኩ፡ አዝእብት፡ ኢ.ርእይዎሙ፡ ለአባግዕ** *wa-'ādihomu 'əlləku 'az'əbt 'i-rə'yəwwomu la-'abāgə'* 'and while those wolves had not yet seen the sheep' (En 89:25).

[190] This adverb usually stands at the beginning of the sentence or immediately after a sentence-introducing conjunction, as in **እመሰ፡ አማን፡ ወልዱ፡ አንተ፡ ለእግዚአብሔር** *'əmma-ssa 'amān waldu 'anta la-'egzi'ab(ə)ḥer* 'if you are truly the son of god' (Mt 4:6).

4.5.1.7. Adverbs of Degree

'very'   **ጥቀ** *ṭəqqa* 'very' (§5.2.8.1.); **ፈድፋደ** *fadfāda* 'greatly, abundantly'
                   (§5.2.8.1.; §5.2.8.3.)
'little'   **ሕቀ** *ḥəqqa* 'little'; **ኅዳጠ** *ḥədāṭa*, **በኅዳጥ** *ba-ḥədāṭ* 'a little'; **ንስቲተ**
                   nəstita 'a little, for a little while'
'much'   **ብዙኀ** *bəzuḫa* 'much'
'completely'   **ገሙራ** *gəmurā* 'completely, entirely'

4.5.1.8. Causal Adverbs

'thus,
therefore'   **በእንተ፡ዝ-** *ba-ʾənta zə-*, **በእንተ፡ዝንቱ** *ba-ʾənta zəntu* 'thus,
                   therefore'; **በበይን** *ba-bayna*, **በበይን፡ዝ-** *ba-bayna zə-* 'because of,
                   therefore'; **እንበይን** *ʾənbayna*, **እምበይን** *ʾəmbayna* 'for the sake of,
                   because of'

4.5.1.9. Other Adverbs

'yes'   **አሆ** *ʾoho* 'certainly, yes!'; **እወ** *ʾəwwa* 'yes, of course'
'no'   **አልቦ** *ʾalbo* 'no' (literally 'it is not')[191]
'perhaps'   **እንዳዒ** *ʾəndāʿi* 'I don't know, perhaps' (< *ʾən [negation] +
                   √ydʿ);[192] **ዮጊ** *yogi* 'perhaps, possibly'
'without
reason'   **ከንቶ** *kanto*, **ለከንቱ** *la-kantu*, **በከንቱ** *ba-kantu* 'without reason,
                   gratis' (**ከንቱ** *kantu* 'nothingness')

4.5.1.10. Interrogative Adverbs

Interrogative adverbs consist of three main types:

---

[191] See, e.g., **እመሂ፡እወ፡እወ፡ወእመሂ፡አልቦ፡አልቦ** *ʾəmma-hi ʾəwwa ʾəwwa wa-ʾəmma-hi ʾalbo ʾalbo* '(let your word be) either 'yes!, yes!' or 'no!, no!'" (Mt 5:37); **አልቦ፡አላ፡ዮሐንስ፡ይሰመይ** *ʾalbo ʾallā yoḥannəs yəssamay* 'No! He is to be called John' (Lk 1:60).

[192] Literally 'the non-existence of my knowing' (*ʾən + dāʿ + 1cs pronominal suffix -i*) or 'I am one who does not know' (*ʾən + dāʿi* agent noun of type *qatāli*).

(a) Compounds containing the interrogative bases **ሚ** *mi* / **ማ** *mā* 'what?' (§4.1.7.2.):

ማእዜ *mā'aze* 'when?' (< *mā* + *ya'aze* 'what now?'); **ሚጊዜ** *mi-gize* 'when?'; **ሚኬ** *mi-ke* 'how?'; **ሚመጠን** *mi-maṭana* 'how much?'

(b) Compounds with the interrogative pronoun **ምንት** *mant* 'what?' (§4.1.7.1.):

በምንት *ba-mant* 'in what way?'; **ለምንት** *la-mant* 'in what way?, why?'; **በእንተ፡ምንት** *ba-'anta mant* 'why?'; **እስከ፡ምንት** *'aska mant* 'how long?'; **ከመ፡ምንቱ** *kama manta-nu* 'how much?'

(c) Other interrogative adverbs:

አይቴ *'ayte*, **በአይቴ** *ba-'ayte* 'where?, whither?'; **እምአይቴ** *'am-'ayte* 'whence?'

እፎ *'affo* 'how?, in what way?' (**እፎ፡ፈድፋደ** *'affo fadfāda* 'how much more')

Note: The interrogative pronouns just mentioned are often extended by the enclitic particles **ኑ** *-nu* and **ሁ** *-hu* (§4.5.9.1.), as in **በምንቱ** *ba-manta-nu* 'in what way?'.

4.5.1.11. Indefinite Adverbs

Indefinite adverbs are formed on the basis of interrogative adverbs by suffixing the enclitic particle **ኒ** *-ni* or **ሂ** *-hi* (§4.5.8.4.). Examples include:

- **አይቴኒ/ሂ** *'ayte-ni/-hi* 'anywhere'
- **ኢአይቴኒ/ሂ** *'i-'ayte-ni/-hi* 'nowhere'
- **በምንትኒ** *ba-manta-ni* 'in any way'

4.5.2. Prepositions

Classical Ethiopic has three main types of prepositions: (a) It has three short, formally monoconsonantal prepositions that are always used proclitically and are written as one unit with the following word. (b) The majority of prepositions constitute independent prepositions. These primarily consist of original nouns that have been grammaticalized into prepositions, including nouns with the preformative *ma–*, as in **ማእከል** *mā'kal* 'center, middle' > **ማእከለ** *mā'kala* 'in the middle of'. Only a small number of prepositions have no noticeable etymology. (c) Classical Ethiopic further has a significant number of compound prepositions that are made up of two prepositions. Particularly frequent are compounds containing proclitic በ– *ba–* or እም– *ʾəm–*.

Prepositions function like nouns in the construct state syntactically and consequently almost always end in *–a*.[193] Before pronominal suffixes, they most commonly end in *–e* (see §4.5.2.4.1.). Some prepositions also use the form with *–e* without pronominal suffixes, such as ዲበ *dibe* besides ዲበ *diba* 'on, upon' and ኀበ *ḫabe* besides ኀበ *ḫaba* 'toward, to'.

All prepositions are followed by a noun in the unmarked case (former genitive).

4.5.2.1. Proclitic Prepositions

4.5.2.1.1. በ– *ba–* 'in, by, with'[194]
This preposition has special forms in combination with pronominal suffixes (§4.5.2.4.3.). For the use of በ– *ba–* with pronominal suffixes in nominal clauses, such as ቦ *bo* 'within him (is)' = 'there is', see §6.1.4. and especially §6.1.4.3.; for constructions with አልቦ *ʾalbo*, see §6.1.4.4.; for በበ *babba* (< *ba+ba*) with distributive meaning, see §5.6.3.

4.5.2.1.2. ለ– *la–* 'to, toward, for, of'[195]
This preposition likewise has special forms when pronominal suffixes are attached (§4.5.2.4.3.). It is also used for periphrastic genitive and accusative constructions (§5.2.3.2.). For the function of ለ– *la–* with pronominal suffixes, see §5.1.1.5.; for ለለ *lalla* (*la+la*) with distributive force, see §5.6.4.; for the lexeme ለሊ– *lalli–* that is likewise based on ለ– *la–*, see §4.1.3.1. and §5.1.3.1.

---

[193] This *–a* could also be interpreted as reflecting an adverbial accusative, which is frequent for marking prepositions in languages with fully productive case systems such as Classical Arabic.

[194] As in በምድር *ba-mədr* 'in the land' and በእደ *ba-ʾəda* 'in/by the hand of'.

[195] As in ወኢይትረከብ፡ ሎሙ፡ አሰር *wa-ʾi-yətrakkab lomu ʾasar* 'no trace of them will be found' (En 48:9).

4.5.2.1.3. እም- ʾəm- 'from, out of, because of, to'[196]

Besides proclitic እም- ʾəm-, Classical Ethiopic also has the independent preposition እምነ ʾəmənna that has the same meaning as እም- ʾəm- (§4.5.2.2.). The proclitic form እም- ʾəm- is not used with pronominal suffixes. When እም- ʾəm- occurs before a noun starting with /m/, only one /m/ is written, as in በአሕቲ፡ እመዋዕል ba-ʾaḥatti ʾəm-mawāʿəl 'on one of the days'.

4.5.2.2. Independent Prepositions (no Compounds)

4.5.2.2.1. Frequently used prepositions include:

(a) Prepositions with primarily local meaning:
- ውስተ wəsta 'in, into'
- ኀበ ḫaba (also ኀቤ ḫabe) 'toward, near to, by, at'
- ዲበ diba (also ዲቤ dibe) 'on, upon, against'
- ላዕለ lāʿla 'above, on, against'
- መልዕልተ malʿəlta 'on, above, upward'
- ቅድመ qədma 'before'
- ታሕተ tāḫta 'below, under'
- እምነ ʾəmənna[197] 'from, out of, because of' (cf. the preposition እም- ʾəm- [§4.5.2.1.3.])
- እንተ ʾənta 'through, by way of, by'[198]
- በይነ bayna, በበይነ ba-bayna, በበይናቲ ba-baynāti 'between, among'
- ማእከለ māʾkala 'in the midst of, among' (noun ማእከል māʾkal 'center, middle')

  The meaning 'between A and B' is, as in other Semitic languages, expressed by the repetition of the preposition, that is በይነ A ወበይነ B bayna A wa-bayna B and ማእከለ A ወማእከለ B māʾkala A wa-māʾkala B, as in ወፈለጠ፡ እግዚአብሔር፡ ማእከለ፡ ብርሃን፡ ወማእከለ፡

---

[196] See, e.g., ዓመት/ተ፡ እም/በዓመት ʿāmat(a) ʾəm/ba-ʿāmat 'year to year/each year'; ዕለተ፡ እም/በዕለት ʿəlata ʾəm/ba-ʿəlat 'day to day/each day' (Jub 49:22). Similarly also እምዓመት፡ በዓመት ʾəm-ʿāmat ba-ʿāmat 'from year to year' (Jub 49:18).

[197] The traditional pronunciation is ʾəmənna, not ʾəmna. It has been suggested that this preposition goes back to original *mənna < *minna, but this derivation requires further proof.

[198] E.g., ወእንተ፡ ካልእ፡ ፍኖት፡ ገብኡ wa-ʾənta kāləʾ fənot gabʾu 'they returned by another road' (Mt 2:12).

ጽልመት wa-falaṭa ʾəgziʾab(ə)her māʾkala bərhān wa-māʾkala ṣəlmat 'and god separated (between) light and darkness' (Gen 1:4); ወይፍልጡ፡ ማእከለ፡ ዕለት፡ ወማእከለ፡ ሌሊት wa-yəfləṭu māʾkala ʿəlat wa-māʾkala lelit 'and let them separate day from night' (Gen 1:14).

(b) Prepositions with primarily temporal meaning:
- አመ ʾama 'at the time of, on'
- እስከ ʾəska (also እስከነ ʾəska-na,[199] እስከኔ ʾəska-ne) 'until, unto, as far as' (note also እስከ፡ ለ- ʾəska la- literally 'until to')

(c) Prepositions with other meanings:
- ምስለ məsla 'with'
- ህየንተ həyyanta 'instead of, in place of, in compensation' (as in ጸጋ፡ ህየንተ፡ ጸጋ ṣaggā həyyanta ṣaggā 'grace for grace' = 'grace upon grace' Jn 1:16)
- ከመ kama 'like, as, just as'
  Semantic specifications do not have to be explicitly expressed with ከመ kama, as in ወክነፊሃኒ፡ ከመ፡ ንስር wa-kənafihā-ni kama (variant ከመዝ kama-za) nəsr 'its wings were like those of an eagle' (literally 'like an eagle' [Dan 7:4]). ከመ kama can also express 'someone like', as in ወናሁ፡ መጽአ፡ ... ከመ፡ ወልደ፡ እጓለ፡ እመ፡ ሕያው wa-nāhu maṣʾa ... kama walda ʾəgʷāla ʾəmma həyāw 'behold, one came ... like a human being' (Dan 7:13).

Note: For the equally frequent prepositions እንበለ ʾənbala 'without' and እንበይነ ʾənbayna 'for the sake of, on account of', see §4.5.2.3.3.

4.5.2.2.2. Less frequently occurring prepositions include:[200]

መቅድመ maqdəma 'before' (cf. ቀድም qədma); ከዋላ kawālā 'behind'; ዐውደ ʿawda 'around'; ፍና fənnā 'towards'; ማዕዶተ māʿdota 'across, beyond, along, to the opposite side'; መትሕተ mathəta 'under, below, beneath' (cf. ታሕተ tāḥta); መንጸረ,

---

[199] The element –na should not be interpreted as a 1cp pronominal suffix (against CDG 380a), but rather as an allomorph of –ne.

[200] For other less frequently occurring prepositions, see DG 357.

አንጸረ *manṣara*, *ʾanṣāra* 'opposite, across, in front of'; ቤዛ *bezā* 'in exchange for, for the sake of'.[201]

4.5.2.3. Compound Prepositions

4.5.2.3.1. Compounds containing በ– *ba–* (§4.5.2.1.1.):

- በእብሬት *ba-ʾəbret* (also በዐብሬት *ba-ʿəbret*) 'on account of, for the sake of'[202]
- በእደ *ba-ʾəda* (before pronominal suffixes በእዴ– *ba-ʾəde-*), በእደወ *ba-ʾədawa* 'by, through, thanks to' (noun እድ *ʾəd* 'hand')
- በእንተ *ba-ʾənta*, ዘበእንተ *za-ba-ʾənta* 'concerning'[203]
- በበይነ *ba-bayna* 1. 'between', 2. 'because of, for the sake of'
- በኀበ *ba-ḫaba* 'among, at, in'
- በላዕለ *ba-lāʿla* 'on, upon' (same meaning as ላዕለ *lāʿla*)
- በታሕተ *ba-tāḥta* 'below'
- በወእደ *ba-waʾ(ə)da*, በውእደ *ba-wəʾda* 'by the side of'
- በማእከለ *ba-māʾkala* 'in the midst of'
- በአፍአ *ba-ʾafʾā*, በአፍአ ፡ እምነ *ba-ʾafʾā ʾəmənna* 'outside of'
- በከመ *ba-kama* 'according to, in accordance with' (as in በከመ ፡ በሰማይ ፡ ወበምድርኒ *ba-kama ba-samāy wa-ba-mədrə-ni* '(your will is done) on earth as it is in heaven' (Mt 6:10)

4.5.2.3.2. Compounds with እም– *ʾəm–* (§4.5.2.1.3.):

- እምአመ *ʾəm-ʾama* 'from the time of/when'; እምዲበ *ʾəm-diba* 'from upon'; እምድኅረ *ʾəm-dəḫra* 'after'; እምኀበ *ʾəm-ḫaba* 'from'; እምላዕለ *ʾəm-lāʿla* 'from above'; እምቅድመ *ʾəm-qədma* 'from before'; እምታሕተ *ʾəm-tāḥta* 'from

---

[201] For the use of the latter, see ዐይን ፡ ቤዛ ፡ ዐይን ፡ ወስን ፡ ቤዛ ፡ ስን *ʿayn bezā ʿayn wa-sənn bezā sənn* 'an eye for an eye and a tooth for a tooth' (Mt 5:38); ቤዛ ፡ ማእስ ፡ ማእስ *bezā māʾs māʾs* 'skin for skin' (Job 2:4); ኵሎ ... ይሁብ ፡ ሰብእ ፡ ቤዛ ፡ ነፍሱ *kʷəllo ... yəhub sabʾ bezā nafsu* 'everything (he owns), man gives for his life' (Job 2:4).

[202] Cf. Hebrew *ba-ʿăbûr* 'on account of'.

[203] በእንተ *ba-ʾənta* is etymologically connected to the preposition እንተ *ʾənta* by Dillmann (DL 355) and the common dictionaries. It is more likely, however, that በእንተ *ba-ʾənta* contains the determinative-relative pronoun of the fs እንተ *ʾənta* (§4.1.5.), while the preposition እንተ *ʾənta* probably has a different etymology (cf. CDG 33a).

below'; እምውስተ ʾəm-wəsta 'out of, from, from within' (እምውስቴቶሙ
ʾəm-wəstetomu 'from among them')

4.5.2.3.3. Compounds with እን– ʾən–:[204]

- እንበለ ʾənbala, ዘእንበለ za-ʾənbala[205] 'without, except', after negations
  mostly in the meaning 'only' (< 'nothing … except');[206] for the
  construction አልቦ … ዘእንበለ ʾalbo … za-ʾənbala, see §6.1.4.5.
- እንብይነ ʾənbayna, እምብይነ ʾəmbayna 'for the sake of, because of'

4.5.2.3.4. Other compound prepositions:

- እንተ፡ዲበ ʾənta diba 'above, over, through'; እንተ፡መንገለ ʾənta mangala
  'by the side of, toward, through'; እንተ፡ውስተ ʾənta wəsta 'at, through';
  እንተ፡ድኅረ ʾənta dəḫra 'behind'; እንተ፡ቅድም ʾənta qədma 'in front';
  እስከ፡አመ ʾəska ʾama 'as long as, until'; እስከ፡ለ– ʾəska la– 'until'; ለአመ la-
  ʾama 'until, at the time of'; ለኀበ la-ḫaba 'away to, unto, toward';
  ውስተ፡ማእከለ wəsta māʾkala 'in the middle of'; ኀበ፡ውእደ ḫaba wəʾda 'at';
  መንገለ፡ውእደ mangala wəʾda 'by the side of'.

4.5.2.4. Prepositions with Pronominal Suffixes

4.5.2.4.1. Most of the non-proclitic prepositions have the vowel -e- as a linking
vowel before pronominal suffixes (§4.2.4.5.6.), such as እምኔየ ʾəmənneya 'from
me'; ዲቤከ dibeka 'on you'; ታሕቴሃ tāḥtehā 'under her'; በማእከሌክሙ ba-

---

[204] እን– ʾən– seems to be the vestige of a preposition that is no longer productive in Classical
Ethiopic and that might be related to Akkadian *ina* 'in, by, with'. It is also possible that it
underlies the conjunction እንዘ ʾənza, although, according to Tropper, the latter might also be
a grammaticalized form of a noun *ḥīn 'time' (cf. Arabic ḥīn 'time') + *da.

[205] ዘእንበለ za-ʾənbala is used in the same way as እንበለ ʾənbala, compare, e.g.,
ወኲሉ፡ነገር፡ሕሙም፡ኢይጻእ፡እምአፉክሙ፡ዘእንበለ፡ሠናይ wa-kʷəllu nagar ḥəśum ʾi-yəḍāʾ ʾəm-
ʾafukəmu za-ʾənbala śannāy 'let no evil word come from your mouth, but only what is good!'
(Eph 4:29); እንዘ፡ሀሎ፡ባሕቲቱ፡ዘእንበለ፡ሠራዊቱ ʾənza hallo bāḥtitu za-ʾənbala śarāwitu 'while he
was alone, without his troops' (ʿAmda Ṣayon 11c).

[206] E.g., ወኢተርፉ፡እምኔሆሙ፡ዘእንበለ፡ኅዳጣን፡ሰብእ wa-ʾi-tarfu ʾəmənnehomu za-ʾənbala ḫədāṭān
sabʾ 'only a few of them remained' (lit. 'and of them did not remain except a few men') (Ləbna
dəngəl 2).

māʔkalekəmu 'among you'; በማእከሌሆሙ *ba-māʔkalehomu* (also ማእከሎሙ *māʔkalomu*) 'in their midst'.[207]

4.5.2.4.2. A few non-proclitic prepositions have special forms before pronominal suffixes:

ከመ *kama* 'like'	ከማ- *kamā-* (ከማሁ *kamāhu*)[208]
ውስተ *wəsta* 'in'	ውስቴት- *wəstet-* (ውስቴትከ *wəstetəka*, ውስቴቱ *wəstetu*)
በእንተ *ba-ʔənta* 'on account of'	በእንቲአ- *ba-ʔəntiʔa-* (በእንቲአሁ *ba-ʔəntiʔahu*)[209]
በበይነ *ba-bayna* 'between'	በበይናቲ- *ba-baynāti-*, በቤናቲ- *ba-benāti-*[210]

4.5.2.4.3. The frequently occurring forms of the proclitic prepositions በ- *ba-* and ለ- *la-* before pronominal suffixes are formed irregularly. To be noted are in particular the forms of the third persons and, in the case of ለ- *la-*, the 1cs ሊተ *lita* 'for me'. If not otherwise indicated, bisyllabic forms are stressed on the penultima.

በ- *ba-* with pronominal suffixes (basic form *bə-* < **bi-*):

	Sing.	Pl.
1	ብየ *bəya*	ብነ *bəna*
2m	ብከ *bəka*	ብክሙ *bəkámu*
2f	ብኪ *bəki*	ብክን *bəkán*
3m	ቦ/ቦቱ *bo/bottú*	ቦሙ *bomu*

---

[207] It is as of yet uncertain why prepositions with pronominal suffixes tend to end in *-e* in Classical Ethiopic. A probable explanation is the contraction of an original diphthong **ay*. For the ending **ay/y* on prepositions compare for example Arabic, Old South Arabian, and Hebrew prepositions that take "plural" suffixes.

[208] From a historical point of view, the preposition ከመ *kama* goes back to *ka+mā*; the final /ā/ was presumably shortened because it was unstressed.

[209] The form **ʔantiʔa-* is identical with that of the fs possessive pronoun with pronominal suffixes (§4.1.6.).

[210] The form **baynāt* is the fem. pl. form of በይነ *bayna*; the final *-i* corresponds to the linking vowel commonly attested before pronominal suffixes on plural nouns (§4.2.4.5.1.).

| 3f | ባ/ባቲ *bā/bātti*[211] | ቦን/ቦንቱ/ቦቶን |
| | | *bon/bonttú/bottón*[212] |

ለ– *la-* with pronominal suffixes (basic form *la-*):

	Sing.	Pl.
1	ሊተ *lita*	ለነ *lana*
2m	ለከ *laka*	ለክሙ *lakə́mu*
2f	ለኪ *laki*	ለክን *lakə́n*
3m	ሎቱ *lottú*	ሎሙ *lomu*
3f	ላቲ *lāttí*	ሎን/ሎንቱ/ሎቶን
		lon/lonttu/lottón

4.5.3. Conjunctions

The border between coordinate and subordinate conjunctions is fluid in Classical Ethiopic since Classical Ethiopic does not always distinguish clearly between main and subordinate clauses.

4.5.3.1. Coordinating Conjunctions

(a) Conjunctive 'and':
The conjunctive function 'and' is expressed by the proclitic conjunction ወ– *wa-*. When more than two sentence-elements are coordinated, *wa-* can either appear before each element or only before the last, as in ዘውእቶሙ፡ ሰማይ፡ ወምድር፡ ወማይ፡ ወነፋስ፡ ወእሳት፡ ወጽልመት፡ ወመላእክት *za-wə'ətomu samāy wa-mədr wa-māy wa-nafās wa-'əsāt wa-ṣəlmat wa-malā'əkt* 'those are heaven, earth, water, wind, fire, darkness, and angels' (*Śəna fəṭrat* 2) as opposed to ዚአከ፡ ይእቲ፡ መንግሥት፡ ኀይል፡ ወስብሓት *zi'aka yə'əti mangəśt ḥayl wa-səbḥāt* 'yours are the kingdom, the power, and the glory' (Mt 6:13).
Semantically closely connected expressions are sometimes connected asyndetically without ወ– *wa-*, as in ሑሩ፡ ንግርዎ፡ ለዮሐንስ *ḥuru nəgar-əwwo la-yoḥannəs* 'go and tell John!' (Lk 7:22).

---

[211] For the endings –*tu* (3ms) and –*ti* (3fs) compare ውእቱ *wə'ətu* 'he' and ይእቲ *yə'əti* 'she' (§4.1.1.). The gemination of /t/ in these forms is most likely secondary (§3.3.2.1.).
[212] Analogical formation based on ቦቱ *bottu*.

The conjunction ወ- wa- is also used for the explicative nuance 'then'. The construction ወ- ... ወ- wa- ... wa- means 'as well as', as in ኩፋሌ፥ ኮሉ፥ መዋዕላት፨ወለሕግ፡ ወለስምዕ kufāle kʷəllu mawāʿəlāt wa-la-ḥəgg wa-la-saməʿ 'the division of all days – both concerning the law and the testimony' (Jub 1:4).

(b) The coordinating function '(and) also' is expressed by ወ- ... -ሂ wa- ... -hi, less frequently by ወ- ... -ኒ wa- ... -ni (§4.5.8.4.), as in ኀድግ፥ ሎቱ፡ ወልብስከኒ ḫədəg lottu wa-ləbsaka-ni 'leave him your cloak as well' (Mt 5:40); በከመ፡ በሰማይ፡ ወበምድርኒ ba-kama ba-samāy wa-ba-mədrə-ni '(your will be done) on earth as it is in heaven' (Mt 6:10).

The construction ወ- ... -ሂ wa- ... -hi further frequently occurs with negated indefinite pronouns (§4.1.8.1.), as in ወኢምንትኒ/ሂ wa-ʾi-məntə-ni/hi 'nothing at all' or ወኢመኑሂ wa-ʾi-mannu-hi 'nobody at all' (cf., e.g., Lk 10:4: ወኢተአምኁ፡ ወኢመነሂ፡ በፍኖት wa-ʾi-taʾamməḫu wa-ʾi-manna-hi ba-fənot 'and greet no one on the road!' [with double negation]).

(c) Disjunctive/alternative '(either) ... or':

- The most frequent disjunctive conjunction is አው ʾaw 'or'.
- Constructions for 'either ... or' are (a) አው ... አው ʾaw ... ʾaw and (b) እመሂ ... አው ʾəmma-hi ... ʾaw (rare in double questions).
- ሚመ mimma 'or' (< *mi 'what' [§4.1.7.2.] + -mma [§4.5.8.6.])
- Frequent constructions for 'either ... or' especially in questions are (a) ሚመ ... ወሚመ mimma ... wa-mimma, (b) ... -ኑ፡ ወሚመ ... -nu wa-mimma (for the question particle -ኑ -nu, see §4.5.9.1.), and (c) ሚመ ... mimma by itself.[213]
- ወ- wa- 'or' (literally 'and') can also function as alternative 'or'.
- እመ ʾəmma 'if' (§4.5.3.2.) is used as a disjunctive/alternative conjunction in the following constructions:

  (a) እመሂ ... ወእመ(ሂ) ʾəmma-hi ... wa-ʾəmma(-hi) 'either ... or'[214]

  (b) እመሂ ... አው ʾəmma-hi ... ʾaw 'either ... or'

  (c) ወእመአኮ wa-ʾəmma-ʾakko and ወእማእኮ wa-ʾəmmāʾəkko 'if not, otherwise, (or) else'[215]

---

[213] As in አሕይዎ፡ ነፍስ፡ ወሚመ፡ ቀቲል ʾaḥyəwwo nafs wa-mimma qatil '(is it lawful) to safe a life or to kill?' (Mk 3:4).

[214] As in እመሂ፡ እወ፡ እወ፡ ወእመሂ፡ አልቦ፡ አልቦ ʾəmma-hi ʾəwwa ʾəwwa wa-ʾəmma-hi ʾalbo ʾalbo '(let your word be) 'yes! yes!' or 'no! no!'" (Mt 5:37).

(d) እመአኮ ... ወእመአኮ ʾəmma-ʾakko ... wa-ʾəmma-ʾakko 'either ... or'[216]

(d) Adversative:

- አላ ʾallā 'but, but rather, on the contrary' (either stressed on the penultima or no stress)[217]
- ዳእሙ dāʾəmú 'merely, but rather, on the contrary'
- እንበለ ዳእሙ ʾənbala dāʾəmu 'never'
- ባሕቱ bāḫ(at)tú, ባሕቲቱ bāḫtitu 'alone, solely, only, but, but rather, however'
- The conjunction ወ- wa- can likewise have an adversative connotation,[218] and so can several enclitic particles, especially –ሰ –ssa (§4.5.8.7.).

(e) Causal:

- እስመ ʾəsma 'because, since, indeed' (also subordinating [§4.5.3.2.])

Note: For other causal and inferential sentence particles such as እንከ ʾənka 'so, then!, therefore' and –ኬ –ke 'now, then, thus', see §4.5.8.1. and §4.5.8.5.

4.5.3.2. Subordinating Conjunctions

(a) Locative (§6.5.4.):

- ኀበ ḫaba '(the place) where' and its compound forms (እምኀበ ʾəm-ḫaba, እንተ ኀበ ʾənta ḫaba)

(b) Temporal (§6.5.5.):

- እንዘ ʾənza 'while, when' (introduces circumstantial clauses [§6.5.5.1.])

---

[215] As in ዘእንበለ በቅድመ ደብተራ እግዚአብሔር ወእመ አኮ በቅድመ ቤት ኀበ ኀደረ ስም ዚአሁ ውስቴቱ za-ʾənbala ba-qədma dabtarā ʾəgziʾab(ə)ḥer wa-ʾəmma ʾakko ba-qədma bet ḫaba ḥadara səma ziʾahu wəstetu '(they shall not celebrate ...) except before the tabernacle of the Lord, or else before the house in which his name has resided' (Jub 49:21).

[216] E.g., እትመየጥ እማእኮ የማነ ወእማእኮ ፀጋም ʾətmayyaṭ ʾəmmāʾəkko yamāna wa-ʾəmmāʾəkko ḍagāma 'so that I may turn either to the right hand or to the left' (Gen 24:49).

[217] According to the traditional pronunciation, the /l/ is not geminated (Mittwoch 1926, 18). The etymology of this lexeme is uncertain (cf. CDG 17b).

[218] E.g., ስዱስ ዕለት ትገብር ግብረ ወእመ ሳብዕት ዕለት ሰንበት sadusa ʿəlata təgabbər gəbra wa-ʾama sābəʿt ʿəlat sanbat 'you will work for six days, but on the seventh day is the Sabbath' (Jub 50:7).

- ሶበ *soba* 'when' (also for conditional 'if')
- አመ *ʾama*, ጊዜ *gize* '(at the time) when'
- እም– *ʾəm–* 'since' in compound forms: እምአመ *ʾəm-ʾama* 'since'; እምከመ *ʾəm-kama*, ለእምከመ *la-ʾəm-kama* 'as soon as, when'; እምድኅረ *ʾəm-dəḫra* 'after that'; እምቅድመ *ʾəm-qədma* 'before'; እምዘ *ʾəm-za* 'when, after that, since'.
- በዘ *ba-za* 'when'
- ለለ– *lalla–* (< *la + la* [§5.6.1.; §5.6.4.]) 'whenever, as often as'
- ድኅረ *dəḫra*, እምድኅረ *ʾəm-dəḫra* 'after'
- እስከ *ʾəska*, እስከ፡አመ *ʾəska ʾama* 'until, as far as'

(c) Conditional and concessive (§6.5.6.):
- እመ *ʾəmma* and its compounds: ለእመ *la-ʾəmma* 'if, whether' (§6.5.6.1.); እመአኮ *ʾəmma-ʾakko* (also እማእኮ *ʾəmmāʾəkko*) 'if not, otherwise, else'; (ለ)እመሂ/ኒ *(la-)ʾəmma-hi/-ni* 'even if, when, although'; እመሰ *ʾəmma-ssa* 'if really, if'.
- ሶበ *soba* 'if'; ሶበ፡እም– *soba ʾəm-* 'even if'

(d) Final/result (§6.5.7.):
- ከመ *kama* 'so that, that'

(e) Comparative (§6.5.8.):
- ከመ *kama* 'like, as' and its compounds (e.g., ዘከመ *za-kama*, እንተ፡ከመ *ʾənta kama* 'as, just as')
- እም–/እምነ *ʾəm(ənna)* '(rather) than' (after comparative constructions)

(f) Causal (§6.5.9.1.):
- እስመ *ʾəsma* 'because, since'
- በእንተ፡ዘ– *ba-ʾənta za–* 'because'

(g) Consecutive (§6.5.9.2.):
- ከመ *kama* 'so that'

(h) 'that' (introduction of object clauses etc.) (§6.5.9.4.):

- ከመ *kama* 'that, so that' (for the introduction of object clauses, see §6.5.3.; for the introduction of direct speech, see §6.5.9.5.)
- እስመ *ʾəsma* 'in that, that is, namely' (also before direct speech [§6.5.9.5.])

(i) Introduction of dependent interrogative clauses:
- እመ *ʾəmma*, ለእመ *la-ʾəmma* 'whether' (§4.5.3.2c; §6.5.10.1.).

(j) Other functions:
- እንበለ *ʾənbala*, ዘእንበለ *za-ʾənbala* 'without, except (for), but also'; compounds with similar meanings include: ዘእንበለ፡ አመ *za-ʾənbala ʾama*, ዘእንበለ፡ ዳእሙ *za-ʾənbala dāʾmu*, ዘእንበለ፡ ከመ *za-ʾənbala kama*, ዘእንበለ፡ ዘ– *za-ʾənbala za–* 'but, except, unless' (§6.1.4.5.)
- መጠነ *maṭana*, አምጣነ *ʾamṭāna*, በአምጣነ *ba-ʾamṭāna* 'as long as, during, as large as'[219]

Note: For relative clauses that are introduced by relative pronouns, see §6.5.1. For other subordinate clauses introduced by ዘ– *za–*, see §6.5.8.–9.

4.5.4. Negative Particles

4.5.4.1. Negative Particle ኢ– *ʾi–*[220]

The main negative particle of Classical Ethiopic is ኢ– *ʾi–*. It is used with verbs (of all moods and tenses) and, less frequently, with nouns. When used before verbs, the particle functions as a sentence-negating particle (§6.2.4.). Before nouns, it is used to negate the individual noun. For emphatic purposes, ኢ– *ʾi–* can occur two or more times in a clause. A few representative examples include:

---

[219] Noun መጠን *maṭan* (pl. አምጣን *ʾamṭān*) 'measure, amount, dimension'.

[220] The etymology of this particle is unclear. It has been suggested that it is derived from *ʾiy* < *ay*, based on Phoenician ʾy and Akkadian ay/ē. Aksumite inscriptions attest to a form ʾəy– and ʾay– (see Goldenberg 1977, 500), which seems to confirm this derivation. See also Tigre/Tigrinya ay–. The problem with a derivation from *ay is that the diphthong /ay/ does not contract into /i/ but into /e/ in Classical Ethiopic.

ኢ.– *ʾi–* before verbs:

- ኢ.ንክል ፡ ሐ ዊ ረ *ʾi-nəkəl ḥawira* 'we are unable to go' (before imperfect)
- ዘኢ.ይትጐለቍ *za-ʾi-yətḫʷellaqʷ* 'innumerable'; ዘኢ.ይማስን *za-ʾi-yəmāssən* 'indestructible' (or *za-ʾiyyətḫʷellaqʷ; za-ʾiyyəmāssən*)[221]
- ኢ.ተእመኑ *ʾi-təʾmanu* 'do not believe!' (with subjunctive as negative imperative)
- ወኢ.ተአምኑ ፡ ወኢ.መነኒ ፡ በፍኖት *wa-ʾi-taʾamməḫu wa-ʾi-manna-hi ba-fənot* 'and greet no one on the road' (Lk 10:4) (§4.5.3.1b)

ኢ.– *ʾi–* before nouns, pronouns, and infinitives:

- ኢ.አማኒ *ʾi-ʾamāni* 'unbeliever'; ኢ.መኑ(ሂ) *ʾi-mannu(-hi)* 'nobody'; ኢ.ለመኑ(ሂ) *ʾi-la-mannu(-hi)* 'for nobody'.
- ኢ.ድው ይ ፡ አነ *ʾi-dəw(w)əy ʾana* 'I am not sick' (ኢ.– *ʾi–* before adjective; in this context, ኢ.– *ʾi–* functions to negate a verbless clause)
- ኢ.ቀቲለ ፡ ነፍስ *ʾi-qatila nafs* 'to kill nobody' (§5.2.4.1.3.)
- እስመ ፡ አምጽአ ፡ ዓለመ ፡ እም ኢ.ሀሎ ፡ ኀበ ፡ ሀሎ *ʾəsma ʾamṣəʾa ʿālama ʾəm-ʾi-halləwo ḫaba halləwo* 'for he brought the world from non-existence into existence' (*Śəna fəṭrat* 1)

ኢ.– ... ወኢ.– *ʾi–* ... *wa-ʾi–* stands for 'neither ... nor':

- ኢ.ትምሐሉ ፡ ግሙራ ፡ ወኢ.ሰማየ ... ወኢ.ምድረ ... ወኢ.በኢ.የሩሳሌም *ʾi-təmḥalu gəmurā wa-ʾi-samāya ... wa-ʾi-mədra ... wa-ʾi-ba-ʾiyarusālem* 'do not swear at all, neither by heaven ... earth ... nor by Jerusalem...' (Mt 5:34)
- ዘነገረ ... ኢ.ኮነ ፡ ለጠቢባን ፡ ወኢ.ለማእምራን ፡ ወኢ.ለሰብአ ፡ ሰገል ፡ ወኢ.ለእለ ፡ ሥራይ ፡ ነገሩ ፡ ለንጉሥ *zə-nagar ... ʾi-kona la-ṭabibān wa-ʾi-la-māʾmərān wa-ʾi-la-sabʾa sagal wa-ʾi-la-ʾəlla śərāy nagaru* (variant ከመ ፡ ይክሀሉ ፡ ይንግ ር ዎ *kama yəkhalu yəngərəwwo*) *la-nəguś* 'neither wise men, enchanters, magicians, nor diviners can tell the king this mystery ...' (Dan 2:27)

For the form of the negative particle before verbal forms beginning with /ʾ/, see §3.6.2.2. (e.g., ኢ.ይነግር *ʾiy ənaggər < *ʾi-ʾ ənaggər* 'I will not speak').

---

[221] For these forms, see the transcriptions in CDG 261b and 366a. According to certain transmitters of the traditional pronunciation, /y/ is pronounced as /yy/ after *ʾi(y)–* (see §3.6.2.2. note).

4.5.4.2. Words with the Element *ʾal (cf. West Semitic *ʾal)

4.5.4.2.1. አልብ-, አልቦ *ʾalbə-, ʾalbo* (negative particle *ʾal + preposition *ba* + pronominal suffix):

አልብ- *ʾalbə-* + pronominal suffix serves to negate verbless clauses, comparable to Hebrew constructions with *ʾēn* and Classical Arabic constructions with *laysa*. The most commonly occurring use of አልቦ *ʾalbo* (< *ʾal-ba-hu*) is in the sense of 'there is not/does not exist (in it/him)', as in አልቦ፡ ኅብስተ *ʾalbo ḥəbəsta* 'there is no bread'. It further negates the positive possessive construction with *bə-* plus pronominal suffix (§6.1.4.), that is አልብየ፡ ኅብስተ *ʾalbəya ḥəbəsta* 'I have no bread'. Other forms with third person suffixes are: 3ms አልቦቱ *ʾalbottu*; 3fs አልባ/አልባቲ *ʾalbā/ʾalbātti*; 3mp አልቦሙ *ʾalbomu*; 3fp አልቦን/አልቦንቱ *ʾalbon/ʾalbontu* (cf. §4.5.2.4.3.). For its syntactic use and examples from texts, see §6.1.4.

4.5.4.2.2. አኮ *ʾakko* (negative particle *ʾal + –ko* [shortened form of ኮነ *kona*]):

አኮ *ʾakko* represents an emphatic negation with the connotation 'by no means, not'. It primarily negates individual sentence elements in mostly unnegated general contexts, especially when a sentence-element is left out (ellipsis) and expresses contrast, as in ወይከውኑ፡ ለበረከት፡ ወአኮ፡ ለመርገም፡ ወይከውኑ፡ ርእሰ፡ ወአኮ፡ ዘነበ *wa-yəkawwənu la-barakat wa-ʾakko la-margam / wa-yəkawwənu rəʾsa wa-ʾakko zanaba* 'they will become a blessing, not a curse; and they will become the head, not the tail' (Jub 1:16), where the verb is left out in the second part of the verse.

አኮ *ʾakko* further serves to negate verbless clauses (§6.1.5.2.) and so-called cleft sentences (§6.4.) with following ዘ– *za–* when these are verbless clauses, as in አኮ፡ ህየ፡ ዘረከብክዎ *ʾakko həyya za-rakabkəwwo* 'it is not there that I found him'.

Lastly, አኮ *ʾakko* negates verbal interrogative clauses with a topicalized sentence-element (§6.2.4.).

4.5.4.3. Words with the Element *ʾən (cf. Arabic ʾin 'not')

The following words are most likely formed with the particle *ʾən, which has the basic meaning of 'non-existence'. This particle is not attested as an independent negator in Classical Ethiopic.

- (a) እንብ- ʾənbə–; always used in combination with pronominal suffixes (< ʾən + ba): እንቢ/እንብየ ʾənbi/ʾənbəya, እንብከ ʾənbəka etc. 'I am not in a position, I am not able, I refuse'; እንብየ ʾənbəya is also used in the sense of 'no'.[222]
- (b) እንበለ ʾənbala 'without' (§4.5.2.3.3.)[223]
- (c) እንዳዒ ʾəndāʿi 'I don't know, perhaps' (§4.5.1.6.)

4.5.5. The Asseverative Particle ለ– la–

The proclitic particle ለ– la– is used before jussives in order to express a stronger wish or command, as in ለይኩን፡ ብርሃን la-yəkun bərhān 'let there be light' (Gen 1:3).

4.5.6. The Presentative Particle ነ– na–

The presentative particle ነ– na–, which is probably related to particles such as Hebrew hinne, hen 'behold!', Arabic ʾinna, and Akkadian anna/annu 'yes', is commonly rendered as 'behold!, as for'. It is most commonly used in combination with pronominal suffixes, in which case it has the basic form *nay–, as in ነየ naya, ነዮ nayo, ነያ nayā, ነየነ nayana, ነዮሙ nayomu, ነዮን nayon 'as for me, there I am!, here I am! behold!' etc., as in ነየ፡ አመተ፡ እግዚአብሔር naya ʾamata ʾəgziʾab(ə)her 'here I am, the maidservant of the Lord' (Lk 1:38).

The same particle ነ– na– is found as an element of the words ነዋ nawā and ናሁ nāhu both meaning 'behold!'. The form እንከሙ ʾən-kəmu that is attested in Mt

---

[222] As in ወአውሥአ፡ ወይቤ፡ እንብየ wa-ʾawśəʾa wa-yəbe ʾənbəya 'and he answered and said: I will not' (Mt 21:29); አሆ፡ በልዎ፡ ለእግዚአብሔር፡ ወእንብየ፡ በልዎ፡ ለጋኔን ʾoho baləwwo la-ʾəgziʾab(ə)her wa-ʾənbəya baləwwo la-gānen 'say 'yes!' to God and say 'no!' (= I refuse) to the devil!' (Jas 4:7).

[223] Alternatively, እንበለ ʾənbala could be derived from the preposition *ina 'with, in' and *bala 'non-existence', corresponding to Akkadian ina balu/i. A preposition *ina, however, cannot be traced to Classical Ethiopic otherwise.

26:26 should also be mentioned in this context. The latter consists of a particle *ʾən* and the pronominal suffix of the 2mp. The element *ʾən* seems to have the meaning 'behold!' (cf. Arabic *ʾinna* and its short form *ʾin*) and might be connected to ነ– *na–* etymologically.

4.5.7. Exclamations and Interjections

4.5.7.1. The connotation 'woe! alas!' is expressed by the lexemes ወይ *way* and አሌ *ʾalle*. Both are most commonly followed by ለ– *la–* + pronominal suffixes, as in ወይ፡ ሊተ *way lita* and ወይልየ *way-ləya* 'woe to me!' or አሌሎ *ʾalle-lo* and አሌ፡ ሎቱ *ʾalle lottu* 'woe to him!'.

4.5.7.2. In order to express pain, danger, and admiration, Classical Ethiopic uses the particle ኦ– *ʾo–* 'o!', as in ኦአብድ *ʾo-ʾabd* 'thou fool!'. The particle is also used as vocative particle (§4.2.4.8.).

4.5.7.3. The interrogative pronoun ሚ *mi* (literally 'what?' [§4.1.7.2.]) can be used as an interjection expressing admiration in the sense of 'how (much/many)'. The same use is attested for the particle ከመ *kama* (ከመ *kama* is otherwise used as a preposition [§4.5.2.2.1c] and a conjunction [§4.5.3.2d]); as in ሚበዝኁ *mi-bazḫu* 'how many they are!'; ሚአዳም *mi-ʾaddām* 'how pleasant!'; ከመ፡ ሠናይ *kama śannāy* 'how beautiful!'.

4.5.8. Logical Sentence-Particles (including Enclitics)

4.5.8. Classical Ethiopic possesses numerous particles that express the logical connection of sentence elements or that put a certain sentence element into focus. Some of these represent independent words (እንከ *ʾanka*, እንጋ *ʾangā*, ከመ *kamma*), while others are enclitics, although they always bear the main stress of the word. Before enclitics, words that end in a consonant exhibit an additional *ə*-vowel, as in ዓለምኒ *ʿālamə-ni* 'as for the world' (§4.2.4.6.), ይከውንኑ *yəkawwənə-nu* 'is it permissible?' (ይከውን *yəkawwən* plus interrogative particle –ኑ *–nu* [§4.5.9.1.]). Two enclitics can follow each other on the same word, as in እመሰከ *ʾəmma-ssa-ke* 'for if/if really' (Gal 2:21). In forms with pronominal suffixes, the enclitic is attached after the suffix, as in ወፍካሬሁስ *wa-fəkkāre-hu-ssa* 'but its interpretation'.

4.5.8.1. እንከ *ʾǝnka* 'so then!, therefore, now then' (after negation 'no longer, no more')

እንከ *ʾǝnka* expresses the logical connection between sentence elements and clauses. It is often used after words with enclitic **–ኬ** *–ke* (§4.5.8.5.). Examples include:

- **ለምንት ፡ እንከ ፡ ሊተ ፡ ትትመዐዑኒ** *la-mǝnt ʾǝnka lita tǝtmaʿaʿu-ni* 'why then are you angry with me?' (Jn 7:23)
- **ግበሩኬ ፡ እንከ ፡ ሠናየ ፡ ፍሬ** *gǝbaru-ke ʾǝnka śannāya fǝre* 'now therefore produce good fruit (of repentance)' (Mt 3:8)

4.5.8.2. እንጋ *ʾǝngā* 'then indeed?, so then, so surely, really'

እንጋ *ʾǝngā* is functionally comparable to the more frequently used particle **እንከ** *ʾǝnka* but is more restricted in use in that it primarily occurs in questions, as in **መኑ ፡ እንጋ ፡ የዐቢ** *mannu ʾǝngā yaʿabbi* 'who then indeed is the greatest?' (Mt 18:1).

4.5.8.3. ከመ *kǝmma* 'thus, also, even, nearly, almost'

ከመ *kǝmma* serves most frequently to emphasize individual words and has to be adjusted in its translation value according to context (cf. the enclitic particle *–መ* *–mma* [§4.5.8.6.] from both a functional and etymological perspective). Examples include:

- **ከማሁ ፡ ከመ ፡ ይቤሉ** *kamāhu kǝmma yǝbelu* 'thus they spoke'
- **ከመ ፡ ምንት ፡ እንከ ፡ ፈድፋደ ፡ ትገብሩ** *kǝmma mǝnta ʾǝnka fadfāda tǝgabbǝru* '... so what more are you doing (than others)?' (Mt 5:47)

4.5.8.4. –ኒ *–ni* and **–ሂ** *–hi* 'also, and further, even, the very'

The enclitic particle **–ኒ** *–ni* emphasizes contrast to a preceding nominal or pronominal sentence-element or whole phrase (when attached to a construct, **–ኒ** *–ni* is suffixed to the last member of the construct chain), as in **ንጉሠኒ** *nǝguśǝ-ni* 'as for the king, even the king'; **ወልደ ፡ እግለ ፡ እመሕያውኒ** *walda ʾǝgʷāla ʾǝmmaḥǝyāw-ni* 'as for the son of man' (Mk 8:38). The particle **–ኒ** *–ni* often occurs twice in the same sentence (**–ኒ** *... –*ኒ *–ni ... –ni*), as in:

- ብዙኅኒ፡ ይክል፡ አውሕዶ፡ ወኀዳጠኒ፡ ይክል፡ አብዝኆ bəzuḫa-ni yəkəl ʾawḥədo wa-ḫədāṭə-ni yəkəl ʾabzəḫo '(as for) the many he can turn (them) into few and (as for) the few he can turn (them) into many' (ʿĀmda Ṣəyon 11c)

The particle –ሂ –hi has functions similar to –ኒ –ni, but expresses less emphasis. It further frequently occurs in the construction ወ– ... –ሂ wa- ... –hi 'and also, further' (§4.5.3.1.). Examples include:

- ኵሉ፡ ዘየኃድግ፡ ብእሲቶ ... ወዘሂ፡ ኃደግታ፡ አውሰበ kʷəllu za-yaḫaddəg bəʾasito ... wa-za-hi ḫədəgta ʾawsaba 'anyone who divorces his wife ...; and further, whoever marries a divorced woman ...' (Mt 5:32)
- ከመ፡ እምጻእ፡ አነሂ፡ ወእስግድ፡ ሎቱ kama ʾəmṣāʾ ʾana-hi wa-ʾəsgəd lottu '... so that also I can come and bow to him' (Mt 2:8)
- ወፈነወ፡ ወቀተለ፡ ኵሎ፡ ሕፃናተ ... ዘክልኤ፡ ዓመት፡ ወዘይንእስሂ wa-fannawa wa-qatala kʷəllo ḫədānāta ... za-kəlʾe ʿāmat wa-za-yənəʾəs-hi 'and he sent and killed all the infants ... who were two years old or younger' (Mt 2:16)

The particles –ኒ –ni and –ሂ –hi can also occur in the same clause, as in ወስማዕተኒ፡ ይቀትሉ፡ ወለእለሂ/ኒ፡ የኅሥሡ፡ ሕገ፡ ይሰድድዎሙ wa-samāʿta-ni yəqattəlu wa-la-ʾəlla-hi (variant -ni) yaḫaśśəśu ḥagga yəsaddədəwwomu '... and they will kill the witnesses; even those who study the law diligently they will persecute' (Jub 1:12).

When suffixed to interrogative pronouns, –ሂ –hi and –ኒ –ni express indefinite nuances, as in መኑሂ manna-hi 'anyone (acc.)' (§4.1.8.1.).

4.5.8.5. –ኬ –ke 'now, then, thus, therefore, indeed'

This particle is often used to render Greek γαρ in translated literature and marks the logical result of a preceding statement, as in ወኵሎንኬ፡ ትውልድ wa-kʷəllona-ke təwlədd 'therefore all the generations are ...' (Mt 1:17).[224]

---

[224] See also Weninger 2015.

4.5.8.6. –መ *–mma* 'precisely, quite, then, the very'

This particle emphasizes the individual words to which it is attached. It primarily occurs after personal pronouns, interrogative pronouns, and adverbs; as in **ውእቱመ** *wəʾətu-mma* 'he himself'; **መኑመ** *mannu-mma* 'who precisely?'.

4.5.8.7. –ስ *–ssa* 'but, however, on the other hand, as for'

This particle primarily occurs attached to the first, usually topicalized sentence-element and expresses a strong contrast to what has been said before. It often occurs to render Greek δέ. Examples include:[225]

- **ንጉሥስ፡ ይፀብእ፡ ኵሎ፡ ምድረ፡ ... ወለንጉሥስ፡ አልቦ፡ ዘይፀብኦ፡ በፈቃዱ** *nəguśa-ssa yəḍabbəʾ kʷəllo mədra ... wa-la-nəguśa-ssa ʾalbo za-yəḍabbəʾo ba-faqādu* 'as for the king, he fights the whole land ... but nobody can fight the king out of his own volition' (ʿĀmda Ṣəyon 11c)
- **ወውስተ፡ ዓለም፡ ሀሎ፡ ወዓለምኒ፡ ቦቱ፡ ኮነ፡ ወዓለምስ፡ ኢያእመሮ** *wa-wəsta ʿālam hallo / wa-ʿālamə-ni bottu kona / wa-ʿālamə-ssa ʾiyāʾmaro* 'and he was in the world, and the world itself came into being through him; yet the world did not know him' (Jn 1:10)

4.5.9. Other Enclitic Particles (–ኑ *–nu*; **–ሁ** *–hu*; **–አ** *–ʾa*; **–ኄ** *–he*)

4.5.9.1. The Enclitic Interrogative Particles **–ኑ** *–nu* and **–ሁ** *–hu*

The interrogative particles **–ኑ** *–nu* (more frequent and stronger in its connotation than *–hu*) and **–ሁ** *–hu* are suffixed to the first sentence-element in a question (with the exception of prepositions and conjunctions) and always bear the stress of the word. They frequently occur after **ቦ** *bo* in rhetorical questions (**ቦኑ/ቦሁ** *bo-nu/bo-hu* 'is this the case?') and after **አኮ** *ʾakko* (**አኮኑ/አኮሁ** *ʾakko-nu/ʾakko-hu* 'not?'). Examples include:

- **አኮሁ፡ ሠናየ፡ ዘርዐ፡ ዘራዕከ፡ ውስተ፡ ገራህትከ** *ʾakko-hu śannāya zarʿa zarāʿka wəsta garāhtəka* 'did you not sow good seed in your field?' (Mt 13:27)

---

[225] See also Weninger 2015.

- እንዘ፡ ምእትኑ፡ ዓመት፡ ሊተ፡ እወልድ፡ ወልደ፡ አነ ʾənza məʾətə-nu ʿāmat lita ʾəwalləd walda ʾana 'can I still beget a child being 100 years old?' (Gen 17:17)

The sequence –ሁ ... –ኑ –hu ... –nu (as well as –ሂ ... –ኒ –hi ... –ni [§4.5.8.4.]) expresses an increasing intensity in the utterance, as in አኮሁ፡ መጸብሓው*ያንሂ*፡ ከማሁ፡ ይገብሩ ʾakko-hu maṣabbəḥāwəyānə-hi kamāhu yəgabbəru 'do not even the tax collectors do the same?' (Mt 5:46), which is followed by አኮኑ፡ አሕዛብኒ፡ ኪያሁስ፡ ይገብሩ ʾakko-nu ʾaḥzābə-ni kiyāhu-ssa yəgabbəru 'and do not even the gentiles do the same?' (Mt 5:47)

4.5.9.2. The Quotation-Particle –አ –ʾa

The enclitic particle –አ –ʾa is used to mark direct speech. It can either be attached to almost every word of the cited direct speech (except for proclitic prepositions and conjunctions) or only after the first (and last) word. Its frequency clearly varies in individual manuscripts. According to Mittwoch (1926, 44), this particle always bears the word stress. Others, however, doubt that this particle was ever pronounced and consider it a purely orthographic device.[226] Examples include:

- ወክልኤቱአ፡ ይሰድድዎሙ፡ ለእልፍ wa-kəlʾetu-ʾa yəsaddədəwwomu la-ʾəlf '... and how can two drive out a thousand?' (Dtn 32:30)
- አንተኑአ፡ ዘይመጽእ ʾanta-nu-ʾa za-yəmaṣṣəʾ 'are you the one who is to come?' (Lk 7:19, 20) (quotation particle –አ –ʾa after enclitic interrogative particle)

4.5.9.3. The Particle –ሄ –he 'there, here, away to'

The enclitic particle –ሄ –he has a local meaning 'here, there, away to', as in ኵሉሄ kʷəllə-he 'everywhere' and ኵለሄ kʷəlla-he (acc.) 'in every direction'.

---

[226] See, e.g., Weninger 2001, 47.

5. Morphosyntax

5.1. Syntax of Pronouns

5.1.1. Personal Pronouns and Pronominal Suffixes

5.1.1.1. Independent personal pronouns are primarily used in verbless clauses to express the subject. In verbal clauses, the subject is incorporated into the finite verbal form and pronominal subjects consequently do not have to be expressed overtly by independent pronouns. When independent pronouns occur to mark the subject of verbal clauses, they usually function to emphasize the pronoun subject, as in:

- ኩኑኬ፡ አንትሙስ፡ ፍጹማን፡ ከም፡ አቡክሙ፡ ሰማያዊ፡ ፍጹም፡ ውእቱ   *kunu-ke ʔantəmu-ssa fəṣṣumāna kama ʔabukəmu samāyāwi fəṣṣum wəʔətu* 'so, *you*, be perfect as your heavenly father is perfect!' (Mt 5:48)
- ከመዝኬ፡ ጸልዩ፡ አንትሙስ፡ *kama-zə-ke ṣalləyu ʔantəmu-ssa* 'but *you*, pray thus!' (Mt 6:9)
- እስመ፡ እምተረፈ፡ ዚአሁ፡ ነሣእነ፡ ንሕነ፡ ኵልነ *ʔəsma ʔəm-tarafa ziʔahu naśāʔna nəḥna kʷəlləna* 'for from his abundance *we* have all received ...' (Jn 1:16)

An independent personal pronoun can also co-occur with a pronominal suffix of the same person. In this case, it emphasizes the suffix, as in በእዴያ፡ አነ፡ ጳውሎስ *ba-ʔədeya ʔana pāwlos* 'I, Paul, (write this ...) with my own hand' (Col 4:18); አስተርአየኒ፡ ራእይ፡ አነ፡ ዳንኤል *ʔastarʔayanni rāʔy ʔana dānəʔel* 'a vision appeared to me, Daniel' (Dan 8:1).

5.1.1.2. Third person personal pronouns often have a demonstrative or a strongly determining function (§5.2.2.1b):

- አላ፡ ወልድ፡ ዋሕድ፡ ዘሀሎ፡ ውስተ፡ ሕፅነ፡ አቡሁ፡ ውእቱ፡ ነገረነ *ʔallā wald wāḥad za-hallo wəsta ḥəḍna ʔabuhu wəʔətu nagaranna* 'but it is the only son who rests in the lap of his father who has told us' (Jn 1:18)
- ወውእቱ፡ ቃል፡ ሥጋ፡ ኮነ *wa-wəʔətu qāl śəgā kona* 'and the (previously mentioned) word became flesh' (Jn 1:14)

The personal pronoun can also occur after a demonstrative or relative pronoun for special emphasis, as in ዝውእቱ za-wəʾətu 'this one (mentioned)'; ዘውእቱ za-wəʾətu 'that is to say, namely', as in ወይሁዳ፡ አስቆሮታዊ፡ ዘውእቱ፡ አግብአ wa-yəhudā ʾasqorotāwi za-wəʾətu ʾagbəʾo 'and Judas Iskariot, that is the one who betrayed him' (Mt 10:4).

5.1.1.3. Personal pronouns of the third person, less often those of the first person, are frequently used as copulas in verbless clauses, as in ዝንቱ፡ ውእቱ፡ ንጉሥ zəntu wəʾətu nəguś 'this is the king' (§6.1.2.).

5.1.1.4. Pronominal suffixes on nouns primarily function as subjective genitives (mostly in the function of expressing possession):

- ታዐብዮ፡ ነፍስየ፡ ለእግዚአብሔር tāʿabbəyo nafsəya la-ʾəgziʾab(ə)ḥer 'my soul exalts the Lord' (Lk 1:46)
- ይትፌሥሐኒ፡ ልብየ፡ በአድኅኖትከ yətfeśśəḥani ləbbəya ba-ʾadḫənotəka 'my heart shall rejoice in your salvation' (Ps 13:5 [12:6])

The same function is exhibited by suffixes on adverbially used nouns, as in ባሕቲቱ bāḥətitu '(he) alone' and ዕራቅየ ʿərāqəya '(in) my nakedness' = 'naked, I' (Job 1:21).

Less frequently, pronominal suffixes function as objective genitives:

- ወወጽአ፡ ስሙዓቱ wa-waḍʾa səmuʿātu 'and the news about him spread ...' (Mt 4:24)
- ዕለት፡ ኰነኔሆሙ ʿəlata kʷənnanehomu 'the day of their judgment' (= 'they being judged') (En 22:4)
- ወከመዝ፡ ትእምርቱ፡ ለከሙ wa-kama-zə təʾəmərtu lakəmu 'and this will be a sign regarding him to you' (Lk 2:12)
- ወኢይትዓደዉ፡ እምትእዛዞሙ wa-ʾi-yətʿāddawu ʾəm-təʾəzāzomu 'and they do not transgress their law' (En 2:1)

5.1.1.5. Pronominal suffixes on verbs mark verbal objects. They primarily express the direct (accusative) object, as in ቀተሎ qatalo 'he killed him', less often the indirect object, as in ወሀበኒ፡ ኅብስት wahabanni ḫəbəsta 'he gave me bread'. For these and other functions, see §5.4.7.3.

Pronominal suffixes on prepositions express the object of the preposition. The preposition ለ– *la*– 'to, for' with pronominal suffix is frequently used to indicate the indirect (dative) object, as in ወሀበ፡ ሊተ፡ ኅብስት *wahaba lita ḫǝbǝsta* 'he gave me bread'. Sometimes, in connection with certain verbs, pronominal suffixes are used in the sense of an "ethical dative," that is they express interest or advantage by marking the person or entity towards which an action is directed. Examples of this use include: ጸሐፍ፡ ለከ *ṣaḥaf laka* 'write down (for yourself)!' (Jub 1:7.26); ለምንት፡ ለከ፡ ትሴአል *la-mǝnt laka tǝsseʾal* 'why do you ask (for yourself)? (Gen 32:30).

Pronominal suffixes can also be attached to interrogative pronouns such as ምንት *mǝnt* 'what?'. In this case they function as datives (§5.1.7.1.).

5.1.1.6. Pronominal suffixes follow the same general agreement rules as attributive adjectives (§5.2.6.). With animate nouns, that is nouns denoting human beings, they show full agreement in gender, number, and person. When they refer to inanimate nouns, agreement in gender and number is often lacking.

Concerning number agreement, the following further has to be noted:

Suffixes referring to an entity in the dual appear in the plural since Classical Ethiopic does not have dual suffixes, as in ወመልኡ፡ ክልኤሆን፡ አሕማረ *wa-malʾu kǝlʾehon ʾaḥmāra* 'and they filled both boats' (Lk 5:7).

For collective nouns that have the morphological form of a singular noun such as ሰብእ *sabʾ* 'men' or ሕዝብ *ḥǝzb* 'people' Classical Ethiopic frequently, but not always, uses plural suffixes (cf. §5.2.6.5.2.), as in ዲቤሆሙ፡ ለሕዝብ *dibehomu la-ḥǝzb* 'concerning the people'; ወተሣሀሎሙ፡ እግዚአብሔር፡ ለሕዝቡ *wa-taśāhalomu ʾǝgziʾab(ǝ)her la-ḥǝzbu* 'and God had mercy on his people' (Lk 7:16). The choice between singular and plural suffixes in these cases reflects semantic agreement. The singular is used when the collective is viewed as an entity as a whole, while the plural is used when the collective is viewed as consisting of multiple members.

Semantic agreement (as opposed to formal agreement) is also found in many other cases, as in ወአእመሮሙ፡ ኢየሱስ፡ ዘይሐልዩ *wa-ʾaʾmaromu ʾiyasus za-yaḥelləyu*[227] 'and Jesus knew what they were pondering' (Lk 5:22).

A plural suffix is further often attached to a formally singular noun with a plural meaning if an entity (e.g., a body part) is attributed to several individual members of the group in question. The suffixed noun is most commonly declined like a plural noun in this case:

- በኮሉ፡ ልቦሙ፡ ወበኮሉ፡ ነፍሶሙ፡ ወበኮሉ፡ ኀይሎሙ *ba-kʷəllu ləbbomu wa-ba-kʷəllu nafsomu wa-ba-kʷəllu ḫaylomu* 'with all their minds, all their souls, and all their strength' (Jub 1:15)
- ምንትኑ፡ ሕዘናን፡ ገጽክሙ፡ ዮም *məntə-nu ḥəzunān gaṣṣəkəmu yom* 'why are your faces downcast today?' (Gen 40:7) (plural predicate)
- ወገጾሙ፡ ይመልእ፡ ኀፍረተ *wa-gaṣṣomu yəmallə ḫāfrata* 'and their face will be filled with shame' (En 62:10) (singular predicate)
- ወልቦሙ፡ ለቅዱሳን፡ ትመልእ፡ ፍሥሓ *wa-ləbbomu la-qəddusān təmallə fəśśəḥā* 'and the heart of the holy ones was full of joy' (En 47:4) (singular predicate)
- ከመ፡ ይፍልጡ፡ መንፈሶሙ፡ ለሙዉታን *kama yəfləṭu manfasomu la-məwwətān* 'so that they might separate the spirits of the dead' (En 22:9)
- ምግባሮሙ *məgbāromu* (also: ምግባሪሆሙ *məgbārihomu* [§4.2.4.5.1.]) and ተግባሮሙ *tagbāromu* 'their deeds'
- ወይገፈትየሙ፡ ለነገሥት ... እመንግሥቶሙ *wa-yəgafattəʿomu la-nagaśt ... ʾəm-mangəśtomu* 'and he will cast down the kings ... from their kingdoms' (En 46:5)
- ኀጢአቶሙ፡ ወኀጣዉአ፡ አበዊሆሙ *ḫāṭiʾatomu wa-ḫāṭāwəʾa ʾabawihomu* 'their sins and the sins of their ancestors' (Jub 1:22) (the first noun with a pronominal suffix is in the singular, the second in the plural)

Particularly frequent is the lack of number agreement in connection with the suffix on the lexeme ኮል– *kʷəll*– 'all, every, each' (§5.1.9.1.3.), as in ኮሉ፡ እኩያን፡ ወረሲዓን *kʷəllu ʾəkkuyān wa-rasiʿān* 'all the wicked and godless' (En 1:1).

5.1.1.7. Third person singular pronominal suffixes can – like independent pronouns (§5.1.1.2.) – have an anaphoric function, that is they refer to a

---

[227] For ዘይኄልዩ *za-yəḫelləyu*.

previously mentioned entity, as in ውስተ፡ኵሎ፡ቤት፡ዘርእዩ፡ውስተ፡አንቀጹ፡ ደም፡በግዕ ... ኢይባኡ፡ውስተ፡ቤቱ *wəsta kʷəllu bet za-rəʾyu wəsta ʾanqaṣu dama baggəʿ* ... *ʾi-yəbāʾu wəsta betu* 'into each house on whose door they saw the blood of a year-old lamb ... they were not to enter that house' (Jub 49:3); ወአርባዕቱ፡አርእስቲሃ፡ለአርዌሁ *wa-ʾarbāʿtu ʾarʾəstihā* (variant አርእስቲሁ *ʾarʾəstihu*) *la-ʾarwehu* 'and that (aforementioned) beast had four heads' (Dan 7:6).

In some cases, especially with adverbial expressions, pronominal suffixes occur without a specific referent (§4.5.1.). In these cases, they are used to determine the situation. The gender of the suffix in these instances can vary; as in አሜሃ *ʾamehā* (less often አሜሁ *ʾamehu*) and ሶቤሃ *sobehā* 'at that time, when'; በጊዜሁ *ba-gizehu* 'at its time' = 'at its proper time'; ድኅሬሁ *dəḫrehu* 'after it' = 'afterwards' (also ድኅሬሁ፡ሎቱ *dəḫrehu lottu* 'after this' [Dan 7:7]); ቅድሜሁ *qədmehu* 'at its front' = 'before'; እምቀዳሚ፡እስከ፡ተፍጻሜቱ *ʾəm-qadāmi ʾəska tafṣāmetu* 'from the beginning to its end' = 'from the beginning to the end' (En 2:2).

5.1.2. Independent Possessive Pronouns

The independent possessive pronouns ዚአ– *ziʾa–* (masc.), እንቲአ– *ʾəntiʾa–* (fem.), and እሊአ– *ʾəlliʾa–* (pl.) (§4.1.6.), which are always used with possessive suffixes, have the following syntactic functions:

(a) After a noun in the construct, they express an (emphasized) genitive attribute:
  - ቤተ፡ዚአሁ *beta ziʾahu* 'his (own) house'
  - ብእሲተ፡እንቲአየ *bəʾəsita ʾəntiʾaya* 'my (own) wife'
  - አግብርተ፡እሊአከ *ʾagbərta ʾəlliʾaka* 'your (own) servants'
  - እምተረፈ፡ዚአሁ *ʾəm-tarafa ziʾahu* 'from his abundance' (Jn 1:16)

(b) After the relative pronoun ዘ– *za–*, they are likewise used as an (emphasized) genitive attribute:
  - መጽሐፍ፡ዘዚአየ *maṣḥaf za-ziʾaya* 'the book of mine/my book'

(c) They are used predicatively:
  - ዝንቱ፡ቤት፡ዚአየ፡ውእቱ *zəntu bet ziʾaya wəʾətu* 'this house is mine' (verbless clause with copula [§6.1.2.])

- እስመ፡ዚአከ፡ይእቲ፡መንግሥት፡ኃይል፡ወስብሐት ʾəsma ziʾaka yəʾati mangəśt ḫayl wa-səbḥāt 'for the kingdom, and the power, and the glory are yours' (Mt 6:13)
- ዚአነ፡ማይ ziʾana māy 'the water is ours' (Gen 26:20) (verbless clause without copula)

(d) They are used to form nominalized relatives (without referent):

- እሊአሁ ʾəlliʾahu 'those of his' = 'his ones'; as in ወእሊአሁስ፡ኢተወክፍዎ wa-ʾəlliʾahu-ssa ʾi-tawakfəwwo 'but his own people (lit. 'those of his') did not accept him' (Jn 1:11)
- ውስተ፡ዚአሁ፡መጽአ wəsta ziʾahu maṣʾa 'he came to what was his own' (Jn 1:11)
- ዘዚአሁ za-ziʾahu 'that which is his' = 'his property'

Note: For the construction ዘዘዚአ– zazza-ziʾa–, see §5.6.5.

5.1.3. The Subject and Direct Object Personal Pronouns ለሊ– lalli– and ኪያ– kiyā–

5.1.3.1. ለሊ– lalli– with pronominal suffixes (§4.1.3.1.) serves to express strong emphasis of the subject and/or contrast, although its use is generally rare. Its main functions are:

(a) The expression of an emphasized subject (in verbal and verbless clauses):

- ርእኪዎ፡ለሊየ rəʾikəwwo lalliya 'I myself saw him'
- ወለሊሁስ፡ኢኮነ፡ብርሃነ wa-lallihu-ssa ʾi-kona bərhāna 'but he himself was not the light' (Jn 1:8)
- ወለሊየኒ፡ኢይደለወኒ፡እምጻእ፡ኀቤከ wa-lalliya-ni ʾi-yədalləwanni ʾəmṣāʾ ḫabeka 'I myself am not worthy to come to you' (Lk 7:7)
- እንዘ፡ይብል፡ለሊሁ፡ፈጣሪ ʾənza yəbəl lallihu faṭāri 'it is the creator himself saying …' (Śəna fəṭrat 25)

(b) The expression of an emphasized subject when it stands in apposition after an independent personal pronoun:

- ውእቱ፡ለሊሁ፡እግዚአነ፡ውእቱ wəʾatu lallihu ʾəgziʾana wəʾatu 'he is our lord (and nobody else)'
- አነ፡ለሊየ፡ፈርዖን ʾana lalliya farʿon 'I am Pharaoh' (Gen 41:44)

(c) To emphasize a noun when it stands in apposition before or after a noun (rare use):

- ለሊሁ፡ ቃልከ *lallihu qāləka* 'your very/own word'
- ብእሲ፡ ለሊሁ *bəʔəsi lallihu* 'that man/the very man'

5.1.3.2. ኪያ– *kiyā*– with pronominal suffixes (§4.1.3.2.) has two main functions. First, it is used to mark a strongly emphasized personal pronoun functioning as a direct object in either independent or attributive position (mostly standing before its referent).

Independent use:

- ኪያከ፡ ርኢነ፡ አኮ፡ ኪያሁ *kiyāka rəʔina ʔakko kiyāhu* 'we saw *you*, not him'
- ወዘኪያየ፡ ተወክፈ፡ ተወክፎ፡ ለዘፈነወኒ *wa-za-kiyāya tawakfa tawakfo la-za-fannawanni* 'who welcomes *me*, welcomes the one who sent me' (Mt 10:40)
- ወኪያሁ፡ ባሕቲቶ፡ ታምልክ *wa-kiyāhu bāḥtito tāmlək* 'him alone you shall worship' (Mt 4:10)
- አኮኑ፡ አሕዛብኒ፡ ኪያሁሰ፡ ይገብሩ *ʔakko-nu ʔaḥzābə-ni kiyāhu-ssa yəgabbəru* 'do not even the gentiles do it (= the very same thing)?' (Mt 5:47)
- ኢትብክያኒ፡ ኪያየሰ፡ አላ፡ ብክያ፡ ላዕለ፡ ርእስክን *ʔi-təbkəyā-ni kiyāya-ssa ʔallā bəkəyā lāʕla rəʔsəkən* 'do not weep for *me*, but weep for yourselves (fp)!' (Lk 23:28)

Attributive use:

- ኮሎ፡ ኪያሁ፡ መጽሐፈ *kʷəllo kiyāhu maṣḥafa* '(he showed) the whole book' (En 89:70) (anaphoric use)
- ኪያሃ፡ ምድረ *kiyāhā mədra* '(Moses gave them) that land' (Josh 12:6)

Second, it functions to express the pronominal direct object of a perfective participle, as in ኪያሁ፡ ቀቲሎ፡ ጐየ *kiyāhu qatilo gʷayya* 'having killed him, he fled'.

Besides these usages, ኪያ– *kiyā*– with third person suffixes can, like *lalli*–, be used attributively with nouns that are not syntactically the object of a clause, as in ኪያሃ፡ ሌሊተ *kiyāhā lelita* 'during that/the very night' (adverbial accusative of time); በኪያሆን፡ መዋዕል *ba-kiyāhon mawāʕəl* 'in those days' (noun after preposition); ብእሲ፡ ኪ.ያሁ * baʾasi kiyāhu* 'the very man/that man' (noun in nominative). In these cases, ኪ.ያ- *kiyā-* serves to emphasize the noun.

5.1.4. Demonstrative Pronouns

5.1.4.1. Demonstrative pronouns primarily function like attributive adjectives and precede the noun they modify, as in ዝብእሲ *za-baʾasi* 'this man'; በውእቱ፡ መዋዕል *ba-waʾatu mawāʿal* 'in those days' (no number agreement); አሐተ፡ እምእላ፡ ትእዛዛት *ʾaḥatta ʾam-ʾallā taʾazāzāt* 'one (acc.) of these commandments' (Mt 5:19); ወበኮሉ፡ ዝነገር *wa-ba-kʷallu za-nagar* 'and in all this affair' (Job 1:22).

5.1.4.2. Demonstrative pronouns can also constitute the subject of a verbless clause. In this case, they are usually followed by a third person pronoun functioning as copula, as in ዛቲ፡ ይእቲ፡ ወለተ፡ ንጉሥ *zātti yaʾati walatta naguś* 'this is the daughter of the king' and እሉ፡ እሙንቱ፡ ውሉደ፡ ንጉሥ *ʾallu ʾamuntu waluda naguś* 'these are the sons of the king'.

5.1.4.3. Demonstrative pronouns can further be used substantivally, as in ወበኮሉዝ *wa-ba-kʷallu-za* 'and in all this' (Job 2:10); ገበርከዝ *gabarka-za* 'you did this'.

The substantival use occurs particularly with lexemes that have been grammaticalized into adverbs, as in እምዝ *ʾam-za* 'thereafter, then'; ከመዝ *kama-za* 'like this, such'; በእንተዝ *baʾanta-za* and በእንተ፡ ዝንቱ *baʾanta zantu* 'thus, therefore'.

5.1.5. Determinative/Relative Pronouns

The basic function of the pronouns ዘ– *za–* (masc.), እንተ *ʾanta* (fem.), and እለ *ʾalla* (pl.) (§4.1.5.) is determinative. Since they introduce relative clauses as well, they are also often referred to as relative pronouns. The main functions of these pronouns are:

(a) They introduce relative clauses (§6.5.1.), as in ብእሲ፡ ዘመጽአ *baʾasi za-maṣʾa* 'the man who came'; ብእሲት፡ እንተ፡ ወለደት፡ ወልደ *baʾasit ʾanta waladat walda* 'the woman who bore a son'; አቡክሙ፡ ዘበሰማያት *ʾabukamu za-ba-samāyāt* 'your father who is in heaven'; ነገር ፡ ዘከመዝ *nagar za-kama-zə* 'an affair that is like this' = 'such an affair'.

(b) They are used for periphrastic genitive constructions (§5.2.4.4.), as in መንበር ፡ ዘወርቅ *manbar za-warq* 'a throne of gold' = 'a golden throne'; ዘኅቡእ *za-ḫəbuʾ* 'mystery' (= 'that which is hidden'); ዘወርቅ/ዘብሩር/ዘብርት *za-warq/za-bərur/za- bərt* 'of gold, golden/of silver/of copper' (Dan 2:32; of figure); ዘጸጉረ ፡ ገመል *za-ṣagʷra gamal* '(clothing of) camel hair' (Mt 3:4); ዘአዲም *za-ʾadim* '(and his belt was) of leather' (Mt 3:4); ዐይንከ ፡ እንተ ፡ የማን *ʿaynəka ʾanta yamān* 'your right eye' (Mt 5:29) (§5.2.6.7.). This use is particularly common for materials.

(c) They are used to express professions etc. when they are not preceded by a head noun and followed by a noun in the genitive, as in እለ ፡ ሰገል *ʾəlla sagal* 'those of magic' = 'magicians'; እለ ፡ ሥራይ *ʾəlla śərāy* 'those of sorcery' = 'sorcerers'; ዘጠቅ *za-ḍarq* 'the one of rags' = 'ragged (one)'; ዘለምጽ *za-lamṣ* 'one of leprosy' = 'leper'; ዘደም *za-dam* 'of blood' (Jn 1:13); ዘሥጋ *za-śəgā* 'of flesh' = 'man' (En 1:9); ዘአምላክ *za-ʾamlāk* 'one of God' (as in ወይከውኑ ፡ ኵሎሙ ፡ ዘአምላክ *wa-yəkawwənu kʷəllomu za-ʾamlāk* 'and all of them will belong to God' En 1:8).

(d) Determinative pronouns that do not have a preceding head noun and that are followed by a third person finite verbal form (most frequently an imperfect, less often a perfect) are used to express the function of an agent noun (§5.5.3.) or verbal adjective, as in እለ ፡ ሞቱ *ʾəlla motu* 'the dead' (= 'those who have died') (Ruth 1:8); ዘይዘርዕ *za-yəzarrəʿ* 'who sows, sower' (Mk 4:2); ዘይሬኢ *za-yəreʾi* 'seer'; ዘይሰርቀኒ *za-yəsarrəq-ni* 'thief' (Eph 4:28); ዘያሜክሮ *za-yāmekkəro* 'the one who tempts him, his tempter' (Mt 4:3); ወእለ ፡ ይሥቅዩኒ *wa-ʾəlla-ssa yəśāqqəyuni* 'those who torment me' = 'my tormentors' (Ps 13:4 [12:5]); ዘይዜንዎ *za-yəzennəwo* 'the one who reports to him' = 'his messenger' (e.g., Job 1:14); በዘሕይወ *ba-za-ḥaywa* '(they found him) alive' (Lk 7:10; with perfect); አነ ፡ ውእቱ ፡ ዘሀሎ *ʾana wəʾətu za-hallo* 'I am the one who is' (Ex 3:14).

(e) With a following finite third person verbal form (imperfect) and most often with a following head noun, determinative pronouns are used to circumscribe an attributive adjective. Examples include: ለዘይመጽኡ ፡ ትውልድ ፡ ርሑቃን *la-za-yəmaṣṣəʾu təwlədd rəhuqān* 'for a distant generation that will come' = 'for a coming distant generation' (En 1:2); ዘየዐቢ ፡ መዓርግ *za-yaʿabbi maʿārəg* 'one of higher rank';

ዘየዐቢ፡ ብርሃን ... ወዘይንእስ፡ ብርሃን *za-yaʿabbi bərhān ... wa-za-yənəʾəs bərhān*
'the greater light ... the lesser light' (Gen 1:16); በቤተ፡ እጐሆሙ፡ ዘይልሀቅ
ba-beta ʾəḫuhomu za-yələhəq 'in the house of the eldest brother' (Job
1:13); ዘያስተርኢ፣/ይትረአይ *za-yāstarəʾi/yətraʾay* 'visible'; ዘኢ.ያስተርኢ./
ኢ.ይትረአይ *za-ʾi-yāstarəʾi/ʾi-yətraʾay* 'invisible'; ዘኢ.ይትኈለቍ *za-ʾi-
yətḫʷellaqʷ* 'innumerable'; ዘኢ.ይማስን *za-ʾi-yəmāssən* 'indestructible'.

(f)   They are used as elements in prepositions and conjunctions (§4.5.2.–3.).

Determinative pronouns commonly agree in gender and number with the
overtly expressed or implicit head noun in all of these cases, except those
mentioned under (b) and (f); for exceptions regarding (a), see §6.5.1.1.6.
Regarding (b), the genitive phrase is commonly introduced by ዘ– *za–*, even with
feminine or plural head nouns.

For ዘ– *za–* in (አል)ቦ፡ ዘ– *(ʾal)bo za–*-constructions, see §6.1.4.4.; for ዘ– *za–* in the
form ዘዘ– *zazza–* (< *za- +za–), see §5.6.5.

5.1.6. Periphrastic Reflexive Expressions

As other Semitic languages, Classical Ethiopic has no specific reflexive pronoun.
In order to express reflexive nuances, Classical Ethiopic uses the nouns ርእስ *rəʾs*
'head' and (less often) ነፍስ *nafs* 'soul' with pronominal suffixes, as in
አላ፡ ብክያ፡ ላዕለ፡ ርእስክን፡ ወላዕለ፡ ውሉድክን *ʾallā bəkəyā lāʿla rəʾ(ə)səkən wa-lāʿla
wəludəkən* '... but weep (fp) for yourselves and for your children' (Lk 23:28);
ከመ፡ ይሑሩ፡ ውስተ፡ አህጉር፡ ወይሣየጡ፡ ለርእሶሙ፡ መብልዐ *kama yəḥuru wəsta ʾahgur
wa-yəśśāyaṭu la-rəʾ(ə)somu mabləʿa* 'so that they may go into the villages and buy
food for themselves' (Mt 14:15); ወአድኅን፡ ነፍስከ፡ ወኢትነጽር፡ ድኅሬከ *wa-ʾadḫən
nafsaka wa-ʾi-tənaṣṣər dəḫreka* 'save yourself and do not look back' (Gen 19:17);
መጠወ፡ ነፍሶ፡ ለሞት *maṭṭawa nafso la-mot* 'he surrendered himself to death'
(liturgical use).

5.1.7. Interrogative Pronouns

5.1.7.1. The following peculiarities have to be noted regarding the use of መኑ
mannu and ምንት *mənt*:

(a) መኑ *mannu* and ምንት *mənt* usually stand at the beginning of the clause, as in ምንተ፡ ረከበ *mənta rakaba* 'what did he find?'; መነ፡ ቀተልከ *manna qatalka* 'whom did you kill?'.

(b) መኑ *mannu*, literally 'who', has to be rendered by other interrogative pronouns in English in certain contexts, as in መኑ፡ ስምከ *mannu səməka* 'what is your name' (literally 'who is your name?').

(c) መኑ *mannu* can also occur in the genitive, as in ወልደ፡ መኑ፡ አንተ *walda mannu ʾanta* 'whose son are you?'; ዝመንፈስ፡ ዘመኑ *zə-manfas za-mannu* 'whose spirit is this?' (En 22:6). Furthermore, መኑ *mannu* can sometimes occur in contexts in which the accusative መነ *manna* is expected, as in መኑ፡ ይብሉኒ፡ ሰብእ *mannu* (as a variant of መነ *manna*) *yəbəluni sabʾ* 'who do the people say I am?' (Mk 8:27).

(d) Sometimes ምንት *mənt* has to be translated adjectivally, as in ወምንትኑ፡ ዛቲ፡ ጥበብ *wa-məntə-nu zātti ṭəbab* 'and what kind of wisdom is this?' (Mk 6:2).

(e) Sentences introduced by መኑ *mannu*, ምንት *mənt* and other interrogative pronouns frequently exhibit the structure of a cleft sentence, as in መኑ፡ ዘቀተሎሙ *mannu za-qatalomu* (instead of መኑ፡ ቀተሎሙ *mannu qatalomu*) and, with an inserted third person pronoun, መኑ፡ ውእቱ፡ ዘቀተሎሙ *mannu wəʾətu za-qatalomu* 'who is it that killed them?' (§6.4.6.).

(f) In some cases, ምንት *mənt* can be accompanied by a pronominal suffix with a dative function, as in ምንትከ፡ ውእቱ፡ ዝንቱ፡ ኮሉ *məntə-ka wəʾətu zəntu kʷəllu* 'what is all this to you?' = 'what do you mean by all this?' (Gen 33:8); ምንትከ፡ እሉ *məntə-ka ʾəllu* 'what are these to you?' = 'who are these (in relation to you)?' (Gen 48:8).

5.1.7.2. The adjectival pronoun አይ *ʾay* always precedes the noun it modifies. It often follows a preposition: አየ፡ ቤተ *ʾaya beta* 'which house (acc.)?'; በአይ፡ ሥልጣን *ba-ʾay śəlṭān* 'by what authority?' (Mt 21:24); ለአይ ... *la-ʾay* ... 'for which ...?'; እምአይ ... *ʾəm-ʾay* ... 'from which?'; መንገለ፡ አይ፡ ዶታ *mangala ʾay ḍotā* 'in which direction?' (Śəna fəṭrat 35).

The use of plural pronominal suffixes with አይ *ʾay* serves to express a partitive connotation, as in አየቶሙ *ʾayatomu* 'which of them?'.

5.1.8. Indefinite Pronouns

The indefinite pronouns that are formed on the basis of the interrogative pronouns መኑ *mannu* and ምንት *mənt* (§4.1.8.1.) are most frequently used in negated sentences. Negative clauses with double negation (that is, with a second negative particle before the indefinite pronoun) express emphatic negation:

- ኢርእየ ፡ (ወኢ.)መኑሂ *ʾi-rəʾya (wa-ʾi-)manna-hi* 'he saw nobody (at all)'
- ኢገብረ ፡ ምንተሂ *ʾi-gabra mənta-hi* 'he did nothing'
- ዘይገብር ፡ ምንተሂ ፡ ግብረ *za-yəgabbər mənta-hi gəbra* 'who performs any work' (Jub 50:8)
- አዘዞሙ ፡ ኢየሱስ ፡ ኢይንግሩ ፡ ወኢለመኑሂ ፡ ዘርእዩ *ʾazzazomu ʾiyasus ʾi-yəngəru wa-ʾi-la-mannu-hi za-rəʾyu* 'Jesus commanded them to tell no one at all about what they had seen' (Mk 9:9)

5.1.9. ኵል– *kʷəll–* and ኵለንታ *kʷəllantā*

5.1.9.1. The quantifier ኵል– *kʷəll–* 'totality, each, every, all' is always used in combination with pronominal suffixes. It can occur in two main constructions, namely with or without a (pro)nominal referent.

5.1.9.1.1. When ኵል– *kʷəll–* is used with plural suffixes and without a referent, it expresses the totality of the persons addressed, as in ኵልነ *kʷəlləna* 'all of us'; ኵልክሙ *kʷəlləkəmu* 'all of you'; ኵሎሙ *kʷəllomu* 'all of them'.

5.1.9.1.2. When ኵል– *kʷəll–* occurs with a third person pronominal suffix but without a referent, it functions to express 'everything, everybody' (lit. 'its totality'). The nom./gen. has the form *kʷəllu* and the acc. the form *kʷəllo* (< *kulla-hu*), as in ወሀብኩ ፡ ሎቱ ፡ ኵሎ *wahabku lottu kʷəllo* 'I gave him everything'; ዝንቱ ፡ ኵሉ *zəntu kʷəllu* 'all this' (nom.); ዘንተ ፡ ኵሎ ፡ እሁበክ *zanta kʷəllo ʾəhubakka* 'all these I will give you' (Mt 4:9).

5.1.9.1.3. When ኵል– *kʷəll–* occurs with a third person suffix and a (pro)nominal referent, it has to be translated adjectivally as 'all, each'. The pronominal suffix usually agrees with its referent in gender and number, as in ውስተ ፡ ኵሉ ፡ ገሊላ *wəsta kʷəllu galilā* 'in all of Galilee'; ውስተ ፡ ኵላ ፡ ሶርያ *wəsta kʷəllā sorəyā* 'in all of

Syria' (ሶርያ *sorəyā* is feminine). Exceptions to this rule, however, occur frequently, especially with inanimate referents. Furthermore, indeclinable ኵሉ *kʷəllu* and ኵሎ *kʷəllo* (with 3ms suffix) are frequently used to refer to both plural and feminine (animate and inanimate) referents:

- ኵሎ፡ ድዉያን፡ ወኵሎ፡ ሕሙማነ *kʷəllo dəwwəyāna wa-kʷəllo ḥəmumāna* '(and they brought to him) all the weak and sick' (Mt 4:24)
- ኵሉ፡ እኩያን፡ ወረሲዓን *kʷəllu ʾakkuyān wa-rasiʿān* 'all the wicked and impious' (En 1:1)
- ኵሉ፡ ነቢያት *kʷəllu nabiyāt* and ኵሎሙ፡ ነቢያት *kʷəllomu nabiyāt* 'all the prophets' (ነቢያት *nabiyāt* is masculine)
- ኵሎ፡ ሕፃናተ *kʷəllo ḥəḍānāta* 'all the children (acc.)' (Mt 2:16) (ሕፃናት *ḥəḍānāt* is masculine)
- ኵሎ፡ ኅቡአተ *kʷəllo ḫabuʾata* 'all the secrets (acc.)' (En 46:2)
- ወኵሎ፡ መዛግብተ፡ ዘኅቡእ *wa-kʷəllo mazāgəbta za-ḫəbuʾ* 'all the hidden treasures' (En 46:3)

The ኵል– *kʷəll*-phrase commonly stands before, but can also follow the referent, as in ኵሎ፡ ብእሲ *kʷəllo baʾasi* = ብእሲ፡ ኵሎ *baʾasi kʷəllo* 'each man, every man (acc.)'; ኵላ፡ ባሕር *kʷəllā bāḥr* 'each sea, all the sea'. Other sentence elements can stand in between ኵል– *kʷəll–* and its referent, as in ኵሎ፡ ዘውስተ፡ ሰማይ፡ ግብረ *kʷəllo za-wəsta samāy gəbra* 'all the events in heaven' (En 2:1).

ኵል– *kʷəll–* can also express indefinite nuances such as 'anything, everybody, any', as in ወይነቡ፡ ኵሎ፡ እከየ፡ ላዕሌክሙ *wa-yənabbu kʷəllo ʾakaya lāʿlekəmu* 'and who say anything evil against you' (Mt 5:11); ለአማስኖ፡ እምኔሆሙ፡ ኵሎ፡ ነፍስ *la-ʾamāsəno ʾamənnehomu kʷəllo nafsa* 'to destroy any of them' (Jub 49:4); ወኢይከውን፡ ጠቢሐቱ፡ በኵሉ፡ ጊዜ፡ ብርሃን *wa-ʾi-yəkawwən ṭabiḥotu ba-kʷəllu gize barhān* 'and it is not to be sacrificed at any hour of the day' (Jub 49:12).

5.1.9.2. The lexeme ኵለንታ *kʷəllantā* 'totality, entirety' is, similar to ኵል– *kʷəll–*, primarily used in combination with third person pronominal suffixes.

When it stands in apposition to a noun it usually precedes the noun in question, as in ኵለንታ፡ ሌሊተ *kʷəllantā lelita* 'the whole night'; ኵለንታሁ፡ ሥጋክ *kʷəllantāhu śagāka* 'your whole body'. The suffix agrees with its referent.

ኮለንታ *kʷəllantā* can further be used adverbially in the sense of 'whole, fully, all together' when it follows its referent, as in ብእሲ፡ ዘለምጽ፡ ኮለንታሁ *bəʾəsi za-lamṣ kʷəllantāhu* 'a man, fully (covered) with leprosy' (Lk 5:12).

5.2. Syntax of the Noun

5.2.1. Gender

Morphological gender-marking often does not correlate to grammatical or natural gender in Classical Ethiopic. There are nouns that are naturally feminine but that exhibit no feminine ending (§4.2.2.2.) and formally masculine or feminine nouns that can be construed as both masculine and feminine when they denote inanimate entities (§4.2.2.3.) – although animate nouns can equally show a lack of correlation between grammatical and morphological gender, as in *nabiyāt* 'prophets (masc.)', where the masc. pl. is expressed by a "fem. pl." marker. In the latter case, however, gender is not variable as in the case of inanimate nouns, there simply exists a formal discrepancy. Furthermore, adjectives occurring in the feminine singular are often used to designate abstract nouns, e.g., ሠናይት *śannāyt* 'goodness'; እኪት *ʾəkkit* 'evil'; ርትዕት *rətəʿt* 'just thing'.

5.2.2. Constructions to Mark a Noun as Definite

5.2.2.1. Classical Ethiopic does not have a definite article, as opposed to most modern Ethiopian languages. It has, however, a number of constructions that mark a noun as definite. These include:

(a) The use of a demonstrative pronoun, as in ዝብእሲ *za-bəʾəsi* 'this man'.

(b) The use of a third person independent personal pronoun in anaphoric function ('that'), as in ውእተ/ይእተ፡ ጊዜ *wəʾəta/yəʾəta gize* 'at that time, suddenly'; ወውእቱ፡ ዮሐንስ *wa-wəʾətu yoḥannəs* 'and that John' (Mt 3:4); ለውእቱ፡ ጠፈር *la-wəʾətu ṭafar* 'that firmament' (Gen 1:8); ወውእቱ፡ ቃል *wa-wəʾətu qāl* 'and that word (became flesh)' (Jn 1:14).

(c) The use of a third person pronominal suffix in the anaphoric sense of 'that (one)'. This use is particularly frequent with temporal expressions, as in በዕለቱ *ba-ʿəlatu* 'on that day'; አሜሃ/ሶቤሃ *ʾamehā/sobehā* 'at that time, then'; ሳኒታ *sānitā* (< *sānit-hā) 'the next day'; በሳኒታ *ba-sānitā* 'on the next day'; ብእሲሁ *bəʾəsihu* 'that man'. This use also occurs in other contexts, such as **ሐለምኩ፡ካልአ፡ ሕልሙ፡ወከመዝ፡ሕልሙ** *ḥalamku kālə'a ḥəlma wa-kama-zə ḥəlmu* 'I have had another dream and this was the dream' (Gen 37:9); **ወይነድድ፡ደብሩ** *wa-yənaddəd dabru* 'and that (aforementioned) mountain burnt' (Dtn 4:11); **ወእምትሕተ፡መንበሩ፡ዓቢይ** *wa-'əm-matḥəta manbaru 'ābiy* 'and from underneath that high throne ...' (En 14:19).

(d) The use of a proleptic possessive suffix on the noun with a following prepositional phrase involving the preposition **ለ**– *la*–. This construction expresses a genitive phrase (§5.2.4.3.), as in **ምሕረቱ፡ ለእግዚአብሔር** *məḥratu la-'əgzi'ab(ə)ḥer* 'the mercy of God'.

(e) The use of a proleptic object suffix on the verb followed by a prepositional phrase involving the preposition **ለ**– *la*– that expresses an accusative phrase (§5.2.3.2.), as in **ርእይዎ፡ለሕፃን** *rə'yəwwo la-ḥəḍān* 'they saw the child' (Mt 2:11).

(f) The use of **ኪያ**– *kiyā*– with a pronominal suffix (§5.1.3.2.), as in **ኪያሃ፡ ሌሊተ** *kiyāhā lelita* 'during that night'.

5.2.2.2. Explicit indefiniteness of a noun can be expressed by a preceding numeral 'one':

- **አሐዱ፡ካህን፡ዘስሙ፡ዘካርያስ** *'aḥadu kāhən za-səmu zakārəyās* 'a priest named Zechariah' (Lk 1:5)
- **አሐቲ፡ሀገር፡ዘገሊላ** *'aḥatti hagar za-galilā* 'a town in Galilee' (Lk 1:26)
- **ወሀሎ፡አሐዱ፡ብእሲ** *wa-hallo 'aḥadu bə'əsi* 'there was once a man ...' (Job 1:1)
- **እዕርግኑ፡ውስተ፡አሐቲ፡እምነ፡አህጉረ፡ይሁዳ** *'ə'rəg-nu wəsta 'aḥatti 'əmənna 'ahgura yəhudā* 'shall I go up into any of the cities of Juda? (2 Sam 2:1)

5.2.3. The Accusative Case and Periphrastic Accusatives

5.2.3.1. Functions of the Accusative

The accusative in Classical Ethiopic has many functions. Besides marking the direct object and the indirect object of certain verb types, it expresses various adverbial functions (e-i) and can have a quasi-nominative function in other constructions (j-n). The most important functions are:

(a) The most basic function of the accusative is to designate the direct object, as in ሐነጸ፡ቤተ ḥanaṣa beta 'he built a house' and ወአምጽኡ፡ ኀቤሁ፡ሕፃናት wa-ʾamṣəʾu ḫabehu ḥəḍānāta 'and they brought children to him' (Mk 10:13). Some verbs in Classical Ethiopic govern an accusative complement that corresponds to a dative or prepositional phrase in English, such as አንከሮ ʾankaro 'he marveled about him'.

(b) After certain verbs, such as መሰለ masala 'to resemble, be like' and ነገረ nagara 'to speak', the accusative marks the indirect object, as in ወምንተ፡ትመስል wa-mənta təmassəl 'what does it (the kingdom of God) resemble?' (Mk 4:30); ይመስል፡ብእሴ፡ ዘ- ... yəmassəl bəʾase za- ... 'that one is like a man who ...' (Lk 6:48, 49); ነጊሮቶሙ nagirotomu '(after he finished) speaking to them, ...' (Lk 7:1).

(c) Certain verbs, such as መልአ malʾa 'to fill (with)' and semantically similar verbs, are construed with two accusatives. In these cases, one accusative has an instrumental function, as in መልአ፡ማየ malʾo māya 'he filled it with water'. Adjectives derived from these verbs equally govern the accusative, such as ምሉእ məluʾ 'full' (as in ዘምሉእ፡ ጸጋ፡ወሞገስ፡ወጽድቀ za-məluʾ ṣaggā wa-mogasa wa-ṣədqa 'the one who is full of kindness, grace, and truth' [Jn 1:14]) and ጽዑን ṣəʿun 'loaded (with)', as in ጽዑን፡አግማሊሆሙ፡አፈዋተ ṣəʿun ʾagmālihomu ʾafawāta 'their camels were loaded with sweet herbs' [Gen 37:25]).

(d) With verbs of motion, the accusative expresses a direction or goal (= allative), as in ሐረ፡አድባረ ḥora ʾadbāra 'he went to the mountains'; ሐረ/ወፅአ፡ጸብአ ḥora/waḍʾa ṣabʾa 'he went into/left for battle'; ቦአ፡ሀገረ boʾa hagara 'he entered the city'; ባእ፡ቤተከ bāʾ betaka 'go into your house!' (Mt 6:6); ወፈነዎሙ፡ቤተልሔምሃ wa-fannawomu betaləhem-hā 'and he sent them to Bethlehem' (Mt 2:8); አዕረገ፡መንፈስ፡ገዳም ʾaʿrago manfas gadāma 'the spirit led him up into the wilderness' (Mt 4:1); ሕልም፡መጽአኒ ḥəlm maṣʾanni 'a dream came to me' (En 13:8). These types of verbs can also be construed with prepositional phrases without any change in meaning (e.g., ቦአ፡ውስተ፡ሀገር boʾa wəsta hagar 'he entered the city').

(e) The accusative further expresses the adverbial functions of manner, time, and location. An adverbial accusative of manner is found when it occurs as predicate of a direct object, as in በከየ፡መሪረ bakaya marira 'he wept bitterly'; ረከቡኒ፡ነቢረየ፡ህየ rakabuni nabirəya ḥəyya 'they found me seated there' (cf. §5.5.2.6.); **ወኢይብልዕዎ፡ ጥራየ፡ አላ፡ ጥቡስ** *wa-ʔi-yəbləʿəwwo ṭərāya ʔallā ṭəbusa* 'and they are not to eat it raw but roasted' (Jub 49:13).

(f) The accusative expresses location in connection with verbs such as **ነበረ** *nabara* 'to sit, stay' and **ኀደረ** *ḫadara* 'to reside, dwell'; as in **ወማርያስ፡ ነበረት፡ ቤተ** *wa-māryā-ssa nabarat beta* 'but Mary stayed at home' (Jn 11:20); **ነበረ፡ ኀበ፡ ሀሎወ፡ ብሔረ፡ ሰኑየ፡ መዋዕለ** *nabara ḫaba hallawa bəḥera sanuya mawāʿəla* 'he stayed at the place where he was for two days' (Jn 11:6).

(g) The accusative serves to express time, both periods and points of time, as in **ወጸዊሞ፡ መዋዕለ፡ አርብዓ፡ ወአርብዓ፡ ለያልየ** *wa-ṣawimo mawāʿəla ʔarbəʿā wa-ʔarbəʿā layāləya* 'having fasted forty days and forty nights ...' (Mt 4:2); **ውእተ/ይእተ፡ ጊዜ** *wəʔəta/yəʔəta gize* 'at that time'; **ዝሉፈ/ዘልፈ** *zəlufa/zalfa* 'forever'; **ምሴተ** *məseta* 'in the evening'; **ጽባሐ** *ṣəbāḥa* 'in the morning' (also **በምሴት** *ba-məset* and **በጽባሕ** *ba-ṣəbāḥ*).

(h) The accusative of a verbal noun is used for paranomastic constructions in order to put the verbal action into focus (§5.5.5.), as in **ወፈርሁ፡ ዐቢየ፡ ፍርሀተ** *wa-farhu ʿabiya fərhata* 'and they were very afraid' (lit. 'they feared a great fear') (Lk 2:9).

(i) The accusative can also express other adverbial notions such as in oaths: **ኢትምሐሉ፡ ግሙራ።ወኢሰማየ ... ወኢምድረ ... ወኢበኢየሩሳሌም** *ʔi-təmḥalu gəmurā wa-ʔi-samāya ... wa-ʔi-mədra ... wa-ʔi-ba-ʔiyarusālem* 'do not swear at all, either by heaven (acc.), or by the earth (acc.), or by Jerusalem ...' (Mt 5:34).

(j) After the verb **ኮነ** *kona* 'to be(come)', the accusative is used to express the predicate of **ኮነ** *kona*, as in **ወኮነ፡ ሌሊተ፡ ወጸብሐ፡ ወኮነ፡ መዓልተ፡ ፩** *wa-kona lelita wa-ṣabḥa wa-kona maʿālta 1* 'and it became night (acc.) and it dawned, and it was the first day (acc.)' (Gen 1:5); **ኩን፡ ጠቢበ** *kun ṭabiba* 'be wise!' (Mt 5:25); **ወዝኩ፡ እብን ... ኮነ፡ ደብረ፡ ዐቢየ** *wa-zəkku ʔəbn ... kona dabra ʿabiya* 'but yonder stone became a big mountain' (Dan 2:35). The subject of **ኮነ** *kona* in the sense of 'to exist', on the other hand, commonly stands in the nominative, as in **ወዓለምኒ፡ ቦቱ፡ ኮነ** *wa-ʿāləmə-ni bottu kona* 'and the world came into being through him' (Jn 1:10); **ለይኩን፡ ብርሃን** *la-yəkun bərhān* 'let there be light!' (Gen 1:3);[228] **ወኮነ፡ ድቀቱ፡ ዐቢየ** *wa-kona dəqatu ʿabiya* 'and its ruin (nom.) was great

---

[228] This corresponds to Arabic *li-yakun nūrun* 'let there be light (nom.)!',

(acc.)' (Lk 6:49). Exceptions can occur, however. The accusative, for example, appears instead of the nominative in sentences such as ወኮነ፡ ፍርሀት፡ ላዕለ፡ ኵሉ፡ ሰብእ *wa-kona fərhata lāʿla kʷəllu sabʾ* 'and fear (acc.) came over all the people' (Lk 1:65); ይኩን፡ ፈቃድከ *yəkun faqādaka* 'your will be done' (Mt 6:10). The nominative can also occur instead of the accusative in sentences such as ኮነ፡ ሌሊት *kona lelit* 'it was night'.

(k) The accusative seems to be used for the syntactic subject (= logical object) in nominal clauses with ብ- *ba-* and አልብ- *ʾalbə-* 'to (not) have' (§6.1.4.), as in ብየ፡ ወዐልት *bəya waʿalta* 'I have soldiers' (Lk 7:8); ብየ፡ ቤት *bəya beta* 'I have a house'; አልብየ፡ ቤት *ʾalbəya beta* 'I do not have a house'; ዐስበ፡ አልብክሙ *ʿasba ʾalbəkəmu* 'you have no reward' (Mt 6:1). This use indicates the verbalization of ብ- *ba-* and አልብ- *ʾalbə-* in possessive constructions and the reinterpretation of the original subject as direct object ('a reward is not for/in you' > 'you have no reward').

(l) The accusative sporadically occurs with infinitives that function as subjects, as in ኢኮነ፡ ሠናየ ... ወውሂበ፡ ለከለባት *ʾi-kona śannaya ... wa-wəhiba la-kalabāt* 'it is not just (to take the children's food) and give it to the dogs' (Mt 15:26), where the accusative is dependent on ኮነ *kona*.

(m) Doubly transitive verbs in passive constructions retain one accusative object, as in ሕጹጸ፡ ይሰመይ *ḥəṣuṣa yəssamay* ... 'he will be called the smallest' (§5.4.8.4.). In some cases, the accusative can stand for the logical subject in passive clauses (§5.4.8.5.).

(n) Further to be noted is the use of the accusative (not of the nominative) in elliptical nominal clauses such as ርዕየ፡ ቅዱስ፡ ዘበሰማያት *rāʿya qəddusa za-ba-samāyāt* '(he saw/this is) a holy vision in the heavens' (En 1:2).

5.2.3.2. Periphrastic Accusative Constructions

5.2.3.2.1. The direct object can also be expressed by periphrastic constructions in Classical Ethiopic that employ a proleptic object suffix on the verb followed by a prepositional phrase. This so-called *qatalo la-nəguś* construction – 'he killed him, the king' = 'he killed the king' – marks the direct object as definite (§5.2.2.1e). The prepositional phrase introduced by *la-* does not always immediately follow the verb with its pronominal suffix. The subject or a second object can stand in between the two members of the construction.

5.2.3.2.2. Examples of the periphrastic accusative construction include:

- ርእዮ፡ ለሕፃን rəʾyəwwo la-ḥəḍān 'they saw the child' (Mt 2:11)
- ዘይሬዕዮሙ፡ ለሕዝብየ za-yəreʿəyyomu la-ḥəzbəya 'the one who will shepherd my people' (Mt 2:6)
- እስመ፡ እሙንቱ፡ ይሬእይዎ፡ ለእግዚአብሔር ʾəsma ʾəmuntu yəreʾəyəwwo la-ʾəgziʾab(ə)ḥer 'for they will see God' (Mt 5:8)
- ወተስእልክዎ፡ ለ፩እመላእክት wa-tasəʾəlkəwwo la-ʾaḥadu ʾəm-malāʾəkt 'and I asked one of the angels' (En 46:2) (The object is not determined in this case because of ፩ ʾaḥadu.)
- ወሰመዮ፡ እግዚአብሔር፡ ለውእቱ፡ ጠፈር፡ ሰማየ wa-samayo ʾəgziʾab(ə)ḥer la-wəʾtu ṭafar samāya 'and God called that dome sky' (Gen 1:8). In this case, the first object is expressed periphrastically and the second by the accusative case (§5.4.7.2b).

5.2.3.2.3. Periphrastic construction expressing the indirect object include:

- ወይሁቦሙ፡ ጥበበ፡ ለጠቢባን wa-yəhubomu ṭəbaba la-ṭabibān 'he gives wisdom to the wise' (Dan 2:21)
- ወአርአዮ፡ ለንጉሥ፡ ናቡከደነጾር፡ ዘሀሎ፡ ይኩን wa-ʾarʾayo la-nəguś nābukadanaṣor za-hallo yəkun 'and he showed the king Nebuchadnezzar what will happen' (Dan 2:28)
- ንጉሥ፡ ይንግሮሙ፡ ሕልሞ፡ ለአግብርቲሁ nəguś yəngəromu ḥəlmo la-ʾagbərtihu 'let the king tell his dream to his servants' (Dan 2:7); the direct object is in the accusative case and the indirect object is expressed periphrastically.

5.2.3.2.4. When the object is focused or topicalized, the prepositional phrase with ለ– la– can appear in topicalized sentence position (§6.2.3.4.) and precede the verb. This phenomenon frequently occurs with አልቦ፡ዘ– ʾalbo za-constructions (§6.1.4.4.):

- ወለብእሲተኒ፡ ይቤላ wa-la-bəʾəsitə-ni yəbelā 'and as for the woman, he said to her' (Gen 3:16)
- ወለዝክቱኒ፡ ሰቀልዎ wa-la-zəktu-ni saqaləwwo 'but as for that one, they hanged him' (Gen 41:13)

- ለውእቱ፡ እምድኅረ፡ ፈጠሮ፡ አዕረጎ፡ ወለያእቲኒ፡ ውስተ፡ ገነት፡ ፈጠራ *la-wəʾatu ʾəm-dəḫra faṭaro ʾaʿrago / wa-la-yəʾati-ni wəsta gannat faṭarā* 'him (Adam), he brought up (to Paradise) after he had created him, but her (Eve), he created in Paradise' (*Śəna fəṭrat* 34)
- ለእግዚአብሔርሰ፡ አልቦ፡ ዘርእዮ፡ ግሙራ *la-ʾəgziʾab(ə)ḥerə-ssa ʾalbo za-rəʾyo gəmurā* 'no one has ever seen God' (Jn 1:18)

5.2.3.2.5. Periphrastic accusative constructions and inflectional accusative case can occur side by side for the purpose of stylistic variation, as in ወኢታስተኃልፍ፡ ዕለተ፡ እምዕለት፡ ወእምወርኅ፡ ለወርኅ *wa-ʾi-tāstaḫāləf ʿəlata ʾəm-ʿəlat wa-ʾəm-warḫ la-warḫ* literally: 'you will not change a day from the day or from month to month' (Jub 49:7) (with chiastic ordering of the sentence elements; cf. also Jub 49:14 ... ዕለተ፡ እምዕለት፡ ወእምወርኅ፡ ወርኅ ... *ʿəlata ʾəm-ʿəlat wa-ʾəm-warḫ warḫa*).

5.2.4. Genitive Constructions and Related Phenomena

5.2.4.1. The Construct

5.2.4.1.1. A construct is the connection of two or more nouns in a modifying, mostly genitival, relationship. It consists of a noun in the construct state followed by a noun in the genitive (standing in the absolute or unbound state). Less often, the noun in the construct is followed by an asyndetically connected attributive relative clause (§6.5.2.). The first member of this construction is commonly called the *nomen regens* (also "bound noun"), while the second noun is called *nomen rectum* (or "unbound noun"). The second noun or *nomen rectum* qualifies or modifies the first noun or *nomen regens*. The second noun can, depending on context, be considered definite or indefinite, while no such distinction can be made for the first noun. This means that the second noun determines the status of definiteness for the whole construction. Besides two nouns in a construct, longer construct chains with three or more members are also attested in Classical Ethiopic.

5.2.4.1.2. The majority of constructs have two members that consist of two nouns, as in ቤት፡ ንጉሥ *beta nəguś* 'the house of the king/ a house of a king'; ጽሒፈ፡ ኦሪት *ṣaḥifa ʾorit* 'the writing of the law'.

Some constructs are treated like compound nouns and can thus also be written as one lexeme, such as እግዚአብሔር ʾəgziʾa-b(ə)ḥer 'lord of the world' = 'God' and እምሕያው ʾəmma-ḥəyāw 'mother of the living one' = 'Eve'.

5.2.4.1.3. The first or "bound" noun can also be a substantivized adjective or an infinitive, as in እኩያን፡ ሀገር ʾəkkuyāna hagar 'the evil ones of the city'; ብፁዓን፡ ገባርያን፡ ሰላም bəḍuʿān gabārəyāna salām 'blessed are the peacemakers' (Mt 5:9); በዊአ፡ ሀገር bawiʾa hagar 'to enter a city' (Mk 1:45); ኢቀቲለ፡ ነፍስ ʾi-qatila nafs 'not to kill anyone' (Mt 19:18).

The *nomen rectum* can also be the possessive pronoun ዚአ– ziʾa– (§5.1.2a), as in ዕበየ፡ ዚአሁ ʿəbaya ziʾahu 'his greatness' (Ps 145:3 [144:3]).

5.2.4.1.4. Construct chains consisting of three or more members are relatively infrequent. They primarily occur when two of the members are perceived as a compound noun.

Examples of construct chains with three members include: ተድባበ፡ ቤተ፡ መቅደስ tadbāba beta maqdas 'the roof of the temple' (literally 'the house of holiness'); እንለ፡ እምሕያው ʾagwāla ʾəmma-ḥəyāw 'man, human race' (lit. 'the offspring of the mother of the living'); አጽባዕተ፡ እደ፡ ሰብእ ʾaṣbāʿta ʾəda sabʾ 'the fingers of a human hand' (Dan 5:5); ወበዕለተ፡ ዓሕበ፡ ዚአሆሙ wa-ba-ʿəlata ḍāḥba ziʾahomu 'on the day of their affliction' (En 48:10); ሞተ፡ ክልኤሆሙ፡ ደቂቀ፡ አሮን mota kəlʾehomu daqiqa ʾaron 'the death of the two sons of Aaron' (Lev 16:1).

Examples of construct chains with four members include: ወልደ፡ እንለ፡ እም፡ ሕያው walda ʾagwāla ʾəmma ḥəyāw 'son of man/human being' (Dan 7:13); ምርገ፡ አረፍተ፡ ቤተ፡ ንጉሥ marga ʾarafta beta nəguś 'the plaster of the wall of the king's palace' (Dan 5:5); ዝንቱ፡ ነገረ፡ ኩፋሌ፡ መዋዕላተ፡ ሕግ፡ ወለሰምዕ zəntu nagara kufāle mawāʿəlāta ḥəgg (variant መዋዕላት፡ ለሕግ mawāʿəlāt la-ḥəgg) wa-la-semʿ 'this is the account of the division of the times of the law and of the testimony' (Jub prologue).

5.2.4.1.5. In a few exceptional cases, the construct chain can exhibit two or more *nomina recta*. The *nomina recta* usually form a semantic unit in these cases, as in አምላከ፡ ሰማይ፡ ወምድር ʾamlāka samāy wa-mədr 'the Lord of heaven and earth'; ፍጥረተ፡ ሰማይ፡ ወምድር faṭrata samāy wa-mədr 'the creation of heaven and

earth' (Gen 2:4); አክብሮ፡ አቡከ፡ ወእምከ *ʾakbəro ʾabuka wa-ʾəmməka* 'to honor your
father and mother' (Mt 19:19); ሕገገ፡ ጊዜ፡ ወጊዜ *ḥəgaga gize wa-gize* 'the laws for
each time' (Jub 50:13); በስመ፡ አብ፡ ወወልድ፡ ወመንፈስ፡ ቅዱስ *ba-səma ʾab wa-wald
wa-manfas qəddus* 'in the name of the father, the son, and the holy spirit'. In
general, however, the use of two or more *nomina recta* is not productive in
Classical Ethiopic.

Construct chains with two or more *nomina regentia* are very rare, as in ወይነግሩ፡
ዕበየ፡ ክብረ፡ ስብሐተ፡ ቅድሳቲከ *wa-yənaggəru ʿəbaya kəbra səbḥata qəddəsātika* 'they
shall relate the greatness, glory, and praise of your holiness' (Ps 145:5 [144:5])
(with asyndetically listed bound nouns). Constructions of this type are more
commonly expressed periphrastically by mentioning the *nomen rectum* twice or
as often as required, as in ለነገደ፡ እስራኤል፡ ወለሕዝብ፡ እስራኤል *la-nagada ʾəsrāʾel wa-
la-ḥəzba ʾəsrāʾel* 'the tribe of Israel and the people of Israel'.

Generally, instead of construct chains with two or more *nomina recta* or *nomina
regentia*, Classical Ethiopic frequently uses periphrastic genitives with ለ– *la–* or
ዘ– *za–* (or እንተ *ʾənta* and እለ *ʾəlla*) (§5.2.4.3.–4.4.).

5.2.4.1.6. The *nomen rectum* can be modified by an attributive adjective or
demonstrative pronoun. The attributive adjective appears at its usual syntactic
position (§5.2.6.), that is, it follows the noun it modifies (as in ውሂዘ፡ ማይ፡ ብዙኅ
wəhiza māy bəzuḫ 'a river with much water' En 89:15). In general, no other
element can stand between the two members of the construct, although a few
important exceptions to this rule occur. Demonstrative pronouns when
modifying a *nomen rectum* can precede the noun they modify and stand
between the *nomen regens* and *nomen rectum*, as in ለዝና፡ ዝንቱሰ፡ ንጉሥ *la-zenā
zəntu-ssa nəguś* 'the story of this king' (*Ləbna dəngəl* Prologue); ነፍስ፡ ዝሕፃን *nafsa
za-ḥəḍān* 'the life of this child'. In fact, this type of construction is fairly
frequent. Similarly, a number that refers to the *nomen rectum* can stand in
between the two members of the construct, as in መጠነ፡ ሠለስቱ፡ አውራኅ *maṭana
śalastu ʾawrāḫ* 'a duration of three months' (Lk 1:56).

5.2.4.1.7. The *nomen regens* can equally be modified by an attributive adjective
or demonstrative pronoun. This attribute either stands after the *nomen rectum*,
that is, after the whole construct chain, or before the *nomen regens*:

- መንፈስ፡እግዚአብሔር፡ቅዱስ *manfasa ʾǝgziʾab(ǝ)her qǝddus* 'the holy spirit of God' (Lk 1:35); ቅዱስ *qǝddus* modifies the first noun, not the second one.
- ሐራውያ፡ገዳም፡ጸሊም *ḥarāwǝyā gadām ṣallima* 'a black wild-boar (acc.)' (En 89:12)
- በአሕቲ፡አይገ፡ማይ *ba-ʾaḥatti ʾayga māy* 'in a stretch of water' (En 89:23)
- ብዙኅ፡ሐራ፡ሰማይ *bǝzuḫ ḥarā samāy* 'a great host of heaven' (Lk 2:13)
- ወብዙኅ፡ሰብእ፡ሀገር *wa-bǝzuḫ sabʾa hagar* 'many people of the city' (Lk 7:12)
- ዐቢየ፡ዜና፡ፍሥሓ *ʿabiya zenā fǝśśǝḥā* '(I am bringing you) news of great joy' (Lk 2:10).

5.2.4.1.8. The semantic functions of the second noun in the construct, which is equivalent to a noun in the genitive, are numerous (cf. §5.1.1.4. [genitive suffixes]).

The genitive most commonly stands for the logical subject and expresses a possessive relationship, as in ቤተ፡ንጉሥ *beta nǝguś* 'the house of the king'. Less often, the genitive stands for the logical object, as in ሰቢከ፡ወንጌል *sabika wangel* 'preaching of the gospel'; ኢቀቲለ፡ነፍስ *ʾi-qatila nafs* 'not to kill anybody' (Mt 19:18).

The genitive can also express various other nuances, e.g., በዊአ፡ሀገር *bawiʾa hagar* 'to enter a town' (Mk 1:45) (direction); በሰይፈ፡እሳት *ba-sayfa ʾǝsāt* 'with a flaming sword' (Gen 3:24); ታቦተ፡እ዁ *tābota ʾǝḍ* 'a wooden ark of the Covenant' (materials); ዕደወ፡ስም *ʿǝdawa sǝm* 'renowned men' (lit. 'men of name') (Gen 6:4); ነፍስ፡ሕይወት *nafsa ḥǝywat* 'a living creature' (Gen 9:12) (manner).

Lastly, the genitive can function in apposition to the *nomen regens* (so-called *genitivus epexegeticus*), as in ምድረ፡ከናአን *mǝdra kanāʾan* 'the land Canaan' (Jub 50:4); በፈለገ፡ዮርዳኖስ *ba-falaga yordanos* 'in the river Jordan' (Mk 1:9); ሀገረ፡ኢየሩሳሌም *hagara ʾiyarusālem* 'the city Jerusalem'; ደብረ፡ሲና *dabra sinā* 'the mountain Sinai'; ደብረ፡ጽዮን *dabra ṣǝyon* 'mount Zion'. The *nomen rectum* is not to be translated as a genitive in these cases.

5.2.4.1.9. To be noted further are attested construct chains that consist of a noun and an adjective and that express the same semantic notion as a noun plus attributive adjective. The adjective can occur in the position of the *nomen regens* (a) or the *nomen rectum* (b):

(a) ሐሳውያን፡ ነቢያት *ḥassāwəyāna nabiyāt* 'false prophets' (Mt 24:11.24) (lit. 'the false ones of the prophets'); ሐሳዌ፡ መሲሕ *ḥassāwe masiḥ* 'false messiah' (1 Jn 2:18); ሐሳውያን፡ መሲሕ *ḥassāwəyāna masiḥ* 'false messiahs' (Mt 24:24; with *nomen rectum* in singular).

(b) አማልክተ፡ ባዕድ *ʾamāləkta bāʿəd* 'other gods' (Jos 23:16) (not: the gods of another'); አማልክተ፡ ነኪር *ʾamāləkta nakir* 'foreign gods' (Gen 35:2); አብ፡ አረጋዊ *ʾaba ʾaragāwi* 'an old father' (Gen 44:20).

5.2.4.2. "Improper" Genitive Construction

An "improper" genitive construction designates a construct chain that has an adjective as *nomen regens* and that is followed by a noun in the genitive. In these constructions, the adjective, despite its position as *nomen regens*, logically functions as an attribute of the *nomen rectum*.

Examples of such constructions with an adjective in the singular include: ሠነየ፡ ገጽ *śannaya gaṣṣ* 'with a beautiful face, good-looking' (ብእሲ፡ ሠነየ፡ ገጽ *bəʾəsi śannaya gaṣṣ* 'a good-looking man');[229] እኩየ፡ ልብ *ʾəkkuya ləbb* 'evil of heart'; ነዊኀ፡ ቆም *nawwiḫa qom* 'of tall stature'; ርሑቀ፡ መዐት *rəḫuqa maʿat* 'slow to anger' (lit. 'remote of anger') (Ps 145:8 [144:8]); ወብዙኀ፡ ምሕረት *wa-bəzuḫa məhrat* 'and merciful' (Ps 145:8 [144:8]); ይቡሰ፡ ክሳድ *yəbusa kəsād* 'stubborn' (lit. 'dry of neck'); ይቡስ/ዕጹብ፡ ልብ *yəbusa/ʿəṣuba ləbb* 'hard-hearted'; ብሉየ፡ መዋዕል *bəluya mawāʿəl* 'an ancient one' (lit. 'old of days') (Dan 7:9).

Examples with an adjective in the plural include: ንጹሓነ፡ ልብ *nəṣuḫāna ləbb* '(people) pure of heart'; ኦዕጹባነ፡ ልብ *ʾo-ʿəṣubāna ləbb* 'o hard-hearted ones!'; እኩያነ፡ ልብ *ʾəkkuyāna ləbb* '(people) of evil heart'; ልዑላነ፡ ዝክር *ləʿulāna zəkr* '(people) of exalted renown'; ርቱዓነ፡ ሃይማኖት *rətuʿāna hāymānot* 'of just faith' (e.g., ነገሥት፡ ርቱዓነ፡ ሃይማኖት *nagaśt rətuʿāna hāymānot* 'kings of just faith' [*Ləbna dəngəl*, Prologue]); ፍጹማነ፡ አበሳ *fəṣṣumāna ʾabbasā* '(people) accomplished in

---

[229] Literally: 'a man, (one) beautiful of face' (not: '... one who is beautiful *with regard to* the face').

wrongdoing' (En 22:13); ትሕታን፡ገጽ *(konu) təḥutāna gaṣṣ* '(they will have) downcast faces' (lit. 'they will be downcast of face') (En 48:8).

5.2.4.3. Periphrastic Genitives with the Preposition ለ- *la-*

Genitives are often expressed periphrastically in Classical Ethiopic by a proleptic pronominal suffix and the preposition ለ- *la-* (the so-called ወልዱ፡ለንጉሥ *waldu la-nəguś* construction). In this construction, the genitive is always definite, as opposed to the construct, which can be definite or indefinite (§5.2.2.1d):

- ቤቱ፡ለንጉሥ *betu la-nəguś* 'the house of the king'; literally 'his house, belonging to the king'
- ቤቱ፡ለዝንቱ፡ንጉሥ *betu la-zəntu nəguś* 'the house of this king' (with a demonstrative pronoun before the head noun [§5.2.6.2.])
- ወልዳ፡ለብእሲት *waldā la-bəʾəsit* 'the son of the woman'
- ምሕረቱ፡ለእግዚአብሔር *məḥratu la-ʾəgziʾab(ə)her* 'the mercy of God'
- ብርሃኑ፡ለዓለም *bərhānu la-ʿālam* '(you are) the light of the world' (Mt 5:14)[230]
- ወእምእዴሆሙ፡ለኮሎሙ፡እለ፡ይጸልኡነ *wa-ʾəm-ʾədehomu la-kʷəllomu ʾəlla yəṣalləʾuna* 'from the hand of all who hate us' (Lk 1:71)
- በኮሉ፡ትእዛዙ፡ወኮነኄሁ፡ለእግዚአብሔር *ba-kʷəllu təʾəzāzu wa-kʷənnanehu la-ʾəgziʾab(ə)her* 'according to all the commandments and regulations of God' (Lk 1:6)
- cf. also ዲቤሆሙ፡ለሕዝብ *dibehomu la-ḥəzb* 'about/concerning the people' (*waldu la-nəguś* construction with prepositional phrase, which has the same meaning as ዲበ፡ሕዝብ *diba ḥəzb*).
- ወለምእላዲሁ፡ለማይ *wa-la-məʾəllādihu la-māy* 'and the gathering place of the water (he called "sea")' (Gen 1:10). In this example, the *waldu la-nəguś* construction follows a prepositional phrase with ለ- *la-* used as a periphrastic expression of the accusative (§5.2.3.2.).

The prepositional phrase with ለ- *la-* often does not immediately follow the noun plus proleptic suffix. The subject (often in the form of a personal

---

[230] Cf. however አንትሙ፡ውእቱ፡ጼው፡ለምድር *ʾantəmu wəʾətu ṣew la-mədr* 'you are the salt of the earth' (Mt 5:13), without proleptic suffix.

pronoun) or a predicate can stand between the two members of the construction:

- ወልዱ፡ አንተ፡ ለንጉሥ *waldu ʾanta la-nəguś* 'you are the son of the king'
- እመ፡ ወልዱሰ፡ አንተ፡ ለእግዚአብሔር *ʾəmma waldu-ssa ʾanta la-ʾəgziʾab(ə)ḥer* 'if you are the son of God …' (Mt 4:3)
- እስመ፡ ሀገሩ፡ ይእቲ፡ ለንጉሥ፡ ዐቢይ *ʾəsma hagaru yəʾəti la-nəguś ʿabiy* 'for it is the city of the great king' (Mt 5:35)
- ወተሣሀሎሙ፡ እግዚአብሔር፡ ለሕዝቡ *wa-taśāhalomu ʾəgziʾab(ə)ḥer la-ḥəzbu* 'and God has mercy on his people' (Lk 7:16)
- ወኮነ፡ ድቀቱ፡ ዐቢየ፡ ለውእቱ፡ ቤት *wa-kona dəqatu ʿabiya la-wəʾətu bet* 'the ruin of that house was great' (Lk 6:49)

For special emphasis, the genitive expression can be topicalized (cf. §6.2.3.5.) and stand before the head noun (type ለንጉሥ ... ወልዱ *la-nəguś ... waldu*):

- እስመ፡ ለእግዚአ፡ መናፍስት፡ ተርእየ፡ ብርሃኑ *ʾəsma la-ʾəgziʾa manāfəst tarəʾya bərhānu* 'for the light of the Lord of Spirits will have appeared' (En 38:4)
- ወለብእሲትየኒ፡ ኀለፈ፡ መዋዕሊሃ *wa-la-bəʾəsitəya-ni ḫalafa mawāʿəlihā* 'and the days of my wife have passed' (that is, she is old) (Lk 1:18)
- ወለላ፡ ፩ምግባሮሙ *wa-lalla ʾaḥadu məgbāromu* '(I wrote down) … the deeds of each one of them' (En 13:6) (distributive connotation)

In some rare cases, the periphrastic genitive with ለ- *la-*, similar to the periphrastic genitive with ዘ- *za-*, occurs without the proleptic pronominal suffix, as in ኩፋሌ፡ መዋዕላተ፡ ሕግ *kufāle mawāʿəlāta ḥəgg* (variant መዋዕላት፡ ለሕግ *mawāʿəlāt la-ḥəgg*) ወለስምዕ *wa-la-səmʿ* (variant ወስምዕ *wa-səmʿ*) 'the divisions of the times of the law and the testimony' (Jub Prologue) (the second genitive of the chain is introduced by ለ- *la-*).

5.2.4.4. Periphrastic Genitives with ዘ- *za-*

A genitive can also be expressed by a periphrastic construction employing the determinative pronoun ዘ- *za-* (formally masculine singular). The masculine sing. form is also often used when the head noun is feminine or plural. The pronouns እንት *ʾanta* (fs) and እለ *ʾəlla* (pl.) occur only rarely.

The construction with ዘ- za- is particularly frequent for designating materials, as in መንበር፡ዘወርቅ manbar za-warq 'a golden throne'; አክሊል፡ዘወርቅ ʾaklil za-warq 'a golden crown'; ቅናት፡ዘአነዳ qanāt za-ʾanadā 'a leather belt'; አማልክቲሆሙ፡ ዘወርቅ፡ወዘብሩር፡ወዘብርት፡ወዘኀጺን፡ወዕፅ፡ወዘለሕኲት amālǝktihomu za-warq wa-za-bǝrur wa-za-bǝrt wa-za-ḫaṣṣin wa-za-ʿǝḍ wa-za-lǝḥakʷt 'their gods of gold, silver, copper, iron, wood, and clay' (Dan 5:4).

The periphrastic construction with ዘ- za- is also used in connection with proper names and to avoid overly complex or long construct chains:

- ዛቲ፡መጽሐፍ፡እንተ፡ፍጥረተ፡ሰማይ፡ወምድር zātti maṣḥaf ʾǝnta fǝṭrata samāy wa-mǝdr 'this is the book of the creation of heaven and earth' (Gen 2:4) (እንተ ʾǝnta used instead of a construct chain with three members)
- ወንጌል፡ቅዱስ፡ዘእግዚእነ wangel qǝddus za-ʾǝgziʾǝna 'the holy gospel of our Lord'
- ወኮኑ፡መራዕየ፡ብዙኃን፡ዘአባግዕ wa-konu marāʿǝya bǝzuḫāna za-ʾabāgǝʿ 'and they became many flocks of sheep' (En 89:14)
- ዓባይ፡ዕለት፡እንተ፡ኮነ፡ወመቅሠፍት፡ወዳዕር ʿābbāy ʿǝlat ʾǝnta kʷǝnnane wa-maqśaft wa-ḍāʿr 'and the great day of judgement, punishment, and torment' (En 22:11) (instead of a construct with several *nomina recta* [§5.2.4.1.5.])
- ክልኤ፡ጽላተ፡እብን፡ዘሕግ፡ወተእዛዝ kǝlʾe (variant ክልኤተ kǝlʾeta) ṣǝllāta ʾǝbn za-ḥǝgg wa-za-tǝʾǝzāz 'the two stone tablets of the law and the commandments' (Jub 1:1)

The genitive phrase can also stand before the head noun in this construction, as in ኮሎ፡ዘውስተ፡ሰማይ፡ግብረ kʷǝllo za-wǝsta samāy gǝbra '(contemplate) all events of heaven' (En 2:1).

5.2.5. Appositions

An apposition is a modification of a noun phrase by a second noun phrase that is on the same syntactic level as the first. Appositions commonly follow the noun to which they refer:

- በኢሳይያስ፡ነቢይ ba-ʾisāyǝyās nabiy 'by the prophet, Isaiah' (Mt 3:3)

- ብእሲ፡ መኰንን *bəʾəsi makʷannən* 'an officer' (lit. 'a man, an officer') (Lk 7:8)
- ወነሥአ፡ ለማርያም፡ ፍኅርቱ *wa-naśʾā la-māryām fəḫərtu* 'and he took Mary, (as) his betrothed' (Mt 1:24) (ፍኅርቱ *fəḫərtu* agrees in case with ማርያም *māryām*)
- ዳኪዮስ፡ ንጉሥ *dākiyos nəguś* 'the king, Dakios'; ቄሳር፡ ንጉሥ *qesār nəguś* 'the king, Cesar (Augustus)'

A construct chain can occur in apposition to a noun phrase as well:

- ነገሥት፡ ርቱዓነ፡ ሃይማኖት *nagaśt rətuʿāna hāymānot* 'the kings, the ones of just (=orthodox) faith' = 'the orthodox kings'
- ንጉሥ፡ መፍቀሬ፡ እግዚአብሔር *nəguś mafqare ʾəgziʾab(ə)her* 'the god-loving king' (lit. 'the king, the lover of God')

The opposite order is generally rare. The appositionally used lexemes ኵል- *kʷəll-* and ኵለንታ *kʷəllantā* (§5.1.9.) form an exception to this rule. These lexemes usually appear before their head noun, as in ኵላ፡ ባሕር *kʷəllā bāḥr* 'each sea'; ኵሎ፡ ምድረ *kʷəllo mədra* 'the whole land, each land (acc.)'; ኵለንታሃ፡ ሌሊተ *kʷəllantāhā lelita* 'the whole night' (but: ዝንቱ፡ ኵሉ *zəntu kʷəllu* 'all this').

Classical Ethiopic sometimes uses a genitive construction in cases in which an apposition is expected, as in the expression ፈለገ፡ ዮርዳኖስ *falaga yordanos* 'the river Jordan' (§5.2.4.1.8.).

The connection of the cardinal number 'one' + counted entity is likewise to be understood as noun + noun in apposition (§5.3.1.1.).

5.2.6. Noun and Attributive Adjective

5.2.6.1. An attributive adjective usually agrees with the noun it modifies in gender, number, and case (for agreement limitations with inanimate nouns, see §5.2.6.5.). In most cases, the attributive adjective follows its head noun, as in the following paradigm:[231]

---

[231] For the position of attributes in Classical Ethiopic, see Schneider 1959 and Gai 1981.

ms	ንጉሥ፡ ክቡር *nəguś kəbur* 'an/the honored king'
ms acc.	ንጉሠ፡ ክቡረ *nəgusa kəbura*
fs	ንግሥት፡ ክብርት *nəgəśt kəbərt* 'an/the honored queen'
mp	ነገሥት፡ ክቡራን *nagaśt kəburān* '(the) honored kings'
fp	ንግሥታት፡ ክቡራት *nəgəśtāt kəburāt* '(the) honored queens'

5.2.6.2. The attributive adjective can also stand before the noun it modifies. This order, which is the normative order in modern Ethiopian languages, is only regularly found with lexemes that have a demonstrative meaning, ordinal numbers, and certain number words such as 'many', 'few', and 'big' in Classical Ethiopic. In most other cases, a preposed adjective expresses focus of the attribute:

- ዜና፡ ዝንቱ፡ ንጉሥ *zenā zəntu nəguś* 'the story of this king'; በዛቲ፡ ልማድ *ba-zātti ləmād* 'according to this custom'; በውእቱ፡ ጊዜ *ba-wəʾətu gize* 'at that time'.

- ውስተ፡ አሐዱ፡ መካን *wəsta ʾaḥadu makān* 'in one place' (Gen 1:9); ወኮነ፡ ካልእት፡ ዕለተ *wa-kona kāləʾta ʿalata* 'and it was the second day' (Gen 1:8); ካልአ፡ ብሔረ *kāləʾa bəḥera* '(they went) to another land'; ሠሉስ፡ ሌሊት *śalus lelit* 'the third night'; ራብዓዊ፡ ብእሲ *rābəʿāwi bəʾsi* 'the fourth man'.

- ኅዳጣን፡ ሰብእ *ḥədāṭān sabʾ* 'few people'

- ብዙኅ፡ ሐራ፡ ሰማይ *bəzuḥ ḥarā samāy* 'a numerous heavenly host' (Lk 2:13); ወበዙኃን፡ አፍላግ፡ መጺአሙ *wa-bəzuḥān ʾaflāg maṣiʾomu* 'and when mighty streams of water had come ...' (Lk 6:48); but also frequently ሰብእ፡ ብዙኅ *sabʾ bəzuḥ* and ሕዝብ፡ ብዙኅ *ḥəzb bəzuḥ* 'many people'.

- ዐቢየ፡ ዜና፡ ፍሥሓ *ʿabiya zenā fəśśəḥā* 'a message of great joy' (Lk 2:10); ዐቢይ፡ ነቢይ *ʿabiy nabiy* 'a great prophet' (Lk 7:16 etc.); በዐቢይ፡ ቃል *ba-ʿabiy qāl* 'with a loud voice' (Lk 1:42 etc.); cf. also ፍሥሓ፡ ዐቢየ *fəśśəḥā ʿabiya* 'great joy' (Mt 2:10).

- ብሉይ፡ ኪዳን/ሐዲስ፡ ኪዳን *bəluy kidān/ḥaddis kidān* 'the Old Testament/ New Testament'.

- ቅዱሳት፡ መጻሕፍት *qəddusāt maṣāḥəft* 'the holy scriptures' (besides: መጻሕፍት፡ ቅዱሳት *maṣāḥəft qəddusāt*).

- ቀዳምያን፡ ነገሥተ፡ ኢትዮጵያ *qadāməyān nagaśta ʾityop(ə)ya* ... 'the former kings of Ethiopia ...'.

- ወበአፈ፡ ክቡራን፡ ካህናት wa-ba-ʾafa kəburān kāhənāt 'and by the word of honored priests' (Ləbna dəngəl Prologue).

5.2.6.3. A noun can govern more than one attributive adjective:

- ወገብረ፡ እግዚአብሔር፡ ብርሃናተ፡ ክልኤተ፡ ዐቢየተ wa-gabra ʾəgziʾab(ə)her bərhānāta kəlʾeta ʿabbayta 'and God made the two great lights' (Gen 1:16)
- ርእየ፡ ካልአነ፡ ክልኤተ፡ አኀወ rəʾya kāləʾāna kəlʾeta ʾaḫawa 'he saw two other brothers' (Mt 4:21)
- ካልእ፡ ቀርን፡ ንኡስ kāləʾ qarn nəʾus 'a second, small(er) horn' (Dan 7:8) (with one attributive adjective before and one after the head noun)

5.2.6.4. In a few cases, an attributive adjective can, at least semantically, refer to more than one head noun, as in ብዙኅ፡ መንክራተ፡ ወመድምማት bəzuḫa mankərāta wa-madməmāta '(he performed) many miracles and wonders' (for the agreement in this clause, see §5.2.6.5.1.)

5.2.6.5. In certain cases, the head noun and attributive adjective do not exhibit strict number agreement.

5.2.6.5.1. Inanimate nouns in the plural can have attributive adjectives in either the singular or plural. Only nouns designating human beings have strict number agreement and regularly have an attribute in the plural with a plural head noun. For the phrase 'many cities', Classical Ethiopic can thus have the following expressions (ሀገር hagar 'city' can have feminine or masculine gender): አህጉር፡ ብዝኅነት / ብዙኅ / ብዙኃት / ብዙኃን ʾahgur bəzəḫt[232] / bəzuḫ / bəzuḫāt / bəzuḫān.

Several nouns that are formally in the plural are often construed as singulars. These nouns include:

- መዋዕል mawāʿəl 'days, time' (pl. of ሞዐልት moʿalt, መዓልት maʿālt): ወበውእቱ፡ መዋዕል wa-ba-wəʾətu mawāʿəl 'and in those days' (En 47:1 etc.;

---

[232] Cf. ወኀጣውኢሆሙ፡ ዐብየት wa-ḫaṭāwəʾihomu ʿabyat 'their sins have become great (fs)' (Gen 18:20).

as opposed to በእማንቱ፡ መዋዕል ba-ʾəmāntu mawāʿəl [En 47:3] and ወበእሉ፡ መዋዕል wa-ba-ʾəllu mawāʿəl [En 47:2])

- ወኮነ፡ መዋዕል፡ ዘነግሠ፡ ዳዊት ... ላዕለ፡ ቤተ፡ ይሁዳ ... wa-kona mawāʿəl za-nagśa dāwit ... lāʿla beta yəhudā ... 'the time that David ruled over Juda was ...' (2 Sam 2:11) ወኈሊፎ፡ ብዙኅ፡ መዋዕል wa-ḫalifo bəzuḫ mawāʿəl 'much time having passed ...' (Job 2:9)
- ሰራዊት sarāwit 'army, hosts' (pl. of ሰርዌ sarwe): ምስለ፡ ብዙኅ፡ ሠራዊት məsla bəzuḫ śarāwit (= ሰራዊት sarāwit) 'with great hosts' (Ləbna dəngəl 2)
- መንክራት mankərāt and መድምማት madməmāt 'miracles, wonders': ብዙኀ፡ መንክራተ፡ ወመድምማተ bəzuḫa mankərāta wa-madməmāta 'many miracles and wonders' (Ləbna dəngəl Prologue)
- ዓሣት ʿāśāt 'fish' (pl. of ዓሣ ʿāśā): ብዙኅ፡ ዓሣት፡ ፈድፋደ bəzuḫ ʿāśāt fadfāda 'a lot of fish' (Lk 5:9)

5.2.6.5.2. Collective nouns that have a singular-looking form are nevertheless most commonly construed as plurals, although in general, collectives in Classical Ethiopic tend to exhibit semantic agreement, that is, they are construed as singular when viewed as a single unit and construed as plural when perceived as consisting of multiple members. This type of noun includes:

- ሰብእ sabʾ 'people, men' (mostly with plural attribute): ኅዳጣን/ ብዙኃን፡ ሰብእ ḫədāṭān /bəzuḫān sabʾ 'few/many people'; ወብዙኅ፡ ሰብአ፡ ሀገር wa-bəzuḫ sabʾa hagar 'and many people of the city' (Lk 7:12); እሙንቱ፡ ሰብእ፡ ኖሎት ʾəmuntu sabʾ nolot 'those shepherds' (Lk 2:15)
- ሕዝብ ḥəzb 'people(s)' (with plural or singular attribute): ብዙኅ፡ ሕዝብ bəzuḫ ḥəzb and ሕዝብ፡ ብዙኅ ḥəzb bəzuḫ 'a great crowd' (Lk 7:11 etc.); ሕዝብ፡ ጽኑዓን ḥəzb ṣənuʿān 'strong people'
- ሐራ ḥarā 'host, army': ወግብተ፡ መጽኡ ... ብዙኅ፡ ሐራ፡ ሰማይ wa-gəbta maṣʾu ... bəzuḫ ḥarā samāy 'and suddenly a great host of heaven arrived' (Lk 2:13) (verb in pl.)
- ትውልድ təwlədd 'generation' (with singular or plural attribute): ወአኮ፡ ለዝ፡ ትውልድ፡ አላ፡ ለዘ፡ ይመጽኡ፡ ትውልድ፡ ርኁቃን wa-ʾakko la-zə təwlədd ʾallā la-za yəmaṣṣəʾu təwlədd rəḫuqān 'not for this generation but for a distant generation to come' (En 1:2)

5.2.6.5.3. When a noun in the singular exhibits the connecting vowel /i/ before pronominal suffixes in analogy with nouns in the plural (§4.2.4.5.1.), the attribute most commonly stands in the singular, as in **ምግባሪክሙ፡ ሠናየ** *məgbārikəmu śannāya* 'your good deed/your good deeds'.

5.2.6.6. Classical Ethiopic, like other Semitic languages, frequently uses a construct chain when European languages would use an attributive adjective, as in **ብርሃነ፡ ጽድቅ** *bərhāna ṣədq* 'the light of truth' = 'the true light' (Jn 1:9).

5.2.6.7. The notion of 'right' and 'left' is likewise most commonly expressed by a noun in the construct or noun plus pronominal suffix. The nouns used are **የማን** *yamān* 'right side, right hand' and **ፀጋም** *ḍagām* 'left side, left hand', as in **መንገለ፡ የማነ፡ ምሥዋዕ** *mangala yamāna məśwāʿ* 'on the right side of the altar' (Lk 1:11); **ኢታእምር፡ ፀጋምከ፡ ዘተገብር፡ የማንከ** *ʾi-tāʾmər ḍagāməka za-təgabbər yamānəka* 'your left shall not know what your right is doing' (Mt 6:3).

Classical Ethiopic further employs a periphrastic construction involving the determinative pronoun **ዘ-/እንተ፡ የማን/ፀጋም** *za-/ʾənta yamān/ḍagām* 'that of the right/left side' for the same notion; as in **እንተ፡ የማን፡ መልታሕተከ** *ʾənta yamān maltāḥtaka* 'your right cheek (acc.)' (Mt 5:39).

The Nisbe-forms (with *-āy* or *-āwi*) of **የማን** *yamān* and **ፀጋም** *ḍagām* are solely used as true attributive adjectives, as in **እምነ፡ የማናይ፡ ገቦሁ** *ʾəmənna yamānāy gabohu* 'from his right side' (Śəna fəṭrat 31).

5.2.7. Adjectives for the Expression of Circumstantial Predicates

5.7.7.1. Adjectives, especially those of the type **qətul* are often used as circumstantial predicates that specify persons or other verbal actions.[233] When the referent is in the accusative, the predicative adjective is likewise in the accusative; when the referent is in the nominative, the predicative adjective can be in either the nominative or accusative:[234]

- **ርኢኩ፡ ኃዋኅወ፡ ሰማይ፡ ፍቱሓተ** *rəʾiku ḫāwāḫəwa samāy fətuḥāta* 'I saw the gates of heaven open' (En 34:2)

---

[233] Other Semitic languages commonly use active participles in the accusative for this notion, as in Classical Arabic *jāʾa rākiban* 'he came, riding'.

[234] Instead with predicative adjectives, Classical Ethiopic can express the same circumstantial notion with subordinate clauses introduced by **እንዘ** *ʾənza* (§6.5.5.1.).

- ወረከብዎ፡ለእግዚአሙ፡ውዱቀ፡ውስተ፡ምድር፡ምዉተ wa-rakabəwwo la-
  ʾəgziʾomu wəduqa wəsta mədr məwuta 'and they found their lord fallen on
  the earth (and) dead' (Judg 3:25).
- ንጉሥኪ፡ይመጽእ፡ኃቤኪ፡የዋህ፡እንዘ፡ይጼዐን፡ዲበ፡እድግት nəguśəki yəmaṣṣəʾ
  ḥabeki yawwāh ʾənza yəṣṣeʿan diba ʾədəgt 'your king comes to you humble,
  riding on a donkey' (Mt 21:5)

5.2.7.2. A particularity of Classical Ethiopic is that circumstantial predicative
adjectives are often extended by a pronominal suffix. In these cases, the
predicative adjective commonly agrees in case, and the pronominal suffix in
person, with the, most commonly, pronominal referent. The pronominal suffix
on the adjective is not usually rendered in the translation. Examples include
(with the referent in either the nominative or accusative):

- ሐርኩ፡ሕዙንየ ḥorku ḥəzunəya 'I went away (being) sad' (lit. 'I went – I
  being a sad one'; the suffix has a nominative, not genitive function);
  ሖረ፡ሕዙኑ ḥora ḥəzunu 'he went away sad'.
- ረከብዎ፡ሕያዎ rakabəwwo ḥəyāwo 'they found him alive'; ኢይነሥኡከ፡
  ሕያወከ ʾi-yənaśśəʾuka ḥəyāwaka 'they will not seize you alive'.

5.2.8. The Elative, Superlative, and Comparative

5.2.8.1. The elative is usually expressed by the use of adverbs such as ጥቀ ṭəqqa
'very', ፈድፋደ fadfāda 'greatly, more' (§4.5.1.4.), as in ጥቀ፡ጠቢብ፡ውእቱ ṭəqqa
ṭabib wəʾətu and ጠቢብ፡ጥቀ፡ውእቱ ṭabib ṭəqqa wəʾətu 'he is very wise'.

5.2.8.2. Classical Ethiopic does not have any morphological means to express
the superlative. A superlative connotation can only be inferred from context,
that is, a simple adjective can be used with a superlative meaning, as in
እግዚአብሔር፡ልዑል ʾəgziʾab(ə)her ləʿul 'God high' = 'God most high' (Lk 1:32).

When an attributive nuance is expressed periphrastically by a relative clause
introduced by ዘ- za- (§5.1.5e), this relative clause can express a superlative
connotation without any further extensions, as in በቤተ፡እኁሆሙ፡ዘይልህቅ ba-
beta ʾəḫuhomu za-yələhəq 'in the house of their oldest brother' (Job 1:13).

5.2.8.3. In comparative constructions, the entity that is compared with another
is usually introduced by the preposition እም- ʾəm- or its biform እምነ ʾəmənna.

(For syntactic constructions in which the compared entity is introduced by a subordinate clause introduced by እም(ነ) *ʾəm(ənna)*, see §6.5.8.2.).

- (a) እም(ነ) *ʾəm(ənna)* after an adjectival nominal phrase:
  - ጠቢብ፡ ውእቱ፡ እምነ፡ ንጉሥ *ṭabib wəʾətu ʾəmənna nəguś* 'he is wiser than the king'
  - ጠቢብ፡ ውእቱ፡ እምእኁሁ *ṭabib wəʾətu ʾəm-ʾəḫuhu* 'he is wiser than his brother'
- (b) እም(ነ) *ʾəm(ənna)* after an adjectival noun phrase modified by ፈድፋደ *fadfāda* 'great, much':
  - ጠቢብ፡ ውእቱ፡ ፈድፋደ፡ እምእኁሁ *ṭabib wəʾətu fadfāda ʾəm-ʾəḫuhu* 'he is much wiser than his brother'
  - እመ፡ ኢፈድፈደ፡ ጽድቅክሙ፡ ፈድፋደ፡ እምጸሐፍት፡ ወእምፈሪሳውያን *ʾəmma ʾi-fadfada ṣədqəkəmu fadfāda ʾəm-ṣaḥaft wa-ʾəm-farisāwəyān* 'if your justice does not very much exceed that of the scribes and Pharisees' (Mt 5:20)
- (c) እም(ነ) *ʾəm(ənna)* besides a verb with a stative meaning:
  - በዝኑ፡ ውእቱ፡ ሕዝብ፡ እምሕዝብነ *bazḫu wəʾətu ḥəzb ʾəm-ḥəzbəna* 'that nation became more numerous than our nation'
  - ይጸንዕ፡ እምኔየ *yəṣannəʿ ʾəmənneya* 'he is more powerful than I' (Mt 3:11)
  - መካነ፡ እምዝ፡ ዘይገርም *makāna ʾəm-zə za-yəgarrəm* '(I went to) a place that is more terrible than this' (En 21:7)
  - በከመ፡ ብርሃን፡ ይኄይስ፡ እምጽልመት፡ ከማሁ፡ እምዝኒ፡ ዓለም፡ ይኄይስ፡ ዓለም፡ ዘይመጽእ፡ ድኅረ *ba-kama bərhān yəḫeyyəs ʾəm-ṣəlmat kamāhu ʾəm-zə-ni ʿālam yəḫeyyəs ʿālam za-yəmaṣṣəʾ dəḫra* 'as light is better than darkness, thus the world that comes later is better than this world' (Śəna fəṭrat 7)

5.2.8.4. Classical Ethiopic also employs comparative constructions without እም(ነ) *ʾəm(ənna)*. In this case, the compared entity is either not explicitly mentioned or expressed indirectly through a dative suffix on a stative verb:

- ከመ፡ ይኩን፡ ኀበ፡ ዘየዓቢ፡ መዓርግ፡ እምዘ፡ ይቴሐት *kama yəkun ḫaba za-yaʿābbi maʿārəg ʾəm-za yətteḥat* 'so that he shall be on a higher rank than the lower ones' (Ləbna dəngəl Prologue)

- ወቀተለ፡ኩሎ፡ሕፃናተ   ...   ዘክልኤ፡ዓመት፡ወዘይንእስ፡ሂ *wa-qatala kʷəllo ḥədānāta ... za-kəlʾe ʿāmat wa-za-yənəʾəs-hi* 'and he killed all the infants ... who were two years old or younger' (Mt 2:16)
- ዘየዐቢ፡ብርሃነ ... ዘይንእስ፡ብርሃነ *za-yaʿabbi bərhān ... za-yənəʾəs bərhān* 'the greater light ... and the small/smaller light' (Gen 1:16)
- በዝገነ፡ውእቱ፡ሕዝብ *bazḫana wəʾətu ḥəzb* 'that nation became more numerous than us' (use of pronominal suffix to express compared entity).

5.3. The Syntax of Numerals

5.3.1. Cardinal Numbers

5.3.1.1. The lexemes expressing the numeral 'one' (masc. አሐዱ *ʾaḥadu*, fem. አሐቲ *ʾaḥatti*) function as adjectives syntactically. All other cardinal numbers are nouns. The connection of 'one' + counted entity corresponds to the construction of "attributive adjective + noun." The syntactic construction of all other cardinal numbers represents "noun (= numeral) + noun in apposition."

5.3.1.2. As in other Semitic languages, Classical Ethiopic connects the formally feminine numbers 3–10 with masculine counted nouns and the corresponding formally masculine numbers with feminine nouns, although this tendency is not as regular as in other Semitic languages (§4.3.1.1.), as in ስድስቱ፡ወርኅ *sədəstu warḫ* 'six months' as opposed to ስሱ፡አንስት *səssu ʾanəst* 'six women' (so-called "chiastic concord").

5.3.1.3. All cardinal numbers (including lexemes of the pattern *qətl [§4.3.1.2.]) commonly stand before the counted entity.

The counted entity/entities are in the singular when following the numeral 'one', most often in the plural in connection with the numeral 'two', and in the singular or plural (less often) in connection with the numerals 3–10 and higher.

Examples include: አሐዱ፡ብእሲ *ʾaḥadu bəʾsi* 'one man, a certain man';[235] አሐቲ፡ብእሲት *ʾaḥatti bəʾsit* 'a certain woman, one woman'; አሐዱ፡አምላክ *ʾaḥadu ʾamlāk* 'one God'; አሐዱ፡ዋሕድ *ʾaḥadu wāḥəd* 'the only one' (Jn 1:14);

---

[235] The lexemes አሐዱ *ʾaḥadu* and አሐቲ *ʾaḥatti* often reflect the nuance 'a certain'.

ክልኤተ፡ አኀወ *kəlʾeta ʾaḫawa* '(he saw) two brothers' (Mt 4:18); ሠለስቱ፡ ወርኀ *śalastu warḫ* 'three months'; ሦልስ፡ ሀገር *śəls hagar* 'three cities'; እሉ፡ አርባዕቱ፡ አራዊት፡ ዐበይት *ʾəllu ʾarbāʿtu ʾarāwit ʿabbayt* 'these four great beasts' (Dan 7:17) (counted entities in pl.); ወላዕሌሃ፡ ኀምስቱ፡ ክንፈ፡ የፍ *wa-lāʿlehā ḫaməstu kənfa ʿof* 'there were five wings of a bird upon it' (Dan 7:6); ስሱ፡ አንስት *səssu ʾanəst* 'six women'; እልክቱ፡ ፲ወ፪፡ አባግዕ *ʾəlləktu ʿaśartu wa-kəlʾetu ʾabāgəʿ* 'those twelve sheep' (En 89:13); ወኮነ፡ ለዮሴፍ፡ ዐሠርቱ፡ ወሰባዕቱ፡ ዓመቱ *wa-kono la-yosef ʿaśartu wa-sabāʿtu ʿāmatu* 'when Josef was 17 years old' (Gen 37:2); ሠላሳ፡ ብሩረ *śalāsā bərura* '(they paid) thirty pieces of silver' (Mt 26:15); አርብዓ፡ ዕለተ፡ ወአርብዓ፡ ሌሊተ *ʾarbəʿā ʿəlata wa-ʾarbəʿā lelita* '40 days and 40 nights' (Jub 1:4); ወዐሠርተ፡ ምእተ፡ ብእሴ፡ አስተየ *wa-ʿaśarta məʾta bəʾse ʾastaya* 'he provided a thousand men with something to drink' (Dan 5:1) (numeral and counted entities in acc.); በትእልፊት፡ ቅዱሳን *ba-təʾəlfit qəddusān* '(he comes) with ten thousand holy ones' (En 1:9).

5.3.1.4. Cardinal numbers infrequently follow the counted entity. When they do, the change in word order is often for stylistic reasons, for example to achieve chiastic word order, as in ወጸዊሞ፡ መዋዕለ፡ አርብዓ፡ ወአርብዓ፡ ለያልየ *wa-ṣawimo mawāʿəla ʾarbəʿā wa-ʾarbəʿā layāləya* 'having fasted for 40 days and 40 nights ...' (Mt 4:2); ወርኢኩ፡ አርባዕተ፡ ነፋሳተ ... ወዐርጉ፡ አራዊት፡ አርባዕቱ፡ ዐበይት *wa-rəʾiku ʾarbāʿta nafāsāta ... wa-ʿargu ʾarāwit ʾarbāʿtu ʿabbayt* 'and I saw the four winds ... and four great beasts came up' (Dan 7:2–3).

5.3.1.5. Since cardinal numbers – except the number 'one' – are nouns, they can occur without the counted entity, as in ካልአነ፡ ሰብዓ *kāləʾāna sabʿā* '(he appointed) 70 others' (Lk 10:1).

When cardinal numbers are used with a pronominal suffix, they exhibit the linking vowel /i/ like nouns in the plural, as in ኀምስቲነ *ḫaməstina* 'the five of us'; ሠለስቲሆሙ *śalastihomu* 'the three of them, those three'.

5.3.2. Ordinal Numbers

Ordinal numbers function like attributive adjectives syntactically and thus agree with the counted entity in gender, number, and case according to the agreement rules given above (§5.2.6.1.). They usually precede the counted entity, as in ምሳሌ፡ ሣልስ፡ ዘሄኖክ *məssāle śāləs za-henok* 'the third parable of

Enoch' (En 69:29); ወአመ፡ ሳብዕት፡ ዕለት፡ ሰንበት wa-ʾama sābəʿt ʿəlat sanbat 'the seventh day is the Sabbath' (Jub 50:7); ሠሉስ፡ ሌሊት śalus lelit 'the third night'; መኮንን፡ ውስተ፡ ሣልስት፡ እደ፡ መንግሥትየ makʷannən wəsta śāləst ʾəda mangəśtəya '(he shall be) a dignitary of the third rank (lit. 'hand') in my kingdom' (Dan 5:7; similar 5:29); ራብዓዊ፡ ብእሲ rābəʿāwi bəʾsi 'the fourth man'.

Only the lexeme ቀዳማዊ qadāmāwi 'first' primarily occurs after the counted entity, as in ክፍል፡ ቀዳማዊ kəfl qadāmāwi 'the first chapter' (but በቀዳማዊ፡ ዓመተ፡ መንግሥቱ፡ ለበልጣሰር ba-qadāmāwi ʿāmata mangəśtu la-balṭāsar 'in the first year of the reign of Belshazzar' (Dan 7:1).

In order to achieve chiastic word order, an ordinal number can occur before and after the respective counted entities, as in አርዌ፡ ራብዕ፡ ራብዕት፡ መንግሥት፡ ይእቲ ʾarwe rābəʿ rābəʿt mangəśt yəʾti 'the fourth beast is the fourth kingdom' (Dan 7:23).

In expressions of dates (cf. §4.3.2.3.), the word 'day' is most often left out, as in (በወርኅ፡ ሣልስ፡)አመ፡ ዐሡሩ፡ ወሰዱሱ፡ ለውእቱ፡ ወርኅ (ba-warḫ śāləs) ʾama ʿaśuru wa-sadusu la-wəʾətu warḫ ('in the third month') on the sixteenth of that month' (Jub 1:1); በወርኀ፡ መጋቢት፡ አመ፡ ጽወዘ፡ በዐለተ፡ እሑድ ba-warḫa maggābit ʾama 20-wa-9 ba-ʿalata ʾəḥud 'in the month Maggābit, on the 29th, on Sunday' (Śəna fəṭrat 2); አመ፡ ኃሙሱ፡ ለሠርቅ ʾama ḫamusu la-śarq 'on the fifth of the month/new moon'.

5.4. Syntax of the Verb

For questions and comments regarding the function of Classical Ethiopic verbal categories cf. Weninger (2001). Weninger also considers influences from other languages such as Greek, Arabic, and Amharic on the syntax of Classical Ethiopic in his study, which are primarily the result of (a) mechanical translations of Greek or Arabic originals and (b) the fact that Amharic was the native language of authors composing Classical Ethiopic texts after the Axumite period. From a methodological point of view, Weninger's analysis is based on the so-called 'noetic analysis', which was developed by E. Koschmieder (Slavicist) and A. Denz (Arabist), and which is also referred to as "Koschmieder-Denz tense-system" Because of this methodological approach, Weninger concludes that the verbal system of Classical Ethiopic as a whole is to be interpreted as a relative tense-system. In this system, *qatala* is used for "relative anteriority" and its opposing form *yəqattəl* for "relative simultaneity and posteriority." According to Weninger, the function and use of a verbal form in Classical Ethiopic is dependent on its contextual reference point, which can coincide with the present tense, but does not have to (Weninger 2001, 336).

The functional analysis presented in the following, however, assumes a twofold interpretation of the Classical Ethiopic verbal system: First, an aspectual understanding of the Classical Ethiopic verbal system with two distinguished verbal aspects, a perfective and an imperfective. Perfective aspect presents the verbal action as a whole and thus as viewed from outside. Imperfective aspect is understood as primarily viewing a situation from within, and as looking at the internal structure of a situation.

Secondly, besides aspect, the Classical Ethiopic verbal system also expresses tense, that is the temporal relation of a given utterance and the action or situation described in that utterance. "Tense" constitutes a system with three degrees which can be viewed as either absolute or relative – the latter being the interpretation adopted by Weninger. The absolute tense categories, which have a reference point that is the present moment, distinguish past (preterite), present, and future actions. In relative tense systems, the categories are anterior, simultaneous, and posterior. Relative and absolute systems often do not correspond in subordinate clauses and direct speech, but in most textual examples these two systems do correspond on the surface since the point of reference is the same, namely the present. In this case, anterior and past actions correspond to each other, as do simultaneous and present, and future and posterior actions. Since the following description primarily deals with the use of verbal forms in main clauses, the terms "past," "present," and "future" are used instead of the relational terms used by Weninger. It is further assumed that the Classical Ethiopic system represents an absolute tense system until further proof is provided in favor of an interpretation as relative tense system.

5.4.1. Function of the Perfect

From an aspectual point of view, the Classical Ethiopic perfect serves to express perfective verbal actions or situations. As a tense value, it expresses past tense actions.

5.4.1.1. Perfects for Past Verbal Actions

5.4.1.1.1. The perfect is commonly used as the normative past tense:

- ወከሠተ፡ አፋሁ፡ ወመሀሮሙ wa-kaśata ʾafāhu wa-maharomu 'and he opened his mouth and taught them' (Mt 5:2)
- ሰሚዕክሙ፡ ከመ፡ ተብህለ፡ ለቀደምት samāʿkəmu kama tabəhla la-qaddamt 'you have heard that it was said to those before' (Mt 5:21)
- እስመ፡ ከመዝ፡ ሰደድዎሙ፡ ለነቢያት፡ እለ፡ እምቅድሜክሙ ʾəsma kama-zə sadadəwwomu la-nabiyāt ʾəlla ʾəm-qədmekəmu 'for in the same way they (already) persecuted the prophets before you' (Mt 5:12)

5.4.1.1.2. The perfect can also express the pluperfect. This nuance can only be deducted from context. Examples from main and subordinate clauses include:

- ወከፈለት፡ ንዋየ፡ እምቅድመ፡ ትሙት wa-kafalat nəwāyā ʾəm-qədma təmut 'she had distributed her property before she died' (Jdt 16:24)
- ወነበረ፡ ያዕቆብ፡ ውስተ፡ ምድር፡ እንተ፡ ውስቴታ፡ ነበረ፡ አቡሁ wa-nabara yāʿqob wəsta mədr ʾənta wəstetā nabara ʾabuhu 'and Jacob settled in the land in which his father had lived (before)' (Gen 37:1)
- ወሶበ፡ ርእየ፡ ሄሮድስ፡ ከመ፡ ተሳለቀ፡ ላዕሌሁ፡ ሰብአ፡ ሰገል፡ ተምዕዐ፡ ጥቀ wa-soba rəʾya herodəs kama tasālaqa lāʿlehu sabʾa sagal tamʿəʿa ṭəqqa 'and when Herod saw that the magicians had ridiculed him, he became very angry' (Mt 2:16).

5.4.1.1.3. It further should be noted that in letters the perfect can express verbal actions that lie in the past from the perspective of the person receiving the letter, but that are in the present from the perspective of the sender. In this context, the perfect is commonly called "epistolary perfect." Such perfect forms are, according to the perspective of the sender, to be rendered as present tense in English:

- ወአማኅኩክሙ፡ ጽሒፍየ፡ በእዴየ፡ አነ፡ ጳውሎስ wa-ʾammāḫkukəmu ṣəḥifəya ba-ʾədeya ʾana ṗāwlos 'and I, Paul, greet you (pf), writing myself' (Col 4:18)
- አምኁከ፡ ኵሎሙ፡ እለ፡ ምስሌየ ʾamməḫuka kʷəllomu ʾəlla məsleya 'all those who are with me send greetings to you (pf)' (Titus 3:15)
- ኵሎ፡ ይጤይቀክሙ፡ ቲኪቆስ … ዘፈኖኩ፡ ኀቤክሙ kʷəllo yəṭeyyəqakkəmu tikiqos ... za-fannoku ḫabekəmu 'Tychicus, whom I am sending (pf) to you, will inform you of all' (Eph 6:21)

5.4.1.2. Perfect for Present Tense Verbal Actions

5.4.1.2.1. Verbal actions of the present are, as expected, primarily expressed by the imperfect in Classical Ethiopic. The perfect is only used in a few specific cases for present tense contexts.

5.4.1.2.2. The perfect is used for the general present with verbs of feeling, thinking, believing, knowing, and the like:[236]

- ነሳሕኩ ፡ እስመ ፡ አንገሥኩዎ ፡ ለሳኦል *nassāḥku ʾəsma ʾangaśkəwwo la-sāʾol* 'I regret that I made Saul king' (1 Sam 15:11)
- ወአነሰ ፡ በምሕረትከ ፡ ተወከልኩ *wa-ʾanə-ssa ba-məḥratəka tawakkalku* 'but I trust in your mercy' (Ps 13:5 [12:5])
- ለእለ ፡ አምኑ ፡ በስሙ *la-ʾəlla ʾamnu ba-səmu* 'to those who believe in his name' (Jn 1:12)
- አማን ፡ አእመርኩ ፡ አነ *ʾamān ʾaʾmarku ʾana* 'I truly know (that) ...' (Dan 2:8)

5.4.1.2.3. The perfect is further used for generic expressions and descriptions, often when the Greek original has an aorist:

- ወገብረ ፡ ኃይለ ፡ በመዝራዕቱ *wa-gabra ḥayla ba-mazrāʿtu* 'he does strength (= shows strength) with his arm' (Lk 1:51 [rendering of the Greek aorist])
- ወነሠቶሙ ፡ ለኃያላን ፡ እምናብርቲሆሙ ፡ ወአዕበዮሙ ፡ ለትሑታን *wa-naśatomu la-ḥayyālān ʾəm-nābərtihomu wa-ʾaʿbayomu la-təḥutān* 'he overthrows the powerful from their thrones and lifts up the lowly' (Lk 1:52 [rendering of the Greek aorist])

5.4.1.2.4. The perfect of the verbs of being ሀሎ/ሀለወ *hallo/hallawa* and ኮነ *kona* often has a present meaning but can also be used to express the past tense. Examples of these verbs used wih a present tense meaning include:

---

[236] Cf. Weninger 2001, 75 and 311. Weninger interprets these uses of the perfect as anterior and paraphrases a sentence such as ነሳሕኩ ፡ በእንተ ፡ ፈጢሮትየ *nassāḥku ba-ʾanta faṭirotəya* (Gen 6:7) as 'regret has come over me regarding my creating', which creates an anterior understanding of the perfect (2001, 312). More likely, these instances indicate the process behind the verbal action, that is 'I came to repent = I repent'.

- ወልድ፡ ዋሕድ፡ ዘሀሎ፡ ውስተ፡ ሕፅን፡ አቡሁ wald wāḥəd za-hallo wəsta ḥəḍna ʾabuhu 'the only son who is in the lap of his father' (Jn 1:18)
- ሀሎ፡ አቡነ፡ አብርሃም hallo ʾabuna ʾabrəhām 'our father Abraham' (Lk 3:8)
- ኢኮነ፡ ሠናይ፡ ለእጓለ፡ እመሕያው፡ ይንበር፡ ባሕቲቱ ʾi-kona śannāy la-ʾəgwāla ʾəmmaḥəyāw yənbar bāḥtitu 'it is not good that the man should dwell/be by himself' (Gen 2:18)

5.4.1.2.5. The perfect further serves to express performative utterances, that is, utterances through which an action is performed (such as 'I declare you man and wife'; 'I promise' etc.).[237] Performatives are most commonly attested for first person forms and verbs of speaking (in their broader sense). The perfect in these cases is frequently preceded by the particle ናሁ nāhu 'behold!' (§4.5.6.). In English, a performative notion can be circumscribed by 'hereby' + present tense:

- መሐልኩ፡ በርእስየ maḥalku ba-rəʾsəya 'I hereby swear by myself' (Gen 22:16)
- ወናሁ፡ ፈኖኩከ wa-nāhu fannokuka 'behold, I hereby send you' (Jud 6:14)
- ወናሁ፡ አማሕፅንኩከ፡ ወለትየ wa-nāhu ʾamāḥḍankuka walattəya 'behold, I hereby entrust my daughter to you' (Tob 10:12)
- ናሁ፡ ወሀብክዎ፡ ለእኁኪ፡ ዐሠርተ፡ ምእተ፡ ጠፋልሐ nāhu wahabkəwwo la-ʾəḫuki ʿaśarta məʾata ṭafāləḥa 'behold, I hereby give your brother a thousand pieces of silver' (Gen 20:16)
- ናሁኪ፡ ኮሎ፡ ዘቦ፡ መጠውኩከ፡ ውስተ፡ እዴከ nāhu-ke kwəllo za-bo maṭṭawkuka wəsta ʾədeka 'behold also, everything that belongs to him, I hereby deliver to you (lit. into your hand)' (Job 1:12)

---

[237] See Weninger 2001, 76–81, 310. Weninger tries to explain this function based on the presumed use of the perfect for anteriority by assuming that the point of reference of the speech act does not lie within the speech act itself, since this would imply simultaneity, but at the end of the utterance (Weninger 2001, 310). He has to admit, however, that the use of qatala for performatives is not necessarily derived from its basic notion of expressing anteriority. A more convincing explanation for the use of the perfect for performatives in Classical Ethiopic and across Semitic is that it is connected to the aspectual functions of the perfect.

Less often, performatives are expressed by the imperfect (§5.4.2.1.2.), as in ናሁ፡ እዜንወክሙ፡ ዐቢየ፡ ዜና፡ ፍሥሓ *nāhu ʾəzenəwakkəmu ʿabiya zenā fəśśəḥā* 'behold, I hereby make known news of great joy' (Lk 2:10).[238]

The performative use of the perfect is to be distinguished from the use of the same form in letters (§5.4.1.1.3.), even though both can be rendered as 'hereby' + present tense in English.

5.4.1.2.6. The perfect is often used in the protasis of a real conditional clause and is then rendered by a present tense verb in English, as in እመ፡ ነበርከ፡ ዝየ፡ (ወ)ይረክቡከ *ʾəmma nabarka zəyya / (wa-)yərakkəbuka* 'if you stay here, they will find you' (for more examples, see §6.5.6.).

5.4.1.3. Perfect for Future Verbal Actions

5.4.1.3.1. Present and future tense are, as in other classical Semitic languages, not strictly differentiated in Classical Ethiopic since Classical Ethiopic has not developed a specific verbal form designating future tense. Verbal actions in the future are typically expressed like present tense actions. Consequently, the imperfect is the most common form to express future tense (§5.4.2.2.). In certain cases, however, the perfect is used for future notions.

5.4.1.3.2. The perfect can express future actions in prophetic speech, for example in descriptions of the end of days.[239] In these cases, the perfect is often preceded by an adverbial expression carrying a future connotation, or by the particle ናሁ *nāhu* 'behold!' (cf. the use of the perfect for performative speech acts of the present after ናሁ *nāhu* [§5.4.1.2.5.]):

---

[238] See Weninger 2000. In translated literature from Greek, the imperfect for performatives in Classical Ethiopic reflects the use of the Greek present. The attestations of the imperfect in Classical Ethiopic in these cases are thus most likely reflecting the Greek Vorlage, not original Classical Ethiopic use.

[239] Cf. the so-called "*perfectum propheticum*" in other West Semitic languages. Weninger (2001, 96–98) derives this function in prophetic speech from the presumed notion of relative anteriority. According to him, these usages reflect a stylistic trick: The prophet presumably shows his audience his certain knowledge of future actions by using a past-tense form (Weninger 2001, 96).

- ሕዝብ፡ ዘይነብር፡ ውስተ፡ ጽልመት፡ ርእዩ፡ ብርሃነ፡ ዐቢየ *ḥəzb za-yənabbər wəsta ṣalmat rə'yu bərhāna ʿabiya* 'the people living in darkness will see a great light' (Isa 9:2)

- ወበውእቱ፡ መዋዕል፡ ዓርገት፡ ጸሎተ፡ ጻድቃን *wa-ba-wə'ətu mawāʿəl ʿārgat ṣalota ṣādəqān* 'in those days, the prayer of the just ones will rise' (En 47:1)

- ወናሁ፡ መጽአ፡ በትእልፊት፡ ቅዱሳን *wa-nāhu maṣʾa ba-təʾəlfit qəddusān* 'and behold, he will come with ten thousand holy ones' (En 1:9) (next to an imperfect with future connotation)

5.4.1.3.3. In the compound verbal construction ሀለወ/ሀሎ *hallawa/hallo* + imperfect/jussive (§5.4.5.3.–5.5.), ሀለወ/ሀሎ *hallawa/hallo* can refer to future actions (cf. §5.4.1.2.4.):

- ወዘይመጽእ፡ ሀሎ *wa-za-yəmaṣṣəʾ hallo* 'and that which is to come' (Job 1:26)

- አቅደምኩ፡ ወነገርኩክሙ፡ ከም፡ ሀለውነ፡ ንሕምም *ʾaqdamku wa-nagarkukəmu kama hallawna nəḥməm* 'I foretold you that we were to suffer persecution' (1 Thess 3:4)

- እስመ፡ ሀለዎ፡ ለሄሮድስ፡ ይኅሥሦ፡ ለሕፃን *ʾasma hallawo la-herodəs yəḫśəśo la-ḥəḍān* 'for Herod will search for the child' (Mt 2:13)

5.4.1.3.4. The perfect can further refer to future actions in temporal or conditional subordinate clauses (§6.5.5.–6.; cf. also §5.4.1.2.6.), as in ወእምከመ፡ ቦኡ ... ውስተ፡ ምድር ... ወይተክሉ፡ ደብተራ፡ እግዚአብሔር *wa-ʾəm-kama boʾu ... wəsta mədr ... / wa-yatakkəlu dabtarā ʾəgziʾab(ə)her* 'and when they come ('will have come') into the land ... they are to set up the tabernacle of God' (Jub 49:18); ዘንተ፡ ኵሎ፡ እሁበከ፡ ለእመ፡ ሰገድከ ... ሊተ *zanta kʷəllo ʾəhubakka / la-ʾəmma sagadka ... lita* 'all this I will give to you if you bow down before me' (Mt 4:9).

The perfect can be used in a similar way in other subordinate clauses, as in ወበኀበ፡ ሞትኪ፡ እመውት *wa-ba-ḫaba motki ʾəmawwət* 'wherever you die, I shall die' (Ruth 1:17).

5.4.1.4. The Perfect for Wishes

The use of the perfect for wishes corresponding to Classical Arabic *raḥimahū llāhu* 'may God have mercy on him!' is not attested with certainty in Classical

Ethiopic. The examples given by Dillmann (DL §199e) might also be interpreted as indicatives (e.g., ይሁዳ፡ ሰብሑ፡ አኀዊከ *yəhudā sabbəḥu ʾaḫawika* 'Juda, your brothers shall praise you' or 'Juda, your brothers praise you' Gen 49:8).

For the perfect used to express unreal wishes (in unreal conditional clauses), see §6.5.6.4.–6.5.

5.4.2. The Function of the Imperfect

The imperfect in Classical Ethiopic serves to express imperfective aspect and is thus the aspectual opposite of the perfect. From a tense point of view, it designates verbal actions in the present and future.

5.4.2.1. Imperfect for Present

5.4.2.1.1. Use of general present in main and subordinate clauses:

- ይጸንዕ፡ እምኔየ *yəṣannəʿ ʾəmənneya* 'he is more powerful than I' (Mt 3:11)
- ኢይደልወኒ *ʾi-yədalləwanni* 'it is not suitable for me (to wear sandals)' (Mt 3:11)
- እፈቅድ *ʾəfaqqəd* 'I want (it)' (Lk 5:13)
- ወታበርህ፡ ለኵሎሙ፡ እለ፡ ውስተ፡ ቤት *wa-tābarrəh la-kʷəllomu ʾəlla wəsta bet* 'and it gives light to all in the house' (Mt 5:15)
- ዘየዐቢ፡ እምኔየ *za-yaʿabbi ʾəmənneya* 'the one who is bigger than I'
- እምነ፡ ዕፅ፡ ዘይፈሪ *ʾəmənna ʿəḍ za-yəfarri* 'from the tree that bears fruit' (Gen 3:2)
- ኵሉ፡ ዘያምዕዕ፡ እኅዋሁ *kʷəllu za-yāməʿəʿ ʾəḫwāhu* 'everyone who angers his brother' (Mt 5:22)
- ... እንዘ፡ ኢያአምር፡ ብእሴ ... *ʾənza ʾi-yāʾammər bəʾse* '(how can I be this) since I do not know any man?' (Lk 1:34)

5.4.2.1.2. Imperfect – instead of perfect – for performative speech acts in main clauses (less frequent than use of perfect):

- ወእምሕል፡ በየማንየ *wa-ʾəməḥəl ba-yamānəya* 'I hereby swear with my right hand' (Dtn 32:40) (as opposed to መሐልኩ *maḥalku* in Gen 22:16)
- አየድዕ፡ ዮም፡ ለእግዚአብሔር፡ አምላከየ *ʾāyaddəʿ yom la-ʾəgziʾab(ə)her ʾamlākəya* ... 'Today, I declare to God, my lord ...' (Dtn 26:3)

- አስተበቍዐክሙ፡ አኀዊነ፡ አነ፡ ጳውሎስ ʾastabaqqʷəʿakkəmu ʾaḫawina ʾana p̄āwlos 'I, Paul, beseech you, my brothers ...' (2 Cor 10:1)
- አሜን፡ ናሁ፡ እቤለክሙ ʾamen / nāhu ʾəbelakkəmu 'truly, behold, I say to you'

5.4.2.2. Imperfect for the Future

Examples from main and subordinate clauses:

- ወዘእምድኅሬየሰ፡ ይመጽእ፡ ይጸንዕ፡ እምኔየ wa-za-ʾəm-dəḫreya-ssa yəmaṣṣəʾ yəṣannəʿ ʾəmənneya 'but the one who will come after me is more powerful than I' (Mt 3:11)
- ወትከውኑ፡ ከመ፡ አማልክት wa-təkawwənu kama ʾamāləkt 'you will be like gods' (Gen 3:5)
- ወእቀትለከ፡ ወእመትር፡ ርእሰከ፡ እምኔከ wa-ʾəqattəlakka wa-ʾəmattər rəʾsaka ʾəmənneka 'and I will kill you and cut off your head' (1 Sam 17:46)
- ወትሰጠም፡ ምድር፡ ወኵሉ ... ይትኃጐል፡ ወይከውን፡ ፍትሕ፡ ላዕለ፡ ኵሉ wa-təssaṭṭam mədr wa-kʷəllu ... yətḫāggʷal wa-yəkawwən fətḥ lāʿla kʷəllu 'and the earth will be submerged and everything ... will be destroyed, and there will be judgement upon all ...' (En 1:7)
- ወብእሲትከኒ፡ ኤልሳቤጥ፡ ትወልድ፡ ለከ፡ ወልደ፡ ወትሰምዮ፡ ስሞ፡ ዮሐንስ wa-bəʾasitəka-ni ʾeləsābeṭ təwalləd laka walda wa-təsamməyo səmo yohannəs 'your wife Elisabeth will bear you a son and you shall name him John' (Lk 1:13) (the second imperfect ትሰምዮ təsamməyo has a modal function)
- እስመ፡ እሙንቱ፡ ይሬእይዎ፡ ለእግዚአብሔር ʾasma ʾəmuntu yəreʾəyawwo la-ʾəgziʾabḥer '(blessed are those pure of heart), for they will see God' (Mt 5:8)
- እመ፡ ኢፈድፈደ፡ ጽድቅክሙ ... ኢትበውኡ፡ ውስተ፡ መንግሥተ፡ ሰማያት ʾəmma ʾi-fadfada ṣədqəkəmu ... ʾi-təbawwəʾu wəsta mangəśta samāyāt 'if your righteousness does not exceed ... you will not enter the kingdom of heaven' (Mt 5:20) (imperfect in apodosis)
- ኢትወፅእ፡ እምህየ፡ እስከ፡ ሶበ፡ ትፈዲ፡ ጥዩቀ፡ ኵሎ ʾi-təwaḍḍəʾ ʾəm-həyya ʾəska soba təfaddi ṭəyyuqa kʷəllo 'you will not leave from there until you pay back everything in full' (Mt 5:26) (ትፈዲ təfaddi expresses anteriority in the future)

- እስከ፡የጎልፍ፡ሰማይ፡ወምድር፡የውጣ   ... ኢተጎልፍ፡እምኦሪት ʾəska yaḥalləf samāy wa-mədr yawṭā ... ʾi-taḥalləf ʾəm-ʾorit 'until heaven and earth perish, not a jota ... will pass from the law' (Mt 5:18)

5.4.2.3. Imperfect for Imperfective Aspect in the Past

5.4.2.3.1. The imperfect is often used to express imperfective actions in the past. In these cases, they primarily express general, habitual, pluralic (iterative), and circumstantial actions. Imperfects that designate circumstantial actions either occur asyndetically after the verb they refer to – comparable to Arabic Ḥāl-sentences – or in subordinate clauses that are introduced by እንዘ ʾənza or ሶበ soba.

5.4.2.3.2. Imperfect for general, habitual, and iterative actions in the past:[240]

- ወምድርሰ፡ኢታስተርኢ   ... ወመንፈሰ፡እግዚአብሔር፡ይጼልል፡መልዕለት፡ማይ wa-mədrə-ssa ʾi-tāstarəʾi ... wa-manfasa ʾəgziʾab(ə)her yəselləl malʿəlta māy 'the earth, however, was not (yet) visible ... and the spirit of God was floating over the water' (Gen 1:2)
- ወይነድድ፡ደብሩ wa-yənaddəd dabru '(you stood under the mountain) and that mountain was burning' (Dtn 4:11; similar Dtn 9:15)
- ዘፈቀደ፡ይቀትል፡ወዘፈቀደ፡ይቀሥፍ፡ወዘፈቀደ፡ያከብር za-faqada yəqattəl wa-za-faqada yəqaśśəf wa-za-faqada yākabbər 'he used to kill whom he wanted and to torment whom he wanted and to honor whom he wanted' (Dan 5:19)
- ወውእቱ፡የዐቢ፡እምኵሉ፡አራዊት፡ዘቅድሜሁ wa-wəʾtu yaʿabbi ʾəm-kʷəllu ʾarāwit za-qədmehu 'and it was taller than all the animals before it' (Dan 7:7)
- ይበልዕ፡ወየሐርጽ፡ወዘተርፈ፡ይከይድ፡በእግሩ yəballəʿ wa-yaḥarrəs wa-za-tarfa yəkayyəd ba-əgru 'it was devouring and crushing (everything), and that which was left, it was trampling down with its foot' (Dan 7:7 and 7:19)
- ወተወፅአ፡ጎቤሁ፡ኵሎ፡ኢየሩሳሌም፡ወኵላ፡ይሁዳ ... ወይጠመቁ፡እምጎቤሁ wa-təwaḍḍəʾ ḥabehu kʷəllā ʾiyarusālem wa-kʷəllā yəhudā ... wa-yəṭṭammaqu ʾəm-

---

[240] Cf. Weninger 2001, 109–12, 315. Weninger assumes that this use of the imperfect is derived from its basic function of denoting "relative simultaneity" and that the imperfect expresses a form of background information in these cases. He admits, however, that this is not a necessary analysis of this use of the imperfect (2001, 316). These usages can, however, also simply be explained through the aspectual functions of the imperfect.

ḥabehu 'and all of Jerusalem and all of Juda used to come out to him ... and used to be baptized by him' (Mt 3:4–5)

- ወናሁ፡ ኮከብ ... ይመርሖሙ· wa-nāhu kokab ... yǝmarrǝhomu 'behold, the star ... was guiding them' (Mt 2:9)
- ወይመጽእ፡ ሰብእ፡ ብዙኅ፡ ይስምዕዎ wa-yǝmaṣṣǝʾ sabʾ bǝzuḫ yǝsmǝʿǝwwo 'many people used to come to hear him' (Lk 5:15)
- ሶበ፡ መጽአ፡ እማንቱ፡ አባግዕ፡ ይስተዩ፡ ይፀንሳ soba maṣʾa ʾǝmāntu ʾabāgǝʿ yǝstayā yǝḍannǝsā 'whenever those sheep came to drink, they conceived' (Gen 30:28)
- ወክልኤሆሙ፡ ጻድቃን፡ እሙንቱ ... ወየሐውሩ፡ በኮሉ፡ ትእዛዙ፡ ወኮነኔሁ፡ ለእግዚአብሔር wa-kǝlʾehomu ṣādǝqān ʾǝmuntu ... wa-yaḥawwǝru ba-kʷǝllu tǝʾǝzāzu wa-kʷǝnnanehu la-ʾǝgziʾab(ǝ)her 'and both of them were righteous ... and they were following all the commandments and regulations of God' (Lk 1:6)
- ይሴብሕዎ፡ ለእግዚአብሔር፡ ወይብሉ yǝsebbǝḥǝwwo la-ʾǝgziʾab(ǝ)her wa-yǝbǝlu '(and suddenly there was with the angel a great host of heaven) praising God and saying' (Lk 2:13)
- ወያፈቅሮሙ፡ ኢየሱስ፡ ለማርታ፡ ወለማርያ፡ እኅታ፡ ወለአልዓዛር wa-yāfaqqǝromu ʾiyasus la-mārtā wa-la-māryā ʾǝḫtā wa-la-ʾalʿāzār 'and Jesus loved Martha and Mary, her sister, and Lazarus' (Jn 11:5)
- ወያመጽኡ፡ ድውያነ፡ በዓራታት፡ ወያነብርዎሙ wa-yāmaṣṣǝʾu dǝwwǝyāna ba-ʿārātāt wa-yānbǝrǝwwomu 'and they were bringing out the sick on cots and put them down (so that the shadow of Peter would fall on them when he came by)' (Acts 5:15)

5.4.2.3.3. The imperfect for the notion 'to be about to happen/begin to happen' (for examples from consecutive እስከ ʾǝska-sentences see [§6.5.9.2.]):

- ተእኅዘ፡ ብዙኅ፡ ዓሣት፡ ፈድፋደ፡ እስከ፡ ይትበተክ፡ መሣግሪሆሙ· taʾǝḫza bǝzuḫ ʿāśat fadfāda ʾǝska yǝtbattak maśāgǝrihomu 'so many fish were caught that (lit. 'until') their nets were about to tear' (Lk 5:6)
- ወመልኡ፡ ክልኤሆን፡ አሕማረ፡ እስከ፡ ይሰጥማ wa-malʾu kǝlʾehon ʾaḥmāra ʾǝska yǝssaṭṭamā 'and they filled their two boats until they were about to sink' (Lk 5:7)

5.4.2.3.4. The imperfect for asyndetically connected circumstantial clauses of the past describing simultaneous accompanying actions that are most commonly of durative nature (most commonly following a perfect):

- ወነበሩ፥የዐቅብዎ፥ህየ wa-nabaru yaʿaqqəbəwwo həyya 'they sat there, guarding him' (Mt 27:36)
- ርእየ፥ካልአነ፥ክልኤተ፥አኀወ ... ይሠርዑ፥መሣግሪሆሙ rəʾya kāləʾāna kəlʾeta ʾaḥawa ... yəśarrəʿu maśāgərihomu 'he saw two other brothers ... preparing their nets' (Mt 4:20)
- ወአንሶሰወ፥ኢየሱስ ... ይሜህር ... ወይሰብክ ... ወይፌውስ wa-ʾansosawa ʾiyasus ... yəmehər ... wa-yəsabbək ... wa-yəfewwəs 'and Jesus walked through (Galilee) ... teaching ... preaching ... and healing' (Mt 4:23)

5.4.2.3.5. Imperfect for circumstantial clauses of the past that are either asyndetically connected, connected by ወ- wa-, or introduced by እንዘ ʾənza or ሶበ soba (§6.5.5.1.–5.2.). These cases express what is called "Inzidenzschema" in German, meaning the accompanying action is more immediate than in the cases described in the previous paragraph (e.g., 'I read when he entered'):

- ወኀደረ፥ውስተ፥መቃብር፤ወይመጽኡ፥መላእክት፥ወይዜንውዎ፥በእንተ፥ኩሉ wa-ḥadara wəsta maqābər wa-yəmaṣṣəʾu malāʾəkt wa-yəzennəwəwwo ba-ʾənta kʷəllu 'he lived among the graves when angels were coming and making everything known to him' (ParJer 5:5)
- ወመሀሮሙ፥እንዘ፥ይብል wa-maharomu ʾənza yəbəl 'he taught them, saying' (Mt 5:2)

5.4.2.3.6. In connection with ኮነ kona and ሀለወ/ሀሎ hallawa/hallo, the imperfect likewise serves to express verbal actions of the past (§5.4.5.2.–5.3.).

5.4.2.4. The Use of the Imperfect ይቤ yəbe(lV) 'He Says/Said'

5.4.2.4.1. The form ይቤ yəbe 'he said', with vocalic suffix ይቤል- yəbel- (from bəhla) primarily expresses past tense. This form most commonly, but not exclusively, occurs to introduce direct speech.

5.4.2.4.2. ይቤ yəbe for introducing direct speech in past contexts (not expressing circumstantial action):

- ከማሁ፥ክመ፥ይቤሉ kamāhu kəmma yəbelu 'they spoke thus'
- ዝውእቱ፥ዘእቤለክሙ፥አነ፥በእንቲአሁ zə-wəʾtu za-ʾəbelakkəmu ʾana ba-ʾəntiʾahu 'this was he of whom I told you (thus)' (Jn 1:15)

- ወትቤ ፡ እፎኑ ፡ ዘከመዝ ፡ አምኃ wa-təbe ʾəffo-nu za-kama-zə ʾamməḥā 'and she pondered what sort of greeting this might be' (Lk 1:29) (indirect speech)
- እስመ ፡ አብደ ፡ ይቤለዎ ʾəsma ʾabda yəbeləwwo 'for they were saying of him "he is insane"' (Mk 3:21) (ይቤለዎ yəbeləwwo following a short direct speech)

5.4.2.4.3. ይቤ yəbe for the introduction of direct speech in past contexts expressing circumstantial action (cf. §5.4.2.3.4.), often in connection with another verb of speaking:

- ወአውሥአ ፡ ኢየሱስ ፡ ወይቤ wa-ʾawśəʾa ʾiyasus wa-yəbe 'Jesus answered saying' (Mt 4:4 etc.)
- ከልሐ ፡ ወይቤ kalḥa wa-yəbe 'he cried out saying' (Jn 1:15)
- ወመሰለ ፡ ሎሙ ፡ ብዙኀ ፡ ወይቤሎሙ ፡ እንዘ ፡ ይሜህሮሙ wa-massala lomu bəzuḫa wa-yəbelomu ʾənza yəmehəromu 'and he taught them through many parables and said to them while teaching them' (Mk 4:2)
- ወአኀዙ ፡ የሐልዩ ... ወይቤሉ wa-ʾaḫazu yaḥalləyu (= የኀልዩ yaḥalləyu) ... wa-yəbelu 'and they began to question ... saying' (Lk 5:21)
- ወቀርበ ፡ ዘያሜክሮ ፡ ወይቤሎ wa-qarba za-yāmekkəro wa-yəbelo 'and the tempter approached him, saying' (Mt 4:3)

5.4.2.4.4. ይቤ yəbe for introducing speech in contexts that are not clearly past tense:

- ከማሁ ፡ ይቤ ፡ መጽሐፍ kamāhu yəbe maṣḥaf 'thus says the scripture' (Rom 15:9 etc.)
- በከመ ፡ ይቤ ፡ መጽሐፍ ba-kama yəbe maṣḥaf 'as the scripture says'
- ወካዕበ ፡ ይቤ ፡ መጽሐፍ/ነቢይ wa-kāʿəba yəbe maṣḥaf/nabiy 'and the scripture/the prophet further says' (Rom 15:10 etc.)
- ቦ/ቦቱ ፡ እለ ፡ ይቤሉ/ይብሉ bo/bottu ʾəlla yəbelu/yəbəlu 'there are those who say'
- ቦዘይቤ ... ወቦ ፡ ዘይቤ bo-za-yəbe ... wa-bo za-yəbe 'some say ... and others say ...'

5.4.2.4.5. Other past tense usages of ይቤ *yəbe*:

- ዘይቤሎሙ፡ ለአበዊነ *za-yəbelomu la-ʔabawina* 'that which he said to our fathers' (Lk 1:55)
- ወይቤ፡ ይቅትልዎሙ፡ ለኵሉ፡ ጠቢባነ፡ ባቢሎን *wa-yəbe yəqtələwwomu la-kʷəllu ṭabibāna bābilon* 'and he commanded to kill all the wise men of Babylon' (Dan 2:12)
- ዘከመ፡ ይቤልዎሙ *za-kama yəbeləwwomu* '... (just) as they were told' (Lk 2:20)
- ወይኩነኒ፡ በከመ፡ ትቤለኒ *wa-yəkunanni ba-kama təbelanni* 'let it be to me as you told me' (Lk 1:38)

Note: For the construction ኮነ፡ ይቤ *kona yəbe* (analogous to ኮነ *kona* + perfect), see §5.4.5.6.

5.4.2.4.6. ይቤ *yəbe* in the protasis of conditional clauses (§6.5.6.1.1.) or in a relative clause with a conditional connotation (§6.5.6.6.) in place of a perfect:

- ወእመ፡ ትቤ ... እብል *wa-ʔəmma təbe ... ʔəbəl* 'and when you ask ... I say' (Śəna fəṭrat 4)
- እመቦ፡ ዘይቤለክሙ *ʔəmma-bo za-yəbelakkəmu* 'if anyone says to you' (Mk 13:21)
- ኵሉ፡ ዘያምዕዕ፡ እኁሁ፡ ረስሐ፡ ውእቱ፡ ለኵነኔ፡ ወዘሂ፡ ይቤ፡ እኁሁ፡ ዘዐርቅ፡ ረስሐ፡ ውእቱ፡ ለዐውድ።ወዘሂ፡ ይቤ፡ አብድ፡ ረስሐ፡ ውእቱ፡ ለገሃነም፡ እሳት። *kʷəllu za-yāməʕəʕ ʔəḫwāhu rasḥa wəʔətu la-kʷənnane / wa-za-hi yəbe ʔəḫwāhu za-darq rasḥa wəʔətu la-ʕawd / wa-za-hi yəbe ʔabd rasḥa wəʔətu la-gahānnama ʔəsāt* 'everyone who angers his brother will be liable to judgement; as for the one who says to his brother '(you) ragged one!', he is subject to the council; as for the one who says '(you) fool!', he is subject to the fire of hell' (Mt 5:22)

5.4.2.5. Modal Usages of the Imperfect

5.4.2.5.1. Besides indicative use, the imperfect can also express the modal nuances 'to be able', 'to be allowed', 'to wish/want', and 'must'. In these cases, it can resemble the functions of the jussive (§5.4.3.1.).

5.4.2.5.2. The nuance 'to be able':

- ወክልኤቱ፡ ይሰድድዎሙ፡ ለእልፍ *wa-kəlʾettu yəsaddədəwwomu la-ʾəlf* '... (how) can two drive out ten thousand?' (Dtn 32:30; direct speech)
- በምንትኑ፡ ይትቄሰም *ba-məntə-nu yətqessam* 'with what can it be seasoned?' (Mt 5:13)
- ወአልቦሙ፡ ዘይበልዑ *wa-ʾalbomu za-yəballəʿu* 'they had nothing they could eat' (Mk 8:1)
- እንዘ፡ ምእትኑ፡ ዓመት፡ ሊተ፡ እወልድ *ʾənza məʾət-nu ʿāmat lita ʾəwallǝd* 'can I (still) beget a child being a hundred years old?' (Gen 17:17)

Similar connotations are otherwise expressed by ክህለ *kəhla* 'to be able' + following infinitive (§5.5.1.2.).

5.4.2.5.3. The nuance 'to be allowed':

- እምነ፡ ዕፅ፡ ዘይፈሪ፡ ውስተ፡ ገነት፡ ንበልዕ *ʾəmənna ʿəḍ za-yəfarri wəsta gannat nəballəʿ* 'we may eat from the tree that bears fruit in the garden' (Gen 3:2)

The connotation 'to be allowed' is also expressed by ይከውን *yəkawwən* (most often with object suffixes), as in ይከውን *yəkawwən* 'it is permitted/allowed' (§5.4.9.); ኢይከውነከ *ʾi-yəkawwənakka* 'it is not permitted to you/ you are not allowed'. For general prohibitions in the sense of 'not being allowed', Classical Ethiopic uses ኢ- *ʾi–* + jussive (§5.4.3. and §5.4.4.3.).

5.4.2.5.4. The nuances 'must' and 'should' (often in laws and prohibitions):

- ወእሳትስ፡ በኵሉ፡ ጊዜ፡ ትነድድ ... ወኢይጠፍእ *wa-ʾəsātə-ssa ba-kʷəllu gize tənaddəd ... wa-ʾi-yəṭaffəʾ* 'the fire has to burn at all times ... and must not be extinguished!' (Lev 6:6)
- ሰዱስ፡ ዕለተ፡ ትገብር፡ ግብረ፡ ወአም፡ ሳብዕት፡ ዕለት፡ ስንበት ... ኢትግብሩ፡ ባቲ፡ ኵሎ፡ ግብረ *sadusa ʿəlata təgabbər gəbra wa-ʾama sābəʿt ʿəlat sanbat ... ʾi-təgbaru bātti kʷəllo gəbra* 'six days you will work (impf.), but on the seventh day is the Sabbath ... do not do any work on it (juss.)!' (Jub 50:7)

- መነ፡ ናጸድቅ፡ እምእሉ፡ ወመነ፡ ናሔሱ manna nāṣaddəq ʾəm-ʾəllu wa-manna nāḥessu 'which of those should we believe and which accuse of lying' (Ləbna dəngəl 2)

5.4.2.5.5. The nuance 'wish/want' and 'become'[241] referring to the first person (quasi cohortative function comparable to that of the jussive [§5.4.3.1.2.]):

- እምግብሩ፡ ደኃራዊ፡ ዘንከሥቶ፡ በጊዜሁ፡ ወንጽሐፎ፡ በበ፡ ገጹ ʾəm-gəbru daḫārāwi za-nəkaśśəto ba-gizehu wa-nəṣəḥəfo babba gaṣṣu 'from his later deeds, which we wish to disclose at its proper time, and write down in detail' (Ləbna dəngəl Prologue)
- ወለእመ፡ ክህለ፡ ተቃትሎተየ፡ ወቀተለኒ፡ ንከውነክሙ፡ አግብርተ   wa-la-ʾəmma kəhla taqātəlotəya wa-qatalanni nəkawwənakkəmu ʾagbərta 'and if he is able to fight me and kill me, we will become your servants' (1 Sam 17:9)
- ወባሕቱ፡ እስመ፡ አዘዝከነ፡ ናወርድ፡ መሣገሪነ wa-bāḥ(ət)tu ʾəsma ʾazzazkana nāwarrəd maśāgərina 'however, because you order us, we will let down our nets' (Lk 5:5)
- እሴብሓ፡ ለእግዚአብሔር፡ በሕይወትየ፤ ወእዜምር፡ ለአምላኪየ፡ በአምጣነ፡ ሀለውኩ ʾasebbəḥo la-ʾəgziʾab(ə)ḥer ba-ḥaywatəya wa-ʾazemmər la-ʾamlākiya ba-ʾamṭāna hallawku 'I shall praise the Lord during my life and will sing praises to my lord as long as I am' (Ps 146:2 [145:1])

5.4.2.5.6. The nuance 'to wish/want' and 'should' in connection with third and second persons, primarily in hymns:

- ተአኮቶ፡ ነፍስየ፡ ለእግዚአብሔር taʾakkʷəto nafsəya la-ʾəgziʾab(ə)ḥer 'my soul wants to praise God' (Ps 146:1 [145:1])
- ይገንዩ፡ ለከ፡ እግዚኦ፡ ኩሉ፡ ተግባርከ፤ ይባርኩከ፡ ጻድቃኒከ yəgannəyu laka ʾəgziʾo kʷəllu tagbārəka yəbārrəkuka ṣādəqānika 'all your works shall praise you, your faithful shall bless you' (Ps 145:10 [144:10])
- ነጊሠኑ፡ ትነግሥ፡ ላዕሌነ nagiśa-nu tənaggəś lāʿlena 'do you truly want to rule as king over us?' (Gen 37:8)

---

[241] Future and volitive actions are semantically close.

5.4.3. Functions of the Jussive

The jussive, which is also commonly called "subjunctive" in grammars of Classical Ethiopic, can be used in two main ways, independently in main clauses (§5.4.3.1.) and dependently in subordinate clauses (§5.4.3.2.–3.3.).

5.4.3.1. The Jussive in Main Clauses

5.4.3.1.1. The jussive expresses wishes when used independently in main clauses (declarative and interrogative sentences), that is, it has injunctive force. It is formed of all persons: in the second and third person it functions like a real jussive, in the first person it is equivalent to the cohortative.

The jussive is negated by **ኢ-** *ʾi-*. The negation **ኢ-** *ʾi-* + jussive of the second person can either express direct prohibitions (= negative imperative) or general prohibitions (e.g., in legal texts).[242] The first usage occurs more frequently than the second usage since the imperative cannot be negated by itself, so that the negated jussive serves as the main means to express negated commands (§5.4.4.3.). Instead of **ኢ-** *ʾi-* + jussive, Classical Ethiopic can also use the functionally equivalent construction **አልቦ፡ ዘ-** *ʾalbo za-* + jussive, as in **አልቦ፡ ዘይምጻእ** *ʾalbo za-yəmṣāʾ* 'nobody shall come' (§6.1.4.4.).

The non-negated jussive can be preceded by the proclitic particle **ለ-** *la-* (§4.5.5.). This particle **ለ-** *la-* is relatively frequent with third person jussives, similarly to Classical Arabic *li-yafʿal*.

5.4.3.1.2. The jussive of the first person ("cohortative"):

- **ዘንተ፡ ኵሎ፡ እሁበከ** *zanta kʷəllo ʾəhubakka* 'all these let me give to you!' (Mt 4:9)
- **እኅድግኑ** *ʾəḫdəg-nu* 'shall I stop (producing my oil)?' (Judg 9:9) (interrogative clause)
- **ንግበር፡ ሰብአ** *nəgbar sabʾa* 'let us make man!' (Gen 1:26)
- **ንግበር፡ ሎቱ፡ ቢጸ** *nəgbar lottu biṣa* 'let us make a companion for him!' (Gen 2:18)

---

[242] Classical Ethiopic **ኢ-** *ʾi-* thus corresponds to Hebrew *ʾal* + jussive and *loʾ* + imperfect.

- ንዑ፡ ንንድቅ፡ ሀገረ *nəˁu nəndəq hagara* 'come on, let us build a city!' (Gen 11:4)
- ወንግበር፡ ሠለስተ፡ መኃድረ *wa-nəgbar śalasta maḥādəra* 'let us build three dwellings here!' (Mk 9:5)
- ንሑር፡ ናንሶሱ፡ እስከ፡ ቤተ፡ ልሔም *nəhur nānsosu ʾəska beta ləḥem* 'come on, let us go to Bethlehem' (Lk 2:15)
- ኢ.ንስከብ *ʾi-nəskab* 'let us not lie down' (negated)

5.4.3.1.3. The jussive of the second person:

- ወኪያሁ፡ ባሕቲቶ፡ ታምልክ *wa-kiyāhu bāḥtito tāmlək* 'him alone you shall serve!' (Mt 4:10)
- ኢ.ትፍራሀ *ʾi-təfrāh* 'do not be afraid!' (negated imperative)
- ኢ.ትቅትል፡ ነፍሰ *ʾi-təqtəl nafsa* 'you shall not murder (a soul)' (Mt 5:21) (general prohibition)

5.4.3.1.4. The jussive of the third person (examples with and without proclitic ለ– *la-*):

- ከማሁ፡ ይብራህ፡ ብርሃንክሙ *kamāhu yəbrāh bərhānəkəmu* 'in the same way, let your light shine!' (Mt 5:16)
- ለይኩን፡ ብርሃን *la-yəkun bərhān* 'let there be light!' (Gen 1:3)
- ለይኩን፡ ጠፈር *la-yəkun ṭafar* 'let there be a dome' (Gen 1:6)
- ለታብቍል፡ ምድር፡ ሐመልማለ፡ ሣዕር *la-tābqʷəl mədr ḥamalmāla śāˁr* 'let the earth put forth green vegetation' (Gen 1:11)
- ከመዝ፡ ለይረስየኒ፡ እግዚአብሔር፡ ወከመዝ፡ ለይኩን *kama-zə la-yərassəyanni ʾəgziʾab(ə)ḥer wa-kama-zə la-yəkun* 'let God act thus upon me and let it be thus!' (Ruth 1:17) (context of oath)
- ለትጥፋእ፡ ይእቲ፡ ዕለት፡ እንተ፡ ባቲ፡ ተወለድኩ *la-təṭfāʾ yəʾəti ˁalat ʾənta bātti tawaladku* 'let the day on which I was born perish!' (Job 3:3)
- ለትጽለም፡ ይእቲ፡ ዕለት *la-təṣlam yəʾəti ˁalat* 'let that day be darkness!' (Job 3:3)
- ዘይፈቅድ፡ ያድኅና፡ ለነፍሱ፡ ይግደፋ *za-yəfaqqəd yādḥannā la-nafsu yəgdəffā* 'the one who wishes to save his life, let him cast it away' (Mk 8:35) (variant ይገድፋ *yəgaddəfā* 'will cast it away' [impf.])

- ወሰብእ፡ ዘይገብር፡ ምንተሂ፡ ግብረ፡ ባቲ፡ ይሙት wa-sabʾ za-yəgabbər mənta-hi gəbra bātti yəmut (variant ይመውት yəmawwət [impf.]) 'the man who does any work on it is to die' (Jub 50:8)

5.4.3.2. The Jussive in Final and Consecutive Subordinate Clauses

5.4.3.2.1. The jussive is further used in subordinate clauses that express purpose (= final clause) or result (= consecutive clause). These two types of subordinate clauses are frequently introduced by the conjunction ከመ kama.[243] The use for final and consecutive clauses is the reason why the jussive is commonly designated as "subjunctive" in the standard grammars. In its use for these types of clauses, the jussive of Classical Ethiopic corresponds to the Classical Arabic subjunctive yafʿala.[244]

The jussive frequently occurs, with or without ከመ kama, after the verb ፈቀደ faqada 'to wish, want', after verbs of beginning[245], such as አኀዘ ʾaḫaza[246], ወጠነ waṭ(ṭ)ana, ቀደመ qadama, and after መጽአ maṣʾa. It further occurs after መከረ makara 'to decide', ኀደገ ḫadaga 'to let, allow', አዘዘ ʾazzaza 'to command' (D), ክህለ kəhla 'to be able', ተደለወ tadallawa 'to be prepared, be found worthy', ደለወ dalawa 'to be suitable, fitting', ረትዐ ratʿa to be right', and መፍትው maftəw 'it is fitting, suitable'. These verbs almost function as auxiliary verbs followed by a jussive. In these cases, the jussive is best rendered as an infinitive in English (as in 'he began to speak').[247] Negated subordinated clauses of this type are commonly introduced by ከመ ፡ ኢ- kama ʾi- ('lest').

---

[243] Not all subordinate clauses introduced by ከመ kama have a verb in the jussive. Classical Ethiopic also has ከመ kama-clauses that contain an imperfect or perfect; see §6.5.3.1. and §6.5.8.

[244] There is, however, no reason to separate the category of "jussive" in main clauses from its use in subordinate clauses from a functional perspective.

[245] After verbs that express the notion of "beginning," Classical Ethiopic also employs እንዘ ʾənza + imperfect (§6.5.5.1.), and, less often, the imperfect by itself.

[246] This meaning of አኀዘ ʾaḫaza is, accidentally, not listed in CDG (p. 14).

[247] These nuances can also be expressed by ለ- la- + infinitive (§5.5.1.3.), although the use of the jussive is more frequent.

5.4.3.2.2. Examples of subordinate clauses without ከመ *kama*:

- ወለዘሂ፡ ይፈቅድ፡ ይትዐገልከ፡ ወመልበሰከ፡ ይንሣእ   *wa-la-za-hi   yəfaqqəd yətʿaggalka wa-malbasaka yənśāʾ* 'and as for the one who wishes to take your garment by force …' (Mt 5:40)
- አኀዘ፡ ኢየሱስ፡ ይስበክ፡ ወይበል   *ʾaḫaza ʾiyasus yəsbak wa-yəbal* 'Jesus began to preach and to say' (Mt 4:17)
- ወአዝእብት፡ አኀዙ፡ የአውይዉ.   *wa-ʾazʾəbt ʾaḫazu yaʾawyəwu* 'and the wolves began to moan' (En 89:20) (textual variant with imperfect የአወይዉ *yaʾawayyəwu*)
- ይደልዎ፡ ትግበር፡ ሎቱ፡ ዘንተ   *yədalləwwo təgbar lottu zanta* 'he is worthy that you do this for him' (Lk 7:4)
- ዘኢይደልወኒ፡ እጹር፡ አሣእኖ   *za-ʾi-yədalləwanni ʾəṣur ʾaśāʾəno* 'it is not appropriate for me (= I am not worthy) to carry his sandals' (Mt 3:11)
- አዕረጎ፡ መንፈስ፡ ገዳመ፡ ይትመከር   *ʾaʿrago manfas gadāma yətmakkar* 'the Spirit led him into the wilderness to be tempted' (Mt 4:1)
- ኢመጻእኩ፡ እስዐሮሙ፡ አላ፡ እፈጽሞሙ   *ʾi-maṣāʾku ʾəsʿaromu ʾallā ʾəfaṣṣəmomu* 'I have not come to abolish them (the laws and prophets) but to fulfill them' (Mt 5:17)
- እስመ፡ ተሐውር፡ ቅድመ፡ እግዚአብሔር፡ ትጺሕ፡ ፍኖቶ   *ʾəsma taḥawwər qədma ʾəgziʾab(ə)ḥer təṣiḥ fənoto* 'for you will go before the Lord to prepare his way' (Lk 1:76)
- ወዕለዋንስ፡ መጽኡ፡ ይዕብእዎ፡ ለንጉሥ   *wa-ʿələwānə-ssa maṣʾu yədbəʾəwwo la-nəguś* 'but the heretics began to fight the king' (ʿĀmda Ṣəyon 11c)
- መኑ፡ አመረክሙ፡ ትጕየዩ፡ እምእንተ፡ ትመጽእ፡ መዐት   *mannu ʾammarakəmu təgʷyayu ʾəm-ʾənta təmaṣṣəʾ maʿat* 'who told you to flee from the coming wrath?' (= 'that you can flee') (Mt 3:7)
- ምንተ፡ ትፈቅድ፡ ይስመይዎ   *mənta təfaqqəd yəsmayəwwo* 'what do you want him to be called?' (Lk 1:62)
- ዘይፈቅድ፡ ይፀመደኒ   *za-yəfaqqəd yəḍḍamadanni* 'the one who wishes to bind himself to me' (Mk 8:34)
- ይኄይሰነ፡ ንንበር፡ ዝየ   *yəḥeyyəsanna nənbar zəya* 'it is good for us to stay here' (Mk 9:5)
- አዘዞሙ፡ ኢየሱስ፡ ኢይንግሩ   *ʾazzazomu ʾiyasus ʾi-yəngəru* 'Jesus commanded them not to speak' (Mk 9:9)

5.4.3.2.3. Examples of subordinate clauses with ከመ *kama*:

- ቀርቡ ፡ ከመ ፡ ይስግዱ ፡ ሎቱ *qarbu kama yəsgədu lottu* 'they approached to bow down to him'
- ፈቀደ ፡ ከመ ፡ ይንበር ፡ ህየ *faqada kama yənbar həyya* 'he wished to stay there'
- ኢ.ይደልወኒ ፡ ከመ ፡ እቅረብ ፡ ሎቱ *ʾi-yədalləwanni kama ʾəqrab lottu* 'it is not fitting for me to approach him'
- መፍትው ፡ ከመ ፡ ንቅብሮ *maftəw kama nəqbəro* 'it is necessary that we bury him'
- ዜንዉኒ ፡ ከመ ፡ እምጻእ ፡ አነሂ ፡ ወእስግድ ፡ ሎቱ *zenəwuni kama ʾəmṣāʾ ʾana-hi wa-ʾəsged lottu* 'report to me, so that I may also go and bow to him' (Mt 2:8)
- አብርሆን ፡ ለአዕይንትየ ፡ ከመ ፡ ኢ.ይኑማ ፡ ለመዊት *ʾabrəhon la-ʾaʿyəntəya kama ʾi-yənumā la-mawit* 'give light to my eyes lest they sleep (the sleep) of death' (Ps 13:3 [12:4]) (negated)

5.4.3.2.4. The following peculiarities further have to be noted:

(a) A main clause can be followed by two subordinated clauses containing jussives. In these cases, one of the subordinate clauses can be introduced by ከመ *kama* while the other is not, as in ወውእቱ ፡ መጽአ ፡ ለስምዕ ፡ ሰማዕተ ፡ ይኩን ፡ በእንተ ፡ ብርሃን ፡ ከመ ፡ ኵሉ ፡ ይእመን ፡ ቦቱ *wa-wəʾətu maṣʾa la-səmʿ samāʿta yəkun baʾənta bərhān kama kʷəllu yəʾman bottu* 'he came as testimony, so that he would be a witness to the light, so that all may believe through him' (Jn 1:7).
(b) The subject of the subordinate clause can be anticipated in the main clause, as in ኀደጎ ፡ ለብእሲ ፡ ከመ ፡ ይንበር *ḫadago la-bəʾəsi kama yənbar* 'he allowed the man to stay'; ይሬስያ ፡ ትዘሙ *yəressəyā təzammu* 'he causes her to commit adultery' (Mt 5:32).
(c) The jussive sometimes occurs in subordinate clauses that are not expressing purpose or result, as in ኢ.ኮነ ፡ ሠናይ ፡ ለእጓለ ፡ እመሕያው ፡ ይንበር ፡ ባሕቲቱ *ʾi-kona śannāy la-ʾəgʷāla ʾəm(m)aḥəyāw yənbar bāḥtitu* 'it is not good that the man should live alone' (Gen 2:18; the jussive-clause has the syntactic function of a subject).
(d) In some contexts, it is difficult to determine whether the jussive is used independently or not, as in ወይእዜኒ ፡ ስምዑ ፡ እንግርክሙ ፡ ካዕባ ... *wa-yəʾəze-ni səməʿu ʾəngərkəmu kāʿəbā ...* 'and now hear: let me tell you again/ that I shall tell you again ...' (ʿĀmda Ṣəyon 11c).

5.4.3.3. The Jussive in Other Subordinate Clauses

5.4.3.3.1. The jussive further occurs in subordinate clauses that are introduced by እም(ነ) ʾəm(ənna) 'than' (after comparative expressions), (ዘ)እንበለ (za-)ʾənbala 'before, without, except', and እምቅድመ ʾəm-qədma 'before'. These types of subordinate clauses express results like consecutive ከመ kama-clauses.

5.4.3.3.2. እም(ነ) ʾəm(ənna)-clauses:

- ይኄይሰከ፡ ነቊርከ፡ ትባእ፡ ውስተ፡ ሕይወት፡ እምእንዘ፡ ክልኤ፡ ዐይነ፡ ብከ፡ ትትወደ
  ይ፡ ውስተ፡ ገሃነመ፡ እሳት yəḫeyyəsakka naqqʷārəka təbāʾ wəsta ḥaywat ʾəm-ʾənza kəlʾe ʿayna bəka tətwaday wəsta gahānnama ʾəsāt 'it is better for you to enter life one-eyed than to have two eyes and to be thrown into the fire of hell' (Mt 18:9). The እም(ነ) ʾəm(ənna)-clause is syntactically on the same level as the preceding subordinate clause containing a jussive.

5.4.3.3.3. (ዘ)እንበለ (za-)ʾənbala-clauses:

- ኵሉ፡ ዘየኀድግ፡ ብእሲቶ፡ ዘእንበለ፡ ትዘሙ kʷəllu za-yaḫaddəg bəʾəsito za-ʾənbala təzammu ... 'anyone who divorces his wife, except in the case that she has comitted adultery ...' (Mt 5:32)
- ሥልስ፡ ትክሕደኒ፡ ዘእንበለ፡ ይነቁ፡ ዶርሆ śəlsa təkəḥədanni za-ʾənbala yənqu dorho 'three times you will deny me before the rooster crows' (Mt 26:75)

5.4.3.3.4. እምቅድመ ʾəm-qədma-clauses:[248]

- ወከፈለት፡ ነዋየ፡ እምቅድመ፡ ትሙት wa-kafalat nawāyā ʾəm-qədma təmut 'she distributed her property before she died' (Jdt 16:24)
- እምቅድመ፡ ይትፈጠር፡ ዓለም፡ ፈጠረኒ ʾəm-qədma yətfaṭar ʿālam / faṭaranni 'before the world was created, he created me' (Sir 24:9)

---

[248] The use of the short form of the prefix conjugation after እምቅድመ ʾəm-qədma could theoretically be a vestige of the Proto Semitic preterite, which is formally identical with the jussive. Compare, for example, the use of the preterite in Akkadian subordinate clauses that are introduced by ādi lā or lāma 'before', or the use of the jussive in Classical Arabic after lam and lammā. Tropper assumes that this analysis is unlikely because there presumably are no traces of the original preterite otherwise; for the verbal form ይቤ yəbe, see §4.4.6.5.2.

5.4.4. Functions of the Imperative

5.4.4.1. The imperative is the form that expresses commands and wishes of the second person. In most cases, it is to be rendered as an imperative in English. Less frequently, a translation as 'should/may' + infinitive is more appropriate. When the subject is emphasized, the imperative is followed by a second person personal pronoun:

- ኩን፡ ጠቢበ *kun ṭabiba* 'be wise!' (Mt 5:25)
- ተፈሥሑ፡ ወተሐሠዩ *tafaśśəḥu wa-taḥaśayu* 'rejoice and be glad!' (Mt 5:12)
- አብርሆን፡ ለአዕይንትየ *ʾabrəhon la-ʾaʿyəntəya* 'give light to my eyes!' (Ps 13:4 [12:4])
- ወሑር፡ ቅድመ፡ ተኳነን፡ ምስለ፡ እኁከ፡ ወእምዝ፡ ገቢአክ፡ አብእ፡ አምኃከ *wa-ḥur qadma takʷānan masla ʾaḫuka wa-ʾam-za gabiʾaka ʾabə ʾammaḫāka* 'first go and get reconciled with your brother, and then, having returned, bring your gift' (Mt 5:24)
- ከመዝከ፡ ጸልዩ፡ አንትሙሰ፡ *kama-za-ke ṣalləyu ʾantəmu-ssa* 'pray (mp) in this way!' (Mt 6:9)

5.4.4.2. The imperatives of certain verbs are semantically bleached and are used as sentence-introducing interjections. The imperatives ነዓ/ንዓ/ነዐ *naʿā/nəʿā/naʿa* 'come!' (§4.4.6.4.) and ተንሥእ *tanśəʾ* 'arise!' (§4.4.7.3.), for example, are used in the sense of 'come now!'. They are most commonly followed by another imperative or a first person jussive:

- ንዑ፡ ትልዉኒ *nəʿu taləwuni* 'come, follow (mp) me!' (Mk 1:17)
- ንዑ፡ ንንድቅ፡ ሀገረ *nəʿu nandəq hagara* 'come, let us build a city!' (Gen 11:4)
- ተንሥኢ፡ ብልዒ፡ ሥጋ፡ ብዙኀ *tanśəʾi bələʿi śagā bazuḫa* 'arise, devour many bodies!' (Dan 7:5)[249]

5.4.4.3. The imperative cannot be negated. Instead, Classical Ethiopic uses the negated form of the jussive in the second person, as in Lk 23:28: ኢትብክያኒ፡ ኪያየሰ፡ አላ፡ ብክያ፡ ላዕለ፡ ርእስክን *ʾi-tabkəyāni kiyāya-ssa ʾallā bəkəyā lāʿla raʾsəkən* 'do not weep for me, but weep for yourselves (fp)!' (negated 2fp jussive followed by fp imperative).

---

[249] The jussive ንሑር *naḥur* ('let us go') is used in a similar manner, as in ንሑር፡ ናንሶሱ፡ እስከ፡ ቤተ፡ ልሔም *naḥur nānsosu ʾaska beta laḥem* 'come, let us go to Bethlehem' (Lk 2:15).

5.4.5. Compound Tenses

5.4.5.1. Classical Ethiopic has several verbal constructions that consist of combinations of a verb of existence, mostly in the perfect, followed by a verb in the perfect, imperfect, or jussive. The form of the verb of existence, that is ኮነ *kona* or ሀሎ/ሀለወ *hallo/hallawa* (§4.4.5.8.3.) – very rarely also ነበረ *nabara* (§5.4.5.7.) – agrees with that of the following verb in gender, number, and person. With the imperfect and jussive, these constructions are used to express certain aspectual and modal functions, while ኮነ *kona* + perfect is only attested in late texts. In addition, Classical Ethiopic has constructions of the type ሀሎ፡ቀቲሎ *hallo qatilo* and ነበረ፡ቀቲሎ *nabara qatilo*, that is, a verb of existence followed by a perfective participle, which are also used like a compound tense (§5.5.2.6.).

5.4.5.2. The construction ኮነ *kona* + agreeing imperfect (type *kona yəqattəl*), which is only attested with relative frequency in post-Axumite texts, primarily serves to express imperfective (mostly general) actions of the past (in texts that are translations from Arabic, this construction is used to render the functionally equivalent Arabic construction *kāna yafʿalu*).[250] The construction *kona yəqattəl* further renders inchoative aspect of the past ('he began to kill') in translations from Arabic, most often rendering Arabic *ṣāra yafʿalu*.[251]

- ወፈድፋደሰ፡በምክረ ... ኮነ፡ይትሜገብ፡አሜሃ፡መንበር፡ንጉሣዊ *wa-fadfāda-ssa ba-məkra ... kona yətmeggab ʾamehā manbar nəguśāwi* 'and especially through the counsel of ... the royal throne was being administered' (Ləbna dəngəl 1)[252]
- ወኮነ፡ይትጋደል፡ተጋድሎተ፡ብዙኀ *wa-kona yətgāddal tagādəlota bəzuḫa* 'and he began to fight many (spiritual) struggles' (Sənk. 21. Ḥədār 338:26) (*kona yəqattəl* for inchoative meaning)

---

[250] This nuance can also be expressed by the imperfect alone (§5.4.2.3.).

[251] See Weninger 2001, 287–301; cf. also Bombeck 1997, 11.

[252] Cf. ወአሜሃ፡ትትሜገብ፡መንግሥት፡በትእዛዘ፡ወላዲቱ *wa-ʾamehā tətmeggab mangəśt ba-təʾəzāza walāditu* ... 'at that time, the kingship was directed through the command of his mother ...' (Ləbna dəngəl 1).

5.4.5.3. The construction ሀለወ/ሀሎ *hallawa/hallo* + imperfect (type *hallo yəqattəl* and *yəqattəl hallo*) has functions similar to the imperfect by itself and designates imperfective actions in all tense contexts, although in most cases, it refers to past actions (mostly of a habitual or progressive nature 'he used to do/was doing') and of the (immediate) future ('he is about to do/going to do'). When the imperfect precedes the verb of existence (*yəqattəl hallo*), the construction always has a future reference. In such constructions, the imperfect of ነበረ *nabara* 'to sit, dwell', is very frequent.[253] Furthermore, this construction renders the Greek verb of existence εἰμί + present participle in half of its attestations.[254] In some cases, the construction ሀለወ/ሀሎ *hallawa/hallo* + imperfect can express intention or obligation like the construction ሀለወ/ሀሎ *hallawa/hallo* + jussive (§5.4.5.4.).

(a) Past actions:

- ወሀሎ፡ ዮሐንስ፡ ያጠምቅ፡ በገዳም *wa-hallo yohannəs yāṭamməq ba-gadām* 'John was baptizing in the wilderness' (Mk 1:4)
- ወኲሎሙ፡ ሕዝብ፡ ሀለዉ፡ በምልኦሙ፡ ይጼልዩ፡ በአፍአ *wa-kʷəllomu ḥəzb hallawu ba-məlʔomu yəṣelləyu ba-ʔafʔa* 'all the people together used to pray outside' (Lk 1:10)
- ሀሎ፡ ይሜህሮሙ፡ ወይነብሩ፡ ፈሪሳውያን *hallo yəmeharomu wa-yənabbəru farisāwəyān* … 'he was teaching them, and the Pharisees were sitting …' (Lk 5:17) (ሀሎ *hallo* relates to both imperfects of the sentence)

(b) Present actions:

- ይጽሕፉ፡ ሀለዉ፡ ኲሎ፡ ኃጢአተከሙ፡ በኲሉ፡ ዕለት *yəṣəḥəfu hallawu kʷəllo ḥāṭiʔatakəmu ba-kʷəllu ʿəlat* 'they are writing down all your sins every day' (En 104:7; similarly 98:7)
- … ውስተ፡ ዛሀገር፡ ኀበ፡ ሀለውክሙ፡ አንትሙ፡ ይእዜ፡ ትነብሩ … *wəsta zā-hagar ḫaba hallawkəmu ʔantəmu yəʔəze tənabbəru* '… in this city, in which you are living now' (Acts 7:4)

(c) Future actions:

- ዘይከውን፡ ሀሎ *za-yəkawwən hallo* 'that which will be' (En 52:2)
- ወትሰጠም፡ ሀለወት *wa-təssaṭṭam hallawat* 'it is about to sink (into the abyss)' (En 83:7)

---

[253] The reason for this use might be that ነበረ *nabara* develops into a semantically bleached verb of existence ('to be') throughout the history of Classical Ethiopic.

[254] See Weninger 2001, 278.

- ሀለዉ፡ ዘርእከ፡ ይነብሩ፡ ፈላስያን፡ ብሔረ፡ ነኪር *hallawu zarʔaka yənabbəru falāsəyān bəḥera nakir* 'your descendants will live as strangers in a foreign land' (Acts 7:6)

5.4.5.4. The construction ሀለወ/ሀሎ *hallawa/hallo* + (dative) object suffix + jussive (type *hallawo yəqtəl*) commonly expresses intention, wish, or an obligation. It is often used to render Greek expressions that are compounds containing μέλλω ('to be about to do, be determined, shall') or δεῖ ('it is necessary').[255] The construction further serves to express prophetic renderings of the future.

(a) Intention

- ኀበ፡ ሀለዎ፡ ይባእ *ḫaba hallawo yəbāʔ* '(he sent disciples to the places) where he himself intended to go' (Lk 10:1)
- እስመ፡ ሀለዎ፡ ለሄሮድስ፡ ይኀሥሦ፡ ለሕፃን፡ ከመ፡ ይቅትሎ *ʔəsma hallawo la-herodəs yəḫśəśo la-ḥəḍān kama yəqtəlo* 'for Herod is about to look for the child to kill him' (Mt 2:13)
- ሚሀለወክሙ፡ ትገብሩ *mi-hallawakkəmu təgbaru* 'what will you (intend to) do?' (En 101:2)

(b) Obligation:

- ሀለዎ፡ ለወልደ፡ እጓለ፡ እመሕያው፡ ብዙኀ፡ ያሕምሞ *hallawo la-walda ʔəgʷāla ʔəmmaḥəyāw bəzuḫa yāḥməməwwo* 'the son of man will have to suffer a lot' (Mk 8:31); literally: 'it is determined for him that they will make him suffer' (impersonal construction; §5.4.8.6.).
- አኮ፡ ትትኃብኡ፡ ሀለወክሙ *ʔakko təthābəʔu hallawakkəmu* 'you will not have to hide (on the great day of judgement)' (En 104:5); the jussive is topicalized in this instance (§6.2.4.)

(c) Prophetic oracles (cf. §5.4.5.5.):

- ሀለዎ፡ ለወልደ፡ እጓለ፡ እመሕያው፡ ይግባእ፡ ውስተ፡ እደ፡ ሰብእ *hallawo la-walda ʔəgʷāla ʔəmmaḥəyāw yəgbāʔ wəsta ʔəda sabʔ* 'the son of man is to be delivered into the hand of men' (Mk 9:31; Lk 9:44)
- እስመ፡ አዳም፡ አምሳሉ፡ ውእቱ፡ ለዘሀለዎ፡ ይምጻእ *ʔəsma ʔaddām ʔamsālu wəʔətu la-za-hallawo yəmṣāʔ* 'for Adam is the likeness of the one who was to come' (Rom 5:14)

---

[255] Weninger 2001, 278.

5.4.5.5. The construction ሀለወ/ሀሎ *hallawa/hallo* (without object suffix) + jussive (type *hallo yəqtəl*), which is attested very rarely,[256] has a function similar to the construction *hallawo yəqtəl* (§5.4.5.4.).[257] It primarily expresses future/posterior actions (often in prophetic oracles):

- ትክሉኑ፡ ሰትየ፡ ዘአነ፡ ሀለውኩ፡ ጽዋዐ፡ እስተዪ *təkəlu-nu satəya za-ʾana hallawku ṣawwāʿa ʾəstay* 'are you able to drink the cup that I am about to drink?' (Mt 20:22)
- አቅደምኩ፡ ወነገርኩክሙ፡ ከመ፡ ሀለውነ፡ ንሕምም *ʾaqdamku wa-nagarkukəmu kama hallawna nəḥməm* 'I previously told you that we were to suffer distress' (1 Thess 3:4)
- እለ፡ ሀለዉ፡ ይኩኑ፡ በዕለተ፡ ምንዳቤ *ʾəlla hallawu yəkunu ba-ʿəlata məndābe* '(the chosen and righteous) who must be present on the day of affliction' (En 1:1)
- ወአርአዮ፡ ለንጉሥ... ዘሎ፡ ይኩን፡ በደኃሪ፡ መዋዕል *wa-ʾarʾayo la-nəguś ... za-hallo yəkun ba-daḫāri mawāʿəl* 'and he showed the king ... that which will happen at the end of days' (Dan 2:28 similar 2:29)

5.4.5.6. The construction ኮነ *kona* + agreeing perfect (type *kona qatala*) only developed in the post-Axumite period, most likely in analogy with Classical Arabic *kāna (qad) faʿala*. It is only used rarely and usually represents a typical characteristic of translation literature.[258] It is used to express anteriority of the past (= pluperfect):

- ወካህነሰ፡ ዘኮነ፡ አቀሞ፡ ናምሩድ ... ፈተወ፡ ከመ፡ ይኩን፡ መምህረ፡ ወጠቢበ *wa-kāhənə-ssa za-kona ʾaqamo nāmrud ... fatawa kama yəkun mamhəra wa-ṭabiba* 'the priest, however, whom Namrud had appointed ... wished to become a teacher and wise one' (Gadla ʾAdām 147:20)[259]

The combination ኮነ፡ ይቤ *kona yəbe* can be used in the same manner since ይቤ *yəbe* ('he said') functionally corresponds to a perfect:

---

[256] Weninger (2001, 271–73) only knows ten attestations of this construction.

[257] Weninger (2001, 278) assumes that there is no difference between the two constructions and that they represent functionally equivalent variants.

[258] See Weninger 1999 and 2001, 283–86.

[259] See Weninger 1999, 175.

- እስመ፡ኮነ፡ይቤ፡እግዚአብሔር፡ለቃየል፡እምቀድመ፡ዝንቱ፡ነገር   *ʾəsma kona yəbe ʾəgziʾab(ə)her la-qāyal ʾəm-qədma zəntu nagar* 'for God had said to Cain before this word ...' (Gadla ʾAdām 90:13)[260]

5.4.5.7. The construction ነበረ *nabara* (with the meaning 'he was') + imperfect (type *nabara yəqattəl*) occurs infrequently and is only attested in late texts. It is used like *kona yəqattəl* (§5.4.5.2.) and probably reflects a construction analogous to Amharic *yəqätəl näbbär(ä)* ('he was doing/used to do').

5.4.6. Linked Verbs

"Linked verbs" describes the paratactic sequence of two agreeing verbal forms of the same conjugation type that form a specific semantic unit with each other. "Linked" verbal forms commonly follow each other asyndetically and are only rarely connected by ወ- *wa-* 'and'. Semantically, these constructions correspond to the sequence verbal form + infinitive and verbal form + (ከመ *kama*) + subordinated jussive. The first verbal form can often be rendered adverbially in English. Examples include:

- ደገመ *dagama* 'to repeat' + verb: 'to do again'; ወደገመት፡ወለደቶ፡ለእጉሁ፡ ለአቤል *wa-dagamat waladato la-ʾəḫuhu la-ʾabel* 'and she gave birth again, to his brother, Abel' (Gen 4:2)[261]
- አፍጠነ *ʾafṭana* 'to be fast' + verb: 'to do quickly, hastily'; ከመ፡ያፍጥኑ፡ ወይፃኡ *kama yāfṭənu wa-yəḍāʾu* 'so that they will leave quickly' (En 62:10)
- ገብአ *gabʾa* 'to return' + verb: 'to do again'; ወገብአ፡ወለአከ *wa-gabʾa wa-laʾaka* 'and he sent again'
- ፈጸመ *faṣṣama* 'to complete' + verb: 'to finish/stop doing'; ወፈጺሞ፡ ነጊሮቶሙ፡ቃሎ፡ለሕዝብ *wa-faṣṣimo nagirotomu qālo la-ḥəzb* 'after he had finished speaking his sayings to the people' (Lk 7:1) (linking of two perfective participles)
- ቀደመ *qadama* 'to precede' + verb: 'to do first/previously'; ቀደምኩ፡ በጻሕኩ *qadamku baṣāḥku* 'I arrived first'; አቅደምኩ፡ወነገርኩክሙ፡ከመ ...

---

[260] See Weninger 1999, 175.

[261] ደገመ *dagama* can also be construed with a following infinitive, as in ደገመ፡መጺአ *dagama maṣiʾa* 'he came again'.

ʾaqdamku wa-nagarkukəmu kama ... 'I told you previously that ...' (1 Thess 3:4); **ቅድሙ ፡ በሉ** qədəmu balu 'first say...!' (Lk 10:5)

- **ወድአ** waddəʾa 'to finish' + verb:[262] 'already'; **ወድአ ፡ ዘመወ ፡ ባቲ ፡ በልቡ** waddəʾa zammawa bātti ba-ləbbu '... he has already committed adultery with her in his heart' (Mt 5:28)[263]

- **ተዐገለ** taʿaggala 'to oppress' + verb: 'to do by force'; **ወለዝሂ ፡ ይፈቅድ ፡ ይትዐገልከ ፡ ወመልበሰከ ፡ ይንሣእ** wa-la-za-hi yəfaqqəd yətʿaggalka wa-malbasaka yənśāʾ 'and as for the one who wishes to take your coat by force ...' (Mt 5:40) (two linked jussives that are dependent on the imperfect **ይፈቅድ** yəfaqqəd)

- **ነሥአ** naśʾa 'to take' + **አውሰበ** ʾawsaba 'to marry': 'to take as a wife'; **ወነሥኡ ፡ አዋልዲሆሙ ፡ አውሰቡ** wa-naśʾu ʾawālədihomu ʾawsabu 'they took their daughters as wives' (Judg 3:6)

5.4.7. Verbal Valency and Object Suffixes on the Verb

5.4.7.1. With regard to syntactic valency, Classical Ethiopic distinguishes three main categories of verbs:

1. Monovalent (= intransitive) verbs (verbs that govern a subject but no object)
2. Bivalent (= singly transitive) verbs (verbs with one object)
3. Trivalent (= doubly transitive) verbs (verbs with two objects)

Classical Ethiopic further has verbs that are construed with a prepositional object that is required by the valency of the respective verb, or that are construed with another adverbial complement.

5.4.7.2. Of note are verbs that are trivalent, and among those in particular verbs that take two direct objects. In these cases, both direct objects can stand in the accusative, or one of the objects can be expressed periphrastically by **ለ**- la- (§5.2.3.2.).

---

[262] The verb **ሰለጠ** salaṭa 'to be whole, finished' + verb is used in a similar way.

[263] Cf. however **እስመ ፡ ናሁ ፡ ወድአ ፡ ማሕጸ ፡ ውስተ ፡ ጕንደ ፡ ዕፀው ፡ ይነብር** ʾasma nāhu waddəʾa māḥḍe wəsta gʷənda ʿəḍaw yənabbər 'for behold, the axe is already at the stem of the trees' (Mt 3:10) (**ወድአ** waddəʾa + agreeing imperfect).

(a) Verbs with two accusatives:

- ወርቱዑ፡ ግበሩ፡ መጽያሕቶ wa-rətuʿa gəbaru maṣyāḥto 'make straight his path!' (Mt 3:3)
- ወትጸውዕ፡ ስሞ፡ ኢየሱስሃ wa-təṣawwəʿ səmo ʾiyasus-hā 'and you are to name him "Jesus"' (Mt 1:21)
- ወይጼውዑ፡ ስሞ፡ አማኑኤል wa-yəṣewwəʾu səmo ʾamānuʾel 'they shall name him "Emmanuel"' (Mt 1:23) (without accusative -hā on the personal name)
- አምሰላ፡ ዘማ ʾamsalā zammā 'he thought her to be a prostitute' (Gen 38:15)
- ወንነሥእ፡ አዋልዲክሙ፡ ለነ፡ አንስቲያ wa-nənaśśəʾ ʾawālədikəmu lana ʾanəstiyā 'we will take your daughters as our wives' (lit. 'as wives for us'; with additional indirect object) (Gen 34:16)

(b) Verbs with one accusative and a second periphrastic accusative:

- ወሰመዮ፡ እግዚአብሔር፡ ለውእቱ፡ ጠፈር፡ ሰማየ wa-samayo ʾəgziʾab(ə)her la-wəʾətu ṭafar samāya 'and God called that dome Sky' (Gen 1:8)
- ወለምእላዲሁ፡ ለማይ፡ ሰመዮ፡ ባሕረ wa-la-məʾəllādihu la-māy samayo bāḥra 'and the gathering place of the water he called Sea' (Gen 1:10)
- ወአልበሰዎ፡ ሜላተ፡ ለዳንኤል wa-ʾalbasəwwo melāta la-dānʾel 'and Daniel was clothed in fine linen' (Dan 5:29)

5.4.7.3. Object suffixes on verbs most commonly function as accusatives and designate the direct object. With some verbs, however, they express the indirect (dative) object or other functions that alternatively can be expressed by prepositional phrases.

The types of verbs that can take dative suffixes or suffixes expressing other prepositional phrases can be divided into several categories: 1. Verbs of giving and surrendering (ወሀበኒ፡ ኅብስት wahabanni ḫəbəsta 'he gave me bread'; corresponds to ወሀበ፡ ሊተ፡ ኅብስት wahaba lita ḫəbəsta); 2. verbs of speaking and addressing (ነገሮ፡ ዘንተ nagaro zanta 'he told him this'); 3. verbs of asking (ሰአለኒ፡ ኅብስት saʾalanni ḫəbəsta 'he asked me for bread'; corresponding to ሰአለ፡ ኅብስተ፡ እምኔየ/ኃቤየ saʾala ḫəbəsta ʾəmənneya/ḫabeya); 4. verbs of motion such as መጽአ maṣʾa 'to come' and በጽሐ baṣḥa 'to arrive' when they mean 'to befall, to happen to' (በጽሐኒ፡ መዋዕለ፡ ምንዳቤ baṣḥanni mawāʿəla məndābe 'days of affliction befell me'), 5. verbs of stealing and depriving (ነሥአኒ ፡ ወርቀየ *naśʾanni warqəya* 'he took my money/gold from me'); 6. the verb ኮነ *kona* (ወእከውኖሙ ፡ አምላክ ፡ ወእሙንቱኒ ፡ ይከውኑኒ ፡ ሕዝብየ *wa-ʾəkawwənomu ʾamlāka wa-ʾəmuntu-ni yəkawwənuni ḥəzbəya* 'and I will become their god [lit. 'their God for them'], and they will become my people [lit. 'my people to/for me']' (Jub 1:17); ይኩንክሙ ፡ ገብረ *yəkunkəmu gabra* 'he must be a slave for you' (Mk 10:43); ኢይከውነከ *ʾi-yəkawwənakka* 'it is not permitted to you' = 'you are not allowed' (Mk 6:18); ኢኮነ ፡ ውሉዳ *ʾi-konəwwā wəludā* 'she had no (more) children' [lit. 'her children did not exist for her'] (Mt 2:18)); and 7. some others, such as በከየቶ *bakayato* 'she mourned over him'.

5.4.7.4. Classical Ethiopic also has verbal forms, like Akkadian and Classical Arabic, which can govern two pronominal suffixes.[264] The first suffix designates the indirect, the second the direct object (for the specific suffix forms, see §4.1.2.3.):

- ናሁ ፡ መጠውኩካሁ *nāhu maṭṭawku-kā-hu* 'behold, I hereby deliver him to you' (Job 2:6)
- ሀበኒየ *hab-anni-yā* 'give her to me!' (Gen 29:21)
- ወሀብኩካሁ *wahabku-kā-hu* 'I have given it to you' (Num 18:8)
- አወፍየኒዮ *ʾawaffəy-anni-yo* 'I will hand him over to you' (Gen 42:37)

5.4.8. Passives and Periphrastic Passive Constructions

5.4.8.1. Passives in Classical Ethiopic are primarily expressed by the *t*-stems (Gt, Dt, Lt). The stems with prefixed *asta-* on the other hand, never have passive function (§4.4.4.5.). Passives are further often circumscribed by impersonal constructions in Classical Ethiopic (§5.4.8.6.).

5.4.8.2. The direct object of an active construction is promoted to subject position in passive constructions and stands in the nominative (= non-accusative; but cf. also §5.4.8.5.). The agent is not commonly expressed in passive constructions:

- ይትቀደስ ፡ ስምከ *yətqaddas səməka* 'hallowed be your name!' (Mt 6:9)

---

[264] See Gensler 1998, 245.

- ... እስመ፡ እሙንቱ፡ ውሉደ፡ እግዚአብሔር፡ ይሰመዩ ... *ʾəsma ʾəmuntu wəluda ʾəgziʾab(ə)ḥer yəssammayu* '... for they will be called the children of God' (Mt 5:9)
- ብፁዓን፡ መሐርያን፡ እስመ፡ እሙንቱ፡ ይትመሐሩ *bəḍuʿān maḥārəyān ʾəsma ʾəmuntu yətmaḥaru* 'blessed are the merciful for they will be shown mercy' (Mt 5:7)

5.4.8.3. When the agent is expressed, it is indicated by a prepositional phrase, usually the preposition እም-/እምነ *ʾəm-/ʾəmənna* or compound prepositions including እም-/እምነ *ʾəm-/ʾəmənna* (such as እምኀበ *ʾəm-ḫaba*, እምላዕለ *ʾəm-lāʿla*). Less often, the agent is expressed by በ- *ba-* or በኀበ *ba-ḫaba*:

- እስከ፡ ሶበ፡ ሐመር፡ ይሴወር፡ እምነ፡ ሞገድ *ʾəska soba ḥamar yəssewar ʾəmənna mogad* '... until the boat was covered by the waves' (Mt 8:24)
- አዕረጎ፡ መንፈስ፡ ገዳመ፡ ይትመከር፡ እምኀበ፡ ዲያብሎስ *ʾaʿrago manfas gadāma yətmakkar ʾəm-ḫaba diyābəlos* 'the spirit led him into the wilderness to be tempted by the devil' (Mt 4:1)
- እስመ፡ ዘእምላዕሌሃ፡ ይትወለድ *ʾəsma za-ʾəm-lāʿlehā yətwallad* 'for (the child) that will be born by her' (Mt 1:20)
- ወይትመሰዉ፡ ከመ፡ መዓረ፡ ግራ፡ እምላህብ *wa-yətmassawu kama maʿāra gərā ʾəm-lāhb* 'they will be melted like wax by a flame' (En 1:6)
- ብርዐኑ፡ ዘይትሐወስ፡ እምነፋስ *bərʿa-nu za-yətḥawwas ʾəm-nafās* '(what did you see?) A reed that is moved by the wind?' (Lk 7:24)
- ተበልዑ፡ እምኵሎሙ፡ አራዊተ፡ ገዳም *tabalʿu ʾəm-kʷəllomu ʾarāwita gadām* 'they were devoured by all the wild animals' (En 89:57)
- ዘተብህለ፡ እምኀበ፡ እግዚአብሔር፡ በነቢይ *za-tabəhla ʾəm-ḫaba ʾəgziʾab(ə)ḥer ba-nabiy* 'that which had been spoken by God through the prophet' (Mt 1:22)
- ወይትወሐጡ፡ ወይትኃጕሉ፡ በውእቱ፡ ማይ *wa-yətwaḥāṭu wa-yətḫāggʷalu* (for ይትህጕሉ *yəthaggʷalu*) *ba-wəʾatu māy* '... and they were swallowed up and destroyed by that water' (En 89:5)
- ... ወኢይትዐቀጹ፡ በኃጢአቶሙ ... *wa-ʾi-yətʿaqaṣu ba-ḫāṭiʾatomu* 'lest they be trapped by their sins' (Jub 1:21)

The preposition ለ- *la-* can have a similar function, as in ዘኢይትመዋእ፡ ለፀር *za-ʾi-yətmawwāʾ la-ḍar* 'the one who is undefeated by the enemy'.

5.4.8.4. Doubly transitive verbs (§5.4.7.2.) retain the second accusative in passive constructions:

- ተመህረ፡ ሕገ *tamahara ḥagga* 'he was taught the law' (as opposed to ተመህረ፡ ሕግ *tamahara ḥagg* 'the law was taught')
- ሕጹጸ፡ ይሰመይ ... ዐቢየ፡ ይሰመይ፡ በመንግሥተ፡ ሰማያት *ḥaṣuṣa yassammay ... ʿabiya yassammay ba-mangaśta samāyāt* 'he will be called the least ... he will be called great in the heavenly kingdom' (Mt 5:19)
- እንተ፡ ላቲ፡ ተሠየምኩ፡ አነ፡ ላእከ *ʾanta lātti taśayamku ʾana lāʾka* '(the church) for which I was appointed servant' (Col 1:25)
- አላ፡ ዮሐንስ፡ ይሰመይ *ʾallā yoḥannas yassammay* 'but he shall be called John (= acc.)' (Lk 1:60)

5.4.8.5. As mentioned above, the direct or indirect object of an active verb is promoted to subject position in the passive and consequently appears in the nominative (cf. §5.4.8.2.). In some cases, however, the accusative occurs in such instances, as in the following examples:

- ወተውህበ፡ ሎቱ፡ መባሕተ *wa-tawahba lottu mabāḥta* (variant መባሕት *mabāḥt*) 'he was given dominion' (lit. 'dominion was given to him') (Dan 7:6)
- ወመንግሥተ፡ ወምኮናን፡ ወዐበየ ... ተውህበ፡ ለቅዱሳነ፡ ልዑል *wa-mangaśta wa-makwannāna wa-ʿabaya ... tawahba la-qaddusāna laʿul* 'kingdom, dominion, and greatness ... were given to the holy ones of the Most High' (Dan 7:27)

5.4.8.6. Classical Ethiopic further frequently employs an impersonal construction containing a 3mp verbal form that stands for an unspecified subject and that is rendered by a passive construction in English. It should be noted, however, that this construction is not passive in Classical Ethiopic in itself, and that its "passive" connotation solely results from its translation value.

- ብእሲት፡ እንተ፡ ደሐረዋ *baʾasit ʾanta daḥarawwā* 'a women they divorced' = 'a divorced woman'
- ብፁዓን፡ አንትሙ፡ ሶበ፡ ይሰድዱክሙ፡ ወይዘነጉጉክሙ *baḍuʿān ʾantamu soba yasaddadukamu wa-yazanaggwagukamu* 'blessed are you when you are

persecuted and reviled' (lit. 'when they persecute and revile you') (Mt 5:11)

- እስመ፡ከመዝ፡ሰደድዎሙ፡ለነቢያት *ʾəsma kama-zə sadadəwwomu la-nabiyāt* 'for in the same way the prophets were persecuted' (Mt 5:12)
- ወይቤ፡ይቅትልዎሙ፡ለኵሉ፡ጠቢባነ፡ባቢሎን *wa-yəbe yəqtələwwomu la-kʷəllu ṭabibāna bābilon* 'and he commanded to have all the wise men of Babylon killed' (Dan 2:12)
- ለእንተ፡ይብልዋ፡መካን *la-ʾənta yəbələwwā makkān* 'for her, who they used to say was barren' (Lk 1:36)
- ሀለዎ፡ለወልደ፡እጓለ፡እመሕያው፡ብዙኅ፡ያሕምምዎ *hallawo la-walda ʾagʷāla ʾəmmaḥəyāw bəzuḫa yāḥməməwwo* 'the son of man will undergo much suffering' (Mk 8:31) (lit. 'it is determined for him that they will make him suffer a lot' [§5.4.5.4b])

5.4.9. Impersonal Usages of 3ms Verbal Forms

Impersonal subjects can further be expressed by a 3ms verbal form in Classical Ethiopic. Examples include: ይጸብሐ *yəṣabbəḥ* 'it became morning'; ኮነ *kona* 'it is' (e.g., ዘኮነ፡ከዊኖ/ከዊና *za-kona kawino/kawinā* 'whatever it is/will be'); ኮነ/ይከውን *kona/yəkawwən* 'it is permitted/allowed' (often with a dative suffix, as in ኢይከውነከ፡ታውስብ፡ብእሲተ፡እኁከ *ʾi-yəkawwənakka tāwsəb bəʾəsita ʾəḫuka* 'you are not allowed to marry your brother's wife' Mk 6:18); ኮነ/ይከውን *kona/yəkawwən* 'it is sufficient' (cf. ኮነየ *konəya* 'it is enough for me'); ይመስል *yəmassəl* and ያስተርኢ *yāstarəʾi* 'it seems'; ይሤኒ *yəśenni* 'it is good'; አከለ/የአክል *ʾakala/ya'akkəl* 'to suffice' (e.g., አከለኒ *ʾakalanni* 'it was enough for me'); ዐጸበ *ʿaṣaba* 'it is difficult' (e.g., ዐጸበኒ *ʿaṣabanni* 'it was (too) difficult for me'); ይሰአን *yəssaʾan* (Gt) 'it is impossible' (often with dative suffix); ይበቍዕ *yəbaqqʷəʿ* 'it is useful'; ይጸሀቀኒ *yəṣəhəqanni* 'I am in want' (lit. 'it is in want for me'); ይደልወኒ *yədalləwanni* 'it is fitting for me'; ሄስ/ይኅይስ/ይኄይስ *hesa/yəḫayyəs/yəḥeyyəs* 'it is suitable' (e.g., ሄሰኒ *hesanni* 'it is suitable for me').

The perfective participle with 3ms pronominal suffix is likewise used impersonally, as in ጸቢሖ *ṣabiḥo* 'when it became morning' (§5.5.2.8.).

5.5. The Functions of Verbal Nouns and Verbal Adjectives

5.5.1. The Infinitive

5.5.1.1. The infinitive is a verbal noun that lies in between the nominal and verbal system from a functional perspective in that it can be construed both nominally and verbally (§5.5.1.5.–1.6.).

5.5.1.2. The infinitive most commonly appears as a verbal complement in the accusative. Verbs that are followed by an infinitive in the accusative include **ክህለ** *kəhla* 'to be able', **ስእነ** *sə'na* 'to be unable', **ከልአ** *kal'a* 'to prevent', **አበየ** *'abaya* 'to refuse', **ረስዐ** *ras'a* 'to forget', **ፈርሀ** *farha* 'to fear', **ኀደገ** *ḫadaga* 'to cease, quit', **አፍቀረ** *'afqara* 'to love', **አስተናሥአ** *'astanāśə'a* 'to provoke, arouse', and **ኀደገ** *ḫadaga* 'to leave, permit'. Other sentence elements can stand in between the verb and infinitive:

- **ወኢክህልኩ፡ ርእዮቶሙ** *wa-'i-kəhəlku rə'əyotomu* 'I was unable to see them' (En 89:6)
- **ወተአቢ፡ ተናዘዞ** *wa-ta'abbi tanāzazo* 'she refuses to be consoled' (Mt 2:18)
- **ብዙኀኒ፡ ይክል፡ አውሕዶ፡ ወኀዳጥኒ፡ ይክል፡ አብዝኆ** *bəzuḫa-ni yəkəl 'awḥədo wa-ḫədāṭa-ni yəkəl 'abzəḫo* 'the many he can make few (lit. one), and the few he can make many'
- **ኢትክል፡ ሀገር፡ ተኀብአ፡ እንተ፡ መልዕልተ፡ ደብር፡ ትነብር** *'i-təkəl hagar taḫabə'o 'ənta mal'əlta dabr tənabbər* 'a city that lies on the top of a mountain cannot be hidden' (Mt 5:14)
- **እስመ፡ ኢትክል፡ አሐተ፡ ሥዕርተ፡ ርእስከ፡ ጸዐዳ፡ ረስዮ፡ ወኢአጽልሞ** *'əsma 'i-təkəl 'aḥatta śə'ərta rə'səka ṣa'adā rassəyo wa-'i-'aṣləmo* 'for you cannot make one hair of your head white or black' (Mt 5:36)
- **ያፈቅሩ፡ በመኳርብት ... ቀዊም፡ ወጸልዮ** *yāfaqqəru ba-mak"ārəbt ... qawima wa-ṣalləyo* 'in the synagogues they love ... to stand and pray' (Mt 6:5)

Certain verbs with a following infinitive are best rendered adverbially in English, such as **ቀደመ** *qadama* 'to do first' (e.g., **ቀደምኩ፡ በጺሐ** *qadamku baṣiḥa* 'I arrived first'), **ደገመ** *dagama* 'to do again' (e.g., **ደገመ፡ መጺአ** *dagama maṣi'a* 'he came again'), **አፍጠነ** *'afṭana* 'to be quick, do quickly', **ኀበረ/ኀብረ** *ḫab(a)ra* 'to do jointly', **አብዝኀ** *'abzəḫa* 'to increase, do often', **ጐንደየ** *g"andaya* 'to be/do late'.

These verbs can also be followed by a second verb of the same verbal conjugation as the main verb instead of an infinitive (see "linked verbs" §5.4.6.), as in ደገመ፡መጽአ *dagama maṣ'a* 'he came again'.

5.5.1.3. After certain verbs, the infinitive is commonly preceded by the preposition ለ- *la-*:

- ዘአስተናሥአነ፡መንፈሰ፡እግዚአብሔር፡ለወጢነ፡ዝንቱ፡መጽሐፍ *za-'astanāśə'-anna manfasa 'əgzi'ab(ə)ḥer la-waṭina zəntu maṣḥaf* 'the spirit of God impelled us to begin this book' (*Ləbna dəngəl* Prologue); the logical object is in the genitive after the preposition (§5.5.1.6.).
- ወይኩኑ፡ለአብርሆ፡ውስተ፡ጠፈረ፡ሰማይ *wa-yəkunu la-'abrəho wəsta ṭafara samāy* 'they shall illuminate the dome of the sky' (Gen 1:15)

The expression ለ- *la-* + infinitive is also used without a main verb, seemingly with ellipsis of the verb ኮነ *kona* 'to be', in the sense of 'to be about to do/happen' (relatively frequent after ሶበ *soba*), as in ዝናም፡ለመጺእ *zənām la-maṣi'* 'rain is about to fall'; ሶበ፡ለሐዊራ፡ይቤላ *soba la-ḥawirā yəbelā* 'when she was about to go, he said to her' (with a pronominal suffix on the infinitive to indicate the subject [cf. §5.5.1.8.]).

5.5.1.4. The infinitive can also follow other prepositions. In this case, it has a stronger nominal function. The use of በ- *ba-* with an infinitive is often encountered for instrumental and similar connotations:

- ወፈጠረ፡ብርሃነ፡በብሂሎቱ *wa-faṭara bərhāna ba-bəhilotu* 'he created the light through (his) speaking' (infinitive with pronominal suffix [§5.5.1.8.])
- እንዘ፡ውእቱ፡ማዕከለ፡ነዊም፡ወነቂህ *'ənza wə'ətu māʿkala nawim wa-naqih* 'as he (Adam) was between sleeping and awakening' (*Śəna fəṭrat* 32)

5.5.1.5. To be noted is further the formulaic expression ዝውእቱ፡ብሂል *za-wə'ətu bəhil* 'that/it means', where the infinitive ብሂል *bəhil* 'to say' functions as the predicate of a nominal clause. ብሂል *bəhil* can also occur twice in such constructions, as in ብሂለ፡ሰኑይኒ፡ብሂል፡ውእቱ *bəhila sanuyə-ni 2 bəhil wə'ətu* 'and *sanuy* (= Monday) means 'two'' (lit. 'the meaning of *sanuy* means 'two'') (*Śəna* *fǝṭrat* 9); ወእሐድ ፡ ብሂል ፡ ፩ብሂል ፡ ውእቱ *wa-ʾǝḥud bǝhil 1 bǝhil wǝʾǝtu* 'and *ʾǝḥud* (= Sunday) means 'one'" (*Śǝna fǝṭrat* 3).

5.5.1.6. Since the infinitive is a verbal noun, the object of a transitive verb is not commonly expressed by the accusative but by a construct chain in which the infinitive is in the construct and is followed by a noun (= direct object) in the genitive (§5.2.4.1.):

- አስተናሥአነ ... ለወጢነ ፡ ዝንቱ ፡ መጽሐፍ *ʾastanāśǝʾanna* ... *la-waṭina zǝntu maṣḥaf* '(the spirit of God) impelled us to begin this book' (*Lǝbna dǝngǝl* Prologue)
- በእንተ ፡ አጠይቆተ ፡ ሠናያቲሁ ... ወበእንተ ፡ አይድዖተ ፡ ኃይል ፡ ወመዊእ *ba-ʾǝnta ʾaṭayyǝqota śannāyātihu* ... *wa-ba-ʾǝnta ʾaydǝʿota ḫāyl wa-mawiʾ* '... to inform about his good works ... and to make known the strength and dominion' (*Lǝbna dǝngǝl* Prologue)

5.5.1.7. When the object precedes the infinitive, however, it does stand in the accusative (verbal use of the infinitive). Similarly, the object tends to be in the accusative when it does not immediately follow the infinitive but occurs later in the sentence:

- ታአምሩ ፡ ሠናየ ፡ ሀብተ ፡ ውሂበ ፡ ለውሉድክሙ *tāʾammǝru śannāya habta wǝhiba la-wǝludǝkǝmu* '(if) ... you know to give good gifts to your children' (Mt 7:11)
- ነፍስክሙ ፡ ኢይክሉ ፡ ቀቲለ *nafsakǝmu ʾi-yǝkǝlu qatila* 'they cannot kill your souls' (Mt 10:28)
- ዘይክል ፡ ወስከ ፡ እምዲበ ፡ ቆሙ ፡ እመተ ፡ አሐተ *za-yǝkǝl wassǝko ʾǝm-diba qomu ʾǝmata ʾaḥatta* 'the one who can add a cubit to his height' (Mt 6:27) (object at end of sentence)

5.5.1.8. Pronominal suffixes on the infinitive most commonly function as objects, as in አበዩ ፡ ቀቲሎቶ *ʾabayu qatiloto* 'they refused to kill him'. In this case, the suffixes have the form of suffixes attached to nouns in the accusative. The object suffix that semantically refers to the infinitive can also be transferred to the verb without any change in meaning, as in አበይዎ ፡ ቀቲለ *ʾabayǝwwo qatila* ('they refused to kill him').

Pronominal suffixes on the infinitive can also, however, express the logical subject. In this case they have the form of suffixes attached to nouns in the nominative (= non-accusative), as in ቀቲሎትከ *qatilotəka* 'your killing', በክዮቱ *bakəyotu* 'his weeping', unless the infinitive is syntactically in the accusative. In the latter case, they have the forms ቀቲሎተከ *qatilotaka*, በክዮቶ *bakəyoto* [§4.4.3.3.2.]), ሶበ፡ ለሐዊራ *soba la-ḥawirā* 'when she was about to go', etc.

5.5.2. The Perfective Participle

5.5.2.1. The perfective participle – also referred to as "gerund" in grammars of Classical Ethiopic – has an active or passive meaning depending on the verbal stem in which it occurs. In translations from Greek, the PP renders the Greek aorist participle, which most commonly has an active meaning. The peculiarity of the Classical Ethiopic PP is that it always occurs in combination with pronominal suffixes that express the Agent.[265]

The PP can only be translated into English periphrastically. In most cases, it is best rendered by a temporal subordinate clause that expresses anteriority (§4.4.3.2.3.).

5.5.2.2. As mentioned in the previous paragraph, the Classical Ethiopic PP primarily expresses anteriority, that is, it expresses the fact that the verbal action denoted by the PP is completed before the verbal action of the following main verb. When the PP is used with verbs designating mental states, such as 'to fear', 'to wish', 'to know', 'to remember', etc., it expresses circumstantiality in the past. This circumstantial notion, however, is the result of its function of denoting anterior actions (e.g., 'he, having known/gotten to know' = 'he knew'). It is further used as a stylistic device for backgrounding.[266] Examples include:

---

[265] Dillmann (DG 398 [§181]) thought that the PP is, in rare cases, attested without a pronominal suffix and referred to Gen 2:2: ወኮሎ፡ ዓለም፡ ፈጸመ፡ እግዚአብሔር፡ ገቢረ፡ ግብሮ *wa-kʷəllo ʿālama faṣṣama ʾəgziʾab(ə)ḥer gabira gəbro* 'the whole world he completed, doing his work'. According to Weninger (2001, 38), the form ገቢረ *gabira* is rather to be interpreted as an infinitive (in the form of an adverbial accusative). As Weninger points out, no other convincing examples of a presumed use of the PP without pronominal suffix have been brought forth (ibid.).

[266] See Weninger 2001, 330.

- ወአንቢበሙ፡ ወፅኡ፡ ውስተ፡ ደብረ፡ ዘይት wa-ʾanbibomu waḍʾu wəsta dabra zayt 'having sung, they went out to the Mount of Olives' (Mk 14:26) (anterior action)
- ወአርመምኩ፡ ፈሪህየ፡ ከመ፡ እንግርከሙ፡ ዘእሔሊ wa-ʾarmamku farihəya kama ʾəngərkəmu za-ʾəḥelli 'I kept silent, having feared to tell you what I was thinking' (Job 32:6)

5.5.2.3. The PP most often stands before an asyndetically following verbal clause. If the subject is indicated by a noun, the noun commonly follows directly after the PP and is syntactically part of the PP clause, not of the following main clause. The direct object and adverbial expressions often precede the PP:

- ወነቢሮ፡ ቀርቡ፡ ኀቤሁ፡ አርዳኢሁ wa-nabiro qarbu ḫabehu ʾardāʾihu 'he, having sat down, his disciples approached him' (Mt 5:1)
- ወተጠሚቆ፡ ኢየሱስ፡ ሶቤሃ፡ ወፅአ፡ እምማይ wa-taṭamiqo ʾiyasus sobehā waḍʾa ʾəm-māy 'Jesus having been baptized, immediately when he came out of the water ...' (Mt 3:16)
- ወዘንተ፡ ሰሚዓ፡ ንግሥት፡ ትቤ wa-zanta samiʿā nəgəśt təbe 'the queen having heard this, she said' (*Kəbra Nagaśt* 20 a 21)

The main clause is only connected by ወ- wa- sporadically, as in ወጸዊሞ፡ መዋዕለ፡ አርብዓ፡ ወአርብዓ፡ ለያልየ፡ ወእምድኀረዝ፡ ርኅበ wa-ṣawimo mawāʿəla ʾarbəʿā wa-ʾarbəʿā layāləya wa-ʾəm-dəḫra-zə rəḥba 'having fasted forty days and forty nights, afterwards he was famished' (Mt 4:2).

5.5.2.4. In fewer cases, the PP occurs asyndetically after a main verbal clause, as in ዐርበ፡ ፀሐይ፡ በጺሐሙ፡ ገባአ ʿarba ḍaḥay baṣiḥomu gabāʾā 'the sun set, they, having arrived at Gibea (= 'after they had arrived')' (Judg 19:14).

5.5.2.5. The PP can further be used predicatively, as a so-called predicative accusative (cf. §5.2.3.1d), as in ረከቡኒ፡ ነቢርየ፡ ህየ rakabuni nabirəya həyya 'they found me as one who sat down there' = 'they found me seated there'.

Special notice has to be given to the predicative use of PPs following ሀለወ/ሀሎ hallawa/hallo, as in ሀለወ፡ ነዊሞ hallawa nawimo 'he was sleeping'. This construction (type *hallo qatilo*), which is only attested in post-Axumite texts, is used like a compound tense, often in the sense of 'he just did something' and 'he already did something' (§5.4.5.1.).[267] The even less frequently occurring construction that is only attested in late texts *nabara qatilo* has a similar function, as in ነበረ፡ ተሪፎ *nabara tarifo* 'he was staying/stayed'. The latter construction is clearly an analogical development based on the Amharic construction PP + *näbbär(ä)*.[268]

5.5.2.6. The PP cannot carry an object suffix in addition to the suffix indicating the subject or Agent of the verbal action. It can, however, govern a direct object, either in the form of an accusative or a prepositional phrase introduced by ለ- *la-*:

- ቀቲሎ፡ ብእሴ *qatilo bəʾəse* 'he, having killed the man …'
- ወበጊዜሃ፡ ኅዲጎሙ፡ ሓመረ፡ ወአባሆሙ፡ ተለዉዎ *wa-ba-gizehā ḫadigomu ḥamara wa-ʾabāhomu talawǝwwo* 'immediately, having left the boat and their father, they followed him' (Mt 4:22)
- በጺሖሙ፡ ገባአ *baṣiḥomu gabāʾā* 'after they arrived at Gibea' (Judg 19:14)

5.5.2.7. PPs are generally not negated. Respective connotations are circumscribed by subordinate clauses introduced by ሶበ *soba* or እንዘ *ʾǝnza* (§6.5.5.1.–5.2.).

5.5.2.8. The PP with a pronominal suffix of the 3ms can, like 3ms finite verbal forms (§5.4.9.), be used impersonally, as in ጸቢሖ *ṣabiḥo* '(it) having dawned …'; መሲዮ *masiyo* 'after it became evening'; ከረምተ፡ ከዊኖ *kǝramta kawino* 'it having become winter/after it had become winter'.

5.5.3. The Agent Noun *qatāli*

5.5.3.1. The agent noun *qatāli* (G-stem) and its corresponding forms in the derived verbal stems are the closest Classical Ethiopic has to an active participle.[269] Agent nouns are primarily used to designate professions and similar connotations. (Classical Ethiopic also uses the pattern *qattāl* [§4.2.14:3] for terms of professions, as in ገባር *gabbār* 'workman'.)

---

[267] See Weninger 2001, 279–82.

[268] Weninger 2001, 306.

[269] The morpheme type *qātəl* < *qātil* (§4.2.1.3:8) that frequently occurs as an active participle in other Semitic languages is not used in this function in Classical Ethiopic.

5.5.3.2. The agent noun is usually construed nominally and only very rarely verbally, unlike real participles. Since it is used as a noun, the logical object follows in the genitive while the agent noun is in the construct, as in ፈጣሬ፡ ምድር *faṭāre mədr* 'the creator of the earth'; ጸሓፌ፡ ዝንቱ፡ መጽሐፍ *ṣaḥāfe zəntu maṣḥaf* 'the scribe of this book'; አምጻኢተ፡ ሞት *ʾamṣāʾita mot* '(Eve,) bringer of death' (*Śəna fəṭrat* 32).

Much less frequently, the agent noun is construed verbally with the object occurring in the accusative, as in ሰአሊ፡ ሕይወተ *saʾāli ḥaywata* 'he who asks for (his) life'.

5.5.3.3. Many verbs do not have a productive form *qatāli* (or its equivalent). In these cases – and also frequently otherwise – a relative clause of the type *za-yəqattəl* (relative pronoun + third person imperfect) is used instead of an agent noun (§5.1.5d).

5.5.4. The Verbal Adjective *qətul*

Substantivized verbal adjectives of the type *qətul* (§4.2.1.3:3) – and their corresponding forms in the derived stems – are always construed nominally, even when their basic meaning is transitive. The logical object follows in the form of a genitive, as in እኁዛነ፡ ወልታ፡ ወኵናት *ʾəḫuzāna waltā wa-kʷināt* 'the carrier of shield and spear'.

5.5.5. Other Verbal Nouns

All verbal nouns, except the infinitive, behave like nouns syntactically. To be further noted is their use in paranomastic constructions ("figura etymologica"). In this construction type, a verbal noun in the adverbial accusative is coordinated with a finite verbal form of the same root and corresponding verbal stem. The verbal noun usually follows the finite verb and is often modified by an adjectival attribute. This construction results in a stronger emphasis on the verbal action:

- ተፈሥሑ፡ ፍሥሓ፡ ዐቢየ *tafaśśəḥu fəśśəḥā ʿabiya* 'they rejoiced greatly' (lit. 'they rejoiced a great joy') (Mt 2:10)
- ወፈርሁ፡ ዐቢየ፡ ፍርሀት *wa-farhu ʿabiya fərhata* 'they were very afraid' (Lk 2:9)

- ተምዕዐ፡ ንጉሥ፡ ዐቢያ፡ መዐተ tamə'ə'a nəguś 'abiya ma'ata 'the king became very angry' (Dan 2:12)

5.6. Expression of Distributive Connotations: በበ babba, ለለ lalla, ዘዘ– zazza–, and others

5.6.1. The lexemes በበ *babba*, ለለ *lalla* and ዘዘ– *zazza–* developed through the repetition of ለ– *la–* (preposition), በ– *ba–* (preposition), and ዘ– *za–* (determinative pronoun). The consonantal gemination is of secondary nature. According to the traditional pronunciation, the first consonant is likewise articulated as geminated when preceded by ወ– *wa–* or ዘ– *za–*, that is ዘበበ *zabbabba*, ዘለለ *zallalla*, ወዘዘ *wazzazza*; this gemination is not indicated in the transliterations in this grammar. በበ *babba* and ለለ *lalla* are considered independent lexemes while ዘዘ– *zazza–* is always treated proclitically in the orthography and written together with the following lexeme.

ለለ *lalla* can take pronominal suffixes, in which case it has the basic form ለሊ–*lalli–*. In this use, the form functions as the emphasizing nominative independent pronoun, as in ለሊሁ *lallihu* 'concerning him, he himself' (§4.1.3.1.).

5.6.2. The lexemes በበ *babba*, ለለ *lalla*, and ዘዘ– *zazza–* express distributive connotations of በ– *ba–*, ለ– *la–*, and ዘ– *za–* respectively: 'in/by each', 'for/to each', '(that) of each'. The basic functions of the particles are not always semantically transparent, however. This is especially true for በበ *babba*. ለለ *lalla* is also used as a conjunction with the meaning 'whenever' (§4.5.3.2.).

5.6.3. Examples of the use of በበ *babba*:

- ወሖረ፡ ኮሉ፡ ሰብእ፡ ይጸሐፍ፡ በበ፡ ሀገሩ *wa-ḥora kʷəllu sabʾ yəṣṣaḥaf babba hagaru* 'and every man went in his own town to be registered' (Lk 2:3)
- ኮሉ፡ በበዘመኑ *kʷəllu babba-zamanu* '(the heavenly luminaries) each at its (proper) time' (En 2:1)
- አሐዘከሙ፡ ሀለዉ፡ በበሕዘቢሆሙ፡ አሐዱአሐዱ፡ በበሥልጣኖሙ፡ ወበበዘመኖሙ *ʾaḥadu ʾaḥadu za-kama hallawu babba-ḥəzabihomu ʾaḥadu ʾaḥadu babba-śəlṭānomu wa-babba-zamanomu* 'each (of the heavenly luminaries), as they are, according to their classes, according to their rule and their times each' (En 72:1)

- ዘይዘራእ ፡ ዘርኡ ፡ ዘበበዘመዱ ፡ ወበበአርአያሁ *za-yǝzzarrā ʔ zarʔu za-babba-zamadu wa-babba -ʔarʔayāhu* '(vegetation) that bears seeds, each according to its kind and each according to its appearance' (Gen 1:12, similar 1:11)
- ወተካሀለ ፡ ምስለ ፡ ገባእት ፡ በበ ፡ ዲናር ፡ ለዕለት *wa-takāhala mǝsla gabāʔt babba dinār la-ʕǝlat* 'he agreed with the workers on one dinar each for the day' (Mt 20:2)
- ወነሥኡ ፡ በበ ፡ ዲናር ፡ እሙንቱሂ *wa-naśʔu babba dinār ʔǝmuntu-hi* 'they received (only) a dinar each' (Mt 20:10)
- ወወሀቦሙ ፡ ዐራዘ ፡ በበ ፡ ክልኤቱ *wa-wahabomu ʕarrāza babba kǝlʔetu* 'he gave them each two garments' (Gen 45:22)

The following frequently occurring phrases require special notice: በበ ፡ አሐዱ *babba ʔaḥadu* 'one after the other' (e.g., ወአኀዙ ፡ ይበሉ ፡ በበ ፡ አሐዱ *wa-ʔaḥazu yǝbalu babba ʔaḥadu* 'they began to speak, one after the other' Mt 26:22); በበ ፡ እብሬቶሙ *babba ʔǝbretomu* 'each in turn'; በበ ፡ ንስቲት *babba-nǝstit* and በበ ፡ ሕቅ *babba-ḥǝqq* 'little by little, gradually'; በበ ፡ ገጹ *babba gaṣṣu* 'in detail' and ('chapter by chapter' =) 'in turn' ; በበ ፡ ጸታሁ *babba ṣotāhu* 'in the right sequence/order'; በበ ፡ መዓርግ *babba maʕārǝg* 'according to the right degree/rank'; በበ ፡ ብሔሩ *babba bǝheru* 'in each of their lands' = 'in many countries'; በበዓመቱ *babba-ʕāmatu* 'each year'; በበዓሙ *babba-ʕāmu* 'yearly'.

Instead of በበ *babba* + noun, Classical Ethiopic can also repeat single በ- *ba-* + noun, as in ፈጠሮሙ ፡ በሠርክ ፡ በሠርክ *faṭaromu ba-śark ba-śark* 'he created each of them in the evening' (*Śǝna faṭrat* 23).

5.6.4. Examples of the use of ለለ *lalla* (except as a conjunction [§4.5.3.2.]) include:

- ሲሳየነ ፡ ዘለለ ፡ ዕለትነ ፡ ሀበነ ፡ ዮም *sisāyana za-lalla ʕǝlatǝna habanna yom* 'our daily bread give us this day!' (Mt 6:11)
- ለለ ፡ አሐዱ ፡ በከመ ፡ ይክሉ *lalla ʔaḥadu ba-kama yǝkǝlu* '(he gave) ... each according to their abilities' (Mt 25:15)
- ወለለ ፡ ፩፩እምኔሆሙ ፡ ዘዚአሁ ፡ ኅብሩ *wa-lalla 1 1 (ʔaḥadu ʔaḥadu) ʔǝmǝnne-homu zazza-ziʔahu ḫǝbru* (= ሕብሩ *ḥǝbru*) 'and each of them had its own appearance' (Dan 7:3)

- ዘለላ፡ ዚአሁ፡ ሕማሞሙ ... *za-lalla ziʾahu ḥəmāmomu* '(they brought all the sick,) each of whom had his own disease' (Mt 4:24)
- ወለላ፡ ፩ምግባሮሙ *wa-lalla ʾaḥadu məgbāromu* 'and the deeds of each of them (I wrote down)' (En 13:6)

5.6.5. Examples of the use of ዘዘ- *zazza-* (ዘዘ- *zazza-* frequently occurs in combination with ዚአ- *ziʾa-* + pronominal suffix 'his own') include:

- አዕኑግ፡ ዘወርቅ፡ ዘዘሕልቅ፡ ድልወቱ *ʾaʿnug za-warq zazza-ḫəlq dəlwatu* 'golden earrings weighing one ounce each' (lit. 'its weight one ounce each')
- ክላሰስቲክሙ፡ ዘዘዚአክሙ *kalāsəstikəmu zazza-ziʾakəmu* 'the sheaves of each of you' (Gen 37:7)
- ወይፈልጦሙ፡ ዘዘ፡ ዚአሆሙ *wa-yəfalləṭomu zazza ziʾahomu* 'he will distinguish them one from another' (Mt 25:32)

5.6.6. Distributive nuances are also expressed by syndetically (ወ- *wa-*) or asyndetically connected repetitions of lexemes. A few examples include:

- Repetition of cardinal numbers, as in አሐዱ፡ አሐዱ *ʾaḥadu ʾaḥadu* 'every one, each one'; ሰባዕት፡ ሰባዕት *sabāʿt sabāʿt* 'seven each' (see §4.3.7.).
- በኵሉ፡ ዓመት፡ ወዓመት *ba-kʷəllu ʿāmat wa-ʿāmat* 'in each and every year' (lit. 'in each year and year') (Jub 49:8)
- ሕገገ፡ ጊዜ፡ ወጊዜ፡ በበ፡ ኩፋሌ፡ መዋዕሊሁ *ḥəgaga gize wa-gize babba kufāle mawāʿəlihu* 'laws for each time in every division of its times' (Jub 50:13)

6. Syntax

6.1. The Nominal Clause

A nominal clause, or better, verbless clause, is a clause that has a non-verbal predicate. The predicate in this case can consist of a noun, a pronoun, a nominal construction (such as a prepositional phrase), or an adverb. Nominal clauses express states. They are usually to be understood as declarative clauses but can also function as interrogative clauses or clauses expressing wishes.

6.1.1. Nominal Clauses Consisting of Two Elements (Clauses without Copula)

6.1.1.1. Nominal clauses in Classical Ethiopic commonly consist of either two or three main elements (§6.1.2.). Less frequent are sentences that only have a single nominal element (§6.1.9.).

A nominal clause with two elements contains a subject (subj. or S) and the nominal predicate (pred. or P). The subject is the given or known information, while the predicate represents the new information, that is, that which is said about the subject. If the predicate is a simple noun or an adjective, it stands in the nominative (or non-accusative) like the subject. A predicative adjective agrees with the subject in gender and number when the subject is animate. Inanimate subjects do not necessarily exhibit strict agreement. The normative and most frequent word order in two-element nominal clauses is P-S. This order occurs significantly more often than the order S-P (§6.1.3.1.). The latter, less frequent order S-P is specifically indicated in the following examples.

6.1.1.2. Nominal clauses with a noun as predicate:

- መሬት፡ አንተ maret ʾanta 'you are dust' (Gen 3:19)
- እስመ፡ መሠግራን፡ እሙንቱ ʾəsma maśaggərān ʾəmuntu 'for they were fishermen' (Mt 4:18)
- አነ፡ ለሊየ፡ ፈርዖን ʾana lalliya farʿon 'I (myself) am Pharaoh' (Gen 41:44) S-P (§5.1.3.1b)
- ወመንፈቃ፡ እገሪሁ፡ ኀጺን፡ ወመንፈቁ፡ ልሕኲት wa-manfaqa ʾəgarihu ḫaṣṣin wa-manfaqu ləḥək*t 'and one part of his feet was (made of) iron and one part was clay' (Dan 2:33) (materials are otherwise more commonly expressed by the determinative pronoun [§6.1.1.7.])

281

6.1.1.3. Nominal clauses with a possessive or interrogative pronoun as predicate:

- ዚአነ፡ ማይ *zi'ana māy* 'the water is ours' (Gen 26:20)
- ምንተ፡ ተግባርክሙ *mənta tagbārəkəmu* 'what is your occupation?' (Gen 46:33)
- መኑ፡ ውእቱ *mannu wə'ətu* 'who is he?' (En 46:2)

6.1.1.4. Nominal clauses with an adjectival predicate:

(a) The subject consists of a personal pronoun that follows the subject:
- ብዙኃን፡ ንሕነ *bəzuḫān nəḥna* 'we are many' (Mk 5:9)
- ብፁዓን፡ አንትሙ *bəḍuʿān 'antəmu* 'blessed are you' (Mt 5:11 etc.)
- እስመ፡ ጕጕአን፡ ንሕነ *'əsma gʷəgguʾān nəḥna* 'for we are zealous'
- ወብፅዕት፡ አንቲ *wa-bəḍəʿt 'anti* 'blessed are you (fs)' (Lk 1:45)

(b) The subject is another nominal phrase:
- ማእረሩ-ስ፡ ብዙኅ፡ ወገባሩ፡ ኅዳጥ *mā'raru-ssa bəzuḫ wa-gabbāru ḫədāṭ* 'his harvest is plentiful, but his laborers are few' (Lk 10:2) S-P
- ዐቢይ፡ እግዚአብሔር፡ ወብዙኅ፡ አኮቴቱ *ʿabiy 'əgzi'ab(ə)ḥer wa-bəzuḫ 'akkʷatetu* 'God is great, and his praise is plentiful' (Ps 145:3 [144:3])
- ምንትኑ፡ ሕዙናን፡ ገጽክሙ፡ ዮም *məntə-nu ḥəzunān gaṣṣəkəmu yom* 'why are your faces so downcast today?' (Gen 40:7)

6.1.1.5. Nominal clauses with a construct chain as predicate:

- ወልደ፡ መኑ፡ አንተ *walda mannu 'anta* 'whose son are you?' (1 Sam 17:58)
- አምላከ፡ ሕያዋንኪ፡ ውእቱ *'amlāka ḥəyāwānə-ke wə'ətu* 'he is the Lord of the living' (Mt 22:32)
- ... ርሑቀ፡ መዐት፡ ወብዙኀ፡ ምሕረት ... *rəḥuqa maʿat wa-bəzuḫa məḥrat* '(God is merciful and compassionate), forbearing and abounding in mercy' (Ps 145:8 [144:8])

6.1.1.6. Nominal clauses with an adverbial (adverb or preposition) predicate:

- ምስሌነ፡ እግዚአብሔር *məslena 'əgzi'ab(ə)ḥer* 'God is with us'
- ወውስቴቱ፡ አዕይንት *wa-wəstetu 'aʿyənt* 'and there were eyes in it' (Dan 7:8)

- ኀቤየ፡ ውእቱ ḫabeya wəʾətu 'he is with me' (Gen 29:34)
- ወሰይፍ፡ ምሉኅ፡ ውስተ፡ እዴሁ wa-sayf məluḫ wəsta ʾədehu 'a drawn sword was in his hand' (Josh 5:13) S-P
- ከመ፡ ኆጻ፡ ባሕር፡ ብዝኆሙ kama ḫoṣā bāḥr bəzḫomu 'their number was like the sand of the sea' (Josh 11:4)
- ወከመዝ፡ ፍካሬሁ wa-kama-zə fəkkārehu 'and this is its interpretation' (Dan 5:26)
- ወክነፊሃኒ፡ ከመ፡ ንስር wa-kənafihā-ni kama (variant: ከመዝ kama-za) nəsr 'and its wings were like those of an eagle' (Dan 7:4) S-P
- አይቴ፡ አንተ ʾayte ʾanta 'where are you?' (Gen 3:9)
- እምአይቴ፡ ሎቱ፡ ዝንቱ፡ ኵሉ ʾəm-ʾayte lottu zəntu kʷəllu 'from where does he have all this?' (Mk 6:2) (basic two-element structure, extended by an element in the dative)

6.1.1.7. Nominal clauses with a determinative phrase as predicate:

- ርእሱ፡ ዘወርቅ rəʾəsu za-warq 'its head was of gold' (Dan 2:32) S-P
- ዘእግዚአብሔር፡ አነ za-ʾəgziʾab(ə)ḥer ʾana 'am I (in the place of) God?' (Gen 50:19)

6.1.1.8. Nominal clauses with several predicates:

- መሓሪ፡ ወመስተሣህል፡ እግዚአብሔር፤ ርሑቅ፡ መዐት፡ ወብዙኅ፡ ምሕረት፡ ወጻድቅ maḥari (for maḥāri) wa-mastaśāḥəl ʾəgziʾab(ə)ḥer rəḥuqa maʿat wa-bəzuḫa məḥrat wa-ṣādəq 'God is merciful and compassionate, forbearing, and abounding in mercy and justice' (Ps 145:8 [144:8])

6.1.2. The nominal Clause with Three Elements (Clauses with a Copula)

6.1.2.1. A nominal clause with three elements consists of a subject, a predicate, and another independent sentence element that is traditionally called a "copula." The copula expresses the predicative relationship, or nexus, between the subject and predicate. Classical Ethiopic primarily uses personal pronouns, most frequently third person singular pronouns (ውእቱ wəʾətu and ይእቲ yəʾəti) as copulae.

The subject can precede or follow the predicate (§6.1.3.2.), that is, both S-P and P-S orders are possible. The copula either stands between the two main sentence elements (subject and predicate) or, less often, at the end of the sentence. The sentence 'John is a prophet' can thus be expressed by ዮሐንስ፡ ውእቱ፡ ነቢይ *yoḥannəs wəʾətu nabiy* or ዮሐንስ፡ ነቢይ፡ ውእቱ *yoḥannəs nabiy wəʾətu*.

Subject and predicate agree in the same manner as in a nominal clause with two elements (§6.1.1.1.). The copula agrees with the subject in gender and number when animate in principle, as in ዝንቱ፡ ውእቱ፡ ወልደ፡ ንጉሥ *zəntu wəʾətu walda nəguś* 'this is the king's son'; ዛቲ፡ ይእቲ፡ ወለተ፡ ንጉሥ *zātti yəʾəti walatta nəguś* 'this is the king's daughter'; እሉ፡ እሙንቱ፡ ውሉደ፡ ንጉሥ *ʾəllu ʾəmuntu wəluda nəguś* 'these are the king's sons', although even in these cases the 3ms pronoun ውእቱ *wəʾətu* has a tendency to appear as a gender and number neutral copula. When the subject is a first or second person pronoun, the copula is usually a third person singular pronoun, as in አነ፡ ውእቱ፡ ንጉሥ *ʾana wəʾətu nəguś* 'I am the king'; አንትሙ፡ ውእቱ፡ ጻድቃን *ʾantəmu wəʾətu ṣādəqān* 'you are just'. Classical Ethiopic also exhibits the sentence-type አነ፡ ንጉሥ፡ አነ *ʾana nəguś ʾana* 'I am the king', where the repetition of the pronoun marks strong emphasis on the subject. This sentence-type can also be understood as a pendens construction (§6.3.) ('as for me, I am the king').

6.1.2.2. Nominal clauses with three elements are more frequent in Classical Ethiopic than those with two elements. They are particularly used when the information conveyed could otherwise be syntactically or semantically ambiguous. Nominal clauses with fronted subjects thus mostly contain three elements. Clauses that have a demonstrative pronoun or relative pronoun as the subject always contain a copula, as in ዝንቱ፡ ውእቱ፡ ንጉሥ *zəntu wəʾətu nəguś* 'this is the king' (as opposed to ዝንቱ፡ ንጉሥ *zəntu nəguś* 'this king'). Nominal clauses that have a personal pronoun as the subject that follows the predicate – often occurring with adjectival predicates – on the other hand, frequently consist of the two-element type (type እኩይ፡ ውእቱ *ʾəkkuy wəʾətu* 'he is evil').

6.1.2.3. Nominal clauses with a noun as predicate:

(a) The subject is a noun:
- ወእግዚአብሔር፡ ውእቱ፡ ቃል *wa-ʾəgziʾab(ə)her wəʾətu qāl* 'and the word was God' (Jn 1:1)
- አንተ፡ ውእቱ፡ ክርስቶስ *ʾanta wəʾətu krəstos* 'you are Christ' (Mk 8:29)

(b) The subject is a personal pronoun:

- አነ፡ ውእቱ፡ ረዳኢከ ʾana wəʾətu radāʾika 'I am your helper' (Ps 35:3 [34:3])
- አነ፡ ውእቱ፡ አምላከ፡ አብርሃም ʾana wəʾətu ʾamlāka ʾabrəhām 'I am the God of Abraham' (Lk 20:37)
- አነኒ፡ ብእሲ፡ መኰንን፡ አነ ʾana-hi bəʾəsi makʷannən ʾana 'also I am a high official' (Lk 7:8)

(c) The subject is a demonstrative pronoun:

- ወዛቲ፡ ይእቲ፡ ሥርዐትየ wa-zātti yəʾəti śərʿatəya 'this is my covenant' (Gen 17:10)
- ዝውእቱ፡ ወልድየ፡ ዘአፈቅር zə-wəʾətu waldəya za-ʾafaqqər 'this is my son whom I love' (Mt 3:17); predicate extended by relative clause
- ተዓይነ፡ እግዚአብሔር፡ ይእቲ፡ ዛቲ taʿāyəna ʾəgziʾab(ə)her yəʾəti zātti 'this is the camp of God' (Gen 32:3) (predicate fronted for emphasis)

(d) The subject is a relative pronoun:

- ዘውእቱ፡ ብርሃነ፡ ጽድቅ za-wəʾətu bərhāna ṣədq 'the one who is the true light' (Jn 1:9)
- ዘውእቶሙ፡ ሴም፡ ወካም፡ ወያፌት za-wəʾətomu sem wa-kām wa-yāfet 'those that are Sem, Ham, and Japheth' (Gen 5:32)

6.1.2.4. Nominal clauses with possessive or interrogative pronouns as predicates:

- ምንትኑ፡ እንጋ፡ ውእቱ፡ ዝንቱ፡ ሕፃን məntə-nu ʾəngā wəʾətu zəntu ḥəḍān 'so what then will this child become?' (Lk 1:66)
- መኑ፡ ውእቱ፡ ዝንቱ mannu wəʾətu zəntu 'who is this?' (Mt 21:10)
- ዝንቱ፡ ምንት፡ ውእቱ፡ ዘአልቦ፡ ዕረፍት zəntu mənt wəʾətu za-ʾalbo ʿəraft 'what is this that has no rest?' (En 23:3); the interrogative pronoun is not in first position
- ወዚአከ፡ ይእቲ፡ ሌሊት wa-ziʾaka yəʾəti lelit 'the night is yours!' (Ps 74:16 [73:17])
- ዚአከ፡ ይእቲ፡ መንግሥት፡ ኃይል፡ ወስብሓት ziʾaka yəʾəti mangəśt ḥayl wa-səbḥāt 'yours is the kingdom, the dominion, and the glory' (Mt 6:13); several subjects; the copula agrees with the first subject

6.1.2.5. Nominal clauses with adjectival predicates:

- እስመ፡ ረሓብ፡ ይእቲ፡ ምድር፡ ቅድሜሆሙ ʾəsma raḥāb yəʾəti mədr qədmehomu 'for the land is large enough before them' (Gen 34:21)
- እስመ፡ አነ፡ ኄር፡ አነ ʾəsma ʾana ḫer ʾana '... for I am good' (Mt 20:15)
- ብዙኃን፡ እሙንቱ፡ ጽዉዓን bəzuḫān ʾəmuntu ṣəwuʿān 'many are summoned' (Mt 20:16)

6.1.2.6. Nominal clauses with a construct chain or genitive phrase as predicate:

- ዝንቱ፡ ውእቱ፡ ቤተ፡ ንጉሥ zəntu wəʾətu beta nəguś 'this is the palace'
- አንትሙ፡ ውእቱ፡ ብርሃኑ፡ ለዓለም ʾantəmu wəʾətu bərhānu la-ʿālam 'you are the light of the world' (Mt 5:14)

6.1.2.7. Nominal clauses with adverbial predicates:

- ፈድፋደሰ፡ እምእሉ፡ እምእኩይ፡ ውእቱ fadfāda-ssa ʾəm-ʾəllu ʾəm-ʾəkkuy wəʾətu 'anything more than these is of the evil one' (Mt 5:37)
- ወውእቱ፡ ቃል፡ ኀበ፡ እግዚአብሔር፡ ውእቱ wa-wəʾətu qāl ḫaba ʾəgziʾab(ə)ḥer wəʾətu 'and that word was with God' (Jn 1:1)
- እስመ፡ ሎሙ፡ ይእቲ፡ መንግሥተ፡ ሰማያት ʾəsma lomu yəʾəti mangəśta samāyāt 'for theirs is the kingdom of heaven' (Mt 5:10); construct chain as subject
- ወከመዝ፡ ውእቱ፡ አስማቲሆሙ wa-kama-zə wəʾətu ʾasmātihomu 'thus are their names' (Gen 46:8)
- ወኀይለ፡ እግዚአብሔር፡ ውእቱ፡ በዘይፌውስ wa-ḫayla ʾəgziʾab(ə)ḥer wəʾətu ba-za-yəfewwəs 'the power of God was there so that he would heal' (Lk 5:17); በ- ba- + relative clause as predicate

6.1.2.8. Nominal clauses with a relative clause as predicate:

- ዝንቱ፡ ውእቱ፡ ዘተብህለ፡ በኢሳይያስ፡ ነቢይ zəntu wəʾətu za-tabəhla ba-ʾisāyəyās nabiy 'this is the one of whom it was said by Isaiah the prophet' (Mt 3:3)
- ዝውእቱ፡ ዘበእንቲአሁ፡ ተጽሕፈ zə-wəʾətu za-ba-ʾəntiʾahu taṣəḥfa 'this is the one of whom it is written' (Lk 7:27)
- አነ፡ ውእቱ፡ ዘሀሎ ʾana wəʾətu za-hallo 'I am the one who is' (Ex 3:14)

6.1.2.9. Nominal clauses with multiple predicates:

- ዝንቱ፡ ውእቱ፡ ኦሪት፡ ወነቢያት zəntu wəʾətu ʾorit wa-nabiyāt 'this is the law and the prophets'

6.1.3. Word Order in Nominal Clauses with Two and Three Elements

6.1.3.1. As seen in §6.1.1., the common word order in nominal clauses with two elements is P-S (as in ጻድቃን፡ አንተሙ ṣādəqān ʾantəmu 'you are just'). The opposite order places focus on the subject, especially when the subject is extended by the enclitic particle –ሰ –ssa.

6.1.3.2. Nominal clauses with three elements, however, exhibit both orders S-P and P-S with about the same frequency. The choice of word order is dependent on the nature of the sentence elements. Interrogative pronouns and interrogative adverbs (as predicates) usually appear in first position, as in መኑ፡ ውእቱ፡ ዝንቱ mannu wəʾətu zəntu 'who is this?'. In declarative clauses, pronouns that function as subjects commonly precede the predicate, as in አንተሙ፡ ውእቱ፡ ጻድቃን ʾantəmu wəʾətu ṣādəqān 'you are just'; ዝንቱ፡ ውእቱ፡ ንጉሥ zəntu wəʾətu naguś 'this is the king' (that is, order S-P).

6.1.4. Nominal Clauses with በ– ba– and አልብ– ʾalbə–

6.1.4.1. Two-element nominal clauses with በ– ba– or (negated) አልብ– ʾalbə– plus pronominal suffix as the first element functioning as the subject require special discussion. Of these, constructions with a pronominal suffix of the 3ms, that is clauses with ቦ bo and አልቦ ʾalbo, furthermore form a particular sub-group.

6.1.4.2. Nominal clauses with በ– ba– and (negated) አልብ– ʾalbə– + pronominal suffix primarily express possessive relationships, as in ብየ bəya '(in) me is' = 'I have/possess'; አልብነ ʾalbəna 'we do not have/possess'. The logical object of this construction usually stands in the accusative (§5.2.3.1k). Tense is not determined in this type of sentence, as is the case with all nominal clauses (§6.1.6.):

- ብየ፡ ቤት bəya beta 'I have/had a house' (cf. ኮኖ፡ ቤት kono beta 'he had a house')
- አልብነ፡ ማየ ʾalbəna māya 'we have/had no water'

- ወአልበሙ፡ ውሉደ wa-ʾalbomu wəluda 'but they had no children' (Lk 1:7)
- ወአልበሙ፡ ዘይበልዑ wa-ʾalbomu za-yəballəʿu 'they had nothing to eat' (Mk 8:1)

When the subject is not pronominal but nominal, it stands before the possessive construction (= casus pendens [§6.3.]), as in ብእሲ፡ ቦቱ፡ ክልኤተ፡ ውሉደ bəʾasi bottu kəlʾeta wəluda 'the man has/had two sons' (lit. 'as for the man, he has/had two sons') and ብእሲት፡ ባቲ፡ ክልኤተ፡ ውሉደ bəʾasit bātti kəlʾeta wəluda 'the woman has/had two sons' (lit. 'as for the woman, she has/had two sons').

A comparable notion can also be expressed by ለ– la– plus pronominal suffix, as in ሎሙ፡ (ይእቲ፡)መንግሥተ፡ ሰማያት lomu (yəʾəti) mangəśta samāyāt 'they have the kingdom of heaven' = 'theirs is the kingdom of heaven' (§6.1.2.7.). The logical object of this sentence-type, however, is in the nominative (= non-accusative).

6.1.4.3. ቦ/ቦቱ bo/bottu and (negated) አልቦ ʾalbo, that is, forms with a 3ms suffix also have the extended meaning 'there is' (< 'within him is'), (and its negated equivalent 'there is not'). In these cases, ቦ/ቦቱ bo/bottu predicates existence. The logical object is either in the accusative or the nominative:

- ቦ፡ ማይ/ማየ bo māy(a) / አልቦ፡ ማይ/ማየ ʾalbo māy(a) 'there is/was (no) water'
- ወአልቦ፡ ቤተ፡ በግብጽ፡ ዘአልቦ፡ በድነ፡ ውስቴታ wa-ʾalbo beta (variant bet) ba-gəbṣ za-ʾalbo badna (variant በድን badn) wəstetā 'and there was no house in Egypt in which there was no corpse' (Jub 49:5)
- ቦኑ፡ በከንቱ ... bo-nu ba-kantu ... '(does Job fear God) without reason?' (Job 1:9) (interrogative clause)
- ብእሲ ... ዘቦ፡ ላዕሌሁ፡ መንፈሰ፡ እግዚአ፡ ብሔር፡ ቅዱስ bəʾasi ... za-bo lāʿlehu manfasa ʾəgziʾa bəḥer qəddusa 'a man ... on whom is the holy spirit of God' (Dan 5:11)

The logical object can be extended by a relative clause:

- አልቦ፡ ሰብአ፡ በዲበ፡ ምድር፡ ዘይክል ʾalbo sabʾa (variant ሰብእ sabʾ) ba-diba mədr za-yəkəl ... 'there is nobody on earth who is able ...' (Dan 2:10)
- ወ(ሚመ)፡ ቦኑ፡ ካልእ፡ ዘንሴፈው wa(-mimma) bo-nu kāləʾ za-nəsseffaw 'or is there another whom we await?' (Lk 7:19.20) (interrogative clause); cf.

Mt 11:3: ወቦኑ፡ካልአ፡ዘንሴፎ *wa-bo-nu kāləʾa za-nəsseffo* (object in the accusative)[270]

These respective clauses can also be extended by a prepositional phrase containing ለ– *la–*. The logical object is always in the nominative in such cases:[271]

- ወአልቦ፡ማኅለቅት፡ለመንግሥቱ *wa-ʾalbo māḥlaqt la-mangəśtu* 'and his kingdom will have no end' (Lk 1:33) (lit. 'there will be no end to his kingdom')
- እስመ፡አልቦ፡ነገር፡ዘይሰአኖ፡ለእግዚአብሔር *ʾasma ʾalbo nagar za-yəssaʾano la-ʾəgziʾab(ə)ḥer* 'for there is nothing that is impossible for God' (Lk 1:37)
- አልቦኬ፡እንከ፡ለዘይበቍዕ *ʾalbo-ke ʾanka la-za-yəbaqqʷəʿ* 'it (the salt) is thus not useful for anything' (Mt 5:13); the logical subject remains unexpressed

6.1.4.4. A relative clause that is most often introduced by ዘ– *za–*, rarely by እንተ *ʾanta* or እለ *ʾalla*, follows immediately after ቦ/ቦቱ *bo/bottu* or አልቦ *ʾalbo* in many cases. The literal translation of this so-called (አል)ቦ፡ዘ (*ʾal)bo za-*construction, which is structurally to be understood as a cleft sentence, is: 'there is somebody/nobody who' and 'there is something/nothing that'. As the translation indicates, the construction itself is equivalent to an indefinite pronoun. (አል)ቦ (*ʾal)bo* mostly represents the logical subject of the clause, but it can also function as the logical object. The clause አልቦ፡ዘበልዐ *ʾalbo za-balʿa*, for example, can mean 'nobody ate' (that is, 'there is/was nobody who ate'), but also 'he ate nothing' (that is, 'there is/was nothing that he ate'). In the latter case, the preposition ለ– *la–* can occur before the relative pronoun (አልቦ፡ለዘ … *ʾalbo la-za* …) to avoid ambiguities and/or to clarify the syntactic relationship of the sentence elements.

---

[270] In this example, ካልአ *kāləʾa* might not necessarily be the logical object of ቦ *bo*. The construction could reflect a relative clause with topicalized object (§6.5.1.8.3.) that would stand for a construction like ወቦኑ፡ዘንሴፎ፡ካልአ *wa-bo-nu za-nəseffo kāləʾa* 'is it the case that we have to await another?'.

[271] The logical object reflects the syntactic subject of the nominal clause 'A *la*-B', that is, 'A is for B' = 'B has/possesses A'.

(a) Examples of ቦ/አልቦ *bo/ʾalbo* as logical subject:

- አልቦ ፡ ዘይክል ፡ ኈልቆቶሙ *ʾalbo za-yəkəl ḫʷalləqotomu* 'nobody was able to count them' (ʿĀmda Ṣəyon 11c)

- ወአልቦ ፡ ዘይሰአኖ *wa-ʾalbo za-yəssaʾano* 'nothing is impossible for him' (ʿĀmda Ṣəyon 11c)

- ወዘእንበሌሁስ ፡ አልቦ ፡ ዘኮነ *wa-za-ʾənbalehu-ssa ʾalbo za-kona* 'without him, there would be nothing that came into being' (Jn 1:3)[272]

- ለእግዚአብሔርስ ፡ አልቦ ፡ ዘርእዮ *la-ʾəgziʾab(ə)ḥerə-ssa ʾalbo za-rəʾyo* 'no one has (ever) seen God' (Jn 1:18); topicalized object

- ወለንጉሥስ ፡ አልቦ ፡ ዘይፀብአ ፡ በፈቃዱ *wa-la-nəguśə-ssa ʾalbo za-yəḍabbəʾo ba-faqādu* 'nobody can fight the king out of his own volition' (ʿĀmda Ṣəyon 11c)

- ወአልቦ ፡ ከማሁ ፡ በዲበ ፡ ምድር *wa-ʾalbo kamāhu ba-diba mədr* 'there is no one like him on earth' (Job 1:8)

- አልቦ ፡ ዘይፈልጠኒ ፡ እምኔኪ ፡ እንበለ ፡ ሞት *ʾalbo za-yəfalləṭanni ʾəmənneki ʾənbala mot* 'nothing but death can separate me from you' (Ruth 1:17)

- ቦዘይቤ ... ወቦ ፡ ዘይቤ ... *bo-za-yəbe ... wa-bo za-yəbe ...* 'there is somebody who says ... and there is another who says ...'; that is 'some say ... but others say ...' (Ləbna dəngəl 1:2); also: ቦ ፡ እለ ፡ ይቤሉ/ይብሉ *bo ʾalla yəbelu/yəbəlu* 'there are those who say'

(b) Examples of ቦ/አልቦ *bo/ʾalbo* as logical object:

- አልቦ ፡ ዘርእየ *ʾalbo za-rəʾya* 'he saw nothing'

- አልቦ ፡ ዘሰምዐ ፡ ቃሎ *ʾalbo za-samʿo qālo* 'he heard nobody's voice'

- ቦ ፡ ዘቀተሉ ፡ ወቦ ፡ ዘኢቀተሉ *bo za-qatalu wa-bo za-ʾi-qatalu* 'some they killed and some they did not kill'

Construction (አል)ቦ ፡ ለዘ (ʾal)bo la-za:

- አልቦ ፡ ለዘ ፡ አዘዘ ... *ʾalbo la-za ʾazzaza* ... 'he commanded nobody (to be wicked)' (Sir 15:20)

6.1.4.5. The construction አልቦ ... ዘእንበለ *ʾalbo ... za-ʾənbala* means 'there is nothing ... except', which can more simply be translated as 'only'. The logical

---

object that follows the preposition እንበለ ʾənbala does not appear in the accusative – except in a few sporadic cases – as in አልብነ፡ ዝየ፡ ዘእንበለ፡ ኃምስ፡ ኅብስት፡ ወክልኤ፡ ዓሣ ʾalbəna zəya za-ʾənbala ḫāms ḫəbəst wa-kəlʾe ʿāśā 'we have only five loaves of bread and two fish here' (Mt 14:17).

6.1.4.6. (አል)ቦኑ፡ ዘ– (ʾal)bo-nu za–, literally: 'is it (not) the case that ...?' and አልቦኑ ʾalbo-nu by itself can – being semantically bleached – be used as simple interrogative particles before nominal and verbal clauses:

- ወቦኑ፡ ዘብክሙ፡ እጐ wa-bo-nu za-bəkəmu ʾəḫʷa 'do you have a brother?' (Gen 43:7)
- ቦኑ፡ ዐቃቢሁ፡ አነ፡ ለእኁየ bo-nu ʿaqqābihu ʾana la-ʾəḫuya 'am I the keeper of my brother?' (Gen 4:9)
- ቦኑ፡ እብነ፡ ይሁቦ bo-nu ʾəbna yəhubo 'will he give him a stone?' (Mt 7:9)

6.1.5. Negation of Nominal Clauses

Nominal clauses in Classical Ethiopic are negated by አልቦ ʾalbo, አኮ ʾakko, and ኢ– ʾi–. Instead of negated nominal clauses, Classical Ethiopic also uses negated verbal clauses containing ኮነ kona or ሀሎ hallo (§6.1.8.3.).

6.1.5.1. Negation by አልቦ ʾalbo

The most frequent type of negation for nominal clauses is አልብ– ʾalbə– (< negation *ʾal + ba– [§4.5.4.2.1.]) plus pronominal suffix, that is አልብየ ʾalbəya, አልብከ ʾalbəka, አልቦ ʾalbo etc., which reflects the negated variant of nominal clauses that contain ብ– ba– plus pronominal suffix (ብየ bəya, ብከ bəka, ቦ bo, etc.). አልቦ፡ ዘ– ʾalbo za– functions as the negated equivalent of ቦዘ bo-za (for examples, see §6.1.4.4.).

6.1.5.2. Negation by አኮ ʾakko

The negative particle አኮ ʾakko (§4.5.4.2.2.) primarily functions to negate individual lexemes. In this function, አኮ ʾakko expresses contrast in declarative clauses. From a semantic point of view, however, it can negate the whole clause, as in አምላከ፡ ሕያዋንኬ፡ ውእቱ፡ ወአኮ፡ አምላከ፡ ምዉታን ʾamlāka ḥayāwānə-ke wəʾətu wa-ʾakko ʾamlāka məwutān 'for he is the God of the living, not the God of the dead' (Mt 22:32);[273] ሰማያዊ፡ አንተ፡ ወአኮ፡ ምድራዊ samāyāwi ʾanta wa-ʾakko mədrāwi 'you are heavenly (of origin) and not earthly' (Śəna fəṭrat 28).

More frequent than the semantic negation of declarative nominal clauses is the use of አኮኑ ʾakko-nu (አኮ ʾakko + interrogative particle) in questions, as in አኮኑ፡ አነ፡ ውእቱ፡ ኢሎፍላዊ ʾakko-nu ʾana wəʾətu ʾiloflāwi 'am I not a Philistine?' (1 Sam 17:8); አኮኑ፡ አኀዊከ፡ ውስተ፡ ሴኬም ʾakko-nu ʾaḫawika wəsta sekem 'are your brothers not in Shechem?' (Gen 37:13).

For the frequent use of አኮዘ ʾakko-za in nominal cleft sentences, see §6.4.

6.1.5.3. Negation by ኢ- ʾi-

In a few cases, the negative particle ኢ- ʾi- is used to negate nominal clauses. As አኮ ʾakko, the particle refers to the immediately following lexeme, but it negates the whole clause from a semantic point of view, as in ኢድውይ፡ አነ ʾi-dəwwəy ʾana 'I am not sick' (ኢ- ʾi- before a predicative adjective).

ኢ- ʾi- further sporadically appears in nominal clauses containing አልቦ ʾalbo (§6.1.4.). The appearance of two negative particles in the same clause places focus on the negation, as in ወኢማይ፡ አልቦ፡ ላዕሌሁ wa-ʾi-māy ʾalbo lāʿlehu 'and there is certainly no water upon it'.

6.1.6. The Expression of Tense in Nominal Clauses

Nominal clauses are not marked for tense. Their temporal relation is solely inferred from context. Most nominal clauses are to be rendered as present tense in English, although there are also clauses that, based on their context, are best rendered as past or future. When a nominal clause has no present tense context, they are often substituted by verbal clauses containing ኮነ kona or ሀሎ hallo as the predicate (§6.1.8.2.).

Examples of nominal clauses with past reference:

---

[273] Cf. Mk 12:27 and Lk 20:38: ኢኮነከ፡ አምላከ፡ ምዉታን፡ አላ፡ አምላከ፡ ሕያዋን፡ ውእቱ ʾi-kona-ke ʾamlāka məwutān ʾallā ʾamlāka ḥəyāwān wəʾətu.

- ወክልኤሆሙ፡ ጻድቃን፡ እሙንቱ   …   ወየሐውሩ፡ በኵሉ፡ ትእዛዙ፡ ወኵነኔሁ፡ ለእግዚአብሔር፡ ወንጹሓን፡ እሙንቱ wa-kəlʾehomu ṣādəqān ʾəmuntu … wa-yahawwəru ba-kʷəllu təʾəzāzu wa-kʷənnanehu la-ʾəgziʾab(ə)her wa-nəṣuḥān ʾəmuntu 'both of them were righteous … and they were following all the commandments and regulations of God, and they were sincere' (Lk 1:6)

Examples of nominal clauses with future reference:

- እስመ፡ ዐስብክሙ፡ ብዙኅ፡ ውእቱ፡ በሰማያት ʾəsma ʿasbəkəmu bəzuḫ wəʾətu ba-samāyāt 'for your reward will be plentiful in heaven' (Mt 5:12)
- ውእቱ፡ ዐቢይ፡ ወይሰመይ፡ ወልደ፡ እግዚአብሔር፡ ልዑል wəʾətu ʿabiy wa-yəssammay walda ʾəgziʾab(ə)her ləʿul 'he will be great and be called Son of God most High' (Lk 1:32)

6.1.7. Expression of Modality in Nominal Clauses

Nominal clauses are unmarked for modality. As with tense, the implied mood can only be inferred from context. Most nominal clauses are to be rendered as indicative statements, as in ብፁዓን፡ መሓርያን bəḍuʿān mahārəyān 'blessed are the merciful' (Mt 5:7); መኑ፡ ውእቱ mannu wəʾətu 'who is he?' (En 46:2) (interrogative clause), but Classical Ethiopic also has nominal clauses with jussive meanings, as in ሰላም፡ ለዝንቱ፡ ቤት salām la-zəntu bet '(let there be) peace to this house!' (Lk 10:5); ሰላም፡ ለክሙ፡ ወጸጋ፡ እግዚአብሔር፡ አቡነ salām lakəmu wa-ṣaggā ʾəgziʾab(ə)her ʾabuna 'peace be with you and the grace of God, our father …!' (Eph 1:2); ሕያው፡ ንጉሥ ḥəyāw nəguś 'may the king be alive!' = 'long live the king!'; ንጉሥ፡ ለዓለም፡ ሕያው፡ አንተ nəguś la-ʿālam ḥəyāw ʾanta '(o) king! May you live forever!' (Dan 2:4).

It is not always possible to determine if a nominal clause is to be understood as indicative or jussive from its context, see, for example, ቡርክት፡ አንቲ፡ እምአንስት፡ ወቡሩክ፡ ፍሬ፡ ከርሥኪ burəkt ʾanti ʾəm-ʾanəst wa-buruk fəre karśəki 'blessed are you among women and blessed is the fruit of your womb' (Lk 1:42).

Instead of nominal clauses with jussive functions, which, as shown, can be ambiguous, Classical Ethiopic tends to employ sentences with the jussive of ኮነ kona or ሀሎ hallo as the predicate in order to avoid ambiguity (§6.1.8.2.).

6.1.8. Nominal Clauses *versus* Clauses with ኮነ *kona* or ሀሎ *hallo* as the Predicate

6.1.8.1. Clauses with ኮነ *kona* or ሀሎ *hallo* (or ሀለወ *hallawa*) as the predicate are verbal clauses since both verbs have fientic basic meanings: ሀሎ *hallo* 'to exist, be there'; ኮነ *kona* 'to be, become, happen'; as in ይኩኑ፡ ብርሃናት *yəkunu bərhānāt* 'may there be lights' (i.e., 'come into existence') (Gen 1:14). These two verbs can also be semantically bleached and act as copulae of nominal clauses. These latter types of clauses are often interchangeable with nominal clauses[274] and tend to correspond to the typical word order of nominal clauses. The use of ኮነ *kona* or ሀሎ *hallo* over simple nominal clauses is preferred in the following environments.

6.1.8.2. When the underlying meaning of an expected nominal clause is jussive, Classical Ethiopic prefers clauses containing the jussive of ኮነ *kona* (less often ሀሎ *hallo*) over an actual nominal clause in order to clearly express the volitive notion.

(a) Clauses with the jussive of ኮነ *kona*:
- ወይኩን፡ ቡሩክ፡ ስሙ፡ ለእግዚአ፤ ብሔር *wa-yəkun buruk səmu la-ʾəgziʾa bəḥer* 'let the name of God be praised' (Job 1:22)
- ወይኩኑ፡ ኵሉ፡ ውሉደ፡ ሰብእ፡ ጻድቃነ *wa-yəkunu kʷəllu wəluda sabʾ ṣādəqāna* 'and all sons of men shall be righteous' (En 10:21)
- ላዕሌየ፡ ይኩን፡ ወልድየ፡ መርገምከ *lāʿleya yəkun waldəya margaməka* 'let your curse be on me, my son' (Gen 27:13)
- በል፡ ከመ፡ እሉ፡ አእባን፡ ኅብስተ፡ ይኩና *bal kama ʾəllu ʾaʾbān ḫəbəsta yəkunā* 'command that these stones may become loaves of bread' (Mt 4:3) (ingressive meaning)
- ለትኩን፡ ሀገሩ፡ በድወ *la-təkun hagaru badwa* 'let his city become a wasteland' (Acts 1:20) (ingressive meaning)

(b) Clause with jussive of ሀሎ *hallo*:
- በረከቱ፡ ወሀብተ፡ ረድእቱ፡ የሀሉ፡ ምስለ፡ ኵልነ *barakatu wa-habta radʾətu yahallu məsla kʷəlləna* 'let his blessing and the gift of his help be with all of us!'.

---

[274] For non-verbal clauses and clauses with verbs of existence, see especially Cohen 1984, 151–232.

6.1.8.3. Non-fientive declarative clauses can likewise be construed with ሀሎ *hallo* and (less often) with ኮነ *kona* as predicates:

- ሀሎ፡ዝየ፡ወልድ *hallo zəya wald* 'there is a boy here' (Jn 6:9); cf. nominal clauses such as አነ፡ዝየ *ʾana zəya* 'I am here'
- ለእለ፡ሀለዉ፡ውስተ፡ቤት *la-ʾəlla hallawu wəsta bet* '(she called to) the ones who were in the house' (Gen 39:14 etc.); cf. however the nominal construction in Mt 5:15: ወታበርህ፡ለኵሎሙ፡እለ፡ውስተ፡ቤት *wa-tābarrəh la-kʷəllomu ʾəlla wəsta bet* 'and it will shine for all who are in the house'.

Furthermore, clauses with negated ኮነ *kona* and ሀሎ *hallo* as predicates tend to be used instead of negated nominal clauses, as in እኁየ፡ጸጓር፡ውእቱ፡ ወአነሰ፡ኢኮንኩ፡ጸጓረ *ʾəhuya ṣaggʷār wəʾətu / wa-ʾanə-ssa ʾi-konku ṣaggʷāra* 'my brother is hairy but I am not hairy' (Gen 27:11); ኢኮነከ፡አምላከ፡ምዉታን፡አላ፡ አምላከ፡ሕያዋን፡ውእቱ *ʾi-kona-ke ʾamlāka məwutān ʾallā ʾamlāka ḥəyāwān wəʾətu* 'for he is not the Lord of the dead but the Lord of the living' (Mk 12:27 and Lk 20:38).

Lastly, clauses with the perfect of ኮነ *kona* and ሀሎ *hallo* as predicates often replace nominal clauses in order to clearly indicate the intended past reference:

- ወሀሎ፡እግዚአብሔር፡ምስለ፡ዮሴፍ *wa-hallo ʾəgziʾab(ə)her məsla Yosef* 'and God was with Joseph' (Gen 39:2); as opposed to ምስሌነ፡እግዚአብሔር *məslena ʾəgziʾab(ə)her* 'God is with us'
- ወኮነ፡ድቀቱ፡ዐቢየ *wa-kona dəqatu ʿabiya* 'its fall was great' (Mt 7:27); as opposed to ወኃጣዉኢሆሙ፡ዐብየት፡ጥቀ *wa-ḫaṭāwəʾihomu ʿabyat ṭəqqa* 'their sins became very great' (Gen 18:20).

6.1.9. One-Element or Incomplete Nominal Clauses

Besides nominal clauses consisting of two elements (without copula) and three elements (with copula), Classical Ethiopic also has constructions that consist of a single nominal element. Most of these clauses can be interpreted as incomplete two-element nominal clauses that only contain the predicate but not the subject.

One-element clauses often reflect exclamations and similar notions, such as
ሠናይ *śannāy* '(it is) good!' (Ruth 3:13); ሕይወተ፡ፈርዖን *ḥaywata farʕon* 'by the life
of Pharaoh!' (Gen 42:15.16; in oath); አባ *ʾabbā* 'o father!' (vocative). Interrogative
pronouns and interrogative adverbs can form a sentence by themselves, as in
እፎ *ʾəffo* 'how?'; እፎ፡ከመ *ʾəffo kama* 'how is it that …?'.

Examples of incomplete three-element nominal clauses include ዝውእቱ *za-
waʾətu* and ዛይእቲ *zā-yaʾəti* in the sense of 'that is to say, namely …' (the
following syntagms functions as predicate).

6.2. The Verbal Clause

A verbal clause has a predicate that is of a verbal nature, most often a finite
verbal form (perfect, imperfect, jussive, imperative), although sentences with a
perfective participle as predicate can be considered verbal clauses in a broader
sense as well (§5.5.2.). Most clauses in Classical Ethiopic are verbal clauses and
tend to express fientive actions in the form of declarations/statements,
questions, and wishes.

6.2.1. The Components of a Verbal Clause

The center of a verbal clause is the verbal predicate. Besides the verb, the
clause can explicitly express one or more subjects in the form of nouns or
independent pronouns. In most cases, however, the subject is implicitly
expressed by the verbal predicate (in the personal affixes on the verb). Verbal
clauses can further contain direct or indirect objects, depending on the valency
of the respective verbal predicate (§5.4.7.). It can further contain adverbial
components (prepositional phrases and others).[275]

The most frequent type of verbal clause in Classical Ethiopic consists of two
elements, either subject + verb (as in ወአውሥአ፡ሄኖክ *wa-ʾawśaʾa henok* 'and
Enoch answered' En 1:2), verb + object (as in ወያደቅቅ፡አስናነ፡ኃጥአን *wa-yādaqqəq
ʾasnāna ḫāṭəʾān* 'he will break the teeth of the sinners' En 46:4), or verb +
adverbial complement (as in ዐርገ፡ውስተ፡ደብር *ʕarga wəsta dabr* 'he went up the
mountain' Mt 5:1).

---

[275] See R. Schneider's detailed investigation of the syntax of verbal complements and the
position of the attributive adjective (Schneider 1959).

Next in frequency are verbal clauses consisting of three elements (verb + object + adverbial complement among others). One-element clauses that only consist of the verb, such as ቆመ *qoma* 'he rose', also occur with relative frequency.

6.2.2. Agreement of Verb and Subject

6.2.2.1. The verb usually agrees with the overtly expressed subject in gender, number, and person independent of its position in the sentence. Subjects with external or internal plural-marking both govern plural verbal forms. These agreement rules primarily apply to animate subjects, however, although inanimate subjects can, but do not have to, follow the same rules. Examples include:

- ወአንሰ፡ እብለክሙ *wa-ʾana-ssa ʾəbəlakkəmu* 'I, however, tell you'
- ወአውሥአ፡ ሄኖክ፡ ወይቤ *wa-ʾawśəʾa henok wa-yəbe* 'and Enoch answered and said' (En 1:2)
- ታዐብዮ፡ ነፍስየ፡ ለእግዚአብሔር *tāʿabbəyo nafsəya la-ʾəgziʾab(ə)her* 'my soul magnifies the Lord' (Lk 1:46) (ነፍስ *nafs* 'soul' is primarily construed as fem.)
- ወያድለቀልቁ፡ ትጉሃን *wa-yādlaqalləqu təguhān* 'and the watchers will shake' (En 1:5)
- ከመ፡ እሉ፡ አእባን፡ ኅብስተ፡ ይኩኑ *kama ʾəllu ʾaʾbān ḫəbəsta yəkunā* '(command) that these stones may become loaves of bread' (Mt 4:3) (እብን *ʾəbn* 'stone' is primarily construed as fem.)

A dual subject governs a plural verb in Classical Ethiopic since there is no dual verbal form, as in ወመልኡ፡ ክልኤሆን፡ አሕማረ፡ እስከ፡ ይሰጠማ *wa-malʾu kəlʾehon ʾaḥmāra ʾəska yəssaṭṭamā* 'and they filled both boats until they were about to sink' (lit. 'to be submerged/sunk') (Lk 5:7).

Exceptions to these agreement rules and special agreement relations are discussed in the following sections.

6.2.2.2. Since nouns not denoting human beings in Classical Ethiopic have no fixed gender, the agreeing verb can have either masculine or feminine gender. Examples of formally feminine subjects with masculine verbal forms (sing. or pl.) include:

- ወኮነ፡ ድቀቱ፡ ዐቢየ *wa-kona dəqatu ʿabiya* 'its fall was great' (Mt 7:27)
- ወራእያት፡ ዲቤየ፡ ወድቁ *wa-rāʾyāt dibeya wadqu* 'and visions fell upon me' (En 13:8)

6.2.2.3. In general, verbs that stand *after* their subject tend to agree more strictly with the subject than those that stand *before* the subject. The verb can further occur in the 3ms when it occurs before a feminine or plural subject, even with animate/human subjects. If the subject in question is followed by other verbs, those verbs tend to agree with the subject, as in ሶበ፡ መጽአ፡ እማንቱ፡ አባግዕ፡ ይስተዩ ... ይፀንሳ *soba maṣʾa ʾəmāntu ʾabāgəʿ yəstayā ... yəḍannəsā* 'whenever those sheep came out (3ms) to drink (3fp) ... they became pregnant (3fp)' (Gen 30:38).

6.2.2.4. Nouns that have a singular-looking form but that are semantically collectives, such as ሰብእ *sabʾ* 'people', ሕዝብ *ḥəzb* 'people, crowd', ዘርእ *zarʾ* 'seed, descendants' (§5.2.6.5.2.) can be construed with a singular or plural verb: ሰትየ፡ ሕዝብ *satya ḥəzb* and ሰትዩ፡ ሕዝብ *satyu ḥəzb* 'the people drank'. The construction with a plural verb, however, occurs more frequently overall.

- ወኮሎሙ፡ ሕዝብ፡ ሀለዉ ... ይጼልዩ *wa-kʷəllomu ḥəzb hallawu ... yəṣelləyu* 'the whole assembly was praying' (Lk 1:10)
- አፅምዑ፡ ሕዝብየ *ʾaḍməʾu ḥəzbəya* 'listen, o my people!' (Ps 78:1 [77:1])
- ሀለዉ፡ ዘርእከ፡ ይነብሩ፡ ፈላስያን፡ ብሔረ፡ ነኪር *hallawu zarʾəka yənabbəru falāsəyān bəhera nakir* 'your descendants will live as strangers in a foreign land' (Acts 7:6)
- ወግብተ፡ መጽኡ ... ብዙኅ፡ ሐራ፡ ሰማይ፡ ይሴብሕዎ፡ ለእግዚአብሔር፡ ወይብሉ *wa-gəbta maṣʾu ... bəzuḫ ḥarā samāy yəsebbəḥəwwo la-ʾəgziʾab(ə)ḥer wa-yəbəlu* 'and suddenly a multitude of the heavenly host came, praising God and saying' (Lk 2:13)
- ወኮሉ፡ ተግባሮሙ፡ ዓመፃ፡ ያርእዩ *wa-kʷəllu tagbāromu ʿāmmaḍā yārəʾəyu* 'and all their deeds show iniquity' (En 46:7)
- ይገንዩ፡ ለከ፡ እግዚአ፡ ኮሉ፡ ተግባርከ *yəgannəyu laka ʾəgziʾo kʷəllu tagbārəka* 'all your works, o Lord, shall praise you' (Ps 145:10 [144:10])
- ከመ፡ ኢይትመየጥ፡ ኮሉ፡ ግብሩ፡ ለአምላክ *kama ʾi-yətmayyaṭ kʷəllu gəbru la-ʾamlāk* 'that no works of the Lord change' (En 2:2)
- ወይፈርሁ፡ ኮሉ *wa-yəfarrəhu kʷəllu* 'and all will be afraid' (En 1:5)

- ለዘ፡ ይመጽኡ፡ ትውልድ፡ ርጕቃን la-za yəmaṣṣəʾu təwlədd rəḥuqān 'for a distant generation that will come' (En 1:2 [1:3])
- ወይሬእዩ፡ መንፈቆሙ፡ ለመንፈቆሙ wa-yəreʾəyu manfaqomu la-manfaqomu 'and one half of them will look at the (other) half' (En 62:5)

When such a subject governs two or more verbs, the verb preceding the subject can occur in the singular and that/those following the subject can be in the plural (cf. §6.2.2.3.), as in ወይመጽእ፡ ሰብእ፡ ብዙኅ፡ ይስምዕዎ wa-yəmaṣṣəʾ sabʾ bəzuḫ yəsmaʿəwwo 'and many people used to come (3ms) to listen to him (3mp)' (Lk 5:15).

6.2.2.5. Plural nouns with collective or singular meaning (cf. §6.2.6.5.2.) can be construed with a plural or singular verb. Verbs that precede the subject most frequently occur in the 3ms, independent of the gender of the following subject. When the verb follows the subject, gender and number agreement is more common (cf. §6.2.2.3.):

- ኀለፈ፡ መዋዕሊሁ ḫalafa mawāʿəlihu '(much) time (pl. form) passed' (Josh 23:1; similarly Lk 1:18)
- ወወፅአ፡ ስሙዓቱ wa-waḍʾa səmuʿātu 'his fame (pl. form) spread' (Mt 4:24)
- ተአኅዘ፡ ብዙኅ፡ ዓሣት፡ ፈድፋደ taʾəḫza bəzuḫ ʿāśāt fadfāda 'very many fish were caught' (Lk 5:6); also the adjective ብዙኅ bəzuḫ is in the singular
- እስከ፡ ተመልኀ፡ ክነፊሃ ʾəska tamalḫa kənafihā '... until its wings (pl.) were torn out (sing.)' (Dan 7:4)

6.2.2.6. When two or more subjects are present, the verb can agree with the sum of all subjects and exhibit the plural or be in the singular. In the latter case, the verb agrees with the first subject when animate nouns are involved.

- ወፍርሀት፡ ወረዓድ፡ ወረደ፡ ላዕሌሁ wa-fərhat wa-raʿād warada lāʿlehu 'and fear and trembling fell upon him (3ms)' (Lk 1:12)
- ወይነሥኦሙ፡ ፍርሃት፡ ወረዓድ፡ ዓቢይ wa-yənaśśəʾomu fərhāt wa-raʿād ʿābiy (for: ፍርሀት fərhat and ዐቢይ ʿabiy) 'and fear and great trembling will seize (3ms) them' (En 1:5)
- ከመ፡ ኢይሙቱ፡ ዳንኤል፡ ወአዕርክቲሁ kama ʾi-yəmutu (variant ኢይሙት ʾi-yəmut) dānəʾel wa-ʾaʿrəktihu 'so that Daniel and his friends might not perish' (Dan 2:18)

6.2.3. Word Order in the Verbal Clause

6.2.3.1. Word order is relatively free in Classical Ethiopic. Because of this syntactic variability, the word order of the original text is often retained in translation literature. In poetic texts, word order variations are deliberately used as a stylistic device.

It is nevertheless possible to notice basic word order types and to distinguish between syntactically marked and unmarked constructions. In many cases, markedness is achieved by fronting a sentence-element that is not usually in first position (topicalization). Sentence-final position can also indicate markedness.

6.2.3.2. In an unmarked verbal clause, the verb usually precedes the other main sentence elements such as subject, object, or adverbial complement. When the subject is overtly expressed by a noun, it commonly follows the verb. Objects (except for object suffixes [§6.2.3.6.]) follow the subject. Longer adverbial complements (such as prepositional phrases and adverbial accusatives) occur after the object and any other complements if these are present in the sentence. Classical Ethiopic thus has – in accordance with other classical West Semitic languages and in contrast to modern Ethiopian languages (SOV throughout) – the basic word order VSO, although this word order is not of the strict type.[276]

The following presents examples for the unmarked order of sentence types that overtly express the subject, that is VSO (verb – subject – object), VSA (verb – subject – adverbial phrase), and VSOA:

VSO   ለታብቊል ፡ ምድር ፡ ሐመልማለ ፡ ሣዕር *la-tābqʷəl mədr ḥamalmāla śāʿr* 'let the earth bring forth green vegetation!' (Gen 1:11); ወገብረ ፡ ኖኅ ፡ ኵሎ *wa-gabra noḫ kʷəllo* 'Noah did all (that the Lord had commanded him)' (Gen 7:5)

VSA   ወአንሶሰወ ፡ ኢየሱስ ፡ ውስተ ፡ ኵሉ ፡ ገሊላ *wa-ʾansosawa ʾiyasus wəsta kʷəllu galilā* 'and Jesus walked through all of Galilee' (Mt 4:23); ወሀሎ ፡ ዮሐንስ ፡ ያጠምቅ ፡ በገዳም *wa-hallo yoḥannəs yāṭamməq ba-gadām* 'John used to baptize in the wilderness' (Mk 1:4) (V_1SV_2A; §5.4.5)

---

[276] See Bulakh 2012 for word order in epigraphic Classical Ethiopic.

VSOA   ወረከበ፡ዮሴፍ፡ሞገሰ፡በቅድም፡እግዚኡ wa-rakaba yosef mogasa ba-qədma
       ʾəgziʾu 'Joseph found favor before his lord' (Gen 39:4)

When the sentence has a direct and indirect object, the indirect object usually
precedes the direct object: ትወልድ፡ለከ፡ወልደ tawalləd laka walda 'she will bear
you a son' (Lk 1:13); ወወሀብኩ፡ከሁ wa-wahabku-kā-hu 'I hereby give it to you'
(Num 18:8 [§5.4.7.4.]). Most verbal clauses do not contain an overtly expressed
subject, that is, a subject noun phrase, since the subject is expressed within the
finite verbal form through personal affixes. The basic word order in these
clauses is thus VO(A) and VA.

6.2.3.3. The placement of the subject before the verb (order SV and SVO[A]),
however, is also frequent:

- እግዚአብሔር፡ወሀበክሙ፡ዘዕለተ፡ሰንበት ʾəgziʾab(ə)ḥer wahabakkəmu za-ʿəlata
  sanbat 'God has given you the Sabbath' (Ex 16:29)
- በልጠሶር፡ንጉሥ፡ገብረ፡ምሳሐ፡ለመገብቱ balṭasor nəguś gabra məsāḥa la-
  maggabtu 'King Belshazzar made a feast for his lords' (Dan 5:1)
- እስመ፡እሙንቱ፡ይሬእይዎ፡ለእግዚአብሔር ʾasma ʾəmuntu yəreʾəyəwwo la-
  ʾəgziʾab(ə)ḥer '... for they will see God' (Mt 5:8)

In many of these cases, the subject is emphasized so that the order SVO, despite
its relative frequency, can be considered marked. The fronted subject is
emphasized for certain when it is extended by a suffixed enclitic particle such
as -ሰ –ssa, -ሂ –hi, or -ኒ –ni (§4.5.8.), the interrogative particle -ኑ/-ሁ –nu/-hu
(§4.5.9.1.), or when it is preceded by a pronoun of demonstrative/anaphoric
force.

Verbal clauses with non-indicative meaning (e.g., clauses with a jussive
[§5.4.3.1.]) only rarely front the subject, the normative word order being verb
first, as in ይገንዩ፡ለከ፡እግዚኦ፡ኩሉ፡ተግባርከ፤ወይባርኩከ፡ጻድቃኒከ yəgannəyu laka
ʾəgziʾo kʷəllu tagbārəka wa-yəbārrəkuka ṣādəqānika 'all your works shall praise you
o Lord, and your righteous shall bless you' (Ps 145:10 [144:10]).

6.2.3.4. The object is only fronted when it is focused or topicalized:

- ሠናየ፡ግበሩ፡ለእለ፡ይጸልኡክሙ śannāya gəbaru la-ʾəlla yəṣalləʾukəmu 'do
  good to those who are hostile toward you' (Mt 5:44)

- ወምኮራብኒ፡ ውእቱ፡ ሐነጸ፡ ለነ *wa-mək^wərāba-ni wəʾətu ḥanaṣa lana* 'and even the synagogue he built for us' (Lk 7:5)

- ሲሳየነ፡ ዘለለ፡ ዕለትነ፡ ሀበነ፡ ዮም *sisāyana za-lalla ʿəlatəna habanna yom* 'our daily bread give us today!' (Mt 6:11)

- ወለምእላዲሁ፡ ለማይ፡ ሰመዮ፡ ባሕረ *wa-la-məʾəllādihu la-māy samayo bāḥra* 'the gathering place of the water he called sea' (Gen 1:10)

- ወለዝክቱኒ፡ ሰቀልዎ *wa-la-zəktu-ni saqaləwwo* 'that one, however, was hanged (lit. 'they hung')' (Gen 41:13) (§5.2.3.2.)

- ለኆእምኔሆሙ፡ መጠውዎ፡ ለአእዱግ *la-ʾaḥadu ʾəmənnehomu maṭṭawəwwo la-ʾaʾdug* '... one of them (i.e., sheep) they handed over to the wild donkeys' (En 89:13)

- ለከ፡ እብለከ፡ ወሬዛ፡ ተንሥእ *laka ʾəbəlakka warezā tanśəʾ* 'I say to you, young man, arise (from the dead)!' (Lk 7:14) (topicalized indirect object)

- ወርቱዐ፡ ግበሩ፡ መጽያሕቶ *wa-rətuʿa gəbaru maṣyāḥto* 'make straight his path!' (Mt 3:3)

The object occurs more often before the verb in subordinate clauses than in main clauses, as in ወእንዘ፡ ዘንተ፡ ይሔሊ *wa-ʾənza zanta yəḥelli* 'while he was thinking (about) this' (Mt 1:20).

6.2.3.5. Longer adverbial phrases, for example prepositional phrases, are likewise only fronted when focused/topicalized:

- ወበውእቱ፡ መዋዕል፡ ዓርገት፡ ጸሎት፡ ጻድቃን *wa-ba-wəʾətu mawāʿəl ʿārgat ṣəlota ṣādəqān* 'and in those days the prayer of the righteous will have risen ...' (En 47:1)

- ወበእማንቱ፡ መዋዕል፡ ርእኩዎ፡ ለርእሰ፡ መዋዕል *wa-ba-ʾəmāntu mawāʿəl rəʾikəwwo la-rəʾsa mawāʿəl* 'and in those days I saw the Head of Days' (En 47:3)

- ወቤት/ወሀገርኒ፡ ኀበ፡ ቦእክሙ *wa-bet / wa-hagarə-ni ḫaba boʾkəmu* 'and whenever you enter a house/a city ...' (Lk 10:5; 10:8); only the nominal element is topicalized, the preposition ኀበ *ḫaba* follows the nominal phrases.

6.2.3.6. The order VOS (object before subject) is the normative order when the object is expressed in the form of a pronominal suffix on the verb, as in አዕረጎ፡ መንፈስ፡ ገዳም *ʾaʿrago manfas gadāma* 'the spirit led him into the wilderness' (Mt 4:1). The object of a *qatalo la-nəguś* construction (§5.2.3.2.) likewise tends to precede the subject, as in ወሶቤሃ፡ ፍጡነ፡ አብኦ፡ ለዳንኤል፡ አርዮክ፡ ቅድመ፡ ንጉሥ *wa-sobehā fəṭuna ʔabəʔo la-dānəʔel ʔaryok qədma nəguś* 'and then Arioch quickly brought Daniel before the king' (Dan 2:25).

The order VOS is further found when the object forms an expression together with the verb, as in ወወለደት፡ ወለደ፡ ይእቲ፡ ብእሲት *wa-waldat walda yəʔəti bəʔəsit* 'that woman bore a son' (Judg 13:24).

In other cases, the order expresses focus of the object or objects, as in ወከሠቶ፡ ለቅዱሳን፡ ወጻድቃን፡ ጠበቡ፡ ለእግዚአ፡ መናፍስት *wa-kaśato la-qəddusān wa-ṣādəqān ṭababu la-ʔəgziʔa manāfəst* 'the wisdom of the Lord of Spirits has revealed him to the holy and righteous' (En 48:7).

6.2.3.7. Other word orders, such as SAV, are rare and always represent marked constructions:

- ወጽድቅ፡ ምስሌሁ፡ ኀደረ *wa-ṣədq məslehu ḫādara* 'righteousness dwells with him' (En 46:3)
- (እስመ፡ ኦሪት፡ በሙሴ፡ ተውህበት፡ ለነ፡)ወጸጋ-ሰ፡ ወጽድቅ፡ በኢየሱስ፡ ክርስቶስ፡ ኮነ *(ʔəsma ʔorit ba-muse tawəhbat lana) wa-ṣaggā-ssa wa-ṣədq ba-ʔiyasus krəstos kona* '(for the law was given to us by Moses), grace and truth came into being through Jesus Christ' (Jn 1:17)
- ወዓለም-ኒ፡ ቦቱ፡ ኮነ *wa-ʕāləmə-ni bottu kona* 'the world, however, came into being through him' (Jn 1:10)
- ወናሁ፡ ሕልም፡ መጽአኒ፡ ወራእያት፡ ዲበየ፡ ወድቁ *wa-nāhu ḥəlm maṣʔanni / wa-rāʔyāt dibeya wadqu* 'and behold, a dream came to me and visions fell upon me' (En 13:8); a poetic text with SAV-order in the second colon.

6.2.4. Negation of Verbal Clauses

Verbal clauses in Classical Ethiopic are usually negated by ኢ- *ʔi–*, which is prefixed to the verb (§4.5.4.1.). In negated interrogative clauses that contain a verb, ኢ- *ʔi–* is prefixed to the verbal form and the interrogative particle -ኑ *–nu* suffixed to it, as in ኢያንበብክሙኑ *ʔi-yānbabkəmu-nu* 'have you not read ...?' (Mk 2:25).

Verbal clauses with a topicalized sentence-element – especially interrogative clauses – on the other hand, use አኮ *ʾakko* or አኮኑ *ʾakko-nu* (§4.5.4.2.2.) before the topicalized element, as in አኮ፡ ትትኃብኡ፡ ሀለወክሙ *ʾakko təthābəʾu hallawakkəmu* 'you will not have to hide' (En 104:5);[277] አኮኑ፡ በእንተ፡ ራሔል፡ ተቀነይኩ *ʾakko-nu ba-ʾənta rāḥel taqanayku* 'did I not serve on account of Rachel?' (Gen 29:25). This type of clause is comparable to negated cleft sentences from a functional perspective (§6.4.5.).

6.3. Casus Pendens

6.3.1. The "casus pendens" – also called "extraposition" – is a construction in which an isolated nominal or pronominal element is placed before a syntactically complete verbal or nominal clause. The extraposed element correlates with a syntactic constituent of the following clause, but, despite its function in the following clause, most commonly appears in the nominative (= non-accusative). The syntactic isolation of the extraposed element is reflected by the fact that it is resumed by either a pronominal or adverbial expression in the following clause. Classical Ethiopic does not usually connect the extraposed element and the following clause by a conjunction.

The extraposed element is in focus. The basic translation value in English is 'as for X, as far as X is concerned'.

Constructions that exhibit a fronted but syntactically integrated sentence element or a following incomplete clause are not to be considered extrapositions, as in ወለዝክቱኒ፡ ሰቀልዎ *wa-la-zəktu-ni saqaləwwo* 'that one, however, they hanged' (§5.2.3.2.) and ወለብእሲትየኒ፡ ኃለፈ፡ መዋዕሊሃ *wa-la-bəʾsitəya-ni ḫalafa mawāʿəlihā* 'and also the days of my wife are advanced (lit. 'passed')' (Lk 1:18) (§5.2.4.3.). This type of sentence reflects a syntactic unit with a topicalized sentence-element. In some cases, the distinction between extraposition and topicalized fronting can be difficult.

6.3.2. The following presents examples of extraposition. The syntactic break between extraposed element and following clause is indicated by a slash in the transliteration.

---

[277] ትትኃብኡ *təthābəʾu* is topicalized in this sentence. The normal word order would be ሀለወክሙ፡ ትትኃብኡ *hallawakkəmu təthābəʾu*.

(a) The extraposed element correlates with the subject of the following clause:

- ውእቱ፡ ብእሲ፡ ዘበላዕሌሁ፡ ተረክበ፡ ኮራየ፡ ውእቱ፡ ይኩነኒ፡ ገብረ *wəʾətu bəʾəsi za-ba-lāʿlehu tarakba korāya / wəʾətu yəkunanni gabra* 'as for the man upon whom my cup was found – he shall be my slave!' (Gen 44:17)

- ወብእሲ፡ እንዘ፡ ንጹሕ፡ ውእቱ፡ ወኢመጽአ ... ወይሠረው፡ ውእቱ፡ ብእሲ *wa-bəʾəsi ʾənza nəṣuḥ wəʾətu wa-ʾi-maṣʾa ... / wa-yəśśarraw wəʾətu bəʾəsi* 'and as for man who is pure but does not come ... - he is to be uprooted' (Jub 49:9)

- አንትሙኬ፡ መነ፡ ትብሉኒ *ʾantəmu-ke / manna təbəluni* 'but you – what do you call me?' (Mk 8:29)

(b) The extraposed element correlates with the direct object of the following clause:

- ወእምዝ፡ ኢየሱስ፡ አዕረጎ፡ መንፈስ፡ ገዳም *wa-ʾəmzə ʾiyasus / ʾaʿrago manfas gadāma* 'and then, as for Jesus – the spirit led him into the wilderness' (Mt 4:1)

(c) The extraposed element correlates with the indirect object of the following clause:

- አንተ፡ አምላከ፡ አበዊነ፡ እገኒ፡ ለከ *ʾanta ʾamlāka ʾabawina / ʾəganni laka* 'you, God of our fathers – I give thanks to you' (Dan 2:23)

- ወአነሂ፡ አኮ፡ በጥበብየ ... ዘተከሥተ፡ ሊተ፡ ዘኅቡእ *wa-ʾana-hi / ʾakko ba-ṭəbabəya ... za-takaśta lita za-ḫəbuʾ* 'but as for me – it is not because of my wisdom that that which is hidden has been revealed to me' (Dan 2:30)

- ለጻድቃንሰ፡ ሰላም፡ ይገብር፡ ሎሙ *la-ṣādəqanə-ssa / salāma yəgabbər lomu* 'but for the righteous – he will make peace' (En 1:8); the extraposed element is preceded by ለ– *la–*.

(d) The extraposed element correlates with a genitive (possessive suffix) in the following clause:

- ወያዕቆብሰ፡ ሕሡም፡ ራእዩ *wa-yāʿqobə-ssa / ḥəśum rāʾyu* 'but as for Jacob – his appearance was ugly' (Gen 25:27)

- ወአዝዕብት፡ ተጸለሉ፡ አዕይንቲሆሙ *wa-ʾazʿəbt / taṣallalu ʾaʿyəntihomu* 'as for the wolves – their eyes were blinded' (En 89:21)

- አኮኑ፡ እሙ፡ ስጋ፡ ማርያም *ʾakko-nu ʾəmmu / səmā māryām* 'as for his mother, is her name not Mary?' (Mt 13:55)

- ወወርቅክሙሰ፡ ካዕቶ፡ ንሥኡ፡ ምስሌክሙ wa-warqakəmu-ssa / kāʿbato nəśəʾu məslekəmu 'but as for your money – take double with you' (Gen 43:12)
- ወውእቱ፡ ዮሐንስ፡ ልብሱ ... ዘጸጕረ፡ ገመል፡ ወቅናቱ፡ ዘአዲም ... ወሲሳዩ፡ አንባጣ፡ ወመዓረ፡ ገዳም wa-wəʾtu yohannəs / ləbsu ... za-ṣagʷra gamal wa-qənātu za-ʾadim ... wa-sisāyu ʾanbaṭā wa-maʿāra gadām 'and as for John – his clothing was of camel's hair and his belt of leather ... and his food was locusts and wild honey' (Mt 3:4)

6.3.3. Nominal clauses of the type ብእሲ፡ ሎቱ፡ ክልኤተ፡ ውሉደ bəʾasi lottu kəlʾeta wəluda 'the man has/had two sons' can also be analyzed as pendens constructions: 'as for the man, he has/had two sons.'

6.4. Cleft Sentences

6.4.1. In order to put a specific sentence-element into focus, a verbal main clause can be transformed ("clefted") into a relative clause that has the structure of a two-element nominal clause (§6.1.1.): the focused element takes on the role of the emphasized predicate, while the following relative clause introduced by ዘ– za– as a whole functions as the subject.

Cleft sentences serve to clearly mark the respective sentence element as focused, especially when the construction serves to express contrast (cf. Kapeliuk 1985). They are particularly frequent in interrogative and negative contexts. The Classical Ethiopic (አል)ቦ፡ ዘ– (ʾal)bo za– construction (§6.1.4.4.–4.5.) likewise has the structure of a cleft sentence.

6.4.2. Cleft sentences in Classical Ethiopic are not negated by ኢ– ʾi– but by the emphasizing negative particle አኮ ʾakko (§4.5.4.2.2.). This negative particle only negates the focused sentence-element, as in አኮ፡ በኅብስት፡ ከመ፡ ዘየሐዩ፡ ሰብእ ʾakko ba-ḫəbəst kəmma za-yaḥayyu sabʾ 'it is not by bread alone that men live' (Mt 4:4).

6.4.3. For a negated verbal clause of the type ኢሐነጸ፡ ንጉሥ፡ ቤቶ፡ ዝየ ʾi-ḥanaṣa nəguś beto zəya 'the king did not build his house here' (VSOA order), Classical Ethiopic has the following possible cleft sentences:

(a) አኮ፡ዝየ፡ዘሐነጸ፡ንጉሥ፡ቤቶ *ʾakko zəya za-ḥanaṣa nəguś beto* (focus on adverbial expression)

(b) አኮ፡ቤቶ፡ዘሐነጸ፡ንጉሥ፡ዝየ *ʾakko betu za-ḥanaṣa nəguś zəya* (focus on object)

(c) አኮ፡ንጉሥ፡ዘሐነጸ፡ቤቶ፡ዝየ *ʾakko nəguś za-ḥanaṣa beto zəya* (focus on subject)

The respective sentences can be translated as follows:

(a) 'It was not here that the king built his house' (i.e., he did not build the house here but somewhere else)
(b) 'It was not his house that the king built here' (i.e., he did not build his house here but something else)
(c) 'It was not the king who built his house here' (i.e., it was not the king but somebody else who built his house here)

6.4.4. Examples for non-negated declarative clauses with cleft-sentence structure:

- ዘውእቱ፡ብርሃነ፡ጽድቅ፡ዘያበርህ፡ለኵሉ፡ሰብእ፡ዘይመጽእ፡ውስተ፡ዓለም   *za-wəʾtu bərhāna ṣədq za-yābarrəh la-kʷəllu sabʾ za-yəmaṣṣəʾ wəsta ʿālam* 'the one who is the true light that illuminates everyone was coming into the world (i.e., 'it was him who came into the world')' (Jn 1:9)

- ወብርሃንሰ፡ዘውስተ፡ጽልመት፡ያበርህ *wa-bərhānə-ssa za-wəsta ṣəlmat yābarrəh* 'but it is the light that shines in the darkness' (Jn 1:5)

6.4.5. Examples of negated declarative clauses with cleft-sentence structure:

- አኮ፡በኅብስት፡ክመ፡ዘየሐዩ፡ሰብእ *ʾakko ba-ḫabəst kəmma za-yaḥayyu sabʾ* 'man does not live by bread alone' (lit. 'it is not by bread alone that men live') (Mt 4:4)

- አኮ፡ኵሉ፡ዘይብለኒ፡እግዚኦ፡እግዚኦ፡ዘይበውእ፡ውስተ፡መንግሥተ፡ሰማያት *ʾakko kʷəllu za-yəbəlanni ʾəgziʾo ʾəgziʾo za-yəbawwəʾ wəsta mangəśta samāyāt* 'not everyone who says to me 'o Lord! o Lord!' will enter the kingdom of heaven' (lit. 'it is not everyone ... who will enter' (Mt 7:21) (basic structure: አኮ፡ኵሉ ... ዘይበውእ *ʾakko kʷəllu ... za-yəbawwəʾ*)

- ወኪያየስ፡ አኮ፡ ዘልፈ፡ ዘትረክቡኒ *wa-kiyāya-ssa ʾakko zalfa za-tərakkəbuni* 'but me, you will not always find me' (lit. 'as for me, it is not always that you will find me' (Mk 14:7)

- ወአነሂ፡ አኮ፡ በጥበብየ ... ዘተከሥተ፡ ሊተ፡ ዘኀቡእ *wa-ʾana-hi / ʾakko ba-ṭəbabəya ... za-takaśta lita za-ḫəbuʾ* 'but as for me – it is not because of my wisdom that that which is hidden has been revealed to me' (Dan 2:30); አኮ፡ ዘ– *ʾakko za-* after extraposition

- አኮ፡ ዘሞተት፡ ሕፃን፡ አላ፡ ትነውም *ʾakko za-motat ḥəḍān ʾallā tənawwəm* 'the child did not die but is (only) sleeping' (Mt 9:24); in this case, the negation itself is the focused element; the sentence is the transformed variant of ኢሞተት *ʾi-motat* 'she did not die' (cf. Mk 5:39 and Lk 8:52: ኢሞተት፡ ሕፃንሰ፡ አላ፡ ትነውም *ʾi-motat ḥəḍānə-ssa ʾallā tənawwəm* 'the child is not dead, it is only sleeping').

6.4.6. Examples of interrogative clauses with cleft-sentence structure:

- መኑ፡ ዘገብረ፡ ዘንተ *mannu za-gabra zanta* or መኑ፡ ውእቱ፡ ዘገብረ፡ ዘንተ *mannu wəʾətu za-gabra zanta* 'who did this?' (lit. 'who was it that ...', transformation of መኑ፡ ገብረ፡ ዘንተ *mannu gabra zanta*)

- እፎ፡ ዘኢትሌብዉ *ʾəffo za-ʾi-təlebbəwu* 'why do you not understand?' (lit. 'why is it that ...') (Mt 16:11)

Questions of this type are frequent in Classical Ethiopic. Although they represent cleft sentences on a syntactic level, they are more commonly translated as simple questions as indicated in the examples above.

6.5. Subordinate Clauses

Subordinate clauses are formally subordinated incomplete sentences. The differentiation of main and subordinate clauses in Classical Ethiopic, however, can be difficult in certain cases since some conjunctions can have both coordinating and subordinating functions. The following subdivision of Classical Ethiopic subordinate clauses is based on their syntactic and semantic functions. Most of the clauses contain a verbal predicate. Verbless subordinate clauses are relatively infrequent.

6.5.1. Relative Clauses

Relative clauses are subordinate clauses that are introduced by a relative pronoun (ዘ– *za*–, እንተ *ʾanta*, እለ *ʾalla* [§4.1.5.]). They most often appear as dependent clauses and have the syntactic function of an attribute to a noun (§6.5.1.1.). They can also, however, appear independently, that is, without a head noun, and can function as the subject (§6.5.1.3.), as the object (§6.5.1.4.), or as another sentence-element (§6.5.1.5.–1.7.).[278]

6.5.1.1. Attributive Relative Clauses

6.5.1.1.1. Attributive relative clauses serve as qualifications of nominal phrases. In this function, they most commonly modify the subject or object of the main clause, less often other sentence-elements. The noun phrase that represents the head of the relative clause (§6.5.1.1.2.), which commonly immediately precedes it, appears in the unbound form:

(a) Subject as head noun:

- ኵሉ፡ዘያምዕዕ፡እኀዋሁ *kʷəllu za-yāməʿəʿ ʾəḫwāhu* 'everyone who provokes his brother' (Mt 5:22)
- ሀገር ... እንተ፡መልዕልተ፡ደብር፡ትነብር *hagar ... ʾanta malʿəlta dabr tənabbər* 'a city that lies on a hill (cannot be hidden)' (Mt 5:14)
- የውጣ፡እንተ፡አሐቲ፡ቅርፀታ *yawṭā ʾanta ʾaḥatti qərḍatā* 'the Iota that is only a single stroke' = 'the Iota that only consists of a stroke' (Mt 5:18); nominal relative clause

(b) Direct object as head noun:

- ወተስእልክዎ፡ለ፩እመላእክት፡ቅዱሳን፡ዘየሐውር፡ምስሌየ *wa-tasəʾalkəwwo la-ʾaḥadu ʾəm-malāʾəkt qəddusān za-yaḥawwər məsleya* 'and I asked one of the holy angels who went with me' (En 46:2)
- ሰደድዎሙ፡ለነቢያት፡እለ፡እምቅድሜክሙ *sadadəwwomu la-nabiyāt ʾalla ʾəm-qədmekəmu* 'the prophets who were before you were persecuted (lit. 'they persecuted the prophets who have come before you') (Mt 5:12); nominal relative clause

(c) Object of preposition as referent:

- ምስሌነ፡ለእለ፡ፀርነ *məslena la-ʾalla ṣorna* 'together with us, who have born the burden (of the heat of the day)' (Mt 20:12)

---

[278] For the function of ዘ– *za*– in Classical Ethiopic, see also Bulakh 2009.

- ዘእንበለ፡ አማልክት፡ እለ፡ ኢኮነ፡ ንብረቶሙ፡ ምስለ፡ ኮሉ፡ ዘሥጋ *za-ʾənbala ʾamāləkt ʾəlla ʾi-kona nəbratomu məsla kʷəllu za-śəgā* '... except for the gods whose dwelling is not with any mortals' (Dan 2:11)

6.5.1.1.2. As mentioned in the previous paragraph, most attributive relative clauses immediately follow their head noun or referent (§6.5.1.1.1.). Short relative clauses, especially those that reflect nominal clauses, and verbal clauses that are used to circumscribe an agent noun or attributive adjective (§5.1.5e), however, can also appear before the head, as in ዘከመዝ፡ ሥልጣን *za-kama-za śəlṭān* 'such power'; ዘመጠነዝ፡ ሃይማኖት *za-maṭana-za hāymānot* 'such faith'; ዘሞተ፡ ብእሲ *za-mota bəʾasi* 'the man who died'; እምእንተ፡ ትመጽእ፡ መዐት *ʾəm-ʾənta təmaṣṣəʾ maʿat* 'before the coming wrath' (Mt 3:7). Relative clauses generally precede their head in modern Ethiopian languages.

6.5.1.1.3. Attributive relative clauses often contain a pronoun or pronominal suffix that resumes the head noun of the main clause, as in ብእሲ፡ ዘርእዮ *bəʾasi za-rəʾyəwwo* (besides ብእሲ፡ ዘርእዩ *bəʾasi za-rəʾyu*) 'the man they saw'. When the head noun is the direct object of its clause, as in the two examples just given, resumption is optional. Resumption is regularly used when the relative clause stands in a genitival or prepositional relationship ('the land in which they dwell', 'a man whose name was John'). No resumption is used when the head noun represents the subject of its clause.

- ብእሲ፡ ዘስሙ፡ ዮሐንስ *bəʾasi za-səmu yoḥannəs* 'a man whose name is John' (besides less frequent ብእሲ፡ ስሙ፡ ዮሐንስ *bəʾasi səmu yoḥannəs* [§6.5.2.])
- ሀገር፡ እንተ፡ ስማ፡ ኢየሩሳሌም *hagar ʾənta səmā ʾiyarusālem* 'a city whose name is Jerusalem'
- አሕዛብ፡ ዘእንትሙ፡ ትትወረስዎሙ *ʾaḥzāb za-ʾantəmu tətwarrasəwwomu* 'the nations from whom you will inherit' (Dtn 12:2)
- ዝመንፈስ፡ ዘመኑ፡ ውእቱ፡ ዘከመዝ፡ ቃሉ፡ ይበጽሕ፡ እስከ፡ ሰማይ፡ ወይሰኪ *zə-manfas za-mannu wəʾətu za-kama-za qālu yəbaṣṣəḥ ʾəska samāy wa-yəsakki* 'whose spirit is this whose voice thus reaches heaven and complains?' (En 22:6) (lit. 'this spirit, whose is it ...')
- በምድር፡ እንተ፡ በውስቴታ፡ ተወልደ *ba-mədr ʾənta ba-wəstetā tawalda* 'in the land in which he was born' (Gen 11:28)

- ወነበረ፡ ያዕቆብ፡ ውስተ፡ ምድር፡ እንተ፡ ውስቴታ፡ ነበረ፡ አቡሁ *wa-nabara yāʕqob wəsta mədr ʾənta wəstetā nabara ʾabuhu* 'Jacob dwelled in a land in which his father had lived' (Gen 37:1)
- (ቤተ፡ ክርስቲያኑ፡)እንተ፡ ላቲ፡ ተሠየምኩ፡ አነ፡ ላእክ (*beta krəstiyānu*) *ʾənta lātti taśayamku ʾana lāʾka* '(his church) over which I was appointed minister' (Col 1:25)
- ለትጥፋእ፡ ይእቲ፡ ዕለት፡ እንተ፡ ባቲ፡ ተወለድኩ *la-təṭfaʾ yəʾəti ʕəlat ʾənta bātti tawaladku* 'let the day perish on which I was born' (Job 3:3)
- ዕለት፡ እንተ፡ ባቲ፡ ገብረ፡ እግዚአብሔር፡ ሰማየ፡ ወምድረ *ʕəlat ʾənta bātti gabra ʾəgziʾab(ə)ḥer samāya wa-mədra* 'the day on which God made heaven and earth' (Gen 2:4)
- ዝውእቱ፡ ዘእቤለክሙ፡ አነ፡ በእንቲአሁ *zə-wəʾətu za-ʾəbelakkəmu ʾana baʾəntiʾahu* 'he was the one of whom I told you (as follows)' (Jn 1:15)
- ፀብእ ... ዘኢኮነ፡ ከማሁ፡ በገብ፡ ቀዳምያን፡ ነገሥተ፡ ኢትዮጵያ *ḍabʾ ... za-ʾi-kona kamāhu ba-ḫaba qadāməyān nagaśta ʾityoṗəyā* '... a battle ... which had no equivalent among the former kings of Ethiopia' (ʕĀmda Ṣəyon 11c)
- ምድር፡ እንተ፡ ኀበ፡ መጻእነ *mədr ʾənta ḫaba maṣāʾna* 'the land into which we have come' (Gen 47:4) (without resumptive pronoun)

6.5.1.1.4. Short (proclitic) prepositions that specify the attribution can also precede the relative pronoun:

- ምስሌነ፡ ለእለ፡ ጸርነ *məslena la-ʾəlla ṣorna* ... 'together with us, who have born the burden (of the heat of the day)' (Mt 20:12)
- ወተጠየቀ፡ እምኀቤሆሙ፡ መዋዕሊሁ፡ በዘ፡ አስተርአዮሙ፡ ኮከብ *wa-taṭayyaqa ʾəm-ḫabehomu mawāʕəlihu ba-za ʾastarʾayomu kokab* 'and he learned from them the time when the star had appeared to them' (Mt 2:7)

6.5.1.1.5. The relative pronoun generally agrees with its head noun in gender and number (cf. §5.1.5.). There are, however, sporadic cases that attest to a gender-neutral use of the pronoun ዘ– *za-* (instead of እንተ *ʾənta* or እለ *ʾəlla*). This use of ዘ– *za-* is, for example, common after a head noun in the plural:

- አሕዛብ፡ ዘእንትሙ፡ ትትወረስዎሙ *ʾaḥzāb za-ʾantəmu tətwarrasəwwomu* 'the nations from whom you will inherit' (Dtn 12:2) (besides አሕዛብ፡ እለ *ʾaḥzāb ʾəlla*)

- ወኮሎ፡ መዛግብት፡ ዘኅቡእ wa-kʷǝllo mazāgǝbta za-ḫǝbuʾ 'and all the treasures of that which is hidden' (En 46:3) (although in this example, also ኩሎ kʷǝllo and ኅቡእ ḫǝbuʾ are in the singular)

6.5.1.1.6. Attributive relative clauses can have causal, conditional, or other adverbial connotations:

- እሴብሐ፡ ለእግዚአብሔር፡ ዘረድአኒ ʾǝsebbǝḥo la-ʾǝgziʾab(ǝ)ḥer za-radʾanni 'I shall praise God who (= because he) has helped me' (Ps 13:6 [12:6])
- ... ከመ፡ ይትፈደዩ፡ እምኔሆሙ፡ ዘገፍዕዎሙ ... kama yǝtfadayu ʾǝmǝnnehomu za-gafʾǝwwomu ... '... so that they may repay those who (= because they) oppressed them (i.e., his children and chosen ones)' (En 62:11)
- ኩሉ፡ ዘያሜዕዕ፡ እኅዋሁ kʷǝllu za-yāmāʿǝʿ ʾǝḫwāhu 'everyone who provokes his brother' = 'if anybody provokes ...' (Mt 5:22); for other relative clauses with conditional connotations, see §6.5.6.6.
- አሐተ፡ እምእላ፡ ትእዛዛት፡ እንተ፡ ተሐጽጽ ʾaḥatta ʾǝm-ʾǝllā tǝʾǝzāzāt ʾǝnta taḥaṣṣǝṣ 'one of these commandments that is the least' = '... even if it is the least' (Mt 5:19)

6.5.1.2. Attributive Relative Clauses without a Head Noun

Of special note are relative clauses that are subject or object clauses syntactically but that have the function of an attributive clause. The logical referent or head of these types of constructions does not stand before the relative clause but usually within the relative clause itself after the verbal predicate and is, syntactically, part of the relative clause. This construction places focus on the head noun:

- ዘአስተናሥአነ፡ መንፈስ፡ እግዚአብሔር፡ ለወጢነ፡ ዝንቱ፡ መጽሐፍ za-ʾastanāśǝʾanna manfasa ʾǝgziʾab(ǝ)ḥer la-waṭina zǝntu maṣḥaf 'the spirit of God, that impelled us to begin this book ...' (literally: 'the one who impelled us, namely the spirit of God ...') (Lǝbna dǝngǝl Prologue)
- እንገርክሙ፡ ካዕበ፡ ዘኮነ፡ ፀብእ፡ በይእቲ፡ ዕለት ʾǝngǝrkǝmu kāʿǝba za-kona ḍabʾ ba-yǝʾǝti ʿǝlat 'I shall tell you again of the battle that happened that day' (ʿĀmda Ṣǝyon 11c); for እንገርክሙ፡ ካዕበ፡ ፀብአ፡ ዘኮነ፡ በይእቲ፡ ዕለት   ... ʾǝngǝrkǝmu kāʿǝba ḍabʾa za-kona ba-yǝʾǝti ʿǝlat ...
- ትክሉኑ፡ ስትየ፡ ዘአነ፡ ሀለውኩ፡ ጽዋዐ፡ እስተይ tǝkǝlu-nu satǝya za-ʾana hallawku ṣǝwwāʿa ʾǝstay 'are you able to drink the cup that I am about to drink?'

(Mt 20:22); for ትክሉኑ፡ ስትየ፡ ጽዋዐ፡ ዘአነ፡ ሀለውኩ፡ እስተይ *təkəlu-nu satəya ṣəwwāʿa za-ʾana hallawku ʾəstay*

6.5.1.3. Independent Relative Clauses Functioning as Subjects

Relative clauses that function as subjects are very frequent among relative clauses that do not function as an attribute to a head noun. Many of these subordinate clauses represent constructions with an imperfective predicate that are used to circumscribe agent nouns (§5.1.5d).

Relative clauses that function as subjects can occupy any position in a sentence that a subject can take. Consequently, they can appear before and after the remainder of the sentence. A few examples include:

The relative clause is the subject of a verbal clause:

- ይመጽእ፡ እምድኅሬየ፡ ዘሀሎ፡ እምቅድሜየ *yəmaṣṣəʾ ʾəm-dəḥreya za-hallo ʾəm-qədmeya* 'the one who was before me comes after me' (Jn 1:15)
- ወዘእምድኅሬሰ፡ ይመጽእ፡ ይጸንዕ፡ እምኔየ *wa-za-ʾəm-dəḥreya-ssa yəmaṣṣəʾ yəṣannəʿ ʾəmənneya* 'but the one who will come after me is more powerful than me' (Mt 3:11)
- ሀለዉ፡ ዝየ ... እለ፡ ኢይጠዕሙዋ፡ ለሞት *hallawu zəya ... ʾəlla ʾi-yəṭəʿməwwā la-mot* 'there are (some) here ... who will not taste death' (Mk 9:1)
- ወዘይከሥት፡ ጐቡአ፡ አርአየከ፡ ዘሀሎ፡ ይኩን *wa-za-yəkaśśət ḥəbuʾa ʾarʾayakka za-hallo yəkun* 'and the revealer of mysteries showed you what is to be' (Dan 2:29)

The relative clause is the subject of a nominal clause:

- ብፁዓን፡ እለ፡ ይርኅቡ፡ ወይጸምኡ፡ ለጽድቅ *bəḍuʿān ʾəlla yərəḥəbu wa-yəṣamməʾu la-ṣədq* 'blessed are those who hunger and thirst for righteousness' (Mt 5:6)
- ብፁዓን፡ እለ፡ ይሰደዱ፡ በእንተ፡ ጽድቅ *bəḍuʿān ʾəlla yəssaddadu baʾanta ṣədq* 'blessed are those who are persecuted on account of righteousness' (Mt 5:10)

For relative clauses that function syntactically as subjects and have a conditional connotation, see §6.5.6.6. Relative clauses that function as subjects can further be found in (አል)ቦ፡ ዘ– (ʾal)bo za– constructions (§6.1.4.4.–4.5.) and in cleft sentences (§6.4.).

6.5.1.4. Independent Relative Clauses that Function as Direct Objects

Relative clauses can function as the direct object of a transitive verb. In this case, they occupy any position in the sentence in which the direct object can appear (usually after the verb and subject):

- ኢታእምር፡ ፀጋምከ፡ ዘትገብር፡ የማንከ ʾi-tāʾmər ḍagāməka za-təgabbər yamānəka 'do not let your left hand know what your right is doing' (Mt 6:3)
- ርኢኩ፡ ዘሎቱ፡ ርእሰ፡ መዋዕል rəʾiku za-lottu rəʾsa mawāʿəl 'I saw one who had a head of days (= who was old)' (En 46:1)
- ዘፈቀደ፡ ይቀትል፡ ወዘፈቀደ፡ ይቀሥፍ፡ ወዘፈቀደ፡ ያከብር za-faqada yəqattəl wa-za-faqada yəqaśśəf wa-za-faqada yākabbər 'he killed whom he wished, he tortured whom he wished, and he honored whom he wished' (Dan 5:19)

For relative clauses that function as direct objects and have a conditional connotation, see §6.5.6.6.

6.5.1.5. Independent Relative Clauses that Function as Indirect Objects

Relative clauses that function as indirect objects are introduced by the preposition ለ– la– followed by a relative pronoun. They take any position in the clause that can be occupied by an indirect object (usually after the verb and subject; fronted for emphasis). Subordinate clauses of this type are often used to circumscribe an agent noun (§5.1.5d):

- ሠናየ፡ ግበሩ፡ ለእለ፡ ይጸልኡክሙ śannāya gəbaru la-ʾəlla yəṣalləʾukəmu 'do good to those who hate you!' (Mt 5:44)
- ለዘ፡ ይስእለከ፡ ሀብ la-za yəsəʾalakka hab 'give to the one who asks of you!' (Mt 5:42)
- ወለእለሰ፡ ተወክፍዎ፡ ወሀቦሙ፡ ሥልጣነ wa-la-ʾəlla-ssa tawakfəwwo wahabomu śəlṭāna 'to those who received him he gave power ...' (Jn 1:12) (with resumptive pronoun)

6.5.1.6. Independent Relative Clauses Functioning as Genitive Attributes

In this type of clause, the head noun is in the bound or construct form followed by the relative pronoun.

- ብእሲተ፡ ዘሞተ *bəʾəsita za-mota* 'the wife of the one who died' = 'the dead man's wife' (cf. §5.1.5d)
- ደመ፡ ዘቀተለ *dama za-qatala* 'the blood of the one he killed' = 'the blood of the slain' (Num 23:24)

6.5.1.7. Independent Relative Clauses that Function Adverbially

Relative clauses that function adverbially (i.e., like the object of an adverbial prepositional phrase) are introduced by a preposition followed by a relative pronoun. Adverbial phrases introduced by the preposition በ– *ba*– are particularly frequent:

- በዘይደሉ *ba-za-yədallu* 'in the manner/way that is appropriate'
- ከመ፡ ተሀቦሙ፡ ያእምሩ፡ መድኃኒቶሙ፡ ለአሕዛብ፡ በዘይትኀደግ፡ ሎሙ፡ ኃጢአቶ ሙ *kama tahabbomu yāʾməru madḫanitomu la-ʾaḥzāb ba-za-yətḫaddag lomu ḫaṭiʾatomu* 'so that you give the people knowledge of their salvation by the forgiveness of their sins' (Lk 1:77)

6.5.1.8. Word Order in Relative Clauses

6.5.1.8.1. The word order in relative clauses does not differ from the word order in verbal or nominal main clauses. Two phenomena, however, have to be noted:

6.5.1.8.2. When the relative pronoun is semantically complemented by a prepositional phrase (with resumptive pronoun) (§6.5.1.1.4.), the prepositional phrase usually follows the relative pronoun directly, as in በምድር፡ እንተ፡ በውስቴታ፡ ተወልደ *ba-mədr ʾənta ba-wəstetā tawalda* 'in the land in which he was born' (Gen 11:28); ይእቲ፡ ዕለት፡ እንተ፡ ባቲ፡ ተወለድኩ *yəʾəti ʿəlat ʾənta bātti tawaladku* 'that day in which I was born' (Job 3:3).

6.5.1.8.3. The relative pronoun ዘ– *za*– does not always stand at the beginning of a relative clause. If a sentence element is topicalized in a verbal relative clause, that is, it is fronted, ዘ– *za*– is usually prefixed to the verbal form that occurs later in the sentence. This prevents the accumulation of several proclitic particles at the beginning of the sentence:

- ከመ፡ ይትፈጸም፡ በነቢይ፡ ዘተብህለ *kama yətfaṣṣam ba-nabiy za-tabəhla* 'so that what had been spoken by the prophet be fulfilled' (Mt 21:4); instead: ዘበነቢይ፡ ተብህለ *za-ba-nabiy tabəhla*, or – without topicalization – ዘተብህለ፡ በነቢይ *za-tabəhla ba-nabiy*.
- ወኵሎ፡ ኅቡአተ፡ ዘአርአየኒ *wa-kʷəllo ḥəbuʾata za-ʾarʾayanni* '(and I asked one of the holy angels who went with me) and who showed me all the secrets' (En 46:2)
- ወኵሎ፡ ዘገብረ፡ ለነ፡ ተአምረ *wa-kʷəllo za-gabra lana taʾamməra* 'and who did all the signs for us' (Josh 24:17); the noun modified by ኵሎ *kʷəllo* follows after the verb
- ወሥጋሁ፡ ዘይከውን *wa-śəgāhu za-yəkawwən* 'and the one who is his (own) kin' (Lev 18:6)
- መካነ፡ እምዝ፡ ዘይጌርም *makāna ʾəm-za za-yəgerrəm* 'to a place that was more terrifying than this' (En 21:7)

The same phenomenon can be observed in በ፡ ዘ– *bo za*-constructions (§6.1.4.4.) that have a topicalized sentence-element, as in ከመቦ፡ እኁከ፡ ዘየሐይሰከ *kama-bo ʾəḫuka za-yahayyəsakka* '(and if you remember) that your brother has a grievance against you' (Mt 5:23); instead of: ከመቦ፡ ዘእኁከ፡ የሐይሰ *kama-bo za-ʾəḫuka yahayyəsakka* or ከመቦ፡ ዘሐይሰከ፡ እኁከ *kama-bo za-yahayyəsakka ʾəḫuka*.

Note: The relative pronoun ዘ– *za*– can also introduce other subordinate clauses, either by itself or in combination with other particles. These clauses are discussed under the respective semantic categories (see especially §6.5.8. and §6.5.9.).

6.5.2. Asyndetic Attributive Subordinate Clauses

6.5.2.1. Besides syndetic relative clauses with an attributive function, that is, those that are introduced by a relative pronoun, (§6.5.1.), local clauses that are introduced by ኀበ *ḫaba* (§6.5.4a), and temporal clauses (§6.5.5.3.) with an attributive function, Classical Ethiopic also has asyndetic, attributive subordinate clauses. This type of clause, however, is less frequent in Classical Ethiopic than in other classical Semitic languages. It seems to have been more frequent in earlier periods of the language. Most attestations consist of more or less formulaic expressions.

Asyndetic attributive clauses immediately follow the head noun. The head noun is in either the unbound or the bound form. When the head noun is in the bound form, the complete subordinate clause functions as a genitive attribute to the head, that is, the head noun and subordinate clause form a construct chain (§5.2.4.1.). Asyndetic subordinate clauses contain a resumptive pronoun cross-referencing the head of the main clause significantly less often than syndetic relative clauses with attributive function (cf. §6.5.1.1.3.–4.).

6.5.2.2. Examples of asyndetic attributive clauses after a head noun in the unbound form:

- በአርአያ፡ አርአይኩክ *ba-ʾarʾayā ʾarʾaykuka* 'according to the plan that I showed you' (Ex 26:30)
- ብእሲ፡ ስሙ፡ ዮሐንስ *bəʾasi səmu yoḥannəs* 'a man whose name is John' = 'a man named John'; sentences of this type are more often introduced by a relative pronoun: ብእሲ፡ ዘስሙ፡ ዮሐንስ *bəʾasi za-səmu yoḥannəs* (§6.5.1.1.3.)

6.5.2.3. Examples of asyndetic attributive relative clauses following a head noun in the bound form (the head noun often represents an expression of time or duration):

- በመዋዕለ፡ ይኴንኑ፡ መሳፍንት *ba-mawāʿəla yək\ᵂennənu masāfənt* 'in the days when the judges ruled' (Ruth 1:1)
- በአምጣነ፡ ሀለውኩ *ba-ʾamṭāna hallawku* '(I shall praise my God) as long as I live' (lit. 'during the time that I live') (Ps 146:1 [145:1])
- ዘመጠነ፡ ጸሐፍኩ *za-maṭana ṣaḥafku* 'that which I have written' (Jub 1:1)
- ወከመ፡ ኢትርግም፡ ዕለተ፡ ተወለድካ *wa-kama ʾi-tərgəm ʿəlata tawaladka* 'lest you curse the day on which you were born' (Sir 23:14)
- ወሶበ፡ ኮነ፡ ጊዜ፡ ይዕረብ፡ ፀሐይ *wa-soba kona gize yəʿrab ḍaḥāy* 'when the time came for the sun to set' (Gen 15:17)
- በጊዜ፡ መጽአ/ይቤሎሰ *ba-gize maṣʾa / yəbelo-ssa* 'at the time when he came / said to him' (Śəna fəṭrat 42/43)

6.5.3. Other Object-Clauses

6.5.3.1. Subordinate clauses introduced by ከመ *kama* serve, besides relative clauses functioning as objects (§6.5.1.4.), as a frequent means to express the syntactic function of a direct object. Examples include (cf. also §5.4.3.2.3.):

- ሰማዕክሙ፡ ከመ፡ ተብህለ፡ ለቀደምት *samāʿkəmu kama tabəhla la-qaddamt* 'you have heard that it was said to the forefathers' (Mt 5:21)
- ወሶበ፡ ርእየ፡ ሄሮድስ፡ ከመ፡ ተሳለቁ፡ ላዕሌሁ፡ ሰብአ፡ ሰገል *wa-soba rəʾya herodəs kama tasālaqu lāʿlehu sabʾa sagal* 'and when Herod saw that the magicians had tricked him' (Mt 2:16)

The logical subject of these subordinate clauses is often already taken up in the main clause in the form of a direct object:

- ርእየ፡ ኖኅ፡ ምድረ፡ ከመ፡ አድነነት *rəʾya noḫ mədra kama ʾadnanat* 'Noah saw the earth, that it had tilted' (En 65:1); in the sense of: ርእየ፡ ኖኅ፡ ከመ፡ ምድር፡ አድነነት *rəʾya noḫ kama mədr ʾadnanat* 'Noah saw that the earth had tilted'
- ወያአምርዎሙ፡ ከመ፡ እሙንቱ፡ ውሉድየ *wa-yāʾammərəwwomu kama ʾəmuntu wəludəya* 'and they will know that they are my children' (Jub 1:25)

Note: The conjunction ከመ *kama* further serves to introduce comparative clauses (§6.5.8.), final clauses (§6.5.7.), and consecutive clauses (§6.5.9.2.).

6.5.3.2. The causal conjunction እስመ *ʾəsma* (besides ከመ *kama*) can likewise serve to introduce subordinate clauses that function as objects after verbs such as አእመረ *ʾaʾmara* 'to know'; as in ወእምይእዜ፡ ተአምሩ፡ እስመ፡ ኵሉ፡ ግፍዕክሙ፡ ዘትገብዑ፡ ይጸሐፍ *wa-ʾəm-yəʾəze taʾamməru* (for ታአምሩ *tāʾamməru*) *ʾəsma kʷəllu gəfʿəkəmu za-təgaffəʿu yəṣṣaḥaf* 'and from now on you know that all your wrongdoing that you do will be written down ...' (En 98:8)

6.5.3.3. Asyndetic clauses that have a jussive as predicate and that are logically subordinate to the preceding clause only rarely function as objects, as in ኢትኃድግ፡ መንፈስ፡ እኩይ፡ ኢይባእ፡ ውስቴቶሙ *ʾi-təḫdəg manfas ʾəkkuy ʾi-yəbāʾ wəstetomu* 'do not allow that an evil spirit enters them!' (lit. 'do not allow – an evil spirit shall not enter them!').

6.5.3.4. Indirect questions introduced by እመ *ʾəmma* 'if' can have the syntactic function of a direct object as well (§6.5.10.1.).

6.5.4. Local Clauses

The lexeme ኀበ *ḫaba* and its compounds እምኀበ *ʾəm-ḫaba*, በኀበ *ba-ḫaba*, and እንተ፡ኀበ *ʾənta ḫaba* introduce adverbial subordinate clauses that express location. In many cases, these clauses are attributively connected to a noun with local meaning such as መካን *makān* 'place' or ብሔር *bəher* 'region'.

(a) Examples of local clauses with an attributive function:
- … ውስተ፡ጀመካን፡ኀበ፡ሀለዉ፡ህየ፡ከመ፡እሳት … *wəsta ʾaḥadu makān ḫaba hallawu həyya kama ʾəsāt* '… at a certain place where there were creatures of fire' (lit. 'where they were like fire') (En 17:1)
- መካን፡ኀበ፡ነበርኩ *makān ḫaba nabarku* 'the place where I sat down'
- ነበረ፡ኀበ፡ሀለወ፡ብሔረ *nabara ḫaba hallawa bəhera* 'he stayed in the place where he was' (Jn 11:6) (local clause before head noun)
- መካን፡ኀበ፡ኖመ፡ህየ *makān ḫaba noma həyya* 'the place where he slept' (with adverbial resumption of head noun)

(b) Examples of local clauses without an attributive function:
- ወኢረከበት፡ኀበ፡ታዐርፍ፡እግራ *wa-ʾi-rakabat ḫaba tāʿarraf ʾagrā* 'it did not find a place to rest its foot' (Gen 8:9)
- ቆመ፡መልዕለተ፡ኀበ፡ሀሎ፡ሕፃን *qoma malʿalata ḫaba hallo ḥaḍān* 'it stopped over the place where the child was' (Mt 2:9)
- ወታስተጋብእ፡እምኀበ፡ኢዘራውክ *wa-tāstagābbə ʾəm-ḫaba ʾi-zarawka* 'you were reaping where you did not sow' (Mt 25:24)
- ወበኀበ፡ሞትኪ፡እመውት፡ወህየ፡እትቀበር *wa-ba-ḫaba motki ʾəmawwət wa-həyya ʾatqabbar* 'and where you die, I will die and there I will be buried' (Ruth 1:17)

6.5.5. Temporal Clauses

Temporal clauses can be introduced by various conjunctions depending on their semantic value. They can stand before and after the main clause. When the temporal clause precedes the main clause, the main clause can be connected asyndetically or by ወ– *wa–*.

The common Classical Ethiopic construction involving the perfective participle has the function of a temporal clause that expresses anteriority, that is, it functions like clauses introduced by ሶበ *soba* or እንዘ *ʾənza*, as in ወረኪቦ ፡ ማየ ፡ ኃለፈ *wa-rakibo māya ḫalafa* 'after he had found water, he departed'. Since the perfective participle is not negated, a corresponding negated subordinate clause has to be used, as in ወእንዘ ፡ ኢረከበ ፡ ማየ ፡ ኃለፈ *wa-ʾənza ʾi-rakaba māya ḫalafa* 'and after he had found no water, he departed'.

6.5.5.1. Circumstantial Clauses with እንዘ *ʾənza*

6.5.5.1.1. The conjunction እንዘ *ʾənza* 'while, when, since' introduces clauses that are simultaneous to the action of the main clause and that express a logically dependent accompanying event/action. The accompanying action can be temporal, modal, or of another type.

6.5.5.1.2. The verbal predicate of this type of subordinate clause, which most commonly has past reference, is typically expressed by the imperfect (§5.4.2.3.5.):

- ወመሀሮሙ ፡ እንዘ ፡ ይብል *wa-maharomu ʾənza yəbəl* 'he taught them, saying' (Mt 5:2)
- ... ሶበ ... ወይነቡ ፡ ኵሎ ፡ እከየ ፡ ላዕሌክሙ ፡ እንዘ ፡ የሐስዉ ... *soba ... wa-yənabbu kʷəllo ʾəkaya lāʿlekəmu ʾənza yaḥassəwu* '... when they say all sorts of evil things about you, lying ...' (Mt 5:11)
- ርእየ ፡ ካልአነ ፡ እንዘ ፡ ይቀውሙ *rəʾya kāləʾāna ʾənza yəqawwəmu* 'he saw others standing'

The same function can also be expressed by an imperfect without a preceding እንዘ *ʾənza*, as in እስከ ፡ ይሬእይዋ ፡ ለመንግሥተ ፡ እግዚአብሔር ፡ ትመጽእ ፡ በኃይል *ʾəska yəreʾəyəwwā la-mangəśta ʾəgziʾab(ə)her təmaṣṣəʾ* (variant: እንዘ ፡ ትመጽእ *ʾənza təmaṣṣəʾ*) *ba-ḫayl* '... until they see that the kingdom of God has come with power' (Mk 9:1).

6.5.5.1.3. For the verbal root √hlw 'to be' (D-stem), Classical Ethiopic usually uses the perfect ሀለወ/ሀሎ *hallawa/hallo* (which also has present meaning [§5.4.1.2.4.]) for circumstantial clauses, as in ... እንዘ ፡ ሀሎ ፡ ባሕቲቱ ... *ʾənza hallo bāḫtitu* '... while (the king) was alone' (ʿĀmda Ṣəyon 11c).

6.5.5.1.4. እንዘ *ʾənza*-clauses can also be nominal:

- ወዳርዮስ ... ነግሠ፡ ህየንቴሁ፡ እንዘ፡ ስሳ፡ ወክልኤ፡ ክረምቱ *wa-dārəyos ... nagśa həyyantehu ʾənza səssā wa-kəlʾe kəramtu* 'and Darius ... became king in his stead when he was 62 years old' (Dan 5:31)
- እንዘ፡ ምእትኑ፡ ዓመት፡ ሊተ፡ እወልድ *ʾənza məʾət-nu ʿāmat lita ʾəwalləd* 'can I (still) beget a child being 100 years old?' (Gen 17:17)

6.5.5.2. Temporal Clauses with ሶበ *soba*

Temporal clauses introduced by ሶበ *soba* that have a perfective predicate most commonly express the nuance 'after, when'. Clauses that have an imperfective predicate on the other hand have the connotation 'whenever, when, as often as':

- ሶበ፡ ረሥአ፡ ሳሙኤል፡ ሤሞሙ፡ ለደቂቁ፡ መኳንንተ፡ ላዕለ፡ እስራኤል *soba raśʾa* (= ረሥዐ *raśʾa*) *sāmuʾel śemomu la-daqiqu makʷānənta lāʿla ʾəsrāʾel* 'when Samuel became old, he appointed his sons judges over Israel' (1 Sam 8:1)
- ሶበ፡ ርእየ፡ ወልዶ፡ ወሮጸ፡ ኀቤሁ *soba rəʾya waldo wa-roṣa ḫabehu* 'when he saw his son, he ran to him' (the main clause is introduced by ወ- *wa-*)
- ወሶበ፡ መጽአ፡ እማንቱ፡ አባግዕ፡ ይስተያ፡ ይፀንሳ *wa-soba maṣʾa ʾəmāntu ʾabāgəʿ yəstayā yəḍannəsā* 'whenever those sheep came out to drink they became pregnant' (Gen 30:38)
- ሶበ፡ ትሰምዕ፡ እንዘ፡ ይጼውዑከ፡ ፍጡነ፡ ተንሥእ *soba təsamməʿ ʾənza yəṣewwəʿuka fəṭuna tanśəʾ* 'when you hear that (lit. 'while') they call you, rise quickly!'

6.5.5.3. Temporal Clauses with አመ *ʾama* and ጊዜ *gize*

Temporal clauses that are introduced by አመ *ʾama* or ጊዜ *gize* have the meaning '(at the time) when'. These clauses can precede or follow the main clause and can in some cases be connected attributively to a noun with temporal meaning:

- ኢያንበብክሙኑ፡ ዘገብረ፡ ዳዊት፡ አመ፡ ርኀበ *ʾi-yānbabkəmu-nu za-gabra dāwit ʾama rəḫba* 'have you not read what David did when he was hungry ...?' (Mt 12:3)

- ወእምዝ፡ አመ፡ ይገብር፡ ግብረ፡ ክህነት wa-ʾǝmza ʾama yǝgabbǝr gǝbra kǝhnat 'and then, when he was serving as a priest ...' (Lk 1:8)
- ውእተ፡ አሚረ፡ አመ፡ ርኢክዎ wǝʾǝta ʾamira ʾama rǝʾikǝwwo 'on that day, when I saw him' (with an attributive function)
- ወጊዜ፡ ፈቀድክሙ፡ ታሤንዩ፡ ላዕሌሆሙ wa-gize faqadkǝmu tāśennǝyu lāʿlehomu 'and whenever you want, you can be gracious to them' (Mk 14:7)

6.5.5.4. Temporal Clauses with እስከ ʾǝska

Temporal clauses introduced by እስከ ʾǝska express the sense of 'until'. The verbal predicate is most commonly in the imperfect (often with the tense-reference of "anterior future"), as in እስከ፡ የኀልፍ፡ ሰማይ፡ ወምድር፡ የውጣ ... ኢተኀልፍ፡ እምኦሪት ʾǝska yaḫalləf samāy wa-mǝdr yawṭā ... ʾi-taḫalləf ʾǝm-ʾorit 'until heaven and earth perish, not (even) a Iota will pass from the law' (Mt 5:18).

Temporal clauses introduced by እስከ፡ ሶበ ʾǝska soba or እስከ፡ አመ ʾǝska ʾama have the same function:

- ወናሁ፡ ኮከብ ... ይመርሐሙ፡ እስከ፡ ሶበ፡ በጺሖ፡ ቆመ wa-nāhu kokab ... yǝmarrǝhomu ʾǝska soba baṣiḥo qoma 'and behold, a star was leading them ... until, having arrived, it stopped' (Mt 2:9)
- እስከ፡ ሶበ፡ ኮሉ፡ ይትገበር ʾǝska soba kʷǝllu yǝtgabbar 'until (= not before) all is accomplished' (Mt 5:18)
- ኢትወፅእ፡ እምህየ፡ እስከ፡ ሶበ፡ ትፈዲ ... ኮሉ ʾi-tǝwaḍḍǝʾ ʾǝm-hǝyya ʾǝska soba tǝfaddi ... kʷǝllo 'you shall not leave from there until you have repaid everything' (Mt 5:26)
- ወሀሉ፡ ህየ፡ እስከ፡ አመ፡ እነግረከ wa-hallu hǝyya ʾǝska ʾama ʾǝnaggǝrakka 'and remain there, until I tell you!' (Mt 2:13)

Note: Clauses introduced by እስከ ʾǝska can also have consecutive meaning (§6.5.9.2.).

6.5.5.5. Temporal Clauses with እምድኅረ ʾǝm-dǝḫra

This type of clause expresses the meaning 'after'. The verbal predicate is in the perfect:

- ወእምድኅረ፡ ኀለፉ፡ ናሁ፡ መልአክ፡ እግዚአብሔር፡ አስተርእዮ፡ በሕልም፡ ለዮሴፍ
  wa-ʾəm-dəḫra ḫalafu nāhu malʾaka ʾəgziʾab(ə)ḥer ʾastarʾayo ba-ḥəlm la-yosef
  'and after they had left, an angel of God appeared to Joseph in a dream'
  (Mt 2:13)

6.5.5.6. Temporal Clauses with እምቅድመ *ʾəm-qədma* and ዘእንበለ *za-ʾənbala*

These temporal clauses express the connotation 'before'. The verbal predicate is always in the jussive (§5.4.3.3.):

- እምቅድመ፡ ይትፈጠር፡ ዓለም፡ ፈጠረኒ *ʾəm-qədma yətfaṭar ʿālam faṭaranni* 'before the world was created, he created me' (Sir 24:9)
- ወዘእንበለ፡ ይትፈጠር፡ ፀሐይ ... ወስሙ፡ ተጸውዐ *wa-za-ʾənbala yətfaṭar ḍaḥay* (= ፀሐይ *ḍaḥāy*) ... *wa-səmu taṣawwəʿa* ... 'even before the sun was created ... his name was named ...' (En 48:3)

6.5.5.7. Other Temporal Subordinate Clauses

በዘ *ba-za* 'as, when', እምዘ *ʾəm-za* 'when, after that, since', ለለ *lalla* 'whenever' (§4.5:3.2), and እመ *ʾəmma* 'when(ever)' can likewise introduce temporal clauses, as in ወለደት፡ ሎቱ፡ ወልደ፡ በዘረስአ *waladat lottu walda ba-za-raśʾa* 'she bore him a son when he had (already) grown old'; ለለ፡ ጸብሐ *lalla ṣabḥa* 'whenever it dawned'; እመ፡ ርኀብኩ፡ ወሀቡኒ፡ ኀብስተ *ʾəmma rəḫəbku wahabuni ḫəbəsta* 'whenever I was hungry, they gave me bread'.

Constructions with (በ)ዕለተ *(ba-)ʿəlata*, እመ፡ ዕለተ *ʾama ʿəlata*, or ጊዜ *gize* with a following asyndetic subordinate clause further function as temporal clauses with the meaning 'on the day, at the time, when' (§6.5.2.3.).

6.5.5.8. Two Main Clauses in the Function of a Temporal Construction

Two paratactically coordinated main clauses (with different tenses) can implicitly express a temporal sequence and should then be translated as such, as in ወኮኖ፡ ለዮሴፍ፡ ዐሠርቱ፡ ወሰባዕቱ፡ ዓመቱ፡ ወይሬዒ፡ ምስለ፡ አኀዊሁ፡ አባጎዐ፡ አቡሁ *wa-kono la-yosef ʿaśartu wa-sabāʿtu ʿāmatu wa-yərəʿi məsla ʾaḫawihu ʾabāgəʿa ʾabuhu* 'when Joseph was 17 years old, he was shepherding the flock of his father with his brothers' (Gen 37:2).

6.5.6. Conditional and Concessive Clauses

Classical Ethiopic has various conjunctions that can introduce subordinate clauses with conditional meaning. In most cases, the conditional subordinate clause (= protasis) precedes the main clause (= apodosis). The apodosis can be introduced by **ወ–** *wa–*. It is further possible to distinguish between real (= possible) and unreal (= impossible) conditional clauses. Concessive clauses (§6.5.6.8.) are a semantic sub-group of conditional clauses. All conditional or concessive subordinate clauses use an indicative perfect or imperfect as the verbal predicate.

6.5.6.1. Real conditional clauses are introduced by **እመ** *ʾəmma* 'if, when'. **እመ** *ʾəmma* either stands by itself or in compounds such as **ለእመ** *la-ʾəmma*,[279] **እመሰ** *ʾəmma-ssa* 'if really, but if', **እምከመ** *ʾəm(mə)-kama* or **ዘእንበለ ፡ እመ** *za-ʾənbala ʾəmma* 'unless'.

6.5.6.1.1. The use of tenses differs in the two clause types. The perfect is used in the protasis in the majority of attestations while the apodosis frequently has an imperfect as the verbal predicate (when the clause expresses volitive nuances, the jussive or imperative can occur as well).

Protasis with perfect – apodosis with imperfect:

- **እመ ፡ ነበርከ ፡ ዝየ ፡ (ወ)ይረክቡክ** *ʾəmma nabarka zəya (wa-)yərakkəbuka* 'if you stay here, they will find you'
- **ወእመሰ ፡ ጼው ፡ ለስነ ፡ በምንትኑ ፡ ይትቄሰም** *wa-ʾəmma-ssa ṣew lasḫa ba-məntə-nu yətqessam* 'if the salt has become tasteless, with what can its saltiness be restored?' (Mt 5:13)

Protasis with perfect – apodosis with imperative:

- **እመ ፡ ረከብከ ፡ ብእሴ ፡ ርኁብ ፡ ሀቦ ፡ መብልዐ** *ʾəmma rakabka bəʾse rəḫuba habo mabləʿa* 'if you find a hungry man, give him food!'

Protasis with **ይቤ** *yəbe* (for the use of this form as perfect, see §5.4.2.4.1.) – apodosis with imperfect:

---

[279] The **ለ–** *la–* in **ለእመ** *la-ʾəmma* is most likely to be analyzed as the affirmative particle **ለ–** *la–* (§4.5.5.), not the preposition **ለ–** *la–*.

- ወእመ፡ ትቤ ... እብል wa-ʾəmma təbe ... ʾəbəl 'and if you say ... I say ...' (Śəna fəṭrat 4)

Protasis with imperfect (with modal nuance [§5.4.2.5.]) – apodosis with imperfect:

- ወእምከመ፡ ኢታየድዑኒ፡ ሕልምየ ... ትመውቱ wa-ʾəm-kama ʾi-tāyaddəʿuni ḥəlməya ... təmawwətu 'and if you cannot tell me my dream, you will die' (Dan 2:5); cf. Dan 2:6, which has a perfect in the protasis: ወእምከመሰ፡ አይዳዕከሙኒ፡ ሕልምየ ... ትነሥኡ wa-ʾəm-kama-ssa ʾaydāʿkəmuni ḥəlməya ... tənaśśəʾu 'if you tell me my dream, you shall receive (gifts)'.

Protasis with imperfect (with modal nuance [§5.4.2.5.]) – apodosis with perfect (for the expression of an unreal condition):

- እመሰኬ፡ በገቢረ፡ ሕገግ፡ ኦሪት፡ ይጸድቁ፡ ለከንቱኬ፡ ሞተ፡ ክርስቶስ ʾəmma-ssa-ke ba-gabira ḥəgaga ʾorit yəṣaddəqu la-kantu-ke mota krəstos 'if one could become just by following the statutes of the law, Christ would have died in vain' (Gal 2:21)

Nominal clause as protasis – apodosis with imperative:

- እመ፡ ወልዱስ፡ አንተ፡ ለእግዚአብሔር፡ በል ... ʾəmma waldu-ssa ʾanta la-ʾəgziʾab(ə)ḥer bal ... 'but if you are the son of God, say ...!' (Mt 4:3)

6.5.6.1.2. Less often, the conditional subordinate clause follows the main clause, as in ዘንተ፡ ኩሎ፡ እሁብከ፡ ለእመ፡ ሰገድክ ... ሊተ zanta kʷəllo ʾəhubakka la-ʾəmma sagadka ... lita 'all this I will give you if you bow down before me' (Mt 4:9) (imperfect – perfect).

6.5.6.1.3. The protasis can be negated by ኢ- ʾi- (that is, እመ፡ ኢ- ʾəmma ʾi-) or, more often, አኮ ʾakko (that is, እመ፡ አኮ ʾəmma ʾakko or እማእኮ ʾəmmāʾəkko 'if not, otherwise').

- ወእፎ፡ ይክል፡ መኑሂ፡ በዊአ፡ ቤተ፡ ኃያል ... ዘእንበለ፡ እመ፡ ኢቀደመ፡ አሢሮቶ፡ ለኃያል wa-ʾəffo yəkəl mannu-hi bawiʾa beta ḥayyāl ... za-ʾənbala ʾəmma ʾi-qadama ʾaśiroto la-ḥayyāl 'how can anybody enter the house of a strong

man (and plunder it), if he does not tie up the strong man before ...?'
(Mt 12:29); note the double negation in the subordinate clause:
ዘእንበለ፡ እመ፡ ኢ.– za-ʾənbala ʾəmma ʾi–, lit. 'except if not'.

- ወለእመሰ፡ ትገብሩ፡ ምሕረተ፡ ወጽድቀ፡ ላዕለ፡ እግዚእየ፡ ንግሩኒ፡ ወእማእኮ፡ እትመ
  የጥ wa-la-ʾəmma-ssa təgabbəru məhrata wa-ṣədqa lāʿla ʾəgziʾəya nəgəruni wa-
  ʾəmmāʾəkko ʾətmayyaṭ 'if you will deal loyally and truly with my lord,
  tell me! And if not, I will turn away ...' (Gen 24.49)

6.5.6.1.4. The disjunctive connotation 'either ... or' in conditional clauses can be
expressed by እመ ... ወእመ፡ አኮ ʾəmma ... wa-ʾəmma ʾakko. The latter part,
ወእመ፡ አኮ wa-ʾəmma ʾakko, lit. 'and if not' stands for 'or', as in
እመቦ፡ ዘተናገረ፡ ወእመ፡ አኮ፡ ሠሐቀ ʾəmma-bo za-tanāgara wa-ʾəmma ʾakko śaḥaqa 'if
somebody speaks or laughs ...'.

6.5.6.2. Unreal conditional clauses are introduced by the conjunction ሶበ soba
(cf. §6.5.5.2.). Finite verbal forms in the apodosis of unreal conditional clauses
exhibit proclitic እም– ʾəm– (እም– ... ወእም– ʾəm– ... wa-ʾəm–), less often non-
proclitic እመ ʾəmma. Both protasis and apodosis have a perfect as the verbal
predicate:

- ወሶበ፡ ነገርከኒ፡ እምፈነውኩከ wa-soba nagarkanni ʾəm-fannawkuka 'if you had
  told me, I would have sent you ...' (Gen 31:27)
- ሶበ፡ በጢሮስ፡ ወበሲዶና፡ ተገብረ፡ ኃይል፡ ዘተገብረ፡ በውስቴትክን፡ ሦቀ፡ እምለብሱ
  ፡ ወውስተ፡ ሐመድ፡ እምነበሩ፡ ወእምነስሑ soba ba-ṭiros wa-ba-sidonā tagabra
  hayl za-tagabra ba-wəstetəkən śaqqa ʾəm-labsu wa-wəsta hamad ʾəm-nabaru
  wa-ʾəm-nassəhu 'if the violent deeds that have been done among you
  would have been committed in Tyre and Sidon, they would have
  clothed themselves in sackcloth, sat down in the dust and repented'
  (Lk 10:13)
- ሶበስ፡ ረከብዎ፡ እኂዞሙ፡ እምአምጽእዎ soba-ssa rakabəwwo ʾəhizomu ʾəm-
  ʾamṣəʾəwwo 'if they had found him, they would have seized him and
  brought him here'[280]
- ወሶበ፡ ነገርኩክ፡ ኍላቍሁ ... እምአምሰልኮ፡ ሐሰተ፡ ወእምረሰይኮ፡ እወ፡ ወአልቦ
  wa-soba nagarkuka ḫʷəlāqʷehu ... ʾəm-ʾamsalko hassata wa-ʾəm-rassayko
  ʾəwwa wa-ʾalbo 'and if I had told you the number ..., you would have

---

[280] If the finite verbal form is preceded by a PP, the particle እም– ʾəm– only occurs on the
finite verbal form.

regarded it as a lie and considered it with doubt (lit. 'as yes and no')' (ʿĀmda Ṣəyon 11c)

- ሶበ፡ አኮ፡ አንተ፡ ዘአበስከ፡ እሙ፡ ኢኮነት፡ ላዕሌነ፡ ዛቲ፡ እኪት soba ʾakko ʾanta za-ʾabbaska ʾəmma ʾi-konat (variant እምኢኮነት ʾəm-ʾi-konat) lāʿlena zātti ʾəkit 'if you had not sinned, this evil would not be upon us' (Ezra-Apocalypse 7:20)

6.5.6.3. Conditional clauses that are introduced by *soba* and that have an imperfect as the verbal predicate commonly express potentiality, as in ብፁዓን፡ አንትሙ፡ ሶበ፡ ይሰድዱክሙ፡ ወይዘነጉጉክሙ *bəḍuʿān ʾantəmu soba yəsaddədukəmu wa-yəzanagg*ʷ*əgukəmu* 'blessed are you if you are persecuted and reviled' (Mt 5:11).

6.5.6.4. Unreal ሶበ *soba*-clauses without an apodosis are used like interjections with the connotation 'would that!':

- ሶበ፡ ሞትነ *soba motna* 'would that we had died!' (Ex 16:3)
- ሶበ፡ ነደርነ *soba ḫadarna* 'would that we had stayed!' (Josh 7:7)

6.5.6.5. A clause in the form of an apodosis of an unreal conditional clause (with እም– *ʾəm–* + perfect) that does not have a protasis can express a similar connotation, as in እምወሀበ፡ ሰብእ፡ ቤዛሃ፡ ለነፍሱ *ʾəm-wahaba sabʾ bezāhā la-nafsu* 'what can a man give in exchange for his life!' (Mk 8:37); እምነሳሕኩ *ʾəm-nassāḥku* 'would that I had repented!'.

The construction እም– *ʾəm–* + perfect can also be embedded into a subordinate clause introduced by ዘ– *za–*, as in ሕቀ፡ ክሙ፡ ዘእምሰከበ *ḥəqqa kəmma za-ʾəm-sakaba* 'somebody might have slept (with your wife)' (Gen 26:10) (lit. 'there was little (left) – almost, that (somebody) slept ...'.

6.5.6.6. Independent relative clauses that are introduced by ኵሎ፡ ዘ– *kʷəllu za–* or with simple ዘ– *za–* commonly imply a conditional meaning: 'whoever does X ...'. The tense used in the relative clause can vary:

Relative clause with imperfect:

- ኵሎ፡ ዘየኀድግ፡ ብእሲቶ ... ይሬስያ፡ ትዘሙ፡ ወዘሂ፡ ነድግተ፡ አውሰበ፡ ዘሙወ *kʷəllu za-yaḫaddəg bəʾsito ... yəressəyā təzammu wa-za-hi ḫədəgta ʾawsaba zammawa* 'anyone who divorces his wife ... causes her to commit adultery; whoever, however, marries a divorced woman commits adultery' (Mt 5:32); the first apodosis has an imperfect, the second a perfect.

- ኮሉ፡ ዘያምዕዕ፡ እኅዋሁ፡ ረስሐ፡ ውእቱ፡ ለኰነኔ *kʷəllu za-yāməʿəʿ ʾəḫwāhu / rasḫa wəʾətu la-kʷənnane* 'whoever provokes his brother is liable to judgement' (Mt 5:22)

- ወለዘሂ፡ ይፈቅድ፡ ይትዐገልክ፡ ወመልበሰክ፡ ይንሣእ፡ ኅድግ፡ ሎቱ፡ ወልብሰክኒ *wa-la-za-hi yəfaqqəd yətʿaggalka wa-malbasaka yənśāʾ ḫədəg lottu wa-ləbsaka-ni* 'whoever wishes to take your coat by force, leave him also your cloak' (Mt 5:40)

- ለዘ፡ ይስእለክ፡ ሀብ *la-za yəsəʾəlakka hab* 'give to whoever asks of you!' (Mt 5:42)

Relative clause with perfect:

- ዘአንበቦ፡ ለዝ፡ መጽሐፍ፡ ወነገረኒ፡ ፍካሬሁ፡ አለብሶ፡ ሜላት *za-ʾanbabo la-zə maṣḥaf wa-nagaranni fəkkārehu ʾālabbəso melāta* ... 'whoever can read this writing and tell me its interpretation I will clothe in purple ...' (Dan 5:7)

- ወዘኪ.ያየ፡ ተወክፈ፡ ተወክፎ፡ ለዘፈነወኒ *wa-za-kiyāya tawakfa tawakfo la-za-fannawanni* 'whoever welcomes me welcomes the one who sent me' (Mt 10:40)

- ወለዘሂ፡ ዐበጠከ፡ ምዕራፈ፡ አሐደ፡ ሑር፡ ምስሌሁ፡ ክልኤተ *wa-la-za-hi ʿabbaṭaka məʿrāfa ʾaḥada ḥur məslehu kəlʾeta* 'and anyone who forces you (to walk) one mile, go the second one with him!' (Mt 5:41)

- ወዘሰ፡ ቀተለ፡ ረስሐ፡ ውእቱ፡ ለኰነኔ *wa-za-ssa qatala rasḫa wəʾətu la-kʷənnane* 'but whoever murders shall be liable to judgement' (Mt 5:21)

- ዘኬ፡ ፈትሐ፡ አሐተ፡ እምእላ፡ ትእዛዛት *za-ke fatḫa ʾaḥatta ʾəm-ʾəllā təʾəzāzāt* 'for whoever breaks one of these commandments' (Mt 5:19)

- ወዘሰ፡ ገደፋ፡ ለነፍሱ ... ወበእንተ፡ ወንጌል፡ ይረክባ *wa-za-ssa gadafā la-nafsu ... wa-ba-ʾənta wangel yərakkəbā* 'but whoever gives up his life on account of the gospel will find it' (Mk 8:35)

6.5.6.7. A paratactic sequence of main clauses can likewise have a conditional meaning:

- ወእብሎ፡ ለዝንቱ፡ ሑር፡ ወየሐውር፡ ወለካልኡ፡ ነዓ፡ ወይመጽእ፡ ወለ1ብርየኒ፡ ግበር ፡ ከመዝ፡ ወይ1ብር *wa-ʾəbəlo la-zəntu ḥur wa-yaḥawwər wa-la-kāləʾu naʿā wa-*

yəmaṣṣəʾ wa-la-gabrəya-ni gəbar kama-zə wa-yəgabbər 'if I say to this one 'go!', he goes; and to another one 'come!', he comes; and to my servant 'do this!', he does (it)' (Lk 7:8)

- ወቤት፡ ጎበ፡ ቦእክሙ፡ ቅድሙ፡ በሉ *wa-bet ḫaba boʾkəmu qədəmu balu* 'and if you enter a house, first say ...!' (Lk 10:5; similarly 10:8)

- ረከብኩ፡ ጸጋ፡ በቅድሜክሙ *rakabku ṣaggā ba-qədmekəmu ...* 'if I have found mercy before you ...' (Gen 34:11)

6.5.6.8. Concessive subordinate clauses are introduced by conditional conjunctions that are commonly extended by enclitic particles or other conjunctions, that is, (ለ)እመሂ *(la-)ʾəmma-hi*, (ለ)እመኒ *(la-)ʾəmma-ni*, እመሙ *ʾəmma-mma*, ወእመ *wa-ʾəmma*, and ሶበ፡ እም- *soba ʾəm-*, all of which have the meaning 'even if, even when'. The use of tenses varies in this type of subordinate clause, although the perfect is more frequent than the imperfect. The conjunction ሶበ፡ እም- *soba ʾəm-* is always followed by the perfect:

- እመሂ፡ ሞትኩ፡ ምስሌከ፡ ኢይክሕደክ *ʾəmma-hi motku məsleka ʾi-yəkəhədakka* 'even when I have to die with you, I will not denounce you' (Mt 26:35)

- እመኒ፡ ሞተ፡ አቡሁ፡ ከመ፡ ዘኢሞተ *ʾəmma-ni mota ʾabuhu kama za-ʾi-mota* 'even if his father should die, it would be as if he had not died' (Sir 30:4)

- እመ፡ ኢይፈርህ፡ እግዚአብሔር፡ ወኢየኃፍር፡ ሰብአ።ከመ፡ ኢታንጠየኒ፡ ዛቲ፡ እበር፡ እኵንና *ʾəmma ʾi-yəfarrəh* (§3.6.2.2.) *ʾəgziʾab(ə)her wa-ʾi-yaḫaffər sabʾa kama ʾi-tānṭəyanni zātti ʾəber ʾəkʷennənā* 'even though I do not fear God and do not revere the people, I shall do justice by this widow lest she be troublesome to me' (Lk 18:4–5); apodosis with imperfect

6.5.7. Final Clauses

6.5.7.1. Subordinate clauses with final meaning, that is clauses expressing purpose, are usually introduced by ከመ *kama* and most commonly have a jussive as the verbal predicate (cf. §5.4.3.2.). In general, the final clause follows the main clause:

- አክብር፡ አባከ፡ ወእመከ።ከመ፡ ሠናየ፡ ይኩንክ፡ ወይኑኅ፡ መዋዕሊከ፡ በዲበ፡ ምድር *ʾakbər ʾabāka wa-ʾəmmaka kama śannāya yəkunka wa-yənuḫ mawāʿəlika ba-diba mədr* 'honor your father and mother – so that you do well and your days on earth may be long' (Eph 6:2)

- ወኢ.ያነትዉ: ማኅቶተ: ከመ: ያንብርዋ: ታሕተ: ከፈር wa-ʾi-yāḫattəwu māḫtota kama yānbərəwwā tāḫta kafar 'you do not light a lamp to put it under a basket' (Mt 5:15)
- ከማሁ: ይብራህ: ብርሃንክሙ: በቅድመ: ሰብእ: ከመ: ይርአዩ: ምግባሪክሙ: ሠናየ kamāhu yəbrāh bərhānəkəmu ba-qədma sabʾ kama yərʾayu məgbārikəmu śannāya 'thus let your light shine before the people, so that they may see your good works' (Mt 5:16)
- ከመ: ኢይሙ‑ቱ: ዳንኤል: ወአዕርክቲሁ kama ʾi-yəmutu (variant: ኢይሙ‑ት ʾi-yəmut) dānəʾel wa-ʾaʿrəktihu 'lest Daniel and his companions die' (Dan 2:18)

The clause introduced by ከመ kama can also have an imperfect as the verbal predicate when it has a modal meaning (§5.4.2.5.), as in ውእቱ: ይከውን: በትረ ... ከመ: ቦቱ: ይትመረጕዙ wəʾətu yəkawwən batra ... kama bottu yətmaraggʷazu ... 'he will be a staff ..., so that they may lean on him ...' (En 48:4) (another textual variant has the jussive ይትመርጕዙ yətmargʷazu instead of the imperfect).

6.5.7.2. Asyndetic subordinate clauses, that is, clauses that are not introduced by ከመ kama and that have a jussive as the verbal predicate can likewise express purpose/result, as in እስመ: ተሐውር: ቅድመ: እግዚአብሔር: ትጺሕ: ፍኖቶ ʾasma taḥawwər qədma ʾəgziʾab(ə)her təṣiḥ fənoto 'for you will go before God to prepare the road for him' (Lk 1:76). For further examples, see §5.4.3.2.1.

6.5.7.3. Lastly, two main clauses that are connected by ወ– wa– can imply purpose/result, as in ወአዘዘ: በልጣሶር: ወአልበስዎ: ሜላተ: ለዳንኤል wa-ʾazzaza balṭāsor wa-ʾalbasəwwo melāta la-dānəʾel 'and Belshazzar commanded to clothe Daniel in purple' (lit. 'and they clothed Daniel ...') (Dan 5:29).

6.5.8. Comparative Clauses

6.5.8.1. The comparative meaning '(just) as, like' is expressed by subordinate clauses that are introduced by ከመ kama and its compounds (such as ዘከመ za-kama, እንተ: ከመ ʾənta kama, በከመ ba-kama). The comparative clause most commonly follows the main clause and can be of a nominal or verbal nature. The verbal predicate stands in an indicative tense, that is, either the perfect or imperfect:

- ኩኑኬ፡ አንተሙሰ፡ ፍጹማነ፡ ከመ፡ አቡክሙ፡ ሰማያዊ፡ ፍጹም፡ ውእቱ *kunu-ke ʾantəmu-ssa fəṣṣumāna kama ʾabukəmu samāyāwi fəṣṣum wəʾətu* 'also you, be as perfect as your heavenly father is perfect' (Mt 5:48) (nominal comparative clause)
- ወኅድግ፡ ለነ፡ አበሳነ፡ ከመ፡ ንሕነኒ፡ ነኅድግ፡ ለዘአበሰ፡ ለነ *wa-ḫədəg lana ʾabbasāna kama nəḥna-ni naḥaddəg la-za-ʾabbasa lana* 'and forgive us our sins, as we forgive those who transgress against us!' (Mt 6:12)
- በእንተ፡ ኩሉ፡ ዘርእዩ፡ ወሰምዑ፡ ዘከመ፡ ይቤልዎሙ *ba-ʾənta kʷəllu za-rəʾyu wa-samʿu za-kama yəbeləwwomu* '... concerning all that they had seen and heard, as they were told' (Lk 2:20)
- በከመ፡ ብርሃን፡ ይኄይስ፡ እምጽልመት፡ ከማሁ፡ እምዝኒ፡ ዓለም፡ ይኄይስ፡ ዓለም፡ ዘ ይመጽእ፡ ድኅረ *ba-kama bərhān yəḫeyyəs ʾəm-ṣəlmat kamāhu ʾəm-zə-ni ʿālam yəḫeyyəs ʿālam za-yəmaṣṣəʾ dəḫra* 'as light is better than darkness, likewise the world to come is better than this world' (Śəna fəṭrat 7) (comparative clause precedes main clause; chiastic word order)

6.5.8.2. The comparative meaning 'more/better than' is expressed by subordinate clauses that are introduced by እም– *ʾəm–* or እምነ *ʾəmənna*. These clauses follow the entity to be compared that is mentioned in the main clause.

- ወያዕቆብሰ፡ ያፈቅሮ፡ ለዮሴፍ፡ እምነ፡ ኩሎሙ፡ ደቂቁ *wa-yāʿqobə-ssa yāfaqqəro la-yosef ʾəmənna kʷəllomu daqiqu* 'but Jacob loved Joseph more than any other of his children' (Gen 37:3)
- ይኄይሰከ፡ ነቍርከ፡ ትባእ፡ ውስተ፡ ሕይወት፡ እምእንዘ፡ ክልኤ፡ ዐይነ፡ ብከ፡ ትትወደ ይ፡ ውስተ፡ ገሃነም፡ እሳት *yəḫeyyəsakka naqqʷārəka təbāʾ wəsta ḥəywat ʾəm-ʾənza kəlʾe ʿayna bəka tətwaday wəsta gahānnam ʾəsāt* 'it is better for you to enter life with one eye than to have two eyes and to be thrown into the hell of fire' (Mt 18:9)

6.5.9. Other Subordinate Clauses

6.5.9.1. Causal Clauses

6.5.9.1.1. Subordinate clauses with causal meaning are most frequently introduced by the conjunction እስመ *ʾəsma* 'because, since', which also introduces main clauses with a causal meaning (the boundaries between causal main and subordinate clauses are often fluid):

- ወእምዝ፡ አኀዘ፡ ኢየሱስ፡ ይሒሶን፡ ለአህጉር ... እስመ፡ ኢነስሑ wa-ʾəm-za ʾaḫaza ʾiyasus yəḥison la-ʾahgur ... ʾəsma ʾi-nassəḥu 'then Jesus began to reproach the cities ... because they did not repent' (Mt 11:20)
- ወእስመ፡ አልቦ፡ ሥርወ፡ የብስ wa-ʾəsma ʾalbo śarwa yabsa 'and since it did not have roots, it withered away' (Mt 13:6)

6.5.9.1.2. በእንተ፡ ዘ– ba-ʾənta za– 'because' and, less often, ዘ– za– by itself can also introduce causal meaning:

- በእንተ፡ ዘሰማዕከ፡ ቃልየ ... ba-ʾənta za-samāʿka qāləya ... 'because you listened to my voice ...'
- ወባረኩ ... በእንተ፡ ዘተከሥተ፡ ሎሙ፡ ስሙ፡ ለውእቱ፡ ወልደ፡ እጓለ፡ እመሕየው wa-bāraku ... ba-ʾənta za-takaśta lomu səmu la-wəʾətu walda ʾəgʷāla ʾəmma-ḥəyaw 'they praised (God) ... because the name of the son of man had been revealed to them' (En 69:26)

6.5.9.1.3. Circumstantial clauses introduced by እንዘ ʾənza (§6.5.5.1.) can sporadically have a causal connotation, as in እፎኑ፡ ይከውነኒ፡ ዝንቱ፡ እንዘ፡ ኢያአምር፡ ብእሴ ʾəffo-nu yəkawwənanni zəntu ʾənza ʾi-yāʾammər bəʾəse 'how can this happen to me since I have known no man?' (Lk 1:34).

6.5.9.2. Consecutive Clauses

Consecutive subordinate clauses, that is those expressing result, are introduced by እስከ ʾəska or እስከ፡ ሶበ ʾəska soba 'until, to the point that, so that'. The verbal predicate stands in the imperfect in most cases:

- ወናሁ፡ ዐቢይ፡ ድልቅልቅ፡ ኮነ፡ በውስተ፡ ባሕር፡ እስከ፡ ሶበ፡ ሐመር፡ ይሴወር፡ እምነ ፡ሞገድ wa-nāhu ʿabiy dələqləq kona ba-wəsta bāḥr ʾəska soba ḥamar yəssewar ʾəmənna mogad 'and behold, a windstorm arose on the sea, so that the boat was swamped by the waves' (Mt 8:24)
- ተእኅዘ፡ ብዙኅ፡ ዓሣት፡ ፈድፋደ፡ እስከ፡ ይትበተክ፡ መሥግሪሆሙ ta'əḥza bəzuḫ ʿāśāt fadfāda ʾəska yətbattak maśāgərihomu 'very many fish were caught, until their nets (almost) broke' (Lk 5:6)
- ወመልኡ፡ ክልኤሆን፡ አሕማረ፡ እስከ፡ ይሰጥማ wa-malʾu kəlʾehon ʾaḥmāra ʾəska yəssaṭṭamā 'and they filled the two boats until they (almost) sunk' (Lk 5:7)

Relative clauses introduced by ዘ– za– and ከመ kama-clauses can likewise have a consecutive meaning; cf., e.g., ወምንትኑ፡ አነ፡ ከመ፡ ትምጽኢ፡ እሙ፡ ለእግዚእየ፡ ኀቤየ wa-mənta-nu ʾana kama təmṣəʾi ʾəmmu la-ʾəgziʾəya ḫabeya 'who am I that the mother of my lord comes to me?' (Lk 1:43).

6.5.9.3. Subordinate Clauses with an Explanatory Meaning

Subordinate clauses with an explanatory meaning are most frequently introduced by እፎ ʾəffo 'how' and በእንተ፡ ዘ– ba-ʾənta za– 'regarding, for the sake of':

- እፎ፡ ኢይመይጡ፡ ፍናዊሆሙ፡ ብርሃናት፡ ዘውስተ፡ ሰማይ   ʾəffo ʾi-yəmayyəṭu fənāwihomu bərhānāt za-wəsta samāy '(contemplate all that happens in heaven), how the lights in heaven do not change their courses' (En 2:1)
- ወነበቦ፡ እግዚአብሔር፡ ለሙሴ፡ እምድኅረ፡ ሞተ፡ ክልኤሆሙ፡ ደቂቀ፡ አሮን፡ በእንተ ፡ ዘአምጽኡ፡ እሳተ፡ እምባዕድ፡ ቅድመ፡ እግዚአብሔር፡ ወሞቱ wa-nababo ʾəgzi-ʾab(ə)ḥer la-muse ʾəm-dəḫra mota kəlʾehomu daqiqa ʾaron ba-ʾənta za-ʾamṣəʾu ʾəsāta ʾəm-bāʿəd qədma ʾəgziʾab(ə)ḥer wa-motu 'and God spoke to Moses after the death of the two sons of Aaron, regarding that they had died when they had brought fire from outside before God' (Lev 16:1)

6.5.9.4. Semantically Unspecified "that"-Clauses

6.5.9.4.1. "That"-clauses that are semantically unspecified, for example after verbs expressing feelings, are primarily introduced by the conjunction ከመ kama 'that' (plus jussive) and እስመ ʾəsma 'namely, that' (with an indicative verbal predicate). After verbs expressing the meaning of being afraid, the ከመ kama-clause usually has a negated jussive as the predicate, which is best rendered without negation in English (cf. also §5.4.3.2.3.):

- እፈርህ፡ አነ፡ እምኔሁ ... ከመ፡ ኢይምጻእ ʾəfarrəh ʾana ʾəmənnehu ... kama ʾi-yəmṣāʾ 'I am afraid of him ... that he may come...' (Gen 32:12)
- ወተፈሥሐ፡ እስመ፡ ተበልዑ wa-tafaśśəḥa ʾəsma tabalʿu 'he rejoiced that they were devoured' (En 89:58)

6.5.9.4.2. Relative clauses introduced by ዘ– *za–* and those introduced by በእንተ፡ዘ– *ba-ʾənta za–* 'regarding, concerning' can have a comparable function. These types of clauses often occur after verbs of speaking, thinking, etc.:

- ኢ.ይምስልክሙ፡ዘመጻእኩ፡እስዐር፡ኦሪተ፡ወነቢያተ *ʾi-yəmsalkəmu za-maṣāʾku ʾasʿar ʾorita wa-nabiyāta* 'it should not seem to you that I have come to abolish the law or the prophets' (Mt 5:17)
- ወመስሎሙ፡ዘተሐውር፡ኀበ፡መቃብሩ *wa-masalomu za-taḥawwər ḥaba maqābəru* 'it appeared to them that she was going to his grave' (Jn 11:31); note that መስለ *masala* is usually followed by ከመ *kama*.

6.5.9.4.3. Verbs of fearing and of guarding oneself are often followed by asyndetic subordinate clauses that contain a negated jussive as the verbal predicate. These clauses have the same function as corresponding ከመ *kama*-clauses (§6.5.9.4.1.). The negation in the subordinate clause is best left untranslated in English:

- ዑቅ፡ርእሰከ፡ኢ.ታግብኦ *ʿuq rəʾsaka / ʾi-tāgbəʾo* 'beware of bringing him back' (Gen 24:6)
- ወባሕቱ፡ዑቁ፡ምጽዋተክሙ፡ኢ.ትግብሩ፡ለዐይነ፡ሰብእ *wa-bāḥtu ʿuqu məṣwā-takəmu ʾi-təgbaru la-ʿayna sabʾ* 'but beware not to give alms before the eyes of the people' (lit. 'beware of your alms-giving, not to do it before ...') (Mt 6:1)

6.5.9.4.4. Verbs of being afraid can also be followed by a formal main clause that is introduced by the adverb ዮጊ *yogi* 'perhaps, possibly' followed by an indicative verbal predicate (most often in the imperfect), as in እፈርህ፡ዮጊ፡ኢ.ትፈቅዱ *ʾəfarrəh yogi ʾi-təfaqqədu* 'I fear, perhaps you might not wish to ...' = 'I fear you do not wish to ...' (En 6:3).

6.5.9.5. The Syntactic Introduction of Direct Speech

Direct speech in Classical Ethiopic does not usually start without any introduction but is connected to the preceding context like "that"-clauses. Most commonly, direct speech is thus introduced by ከመ *kama* ('that') (cf. Greek ὅτι with the same function). Less often, the relative pronoun ዘ– *za–* or an እስመ *ʾəsma*-clause have the same function. In English, these lexemes are best left untranslated:

- ከመ ፡ ይትፈጸም ፡ ዘተብህለ ፡ በነቢይ ፡ ከመ ፡ ናዝራዊ ፡ ይሰመይ ፡ ወልድየ *kama yətfaṣ-ṣam za-tabəhla ba-nabiy kama nāzərāwi yəssamay waldəya* '... so that what was said by the prophet might be fulfilled: my son will be called a Nazorean' (Mt 2:23)

- ናሁ ፡ እብለክሙ ፡ ከመ ፡ እመ ፡ ኢፈድፈደ ፡ ጽድቅክሙ *nāhu ʾəbəlakkəmu kama ʾəmma ʾi-fadfada ṣədqəkəmu* 'behold, I tell you: unless your righteousness does not surpass ...' (Mt 5:20)

- ወይጸርሑ   ...   እስመ ፡ ኢንክል ፡ ቀዊመ ፡ ቅድመ ፡ እግዚእነ ፡ ወኢነጽሮቶ   *wa-yəṣarrəhu ... ʾəsma ʾi-nəkəl qawima qədma ʾəgziʾəna wa-ʾi-naṣṣəroto* '... and they cried out ...: we cannot stand before our Lord nor look at him!' (En 89:31)

6.5.10. Indirect Questions

6.5.10.1. Indirect interrogative clauses are introduced by the conditional conjunctions እመ *ʾəmma* or ለእመ *la-ʾəmma* (§4.5.3.2i) in the sense of 'if', as in ንግርኒ ፡ ለእመ ፡ ቦቱ ፡ ማኅደረ ፡ ቤተ ፡ አቡኪ ፡ ለነ *nəgərənni la-ʾəmma bottu māḫdara beta ʾabuki lana* 'tell me if there is lodging in the house of your father for us' (Gen 24:23).

6.5.10.2. Indirect wh-questions are introduced by the various interrogative pronouns and interrogative adverbs, as in ኀለይከ ፡ ምንተ ፡ ይከውን ፡ እምድኅሬከ *ḫallayka mənta yəkawwən ʾəm-dəḫreka* 'you thought about what would be after you' (Dan 2:29).

Abbreviations and Bibliography

Abbreviations

A	adverbial phrase		masc.	masculine
abs.	absolute state		nom.	nominative
acc.	accusative		O	object
AN	agent noun		OB	Old Babylonian
Aram.	Aramaic		OSA	Old South Arabian
c.	communis		p	plural
C	consonant		P	predicate
CA	Classical Arabic		perf.	perfect
CE	Classical Ethiopic		pf.	perfect
com.	communis		pl.	plural
cstr.	construct state		PP	perfective participle
f	feminine		pron.	pronominal
fem.	feminine		PS	Proto-Semitic
G	guttural		quadr.	quadriliteral
gem.	geminated		quinq.	quinquiliteral
gen.	genitive		s	singular
gutt.	guttural		S	subject
Heb.	Hebrew		sing.	singular
imp.	imperative		trad.	traditional pronunciation
impf.	imperfect		Ug.	Ugaritic
inf.	infinitive		V	vowel
juss.	jussive		V:	long vowel
m	masculine			

Abbreviations of Biblical Books and Other Literary Works

Old Testament

Gen, Ex, Lev, Num, Deut, Josh, Judg, Ruth, 1 Sam, 2 Sam, 1 Kings, 2 Kings, 1 Chr, 2 Chr, Ezra Neh, Esth, Job, Ps,[281] Prov, Eccl, Song, Isa, Jer, Lam, Ezek, Dan, Hos, Joel, Am, Ob, Jon, Mic, Nah, Hab, Zeph, Hag, Zech, Mal.

---

[281] The verse numbers are cited according to the Hebrew enumeration with the Ethioipic-Greek enumeration given in square brackets.

New Testament

Mt, Mk, Lk, Jn, Acts, Rom, 1 Cor, 2 Cor, Gal, Eph, Phil, Col, 1 Thess, 2 Thess, 1 Tim, 2 Tim, Titus, Philem, Heb, Jas, 1 Pet, 2 Pet, 1 Jn, 2 Jn, 3 Jn, Jude, Rev.

Others

ʿĀmda Ṣəyon (Kropp, M. 1994. *Der siegreiche Feldzug des Königs ʿĀmda-Ṣəyon gegen die Muslime in Adal im Jahre 1332 n. Chr.* 2 vols. Leuven.)

En = Enoch (Knibb, Michael A. 1978. *The Ethiopic Book of Enoch: A New Edition in the Light of the Aramaic Dead Sea Fragments.* Oxford.)

Jub = Jubilees (Vanderkam, James C. 1989. *The Book of Jubilees: A Critical Text* [2 vols]. Leuven.)

Kəbra Nagaśt (Bezold, Carl. 1909. *Kebra Nagast – Die Herrlichkeit der Könige.* Abhandlungen der Philosophisch-Philologischen Klasse der Königlich Bayerischen Akademie der Wissenschaften 23. München.)

Ləbna Dəngəl (Kropp, M. 1988. *Die Geschichte des Lebna-Dengel, Claudius und Minās* [2 vols]. Leuven.)

ParJer = Paralipomena Jeremiae (Dillmann, A. 1941. *Chrestomathia Aethiopica, edita et glossario explanata.* Reprint, Amsterdam, 1974.)

Səna fəṭrat (Haile, G., and M. Amare. 1991. *Beauty of Creation.* Manchester.)

Sənkəssār Ḫədār (Colin, G. 1988. "Le synaxaire éthiopien mois de Ḫedār." *Patrologia Orientalis* 44:3.)

Bibliographical Abbreviations

CDG   Leslau, W. 1987. *Comparative Dictionary of Geʿez (Classical Ethiopic).* Wiesbaden.

DG   Dillmann, A. 1899. *Grammatik der äthiopischen Sprache.* Second edition. Leipzig.

DL   Dillmann, A. 1865. *Lexikon linguae aethiopicae cum indice latino.* Leipzig.

RIÉ Bernard, E., A.J. Drewes, R. Schneider. 1991. *Recueil des inscriptions de l'Éthiopie des périodes pré-axoumite et axoumite*. 3 vols. Paris.

SED I Militarev, A., and L. Kogan. 2000. *Semitic Etymological Dictionary*, vol. 1, *Anatomy of Man and Animals* (Alter Orient und Altes Testament 278/1). Münster.

Bibliography

Bombeck, S. 1997. "*hallo* und *kona* im altäthiopischen Markusevangelium." *Biblische Notizen* 87:5–12.

Brockelmann, C. 1908. *Grundriß der vergleichenden Grammatik der semitischen Sprachen*, vol. 1, *Laut- und Formenlehre*. Berlin.

Bulakh, M. 2009. "Nota genitivi *za-* in Epigraphic Geez." *Journal of Semitic Studies* 54:393–419.

———. 2012. "Word Order in Epigraphic Gəʿəz." *Aethiopica* 15:136–75.

———. 2016. "Some Problems of Transcribing Geez." Pages 103–37 in *150 Years after Dillmann's* Lexicon: *Perspectives and Challenges of Gəʿəz Studies*. Edited by A. Bausi with assistance from E. Sokolinski. Wiesbaden.

Bulakh, M., and L. Kogan. 2010. "The Genealogical Position of Tigre and the Problem of North Ethio-Semitic Unity." *Zeitschrift der Deutschen Morgenländischen Gesellschaft* 160:273–302.

———. 2013. "More on Genealogical Classification of Ethiopian Semitic." *Babel und Bibel* 7:600–608.

Butts, A.M. 2011. "Ethiopic Christianity, Syriac Contacts with." Pages 148–53 in *Gorgias Encyclopedic Dictionary of the Syriac Heritage*. Edited by S.P. Brock, A.M. Butts, and. G.A. Kiraz. Piscataway.

Chaîne, M. 1938. *Grammaire éthiopienne, Nouvelle Édition*. Beirut.

Cohen, D. 1984. *La phrase nominale et l'évolution du système verbal en sémitique: Études des syntaxes historique*. Collection linguistique 72. Leuven.

Conti Rossini, C. 1941. *Grammatica elementare della lingua etiopica*. Rome. Reprint, Rome, 1967.

Corriente, F. 1996. *Introducción a la gramática comparanda del semítico meridional*. Centro de Estudios del Próximo Oriente: Lenguas y Culturas del Antiquo Oriente Próximo 1. Madrid.

Daniels, P.T. 1991. "Ha, La, Ḥa or Hōi, Lawe, Ḥaut. The Ethiopic Letter Names." Pages 275–88 in vol. 1 of *Semitic Studies in Honor of Wolf Leslau on the Occasion of His Eighty-Fifth Birthday*. Edited by A.S. Kaye. Wiesbaden.

Diem, W. 1988. "Laryngalgesetz und Vokalismus: Ein Beitrag zur Geschichte des Altäthiopischen." *Zeitschriften der Deutschen Morgenländischen Gesellschaft* 138:236–62.

Dillmann, A. 1857. *Grammatik der äthiopischen Sprache.* First edition. Leipzig.

———. 1865. *Lexicon linguae aethiopicae cum indice latino.* Leipzig. (= DL)

———. 1899. *Grammatik der äthiopischen Sprache.* Second edition. Leipzig. (= DG)

———. 1907. *Ethiopic Grammar.* Second edition. Translated by J.A. Crichton. London.

———. 1941. *Chrestomathia Aethiopica, edita et glossario explanata.* Reprint, Amsterdam, 1974.

Dolgopolsky, A. 1999. *From Proto-Semitic to Hebrew. Etymological Approach in a Hamito-Semitic Perspective.* Studi Camito-Semitici 2. Milano.

El-Antony, M., J. Blid., and A.M. Butts. 2016. "An Early Ethiopic Manuscript Fragment (12th–13th cent.) from the Monastery of St. Antony (Egypt)." *Aethiopica* 19:27–51.

Fox, J. 2003. *Semitic Noun Patterns.* Winona Lake.

Gai, A. 1981. "The Place of the Attribute in Geʿez." *Journal of Semitic Studies* 26:257–65.

Gensler, O.D. 1997. "Reconstructing Quadriliteral Verb Inflection: Ethiopic, Akkadian, Proto Semitic." *Journal of Semitic Studies* 42:229–57.

———. 1998. "Verbs with Two Object Suffixes: A Semitic Archaism in Its Afroasiatic Context." *Diachronica* 15:231–84.

Goldenberg, G. 1977. "The Semitic Languages of Ethiopia and Their Classification." *Bulletin of the School of Oriental and African Studies* 40:461–507.

Gragg, G. 1997. "Geʿez (Ethiopic)." Pages 242–60 in *The Semitic Languages.* Edited by R. Hetzron. New York.

———. 2004. "Geʾez (Aksum)." Pages 427–53 in *The Cambridge Encyclopedia of the World's Ancient Languages.* Edited by R.D. Woodard. Cambridge.

Grébaut, S. 1952. *Supplément au Lexicon Linguae Aethiopicae de August Dillmann (1865) et édition du lexique de Juste d'Urbin (1859–1855).* Paris.

Hartmann, J. 1980. *Amharische Grammatik.* Äthiopistische Forschungen 3. Wiesbaden.

Heide, M. 2006. "Some Possible Traces of the Dual in Gəʿəz." Pages 769–76 in *Proceedings of the XVth International Conference of Ethiopian Studies, Hamburg, July 20–25, 2003.* Edited by S. Uhlig. Wiesbaden.

Hetzron, R. 1972. *Ethiopian Semitic: Studies in Classification.* Journal of Semitic Studies Monograph 2. Manchester.

Kapeliuk, O. 1995. "La phrase coupée en Guèze." Pages 191–204 in *Mélanges linguistiques offerts à Maxime Rodinson.* Edited by C. Robin. Comptes rendus du Groupe Linguistique d'Études Chamito-Sémitique. Paris.

Kogan, L. 2005. "γ in Ethiopian." Pages 183–216 in *Studia Semitica et Semitohamitica: Festschrift für Rainer Voigt anläßlich seines 60. Geburtstags am 17. Januar 2004.* Edited by B. Burtea, J. Tropper, and H. Younansardaroud. Münster.

———. 2006."Ethiopian Cognates to the Akkadian and Ugaritic Lexicon." *Šapal tibnim mû illkū: Studies Presented to Joaquín Sanmartín on the Occasion of His 65th Birthday.* Edited by G. del Olmo Lete, L. Feliu, and A. Millet Albà. Barcelona.

———. 2015. *Genealogical Classification of Semitic: The Lexical Isoglosses.* Berlin.

Kouwenberg, N.J.C. 2010. *The Akkadian Verb and Its Semitic Background.* Winona Lake.

Lambdin, T.O. 1978. *Introduction to Classical Ethiopic (Geʿez).* Harvard Semitic Studies 24. Missoula.

Leslau, W. 1987. *Comparative Dictionary of Geʿez (Classical Ethiopic).* Wiesbaden. (= CDG)

———. 1989. *Concise Dictionary of Geʿez (Classical Ethiopic).* Wiesbaden.

———. 1990. *Arabic Loanwords in Ethiopian Semitic.* Wiesbaden.

———. 1995. *Reference Grammar of Amharic.* Wiesbaden.

Littmann, E. 1954. "Die äthiopische Literatur." Pages 375–85 in *Semitistik.* Edited by B. Spuler. Handbuch der Orientalistik I/3.

Marrassini, P. 1990. "Some Considerations on the Problem of the 'Syriac Influences' on Aksumite Ethiopia." *Journal of Ethiopian Studies* 23:35–46.

McKenzie, J., and F. Watson. 2016. *The Garima Gospels: Early Illuminated Gospel Books from Ethiopia.* Oxford.

Mercier, J. 2000. "La peinture éthiopienne à l'époque axoumite et au XVIIIe siècle." *Comptes rendus des séances de l'Académie des Inscriptions et Belles-Lettres* 144:35–71.

Militarev, A., and L. Kogan. 2000. *Semitic Etymological Dictionary,* vol. 1, *Anatomy of Man and Animals.* Alter Orient und Altes Testament 278/1. Münster. (= SED I)

Phillipson, D.W. 2012. *Foundations of an African Civilization¨ Aksum and the Northern Horn, 1000 BC–AD 1300.* Suffolk.

Porkhomovsky, V. 1997. "Modern South Arabian Languages from a Semitic and Hamito-Semitic Perspective." *Proceedings of the Seminar for Arabian Studies* 27:219–23.

Praetorius, F. 1886. *Aethiopische Grammatik mit Paradigmen, Litteratur, Chrestomathie und Glossar.* Porta Linguarum Orientalium 7. Karlsruhe.

Schneider, R. 1959. *L'expression des complements de verbe et de nom et la place de l'adjectif épithète en guèze.* Bibliothèque de l'École des Hautes Études 312. Paris.

Soden, W. von. 1987. "Äthiopisch-Akkadische Isoglossen." Pages 559–67 in *Proceedings of the Fourth International Hamito-Semitic Congress, Marburg, 20–22 September, 1983.* Edited by H. Jungraithmayr and W.W. Müller. Amsterdam.

Tropper, J. 2000. "Der altäthiopische Status constructus auf -*a* aus sprachvergleichender Sicht." *Wiener Zeitschrift für die Kunde des Morgenlandes* 90:201–18.

Trumpp, E. 1874. "Ueber den Accent im Aethiopischen." *Zeitschrift der Deutschen Morgenländischen Gesellschaft* 28:515–61

Uhlig, S. 1988. *Äthiopische Paläographie.* Äthiopische Forschungen 22. Stuttgart.

Ullendorff, E. 1955. *The Semitic Languages of Ethiopia: A Comparative Phonology.* London.

———. 1973. *The Ethiopians: An Introduction to Country and People.* Third edition. Oxford.

Voigt, R.M. 1983. "The Vowel System of Gəʿz." Pages 355–62 in *Ethiopian Studies Dedicated to Wolf Leslau.* Edited by S. Segert and A.J.E. Bodrogligeti. Wiesbaden.

———. 1989. "The Development of the Old Ethiopic Consonantal System." Pages 633–47 in vol. 2 of *Proceedings of the Eighth International Conference of Ethiopian Studies.* Edited by Taddese Beyene. Addis Ababa.

———. 1990. "The Gemination of the Present-Imperfect Forms in Old Ethiopic." *Journal of Semitic Studies* 35:1–18.

———. 1994. "Die Entsprechung der ursemitischen Interdentale im Altäthiopischen." Pages 102–17 in *Festschrift Ewald Wagner zum 65. Geburtstag.* Edited by W. Heinrichs and G. Schoeler. Beiruter Texte und Studien 54. Beirut.

———. 1997. "On the Irregular Form *yəbe* in Classical Ethiopic." Pages 583–95 in vol. 1 of *Ethiopia in Broader Perspective: Papers of the XIIIth International Conference of Ethiopic Studies (Kyoto 1997).* Edited by K. Fukui and E. Kurimoto. Kyoto.

———. 1998. "'Fuß' (und 'Hand') im Äthiopischen, Syroarabischen und Hebräischen." *Zeitschrift für Althebraistik* 11:191–99.

———. 1999. "Rezension von R. Hetzron (ed.), *The Semitic Languages* (London/New York 1997)." *Aethiopica* 2:206–29.

———. 2000. "Über die unregelmäßige Form *yəbe* im Altäthiopischen. II." *Aethiopica* 3:120–31.

———. 2009. "North vs. South Ethiopian Semitic." Pages 1375–87 in *Proceedings of the 16ᵗʰ International Conference of Ethiopian Studies*. Edited by S. Ege and H. Aspen et al. Trondheim.

Waltisberg, M. 2000. "Die Funktion der Ast-Stämme im System der Altäthiopischen Verbalderivation." Unpublished MA thesis, München: Ludwig-Maximilian Universität..

Weninger, S. 1993. *Gǝʕǝz*. Languages of the World/Materials 1. München.

———. 1998. "Zur Realisation des ḍ (<*ḏ) im Altäthiopischen." *Welt des Orients* 29:147–48.

———. 1999. "*kona qatala* zum Ausdruck der Vorvergangenheit im Gǝʕǝz?" Pages 171–83 in *Tempus und Aspekt in den semitischen Sprachen: Jenaer Kolloquium zur semitischen Sprachwissenschaft*. Edited by N. Nebes. Wiesbaden.

———. 2000. "On Performatives in Classical Ethiopic." *Journal of Semitic Studies* 45:91–101.

———. 2001. *Das Verbalsystem des Altäthiopischen: Eine Untersuchung seiner Verwendung und Funktion unter Berücksichtigung des Interferenzproblems*. Akademie der Wissenschaften und der Literatur, Mainz: Veröffentlichungen der Orientalischen Kommission 47. Wiesbaden.

———. 2002. "Was wurde aus *ǧ im Altäthiopischen?" Pages 289–98 in *Neue Beiträge zur Semitistik: Erstes Arbeitstreffen der Arbeitsgemeinschaft Semitistik der Deutschen Morgenländischen Gesellschaft vom 11. bis 13. September 2000 an der Friedrich-Schiller-Universität Jena*. Edited by N. Nebes. Wiesbaden.

———. 2010. "Sounds of Geʕez – How to Study the Phonetics and Phonology of an Ancient Language." *Aethiopica* 13:75–88.

———. 2011. "Old Ethiopic." Pages 1124–41 in *The Semitic Languages: An International Handbook*. Edited by S. Weninger. Berlin.

———. 2015. "Zur Funktion altäthiopischer Diskurspartikel: -*ke* und -(*ǝ*)*ssä*." Pages 323–34 in *Neue Beiträge zur Semitistik: Fünftes Treffen der Arbeitsgemeinschaft Semitistik in der Deutschen Morgenländischen Gesellschaft vom 15.-17. Februar 2012 an der Universität Basel*. Edited by V. Golinets. Münster.

Zaborski, A. 2005. "The Decay of *qattala/qātala* in Gǝʕǝz." Pages 26–50 in *Semitic Studies in Honour of Edward Ullendorff*. Edited by G. Khan. Leiden.

Appendix A: Sample Texts in Original Script and Transliteration

Text 1: John 1: 1–18

ወንጌል ፡ ዘዮሐንስ ።

ምዕራፍ ፡ ፩ ፤

፩ ፤   ቀዳሚሁ ፡ ቃል ፡ ውእቱ ፡ ወውእቱ ፡ ቃል ፡ ኀበ ፡ እግዚአብሔር ፡

፪ ፤ ውእቱ ፡ ወእግዚአብሔር ፡ ውእቱ ፡ ቃል ። ወዝንቱ ፡ እምቀዲሙ ፡ ኀበ ፡

፫ ፤ እግዚአብሔር ፡ ውእቱ ፡ ኵሉ ፡ ቦቱ ፡ ኮነ ፡ ወዘእንበሌሁሰ ፡ አልቦ ፡ ዘከ

፬ ፤ ነ ፡ ወኢምንትኒ ፡ እምዘኮነ ፡ ቦቱ ፡ ሕይወት ፡ ውእቱ ፡ ወሕይወትሰ ፡ ብር

፭ ፤ ሃኑ ፡ ለእጓለ ፡ እመሕያው ፡ ውእቱ ፡ ወብርሃንሰ ፡ ዘውስተ ፡ ጽልመት ፡ ያ

፮ ፤ በርህ ፡ ወያርኢ ፡ ወጽልመትኒ ፡ ኢይረክቦ ። ወሀሎ ፡ አሐዱ ፡ ብእሲ ፡ ዘ

፯ ፤ ተፈነወ ፡ እምኀበ ፡ እግዚአብሔር ፡ ዘስሙ ፡ ዮሐንስ ። ወውእቱ ፡ መጽአ ፡ ለስምዕ ፡ ሰማዕተ ፡ ይኩን ፡ በእንተ ፡ ብርሃን ፡ ከመ ፡ ኵሉ ፡ ይእመን ፡ ቦ

፰ ፤ ቱ ። ወለሊሁሰ ፡ ኢኮነ ፡ ብርሃን ፡ ዳእሙ ፡ ሰማዕተ ፡ ይኩን ፡ በእንተ ፡ ብር

፱ ፤ ሃን ። ዘውእቱ ፡ ብርሃን ፡ ጽድቅ ፡ ዘያበርሁ ፡ ለኵሉ ፡ ሰብእ ፡ ዘይመጽእ ፡ ው

፲ ፤ ስተ ፡ ዓለም ። ወውስተ ፡ ዓለም ፡ ሀሎ ፡ ወዓለምኒ ፡ ቦቱ ፡ ኮነ ፡ ወዓለምሰ ፡

፲፩ ፤ ኢያእመር ። ውስተ ፡ ዚአሁ ፡ መጽአ ፡ ወእሊአሁሰ ፡ ኢተወክፍዎ ። ወ

፲፪ ፤ ለእለሰ ፡ ተወክፍዎ ፡ ወሀበሙ ፡ ሥልጣነ ፡ ውሉደ ፡ እግዚአብሔር ፡ ይኩ

፲፫ ፤ ኑ ፡ ለእለ ፡ አምኑ ፡ በስሙ ። እለ ፡ ኢኮኑ ፡ እምነ ፡ ዘደም ፡ ወኢእምፈቃ ደ ፡ ፍትወት ፡ ዘሥጋ ፡ ወኢእምሥምረተ ፡ ብእሲ ፡ አላ ፡ እምእግዚአብሔ

፲፬ ፤ ር ፡ ተወልዱ ። ወውእቱ ፡ ቃል ፡ ሥጋ ፡ ኮነ ፡ ወኀደረ ፡ ላዕሌነ ፡ ወርኢነ ፡ ስብሓቲሁ ፡ ከመ ፡ ስብሓተ ፡ አሐዱ ፡ ዋሕድ ፡ ለአቡሁ ፡ ዘምሉእ ፡ ጸጋ ፡

፲፭ ፤ ወሞገሰ ፡ ወጽድቀ ፡ ዮሐንስ ፡ ሰማዕቱ ፡ በእንቲአሁ ፡ ክልሐ ፡ ወይቤ ፡ ዝ ውእቱ ፡ ዘእቤለክሙ ፡ አነ ፡ በእንቲአሁ ፡ ይመጽእ ፡ እምድኅሬየ ፡ ዘሀሎ ፡

፲፮ ፤ እምቅድሜየ ፡ እስመ ፡ ውእቱ ፡ ቀዳሚ ። እስመ ፡ እምተረፈ ፡ ዚአሁ ፡

፲፯ ፤ ነሣእነ ፡ ንሕነ ፡ ኵልነ ፡ ጸጋ ፡ ህየንተ ፡ ጸጋ ። እስመ ፡ ኦሪት ፡ በሙሴ ፡ ተውህበት ፡ ለነ ፡ ወጸጋሰ ፡ ወጽድቅ ፡ በኢየሱስ ፡ ክርስቶስ ፡ ኮነ ።

፲፰ ፤ ለእግዚአብሔርሰ ፡ አልቦ ፡ ዘርእዮ ፡ ግሙራ ፡ እላ ፡ ወልድ ፡ ዋሕድ ፡ ዘሀ ሎ ፡ ውስተ ፡ ሕፅነ ፡ አቡሁ ፡ ውእቱ ፡ ነገረነ ።

wangel za-yoḥannəs məʿrāf 1

1. *qadāmihu qāl wəʾətu wa-wəʾətu qāl ḥaba ʾəgziʾab(ə)her wəʾətu wa-ʾəgziʾab(ə)her wəʾətu qāl;*

2. *wa-zəntu ʾəm-qadimu ḫaba ʾəgziʾab(ə)her wəʾətu;*

3. *kʷəllu bottu kona wa-za-ʾənbalehu-ssa ʾalbo za-kona wa-ʾi-məntə-ni ʾəm-za-kona;*

4. *bottu ḥəywat wəʾətu wa-ḥəywatə-ssa bərhānu la-ʾəgʷāla ʾəmmaḥəyāw wəʾətu;*

5. *wa-bərhānə-ssa za-wəsta ṣəlmat yābarrəh wa-yārəʾi wa-ṣəlmatə-ni ʾi-yərakkəbo;*

6. *wa-hallo ʾaḥadu bəʾsi za-tafannawa ʾəm-ḫaba ʾəgziʾab(ə)her za-səmu yoḥannəs;*

7. *wa-wəʾətu maṣʾa la-səmʿ samāʿta yəkun baʾənta bərhān kama kʷəllu yəʾman bottu;*

8. *wa-lallihu-ssa ʾi-kona bərhāna dāʾmu samāʿta yəkun ba-ʾənta bərhān;*

9. *za-wəʾətu bərhāna ṣədq za-yābarrəh la-kʷəllu sabʾ za-yəmaṣṣəʾ wəsta ʿālam;*

10. *wa-wəsta ʿālam hallo wa-ʿāləmə-ni bottu kona wa-ʿāləmə-ssa ʾi-yāʾmaro (< *ʾi-ʾaʾmaro);*

11. *wəsta ziʾahu maṣʾa wa-ʾəlliʾahu-ssa ʾi-tawakfəwwo;*

12. *wa-la-ʾəlla-ssa tawakfəwwo wahabomu śəlṭāna wəluda ʾəgziʾab(ə)her yəkunu la-ʾəlla ʾamnu ba-səmu;*

13. *ʾəlla ʾi-konu ʾəmənna za-dam wa-ʾi-ʾəm-faqāda fətwat za-śəgā wa-ʾi-ʾəm-śəmrata bəʾsi ʾallā ʾəm-ʾəgziʾab(ə)her tawaldu;*

14. *wa-wəʾətu qāl śəgā kona wa-ḥadara lāʿlena wa-rəʾina səbḥātihu kama səbḥāta ʾaḥadu wāḥəd la-ʾabuhu za-məluʾ ṣaggā wa-mogasa wa-ṣədqa;*

15. *yoḥannəs samāʿtu ba-ʾəntiʾahu kalḥa wa-yəbe zə-wəʾətu za-ʾəbelakkəmu ʾana ba-ʾəntiʾahu yəmaṣṣəʾ ʾəm-dəḥreya za-hallo ʾəm-qədmeya ʾəsma wəʾətu qadamanni;*

16. *ʾəsma ʾəm-tarafa ziʾahu naśāʾna nəḥna kʷəlləna ṣaggā həyyanta ṣaggā ba-diba ṣaggā;*

17. *ʾəsma ʾorit ba-muse tawəhbat lana wa-ṣaggā-ssa wa-ṣədq ba-ʾiyasus krəstos kona;*

18. *la-ʾəgziʾab(ə)herə-ssa ʾalbo za-rəʾəyo gəmurā ʾallā wald wāḥəd za-hallo wəsta ḥəḍna ʾabuhu wəʾətu nagaranna.*

Text 2: Matthew 6: 9–13 (The Lord's Prayer)

∷ ከመዝኬ ፡ ፱ ፩

ጸልዩ ፡ አንትሙስ ∷ አቡነ ፡ ዘበሰማያት ፡ ይትቀደስ ፡ ስምክ ∷ ትምጻእ ፡ መ ፲ ፩

ንግሥትክ ∷ ይኩን ፡ ፈቃደክ ፡ በከመ ፡ በሰማይ ፡ ወበምድርኒ ፡ ሲሳየነ ፡ ዘ ፲፩ ፩

ለለ ፡ ዕለትነ ፡ ሀበነ ፡ ዮም ∷ ወኀድግ ፡ ለነ ፡ አበሳነ ፡ ከመ ፡ ንሕነኒ ፡ ነኀድ ፲፪ ፩

ግ ፡ ለዘአበሰ ፡ ለነ ∷ ወኢታብአነ ፡ ውስተ ፡ መንሱት ፡ አላ ፡ አድኅነነ ፡ ወ ፲፫ ፩

ባልሐነ ፡ እምኵሉ ፡ እኩይ ∷ እስመ ፡ ዚአከ ፡ ይእቲ ፡ መንግሥት ፡ ኀይል ፡

ወስብሐት ፡ ለዓለመ ፡ ዓለም ፡ አሜን ∷

1. kama-za-ke ṣalləyu ʾantəmu-ssa; ʾabuna za-ba-samāyāt yətqaddas səməka;
2. təmṣāʾ mangəśtəka; yəkun faqādaka ba-kama ba-samāy wa-ba-mədrə-ni;
3. sisāyana za-lalla ʿəlatəna habanna yom;
4. wa-ḫədəg lana ʾabbasāna kama nəḥna-ni naḫaddəg la-za-ʾabbasa lana;
5. wa-ʾi-tābəʾanna wəsta mansut ʾallā ʾadḫananna wa-bāləḥanna ʾəm-kʷəllu ʾəkkuy; ʾəsma ziʾaka yəʾəti mangəśt ḥayl wa-səbḥāt la-ʿālama ʿālam ʾamen.

Text 3: Matthew 5 (so-called "text B")

ምዕራፍ ፡ ፭ ፤

፩ ፤　　　　　፭ ፤ በእንተ ፡ ብፁዓን ። ወርእዮ ፡ አሕዛበ ፡ ዐርገ ፡ ውስተ ፡ ደብር ፡
፪ ፤　ወነቢሮ ፡ ቀርቡ ፡ ኀቤሁ ፡ አርዳኢሁ ። ወከሠተ ፡ አፉሁ ፡ ወመህሮሙ ፡ እ
፫ ፤　ንዘ ፡ ይብል ። ብፁዓን ፡ ነዳያን ፡ በመንፈስ ፡ እስመ ፡ ሎሙ ፡ ይእቲ ፡ መን
፬ ፤　ግሥተ ፡ ሰማያት ። ብፁዓን ፡ እለ ፡ ይላሕዉ ፡ ይእዜ ፡ እስመ ፡ እሙንቱ ፡
፭ ፤　ይትፌሥሑ ። ብፁዓን ፡ የዋሃን ፡ እስመ ፡ እሙንቱ ፡ ይወርስዋ ፡ ለምድ
፮ ፤　ር ። ብፁዓን ፡ እለ ፡ ይርኀቡ ፡ ወይጸምኡ ፡ ለጽድቅ ፡ እስመ ፡ እሙንቱ ፡
፯ ፤　ይጸግቡ ። ብፁዓን ፡ መሓርያን ፡ እስመ ፡ እሙንቱ ፡ ይትመሐሩ ። ብፁዓ
፰ ፤　ን ፡ ንጹሓነ ፡ ልብ ፡ እስመ ፡ እሙንቱ ፡ ይሬእይም ፡ ለእግዚአብሔር ። ብፁ
፱ ፤　ዓን ፡ ገባርያነ ፡ ሰላም ፡ እስመ ፡ እሙንቱ ፡ ውሉደ ፡ እግዚአብሔር ፡ ይሰ
፲ ፤　መዩ ። ብፁዓን ፡ እለ ፡ ይሰደዱ ፡ በእንተ ፡ ጽድቅ ፡ እስመ ፡ ሎሙ ፡ ይእቲ ፡
፲፩ ፤　መንግሥተ ፡ ሰማያት ። ብፁዓን ፡ አንትሙ ፡ ሶበ ፡ ይሰድዱክሙ ፡ ወይዘነ
　　　ጕቱክሙ ፡ ወይነቡ ፡ ኵሎ ፡ እከየ ፡ ላዕሌክሙ ፡ እንዘ ፡ ይሔስዉ ፡ በእንቲ
፲፪ ፤　አየ ። ተፈሥሑ ፡ ወተሓሠዩ ፡ እስመ ፡ ዐስብክሙ ፡ ብዙኅ ፡ ውእቱ ፡ በሰ
　　　ማያት ። እስመ ፡ ከመዝ ፡ ሰደድዎሙ ፡ ለነቢያት ፡ እለ ፡ እምቅድሜክሙ ።
፲፫ ፤　አንትሙ ፡ ውእቱ ፡ ጼው ፡ ለምድር ፡ ወእመሰ ፡ ጼው ፡ ለስጎ ፡ በምንትኑ ፡
　　　ይትቄሰም ። አልቦኬ ፡ እንከ ፡ ለዘይበቍዕ ፡ ዘእንበለ ፡ ለገዲፍ ፡ አፍአ ፡ ወ
፲፬ ፤　ይከይዶ ፡ ሰብእ ። አንትሙ ፡ ውእቱ ፡ ብርሃን ፡ ለዓለም ። ኢትክል ፡ ሀገ
፲፭ ፤　ር ፡ ተኀብአ ፡ እንተ ፡ መልዕልተ ፡ ደብር ፡ ትነብር ። ወኢያኀትዉ ፡ ማኅቶ
　　　ት ፡ ከመ ፡ ያንብርዋ ፡ ታሕተ ፡ ከፈር ፡ እላ ፡ ዲበ ፡ ተቀዋማ ፡ ወታበርህ ፡
፲፮ ፤　ለኵሎሙ ፡ እለ ፡ ውስተ ፡ ቤት ። ከማሁ ፡ ይብራህ ፡ ብርሃንክሙ ፡ በቅድ
　　　መ ፡ ሰብእ ፡ ከመ ፡ ይርአዩ ፡ ምግባሪክሙ ፡ ሠናየ ፡ ወይሰብሕዎ ፡ ለአቡክ
　　　ሙ ፡ ዘበሰማያት ።

ኢ_ይምሰልክሙ ፡ ዘመጻእኩ ፡ እስዐር ፡ ኦሪተ ፡ ወነቢያ ፡ ፲፯ ።
ተ ። ኢ_መጻእኩ ፡ እስዐርሙ ፡ አላ ፡ እፈጽሞሙ ። አማን ፡ እብለክሙ ፡ ፲፰ ።
እስከ ፡ የኅልፍ ፡ ሰማይ ፡ ወምድር ፡ የውጣ ፡ እንተ ፡ አሐቲ ፡ ቅርፀታ ፡ ኢ_
ተኅልፍ ፡ እምኦሪት ፡ እስከ ፡ ሶበ ፡ ኵሉ ፡ ይትገበር ። ዘኬ ፡ ፈትሐ ፡ አሐ ፡ ፲፱ ።
ተ ፡ እምእላ ፡ ትእዛዛት ፡ እንተ ፡ ተሐጽጽ ፡ ወይሜህር ፡ ከመጝ ፡ ለሰብእ ፡
ሕጹጽ ፡ ይሰመይ ፡ በመንግሥተ ፡ ሰማያት ፡ ወዘሰ ፡ ይሜህር ፡ ወይገብር ፡
ውእቱ ፡ ዐቢየ ፡ ይሰመይ ፡ በመንግሥተ ፡ ሰማያት ። ናሁ ፡ እብለክሙ ፡ ከ ፡ ፳ ።
መ ፡ እመ ፡ ኢ_ፈድፈደ ፡ ጽድቅክሙ ፡ ፈድፋደ ፡ እምጸሐፍት ፡ ወእምፈሪ
ሳውያን ፡ ኢ_ትበውኡ ፡ ውስተ ፡ መንግሥተ ፡ ሰማያት ። ሰማዕክሙ ፡ ከ ፡ ፳፩ ።
መ ፡ ተብህለ ፡ ለቀደምት ፡ ኢ_ትቅትል ፡ ነፍስ ፡ ወዘሰ ፡ ቀተለ ፡ ረስሐ ፡ ው
እቱ ፡ ለኵነኔ ። ወአነ ፡ እብለክሙ ፡ ኵሉ ፡ ዘያምዕዕ ፡ እኁሁ ፡ ረስሐ ፡ ፳፪ ።
ውእቱ ፡ ለኵነኔ ። ወዘሂ ፡ ይቤ ፡ እኁሁ ፡ ዘዐርቅ ፡ ረስሐ ፡ ውእቱ ፡ ለዐው
ድ ። ወዘሂ ፡ ይቤ ፡ አብድ ፡ ረስሐ ፡ ውእቱ ፡ ለገሃነም ፡ እሳት ። ወእምከመ ፡ ፳፫ ።
ኬ ፡ ታበውእ ፡ አምኃከ ፡ ውስተ ፡ ምሥዋዕ ፡ ወበህየ ፡ ተዘከርከ ፡ ከመዐ
እኁክ ፡ ዘየሐይሰከ ፡ ኃድግ ፡ ህየ ፡ መባአከ ፡ ቅድመ ፡ ምሥዋዕ ፡ ወሑር ፡ ፳፬ ።
ቅድመ ፡ ተኳነን ፡ ምስለ ፡ እኁክ ፡ ወእምዝ ፡ ገቢአክ ፡ አብእ ፡ አምኃክ ።
ኩን ፡ ጠቢበ ፡ ለዐድውክ ፡ ፍጡነ ፡ እንዘ ፡ ሀለውክ ፡ ምስሌሁ ፡ ውስተ ፡ ፍ ፡ ፳፭ ።
ኖት ፡ ከመ ፡ ኢ_ይመጡክ ፡ ዐድውክ ፡ ለመኰንን ፡ ወመኰንን ፡ ለላእኩ ፡
ወውስተ ፡ ሞቅሕ ፡ ትትወፈይ ፡ አማን ፡ እብለከ ፡ ኢ_ትወፅእ ፡ እምህየ ፡ እ ፡ ፳፮ ።
ስከ ፡ ሶበ ፡ ትፈዲ ፡ ጥዩቀ ፡ ኵሎ ። ሰማዕክሙ ፡ ከመ ፡ ተብህለ ፡ ኢ_ትዘም ፡ ፳፯ ።
ው ። ወአንሰ ፡ እብለክሙ ፡ ኵሉ ፡ ዘይሬኢ ፡ ብእሲተ ፡ ወይፈትዋ ፡ ወዲ ፡ ፳፰ ።
አ ፡ ዘመወ ፡ ባቲ ፡ በልቡ ። እመ ፡ ዐይንክ ፡ እንተ ፡ የማን ፡ ታስሕተከ ፡ ም ፡ ፳፱ ።
ልኃ ፡ ወአውፅአ ፡ እምላዕሌክ ፡ እስመ ፡ ይኄይሰክ ፡ ከመ ፡ ይትሐጎል ፡ አ
ሐዱ ፡ እምን ፡ አባልክ ፡ እምኵሉ ፡ ሥጋክ ፡ ይትወደይ ፡ ውስተ ፡ ገሃነም ።
ወእመ ፡ እንተ ፡ የማን ፡ እዴክ ፡ ታስሕተከ ፡ ምትራ ፡ ወአውፅአ ፡ እምላዕ ፡ ፴ ።
ሌክ ። እስመ ፡ ይኄይሰክ ፡ ይትሐጎል ፡ አሐዱ ፡ እምን ፡ አባልክ ፡ እምኵለ
ንታሁ ፡ ሥጋክ ፡ ውስተ ፡ ገሃነም ፡ ይትወደይ ። ወተብህለ ፡ ዘኀደገ ፡ ብእሲ ፡ ፴፩ ።
ቶ ፡ የሀባ ፡ መጽሐፈ ፡ ኃድጋቲሃ ። ወአንሰ ፡ እብለክሙ ፡ ከመ ፡ ኵሉ ፡ ዘየ ፡ ፴፪ ።
ኃድግ ፡ ብእሲቶ ፡ ዘእንበለ ፡ ትዝሙ ፡ ይሬስያ ፡ ትዘሙ ። ወዘሂ ፡ ኃድግተ ፡ ፴፫ ።
አውሰበ ፡ ዘመወ ። ወካዕበ ፡ ሰማዕክሙ ፡ ከመ ፡ ተብህለ ፡ ለቀደምት ፡ ኢ_
ትምሐል ፡ በሐሰት ፡ አግብኡ ፡ ባሕቱ ፡ ለእግዚአብሔር ፡ መሐላክሙ ።
ወአንሰ ፡ እብለክሙ ፡ ኢ_ትምሐሉ ፡ ግሙራ ። ወኢ_ሰማየ ፡ እስመ ፡ መንበ ፡ ፴፬ ።
ሩ ፡ ለእግዚአብሔር ፡ ውእቱ ። ወኢ_ምድረ ፡ እስመ ፡ መከየደ ፡ እገሪሁ ፡ ፴፭ ።
ይእቲ ። ወኢ_በኢየሩሳሌም ፡ እስመ ፡ ሀገሩ ፡ ይእቲ ፡ ለንጉሥ ፡ ዐቢይ ።

፶፰፤ ወኢ.ቦርእስከ ፡ ትምሐል ፡ እስመ ፡ ኢ.ትክል ፡ አሐተ ፡ ሥዕርተ ፡ ርእስከ ፡

፶፱፤ ጸዐዳ ፡ ረስዮ ፡ ወኢአጽልሞ ፡ ይኩን ፡ ባሕቱ ፡ ነገርክሙ ፡ እመሂ ፡ እወ ፡

፷፤ እወ ፡ ወእመሂ ፡ አልቦ ፡ አልቦ ፡ ወፈድፋደሰ ፡ እምእሉ ፡ እምእኩይ ፡ ው

፷፩፤ እቱ ፡ ሰማዕክሙ ፡ ከመ ፡ ተብህለ ፡ ዐይን ፡ ቤዛ ፡ ዐይን ፡ ወስን ፡ ቤዛ ፡ ስ
ን ፡ ወአንሰ ፡ እብለክሙ ፡ ኢ.ትትቃወምዎ ፡ ለእኩይ ፡ ወለዘሂ ፡ ጸፍዐከ ፡

፷፤ እንተ ፡ የማን ፡ መልታሕተከ ፡ ሚጥ ፡ ሎቱ ፡ ካልእታሂ ፡ ወለዘሂ ፡ ይፈቅ

፷፮፤ ደ ፡ ይትዐገልከ ፡ ወመልበሰከ ፡ ይንሣእ ፡ ኅድግ ፡ ሎቱ ፡ ወልብሰከኒ ፡ ወ

፷፯፤ ለዘሂ ፡ ዐበጠከ ፡ ምዕራፈ ፡ አሐደ ፡ ሑር ፡ ምስሌሁ ፡ ክልኤተ ፡ ለዘ ፡ ይስ

፷፬፤ እለከ ፡ ሀብ ፡ ወለዘ ፡ ይፈቅድ ፡ እምኀቤከ ፡ ይትለቃሕ ፡ ኢ.ትክልአ ፡ ሰማ

፷፭፤ ዕክሙ ፡ ከመ ፡ ተብህለ ፡ አፍቅር ፡ ቢጸከ ፡ ወጽላእ ፡ ጸላኤከ ፡ ወአንሰ ፡ እ
ብለክሙ ፡ አፍቅሩ ፡ ጸላእተክሙ ፡ ባርክዎሙ ፡ ለእለ ፡ ይረግሙክሙ ፡ ሠ
ናየ ፡ ግበሩ ፡ ለእለ ፡ ይጸልኡክሙ ፡ ወጸልዩ ፡ በእንተ ፡ እለ ፡ ይሰድዱክ

፷፮፤ ሙ ፡ ከመ ፡ ትኩኑ ፡ ውሉደ ፡ ለአቡክሙ ፡ ዘበሰማያት ፡ እስመ ፡ ፀሐየ ፡ ያ
ሠርቅ ፡ ላዕለ ፡ እኩያን ፡ ወኄራን ፡ ወያዘንም ፡ ዝናመ ፡ ላዕለ ፡ ጻድቃን ፡ ወ

፷፯፤ ዐማፅያን ፡ ወእመሰ ፡ ታፈቅሩ ፡ ዘያፈቅረክሙ ፡ ምንት ፡ ዐሰብ ፡ ብክሙ ፡

፷፰፤ አኮሁ ፡ መጸብሓውያንኒ ፡ ከማሁ ፡ ይገብሩ ፡ ወእመ ፡ ተአማኅክሙ ፡ አኃ
ዊክሙ ፡ ከመ ፡ ምንት ፡ እንከ ፡ ፈድፋደ ፡ ትገብሩ ፡ አኮኑ ፡ አሕዛብኒ ፡ ኪ.

፷፱፤ ያሁስ ፡ ይገብሩ ፡ ኩኑኬ ፡ አንትሙሰ ፡ ፍጹማን ፡ ከመ ፡ አቡክሙ ፡ ሰማያ
ዊ ፡ ፍጹም ፡ ውእቱ ።

məʿrāf 5

5: ba-ʾənta bəḍuʿān;

1. wa-rəʾəyo ʾaḥzāba ʿarga wəsta dabr wa-nabiro qarbu ḫabehu ʾardāʾihu;

2. wa-kaśata ʾafāhu wa-maharomu ʾənza yəbəl;

3. bəḍuʿān naddāyān ba-manfas ʾəsma lomu yəʾəti mangəśta samāyāt;

4. bəḍuʿān ʾəlla yəlāḥəwu yəʾəze ʾəsma ʾəmuntu yətfeśśəḥu;

5. bəḍuʿān yawwāhān ʾəsma ʾəmuntu yəwarrəsəwwā la-mədr;

6. bəḍuʿān ʾəlla yərəḥəbu wa-yəṣamməʾu la-ṣədq ʾəsma ʾəmuntu yəṣaggəbu;

7. bəḍuʿān maḥārəyān ʾəsma ʾəmuntu yətmaḥaru;

8. bəḍuʿān naṣuḥāna ləbb ʾəsma ʾəmuntu yəreʾəyəwwo la-ʾəgziʾab(ə)ḥer;

9. bəḍuʿān gabārəyāna salām ʾəsma ʾəmuntu wəluda ʾəgziʾab(ə)ḥer
   yəssammayu;

10. bəḍuʿān ʾəlla yəssaddadu ba-ʾənta ṣədq ʾəsma lomu yəʾəti mangəśta samāyāt;

11. bəḍuʿān ʾantəmu soba yəsaddədukəmu wa-yəzanaggʷəgukəmu wa-yənabbu
    kʷəllo ʾəkaya lāʿlekəmu ʾənza yəḥessəwu ba-ʾəntiʾaya;

12. tafaśśəḥu wa-taḥaśayu ʾəsma ʿasbəkəmu bəzuḫ wəʾətu ba-samāyāt; ʾəsma
    kama-za sadadəwwomu la-nabiyāt ʾəlla ʾəm-qədmekəmu;

13. ʾantəmu wəʾətu ṣew la-mədr wa-ʾəmma-ssa ṣew lasḥa ba-məntə-nu yətqessam;
ʾalbo-ke ʾənka la-za-yəbaqqʷəʿ za-ʾənbala la-gadif ʾafʾa wa-yəkayyədo sabʾ;

14. ʾantəmu wəʾətu bərhānu la-ʿālam; ʾi-təkəl hagar taḥabəʾo ʾənta malʿəlta dabr
tənabbər;

15. wa-ʾi-yāḥattəwu māḥtota kama yānbərəwwā tāḥta kafar ʾallā diba taqwāmā
wa-tābarrəḥ la-kʷəllomu ʾəlla wəsta bet;

16. kamāhu yəbrāḥ bərhānəkəmu ba-qədma sabʾ kama yərʾayu məgbārikəmu
šannāya wa-yəsabbəḥəwwo la-ʾabukəmu za-ba-samāyāt;

17. ʾi-yəmsalkəmu za-maṣāʾku ʾəsʿar ʾorita wa-nabiyāta; ʾi-maṣāʾku ʾəsʿaromu
ʾallā ʾəfaṣṣəmmomu;

18. ʾamān ʾəbəlakkəmu ʾəska yaḥalləf samāy wa-mədr yawṭā ʾənta ʾaḥatti qərḍatā
ʾi-taḥalləf ʾəm-ʾorit ʾəska soba kʷəllu yətgabbar;

19. za-ke fatḥa ʾaḥatta ʾəm-ʾəllā təʾəzāzāt ʾənta taḥaṣṣəṣ wa-yəmehər kama-zə la-
sabʾ ḥəṣuṣa yəssammay ba-mangəsta samāyāt wa-za-ssa yəmehər wa-
yəgabbar wəʾətu ʿabiya yəssammay ba-mangəsta samāyāt;

20. nāhu ʾəbəlakkəmu kama ʾəmma ʾi-fadfada ṣədqəkəmu fadfāda ʾəm-ṣaḥaft wa-
ʾəm-farisāwəyān ʾi-təbawwəʾu wəsta mangəsta samāyāt;

21. samāʿkəmu kama tabəhla la-qaddamt ʾi-təqtəl nafsa wa-za-ssa qatala rasḥa
wəʾətu la-kʷənnane;

22. wa-ʾanə-ssa ʾəbəlakkəmu kʷəllu za-yāməʾəʿ ʾəḥwāhu rasḥa wəʾətu la-kʷənnane
wa-za-hi yəbe ʾəḥwāhu za-ḍarq rasḥa wəʾətu la-ʿawd; wa-za-hi yəbe ʾabd
rasḥa wəʾətu la-gahānnama ʾəssāt;

23. wa-ʾəm-kama-ke tābawwəʾ ʾamməḥāka wəsta məśwāʿ wa-ba-həy(y)a
tazakkarka kama-bo ʾəḥuka za-yaḥayyəsaka;

24. ḥədəg həy(y)a mabāʾaka qədma məśwāʿ wa-ḥur qədma takʷānan məsla ʾəḥuka
wa-ʾəm-zə gabiʾaka ʾabəʾ ʾamməḥāka;

25. kun ṭabiba la-ʿədəwəka fəṭuna ʾənza hallawka məslehu wəsta fənot kama ʾi-
yəmaṭṭuka ʿədəwəka la-makʷannən wa-makʷannən la-lāʾku wa-wəsta moqəḥ
tətwaday;

26. ʾamān ʾəbəlakka ʾi-təwaḍḍəʾ ʾəm-həy(y)a ʾəska soba təfaddi ṭəyyuqa kʷəllo;

27. samāʿkəmu kama tabəhla ʾi-təzamməw;

28. wa-ʾanə-ssa ʾəbəlakkəmu kʷəllu za-yəreʾi bəʾəsita wa-yəfattəwwā waddəʾa
zammawa bātti ba-ləbbu;

29. ʾəmma ʿaynəka ʾənta yamān tāsəḥətakka mələḥā wa-ʾawḍəʾā ʾəm-lāʿleka;
ʾəsma yəḥeyyəsakka kama yəthagʷal ʾaḥadu ʾəmənna ʾabāləka ʾəm-kʷəllu
šəgāka yətwaday wəsta gahānnam;

30. wa-ʾəmma ʾənta yamān ʾədeka tāsəḥətakka mətərrā wa-ʾawḍəʾā ʾəm-lāʿleka;
ʾəsma yəḥeyyəsakka yəthagʷal ʾaḥadu ʾəmənna ʾabāləka ʾəm-kʷəllantā-hu
šəgāka wəsta gahānnam yətwaday;

31. wa-tabəhla za-ḥadaga bəʾəsito yahabbā maṣḥafa ḥəd(də)gātihā;

32. wa-ʾanə-ssa ʾəbəlakkəmu kama kʷəllu za-yaḥaddəg bəʾəsito za-ʾənbala
    təzammu yəressəyā təzammu; wa-za-hi ḥədəgta ʾawsaba zammawa;

33. wa-kāʿəba samāʿkəmu kama tabəhla la-qad(d)amt ʾi-təmḥalu ba-ḥassat
    ʾagbəʾu bāḥ(ət)tu la-ʾəgziʾab(ə)ḥer maḥalākəmu;

34. wa-ʾanə-ssa ʾəbəlakkəmu ʾi-təmḥalu gəmurā; wa-ʾi-samāya ʾəsma manbaru
    la-ʾəgziʾab(ə)ḥer wəʾətu;

35. wa-ʾi-mədra ʾəsma makayada ʾəgarihu yəʾəti; wa-ʾi-ba-ʾiyarusālem ʾəsma
    hagaru yəʾəti la-nəguś ʿabiy;

36. wa-ʾi-ba-rəʾsəka təmḥal ʾəsma ʾi-təkəl ʾaḥatta śəʿərta rəʾsəka ṣaʿadā rassəyo
    wa-ʾi-ʾaṣləmo;

37. yəkun bāḥ(ət)tu nagarəkəmu ʾəmma-hi ʾəwwa ʾəwwa wa-ʾəmma-hi ʾalbo
    ʾalbo; wa-fadfāda-ssa ʾəm-ʾəllu ʾəm-ʾəkkuy wəʾətu;

38. samāʿkəmu kama tabəhla ʿayn bezā ʿayn wa-sənn bezā sənn;

39. wa-ʾanə-ssa ʾəbəlakkəmu ʾi-tətqāwaməwwo la-ʾəkkuy; wa-la-za-hi ṣafʿa-ka
    ʾənta yamān maltāḥtaka miṭ lottu kāləʾtā-hi;

40. wa-la-za-hi yəfaqqəd yətʿaggalka wa-malbasaka yənśāʾ ḥədəg lottu wa-
    ləbsaka-ni;

41. wa-la-za-hi ʿabbaṭaka məʿrāfa ʾaḥada ḥur məslehu kələʾeta;

42. la-za yəsəʾəlakka hab wa-la-za yəfaqqəd ʾəm-ḫabeka yətlaqqāḥ ʾi-təkləʾo;

43. samāʿkəmu kama tabəhla ʾafqər biṣa-ka wa-ṣəlāʾ ṣalāʾeka;

44. wa-ʾanə-ssa ʾəbəlakkəmu ʾafqəru ṣalāʾtakəmu bārəkəwwomu la-ʾəlla
    yəraggəmukəmu śannāya gəbaru la-ʾəlla yəṣalləʾukəmu wa-ṣalləyu ba-ʾənta
    ʾəlla yəsaddədukəmu;

45. kama təkunu wəluda la-ʾabukəmu za-ba-samāyāt ʾəsma ḍaḥāya yāśarrəq lāʿla
    ʾəkkuyān wa-ḫerān wa-yāzannəm zənāma lāʿla ṣādəqān wa-ʿammāḍəyān;

46. wa-ʾəmma-ssa tāfaqqəru za-yāfaqqərakkəmu mənta ʿasba bəkəmu; ʾakko-hu
    maṣabbəḥāwəyānə-hi kamāhu yəgabbəru;

47. wa-ʾəmma taʾamāḫkəmu ʾaḥawikəmu kəmma mənta ʾənka fadfāda təgabbəru;
    ʾakko-nu ʾaḥzābə-ni kiyāhu-ssa yəgabbəru;

48. kunu-ke ʾantəmu-ssa fəṣṣumāna kama ʾabukəmu samāyāwi fəṣṣum wəʾətu.

Text 4: Enoch 1:1–9

The verse count in the text edition and transliteration vary. The latter follows M.A. Knibb *The Ethiopic Book of Enoch* (Oxford 1979).

A note on the orthography: after gutturals, /a/ and /ā/ are used interchangeably.

ምዕራፍ ፩ ፥

፩ ቃለ በረከት ዘሄኖክ ዘከመ ባረከ ኅሩያነ ወጻድቃነ እለ ሀለዉ ይኩኑ በዕለት ምንዳቤ ለአሰስሎ ኵሉ እኩ ያን ወረሲዓን ፥

፪ ወአውሥአ ሄኖክ ወይቤ ፡ ብእሲ ጻድቅ ዘእምኀበ እግዚአብሔር እንዘ አዕይንቲሁ ክሡታት ወይሬኢ ራእየ ቅዱሰ ዘበሰማያት ፡ ዘእርአዩኒ መላእ ክት ፡ ወሰማዕኩ ዘእምኀቤሆሙ ኵሎ ወአእመርኩ አነ ዘእሬኢ ፥

፫ ወአነ ለዝ ትኡልድ ፡ አላ ለዘይመ ጽእ ትኡልድ ርኁቃን ፡ በእንተ ኅሩ ያን እቤ ፡ ወአውሣእኩ በእንቲአሆሙ ምስለ ዘይወፅእ ቅዱስ ወዓቢይ እማኅ ደሩ ወአምላክ ዓለም ፥

፬ ወእምህየ ይከይድ ዲበ ሲና ደብር ወያስተርኢ በተዕይንት ፡ ወያስተርኢ በጽንዐ ኃይሉ እምሰማይ ፡ ወይፈርሁ ኵሉ ፡ ወያድለቀልቁ ትጉኃን ፡ ወይነሥ አሙ ፍርሃት ወረዓድ ዓቢይ እስከ አጽናፈ ዓለም ፥

፭ ወይደነግፁ አድባር ነዋነን ፡ ወይ
ቴሐቱ አውግር ነዋነን ፡ ወይትመሰዉ
ከመ መዓረ ግራ እምላህብ ፡ ወትሰጠም
ምድር ፡ ወኮሉ ዘውስተ ምድር ይት
ኃጎል ፡ ወይከውን ፍትሕ ላዕለ ኮሉ ፡
ወላዕለ ጻድቃን ኮሎሙ ።

፮ ለጻድቃንሰ ሰላም ይገብር ሎሙ ፡
ወየዓቅቦሙ ለነሩያን ፡ ወይከውን
ሣህል ላዕሌሆሙ ፡ ወይከውኑ ኮሎሙ
ዘእምላክ ፡ ወይሤርሑ ወይትባረኩ
ወይበርህ ሎሙ ብርሃነ እምላክ ።

፯ ወናሁ መጽአ በትእልፊት ቅዱ
ሳን ፡ ከመ ይግበር ፍትሐ ላዕሌሆሙ ፡
ወያናጕሎሙ ለረሲዓን ፡ ወይትዋቀስ
ኮሎ ዘሥጋ ፡ በእንተ ኮሉ ዘገብሩ ወረ
ሰዩ ላዕሌሁ ኃጥአን ወረሲዓን ።

məʕrāf 1

1. qāla barakat za-henok
   za-kama bāraka ḫaruyāna wa-ṣādəqāna
   ʾəlla hallawu yəkunu ba-ʕəlata məndābe
   la-ʾasassəlo kʷəllu ʾəkkuyān wa-rasiʕān;
2. wa-ʾawśəʾa henok wa-yəbe
   baʾəsi ṣādəq za-ʾəm-ḫaba ʾəgziʾab(ə)ḥer
   ʾənza ʾaʕyəntihu kəśutāt wa-yəreʾi
   rāʾya qəddusa za-ba-samāyāt
   za-ʾarʾayuni malāʾəkt
   wa-samāʕku za-ʾəm-ḫabehomu kʷəllo
   wa-ʾaʾmarku ʾana za-ʾəreʾi;
   wa-ʾakko la-zə təwlədd
   ʾallā la-za-yəmaṣṣəʾu təwlədd rəḫuqān
3. baʾənta ḫəruyān ʾəbe

wa-ʾawśāʾku baʾəntiʾahomu məsla[282]
za-yəwaḍḍəʾ qəddus wa-ʿābiy ʾəm-māḫdaru wa-ʾamlāka ʿālam;

4. wa-ʾəm-həy(y)a yəkayyəd diba sinā dabr
wa-yāstarəʾi ba-təʿyəntu
wa-yāstarəʾi ba-ṣənʿa ḫāylu ʾəm-samāy

5. wa-yəfarrəhu kʷəllu
wa-yādlaqalləqu təguhān
wa-yənaśśəʾomu fərhāt wa-raʿād ʿābiy
ʾəska ʾaṣnāfa ʿālam;

6. wa-yədanaggəḍu ʾadbār nawwāḫan (= nawwāḫān)
wa-yəttehatu ʾawgər nawiḫan (= nawiḫān)
wa-yətmassawu kama maʿāra gərā ʾəm-lāhb

7. wa-təssaṭṭam mədr
wa-kʷəllu za-wəsta mədr yətḫāggʷal (= yəthaggʷal)
wa-yəkawwən fətḥ lāʿla kʷəllu
wa-lāʿla ṣādəqān kʷəllomu;

8. la-ṣādəqānə-ssa salāma yəgabbər lomu
wa-yaʿāqqəbomu la-ḫəruyān
wa-yəkawwən śāhl lāʿlehomu
wa-yəkawwənu kʷəllomu za-ʾamlāk
wa-yəśerrəhu wa-yətbārraku
wa-yəbarrəh lomu bərhāna ʾamlāk;

9. wa-nāhu maṣ'a ba-təʾəlfit qəddusān
kama yəgbar fətḥa lāʿlehomu
wa-yāḫgʷəlomu (= yāhgʷəlomu) la-rasiʿān
wa-yətwāqas kʷəllo za-śəgā
ba-ʾənta kʷəllu za-gabru wa-rassayu lāʿlehu ḫāṭəʾān wa-rasiʿān.

---

[282] Other text variants have məsāle or məsla məsāle instead of məsla.

Text 5: *Śəna fəṭrat* ("Beauty of Creation"), sections 1–7

The handwritten version of the text is taken from Getatchew Haile – Misrak Amare, *Beauty of Creation*, Manchester (1991). Gutturals are used interchangeably in this text, as are /a/ and /ā/ after gutturals.

1. በስመ፡ አግዚአብሔር ፡ መሕሌ፡ ወመሰተ፡ ሥህል፡(sic) ንጽሐፍ ፡ ሰነ፡ ፍጥረታቲሁ፡ ለአግዚአ ብሔር ፡ ዘመሀራነ፡ ኪያሁ፡ አቦዊነ፡ መጥዐሃራነ፡ ቅድስት፡ ቤተ፡ ክርስቲያነ፡ ኣቢያሙ፡ አፃኦኤ ተ፡ ሙሴ፡ ነቢይ፡ አስመ፡ይኣቲ፡ ትዜኑ፡ ጸዋት ወ፡ ፍጥረታቲሁ፡ ለዝንቱ፡ ፈጣሬ፡ ነጐሉ፡ አምላ ክነ፡ ይትገሬነ፡ ስሙ፡ ወይትሌዓል፡ ዝኽሬ፡ አስ መ፡ አምጽኦ፡ ዓለመ፡ አምኒሀልዎ፡ ኃበ፡ ሀልዎ ፡ በኒሩቱ፡ ገመ፡ይኩነነ፡ ሬገሕ፡ ወነገመ፡ይትዳወቅ ክሄሎቱ፡ በኃበ፡ ሰብኦ፡ ወመሳእክት፡ ወነገመ ፡ ይሰባሕ፡ በኣሬ፡ አሉ፡ ሰዒለመ፡ ዓለጥዐ፡ አሜን።

2. አጥዐቅድመ፡ ዓለማት፡ ቅድመ፡ ሀሉ፡ አ ግዚአብሔር ፡ በትሥልስት፡ አካላቱ፡ ወበተዋሕ ዴተ፡ መስኮቱ።ወሰበ፡ ፈቀደ፡ በዘባሕቲቱ፡ ፈቃይ፡ ነገመ ፡ ይፍጥር ፡ ፍጥረታተ፡ በወርኅ፡ መጋቢት፡ አጠ ኾወዩ በዕሬተ፡ አሁድ፡ ፲ ፍጥረታተ፡ ፈጠሬ፡ ፯ በአ ርየጥዐ፡ ወ፮ በነቡብ ፡ ዘውኦጹሙ፡ ሰማይ፡ ወጥዐይ ር ፡ ወማይ፡ ወነፉስ፡ ወአሳት፡ ወጽልመት፡ ወመሳእክት፡ ወአሶንት፡ ፯ ፍጥረታተ፡ ፈጠሬ፡ በኒ ዘ፡ ሰርነበ፡ አጥዐባ፡ አልበ።ወአጥዐዝ፡ ሰበ፡ ስሕቲ ዴያብሎስ፡ በተዐቢተ፡ ርአሱ፡ ፈጠሬ፡ ነዐበ፡ ዘክቱ፡ ሳጥዐየ ፡ ፍጥሬት፡ አጥዐባ ፡ አልበ።ዘውኦቹ ፡ በርሃ ኅ ፡ ኣኣዘ ፡ ይብል፡ ሉየኩነ፡ ብርሃኅ፡

3. እሉ፡ አሙንቱ፡ ፍኖ (c f.87ᵇ) ረታተ፡
እሑድ፡፡ ወእሑድ፡ በሂል፡ ፩፡በሂል፡ ውእቱ፡፡
አግዚእብሔርነ፡ ብሂል፡ ውእቱ፡ ኦሪትኒ፡በ
ሂል፡ ዜና፡ በሂል፡ ውእቱ፡፡

4. ወእ (D f.7ᵇ) መ፡ ትቤ፡ ምንት፡ አጽሐፎ፡
ሶአግዚአብሔር፡ ይፍጣር፡ ፍጥረታተ፡ ኦብል፡
በእንተ፡ ፪፡ነገር፡ ውእቱ፡ አሰመ፡አግዚእብሔር፡
ሰሃሊ፡ ውእቱ፡፡ ወገበሬ፡ ወፈታሒ፡ ወርኩብ፡ ዘኢ
ይትረከብ፡ ውእቱ፡፡ ወበእንተዝ፡ አንዘ፡ያጠይቅ
ከመ፡እሉ፡ ፪፡ ያታ፡ ህሊዋና፡ ዮቱ፡ ጽሕቀ፡ ፈጢሪ፡
ፍጥረታት፡፡

5. ወእመ፡ ትቤ፡ ካዕበ፡በእንተ፡ምንት፡   በአ
ርሞሞ፡ ፈጠሪ፡ አሎንተ፡ ፮፡ ጸዋትወ፡ ኦብል፡
በእንተ፡ ዘኢሀሎ፡ አሜሃ፡ ሰማዕያን፡፡

6. ⌜በነቢብሬ፡ ፈጢሮቱ፡ ብርሃነ፡ አሰመ፡ዘሀለ
ወ፡ አሜሃ፡ ሰማዕያን፡ መሳእክተ፡ ወበእንተዝ፡ክ
መ፡ ይሳመሬ፡ አሙንቱ፡ አምሳእናሁ፡ በነቢብ፡ፈ
ጠሪ፡ ብርሃን፡፡

7. ወእመ፡ ትቤ፡ ዓዲ፡ በእንተ፡ምንት፡ አስ
ተደኃረ፡ ተፈጥሮተ፡በርሃን፡አሞሃ፡እሉ፡ ፮፡፡ ኡብል፡ከ
መ፡ይኩን፡ አሞሳ፡ መንግሥተ፡ ሰማያት፡፡ በከመ፡ብ
ርሃን፡ ይኔይስ፡ አምጽልመት፡ ከማሁ፡ አሞዝኒ፡ዓሰ
ሞ፡ ይኔይስ፡ ዓሰሞ፡ ዘየመጽእ፡ ድኃሪ፡ አንዘ፡ይብል፡
ፈጠሪ፡   በእንተ፡ዝንቱ፡ አስተደኃሮ፡ ሎብርሃን፡አሞነ፲፡

1. *ba-səma ʔəgziʔab(ə)ḥer maḥari wa-mastaśāḥəl*
   nəṣḥəf səna fəṭratātihu la-ʔəgziʔab(ə)ḥer
   za-maharuna kiyāhu ʔabawina mamhərāna qəddəst beta krəstiyān
   labbiwomu ʔəm-ʔorita muse nabiy
   ʔəsma yəʔəti təzenu ṣawātəwa fəṭratātihu la-zəntu faṭāre kʷəllu
   ʔamlākəna
   yətbārak səmu wa-yətleʕāl zəkru
   ʔəsma ʔamṣəʔa ʕālama ʔəm-ʔi-halləwo ḫaba halləwo ba-ḫirutu
   kama yənunanna rabāḥa
   wa-kama yətʕāw(w)aq (= G or D respectively) kəhilotu ba-ḫaba sabʔ wa-
   malāʔəkt
   wa-kama yəsbāḥ ba-ʔafa ʔəllu la-ʕālamaʕālam ʔamən;
2. *ʔəm-qədma ʕālamāt qədma hallo ʔəgziʔab(ə)ḥer*
   ba-təśləsta ʔakālātihu wa-ba-tawāḥədota malakotu;
   wa-soba faqada ba-za-bāḥtitu faqād
   kama yəfṭər fəṭratāta
   ba-warḫā maggābit ʔama 20-wa-9 ba-ʕalata ʔəhud
   8 fəṭratāta faṭara 7 ba-ʔarməmo wa-1 ba-nabib
   za-wəʔətomu samāy wa-mədr wa-māy wa-nafās wa-ʔəsāt wa-ṣəlmat wa-
   malāʔəkt
   wa-ʔəllontu 7 fəṭratāta faṭara ba-gize sark ʔəm-ḫaba ʔalbo;
   wa-ʔəm-zə soba səḥta diyābəlos ba-təʕabita rəʔsu
   faṭara kāʕaba zəkta sāmənāya fəṭrata ʔəm-ḫaba ʔalbo;
   za-wəʔətu bərhān
   ʔənza yəbəl la-yəkun bərhān
3. *ʔəllu ʔəmuntu fəṭratāta ʔəhud;*
   wa-ʔəhud bəhil 1 bəhil wəʔətu;
   ʔəgziʔab(ə)ḥerə-ni bəhil wəʔətu
   ʔoritə-ni bəhil zenā bəhil wəʔətu;
4. *wa-ʔəmma təbe*
   mənt ʔaṣḥaqo la-ʔəgziʔab(ə)ḥer yəfṭər fəṭratāta
   ʔəbəl ba-ʔənta 4 nagar wəʔətu
   ʔəsma ʔəgziʔab(ə)ḥer kahāli wəʔətu;
   wa-bāʕəl wa-fatāḥi wa-rəkub za-ʔi-yətrakkab wəʔətu;
   wa-ba-ʔənta-zə ʔənza yāṭeyyəq
   kama ʔəllu 4 ḍotā halləwān bottu
   ṣəḥqa faṭira fəṭratāt;
5. *wa-ʔəmma təbe kāʕaba*
   ba-ʔənta mənt ba-ʔarməmo faṭara ʔəllonta 7 ṣawātəwa
   ʔəbəl ba-ʔənta za-ʔi-hallawu ʔamehā samāʕəyān;

6. *ba-nabibə-hi faṭirotu bərhāna*
   ʾəsma za-hallawu ʾamehā samāʿəyān malāʾəkt
   wa-ba-ʾənta-zə kama yāʾməru ʾəmuntu ʾamlākənnāhu
   ba-nabib faṭara bərhāna;
7. *wa-ʾəmma təbe ʿādi*
   ba-ʾənta mənt ʾastadaḫāra tafaṭrota bərhān ʾəmənna ʾəllu 7;
   ʾəbəl kama yəkun ʾamsāla mangəśta samāyāt;
   ba-kama bərhān yəḫeyyəs ʾəm-ṣəlmat
   kamāhu ʾəm-zə-ni ʿālam yəḫeyyəs ʿālam za-yəmaṣṣəʾ dəḫra
   ʾənza yəbəl faṭāri
   ba-ʾənta zəntu ʾastadaḫāro la-bərhān ʾəmənna 7.

Text 6: Jubilees 50:12–13

The following text represents the last verses of the book of Jubilees (following J.C. Vanderkam *The Book of Jubilees* [CSCO 510/87]). They are only given in Ethiopic script.

50:12 ወኵሎ ፡ ሰብእ ፡ ዘይገብር ፡ ግብረ ፡ ወዘሂ ፡ የሐ
ዉ፦ር ፡ መንገደ ፡ ወዘሂ ፡ ይትቀነይ ፡ ወፍሬ ፡ ወእሞሂ ፡ በቤቱ ፡
ወእሞሂ ፡ በኵሎ ፡ መካን ፡፡ ወዘሂ ፡ ያነጽድ ፡ እሳተ ፡ ወዘሂ ፡ ይጼዐን ፡
ዲበ ፡ ኵሉ ፡ እንስሳ ፡፡ ወዘሂ ፡ ይነግድ ፡ በሐመር ፡ ባሕረ ፡ ወኵሎ ፡
ሰብእ ፡ ዘይዘብጥ ፡ ወይቀትል ፡ ምንተሂ ፡ ወዘሂ ፡ የሐርድ ፡ እንስሳ ፡
ወፍሬ ፡ ወዘሂ ፡ አሥገረ ፡ እሞሂ ፡ አርዌ ፡ ወፍሬ ፡ ወእሞሂ ፡ ዓሣ ፡
ወዘሂ ፡ ይጸውም ፡ ወይገብር ፡ ፀብአ ፡ በዕለተ ፡ ሰንበት ፡ 50:13 ወሰ
ብእ ፡ ዘይገብር ፡ ኵሎ ፡ ዘእምዝ ፡ በዕለተ ፡ ሰንበት ፡ ይሙት ፡፡ ከመ ፡
ይኩኑ ፡ ውሉደ ፡ እስራኤል ፡ እንዘ ፡ ያስነብቱ ፡ በከመ ፡ ትእዛዛተ ፡
ሰንበታት ፡ ምድር ፡ በከመ ፡ ተጽሕፈ ፡ እምውስተ ፡ ጽላት ፡ ዘወሀ
በኒ ፡ ውስተ ፡ እደዊየ ፡ ከመ ፡ እጽሐፍ ፡ ለከ ፡ ሕገገ ፡ ጊዜ ፡ ወጊዜ ፡
በበ ፡ ኩፋሌ ፡ መዋዕሊሁ ፡፡

Grammatical notes:

- Syntactic structure (12–13a): *kʷəllu sabʾ za– … wa-za-hi … wa-za-hi … wa-za-hi … wa-za-hi … wa-kʷəllu sabʾ za– … wa-za-hi … wa-za-hi … wa-za-*

hi ... (13) *wa-sabʾ za-yəgabbər kʷəllo za-ʾəm-zə ba-ʿəlata sanbat yəmut* 'whoever ... whoever does anything of these things on a Sabbath shall die' (§6.5.6.6.).

- *ba-kʷəllu makān* 'at any place' (§5.1.9.1.3.).
- *yəṣṣeʿan < *yətṣeʿan* (§3.6.5.1.) 'he rides'; irregular imperfect of the Gt-stem modeled after the Dt-stem (§4.4.6.3.1.).
- *mənta-hi* (§4.1.8.1.); *wa-za-hi ʾaśgana* 'and whoever catches (an animal)': note the use of the perfect. After *wa-za-hi*, the text usually uses the imperfect.
- *yāsanabbətu* 'they keep the Sabbath': CG imperfect (§4.4.7.3.).
- *taṣəḥfa* '(as) it is written': Gt perfect (§4.4.5.3.2.).
- *ḥəgaga gize wa-gize babba kufāle mawāʿəlihu* (§5.6.6.).

Text 7: Kəbra Nagaśt Chapter 1, "The Glory of Kings Chapter 1"

The following chapters from Kəbra Nagaśt follow Carl Bezold's edition (Bezold, Carl. 1909. *Kebra Nagast – Die Herrlichkeit der Könige*. Abhandlungen der Philosophisch-Philologischen Klasse der Königlich Bayerischen Akademie der Wissenschaften 23. München, Verlag der K.B. Akademie der Wissenschaften).

፩፡ በእንተ፡ ክብረ፡ ነገሥት።

ፍካሬ፡ ወዜና፡ ዘየ፯፻ወ፳፡ ርቱዓነ፡ ሃይማኖት፡ በእንተ፡ ክብር፡ ወዕበይ፡ ወተድላ፡ ዘከመ፡ ወሀበ፡ እግዚአብሔር፡ ለደቂቀ፡ አዳም፤ ወፈድፋደሰ፡ ዘበእንተ፡ ዕበያ፡ ወክብራ፡ ለጽዮን፡ ታቦተ፡ ሕጉ፡ ለእግዚአብሔር፡ እንተ፡ ገባርያ፡ ወኬንያ፡ ለሊሁ፡ በውስተ፡ ጽርሐ፡ መቅደሱ፡ እምቅድመ፡ ኮሉ፡ ፍጥረት፡ መላእክት፡ ወሰብእ።

እስመ፡ በገብረት፡ ወበሥምረት፡ ወበዕሪና፡ ገብርዋ፡ አብ፡ ወወልድ፡ ወመንፈስ፡ ቅዱስ፡ ለጽዮን፡ ሰማያዊት፡ ለማኅደረ፡ ስብሐቲሆሙ።

ወእምዝ፡ ይቤ፡ አብ፡ ለወልድ፡ ወለመንፈስ፡ ቅዱስ፡ ንግበር፡ ሰብአ፡ በአርአያነ፡ ወበአምሳለነ፤ ወኑብሩ፡ ወሠምሩ፡ በዝ፡ ምክር።

ወይቤ፡ ወልድ፡ አነ፡ እለብስ፡ ሥጋሁ፡ ለአዳም፤ ወይቤ፡ መንፈስ፡ ቅዱስ፡ አነ፡ አኀድር፡ ውስተ፡ ልበ፡ ነቢያት፡ ወጻድቃን።

ወዛቲ፡ ኅብረተ፡ ወኪዳን፡ ተገብረት፡ በውስተ፡ ጽዮን፡ ማኅደረ፡ ስብሐቲሆሙ።

ወዳዊትኒ፡ ይቤ፡ ተዘከር፡ ማኅበረከ፡ ዘአቅደምከ፡ ፈጢረ፡ ለመድኅኒተ፡ በትረ፡ ርስትከ፡ በደብረ፡ ጽዮን፡ ዘኀደርከ፡ ውስቴታ።

ወገብሮ፡ ለአዳም፡ በዘዚአሁ፡ አርአያ፡ ወአምሳለ፡ ከመ፡ ይንሥቶ፡ ለሰይጣን፡ በእንተ፡ ትዕቢቱ፡ ምስለ፡ ሰራዊቱ፤ ወያቅም፡ ለአዳም፡ ተክለ፡ ዚአሁ፡ ምስለ፡ ኤራን፡ ደቂቁ፡ ለስብሐቲሁ።

እስመ፡ ኅሉቅ፡ ወምቱር፡ ምክረ፡ እግዚአብሔር፡ እንተ፡ ይቤ፡ እከውን፡ ሰብአ፡ ወአስተርእኢ፡ ለ
ኵሉ፡ ዘፈጠርኩ፡ በሥጋ፡ እትገሰስ፤ ወበደኃሪ፡ መዋዕል፡ በሥምረቱ፡ ተወልደ፡ በሥጋ፡ እምዳግ
ማዊት፡ ጽዮን፡ ዳግማዊ፡ አዳም፡ ዝውእቱ፡ መድኀኒነ፡ ክርስቶስ፡ ዛቲ፡ ይእቲ፡ ምክሕነ፡ ወሃይማ
ኖትነ፡ ተስፋነ፡ ወሕይወትነ፡ ጽዮን፡ ሰማያዊት።

1: ba-ʾənta kəbra nagaśt

fəkkāre wa-zenā za–310wa–8 rətuʿāna hāymānot baʾənta kəbr wa-ʿəbay wa-tadlā za-
kama wahaba ʾəgziʾābḥer la-daqiqa ʾādām; wa-fadfāda-sa za-baʾənta ʿəbayā wa-kəbrā
la-ṣəyon tābota ḥəggu la-ʾəgziʾābḥer ʾənta gabārihā wa-kenəyāhā lallihu ba-wəsta
ṣərḥa maqdasu ʾəm-qədma kʷəllu fəṭrat malāʾəkt wa-sabʾ.
ʾəsma ba-ḥəbrat wa-ba-śəmrat wa-ba-ʾərinā gabrəwwā ʾab wa-wald wa-manfas qəddus
la-ṣəyon samāyāwit la-māḫdara səbḥatihomu.
wa-ʾəmzə yəbe ʾab la-wald wa-la-manfas qəddus nəgbar sabʾa ba-ʾarʾayāna wa-ba-
ʾamsālina; wa-ḥabru wa-śamru ba-zə məkr.
wa-yəbe wald ʾana ʾəlabbəs śəgāhu la-ʾadām; wa-yəbe manfas qəddus ʾana ʾaḥaddər
wəsta ləbba nabiyāt wa-ṣādəqān.
wa-zāti ḥəbrat wa-kidān tagabrat ba-wəsta ṣəyon māḫdara səbḥatihomu.
wa-dāwit-əni yəbe tazakkar māḫbaraka za-ʾaqdamka faṭira la-madḫanita batra rəstəka
ba-dabra ṣəyon za-ḫadarka wəstetā.
wa-gabro la-ʾadām ba-za-ziʾahu ʾarʾayā wa-ʾamsāl kama yənśəto la-sayṭān ba-ʾənta
təʿbitu məsla sarāwitu; wa-yāqəmo la-ʾadām takla ziʾahu məsla ḫerān daqiqu la-
səbḥatihu.
ʾəsma ḫəluq wa-mətur məkra ʾəgziʾābḥer ʾənta yəbe ʾəkawwən sabʾa wa-ʾāstarəʾi la-
kʷəllu za-faṭarku ba-śəgā ʾətgassas; wa-ba-daḫāri mawāʿəl ba-śəmratu tawalda ba-śəgā
ʾəm-dāgəmāwit ṣəyon dāgəmāwi ʾadām zə-wəʾətu madḫanina kərəstos zāti yəʾəti
məkḫana wa-hāymānotəna tasfāna wa-ḥəywatəna ṣəyon samāyāwit.

Text 8: Kəbra Nagaśt Chapter 22

፳፪፡ በእንተ፡ ታምሪን፡ ነጋዲ።

ወሀለወ፡ ፩፡ ልብው፡ ሊቀ፡ ነጋድያን፡ ዘስሙ፡ ተምሪን፡ ወይጸዖን፡ ፳፪፡ ወ፮፡ አግማለ፡ ወአሕጋ
ረኒ፡ ቦቱ፡ መጠነ፡ መወጅ።

ወሰሎሞን፡ ንጉሥ፡ አሜሃ፡ ፈቀደ፡ ከመ፡ ይሕንጽ፡ ቤተ፡ እግዚአብሔር፡ ወለአከ፡ ውስተ፡ ኵሉ
፡ ነጋድያን፡ ለምሥራቅ፡ ወለምዕራብ፡ ለደቡብ፡ ወለሰሜን፡ ከመ፡ ይምጽኡ፡ ነጋድያን፡ ወይንሥ
ኡ፡ በጊቤሁ፡ ወርቀ፡ ወብሩረ፡ ወውእቱኒ፡ ይንሣእ፡ ዘይትፈቀድ፡ ለገብር።

ወነገርዎ፡ በእንተ፡ ውእቱ፡ ነጋዲ፡ ኢትዮጵያዊ፡ ባዕል፡ ወለአከ፡ ከመ፡ ያምጽእ፡ ሎቱ፡ ዘይትፈቀ
ድ፡ እምብሔረ፡ ዐረብ፡ ወርቀ፡ ቀዩሐ፡ ወዕፀ፡ ዘኢይነቅዝ፡ ጸሊመ፡ ወሰንፔረ።

ወሐረ፡ ውእቱ፡ ነጋዲ፡ ዘበስሙ፡ ተምሪን፡ ነጋዲሃ፡ ለንግሥተ፡ ኢትዮጵያ፡ ኀበ፡ ሰሎሞን፡ ንጉሥ ፤ ወነሥአ፡ ኵሎ፡ ዘፈቀደ፡ እምኔሁ፡ ወወሀቦ፡ ለነጋዲ፡ ዘይፈቅድ፡ አፈድፍዶ፡ እምንዋዩ።

ወውእቱሰ፡ ነጋዲ፡ ልብው፡ ፈድፋደ፡ ወየሬኢ፡ ጥበቢሁ፡ ለሰሎሞን፡ ወያነክር፡ ወይተዐቀብ፡ ከ ማ፡ ይጠይቅ፡ አውሥኦተ፡ ቃሉ፡ ወፈትሐ፡ ወሣእሣእ፡ አፉሁ፡ ወጣዐመ፡ ነገሩ፡ ወሐረቶ፡ ወን ብረቶ፡ ወተንሥኦቶ፡ ወገብሮ፡ ወፍቅሮ፡ ወሥርዐቶ፡ ወማእዶ፡ ወሕጎ።

ወለእለኒ፡ ይኤዝዙሙ፡ ምስለ፡ ትሕትና፡ ወየውሀት ፤ ወሰበኒ፡ አበሱ፡ ይምሕሮሙ፡ እስመ፡ በጥበ ብ፡ ወበፍርሀት፡ እግዚአብሔር፡ ይሞርሕ፡ ቤቶ፡ ወያከምስሙ፡ በየውሀት፡ ለአብዳን፡ ወይሜር ሓን፡ በየውሀት፡ ለአእማት፡ ወይከሥት፡ አፉሁ፡ በአምሳል፡ ወይጠዕም፡ ቃሉ፡ እምጸቃውዕ፡ መ ዓር፡ ወኮሉ፡ ግብሩ፡ ፍትው፡ ወኮሉ፡ ርእየቱ፡ አዳም ፤ እስመ፡ ትትፈቀር፡ ጥበብ፡ በኀበ፡ ማእም ራን፡ ወትትሜነን፡ በኀበ፡ አብዳን።

ወዘንተ፡ ኵሎ፡ ርእዮ፡ ያስተዐጽብ፡ ውእቱ፡ ነጋዲ፡ ወያነክር፡ ፈድፋደ፡ እስመ፡ ለእለ፡ ይሬአይ ዎ፡ ኮለንታሁ፡ መፍትው፡ ወመምህር፡ ውእቱ ፤ ወእለኒ፡ በጽሑ፡ ኀቤሁ፡ ኢይፈቅዱ፡ ይእትቱ፡ ወይትገሐሡ፡ እምኔሁ፡ በእንተ፡ ጥበቡ፡ ወላሕዩ፡ ወጣዐሙ፡ ነገሩ፡ ከመ፡ ማይ፡ ለጽሙእ፡ ወከመ ፡ ኀብስት፡ ለርኁብ፡ ወከመ፡ ፈውስ፡ ለድዉይ፡ ወከመ፡ ልብስ፡ ለዕሩቅ፡ ወከመ፡ አብ፡ ለእንጋ፡ ማውታ ፤ ወይፈትሕ፡ በጽድቅ፡ ወኢያደሉ፡ ለገጽ ፤ ወቱ፡ ክብር፡ ወብዕለ፡ ዘወሀበ፡ እግዚአብሔ ር፡ ፈድፋደ፡ ወርቀ፡ ወብሩረ፡ ወዕንቄ፡ ወአልባሰ፡ ክቡረ፡ ወእንስሳ፡ ወአራዊት፡ ዘአልቦ፡ ኍልቄ ።

ወበመዋዕሊሁሰ፡ ለሰሎሞን፡ ንጉሥ፡ ኮነ፡ ወርቅ፡ ከመ፡ ብርት፡ ወብሩር፡ ከመ፡ ዐረር፡ ወብርትስ ፡ ወዐረር፡ ወኀጺን፡ ኮነ፡ ብዝኁት፡ ከመ፡ ዕፀ፡ ባሕሩስ፡ ወከመ፡ ብርዐ፡ ገዳም፡ ወዕፀ፡ ቄድሮስኒ፡ ብ ዙኅ፡ ኮነ ፤ በዘ፡ ወሀቦ፡ እግዚአብሔር፡ ክብረ፡ ወብዕለ፡ ወጥበበ፡ ወሞገሰ፡ ዘኢኮነ፡ ከማሁ፡ እለ፡ እምቅድሜሁ፡ ወኢይከውኑ፡ እምድኅሬሁ፡ ዘከማሁ።

ba'ənta tāmrin nagādi
wa-hallawa 1 ləbbəw liqa nagādəyān za-səmu tamrin wa-yəṣə'ən 500-wa-20 'agmāla
wa-'aḥmāra-ni botu maṭana 70-wa-3;
wa-salomon naguś 'amehā faqada kama yəḥnəṣ beta 'əgzi'ābḥer wa-la'aka wəsta kʷəllu
nagādəyān la-məśrāq wa-la-mə'rāb la-dabub wa-la-samen kama yəmṣə'u nagādəyān
wa-yənśə'u ba-ḫabehu warqa wa-bərura wa-wə'ətu-ni yənśā' za-yətfaqqad la-gəbr;
wa-nagarəwwo ba'ənta wə'ətu nagādi 'ityopyāwi bā'əl wa-la'aka kama yāmṣə' lotu za-
yətfaqqad 'əm-bəhera 'arab warqa qayyiḥa wa-'əda za-'i-yənaqqəz ṣallima wa-sanpera;
wa-ḥora wə'ətu nagādi za-səmu tamrin nagādihā la-nəgəśta 'ityopyā ḫaba salomon
naguś; wa-naś'a kʷəllo za-faqada 'əmənnehu wa-wahabo la-nagādi za-yəfaqqəd
'afadfədo 'əm-nəwāyu;
wa-wə'ətu-sa nagādi ləbbəw fadfāda wa-yəre'i ṭəbabihu la-salomon wa-yānakkər wa-
yət'aqqab kama yəṭayyəq 'awśə'ota qālu wa-fətḥo wa-śā'śā'a 'afuhu wa-ṭā'ma nagaru
wa-ḥurato wa-nəbrato wa-tanśə'oto wa-gəbro wa-fəqro wa-śər'ato wa-mā'əddo wa-
ḥəggo;

wa-la-ʾəlla-ni yəʾezzəzomu məsla təḥtənnā wa-yawwəhat; wa-soba-ni ʾabbasu yəməḥəromu ʾəsma ba-ṭəbab wa-ba-fərhata ʾəgziʾābḥer yəśarrəʿ beto; wa-yākmossəsomu ba-yawwəhat la-ʾabdān wa-yəśerrəḥon ba-yawwəhat la-ʾaʾəmāt wa-yəkaśśət ʾafuhu ba-ʾamsāl wa-yəṭəʿəm qālu ʾəm-ṣaqāwəʿa maʿār wa-kʷəllu gəbru fətəw wa-kʷəllu rəʾyatu ʾaddām; ʾəsma tətfaqqar ṭəbab ba-ḫaba māʾmərān wa-tətmennan ba-ḫaba ʾabdān;

wa-zanta kʷəllo rəʾiyo yāstaʿaṣṣəb wəʾətu nagādi wa-yānakkər fadfāda ʾəsma la-ʾəlla yəreʾəyəwwo kʷəllantāhu maftəw wa-mamhər wəʾətu; wa-ʾəlla-ni baṣḥu ḫabehu ʾi-yəfaqqədu yəʾtətu wa-yətgaḥaśu ʾəmənnehu baʾənta ṭəbabu wa-lāḥəyu; wa-ṭāʿma nagaru kama māy la-ṣəmuʾ wa-kama ḫəbəst la-rəḫub wa-kama faws la-dəwuy wa-kama ləbs la-ʿəruq wa-kama ʾab la-ʾəgʷāla māwtā; wa-yəfattəḥ ba-ṣədq wa-ʾi-yādallu la-gaṣṣ; wa-botu kəbra wa-bəʿla za-wahabo ʾəgziʾābḥer fadfāda warqa wa-bərura wa-ʿənqʷa wa-ʾalbāsa kəbura wa-ʾənsəsā wa-ʾarāwit za-ʾalbo ḫolqʷa;

wa-ba-mawāʿəlihu-sa la-salomon nəguś kona warq kama bərt wa-bərur kama ʿarar wa-bərt-sa wa-ʿarar wa-ḫaṣṣin kona bəzḫu (sic!) *kama ʿəḍa bāḥrus wa-kama bərʿa gadām wa-ʿəḍa qedros-ni bəzuḫa kona; ba-za wahabo ʾəgziʾābḥer kəbra wa-bəʿla wa-ṭababa wa-mogasa za-ʾi-konu kamāhu ʾəlla ʾəm-qədmehu wa-ʾi-yəkawwənu ʾəm-dəḫrehu za-kamāhu.*

Text 9: Kəbra Nagaśt Chapter 23

፳፫፡ ኀበ፡ ገብአ፡ ነጋዲ፡ ኢትዮጵያ።

ወእምዝ፡ ፈተወ፡ ነጋዲ፡ ተምሪን፡ ከመ፡ ይግባእ፡ ብሔሮ፡ ወሖረ፡ ኀቤሁ፡ ለሰሎሞን፡ ወሰገደ፡ ሎቱ፡ ወአምኆ፡ ወይቤሎ፤ ሰላም፡ ለዕበይከ፡ ፈንወኒ፡ እሖር፡ ብሔርየ፡ ኀበ፡ እግዝእትየ፡ እስመ፡ ጐንደይኩ፡ በርኢየ፡ ክብርከ፡ ወጥበብከ፡ ወበብዙኅ፡ መባልዕት፡ ዘትጼግወኒ፤ ወይእዜሰ፡ አሐውር፡ ኀበ፡ እግዝእትየ፤ እስመ፡ እምፈተውኩ፡ እንበር፡ ምስሌከ፡ ከመ፡ ፩፡ እምአግብርቲከ፡ እምእለ፡ ይቴሐቱ፤ ብፁዓንሰ፡ እለ፡ ይሰምዑ፡ ቃለከ፡ ወይገብሩ፡ ትእዛዘከ፤ እስመ፡ እምፈተውኩ፡ እንበር፡ ዝየ፡ ወኢይትፈለጥ፡ እምኔከ፤ አላ፡ ባሕቱ፡ ፈንወኒ፡ ኀበ፡ እግዝእትየ፡ በእንተ፡ ምዕቅብና፡ ዘላዕሌየ፡ ከመ፡ አህባ፡ ንዋያ፡ ወለሊየኒ፡ ገብር፡ ላቲ።

ወቦአ፡ ሰሎሞን፡ ቤቶ፡ ወወሀቦ፡ ኵሎ፡ ዘይትፈቀድ፡ ክብረ፡ ለብሔረ፡ ኢትዮጵያ፡ ወፈነዎ፡ በሰላም፤ ወሰገደ፡ ወወፅአ፡ ወሖረ፡ ፍኖቶ፡ ወበጽሐ፡ ኀበ፡ እግዝእቱ፡ ወአወፈያ፡ ኵሎ፡ ንዋየ፡ ዘአእተወ።

ወነገራ፡ ዘከመ፡ በጽሐ፡ ሀገረ፡ ይሁዳ፡ ኢየሩሳሌም፡ ኀበ፡ ሰሎሞን፡ ንጉሥ፡ ወኵሎ፡ ዘሰምዐ፡ ወዘርእየ፡ ነገራ፡ ዘከመ፡ ይገብር፡ ፍትሐ፡ ወዘከመ፡ ይትናገር፡ ንጽሐ፡ ወዘከመ፡ ይኤዝዝ፡ ርትዐ፡ በኵሉ፡ ዘሐተቶ፡ ያወሥእ፡ በየውሀት፡ ወአልቦ፡ ሐሰት፡ በኀቤሁ፡ ወዘከመኒ፡ ሜመ፡ ነዳእተ፡ ገባር፡ እለ፡ ይጸውሩ፡ ዕፀ፡ አርሶን፡ በበ፲፻ወወቀርተ፡ እብን፡ ፰፻፡ እምነ፡ ኵሉ፡ ነጋድያን፡ ወሠያጥያን፡

ዘከመ፡የጎሥሥ፡ለኪነ፡ጥበብ፡ወምግባር፡ወዘከመ፡ይነሥእ፡ወይሁብ፡በካዕበት፡ወኮሉ፡ኪኑ
፡ወግብሩ፡በጥበብ።

ወይነግራ፡ለለጸብሐት፡ኮሉ፡ጥበ፡ሰሎሞን፡ከመ፡ይገብር፡ፍትሐ፡ወዘከመ፡ይገብር፡ርትዐ
፡ወዘከመ፡ይሠርዕ፡ማእደ፡ወዘከመ፡ይገብር፡ምሳሐ፡ወዘከመ፡ይሜህር፡ጥበ፡ወዘከመ፡ይኤ
ዝዝ፡አግብርቲሁ፡ወኮሉ፡ሥሩዕ፡በምክር፡ወየሐውሩ፡በቃሉ፡ወአልቦ፡ዘይትዔገል፡ካልኡ፡
ወአልቦ፡ዘይዔምፅ፡ንዋየ፡ቢጹ፡ወአልቦ፡ሀያዲ፡ወኢሰራቂ፡በመዋዕሊሁ፤እስመ፡በጥበብ፡ያ
አምር፡ለለ፡ስሕቱ፡ወይቀሥፎሙ፡ወያፈርሆሙ፡ወኢይደግሙ፡እኩየ፡አላ፡በሰላም፡ይነብ
ሩ፡ምስለ፡ፍርሀተ፡ንጉሥ።

ወዘንተ፡ኮሉ፡ይነግራ፡ወለለ፡ጸብሐት፡ይዜክር፡ዘርእያ፡በጎብ፡ንጉሥ፡ወይነግራ፤ወታስተደ
ምም፡በዘ፡ሰምዐት፡እምነበ፡ነጋዲ፡ገብራ፡ወትኔሊ፡በልባ፡ከመ፡ትሐር፡ጎቤሁ፡ወትበኪ፡እ
ምብዝጎን፡ፍቅር፡በዘ፡ነገራ፡ወታፈቅር፡ፈድፋደ፡ሐዊረ፡ጎቤሁ፡ወትኔሊ፡ኅሊና፡ሐዊረ፡ጎቤ
ሁ፡ወታስተራሕቅ፡ወታስተዐጽብ።

ወካዕበ፡ተሐትት፡ወይነግራ፡ካዕበ፡ትፈቱ፡ወታስተአድም፡ሐዊረ፡ከመ፡ትስማዕ፡ጥበቢሁ፡ወ
ትርኢ፡ገጹ፡ወተአምኖ፡ኪያሁ፡ወትግነይ፡ለመንግሥቱ፤ወአጥበዐት፡ልባ፡ከመ፡ትሐር፡ጎ
ቤሁ፡ወእግዚአብሔርኒ፡አጥብዐ፡ልባ፡ከመ፡ትሐር፡ወአፍተዋ።

ወእምዝ፡አኀዘት፡ትሥራዕ፡ቤታ፡ወተአዘዘ፡አግብርቲሃ፡ወትዕዐድ፡አጋዕዝቲሃ፡ወታስተሣኒ
፡ንዋየ፤ወተጎሥሥ፡ዘይትፈቀድ፡ለፍኖት፡ወለአምኃ፡ለንጉሥ፡ወለውሂብ፡ለመኳንንቲሃ፡ወ
ለዕሴተ፡አጋዕዚሃ።

ወአስተጋብአት፡ራኩባተ፡ወአብቅልተ፡ወአፍራስ፡ወአእዱገ፡ወአሕማረ፡ወአርማሰ፡ወመጸፍ
ነ፡ወአሕስለ፡ወመሣንቀ፡ወመሳተየ፡ወመጸውረ፤ወተደለወት፡ከመ፡ትሐር፡ወአዘዘት፡ለኮሉ
፡መኳንንቲሃ፡እለ፡እምታሕቴሃ፡ከመ፡ይደለዉ፡ለፍኖት፡እስከ፤አውራኅ፡ወይነሥኡ፡መሣ
ንቀ፡ወይሥርዑ፡አብያቲሆሙ፡እስመ፡ርሑቅ፡ብሔር፡ጎበ፡የሐውሩ※

23. ḫaba gabʾa nagādi ʾityoṗyā

wa-ʾəmzə fatawa nagādi tamrin kama yəgbāʾ bəḥero wa-ḥora ḫabehu la-salomon wa-sagada lotu wa-ʾamməḫo wa-yəbəlo; salām la-ʿabayəka fannəwanni ʾəḫor bəḥerəya ḫaba ʾəgzəʾtəya ʾasma gʷandayku ba-rəʾiya kəbrəka wa-ṭəbabəka wa-ba-bəzuḫ mabāləʾt za-təṣeggəwanni; wa-yəʾze-sa ʾaḥawwər ḫaba ʾəgzəʾtəya; ʾasma ʾəm-fatawku ʾənbar məsleka kama 1 ʾəm-ʾagbərtika ʾəm-ʾəlla yəttəḥatu; bəḍuʿānə-ssa ʾəlla yəsamməʾu qālaka wa-yəgabbəru təʾəzāzaka; ʾasma ʾəm-fatawku ʾənbar zəya wa-ʾi-yətfalaṭ ʾəmənneka; ʾallā bāḥəttu fannəwanni ḫaba ʾəgzəʾtəya ba-ʾənta məʿqəbənnā za-lāʿleya kama ʾahabā nəwāyā wa-lalliya-ni gabr lātti;
wa-boʾa salomon beto wa-wahabo kʷəllo za-yətfaqqad kəbra la-bəḥera ʾityoṗyā wa-fannawo ba-salām; wa-sagada wa-waḍʾa wa-ḥora fənoto wa-bašḥa ḫaba ʾəgzəʾtu wa-ʾawaffayā kʷəllo nəwāya za-ʾaʾtawa;

wa-nagarā za-kama baṣḥa hagara yəhudā ʾiyarusālem ḥaba salomon nəguś wa-kʷəllo
za-samʿa wa-za-rəʾya nagarā za-kama yəgabbər fətḥa wa-za-kama yətnāggar nəṣḥa
wa-za-kama yəʾezzəz rətʿa ba-kʷəllu za-ḥatato yāwaśśəʾ ba-yawwəhat wa-ʾalbo ḥassat
ba-ḥabehu wa-za-kama-ni śema nadāʾta gabbār ʾəlla yəṣawwəru ʿəḍa ʾārson baba 700
wa-waqarta ʾəbn 800 ʾəmənna kʷəllu nagādəyān wa-śayāṭəyān za-kama yaḥaśśəś la-
kina ṭabab wa-məgbār wa-za-kama yənaśśəʾ wa-yəhub ba-kāʿəbat wa-kʷəllu kinu wa-
gəbru ba-ṭabab;

wa-yənaggərā lalla-ṣabḥat kʷəllo ṭababa salomon kama yəgabbər fətḥa wa-za-kama
yəgabbər rətʿa wa-za-kama yəśarrəʿ māʾədda wa-za-kama yəgabbər məsāḥa wa-za-
kama yəmehr ṭababa wa-za-kama yəʾezzəz ʾagbərtihu wa-kʷəllo śəruʿ ba-məkr wa-
yaḥawwəru ba-qālu wa-ʾalbo za-yətʿeggal kāləʾu wa-ʾalbo za-yəʾemməḍ nəwāya biṣu
wa-ʾalbo hayyādi wa-ʾi-sarāqi ba-mawāʿəlihu; ʾəsma ba-ṭabab yāʾammər la-ʾəlla səḥtu
wa-yəqaśśəfomu wa-yāfarrəhomu wa-ʾi-yədaggəmu ʾəkkuya ʾallā ba-salām yənabbəru
məsla fərḥata nəguś;

wa-zanta kʷəllo yənaggərā wa-lalla ṣabḥat yəzekkər za-rəʾya ba-ḥaba nəguś wa-
yənaggərā; wa-tāstadamməm ba-za samʿat ʾəm-ḥaba nagādi gabrā wa-təḥelli ba-ləbbā
kama təḥor ḥabehu wa-təbakki ʾəm-bəzha fəqrā ba-za nagarā wa-tāfaqqər fadfāda
ḥawira ḥabehu wa-təḥelli ḥəllinā ḥawira ḥabehu wa-tāstarāḥəq wa-tāstaʿaṣṣəb;

wa-kāʿəba taḥattət wa-yənaggərā kāʿəba təfattu wa-tāstaʾaddəm ḥawira kama təsmāʿ
ṭababihu wa-tərʾay gaṣṣo wa-taʾamməḥ kiyāhu wa-təgnay la-mangəśtu; wa-ʾaṭbəʿat
ləbbā kama təḥor ḥabehu wa-ʾəgziʾābḥerə-ni ʾaṭbəʿa ləbbā kama təḥor wa-ʾaftawā.

wa-ʾəmzə ʾaḥazat taśrāʿ betā wa-taʾazzəz ʾagbərtihā wa-təmʿad ʾaʾəmātihā wa-
tāstaśānni nəwāyā; wa-taḥaśśəś za-yətfaqqad la-fənot wa-la-ʿamməḥā la-nəguś wa-la-
wahib la-makʷānəntihā wa-la-ʿəsseta ʾaʾəmātihā;

wa-ʾastagābəʾat rākubāta wa-ʾabqalta wa-ʾafrāsa wa-ʾaʾduga wa-ʾaḥmāra wa-ʾarmāsa
wa-maṣāfəna wa-ʾaḥsəla wa-maśānəqa wa-masātəya wa-maṣāwəra; wa-tadallawat
kama təḥor wa-ʾazzazat la-kʷəllu makʷānəntihā ʾəlla ʾəm-tāḥtehā kama yəddallawu la-
fənot ʾəska 6-ʿawrāḥ wa-yənśəʾu masānəqa wa-yəśrəʾu ʾabyātihomu ʾəsma rəḥuq bəḥer
ḥaba yaḥawwəru.

Text 10: Jubilees Chapter 12

The following chapter of Jubilees follows Vanderkam's edition (Vanderkam,
James C. 1989. *The Book of Jubilees: A Critical Text* (2 vols). Leuven: Peeters.)

1

**ወኮነ፡ በሱባዔ፡ ሳድስ፡ በሳብዕ፡ ዓመቱ፡ ሎቱ፡ ይቤ፡ አብራም፡ ለታራ፡ አቡሁ፡ እንዘ፡ ይብል፡ አ
ባ፡ ወይቤ፡ ነየ፡ አነ፡ ወልድየ።**

2

ወይቤ ፡ ምንተ ፡ ረድኤተ ፡ ወተድላ ፡ ለነ ፡ እምእሱ ፡ ጣዖት ፡ ዘአንተ ፡ ታመልክ ፡ ወትሰግድ ፡ ቅድ ሜሆሙ ፡

3

እስመ ፡ አልቦ ፡ ላዕሌሆሙ ፡ ምንተኒ ፡ መንፈስ ፡ እስመ ፡ ስግመት ፡ እሙንቱ ፡ ወስሕተት ፡ ልብ ፡ እ ሙንቱ ፡ ኢታምልክዎሙ ።

4

አምልኩ ፡ አምላከ ፡ ሰማይ ፡ ዘያወርድ ፡ ዝናመ ። ወጠለ ፡ ላዕለ ፡ ምድር ፡ ወይገብር ፡ ኩሎ ፡ ላዕለ ፡ ም ድር ፡ ወኩሎ ፡ ፈጠረ ፡ በቃሉ ። ወኩሎ ፡ ሕይወት ፡ እምቅድመ ፡ ገጹ ።

5

ለምንት ፡ አንትሙ ፡ ታመልኩ ፡ እለ ፡ አልቦሙ ፡ መንፈስ ፡ ላዕሌሙ ፡ እስመ ፡ ግብረ ፡ እደው ፡ እ ሙንቱ ፡ ወዲበ ፡ መታክፍቲሙ ፡ አንትሙ ፡ ትጸውርዎሙ ፡ ወአልቦ ፡ እምኔሆሙ ፡ ለከሙ ፡ ረድ ኤተ ፡ ዘእንበለ ፡ ኃሣር ፡ ዐቢይ ፡ ለእለ ፡ ይገብርዎሙ ፡ ወስሕተት ፡ ልብ ፡ ለእለ ፡ ያመልክዎሙ ፡ ኢ ታምልክዎሙ ፡

6

ወይቤሎ ፡ አነሂ ፡ አአምር ፡ ወልድየ ፡ ምንተ ፡ እሬሲ ፡ ለሕዝብ ፡ እለ ፡ አዘዙኒ ፡ እትለአክ ፡ ቅድሜሆ ሙ ፡

7

ወእም ፡ ነገርክዎሙ ፡ ጽድቀ ፡ ይቀትሉኒ ፡ እስመ ፡ ተለወት ፡ ነፍሶሙ ፡ ኀቤሆሙ ፡ ከመ ፡ ያምልክ ዎሙ ፡ ወይሰብሕዎሙ ። አርምም ፡ ወልድየ ፡ ኢይቅትሉከ ፡

8

ወነገረ ፡ ዘንተ ፡ ነገረ ፡ ለክልኤ ፡ አጓዊሁ ፡ ወተምዕዑ ፡ ላዕሌሁ ፡ ወአርመሙ ።

9

ወበአርባዕ ፡ ኢዮቤልዉ ፡ በሱባዔ ፡ ካልእ ፡ በሳብዕ ፡ ዓመቱ ፡ ሎቱ ፡ ነሥአ ፡ ሎቱ ፡ አብራም ፡ ብእሲ ተ ፡ ወስማ ፡ ሶራ ፡ ወለተ ፡ አቡሁ ፡ ወኮነቶ ፡ ሎቱ ፡ ቡእሲተ ።

10

ወአራን ፡ እኁሁ ፡ ነሥአ ፡ ሎቱ ፡ በዓመት ፡ ሣልስ ፡ ዘሱባዔ ፡ ሣልስ ፡ ወወለደት ፡ ሎቱ ፡ ወልደ ፡ በዓ መት ፡ ሳብዕ ፡ ዘሱባዔ ፡ ዝንቱ ፡ ወጸውዐ ፡ ስሞ ፡ ሎጥ ።

11

ወናኮርኒ ፡ እኁሁ ፡ ነሥአ ፡ ሎቱ ፡ ብእሲተ ።

12

ወበዓመት ፡ ዘስሳ ፡ ዘሕይወተ ፡ አብራም ፡ ውእቱ ፡ ሱባዔ ፡ ራብዕ ። በዓመት ፡ ራብዑ ፡ ሎቱ ፡ ተንሥ አ ፡ አብራም ፡ በሌሊት ፡ ወአውዐየ ፡ ቤተ ፡ ጣዖታት ፡ ወአውዐየ ፡ ኩሎ ፡ በውስተ ፡ ቤት ፡ ወሰብእ ፡ አ ልቦ ፡ ዘአእመረ ።

13

ወተንሥኡ ፡ ሌሊተ ፡ ወፈቀዱ ፡ ያድኅኑ ፡ አማልክቲሆሙ ፡ እማእከለ ፡ እሳት ፡

14

ወሰረረ፡ አራን፡ ከመ፡ ያድኅኖሙ፡ ወነደደ፡ እሳት፡ ላዕሌሁ፡ ወውዕየ፡ በእሳት፡ ወሞተ፡ በኤሮ፡ ዘከላዴዎን፡ በቅድመ፡ ታራ፡ አቡሁ፡ ወቀበርዎ፡ በኤሮ፡ ዘከላዴዎን።

15

ወወፅአ፡ ታራ፡ እምነ፡ ኡር፡ ዘከለዳዊያን፡ ውእቱ፡ ወወሉዱ፡ ከመ፡ ይምጽኡ፡ ውስተ፡ ምድረ፡ ሊባኖስ፡ ወውስተ፡ ምድረ፡ ክናኦን፡ ወኀደረ፡ ውስተ፡ ካራን።ወኀደረ፡ አብራም፡ ምስለ፡ አቡሁ፡ ውስተ፡ ካራን፡ ክልኤ፡ ሱባኤ፡ ዓመታተ።

16

ወበሳድስ፡ ሱባኤ፡ በዓመት፡ ኃምሱ፡ ሎቱ፡ ነበረ፡ አብራም፡ በሌሊት፡ በሠርቀ፡ ወርኅ፡ ሳብዕ፡ ከመ፡ ያበይን፡ ከዋክብተ፡ እምሰርክ፡ እስከ፡ ነግህ፡ ከመ፡ ይርአይ፡ ምንተ፡ ግብረ፡ ዓመት፡ በዝናማ ት፡ ወሀሎ፡ ውእቱ፡ ባሕቲቱ፡ ይነብር፡ ወያቤይን፡

17

ወመጽአ፡ ውስተ፡ ልቡ፡ ቃል፡ ወይቤ፡ ኩሉ፡ ተአምረ፡ ከዋክብት፡ ወተአምሪሃ፡ ለወርኅ፡ ወለፀሐ ይ፡ ኩሉ፡ በእደ፡ እግዚአብሔር።ለምንት፡ አነ፡ እትኃሠሥ፡

18

ለእመ፡ ፈቀደ፡ ያዘንም፡ ነግህ፡ ወሰርክ፡ ወእመ፡ ፈቀደ፡ ኢያወርድ፡ ወኩሉ፡ ውስተ፡ እዴሁ።

19

ወጸለየ፡ በዛቲ፡ ሌሊት፡ ወይቤ፡ አምላኪየ፡ አምላኪየ፡ አምላክ፡ ልዑል፡ አንተ፡ ባሕቲትክ፡ ሊተ ፡ አምላክ፡ ወአንተ፡ ኩሉ፡ ፈጠርክ፡ ወግብረ፡ እደዊከ፡ ኩሉ፡ ኮነ፡ ወሀለወ፡ ወኪያከ፡ ወመለኮትክ ፡ ኃረይኩ።

20

አድኅነኒ፡ እምእደ፡ መናፍስት፡ እኩያን፡ እለ፡ ይሴለጡ፡ ውስተ፡ ኅሊና፡ ልበ፡ ሰብእ፡ ወኢያስሐ ቱኒ፡ እምድኅሬከ፡ አምላኪየ፡ ወተረስዖኒ፡ ኪያየ፡ ወዘርእየ፡ አንተ፡ ለዓለም።ወኢንስሐት፡ እምይ እዜ፡ ወእስከ፡ ለዓለም።

21

ወይቤ፡ እመ፡ እገብእኑ፡ ውስተ፡ ኡር፡ ዘከለዳዊያን፡ እለ፡ እሙንቱ፡ የኃሡሡ፡ ገጽየ፡ ከመ፡ እግ ባእ፡ ኀቤሆሙ፡ ወሚመ፡ እንበር፡ ዝየ፡ በዝ፡ መካን፡ ፍኖተ፡ ርቱዕ፡ ቅድሜከ፡ ኪያሃ፡ ሰርሕ፡ በእ ደ፡ ገብርከ፡ ይግበር፡ ወኢይሑር፡ በስሕተተ፡ ልብየ፡ አምላኪየ፡

22

ወውእቱ፡ ሶበ፡ ፈጸመ፡ ተናግሮ፡ ወጸለየ።ወናሁ፡ ቃለ፡ እግዚአብሔር፡ ተፈነወ፡ ኀቤሁ፡ በእዴየ ፡ እንዘ፡ ይብል፡ ነዓ፡ አንተ፡ እምድርክ፡ ወእምነ፡ ትዝምድክ፡ ወእምነ፡ ቤተ፡ አቡከ፡ ውስተ፡ ም ድር፡ እንተ፡ አርእየከ።ወእሬስየክ፡ ሕዝበ፡ ዐቢየ፡ ወብዙኀ፡

23

ወእባርከከ፡ ወአዐቢ፡ ስመክ፡ ወትከውን፡ ቡሩክ፡ ውስተ፡ ምድር።ወይትባረኩ፡ ብከ፡ ኩሎሙ፡ አሕዛበ፡ ምድር፡ ወለእለ፡ ይባርኩከ፡ እባርከሙ።ወለእለ፡ ይረግሙክ፡ እረግሞሙ፡

24
ወእከውነከ፡ለከ፡ወለወልድከ፡ወለወለደ፡ወልድከ፡ወለኮሉ፡ዘርእከ፡አምላከ፡ኢትፍራህ፡እ
ምይእዜ፡ወእስከ፡ኮሉ፡ትዝምደ፡ምድር፡አነ፡አምላከክ።

25
ወይቤለኒ፡እግዚአብሔር፡አምላክ፡ፍታሕ፡አፉሁ፡ወእዘኒሁ፡ይስማዕ፡ወይንብብ፡በልሳኑ፡በ
ልሳን፡እንተ፡ታስተርኢ፡እስመ፡አዕረፈ፡እምአፉ፡ኮሉ፡ውሉደ፡ሰብእ፡እምዕለተ፡ድቀት፡

26
ወፈታሕኩ፡አፉሁ፡ወእዘኒሁ፡ወከናፍሪሁ፡ወአንዘብኩ፡እትናገር፡ምስሌሁ፡ዕብራይስጥ፡በልሳ
ነ፡ፍጥረት።

27
ወነሥአ፡መጻሕፍተ፡አበዊሁ፡ወጽሑፋት፡እማንቱ፡ዕብራይስጥ፡ወደገሞን፡ወአንዘ፡ይትመሀ
ሮን፡እምአጌሃ፡ወአነ፡አየድዖ፡ኮሉ፡ዘይስአኖ።ወተምህሮን፡ስድስተ፡ወርኀ፡ዝናም።

28
ወኮነ፡በዓመት፡ሳብዕ፡ዘሱባዔ፡ሳድስ፡ወተናገሩ፡ምስለ፡አቡሁ፡ወአይድያ፡ከመ፡የሐውር፡
ውእቱ፡እምካራን፡ለሐዊረ፡ምድረ፡ከናአን፡ይርአያ፡ወይግባእ፡ኀቤሁ፡

29
ወይቤሎ፡ታራ፡አቡሁ፡ሐር፡በሰላም፡አምላከ፡ዓለም፡ያርትዕ፡ፍኖተከ፡ወእግዚአብሔር፡ም
ስሌከ፡ወይትማነፀንከ፡እምኮሉ፡እኩይ።ወየሀብ፡ላዕሌከ፡ሣህለ፡ወምሕረተ፡ወሞገሰ፡በቅድ
መ፡እለ፡ይሬእዩከ፡ወኢኩኑንከ፡ኮሉ፡ውሉደ፡ሰብእ፡ለአእክዮ፡ዲቤከ፡ሐር፡በሰላም።

30
ወእም፡ርኢከ፡ምድረ፡አዳም፡ለአዕይንቲከ፡ለጐዲር፡ውስቴታ፡ነዓ፡ወንሥአኒ፡ኀቤከ፡ወንሥ
አ፡ለሎጥ፡ምስሌከ፡ወልደ፡አራን፡እጐከ፡ለከ፡ለወልድ፡እግዚአብሔር፡ምስሌከ፡

31
ወናኮርሃ፡እንዋ፡ኀድግ፡ኀቢየ፡እስከ፡ትገብእ፡በሰላም፡ወነሐውር፡ኩልነ፡ኀቡረ፡ምስሌከ።

1 *wa-kona ba-subāᶜe sādəs ba-sābəᶜ ᶜāmatu lottu yəbe ʾabrām la-tārā ʾabuhu ʾənza yəbəl ʾabbā wa-yəbe naya ʾana waldəya;*

2 *wa-yəbe mənta radʾeta wa-tadlā lana ʾəm-ʾəllu ṭāᶜot za-ʾanta tāmallək wa-təsaggəd qədmehomu*

3 *ʾəsma ʾalbo lāᶜlehomu mənta-ni manfasa ʾəsma səgmat ʾəmuntu wa-səḥtata ləbb ʾəmuntu ʾi-tāmləkəwwomu;*

4 *ʾamləku ʾamlāka samāy za-yāwarrəd zənāma; wa-ṭalla lāᶜla mədr wa-yəgabbər kʷəllo lāᶜla mədr wa-kʷəllo faṭara ba-qālu; wa-kʷəllu ḥəywat ʾəm-qədma gaṣṣu;*

5 *la-mənt ʾantəmu tāmalləku ʾəlla ʾalbomu manfasa lāᶜlehomu ʾəsma gəbra ʾədaw ʾəmuntu wa-diba matākəftikəmu ʾantəmu təsawwərəwwomu wa-ʾalbo ʾəmannehomu lakəmu radʾeta za-ʾənbala ḥasār ᶜabiy la-ʾəlla yəgabbərəwwomu wa-səḥtata ləbb la-ʾəlla yāmalləkəwwomu ʾi-tāmləkəwwomu*

6 wa-yəbelo ʾana-hi ʾaʾammər waldəya mənta ʾəressi la-ḥəzb ʾəlla ʾazzazuni ʾətlaʾak qədmehomu

7 wa-ʾəmma nagarkəwwomu ṣədqa yəqattəluni ʾəsma talawat nafsomu ḥabehomu kama yāmləkəwwomu wa-yəsabbəḥəwwomu; ʾarməm waldəya ʾi-yəqtəluka

8 wa-nagara zanta nagara la-kəlʾe ʾaḫāwihu wa-taməʾəʿu lāʿlehu wa-ʾarmama;

9 wa-ba-ʾarbəʿā ʾiyyobelwu ba-subāʿe kāləʾ ba-sābəʿ ʿāmatu lottu naśʾa lottu ʾabrām bəʾsita wa-səmā sorā walatta ʾabuhu wa-konato lottu bəʾsita;

10 wa-ʾarān ʾəḫuhu naśʾa lottu ba-ʿāmat śāləs za-subāʿe śāləs wa-waladat lottu walda ba-ʿāmat sābəʿ za-subāʿe zəntu wa-ṣawwəʿa səmo loṭ;

11 wa-nākorə-ni ʾəḫuhu naśʾa lottu bəʾsita;

12 wa-ba-ʿāmat za-səssā za-ḥəywata ʾabrām wəʾtu subāʿe rābəʿ; ba-ʿāmat rābəʿu lottu tanśəʾa ʾabrām ba-lelit wa-ʾawʿaya beta ṭāʿotāt wa-ʾawʿaya kʷəllo ba-wəsta bet wa-sabʾ ʾalbo za-ʾaʾmara;

13 wa-tanśəʾu lelita wa-faqadu yādḫənu ʾamāləktihomu ʾəm-māʾkala ʾəsāt

14 wa-sarara ʾarān kama yādḫənomu wa-nadada ʾəsāt lāʿlehu wa-wəʾya ba-ʾəsāt wa-mota ba-ʾenur za-kalādewon ba-qədma tārā ʾabuhu wa-qabarəwwo ba-ʾenur za-kalādewon;

15 wa-waḍʾa tārā ʾəmənna ʾur za-kaladāwiyān wəʾtu wa-waludu (sic!) kama yəmṣəʾu wəsta mədra libānos wa-wəsta mədra kanāʾan wa-ḥadara wəsta kārān; wa-ḥadara ʾabrām məsla ʾabuhu wəsta kārān kəlʾe subāʿe ʿāmatāta;

16 wa-ba-sādəs subāʿe ba-ʿāmat ḫāmsu lottu nabara ʾabrām ba-lelit ba-śarqa warḫ sābəʿ kama yābayyən kawākəbta ʾəm-sark ʾəska nagh kama yərʾay mənta gəbra ʿāmat ba-zənāmāt wa-hallo wəʾtu baḥtitu yənabbər wa-yābeyyən

17 wa-maśʾa wəsta ləbbu qāl wa-yəbe kʷəllu taʾamməra kawākəbt wa-taʾammərihā la-warḫ wa-la-ḍaḥay kʷəllu ba-ʾəda ʾəgziʾabḥer; la-mənt ʾana ʾətḫāśśaś;

18 la-ʾəmma faqada yāzannəm nagha wa-sarka wa-ʾəmma faqada ʾi-yāwarrəd wa-kʷəllu wəsta ʾədehu;

19 wa-ṣallaya ba-zātti lelit wa-yəbe ʾamlākiya ʾamlākiya ʾamlāk ləʿul ʾanta bāḥtitəka lita ʾamlāk wa-ʾanta kʷəllo faṭarka wa-gəbra ʾədawika kʷəllu kona wa-hallawa wa-kiyāka wa-malakotəka ḫarayku;

20 ʾadḫananni ʾəm-ʾəda manāfəst ʾəkkuyān ʾəlla yəsellaṭu wəsta ḥəllinā ləbba sabʾ wa-ʾi-yāsḫatuni ʾəm-dəḫreka ʾamlākiya wa-tərassəyanni kiyāya wa-zarʾəya ʾanta la-ʿālam; wa-ʾi-nəsḫat ʾəm-yəʾəze wa-ʾəska la-ʿālam;

21 wa-yəbe ʾəmma ʾəgabbəʾ-hu wəsta ʾur za-kaladāwiyān ʾəlla ʾəmuntu yaḥaśśəśu gaṣṣəya kama ʾəgbāʾ ḥabehomu wa-mimma ʾənbar zəya ba-zə makān fənota rətuʿa qədmeka kiyāhā sarrəḥ ba-ʾəda gabrəka yəgbar wa-ʾi-yəḫor ba-səḥtata ləbbəya ʾamlākiya

22 wa-wəʾtu soba faṣṣama tanāgəro wa-ṣalləyo; wa-nāhu qāla ʾəgziʾabḥer tafannawa ḥabehu ba-ʾədeya ʾənza yəbəl naʿā ʾanta ʾəm-mədrəka wa-ʾəmənna təzməddəka wa-

ʾəmənna beta ʾabuka wəsta mədr ʾənta ʾarəʾəyaka; wa-ʾəressəyaka ḥəzba ʿabiya wa-
bəzuḫa

23 wa-ʾəbārrəkaka wa-ʾaʿabbi səmaka wa-təkawwən buruka wəsta mədr; wa-
yətbārraku bəka kʷəllomu ʾaḥzāba mədr wa-la-ʾəlla yəbārrəkuka ʾəbārrəkomu; wa-la-
ʾəlla yəraggəmuka ʾəraggəmomu

24 wa-ʾəkawwənakka laka wa-la-waldəka wa-la-walda waldəka wa-la-kʷəllu zarʾəka
ʾamlāka ʾi-təfrāḥ ʾəm-yəʾəze wa-ʾəska kʷəllu təzmədda mədr ʾana ʾamlākəka;

25 wa-yəbelanni ʾəgziʾabḥer ʾamlāk fətāḥ ʾafuhu wa-ʾəzanihu yəsmāʿ wa-yənbəb ba-
ləssānu ba-ləssān ʾənta tāstarəʾi ʾəsma ʾaʿrafa ʾəm-ʾafa kʷəllu wəluda sabʾ ʾəm-ʿəlata
dəqat

26 wa-fatāḥku ʾafuhu wa-ʾəzanihu wa-kanāfərihu wa-ʾaḥazku ʾətnāgar məslehu
ʿəbrāyəṣt ba-ləssāna fəṭrat;

27 wa-naśʾa maṣāḥəfta ʾabawihu wa-ṣəḥufāt ʾəmāntu ʿəbrāyəṣt wa-dagamon wa-
ʾaḥaza yətmaharon ʾəm-ʾamehā wa-ʾana ʾayaddəʿo kʷəllo za-yəssaʾano; wa-taməharon
sədəsta warḫa zənām;

28 wa-kona ba-ʿāmat sābəʿ za-subāʿe sādəs wa-tanāgara məsla ʾabuhu wa-ʾaydəʿo
kama yaḥawwər wəʾətu ʾəm-kārān la-ḥawira mədra kanāʾan yərʾayā wa-yəgbāʾ ḥabehu

29 wa-yəbelo tārā ʾabuhu ḥor ba-salām ʾamlāka ʿālam yārtəʿ fənotaka wa-ʾəgziʾabḥer
məsleka wa-yətmāḥdanka ʾəm-kʷəllu ʾəkkuy; wa-yahab lāʿleka śāhla wa-məhrata wa-
mogasa ba-qədma ʾəlla yəreʾəyuka wa-ʾi-yəkʷannənka kʷəllu wəluda sabʾ la-ʾaʾkəyo
dibeka ḥor ba-salām;

30 wa-ʾəmma rəʾika mədra ʾaddām la-ʾaʿyəntika la-ḥadir wəstetā naʿā wa-nəśəʾanni
ḥabeka wa-nəśəʾo la-loṭ məsleka walda ʾarān ʾəḫuka laka la-wald ʾəgziʾabḥer məsleka;

31 wa-nākor-hā ʾəḥwāka ḥədəg ḥabeya ʾəska təgabbəʾ ba-salām wa-naḥawwər kʷəlləna
ḥabura məsleka.

Text 11: Enoch 12:1–13:6

The following verses of Enoch follow the edition of Knibb (Knibb, Michael A.
1978. *The Ethiopic Book of Enoch: A New Edition in the Light of the Aramaic Dead Sea
Fragments*. Oxford: Clarendon.)

In the edition presented by Knibb, gutturals and certain sibilant phonemes are
confused. In the text given below, these have been adjusted to reflect the
etymologies of the words in question in order to make it easier to find the
lexemes in the glossary. What has not been changed is the frequent use of /ā/
instead of /a/ around gutturals.

12:1

ወእምቅድመ ፡ ኮሉ ፡ ነገር ፡ ተከብተ ፡ ሄኖክ ፡ ወአልቦ ፡ ዘየአምሮ ፡ እምውሉደ ፡ ሰብእ ፡ በገበ ፡ ተከ
ብተ ፡ ወገበ ፡ ሀሎ ፡ ወምንተ ፡ ኮነ ፡

12:2

ወኮሉ ፡ ግብሩ ፡ ምስለ ፡ ቅዱሳን ፡ ወምስለ ፡ ትጉኃን ፡ በመዋዕለ ፡ ዚአሁ ፡

12:3

ወአነ ፡ ሄኖክ ፡ ኮንኩ ፡ እባርክ ፡ ለእግዚእ ፡ ዐቢይ ፡ ወለንጉሠ ፡ ዓለም ፨ ወናሁ ፡ ትጉኃን ፡ ይጼውዑኒ ፡
ሊተ ፡ ለሄኖክ ፡ ጸሐፊ ፨ ወይቤሉኒ ፡

12:4

ሄኖክ ፡ ጸሐፌ ፡ ጽድቅ ፡ ሐር ፡ አይድዕ ፡ ለትጉኃን ፡ ሰማይ ፡ እለ ፡ ኃደጉ ፡ ሰማየ ፡ ልዑለ ፡ ወምቅዋመ
፡ ቅዱሰ ፡ ዘለዓለም ፡ ወምስለ ፡ አንስት ፡ ማሰኑ ፡ ወገብሩ ፡ ዘከመ ፡ ይገብሩ ፡ ውሉደ ፡ ሰብእ ፨ ወነሥ
ኡ ፡ ሎሙ ፡ አንስተ ፡ ወማሰኑ ፡ ዓቢየ ፡ ሙስና ፡ በዲበ ፡ ምድር ፨

12:5

ወኢይከውን ፡ ሎሙ ፡ በዲበ ፡ ምድር ፡ ሰላም ፡ ወኅድገተ ፡ ኃጢአት ፨

12:6

እስመ ፡ ኢይትፌሥሑ ፡ በውሉዶሙ ፡ ቀትለ ፡ ፍቁራኒሆሙ ፡ ይሬእዩ ፡ ወዲበ ፡ ሃጉለ ፡ ውሉዶሙ
፡ ይገብሩ ፡ ወይስእሉ ፡ ለዓለም ፡ ወኢይከውን ፡ ሎሙ ፡ ምሕረት ፡ ወኢሰላም ፨

13:1

ወሄኖክ ፡ ኃሊፈ ፡ ይቤሎ ፡ ለአዘዝኤል ፡ ኢይከውነከ ፡ ሰላም ፡ ዓቢይ ፡ ኮነ ፡ ወፀአ ፡ ላዕሌከ ፡ ይእሥ
ርክ ፡

13:2

ወኃጢ ፡ ወምሕረት ፡ ወስእለት ፡ ኢይከውነከ ፡ በእንተ ፡ ዘመሀርከ ፡ ግፍዐ ፡ ወበእንተ ፡ ኮሉ ፡ ምግ
ባረ ፡ ዕርፈት ፡ ወግፍዕ ፡ ወኃጢአት ፡ ዘአርአይከ ፡ ለውሉደ ፡ ሰብእ ፡

13:3

አሜሃ ፡ ሐዊርየ ፡ ነገርኩዎሙ ፡ ለኮሎሙ ፡ ኅቡረ ፡ ወእሙንቱ ፡ ፈርሁ ፡ ኮሎሙ ፡ ፍርሃት ፡ ወረዓ
ድ ፡ ነሥአሙ ፡

13:4

ወተስእሉኒ ፡ ተዝካረ ፡ ዕለት ፡ ከመ ፡ እጽሐፍ ፡ ሎሙ ፡ ከመ ፡ ይኩኖሙ ፡ ኃድገተ ፡ ወከመ ፡ አነ ፡ አዕ
ርግ ፡ ተዝካረ ፡ ስእለቶሙ ፡ ኀበ ፡ እግዚአብሔር ፡ ሰማየ ፨

13:5

እስመ ፡ ኢይክሉ ፡ እሙንቱ ፡ እምይእዜ ፡ ተናግሮ ፡ ወኢያነሥኡ ፡ አዕይንቲሆሙ ፡ ውስተ ፡ ሰማይ
፡ እምኃፍረተ ፡ አበሳሆሙ ፡ ዘተኩነኑ ፡

13:6

ወአሜሃ ፡ ጸሐፍኩ ፡ ተዝካረ ፡ ስእለቶሙ ፡ ወአስተብቍኦ ያቶሙ ፡ በእንተ ፡ መንፈሶሙ ፡ ወለለ ፡ ጅም
ግባሮሙ ፡ ወበእንተ ፡ ዘይስእሉ ፡ ከመ ፡ ይኩኖሙ ፡ ስርየተ ፡ ወኑኃተ ፨

12.1 wa-ʾəm-qədma kʷəllu nagar takabta henok wa-ʾalbo za-yaʾamməro ʾəm-wəluda sabʾ ba-ḫaba takabta wa-ḫaba hallo wa-mənta kona;

12:2 wa-kʷəllu gəbru məsla qəddusān wa-məsla təguhān ba-mawāʿəla ziʾahu;

12:3 wa-ʾana henok konku ʾəbārrəko la-ʾəgziʾ ʿābiy wa-la-nəguśa ʿālam; wa-nāhu təguhān yəṣewwəʿuni lita la-henok ṣaḥāfi; wa-yəbeluni

12.4 henok ṣaḥāfe ṣədq ḥur ʾāydeʿ la-təguhāna samāy ʾəlla ḫādagu samāya ləʿula wa-məqwāma qəddusa za-la-ʿālam wa-məsla ʾanəst māsanu wa-gabru za-kama yəgabbəru wəluda sabʾ; wa-naśʾu lomu ʾanəsta wa-māsanu ʿābiya musənnā ba-diba mədr;

12.5 wa-ʾi-yəkawwən lomu ba-diba mədr salām wa-ḥədgata ḫāṭiʾat;

12.6 ʾəsma ʾi-yətfeśśəḥu ba-wəludomu qatla fəqurānihomu yəreʾəyu wa-diba hagʷla wəludomu yəgəʿəru wa-yəsəʾəlu la-ʿālam wa-ʾi-yəkawwən lomu məḥrat wa-ʾi-salām;

13.1 wa-henok ḫālifo yəbelo la-ʾazzazʾel ʾi-yəkawwənaka salām ʿābiy kʷənnane waḍʾa lāʿleka yəʾśərka ;

13.2 wa-śāḥt wa-məḥrat wa-səʾlat ʾi-yəkawwənaka ba-ʾənta za-maharka gəfʿā wa-ba-ʾənta kʷəllu məgbāra ḍərfat wa-gəf wa-ḫāṭiʾat za-ʾarʾayka la-wəluda sabʾ;

13.3 ʾamehā ḥawirəya nagarkəwwomu la-kʷəllomu ḥəbura wa-ʾəmuntu farhu kʷəllomu fərhāt wa-raʿād naśʾomu;

13.4 wa-tasəʾluni tazkāra ʿəlat kama ʾəṣḥaf lomu kama yəkunomu ḥədgata wa-kama ʾana ʾāʿrəg tazkāra səʾlatomu ḫaba ʾəgziʾabḥer samāya;

13.5 ʾəsma ʾi-yəkəlu ʾəmuntu ʾəm-yəʾəze tanāgəro wa-ʾi-yānaśśəʾu ʾaʿyəntihomu wəsta samāy ʾəm-ḫāfrata ʾabbasāhomu za-takʷannanu;

13.6 wa-ʾamehā ṣaḥafku tazkāra səʾlatomu wa-ʾastabqʷəʿotomu ba-ʾənta manfasomu wa-lala 1 məgbāromu wa-ba-ʾənta za-yəsəʾəlu kama yəkunomu səryata wa-nuḥāta.

Appendix B: List of Signs

Vowels are given according to the traditional pronunciation.

1st	2nd	3rd	4th	5th	6th	7th
ሀ *ha*	ሁ *hu*	ሂ *hi*	ሃ *ha*	ሄ *he*	ህ *h, hə*	ሆ *ho*
ለ *lä*	ሉ *lu*	ሊ *li*	ላ *la*	ሌ *le*	ል *l, lə*	ሎ *lo*
ሐ *ḥa*	ሑ *ḥu*	ሒ *ḥi*	ሓ *ḥa*	ሔ *ḥe*	ሕ *ḥ, ḥə*	ሖ *ḥo*
መ *mä*	ሙ *mu*	ሚ *mi*	ማ *ma*	ሜ *me*	ም *m, mə*	ሞ *mo*
ሠ *śä*	ሡ *śu*	ሢ *śi*	ሣ *śa*	ሤ *śe*	ሥ *ś, śə*	ሦ *śo*
ረ *rä*	ሩ *ru*	ሪ *ri*	ራ *ra*	ሬ *re*	ር *r, rə*	ሮ *ro*
ሰ *sä*	ሱ *su*	ሲ *si*	ሳ *sa*	ሴ *se*	ስ *s, sə*	ሶ *so*
ቀ *qä*	ቁ *qu*	ቂ *qi*	ቃ *qa*	ቄ *qe*	ቅ *q, qə*	ቆ *qo*
በ *bä*	ቡ *bu*	ቢ *bi*	ባ *ba*	ቤ *be*	ብ *b, bə*	ቦ *bo*
ተ *tä*	ቱ *tu*	ቲ *ti*	ታ *ta*	ቴ *te*	ት *t, tə*	ቶ *to*
ኀ *ḫa*	ኁ *ḫu*	ኂ *ḫi*	ኃ *ḫa*	ኄ *ḫe*	ኅ *ḫ, ḫə*	ኆ *ḫo*
ነ *nä*	ኑ *nu*	ኒ *ni*	ና *na*	ኔ *ne*	ን *n, nə*	ኖ *no*
አ *ʾa*	ኡ *ʾu*	ኢ *ʾi*	ኣ *ʾa*	ኤ *ʾe*	እ *ʾ, ʾə*	ኦ *ʾo*
ከ *kä*	ኩ *ku*	ኪ *ki*	ካ *ka*	ኬ *ke*	ክ *k, kə*	ኮ *ko*
ወ *wä*	ዉ *wu*	ዊ *wi*	ዋ *wa*	ዌ *we*	ው *w, wə*	ዎ *wo*
ዐ *ʿa*	ዑ *ʿu*	ዒ *ʿi*	ዓ *ʿa*	ዔ *ʿe*	ዕ *ʿ, ʿə*	ዖ *ʿo*
ዘ *zä*	ዙ *zu*	ዚ *zi*	ዛ *za*	ዜ *ze*	ዝ *z, zə*	ዞ *zo*
የ *yä*	ዩ *yu*	ዪ *yi*	ያ *ya*	ዬ *ye*	ይ *y, yə*	ዮ *yo*
ደ *dä*	ዱ *du*	ዲ *di*	ዳ *da*	ዴ *de*	ድ *d, də*	ዶ *do*
ገ *gä*	ጉ *gu*	ጊ *gi*	ጋ *ga*	ጌ *ge*	ግ *g, gə*	ጎ *go*
ጠ *ṭä*	ጡ *ṭu*	ጢ *ṭi*	ጣ *ṭa*	ጤ *ṭe*	ጥ *ṭ, ṭə*	ጦ *ṭo*
ጰ *ṗä*	ጱ *ṗu*	ጲ *ṗi*	ጳ *ṗa*	ጴ *ṗe*	ጵ *ṗ, ṗə*	ጶ *ṗo*
ጸ *ṣä*	ጹ *ṣu*	ጺ *ṣi*	ጻ *ṣa*	ጼ *ṣe*	ጽ *ṣ, ṣə*	ጾ *ṣo*
ፀ *ḍä*	ፁ *ḍu*	ፂ *ḍi*	ፃ *ḍa*	ፄ *ḍe*	ፅ *ḍ, ḍə*	ፆ *ḍo*
ፈ *fä*	ፉ *fu*	ፊ *fi*	ፋ *fa*	ፌ *fe*	ፍ *f, fə*	ፎ *fo*
ፐ *pä*	ፑ *pu*	ፒ *pi*	ፓ *pa*	ፔ *pe*	ፕ *p, pə*	ፖ *po*

Labiovelars

First order	Third order	Fourth order	Fifth order	Sixth order
ቈ $q^wä$	ቊ q^wi	ቋ q^wa	ቌ q^we	ቍ $q^wə$
ኈ $\underline{h}^wä$	ኊ $\underline{h}^wi$	ኋ $\underline{h}^wa$	ኌ $\underline{h}^we$	ኍ $\underline{h}^wə$
ኰ $k^wä$	ኲ k^wi	ኳ k^wa	ኴ k^we	ኵ $k^wə$
ጐ $g^wä$	ጒ g^wi	ጓ g^wa	ጔ g^we	ጕ $g^wə$

Appendix C: Main Paradigms

Independent Personal Pronouns (§4.1.1.)

	Singular		Plural	
1c	ʾana	'I'	nəḥna	'we'
2m	ʾanta	'you'	ʾantəmu	'you'
2f	ʾanti	'you'	ʾantən	'you'
3m	wəʾətu	'he'	ʾəmuntu, wəʾətomu	'they'
3f	yəʾəti	'she'	ʾəmāntu, wəʾəton	'they'

Pronominal Suffixes (after Nouns Ending in a Vowel; §4.1.2.)

	Singular	Plural
1c	–ya, –ni	–na
2m	–ka	–kəmu (trad. –kkəmu)
2f	–ki	–kən (trad. –(k)kən)
3m	–hu	–homu
3f	–hā	–hon

Pronominal Suffixes (after Nouns Ending in a Consonant and in the Accusative; §4.1.2.2.)

	Nom./Gen.	Acc.
1cs	–əya	–əya
2ms	–əka	–aka
2fs	–əki	–aki
3ms	–u (< *–əhu)	–o (< *–ahu)
3fs	–ā (< *–əhā)	–ā (< *–ahā)
1cp	–əna	–ana
2mp	–əkəmu	–akəmu
2fp	–əkən	–akən
3mp	–omu (< *–əhomu)	–omu (< *–ahomu)
3fp	–on (< *–əhon)	–on (< *–ahon)

Demonstrative Pronouns (§4.1.4.)

'this' (type I)			
Masc. sing.	*zə–* (acc. *za–*)	Masc. pl.	*ʔəllu* (= acc.)
Fem. sing.	*zā–* (= acc.)	Fem. pl.	*ʔəllā* (= acc.)

'this' (type II)			
Masc. sing.	*zəntu* (acc. *zanta*)	Masc. pl.	*ʔəllontu* (acc. *ʔəllonta*)
Fem. sing.	*zātti* (acc. *zātta*)	Fem. pl.	*ʔəllāntu* (acc. *ʔəllānta*)

'that' (type I)			
Masc. sing.	*zək(k)u* (acc. *zə(k)kʷa*)	Com. pl.	*ʔəllə(k)ku*
Fem. sing.	*ʔəntə(k)ku* (acc. *ʔənta(k)kʷa*		

'that' (type II)			
Masc. sing.	*wəʔətu*	Masc. pl.	*ʔəmuntu*
Fem. sing.	*yəʔəti*	Fem. pl.	*ʔəmāntu*

Determinative and Relative Pronoun (§4.1.5.)

Masc. sing.	Fem. sing.	Com. pl.
za–	*ʔənta*	*ʔəlla* (also *za–*)

Regular Nominal Declension (§4.2.7.)

	Singular		Plural	
	Nom./Gen.	Acc.	Nom./Gen.	Acc.
Masc. noun				
Unbound	*liq*	*liqa*	*liqān*	*liqāna*
With pronominal suffixes	*liqə–*	*liqa–*	*liqāni–*	*liqāni–*
Bound	*liqa*	*liqa*	*liqāna*	*liqāna*

Fem. noun				
Unbound	ʿazaqt	ʿazaqta	ʿazaqāt	ʿazaqāta
With pronominal suffixes	ʿazaqtə–	ʿazaqta–	ʿazaqāti–	ʿazaqāti–
Bound	ʿazaqta	ʿazaqta	ʿazaqāta	ʿazaqāta

Cardinal Numbers (Simplified Paradigm; cf. §4.3.1.)

	Form with masculine counted noun		Form with feminine counted noun	
	Nom./Gen.	Acc.	Nom./Gen.	Acc.
1	ʾaḥadu	ʾaḥada	ʾaḥatti	ʾaḥatta
2	kəlʾetu kəlʾe	kəlʾeta	kəlʾeti kəlʾe	kəlʾeta
3	śalastu	śalasta	śalās	śalāsa
4	ʾarbāʿtu	ʾarbāʿta	ʾarbāʿ	ʾarbāʿa
5	ḥaməstu	ḥaməsta	ḥams	ḥamsa
6	sədəstu	sədəsta	səssu	səssu
7	sabʿatu sabāʿtu	sabʿata sabāʿta	sabʿu sabʿ, səbʿ	sabʿu
8	samā/antu samānitu	samā/anta samānita	samāni	samāni
9	tə/asʿatu	tə/asʿata	tə/asʿu	tə/asʿu
10	ʿaśartu	ʿaśarta	ʿaśru	ʿaśru

Perfect: Strong Root (§4.4.1.2.)

	Singular		Plural	
3m	nagara	labsa	nagaru	labsu
3f	nagarat	labsat	nagarā	labsā
2m	nagarka	labaska	nagarkəmu	labaskəmu
2f	nagarki	labaski	nagarkən	labaskən
1c	nagarku	labasku	nagarna	labasna

Imperfect: Strong Root (§4.4.1.3.)

	Singular	Plural
3m	yənaggər	yənaggəru
3f	tənaggər	yənaggərā
2m	tənaggər	tənaggəru
2f	tənaggəri	tənaggərā
1c	ʔənaggər	nənaggər

Jussive: Strong Root (§4.4.1.4.)

	Singular		Plural	
3m	yəngər	yəlbas	yəngəru	yəlbasu
3f	təngər	təlbas	yəngərā	yəlbasā
2m	təngər	təlbas	təngəru	təlbasu
2f	təngəri	təlbasi	təngərā	təlbasā
1c	ʔəngər	ʔəlbas	nəngər	nəlbas

Imperative: Strong Root (§4.4.1.5.)

Masc. sing.	Fem.sing.	Masc. pl.	Fem. pl.
nəgər	nəgəri	nəgəru	nəgərā
ləbas	ləbasi	ləbasu	ləbasā

Verbal Stems (Strong Triradical Root; §4.4.4.4.)

	G-stem		D-stem	L-stem
Perf.	nagara	labsa	naggara	nāgara
Impf.	yənaggər	yəlabbəs	yəneggər	yənāggər
Juss.	yəngər	yəlbas	yənaggər	yənāgər
Imp.	nəgər	ləbas	naggər	nāgər
PP	nagir–	labis–	naggir–	nāgir–
Inf.	nagir(ot)	labis(ot)	naggəro(t)	nāgəro(t)

	CG	CD	CL
Perf.	ʔangara	ʔanaggara	ʔanāgara
Impf.	yānaggər	yāneggər	yānāggər
Juss.	yāngər	yānaggər	yānāgər

Imp.	ʔangər	ʔanaggər	ʔanāgər
PP	ʔangir–	ʔanaggir–	ʔanāgir–
Inf.	ʔangəro(t)	ʔanaggəro(t)	ʔanāgəro(t)

	Gt	Dt	Lt
Perf.	tanag(a)ra	tanaggara	tanāgara
Impf.	yətnaggar	yətneggar	yətnāggar
Juss.	yətnagar	yətnaggar	yətnāgar
Imp.	tanagar	tanaggar	tanāgar
PP	tanagir–	tanaggir–	tanāgir–
Inf.	tanagəro(t)	tanaggəro(t)	tanāgəro(t)

	CGt	CDt	CLt
Perf.	ʔastangara	ʔastanaggara	ʔastanāgara
Impf.	yāstanaggər	yāstaneggər	yāstanāggər
Juss.	yāstangər	yāstanaggər	yāstanāgər
Imp.	ʔastangər	ʔastanaggər	ʔastanāgər
PP	ʔastangir–	ʔastanaggir–	ʔastanāgir–
Inf.	ʔastangəro(t)	ʔastanaggəro(t)	ʔastanāgəro(t)

Quadriliteral Verbal Roots (§4.4.7.)

	G	II-guttural	Reduplicated	L
Perf.	targʷama		fadfada	
Impf.	yətraggʷəm		yəfadaffəd	
Juss.	yətargʷəm		yəfadfəd	
Imp.	targʷəm		fadfəd	
PP	targʷim–		fadfid–	
Inf.	targʷəmo(t)		fadfədo(t)	

C-stems				
Perf.	ʔamandaba	ʔamāḫbara	ʔafadfada	
Impf.	yāmanaddəb		yāfadaffəd	
Juss.	yāmandəb		yāfadfəd	
Imp.	ʔamandəb		ʔafadfəd	
PP	ʔamandib–		ʔafadfid–	
Inf.	ʔamandəbo(t)		ʔafadfədo(t)	

t-stems				
Perf.	tamandaba	tamāḫbara	tafadfada	tasanāsala
Impf.	yətmanaddab		yətfadaffad	yəssanāssal
Juss.	yətmandab		yətfadfad	yəssanāsal
Impv.	tamandab		tafadfad	tasanāsal
PP	tatargʷim–		tafadfid–	tasanāsil–
Inf.	tatargʷəmo(t)		tafadfədo(t)	tasanāsəlo(t)

Ct/asta-stems				
Perf.	ʾastasanbata			ʾastagʷanādaya
Impf.	yāstasanabbət			yāstagʷanāddi, –əyu
Juss.	yāstasanbət			yāstagʷanādi, –əyu
Imp.	ʾastasanbət			ʾastagʷanādi, –əyu
PP	ʾastasanbit–			ʾastagʷanādə/iy–
Inf.	ʾastasanbəto(t)			ʾastagʷanādə/iyo(t)

Appendix D: Glossary

The following lexemes, which reflect the basic forms of verbs, nouns, and particles used in the grammar and sample texts, are ordered alphabetically according to the Latin transcription of the Geʿez script including its vowels. The vowel /ə/ follows the vowel /e/ while /a/ and /ā/ are not distinguished, that is /ā/ is listed in the same alphabetic slot as /a/. The labialized consonants /gʷ/, /ḫʷ/, /kʷ/, and /qʷ/ are ordered like their unlabialized counterparts followed by /w/. This results in the following ordering of phonemes (vowels are indicated in bold script):

ʔ, ʕ, **a/ā**, b, d, ḍ, **e, ə**, f, g, gʷ, h, ḥ, ḫ, ḫʷ, **i**, k, kʷ, l, m, n, **o**, p, ṗ, q, qʷ, r, s, ś, ṣ, t, ṭ, **u**, w, y, z

The listed meanings of the words in this glossary are based on the basic entries found in Leslau (CDG). In the translations found throughout the grammar, these might have been adjusted slightly based on context. Since the glossary is ordered according to the Latin alphabet, the words in Ethiopic script follow the transliterated ones.

–ʔa -አ quotation particle used whenever exact words of messages, letters, utterances are quoted

ʔaʔkaya አእከየ (CG) 'to make bad, do harm, afflict'

ʔaʔmara አእመረ (CG) 'to know, understand, discern'

ʔaʔnus አእኑስ (pl. of ʔanəst አንስት) 'women'

ʔaʔtawa አእተወ (CG) 'to bring, bring home'

ʔaʕbaya አዕበየ (CG) 'to make great, magnify, enlarge'

ʔaʕrafa አዕረፈ (CG) 'to rest, find rest, cease'

ʔaʕraga አዕረገ (CG) 'to raise, take up, offer'

ʔaʕyənt አዕይንት (pl. of ʕayn ዐይን) 'eyes'

ʔab አብ (with suffix ʔabu- አቡ-, ʔabā- አባ-) 'father'

ʔabadbid አበድቢድ 'foolish, inept'

ʔabāgəʕ አባግዕ (pl. of baggəʕ በግዕ) 'sheep'

ʔabala አበለ < *abhala (CG) 'to cause to say, announce'

ʔabawənnā አበውና 'fatherhood, paternity'

ʔabawəya አበውየ (besides ʔabawiya አበዊየ) 'my fathers/forefathers'

ʾabawḥa አበው‧ሐ, ʾabəḥa አብሐ (√bwḥ CG) 'to permit, allow, authorize'

ʾabaya አበየ (G) 'to refuse, disobey'

ʾabayyana አበየነ (CD) 'to decide, make clear'

ʾabbā አባ 'father!'

ʾabbasa አበሰ (D) 'to sin, transgress, do wrong'

ʾabbasā አበሳ 'transgression, offense, sin'

ʾabbāsi አባሲ (pl. ʾabbāsəyān አባስያን) 'sinner, offender'

ʾabd አብድ (pl. ʾabdān አብዳን) 'fool, foolish'

ʾabəʾa አብአ, ʾaboʾa አቦአ (√bwʾ CG) 'to bring'

ʾabədd አብድ (fem.) 'fool, foolish'

ʾabzəḫa አብዝነ (CG) 'to multiply, increase'

ʾaddām አዳም 'pleasant, agreeable'

ʾadəgt አድግት, ʾədəgt እድግት 'female donkey'

ʾadg አድግ (pl. አእዱግ ʾaʾdug) 'donkey'

ʾadḫana አድነነ (CG) 'to save, keep safe, rescue'

ʾadkama አድከመ (CG) 'to weaken, make soft'

ʾadlaqlaqa አድለቅለቀ (quinq.) 'to shake (intr.), quake, tremble'

ʾadlawa አድለወ (CG) 'to please, respect, show partiality'

ʾaḍrara አፀረረ (also ʾaṣrara አጽረረ, CG) 'to become an enemy, be hostile, revolt'

ʾaf አፍ (with suffix ʾafu– አፉ–, ʾafā– አፋ–) 'mouth'

ʾafadfada አፈድፈደ (C quadr.) 'to multiply (tr.), augment, give in abundance'

ʾafʾa አፍአ/ʾafʾā አፍአ 'out, outside, outwards'

ʾafqara አፍቀረ (CG) 'to love'

ʾafrəha አፍርሀ (CG) 'to make afraid, frighten'

ʾaftawa አፍተወ (CG) 'to cause sb. to desire; to please, satisfy'

ʾafṭana አፍጠነ (CG) 'to make haste, hasten, to do quickly'

ʾagabbāri አገባሪ 'compelling, coercing'

ʾagbāri አግባሪ 'causing to make, work'

ʾagbəʾa አግብአ (CG) 'to make return, give back'

ʾaggār አጋር 'pedestrian, infantry'

ʾaḥadu አሐዱ (masc.) 'one'

ʾaḥadu ʾaḥadu አሐዱ፡ አሐዱ 'every one, each one'

ʾaḥatta አሐተ 'one time, once'

ʾaḥatti አሐቲ (fem.) 'one'

ʾaḥmalmala አሕመልመለ (quinq.) 'to grow green, be greenish'

ʾaḥyawa አሕየወ (CG) 'to keep alive, let live, cure'

ʾaḫaza አኀዘ (G) 'to seize; to begin'

ʾaḫsarsara አኀሰርሰረ (quinq.) 'to revile repeatedly'

ʾakala አከለ, yaʾakkəl የአክል (G) 'to be equal, enough'

ʾakaya አከየ/ʾakya አክየ (G) 'to be evil, bad'

ʾakko አኮ negative particle

     ʾakko-nu አኮኑ, ʾakko-hu አኮሁ 'not?'

ʾakkʷatet አኰትት 'praise, glorification, gratitude'

ʾakmosasa አክሞሰሰ (quinq.) 'to rebuke in a mild manner, smile'

ʾalbə– አልብ–, ʾalbo አልቦ negative particle

     ʾalbo አልቦ 'no!' (lit. 'it is not')

     ʾalbo za– አልቦ ፥ ዘ– 'no one, none of'

ʾalelaya አሌለየ (denominative, C quadr.) 'to spend the night'

ʾallā አላ 'but, but rather'

ʾalle la– አሌ ፥ ለ– 'woe to!'

ʾama አመ (conjunction) 'when, at the time when'

ʾama አመ (preposition) 'at the time of, on'

ʾamāḫbara አማኅበረ (denominative, C quadr.) 'to assemble together, associate, join'

ʾamān አማን 'verily; truth'

ʾamāna አማነ 'truly, surely, really'

ʾamandaba አመንደበ (C quadr.) 'to torment, afflict'

ʾamāsana አማሰነ (CL) 'to spoil, ruin, demolish'

ʾamāsāni አማሳኒ 'destroyer'

ʾamasṭara አመስጠረ (C quadr.) 'to write in mysteries, speak mysteriously'

ʾamat አመት (pl. ʾaʾəmāt አእማት) 'maid'

ʾamehā አሜሃ, less often ʾamehu አሜሁ 'when, at that time'

ʾamin አሚን 'belief, faith'

ʾamir አሚር 'sun, day, time'

ʾamlāk አምላክ (pl. ʾamāləkt አማልክት) 'God'

ʾamlaka አምለከ (CG) 'to worship (God or idols)'

ʾamlākənnā አምላክና 'authority of God'

ʾamlākiya አምላኪየ 'my God'

ʾamləko(t) አምልኮ(ት) 'cult, godliness, divine worship'

ʾamməḫā አምኃ 'kiss, salute, greetings, gift'

ʾamṣəʾa አምጽአ (CG) 'to bring, offer, bring about'

ʾamṭāna አምጣነ 'as long as, as large as, in accordance with'

ʾana አነ 'I'

ʾanassəḥa አነስሐ (CD) 'to cause to repent, regret'

ʾanbābi አንባቢ 'reader, lector'

ʾanbalbala አንበልበለ (quinq.) 'to blaze, emit flames'

ʾanbəʿ አንብዕ 'tear'

ʾanəst አንስት (pl. አእኑስ ʾaʾnus) 'woman'

ʾanəstə/iyā አንስትየ/አንስቲየ 'women folk, wives'

ʾanfarʿaṣa አንፈርዐጸ (quinq.) 'to exult, spring, leap'

ʾangargara አንገርገረ (quinq.) 'to revolve, roll, spin'

ʾangargāri አንገርጋሪ 'one who rolls, spins'

ʾangegaya አንጌገየ (quinq.) 'to cause to go astray, sin'

ʾangogawa አንጎገወ (quinq.) 'to wander, wander about restlessly'

ʾangʷadgʷada አንጐድጐደ (quinq.) 'to thunder'

ʾangʷargʷara አጐርጐረ (quinq.) 'to murmur, mutter, complain'

ʾangʷargʷāri አንጐርጓሪ 'one who murmurs, grumbles'

ʾangʷəʿ አንጒዕ 'marrow, soft fat of animals'

ʾankara አንከረ (CG) 'to marvel, admire, be amazed'

ʾanqaṣ አንቀጽ 'door, gate'

ʾanqalqala አንቀልቀለ (quinq.) 'to move, shake'; t-stem 'to totter'

ʾansāḥsəḥa አንሳሕስሐ, ʾansəhasha አንስሕስሐ (quinq.) 'to be in motion, stir'

ʾansosawa አንሶሰወ (quinq.) 'to move, walk'

ʾanśəʾa አንሥአ (CG) 'to take up, raise up'

ʾanṣafṣafa አንጸፍጸፈ (quinq.) 'to ooze, drip'

ʾanṣāra አንጻረ 'opposite, across'

ʾanta አንተ 'you' (ms)

ʾantəmu አንትሙ 'you' (mp)

ʾanzāhlala አንዛህለለ (quinq.) 'to grow weak, be indolent'

ʾaqdama አቅደም (CG) 'to place first, happen first; to do first, do previously'

ʾaqoma አቆም (CG) 'to establish, set up'

ʾaqraba አቅረበ (CG) 'to cause to approach, bring near'

ʾaqtala አቅተለ (CG) 'to cause to kill'

ʾaqyāḥyəḥa አቅያሕይሐ (quinq.) 'to gleam red, become reddish'

ʾarʾaya አርአየ (CG) 'to show'

ʾarʾayā የአርአያ 'likeness, image'

ʾaraft አረፍት 'wall'

ʾaragāwi አረጋዊ 'old, old person'

ʾarassaya አረሰየ (CD) 'to cause to put, place'

ʾarbāʿ አርባዕ 'four'

ʾarbāʿtu አርባዕቱ 'four'

ʾarbəʿā አርብዓ '40'

ʾarmama አርመመ (CG) 'to keep silence/silent, be quiet'

ʾarmasmasa አርመስመሰ (quinq.) 'to grope, feel the way'

ʾaroṣa አሮጸ (CG) 'to cause to run'

ʾarsāḥsəḥa አርሳሕስሐ (quinq.) 'to render impure, accuse, prove guilty'

ʾarson አርሶን 'load, weight, board'

ʾartəʿa አርትዐ (CG) 'to straighten, make right, render straight'

ʾarwe አርዌ (pl. ʾarāwit አራዊት) '(wild) animal, beast'

ʾasaffawa አሰፈወ (CD) 'to give hope, promise'

ʾasanbata አሰንበተ (C quadr.) 'to keep the Sabbath'

ʾasara አሰረ (G) 'to bind'

ʾaśara አሠረ (G) 'to follow, look for tracks'

ʾasargawa አሰርገወ (C quadr.) 'to adorn, decorate'

ʾasgala አስገለ (CG) 'to practice magic, use divination'

ʾashata አስሐተ (CG) 'to lead astray, lead into sin'

ʾaskaba አስከበ (CG) 'to lay, lay down'

ʾasmaya አስመየ (CG) 'to become renowned, become famous'

ʾasot አሶት 'healing, remedy'

ʾasqoqawa አስቆቀወ (quinq.) 'to howl, lament, wail'

ʾasqoqara አስቆቀረ (quinq.) 'to feel horror, loathe'

ʾastaʾaddama አስተአደመ (CDt) 'to be pleased with, delight in'

ʾastaʾākaya አስተአከየ (CLt) 'to despise, scorn'

ʾastaʿaṣaba አስተዐጸበ (CGt) 'to consider difficult, strange; admire, wonder'

ʾastabawəḥa አስተበውሐ (CGt) 'to give permission, give power'

ʾastabqʷəʿa አስተብቍዐ (CGt) 'to ask for a favor, beseech'

ʾastabqʷəʿot አስተብቍዖት 'entreaty'

ʾastadāḫara አስተዳኅረ (CLt) 'to preserve to the last, keep back'

ʾastadamama አስተደመመ (CGt) 'to be surprised, wonder'

ʾastagābāʾi አስተጋባኢ 'who gathers, magician'

ʾastagābəʾa አስተጋብአ (CLt) 'to gather, collect, bring together'

ʾastagʷāḥlawa አስተጓሕለወ (CGt/CLt) 'to cause to commit fraud'

ʾastagʷanādaya አስተጕናደየ (CLt quadr.) 'to think that one has come too late, to defer, delay'

ʾastaḥāmama አስተሐመመ (CLt) 'to trouble oneself, take care of'

ʾastaḥawra አስተሐወረ (CGt) 'to bring back, report to, send'

ʾastaḫayyasa አስተኅየሰ (CDt) 'to prefer, regard as better, praise'

ʾastalaḥafa አስተለሐፈ (CGt) 'to cause concern, give worries'

ʾastalāṣāqi አስተላጻቂ 'one who unites'

ʾastalāṣaya አስተላጸየ (CLt) 'to cause to shave, cause to shave oneself'

ʾastamakkəḥa አስተመክሐ (CDt) 'to cause to praise oneself, embellish'

ʾastamāləḫa አስተማልኀ (CLt) 'to cause to draw swords on one another'

ʾastamalḫa አስተመልኀ (CGt) 'to cause to draw (a sword)'

ʾastamāwaṣa አስተማወጸ CLt) 'to reconcile'

ʾastamḥara አስተምሐረ (CGt) 'to implore pity, seek mercy'

ʾastanassəḥa አስተነስሐ (CDt) 'to make do penance'

ʾastanāśəʾa አስተናሥአ (CLt) 'to cause to rise up, reestablish, stir up, provoke'

ʾastanāṣəḥa አስተናጽሐ (CLt) 'to purify, cleanse, declare pure'

ʾastaqaddasa አስተቀደሰ (CDt) 'to make to be consecrated'

ʾastaqʷarara አስተቈረረ (CGt) 'to hold in abomination'

ʾastarāḥaqa አስተራሐቀ (CLt) 'to consider far away'

ʾastarʾaya አስተርአየ (CGt) 'to become visible, show oneself, be manifested'

ʾastarḥaqa አስተርሐቀ (CGt) 'to remove, lengthen'

ʾastasanʾala አስተሰንአለ (CGt quadr.) 'to grant leave, dismiss'

ʾastasānaʾawa አስተሳነአወ (CGt quadr.) 'to cause to/let live in peace'

ʾastaśannaya አስተሠነየ (CDt) 'to beautify, restore, adjust'

ʾastaṣādala አስተጻደለ (CLt) 'to cause to shine, illuminate'

ʾaśāʾən አሣእን (pl. of ሣእን śāʾn) 'shoes, sandals'

ʾaśalṭana አሠልጠነ (C quadr.) 'to give full power, give authority'

ʾaśannaya አሠነየ (CD) 'to beautify, adorn, do good'

ʾaśartu ʾəlf አሠርቱ፡ እልፍ '100,000'

ʾaśema አሤመ (also ʾaśyama አሥየመ CG) 'to cause to set/place'

ʾaṣbāʿt አጽባዕት 'finger'

ʾaṣnəʿa አጽነዐ (CG) 'to fortify, strengthen, consolidate'

ʾatata አተተ (G) 'to be removed, withdraw'

ʾatawa አተወ (G) 'to come home, go home'

ʾaṭbəʿa አጥብዐ (CG) 'to make ready, decide upon, encourage'

ʾaṭwaqa አጥወቀ (besides ʾaṭaqa አጠቀ CG) 'to oppress, compress, force'

ʾaw አው 'or'

ʾaw ... ʾaw አው ... አው 'either ... or'

ʾawʿaya አውዐየ (CG) 'to burn (tr.), scorch, set on fire'

ʾawaffaya አወፈየ (CD) 'to hand over, deliver, receive'

ʾawāḥada አዋሐደ (CL) 'to unite one thing to another, add'

ʾawrada አውረደ (CG) 'to make go down, send down'

ʾawsaba አውሰበ (CG) 'to marry, take a wife'

ʾawśəʿa አውሥአ (CG) 'to answer, respond'

ʾawśəʿo(t) አውሥአ(ት) 'answer'

ʾay አይ (acc. ʾaya አየ) 'which?, what?'

ʾaydəʿa አይድዐ (CG) 'to make known, inform'

ʾayte አይቴ 'where?'

ʾayte-ni አይቴኒ, ʾayte-hi አይቴሂ 'anywhere'

ʾazeb አዜብ 'south, south wind'

ʾazmar አዝመር 'purple, scarlet'

ʾaznama አዝነመ (CG) 'cause to rain, send rain'

ʾazzaza አዘዘ (D) 'to command, order, rule'

ʾəbn እብን 'stone'

ʾəd እድ (pl. ʾədaw እደው) 'hand'

ʾəde- እዴ- (+ pronominal suffix) 'hand'

ʾəffo እፎ 'how?, in what way?, why?'

ʾəgaleyāwi እገሌያዊ 'so-and-so, a certain (place)'

ʾəgr እግር 'foot, measure'

ʾəgʷāl እጓል 'the young of any animal, fowl, or human; child'

ʾəgʷalt እጓልት, ʾəgʷəlt እጉልት 'calf, heifer'

ʾəgʷl እጉል 'the young of any animal or fowl' (less often for humans)

ʾəgzəʾt እግዝእት, ʾəgziʾt እግዚእት 'mistress, lady'

ʾəgziʾ እግዚእ 'master, lord'

ʾəgziʾ-o እግዚኦ 'o lord!'

ʾəgziʾab(ə)ḥer እግዚአብሔር 'God'

ʾəhud እሑድ, ʿəlata ʾəhud ዕለተ፡ እሑድ 'Sunday, first day of the week'

ʾəḫat እኅት (pl. ʾaḫāt አኃት) 'sister'

ʾəḫəw እኍ, ʾəḫʷ እኍ (with pronominal suffix ʾəḫu– እኍ–, ʾəḫʷā– እኋ–; pl. ʾaḫaw
     አኀው) 'brother'

ʾəḫuz እኍዝ 'captive, joined' also: 'who holds, holding'

ʾəkay እከይ 'evil thing, wickedness'

ʾəkkuy እኩይ 'bad, evil; evil thing, wickedness'

ʾəkkuyāna ləbb እኩያነ፡ ልብ 'those of evil heart = evil people'

ʾəkkʷāte እኳቴ 'glorification'

ʾəlf እልፍ '10,000'

ʾəlla እለ relative pronoun (pl.)

ʾəlliʾa– እሊአ– (+ pronominal suffix) possessive pronoun

ʾəlləkku እልኩ 'those'

ʾəm– እም–, ʾəmenna እምነ 'from, out of, since'

ʾəm– እም–, ʾəmenna እምነ 'than' (after comparative)

     ʾəm-ʾama እምአመ 'since'

     ʾəm-ʾayte እምአይቴ 'from where?'

     ʾəm-bayna እምበይነ, ʾən-bayna እንበይነ 'for the sake of, on account of,
     because of'

     ʾəm-bayna-zə እምበይነዝ, ʾəm-bayna-zəntu እምበይነ፡ ዝንቱ 'on account of this'

     ʾəm-diba እምዲበ 'from above'

     ʾəm-dəḫra እምድኅረ (prep.) 'from behind, after'

     ʾəm-dəḫra እምድኅረ (conj.) 'after'

     ʾəm-dəḫra zəntu እምድኅረ፡ ዝንቱ 'after this'

     ʾəm-həyya እምህየ 'thence, from that place'

     ʾəm-ḫaba እምኀበ 'from'

     ʾəm-ḫaba mannu እምኀበ፡ መኑ 'of whom?'

     ʾəm-kama እምከመ 'as soon as, when'

     ʾəm-lāʿla እምላዕለ 'from above'

     ʾəm-lafe እምለፌ 'from this side'

ʾəm-qədma እምቅድመ 'from before, from the presence of'

ʾəm-qədma እምቅድመ (conj.) 'before'

ʾəm-tāḥta እምታሕተ 'from under'

ʾəm-wəsta እምውስተ 'out of, from'

ʾəmza- እምዘ- 'when, after that, since'

ʾəm-zə እምዝ 'thereafter, after this, then'

ʾəm- እም- particle used on verbs in the apodosis of unreal conditional clauses
   and on verbs used as optatives

ʾəmāntu እማንቱ (fp) 'they'

ʾəmm እም (pl. ʾəmmāt እማት) 'mother'

ʾəmma እመ 'if, suppose that'

ʾəmma እመ 'whether'

ʾəm(mə)-kama እምከመ 'if, when, whenever'

   ʾəmma ... wa-ʾəmma ʾakko እመ ... ወእመ፡ አኮ 'either ... or'

   ʾəmma-ʾakko እመአኮ (also ʾəmmāʾəkko እማእኮ) 'otherwise, else, if not'

   ʾəmma-ʾakko ... wa-ʾəmma-ʾakko እመአኮ ... ወእመአኮ 'either ... or'

   ʾəmma-hi እመሂ, ʾəmma-ni እመኒ 'even if, even when, although'

   ʾəmma(-hi/-ni) ... ʾaw እመሂ/ኒ ... አው 'either ... or'

   ʾəmma(-hi) ... wa-ʾəmma(-hi) እመ(ሂ) ... ወእመ(ሂ) 'be it ... or'

   ʾəmma-ssa እመሰ 'if really, if'

ʾəmmāḫe እማኄ 'greeting, salutation'

ʾəmmāre እማሬ 'sign, demonstration, revelation'

ʾəmənna እምነ 'from, out of, since'

ʾəmənna እምነ 'than' (after comparative)

   ʾəmənnehu እምኔሁ 'thereafter'

   ʾəmənnehu እምኔሁ 'from him'

   ʾəmənneya እምኔየ 'from me'

ʾəmuntu እሙንቱ (mp) 'they'

ʾənbala እንበለ 'without'

ʾənbala እንበለ, za-ʾənbala ዘእንበለ 'without, save, except for, before'

ʾənbala dāʾəmu እንበለ፡ ዳእሙ 'never'

ʾənbayna እንበይነ, ʾəmbayna እምበይነ 'for the sake of, on account of, because of'

ʾənbayna-zə እንበይነዝ, ʾənbayna zəntu እንበይነ፡ ዝንቱ 'on account of this'

ʾənb- እንብ– negative particle (with pronominal suffixes, as in ʾənbi እንቢ,
   ʾənbəya እንብየ 'I am not in the position, I refuse')

ʾəndāʿi እንዳዒ 'I do not know, perhaps, probably'

ʾəngā እንጋ 'so then, so, surely, really'

ʾəngegāy እንጌጋይ 'aberration, absent-mindedness'

ʾəngədā እንግዳ 'foreigner, stranger, guest'

ʾəngogāwi እንጎጋዊ 'vagabond'

ʾəngugāw እንጉጋው 'aberration, wandering'

ʾəngugəw እንጉግው 'erring, wandering'

ʾənka እንክ 'so then!, therefore, now then, yet'; with negation 'no longer, no
   more'

ʾənmo እንሞ 'texture, web'

ʾənsəsā እንሰሳ 'cattle, livestock'

ʾənta እንተ (fs) relative pronoun

ʾənta እንተ 'through, by way of, into'
   ʾənta dəḫra እንተ፡ ድኅረ 'behind'
   ʾənta diba እንተ፡ ዲበ 'on, over'
   ʾənta kama እንተ፡ ከመ 'just as, as'
   ʾənta mangala እንተ፡ መንገለ 'through'

ʾəntəkku እንትኩ 'that' (fem.)

ʾəntiʾa– እንቲአ– possessive pronoun

ʾənza እንዘ 'while, whereas, when'

ʾəsāt እሳት 'fire'

ʾəska እስክ 'until, unto, as far as'

ʾəska እስክ (conj.) 'so that, until, insomuch as'
   ʾəska ʾama እስክ፡ አመ 'until'
   ʾəska la– እስክ፡ ለ– 'until, to'
   ʾəska mənt እስክ፡ ምንት 'how long?'
   ʾəska soba እስክ፡ ሶበ 'till, so that'

ʾəsma እስመ 'because, since, indeed'

ʾəwwa እወ 'yes, of course, certainly'

ʾəzn እዝን (pl. ʾəzan እዘን) 'ear'

ʾəzzuz እዙዝ 'commanded, ordered, obedient'

ʾi– ኢ.– negative particle

ʾi-ʾamāni **ኢ.አማኒ** 'unbeliever'

ʾi-ʾayte-ni/-hi **ኢ.አይቴኒ/ሂ** 'nowhere'

ʾi-mannu(-hi) **ኢ.መኑ(ሂ)**, ʾi-la-mannu(-hi) **ኢ.ለመኑ(ሂ)** 'no one'

ʾi-təngər **ኢ.ትንግር** 'do not speak!'

ʾityopəya **ኢ.ትዮጵየ** 'Ethiopia'

ʾiyafqara **ኢ.የፍቀረ** (< *ʾi-ʾafqara) 'he did not love'

ʾiyənaggər **ኢ.ይነግር** (< *ʾi-ʾənaggər) 'I will not speak'

ʾiyyobelwu **ኢ.ዮቤልዉ** 'jubilee year'

ʾo– **አ–** vocative particle 'o!'

ʾo-bəʾəsit-o **አብእሲቶ** 'o woman!'

ʾoho **አሆ** 'certainly!, yes, all right'

ʿabiy **ዐቢይ** (f. ʿabbāy **ዐባይ**, pl. ʿabbayt **ዐበይት**) 'big, great, large'

ʿadawa **ዐደወ** (G) 'to cross, transgress'

ʿabra **ዐብረ**, ʿabara **ዐበረ** (G) 'to dry up, be arid'

ʿādi **ዓዲ** 'still, again, further'

ʿaḍḍa **ዐፀ**, ʿaḍaḍa **ዐፀፀ** (G) 'to deprive, cause harm'

ʿalʿala **ዐልዐለ** (quadr.) 'to lift up, raise, elevate'

ʿālam **ዓለም** 'world, this world, eternity'

ʿalawa **ዐለወ**, ʿalwa **ዐልወ** (G) 'to conspire, corrupt, rebel'

ʿām **ዓም**, ʿāmat **ዓመት** (pl. ʿāmatāt **ዓመታት**) 'year'

ʿammaḍa **ዐመፀ** (D) 'to act unjustly, do wrong'

ʿamaḍā **ዐመፃ** 'injustice, violence'

ʿarab **ዐረብ** 'west; Arabia'

ʿarabi **ዐረቢ** 1. 'western'; 2. 'Arabian, Arabic'

ʿarar **ዐረር** 'lead'

ʿarb **ዐርብ** 'Friday'

ʿarrāz **ዐራዝ** 'clothing, garment'

ʿāśā **ዓሣ** 'fish'

ʿaśartu **ዐሠርቱ** 'ten'

ʿaśartu məʾət **ዐሠርቱ፡ ምእት** '1000'

ʿāśāt **ዓሣት** 'fish' (pl. of ʿāśā **ዓሣ**)

ʿaśrāt **ዐሥራት** (also ʿaśrāt ʾəd **ዐሥራት፡ እድ**) 'tithe, a tenth'

ʿaśru **ዐሥሩ** 'ten'

ʿaṣaba **ዐጸበ**, ʿaṣba **ዐጽበ** (G) 'to be difficult, hard, grievous'

ʿaṣawa **ዐጸወ** (G) 'to close, shut, block'

ʿawda **ዐውደ** 'around'

ʿawyāt **ዐውያት** 'wailing, lamentation'

ʿawyawa **ዐውየወ** (quadr.) 'to wail in mourning, moan, lament'

ʿayn **ዐይን** (pl. **አዕይንት** ʾaʿyənt/ ʾaʿəyyənt) 'eye, spring'

ʿayaya **ዐየየ** (G) 'to err, stray, be ignorant'

ʿazaqt **ዐዘቅት** 'well, cistern, pit'

ʿela **ጔላ** (G) 'to go astray, ramble, err'

ʿəbay **ዕበይ** 'greatness, size, majesty'

ʿəbbuy **ዕቡይ** (f. ʿəbbit **ዕቢት**) 'proud, arrogant'

ʿədā **ዕዳ** 'debt, guilt'

ʿədəw **ዕድው** 'enemy, adversary'

ʿəḍ **ዕፀ** 'tree, bush, wood'

ʿəlat **ዕለት** 'day, time'

ʿələw **ዕልው** (f. ʿəlut **ዕሉት**) 'crooked, perverse, evil'

ʿənqʷ **ዕንቈ** 'precious stone, pearl'

ʿəraft **ዕረፍት** 'rest, peace, quiet'

ʿərāq **ዕራቅ** 'emptiness, nakedness'

ʿərinā **ዕሪና** 'equality, agreement'

ʿərqān **ዕርቃን** 'nakedness'

ʿəruq **ዕሩቅ** 'naked, bare, empty'

ʿəruy **ዕሩይ** 'equal, the same'

ʿəsset **ዕሴት** 'wages, recompense'

ʿəśrā **ዕስራ** '20'

ʿəśrā məʾət **ዕስራ ፡ ምእት** '2000'

ʿəśrāwi **ዕስራዊ** 'twentieth'

ʿoda **ዖደ** (G) 'to go around, turn around, encircle'

ʿof **ዖፍ** (pl. ʾaʿwāf **አዕዋፍ**) 'bird, fowl'

ʿoqa **ዖቀ** (G) 'to know, understand, take heed'

ʿudat **ዑደት** 'circle, orbit'

ba– **በ**– 'in, at, into, by'

    ba-ʾafʾā **በአፍአ**, ba-ʾafʾā ʾəm(ənna) **በአፍአ ፡ እም(ነ)** 'outside (of)' ba-ʾəbret በእብሬት (also ba-ʿəbret በዕብሬት) 'on account of, for the sake of'

ba-ʾədawa በእደወ 'by, through, thanks to'

ba-ʾəgr በእግር 'on foot'

ba-ʾamṭāna በአምጣነ 'as long as, as often as'

ba-ʾənta በእንተ 'about, concerning, regarding'

ba-ʾənta mannu በእንተ፡ መኑ 'on account of whom?'

ba-ʾənta mənt በእንተ፡ ምንት 'why?'

ba-ʾənta za- በእንተ፡ ዘ- 'because'

ba-ʾənta zə- በእንተ፡ ዝ- 'thus, therefore'

ba-ʾənta zəntu በእንተ፡ ዝንቱ 'thus, therefore'

ba-ʾayte በአይቴ 'where?, in what way?, how?'

ba-bayna በበይነ 1. 'between'; 2. 'for, because of, on account of'

ba-bayna mənt በበይነ፡ ምንት 'why?'

ba-bayna zə- በበይነ፡ ዝ- 'because of this, therefore'

ba-baynāti- በበይናቲ- 'between, among'

ba-gizehā በጊዜሃ 'straightaway, at once, immediately'

ba-gizehu በጊዜሁ 'at its proper time, in due time'

ba-həyya በህየ 'there'

ba-ḫaba በኀበ 'among, at, to, toward, in the presence of'

ba-kaḥa በከሐ 'yonder, thither'

ba-kama በከመ 'according to, as, like'

ba-kantu በከንቱ 'for nothing, gratis, freely'

ba-lāʿla በላዕለ 'above, on, upon'

ba-māʾkala በማእከለ 'in the midst of, among'

ba-mənt በምንት 'in what way?, why?'

ba-məntə-ni በምንትኒ 'in any way'

ba-məntə-nu በምንትኑ 'in what way?'

ba-śāləs በሥልስ 'for the third time'

ba-tāḥta በታሕተ 'below, under'

ba-waʾəda/waʾəda በወእደ/በውእደ 'by the side of'

ba-za በዘ 'with which, at which'

ba-zəya በዝየ 'here'

bāʿəl ባዕል 'owner, possessor, rich, wealthy'

baʿāl በዓል 'festival, feast'

bāʿəd ባዕድ 'other, different, strange'

bāʿəlt ባዕልት 'mistress'

babba በበ (< ba– + ba–) 'each'

badbada በድበደ (quadr.) 'to perish, disappear, get sick'

badn በድን (pl. ʾabdənt አብድንት) 'corpse, dead person'

badw በድው 'desert, wasteland'

badwa በድወ (G) 'to be a desert, be desolate'

bahām በሃም 'mute, dumb'

bāḥr ባሕር (pl. ʾabḥərt አብሕርት) 'sea, lake, ocean'

bāḥtawa ባሕተወ (quadr.) 'to be alone, be solitary'

bāḥtāwi ባሕታዊ 'hermit'

bāḥ(ə)tit ባሕቲት 'solitude'

bāḥ(ət)tu ባሕቱ 'only, but, alone'

bāḥ(ə)titu ባሕቲቱ 'alone, only, merely'

bāḥrus ባሕሩስ 'reed, cane'

bakaya በከየ (G) 'to weep, mourn'

bakāyi በካዪ, biform bakāy በካይ 'one who weeps'

bālāḥi ባላሒ 'liberator'

bāləḥa ባልሐ (L) 'to liberate, rescue'

baliḥ በሊኅ '(f. ballāḫ በላኅ, pl. ballāḫt በላኅት) 'sharp, quick, violent, smart'

baql በቅል (pl. ʾabqəlt አብቅልት) 'mule'

barad በረድ 'hail, snow'

barāhrəht በራህርህት 'glittering, sparkling'

bāraka ባረከ (L) 'to bless, praise'

barakat በረከት 'blessing'

barha በርሀ (G) 'to shine, be bright'

barra በረ (G) 'to purify, make white'

baṣḥa በጽሐ (G) 'to arrive, befall'

batr በትር 'branch, rod, scepter, tribe'

bātti ባቲ (see under ba– በ–)

bayna በይን 'between'

bayyana በየነ (D) 'to discern, distinguish'

bazḫa በዝኀ (G) 'to be numerous, abundant, be much, many'

bet ቤት (pl. ʾabyāt አብያት) 'house'

bezā ቤዛ 'in exchange for, for the sake of; ransom, redemption'

bezawa ቤዘወ (quadr.) 'to redeem, save'

bəʾsa ብእሰ (G) 'to be bad, be vicious, harmful'

bəʾəsi ብእሲ (acc. bəʾəse ብእሴ) 'man, male, husband'

bəʾəsit ብእሲት (pl. አንስት ʾanəst) 'woman, wife, female'

bəʾəsit-o ብእሲቶ 'o woman!'

bəʿl ብዕል 'wealth, riches'

bədbəd ብድብድ 'plague, pestilence'

bədʿān ብዕዓን 'blessedness, happiness'

bəḍuʿ ብፁዕ 'fortunate, blessed'

bəhla ብህለ (G) 'to say, speak'

bəhil ብሂል infinitive of bəhla ብህለ

bəher ብሔር 'region, district, country'

bəkāy ብካይ 'weeping, lamentation'

bəlit ብሊት (f. of bəluy ብሉይ) 'old, ancient'

bəluy ብሉይ (f. bəlit ብሊት) 'old, ancient'

bərʿ ብርዕ 'reed, stubble'

bərhān ብርሃን 'light, brightness'

bərhānāwi ብርሃናዊ 'luminous, radiant'

bərt ብርት 'copper, brass'

bərur ብሩር 'silver, money'

bəslo ብስሎ 'cooked food'

bətkat ብትከት 'fracture, breaking'

bətuk ብቱክ 'broken, torn apart'

bəwuḥ ብዉሕ, bəwwəḥ ብውሕ (f. bəwwəḥt ብውሕት) 'one who has power;
    allowable, permitted'

bəya ብየ 'in me'

bəzḫ ብዝኅ 'multitude, large number'

bəzuḫ ብዙኅ 'many, much, numerous'

bəzuḫa ብዙኀ 'much, in large numbers'

bəzuḫa məhrat ብዙኀ፡ ምሕረት 'merciful'

biṣ ቢጽ 'fellow, companion, individual'

bo ቦ 'in it/him'

boʾa ቦአ (G) 'to enter, proceed'

boḥa ቦሐ (G) 'to receive authority, receive permission'

bomu ቦሙ 'in them (3mp)'

bonttu ቦንቱ 'in them (3fp)'

botton ቦቶን 'in them (3fp)'

bottu ቦቱ 'in it/him (3ms)'

burāke ቡራኬ 'blessing, benediction'

buruk ቡሩክ (f. burəkt ቡርክት) 'blessed, praised'

dāʾəmu ዳእሙ 'verily, really, moreover, however'

dabr ደብር 'mountain'

dabub ደቡብ 'north, south'

dādaqa ዳደቀ (L) 'to knock down, strike'

dagama ደገመ (G) 'to repeat, do a second time'

dāgəm ዳግም, dāgəmāwi ዳግማዊ, dāgəmāy ዳግማይ 'second'

dāgəma ዳግመ 'twice, for the second time'

dāgəmāwi ዳግማዊ 'second'

dāḫən ዳኅን 'safe, sound, whole'

daḫāri ደኃሪ 'last, latest'

daḫ(ā)rāwi ደኃራዊ/ደኃራዊ, daḫ(ā)rāy ደኃራይ/ደኃራይ 'last, late, farthest'

dāḫnā ዳኅና, dəḫnā ድኅና 'health, safety'

dāḫra ዳኅረ, dəḫra ድኅረ 'then, afterwards'

dakma ደክመ (G) 'to become weak, weary, feeble'

damanmin ደመንሚን 'obscure, very gloomy'

dammana ደመነ (D) 'to be clouded, be dark'

dammanā ደመና 'cloud'

damsasa ደምሰሰ (quadr.) 'to abolish, obliterate, destroy'

dangaḍa ደንገፀ (quadr.) 'to be terrified, shocked, alarmed'

daqiq ደቂቅ 'child; young, small'

dayyana ደየነ (D) 'to judge, punish, condemn'

degana ዴገነ (quadr.) 'to pursue, chase, persecute'

degāni ዴጋኒ 'one who pursues'

dəbʿənkʷəl ድብዕንኩል 'snare, trap'

dəgdāge ድግዳጌ 'leanness, meagerness'

dəgdug ድግዱግ 'meager, thin'

də(g)gəl ድግል, besides dəngəl ድንግል 'virgin, celibate'

dəḫra ድኅረ, ʔəm-dəḫra እምድኅረ 'behind, after that, afterwards'

dəḫrehu ድኅሬሁ, dāḫra ዳኅረ, dəḫra ድኅረ 'afterwards, thereafter'

dəḫreya ድኅሬየ 'behind me'

dəkām ድካም 'weakness, weariness'

dələqləq ድልቅልቅ 'shaking, trembling, quaking'

dəlləw ድልው (f. dəllut ድሉት) 'fitting, proper, ready, prepared'

dəmāḫ/ḥ ድማኅ/ድማሕ 'head, skull, summit'

dəngāg ድንጋግ 'edge, border, rim'

dəngāle ድንጋሌ 'virginity'

dəngəl ድንግል (pl. danāgəl ደናግል) 'virgin, celibate'

dəngələnnā ድንግልና 'virginity, chastity'

dənguḍ ድንጉፅ 'frightened, astonished'

dəqat ድቀት 'fall, ruin, downfall'

dəqʷəndəqʷ ድቍንድቍ 'axe, crowbar'

dəwuy ድዉይ, dəwwəy ድውይ (f. dəwwəyt ድውይት) 'sick, ill'

diba ዲበ (also dibe ዲቤ; with pronominal suffix dibe– ዲቤ–) 'on, upon, above'

ḍaʔat ፀአት 'exit, going out, origin'

ḍagām ፀጋም 'left, left hand'

ḍaḥāy ፀሓይ 'sun'

ḍar ፀር 'enemy, adversary'

ḍewāwe ፄዋዌ, ḍiwāwe ፂዋዌ 'captivity, imprisonment, exile'

ḍərfat ፀርፈት 'blasphemy, abuse'

ḍənəst ፅንስት 'pregnant'

ḍəwaw ፀዉዉ, ḍiwaw ፂዉዉ 'captive, prisoner, exiled'

fadfada ፈድፈደ (quadr.) 'to become numerous, increase'

fadfāda ፈድፋደ 'abundantly, exceedingly'

faḫara ፈኀረ (G) 'to engage, betroth'

falaṣa ፈለጸ (G) 'to split, separate'

fannawa ፈነወ (D) 'to send, send away, dismiss'

faqād ፈቃድ 'wish, desire'

faqada ፈቀደ (G) 'to wish, desire, seek'

faras ፈረስ (pl. ʔafrās አፍራስ) 'horse'

farha **ፈርሀ** (G) 'to be afraid, fear, revere'

farrāh **ፈራሀ** 'fearful, coward'

faṣṣama **ፈጸመ** (D) 'to complete, finish, fulfill'

    faṣṣama **ፈጸመ** + verb 'to finish to do'

fatāḥi **ፈታሒ** 'judge'

fatḥa **ፈትሐ** (G) 'to open, loose, release; to judge, pass judgement'

fat(a)wa **ፈትወ/ፈተወ** (G) 'to desire, wish, covet'

faṭara **ፈጠረ** (G) 'to create, fashion, produce'

faṭāre mədr **ፈታሬ፡ምድር** 'creator of the world'

faṭāri **ፈታሪ** 'creator'

fawwasa **ፈወሰ** (D) 'to cure, heal'

faws **ፈውስ** 'healing, cure, medicine'

fəkkāre **ፍካሬ** 'interpretation, explanation, commentary'

fəlsat **ፍልሰት** 'departure, exile'

fəlṭān **ፍልጣን** 'separation, divorce, difference'

fənnā **ፍና** 'way, path; towards'

fənnəw **ፍንው** (f. fənnut **ፍኑት**) 'sent'

fənot **ፍኖት** 'way, path, road'

fəqr **ፍቅር** 'love, affection'

fəqur **ፍቁር** (pl. fəqurān **ፍቁራን**) 'loved, beloved'

fəre **ፍሬ** 'fruit'

fərhat **ፍርሀት** 'fear, terror, awe'

fəśśəḥā **ፍሥሓ** 'joy, gladness, happiness'

fəśśuḥ **ፍሡሕ** 'glad, joyful, happy'

fəṣṣəmənnā **ፍጽምና** 'perfection, integrity'

fəṣṣum **ፍጹም** 'completed, finished'

fətəw **ፍትው** 'desired, pleasing, pleasant'

fətḥ **ፍትሕ** 'law, judgement, verdict'

fətot **ፍቶት** (besides fətwat **ፍትወት**) 'desire, wish'

fətwat **ፍትወት** (besides fətot **ፍቶት**) 'desire, wish'

fəṭrat **ፍጥረት** 'creation, act of creation'

fəṭuna **ፍጡነ** 'quickly, immediately'

fəwwāse **ፍዋሴ** 'healing'

fəwwəs **ፍውስ** 'healed, cured'

gabʾa ገብአ (G) 'to return, leave, turn back'; gābəʾa ጋብአ (L) 'to collect, gather';
  tagābəʾa ተጋብአ (Lt) 'to be collected, be compiled'
  gabʾa ገብአ + verb 'to do again'

gabāʾi ገባኢ 'hireling, hired servant, mercenary'

gabāri ገባሪ 'craftsman'

gabbār ገባር 'workman, farmer'

gabbārāwi ገባራዊ 'workman, farmer'

gabr ገብር (pl. ʾagbərt አግብርት) 'slave, servant'

gabra ገብረ (G) 'to act, work, make'

gadām ገዳም 'wilderness, desert'

gamal ገመል (pl. ʾagmāl አግማል) 'camel'

ganaya ገነየ (G) 'to bow down, praise, thanks'

gānən ጋንን 'demon, ghost, evil spirit'

gannat ገነት (pl. gannatāt ገነታት) 'garden, the Garden of Eden'

garāht ገራህት 'field, arable land, farm'

gaṣṣ ገጽ 'face, appearance'

gays ገይስ 'journey'

gazʾa ገዝአ (G) 'to dominate, master'

gegāy ጌጋይ 'iniquity, sin, error'

gegaya ጌገየ (quadr.) 'to err, go astray, sin'

gegāyi ጌጋዪ 'sinner'

gesam ጌሰም, geśam ጌሠም 'tomorrow, the morrow'

gəʿra ግዕረ (G) 'to cry out, wail, lament'

gəbr ግብር 'affair, matter, thing'

gəbrat ግብረት 'work, working'

gəbrənnā ግብርና 'service, servitude'

gəbrənnāt ግብርናት 'service, servitude'

gəbta ግብት 'suddenly, accidentally'

gəfʿ ግፍዕ 'oppression, violence, wrong, injustice'

gəfʿa ግፍዐ 'wrongfully, unjustly'

gəlfo ግልፎ 'carved work, carved idol'

gəmmāne ግማኔ 'pollution, defiling'

gəmurā ግሙራ, la-gəmurā ለግሙራ 'certainly, utterly, always, forever' gənfāl **ግንፋል** 'brick, tile'

gəramt **ግረምት** 'terror, dread'

gəz²at **ግዝአት** 'dominion, ownership'

giguy **ጊጉይ** 'guilty, erring, sinner'

gize **ጊዜ** 'time, season'

gize **ጊዜ** 'when'

gogawa **ጎጎወ** (quadr.) 'to err'

gʷadgʷada **ጐድጐደ** (quadr.) 'to knock, strike'

gʷa/āḥlawa **ጐሕለወ/ኋሕለወ** (quadr.) 'to be crafty, be cunning, cheat'

gʷandaya **ጐንደየ** (quadr.) 'to delay, wait, be late in doing something'

gʷayya **ጐየ** (G) 'to flee, run away'

gʷazgʷaz **ጐዝጐዝ** 'covering, carpet, mat'

gʷəhān **ጕኃን** 'mystery, sacred secret'

habanniya **ሀበኒየ** 'give it to me!' (with two object suffixes)

habənni **ሀብኒ** 'give (f.) me!'

habt **ሀብት** 'gift'

hagar **ሀገር** 'city, town'

hagʷl **ሀጕል** 'destruction, loss, end'

hagʷla **ሀጕለ**, ḥagʷla **ሐጕለ** (G) 'to be destroyed, perish'

hallawa **ሀለወ**, hallo **ሀሎ** (D) 'to be, exist, live'

hallo **ሀሎ**, see hallawa **ሀለወ**

hāymānot **ሃይማኖት** 'faith, belief, religion'

hayyādi **ሀያዲ** 'robber, thief'

–he **–ሄ** 'there, here, away to'

həgʷəl **ሀጕል**, həgul **ሀጉል** 'lost, destroyed, ruined'

həllāwe **ሀላዌ** 'substance, essence, nature'

hə(y)ya **ሀየ**, hi(y)ya **ሒየ** 'there, thither'

həyyanta **ሀየንተ** 'instead of, in place of, because of'

–hi **–ሂ** 'also, and, further, the very'

hoka **ሆከ** (G) 'to stir up, disturb, trouble'

–hu **–ሁ** 3ms pronominal suffix

–hu **–ሁ** interrogative particle

ḥaw **ሐው**, haw **ሀው** 'fire'

ḥablaka ሐብለከ (quadr.) 'to vanish from sight, go away for good'

ḥablāt ሐብላት 'plaited work, anything pendent'

ḥabq(w)aq(w)a ሐብቀቀ/ሐብቈቈ (quadr.) 'to bedaub oneself, stain, make dirty'

ḥaddəs ሐድስ 'excellent'

ḥaddis ሐዲስ 'new, recent'

ḥaddiso ሐዲሶ 'he, having restored'

ḥagʷla ሐጕለ, ḥagʷla ህጕለ (G) 'to be destroyed, perish'

ḥalaya ሐለየ (G) 'to sing'

ḥalāyi ሐላዪ 'singer'

ḥalāyt ሐላይት 'singer (f.)'

ḥam ሐም (ḥamu- ሐሙ- with pronominal suffixes) 'father-in-law, son-in-law'

ḥamadā ሐመዳ 'snow, frost'

ḥamalmil ሐመልሚል 'green, verdant'

ḥamar ሐመር (pl. ʔaḥmār አሕማር) 'ship, boat'

ḥamāt ሐማት 'mother-in-law, daughter-in-law'

ḥaml ሐምል 'vegetation, herbs'

ḥanaṣa ሐነጸ (G) 'to build, construct'

ḥanzar ሐንዘር 'pig, wild boar'

ḥaqafa ሐቀፈ (G) 'to hug, embrace'

ḥaqʷe ሐቈ 'hip, loin'

ḥarā ሐራ 'army, troops'

ḥargaṣ ሐርገጽ 'crocodile'

ḥasl ሐስል (pl. ʔaḥsəl አሕስል) 'sack'

ḥassat ሐሰት 'lie, falsehood'

ḥaṣṣa ሐጸ (G) 'to be wanting, be less, decrease'

ḥaṣur ሐጹር 'fence, wall, enclosure'

ḥatata ሐተተ (G) 'to search, inquire, examine, explore'

ḥatatā ሐተታ 'inquiry, searching, investigation'

ḥawāri ሐዋሪ 'traveler, apostle'

ḥawārəyā ሐዋርያ 'traveler, messenger, apostle'

ḥawwāṣi ሐዋጺ 'overseer, watchman'

ḥayq ሐይቅ 'shore, seashore'

ḥaywa ሐይወ (G) 'to live, be alive, be well'

ḥazan ሐዘን 'sadness, grief'

ḥazḥaz ሐዝሐዝ 'swamp, pool'

ḥesa ሔሰ (G) 'to blame, reprove'

ḥəddāse ሕዳሴ 'renewal, restoration'

ḥəgg ሕግ 'law, decree, rule'

ḥəlm ሕልም 'dream, vision'

ḥəlqat ሕልቀት 'ring'

ḥəqqa ሕቀ 'a little, a little while'

ḥəwwāṣe ሕዋጼ 'watching, inspection, visitation'

ḥəyāw ሕያው (f. ḥəyāwt ሕያውት) 'alive, living, healed'

ḥəywat ሕይወት 'life, lifetime'

ḥəzb ሕዝብ (pl. ʾaḥzāb አሕዛብ) 'nation, people, tribe'

ḥəzun ሕዙን 'sad, sorrowful, distressed'

ḥora ሖረ (G) 'to go, go forth'

ḥosa ሖሰ (G) 'to move, shake'

ḥurat ሑረት 'course, walking, way of life, manners, behavior'

ḫabz ኅብዝ, ḫəbz ኅብዝ 'bread'

ḫab(a)ra ኅበረ/ኅብረ (G) 'to be associate with, join, do together'

ḫaba ኀበ (also ḫabe ኀቤ) 'toward, near to, by, at'

ḫaba ኀበ '(the place) where'

    ḫaba waʾəda ኀበ ፡ ውእደ, mangala waʾəda መንገለ ፡ ውእደ 'at'

    ḫaba mannu ኀበ ፡ መኑ 'to whom?'

ḫadaga ኀደገ (G) 'to abandon, leave, allow, permit'

ḫadara ኀደረ (G) 'to reside, dwell'

ḫafrat ኀፍረት 'shame, impropriety, disgrace'

ḫalafa ኀለፈ (G) 'to pass, pass by'

ḫalāfit ኀላፊት 'people travelling or passing by, crowd'

ḫallaya ኀለየ (D) 'to think, consider'

ḫaməstu ኀምስቱ 'five'

ḫams ኀምስ 'five'

ḫamsā ኀምሳ 'fifty'

ḫamus ኀሙስ 'the fifth day, Thursday'

ḫar(a)ya ኀረየ/ኀርየ (G) 'to choose, elect'

ḫasār ኀሳር 'dishonor, wretchedness, misery'

ḥasarsara ኀሰርሰረ (quinq.) 'to be reviled, humiliated'

ḥasra ኀስረ (G) 'to be disgraced, be vilified'

ḥaśaśa ኀሠሠ (G) 'to seek, search, explore'

ḥaśaśā ኀሠሣ 'inquiry, searching, wish'

ḥaṣṣin ኀጺን 'iron, sword'

ḫāṭə' ኃጥእ 'sinner'

ḫaṭi'at ኀጢአት 'fault, offense, sin'

ḫayl ኀይል 'power, strength, might'

ḫayyāl ኀያል 'strong, powerful, mighty'

ḥela ኄለ (G) 'to become strong, be mighty'

ḥer ኄር 'good, excellent'

ḥesa ኄሰ (G) 'to be suitable'

ḥeṭa ኄጠ, heṭa ፄጠ (G) 'to deceive, cheat, seduce'

ḫəbəst ኅብስት (< *ḫəbəzt) 'bread'

ḫəbrat ኅብረት 'union, joining, accord'

ḫəbura ኅቡረ 'together, jointly'

ḫəbz ኅብዝ, ḫabz ኀብዝ 'bread'

ḫədāṭ ኅዳጥ 'a small amount, little'

ḫədāṭa ኅዳጠ, ba-ḫədāṭ በኅዳጥ 'a little, a little bit'

ḫədgat ኅድገት 'release, remission, forgiveness'

ḫəllinā ኅሊና 'thinking, mind, thought'

ḫəluq ኅሉቅ 'finished, accomplished, destroyed'

ḫəmmāse ኅማሴ 'the five, reunion of five'

ḫəruy ኅሩይ (f. ḫarit ኀሪት) 'chosen, selected'

ḫoḫət ኆኅት 'door, doorway, gate'

ḫolləqotomu ኆልቆቶሙ 'in order to count them'

ḫolqʷ ኆልቍ 'number, sum'

ḫʷallaqʷa ኍለቈ (D) 'to count, number'

ḫʷalqʷ ኍልቍ 'number, sum'

ḫʷəlqʷ ኍልቍ 'number, sum'

ka'awa ከዐወ (G) 'to pour, pour out, disperse'

kā'əba ካዕበ 'secondly, another time, twice'

kā'əbat ካዕበት 'double, double amount'

kāʿəbata ካዕበት 'doubly, twofold'

kabaro ከበሮ 'drum'

kabkāb ከብካብ 'wedding, nuptials'

kadana ከደነ (G) 'to cover, wrap, hide'

kaḥa/ā ከሐ/ከሓ, ba-kaḥa በከሓ, kaḥak(a) ከሐከ/ከሓከ 'yonder, away, beyond'

kaḥad ከሐድ 'lack of faith, impiety, heresy'

kāḥd ካሕድ 'lack of faith, impiety, heresy'

kalʾa ከልአ (G) 'to hinder, prohibit'

kalb ከልብ 'dog'

kāləʾ ካልእ 'other, another, second'

kama ከመ 'as, just as, like, as if'

kama ከመ 'that, so that, in order that'

    kama ከመ 'how much!'

    kamāhu ከማሁ 'such a one, such a thing'

    kama mənt ከመ፡ ምንት, kama məntə-nu ከመ፡ ምንትኑ 'how much?'

    kama śannāy ከመ፡ ሠናይ 'how beautiful!'

    kama-zə ከመዝ 'such, like this, thus'

kanfar ከንፈር (pl. kanāfər ከናፍር) 'lip, language'

kanfif ከንፊፍ 'border, limit'

kanto ከንቶ 'without reason, in vain, for nothing, gratis'

kantu ከንቱ 'nothingness, emptiness, vanity'

karabo ከረቦ 'woven basket'

karaya ከረየ (G) 'to dig, dig up'

karś ከርሥ 'belly, stomach, womb'

kaśata ከሠተ (G) 'to uncover, reveal, open (eyes, mouth, box)'

kawālā ከዋላ 'behind, hind part'

–ke –ኬ 'now, then, thus, therefore'

keda ኬደ (G) 'to tread, trample'

kəʿub ክዑብ 'double, doubly twined'

kəbədd ክብድ (f. of kəbud ክቡድ) 'heavy, burdensome'

kəbərt ክብርት (f. of kəbur ክቡር) 'honored, glorious'

kəbərtāwi ክብርታዊ 'revered'

kəbr ክብር 'honor, glory, splendor'

kəbrat ክብረት 'glory'

kəbud ከቡድ 'heavy, burdensome'

kəbur ከቡር 'honored, glorious'

kəhla ከህለ (G) 'to be able, overcome'

kəḥda ከሕደ (G) 'to deny, denounce, repudiate'

kəlʾe ክልኤ 'two, double, twofold'

kəlʾe kəlʾe ክልኤ ፡ ክልኤ 'two each'

kəlʾeti ክልኤቲ 'two' (with feminine nouns)

kəlʾetu ክልኤቱ 'two' (with masculine and feminine nouns)

kəlʾetu məʾət ክልኤቱ ፡ ምእት '200'

kəmma ከመ 'thus, nearly, almost, also, even'

kenəyā ኬንያ 'artisan, craftsman, workman'

kənf ክንፍ 'wing, border'

kərəstənnā ክርስትና 'Christianity'

kəsād ክሳድ 'neck'

kətāb ከታብ 'writing, message, book, text'

kəwwāne ከዋኔ 'being, origin, essence'

kidān ኪዳን 'covenant, pact, testament'

kin ኪን 'art, skill, workmanship'

kiyā– ኪያ– (with pronominal suffix) independent object pronoun

kokab ኮከብ (pl. kawākəbt ከዋክብት) 'star'

kona ኮነ (G) 'to be, become, exist, happen'

    kona ኮነ, yəkawwən ይከውን 'to be permissible'

    kona ኮነ in: za-kona kawino/kawinā ዘኮነ ፡ ከዊኖ/ከዊና 'whoever, whatsoever, whosoever he may be'

    kona yəbe ኮነ ፡ ይቤ 'he had said'

kufāle ኩፋሌ 'partition, division'

kʷannana ኰነነ (D) 'to rule over, govern, judge'

kʷannāni ኰናኒ 'ruler, governor'

kʷəḥl ኵሕል 'antimony, dye for the eyelid'

kʷəll– ኵል– 'all, every, each'

kʷəllantā ኵለንታ 'totality, entirety'

kʷəllantāwi ኵለንታዊ 'total'

kʷəllo ኵሉ 'altogether, completely'

kʷəllomu ኵሎሙ 'all of them, each of them (mp)'

kʷəllə-he **ኩልዬ** 'everywhere, wherever'

kʷəlləna **ኩልነ** 'all of us, each of us'

kʷənnāne **ኩናኔ** 'rule, judgment, trial'

kʷināt **ኩናት** 'spear, sword'

la– **ለ**– 'to, toward, for, according to'

    la-ʾama **ለአመ** 'until, at the time when'

    la-ʾəm kama **ለእም፡ከመ** 'as soon as, when'

    la-ʾəmma **ለእመ** 'if, even if'

    la-ḫaba **ለኀበ** 'away to, unto, at'

    la-kantu **ለከንቱ** 'without reason, gratis, freely'

    la-mannu **ለመኑ** 'for whom?'

    la-mənt **ለምንት**, ba-mənt **በምንት** 'why?'

    la-zallāfu **ለዘላፉ** 'continuously, forever, always'

    la-zəlufu **ለዝሉፉ** 'continuously, forever, always'

la– **ለ**– affirmative particle

laʾaka **ለአከ** (G) 'to send'

laʿala **ለዐለ**, ləʿla **ልዕለ** (G) 'to be high, superior, elevated'

lāʿla **ላዕለ** 'above, against, on, upon'

lāʿlāy **ላዕላይ** 'upper, high, superior'

lāʿlu **ላዕሉ**, ba-lāʿlu **በላዕሉ** 'above, upward'

labbawa **ለበወ** (D) 'to understand, be clever'

labsa **ለብሰ** (G) 'to clothe oneself, wear'

la-fe **ለፌ**, ʾəm-la-fe **እምለፌ** 'on this side'

lāhm **ላህም** 'ox, bull, cow'

lāḫ **ላሕ** (< *lāḫw) 'mourning, grief'

laḥakʷa **ለሐኰ** (G) 'to fashion, form, create'

lāḥawa **ላሐወ** (L) 'to mourn for, lament'

laḥāy **ለሓይ** (f. lāḥəyt **ላሕይት**, lāḥit **ላሒት**) 'beautiful'

lāḥəy **ላሕይ** 'beauty, splendor; beautiful, handsome'

lalla– **ለለ**– 'every, each'

lalli– **ለሊ**– (with pronominal suffix) independent subject pronoun

lamlama **ለምለመ** (quadr.) 'to be verdant, mild, smooth, fresh'

laṣlaṣa **ለጽለጸ** (quadr.) 'to weigh, measure, to move to and fro'

laṣliṣ ለጽሊጽ 'tongue of a scale, pointer of a scale'

lātti ላቲ 'to/for her'

layāləy ለያልይ (pl. of lelit ሌሊት) 'nights'

lelaya ሌለየ (quadr.) 'to separate, divide'

lelit ሌሊት 'night'

lelita ሌሊተ 'at night'

lə'ul ልዑል 'high, Most High'

lə'ulāna zəkr ልዑላነ፡ ዝክር 'those of exalted memory'

ləbb ልብ 'heart, mind'

ləbbāwe ልባዌ 'intelligence, mind, intellect'

ləbbəw ልብው 'wise, intelligent, skilled'

ləbs ልብስ (pl. ʾalbās አልባስ) 'clothes, garment, tunic'

ləd ልድ 'son, child'

lədat ልደት 'birth'

ləhəqt ለሀቅት (f.) 'grown-up, old; old woman'

ləhiq ለሂቅ 'grown-up, old'

ləhqa ለሀቀ (G) 'to grow up, grow old'

ləhqān ለሀቃን 'seniority, old age'

ləhqāt ለሀቃት 'old age, mature age'

ləhqənnā ለሀቅና 'old age, principality'

ləmlum ልምሉም 'soft, tender, fresh'

ləssān ልሳን 'tongue, language'

lilāy ሊላይ 'separation, distinction'

liq ሊቅ 'chief, elder, old man'

lita ሊተ 'to/for me'

–(m)ma –መ emphasizes word to which it is attached

māʾədd ማእድ 'table, food, banquet'

māʾəze ማእዜ 'when?'

māʾkal ማእከል 'center, middle'

māʾkala ማእከለ 'in the midst of, in the middle of, among'

māʾman ማእመን 'faithful, believer, devout'

māʾmari ማእመሪ 'knower of, who possesses knowledge'

māʾmər ማእምር 'learned, skilled, diviner'

māʾs ማእስ, māʿs ማዕስ 'skin, leather, hide'

maʿada, məʿda መዐደ/ምዐደ (G) 'to counsel, admonish'

maʿālt መዓልት (pl. mawāʿəl መዋዕል) 'day, daytime'

maʿār መዓር 'honey'

maʿārʿir መዓርጊር 'sweet, sweet-tasting'

māʿbal ማዕበል 'flood, wave'

māʿdota ማዕዶተ 'across, to the opposite side, beyond'

mabkəy መብክይ 'mourner'

mabləʿ መብልዕ (pl. mabāləʿt መባልዕት) 'food, provisions'

madḫani መድኃኒ 'redeemer, savior'

madḫanit መድኃኒት 'salvation, redemption'

madməm መድምም 'wonderful, wonder, miracle'

mafawwəs መፈውስ 'physician, healer'

mafqare ʾəgziʾab(ə)ḥer መፍቀሬ፡እግዚአብሔር 'loving god'

mafqari መፍቀሪ 'lover, friend'

mafrəh መፍርህ 'fearful, terrifying, frightening'

maftəw 'fitting, suitable, pleasant, pleasing'

magaśśəṣ መገሥጽ 'teacher'

magramt መግረምት 'terror'

mahara መህረ (D) and məhra ምህረ (G) 'to teach, instruct'

maḥara መሐረ (G) 'have mercy, be compassionate, show mercy'

maḥāri መሐሪ 'merciful, compassionate'

māḥlet ማሕሌት 'song, hymn'

māḥyawi ማሕየዊ 'life-giving, savior'

māḥzani ማሕዘኒ 'saddening, sorrowful'

māḫbar ማኅበር 'association, assembly, council'

māḫdar ማኅደር 'dwelling, abode, resting place, tabernacle'

māḫlaqt ማኅለቅት 'ceasing, end, death'

makān መካን 'place, space'

makkarā መከራ 'trial, testing, temptation'

makʷannən መኮንን (pl. makʷānənt መኳንንት) 'ruler, governor, judge, high official'

malʾa መልአ (G) 'to fill, be full, be filled'

malʾak መልአክ (pl. malāʾəkt መላእክት) 'messenger, angel'

mal(ə)ʾəkt መልእክት 'letter, message, service'

malʿəlt መልዕልት 'upper part, height, top'

malʿəlta መልዕልተ 'on, above, on top of'

malakot መለኮት 'lordship, kingdom'

malhəqt መልህቅት 'elder, senior'

mam(ə)hər መምህር 'teacher, superior'

mamkər መምክር (pl. mamākərt መማክርት) 'counselor'

manāfəq መናፍቅ 'heretic, hypocrite'

manāzəz መናዝዝ 'consoling, comforting'

manbar መንበር (pl. manābərt መናብርት) 'seat, throne'

manbart መንበርት 'state, condition, mode of life'

mandad መንደድ 'kitchen'

manfaq መንፈቅ 'half, part'

manfas መንፈስ (pl. manāfəst መናፍስት) 'spirit, breath'

mangala መንገለ 'toward, to, with regard to'

mangala waʾəda መንገለ፡ ውእደ 'by the side of'

mangəśt መንግሥት 'kingdom, kingship'

mangogəw መንጎጋው 'vagabond'

mangʷarāgʷər መንጐራጐር 'who murmurs, who mutters'

mangʷargʷər መንጐርጐር 'who murmurs, who mutters'

mankər መንክር (pl. mankərāt መንክራት) 'wonder, miracle; marvelous'

mankʷasa መንኩሰ (quadr.) 'to become a monk, live a monastic life'

manna መነ 'whom?'

mannu መኑ 'who?'

mannu-hi መኑኒ, manna-hi መነኒ (acc.) 'anyone'

mansawa መንሰወ (quadr.) 'to be in danger, be led to temptation'

mansut መንሱት 'temptation, test, peril'

maqbart መቅበርት 'grave, tomb'

maqdas መቅደስ 'sanctuary, temple'

maqdəma መቅድመ 'first, beforehand, before'

maqśaft መቅሠፍት 'punishment, whipping'

marābəʿt መራብዕት 'square'

marḥ መርሕ 'leader, guide'

marḥa መርሐ (G) 'to lead, guide'

marir መሪር (f. marrār መራር) 'bitter, grievous'

marira መሪረ 'bitterly'

marḫo መርኆ (pl. marāḫut መራኁት) 'key'

marrāḥ መራሕ 'guide, leader'

masaggəl መሰግል 'magician, diviner'

māsana ማሰነ (L) 'to decay, be corrupt, be ruined'

masfən መስፍን 'ruler, governor, prince'

masḫənt መስኀንት 'oven'

mastaʿaggəś መስተዐግሥ 'patient'

mastaḫaśəś መስተኀሥሥ 'inventor, discoverer'

mastaśāhəl መስተሣህል 'compassionate, merciful'

mastasrəy መስተስርይ, mastasri መስተስሪ 'asking for forgiveness, causing to forgive'

maśʿərt መሥዕርት 'comb'

maśaggər መሠግር 'fisherman'

maśannəy መሠንይ 'beautiful, fair, the best (of)'

maśgart መሥገርት (pl. maśāgər መሣግር) 'snare, trap, net'

maślast መሥለስት 'triple, threefold'

maśləst መሥልስት 'triple, third rank'

maśnaq መሥነቅ (pl. maśānəq መሣንቅ) 'bag of provisions, pouch'

maṣ'a መጽአ 'to come, happen, occur'

*maṣfan መጽፈን (pl. maṣāfən መጻፍን) 'satchel'

maṣḥaf መጽሐፍ (pl. maṣāḥəft መጻሕፍት) 'book, written document'

maṣwart መጽወርት (pl. maṣāwər(t) መጻውC(ት)) 'pole, means of carrying a load'

maṣwata መጽወተ 'to give alms'

maṣyāḫt መጽያሕት 'beaten path, paved road'

matḫata መትሕተ 'under, below, beneath'

matkaf(t) መትከፍ(ት) (pl. matākəft መታከፍት) 'shoulder'

matkal መትከል 'peg, nail'

maṭana መጠነ 'as long as, as often as, as great as'

maṭməq መጥምቅ 'who baptizes'

mawā'i መዋኢ 'victor, conqueror; victorious'

mawāʿəl መዋዕል 'days, daytime' (pl. of moʿalt ሞዐልት, maʿālt መዓልት)

mawāti መሞቲ 'mortal, dead'

māwtā **ማውታ** 'corpse, dead body'

māy **ማይ** 'water, liquid'

mazenāwi **መዜናዊ**, mazenəw **መዜነው** 'announcer, messenger'

meṭa **ሜጠ** (G) 'to turn, turn aside, turn back'

məʾəllād **ምእላድ** 'gathering place, receptacle'

məʾəmān **ምእማን** 'faithful, believing'

məʾət **ምእት** 'hundred'

məʿqəbənnā **ምዕቅብና** 'deposit'

məʿr **ምዕር** 'moment, time'

məʿra **ምዕረ** 'once, at once'

məʿrāb **ምዕራብ** 'west'

mədr **ምድር** 'land, ground, district'

mədrāwi **ምድራዊ** ''earthly, worldly'

məgbār **ምግባር** 'action(s), deed(s), achievement(s)'

məhəllāw **ምህላው** 'dwelling place, domicile'

məḥra **ምሕረ** (G) 'to have compassion, show mercy'

məḥrat **ምሕረት** 'compassion, mercy'

məkʷənnān **ምኵናን** 'court of justice, hall of judgement'

məkḥ **ምክሕ** 'boasting, glory, praise'

məkr **ምክር** 'plan, counsel, advice'

məlkot **ምልኮት** 'property, possession'

məmməʿā **ምምዓ** 'anxiety, terror, fear'

mənbāb **ምንባብ** 'passage (of a book), place of reading'

mənbār **ምንባር** 'seat, dwelling, base'

məndād **ምንዳድ** 'fireplace, oven'

məndub **ምንዱብ** 'tormented, afflicted'

mənsāwe **ምንሳዌ** 'temptation, peril, affliction'

mənsəw **ምንስው** 'tempted, tried'

mənt **ምንት** 'what?'

mənta-hi **ምንተሂ** 'anything, whatever' (acc.)

məntə-hu **ምንትሁ** 'what?'

məqwām **ምቅዋም** 'place, position, pedestal'

məsāḥ **ምሳሕ** 'meal, dinner, supper'

məsəwwār **ምስዋር** 'hiding place, shelter, refuge'

məsfənnā ም**ስፍና** 'leadership, governance, ruling'

məskāb ም**ስካብ** 'couch, bed'

məsl ም**ስል** (pl. ʔamsāl **አምሳል**) 'likeness, image, parable, proverb'

məsla ም**ስለ** (with pronominal suffixes məsle– ም**ስሌ**–) 'with, in the company of'

məsmənit ም**ስምኒት** 'eightfold'

məsyat ም**ስየት**, məset ም**ሴት** 'evening, twilight'

məśrāq ም**ሥራቅ** 'east'

məṣəllāy ም**ጸላይ** 'place of prayer, chapel'

məthat ም**ትሀት** 'specter, ghost'

mətur ም**ቱር** 'cut, removed, decided, absolute'

məṭṭəw ም**ጡው** 'handed over, delivered, surrendered'

məwut ም**ዉት**, məwwət ም**ውት** (f. məwwətt ም**ውት**; pl. məwwətān ም**ውታን** and mutān **ሙታን**) 'dead'

məzrāʔ ም**ዝራዕ** 'sowed field'

mi **ሚ** 'what?'

mi– **ሚ**– used as exclamation 'how (much)!'

    mi-ʔaddām **ሚአዳም** 'how pleasant!'

    mi-bazḫu **ሚበዝኁ** 'how many they are!'

    mi-gize **ሚጊዜ** 'when?'

    mi-ke **ሚኬ** 'how?'

    mi-maṭana **ሚመጠነ** 'how much?'

mimma **ሚመ** 'or?'

miṭat **ሚጠት** 'turning, returning, answer'

moʔa **ሞአ** (G) 'to conquer, defeat'

moʕalt **ሞዐልት** (pl. mawāʕəl **መዋዕል**) 'day, daytime'

moḍā **ሞፃ** (√wḍʔ) 'offering, gift'

mogas **ሞገስ** 'favor, grace, benevolence'

moqa **ሞቀ** (G) 'to grow hot, be warm'

moqəḥa **ሞቅሐ** (quadr.) 'to put in chains, take prisoner'

mot **ሞት** 'death'

mota **ሞተ** (G) 'to die'

mulād **ሙላድ** 'birthplace, native land'

muqāḫe **ሙቃሐ** 'imprisonment'

muquḥ **ሙቁሕ** 'captive, prisoner; chained, bound'

musənnā **ሙስና**, musunnā **ሙሱና** 'spoiling, ruin, devastation'

musun **ሙሱን** (f. musənt **ሙስንት**) 'corrupt, spoilt, destroyed'

na– **ነ**– 'behold!, as for'

naʿā **ነዓ** (also nəʿā **ንዓ** and naʿa **ነዐ**) 'come!, come now!'

nababa **ነበበ** (G) 'to talk, speak, proclaim'

nabalbāl **ነበልባል** 'flame'

nabara **ነበረ** (G) 'to sit, sit down, remain, dwell'

nabiy **ነቢይ** (pl. nabiyāt **ነቢያት**) 'prophet'

nadāʾi **ነዳኢ** (pl. nadāʾt **ነዳእት**) 'driver, overseer'

nadada **ነደደ** (G) 'to burn, blaze, be on fire'

nadd **ነድ** 'flame, fever'

nadda **ነደ** 'to burn, blaze'

naddāy **ነዳይ** 'poor, needy'

nadifa qast **ነዲፈ ፡ ቀስት** 'archery'

nafaqa **ነፈቀ** (G) 'to tear off, divide, separate'

nāfaqa **ናፈቀ** (L) 'to divide, doubt'

nafās **ነፋስ** 'wind, air'

nāfəqo(t) **ናፍቆ(ት)** 'heresy'

nafs **ነፍስ** (pl. nafsāt **ነፍሳት**) 'soul, spirit, self'

nagādi **ነጋዲ** (pl. nagādəyān **ነጋድያን**) 'traveler, merchant'

nagar **ነገር** 'speech, talk, word, thing, affair, matter'

nagara **ነገረ** (G) 'to say, tell, speak'

nagh **ነግህ** 'early morning, dawn'

nagogāw **ነነጋው** 'hesitation, erring, moving about restlessly'

nagʷadgʷād **ነጐድጓድ** 'thunder'

nāhu **ናሁ** 'behold!, now that'

nakir **ነኪር** (f. nakkār **ነካር**) 'strange, foreign; stranger'

naqqʷār **ነቝር** 'one-eyed, cross-eyed, blind'

naqza **ነቅዘ** (G) 'to be worm-eaten, spoiled'

naśʾa **ነሥአ** (G) 'to take, receive, accept, raise'

    naśʾa **ነሥአ** 'to take' + ʾawsaba **አውሰበ** 'to marry' (lit. 'to take as a wife')

nasawa **ነሰወ** (G) 'to try, tempt'

nassāḥi **ነሳሒ** 'one who is repentant, penitent'

naśata ነሠተ (G) 'to destroy, ruin, overturn'

nassəḥa ነስሐ (D) 'to repent, do penance'

nāśəʾa ናሥአ (L) 'to take away, carry off'

naṣafṣāf ነጸፍጻፍ 'drops, falling in drops'

naṣṣara ነጸረ (D) 'to look, view, watch'

naw(w)iḫa qom ነዊኀ፡ ቆም 'high of stature' = 'tall'

nawā ነዋ 'behold!'

naw(w)iḫ ነዊኅ (f. nawwāḫ ነዋኅ) 'long, high, lofty'

naya ነየ 'as for me, here I am, behold'

nāzaza ናዘዘ (L) 'to console, comfort'

nāzāzi ናዛዚ 'consoler, comforter'

nəʾus ንኡስ 'small, little, young'

nəʿiwa ʾarāwit ንዒወ፡ አራዊት 'hunting of animals'

nəbāb ንባብ 'speech, utterance, discourse'

nəbrat ንብረት 'position, dwelling, state'

nəbur ንቡር 'who sits down, sitting, seated'

nədād ንዳድ 'fever'

nəddat ንደት 'flame, fever'

nədyat ንድየት, nədet ንዬት 'poverty, want'

nəfq ንፍቅ, nəfqā ንፍቃ, nəfqat ንፍቀት 'half, middle'

nəgəśt ንግሥት 'queen'

nəgś ንግሥ 'reign, rule'

nəguś ንጉሥ (pl. nagaś t ነገሥት) 'king, ruler'

nəḥna ንሕነ 'we'

nəsr ንስር 'eagle'

nəssəḥā ንስሓ 'penitence, repentance, regret'

nəstit ንስቲት 'small, little, young' (√nʾs)

nəstita ንስቲተ 'a little, for a little while'

nəṣḥ ንጽሕ 'purity, sincerity, chastity'

nəṣṣāre ንጻሬ 'view, look, gaze'

nəṣuḥāna ləbb ንጹሓነ፡ ልብ 'those pure of heart'

nəwāy ንዋይ 'vessel, utensil, object'

nəzəhlul ንዝህሉል 'careless, immoral, dissolute'

–ni –ኒ 'too, also, even, likewise'

noḫa ኖኀ (G) 'to be high, be tall, be long'

nolawa ኖለወ (quadr.) 'to be a shepherd, tend flocks'

nolāwi ኖላዊ 'shepherd, herder'

noma ኖመ (G) 'to sleep, fall asleep, die'

–nu –ኑ interrogative particle

nufāqe ኑፋቄ 'division, dissension, heresy'

nufāqeyāt ኑፋቄያት 'heresy'

nuḫ ኑኅ, nuḫat ኑኃት 'length'

nuzāze ኑዛዜ 'consolation, comfort'

ṗāṗṗās ጳጳስ (pl. ṗāṗṗāsāt ጳጳሳት) 'metropolitan, patriarch, bishop'

qabar ቀብር 'burial, funeral, grave'

qabara ቀበረ (G) 'to bury'

qabbalā ቀበላ 'meeting, encounter'

qadama ቀደመ (G) 'to go before, precede, begin'; with another verb 'to do first'

qadāmāwi ቀዳማዊ (f. qadāmāwit ቀዳማዊት) 'first, former, ancient'

qadāmi ቀዳሚ 'first, predecessor, beginning; at first, in the beginning, before'

qaddamt ቀደምት (pl.) 'forefathers, ancestors'

qaddasa ቀደሰ (D) 'to sanctify, make holy, consecrate'

qadima ቀዲመ 'in the first place, before, formerly'

qadimu ቀዲሙ 'first, at the beginning, previously'

qāl ቃል 'voice, word'

qalāy ቀላይ 'depth (of river, sea), abyss, underworld'

qalqal ቀልቀል 'sloping place, cliff'

qarba ቀርበ, qaraba ቀረበ (G) 'to draw near, approach'

qast ቀስት 'bow'

qaśafa ቀሠፈ (G) 'to discipline, inflict punishment'

qatala ቀተለ (G) 'to kill, slay, murder'

qatl ቀትል 'murder, killing, battle, fight'

qaṭqaṭa ቀጥቀጠ (quadr.) 'to smash, crush, break'

qaṭṭin ቀጢን 'fine, thin'

qawwām ቀዋም 'tall, high'

qayyəḥ ቀይሕ, qayyiḥ ቀዪሕ 'red'

qedros ቄድሮስ 'cedar'

qəbur ቅቡር 'buried'

qəddāse ቅዳሴ 'sanctification, holiness'

qəddəsāt ቅድሳት 'holiness, sanctuary, divine service'

qəddəst ቅድስት (f. of qəddus ቅዱስ) 'holy, sacred, saint'

qəddus ቅዱስ (pl. qəddusān ቅዱሳን) 'holy (one), sacred, saint'

qədma ቅድም 'before, in front; beforehand, previously'

qənyat ቅንየት, qənet ቅኔት 'dominion, service, servitude, slavery'

qənyāt ቅንያት 'servitude, slavery'

qəruṣ ቅሩጽ, qʷəruṣ ቁሩጽ 'incised, engraved'

qətul ቅቱል 'killed, slain, murdered'

qiḥat ቂሐት 'redness'

qom ቆም 'height, growth, stature'

qoma ቆመ (G) 'to stand, rise, remain'

qumat ቁመት 'state, stature, condition'

qʷənfəz ቁንፍዝ 'hedgehog'

qʷənṣəl ቁንጽል 'fox, jackal'

rāʔ(ə)y ራእይ 'vision, gaze, image'

raʕād ረዓድ 'trembling, tremor'

raʕām ረዓም, rəʕām ርዓም 'thunder, noise, roar'

rābəʕ(t) ራብዕ(ት) 'fourth'

rābəʕāwi ራብዓዊ, rābəʕāy ራብዓይ 'fourth'

rābəʕta ራብዕተ 'for the fourth time'

    rābəʕta ʔəd ራብዕተ፡እድ 'a fourth'

rābəʕə-mma ራብዕመ 'fourthly'

rabuʕ ረቡዕ 'fourth day of the week, Wednesday;

radʔ ረድእ (pl. ʔardāʔ አርዳእ, ʔardəʔət አርድእት) 'help, helper, assistant'

radʔa ረድአ 'to give help, aid, assist'

radʔet ረድኤት 'help, assistance'

radāʔi ረዳኢ 'helper, assistant'

ragama ረገመ (G) 'to curse, insult, excommunicate'

raḫāṣ ረኃጽ (also raḫaṣ ረኀጽ and rāḫṣ ራኅጽ) 'tender, delicate'

rākub/rākubāt ራኩብ/ራኩባት 'female camels'

rams ረምስ (pl. ʔarmās አርማስ) 'raft'

ramsasa ረምሰሰ (quadr.) 'to grope, feel the way'

rasˁa ረስዐ (G) 'to forget, overlook'

rasiˁ ረሲዕ (f. rassāˁ ረሳዕ) 'godless, impious'

rasiˁān ረሲዓን 'the godless (people)'

rassaya ረሰየ (D) 'to put, place'

rātəˁ ራትዕ 'upright, just, honest'

rayama ረየመ (G) 'to be high, long, raised'

rəˀ(ə)s ርእስ 'head, top, chief'

rəˀya ርእየ (impf. yəreˀi ይሬኢ) (G) 'to see, look, observe'

rəˀyat ርእየት 'appearance, vision, image'

rəˁya ርዕየ (impf. yəreˁi ይሬዒ) (G) 'to herd, tend, graze'

rəbbuˁ ርቡዕ 'square, fourfold'

rəbub ርቡብ 'unrolled, hovering'

rəḥqa ርሕቀ (G) 'to be far off, keep away'

rəḥe ርሔ 'perfume, flavor, odor'

rəḥib ርሒብ (f. raḥab ረሓብ, raḥāb ረሓብ) 'broad, wide, spacious'

rəḥuq ርሑቅ 'far, far away, distant'

    rəḥuqa maˁāt ርሑቀ፡ መዓት 'long-suffering, forbearing'

rəḫba ርኅበ (G) 'to be hungry'

rəḫub ርኁብ 'hungry, starving'

rəkbat ርክበት 'discovery, finding, acquisition'

rəmḥ ርምሕ 'spear'

rəsˁənnat ርስዐነት 'forgetfulness, impiety'

rəst ርስት 'inheritance'

rəśˀān ርሥአን 'old age'

rəśˀənnā ርሥእና 'old age'

rətˁ ርትዕ 'righteousness, justice, honesty'

rətuˁ ርቱዕ 'upright, righteous, right, proper'

    rətuˁāna hāymānot ርቱዓነ፡ ሃይማኖት 'those of just/orthodox faith'

roṣa ሮጸ (G) 'to run'

ruṣat ሩጸት 'running, course, pathway'

–sa –ሰ, see under –ssa

saˀala ሰአለ (G) 'to ask, enquire, petition'

saʿara ሰዐረ, səʿra ስዐረ (G) 'to remove, withdraw'

sabʾ ሰብእ 'people, mankind, man'

sabʿā ሰብዓ 'seventy'

sabʿā məʾət ሰብዓ ፡ ምእት '7000'

sabʿatu ሰብዐቱ, sabāʿtu ሰባዕቱ 'seven'

sabʿu ሰብዑ 'seven (days), the seventh day (of a week), week'

sabāʿt sabāʿt ሰባዕት ፡ ሰባዕት 'seven each'

sabāʿtu ሰባዕቱ 'seven'

sabbəḥa ሰብሐ (D) 'to praise, extol, laud'

sābəʿ ሳብዕ 'seventh'

sādəs ሳድስ 'sixth'

safaya ሰፈየ (G) 'to sew, stitch, mend'

sagada ሰገደ (G) 'to bow, bow down'

sagal ሰገል 'divination, magic, omen'

saḥaṭa ሰሐጠ, səḥṭa ስሕጠ (G) 'to wound, injure, do harm'

sāḥsəḥa ሳሕስሐ (quadr.) 'to move backward and forward, agitate'

saḫana ሰኀነ, səḫna ስኀነ (G) 'to warm oneself, become warm'

sakaba ሰከበ, sakba ሰክበ (G) 'to lie, lie down, be asleep'

saktata ሰክተተ (quadr.) 'to cook on a griddle'

sakʷat ሰኩት, sakot ሰኮት 'street, lane'

sākʷaya ሳኩየ (L), sakʷaya ሰኩየ (G) 'to go astray, rush about'

salām ሰላም 'peace, salutation'

salaṭa ሰለጠ (G) 'to be whole, be perfect'

samʿa ሰምዐ (G) 'to hear, listen, obey'

samantu ሰመንቱ 'eight'

samāni ሰማኒ 'eight'

samānitu ሰማኒቱ 'eight'

samānəyā ሰማንያ 'eighty'

samāy ሰማይ 'heaven, sky'

samāyāwi ሰማያዊ 'heavenly, divine'

samen ሰሜን 'south, north, north wind'

sanbat ሰንበት 'Sabbath'

sandada ሰንደደ (quadr.) 'to throw, forget'

sānəy ሳንይ, sānit ሳኒት 'the next day, the day after'

sānitā ሳኒታ 'the next day'

sanper ሰንፔር 'sapphire'

sansal ሰንሰል 'chain'

sanuy ሰኑይ 'the second day of the week or month, Monday'

saqalā ሰቀላ 'tent, house, shed'

sarāqi ሰራቂ 'thief, robber'

sarara ሰረረ (G) 'to fly, rush, flee'

sarāwit ሰራዊት (pl. of sarwe ሰርዌ) 'army, troops'

saraya ሰረየ (G) 'to pardon, absolve, forgive'

sark ሰርክ 'evening, twilight'

sarwe ሰረዌ 'army, troops'

sattāy ሰታይ 'drinker'

satya ሰትየ (G) 'to drink'

sayf ሰይፍ 'sword'

saytān ሰይጣን 'Satan, devil, demon'

sesaya ሴሰየ (quadr.) 'to feed, nourish, sustain'

səʾla ስእለ (G) 'to ask, inquire'

səʾlat ስእለት 'request, petition, entreaty'

səʾna ስእነ (G) 'to be unable, be powerless'

səbbuʿ ስቡዕ 'sevenfold'

səbbuḥ ስቡሕ 'praised, glorified, honored'

səbḥatihu ስብሐቲሁ 'his majesty'

səbkat ስብከት 'preaching, sermon'

səbko ስብኮ, śəbko ሥብኮ 'casting, smelting, molten metal'

sədəstu ስድስቱ 'six'

səgdat ስግደት 'worship, prostration'

səgmat ስግመት 'dumbness'

səḥta ስሕተ (G) 'to make a mistake, err, sin'

səḥtat ስሕተት 'error, transgression, seduction'

səḥta ስሕጠ, saḥaṭa ሰሐጠ (G) 'to wound, injure, hurt'

səḥit ስሒት 'error, deceit'

səkub ስኩብ 'lying, lying down'

səm ስም 'name, fame, reputation'

səmn ስምን 'eight'

səmuy ሰሙይ 'named, one of renown, honored'

sənn ስን 'tooth'

səqul ስቁል 'hung up, hanging, crucified'

səryat ስርየት 'remission of sins, forgiveness'

səssā ስሳ 'sixty'

səssu ስሱ 'six'

səte ስቴ 'drink, beverage'

sisāy ሲሳይ 'food, nourishment'

soba ሶበ 'when, then, at the time'

    soba ʾəm ሶበ ፡ እም 'even if'

sobehā ሶቤሃ 'then, instantly, immediately'

sor ሶር (pl. ʾaswār አስዋር) 'ox, bull'

–ssa –ስ 'but, however, on the other hand'

subāʿe ሱባዔ 'week, seven-year cycle'

sutāf(e) ሱታፍ/ሱታፈ 'companion, partner'

sutuf ሱቱፍ 'companion, partaker, associate'

śāʾn ሣእን 'shoe, sandal'

śāʾśāʾ ሣእሣእ 'eloquence, pleasantness of speech'

śāʿr ሣዕር 'herb, grass, vegetation'

śāhl ሣህል 'grace, compassion, mercy'

śaḥaq ሠሐቅ 'laughter, mockery'

śaḥt ሣሕት 'rest, comfort, relief'

śalās ሠላስ 'three'

śalāsā ሠላሳ 'thirty'

śalāsā məʾət ሠላሳ ፡ ምእት '3000'

śalāsāwi ሠላሳዊ 'thirtieth'

śalastu ሠለስቱ, śalasta ሠለስተ (acc.) 'three'

śallasa ሠለሰ (D) 'to triple, do for the third time'

śāləs ሣልስ 'third'

śāləsāwi ሣልሳዊ 'third'

śāləsāy ሣልሳይ (f. śāləsit ሣልሲት) 'third'

śāləsit ሣልሲት 'the third (f.), third time'

śāləsta ʾəd ሣልስተ ፡ እድ 'a third'

śalus **ሡሉስ** 'the third day of the week or month, Tuesday'

śam(a)ra **ሠምረ/ሠመረ** (G) 'to delight in, be pleased, agree'

śannāy **ሠናይ** (f. śannāyt **ሠናይት**) 'beautiful, good'

     śannāya ga ṣṣ **ሠናየ፡ ገጽ** 'beautiful of appearance'

śannaya **ሠነየ** (D) 'to be beautiful, be good, be appropriate'

śannayt **ሠነይት** (besides śannāyt **ሠናይት**) 'beautiful, good (f.)'

śāqaya **ሣቀየ** (L) 'to afflict, torture'

śarʿa **ሠርዐ** (G) 'to set in order, arrange, stipulate'

śārara **ሣረረ** (L) 'to lay a foundation, found, establish'

śārāri **ሣራሪ** 'founder'

śarq **ሠርቅ** 'rising, day of a new moon'

śarraḥa **ሠርሐ** (D) 'to prosper, make prosper'

śawʿa **ሠውዐ** (G) 'to sacrifice, slaughter'

śawāʿi **ሠዋዒ** 'priest, sacrificer'

śayāṭi **ሠያጢ** (pl. śayāṭǝyān **ሠያጥያን**) 'merchant, vendor, seller'

śema **ሤመ** (G) 'to set, place, appoint'

śeṭ **ሤጥ** 'sale, value, price'

śeṭa **ሤጠ** (G) 'to sell'

śǝʿǝrt **ሥዕርት** 'hair'

śǝgā **ሥጋ** 'flesh, meat, body'

śǝllāse **ሥላሴ** 'triad, Trinity'

śǝllus **ሥሉስ** 'threefold, triple'

śǝls **ሥልስ** 'a third part'

śǝlsa **ሥልስ** 'thrice, three times'

śǝlsa-mma **ሥልስም** 'thirdly'

śǝlṭān **ሥልጣን** 'dominion, authority, power'

śǝmrat **ሥምረት** 'will, good will, benevolence, consent'

śǝn **ሥን** 'beauty, goodness, grace' (√śny)

śǝnnuy **ሥኑይ** (f. śǝnnit **ሥኒት**) 'adorned, lovely'

śǝrʿat **ሥርዐት** 'ordering, arrangement, manner'

śǝrāy **ሥራይ** 'incantation, medicine, cure'

śǝruʿ **ሥሩዕ** 'ordered, established, arranged'

śǝrur **ሥሩር** 'flying'

śǝṭuṭ **ሥጡጥ** (f. śǝṭaṭṭ **ሥጣጥ**) 'torn, split'

śəṭṭat ሥጠት 'tearing, tear'

śuʿat ሡዐት 'act of sacrificing'

śurāre ሡራሬ 'foundation, founding'

ṣāʿdā ጸዕዳ, ṣaʿadā ጸዐዳ 'white, bright'

ṣaʿadʿid ጸዐድዒድ 'whitish'

ṣāʿdawa ጸዕደወ (quadr.) 'to be white, be bright'

ṣabʾ ጸብእ 'warfare, battle, attack'

ṣabʾa ጸብአ (G) 'to make war, fight, attack'

ṣabḥa ጸብሐ (G) 'to become morning, dawn'

ṣabḫa ጸብኀ (G) 'to dip (into a sauce)'

ṣādəq ጸድቅ 'just, righteous'

ṣafṣāf ጸፍጸፍ 'drops'

ṣaggā ጸጋ (√ṣgw) 'grace, favor, kindness'

ṣaggawa ጸገወ (D) 'to bestow favor, give graciously, grant'

ṣaggʷār ጸጓር 'hairy'

ṣahāq ጸሃቅ 'longing, care'

ṣaḥafa ጸሐፈ (G) 'to write, inscribe'

ṣaḥāfi ጸሓፊ (acc. ṣaḥāfe ጸሓፌ) 'scribe, copyist'

ṣalbo ጸልቦ 'cross'

ṣallaya ጸለየ (D) 'to pray, plead'

ṣallim ጸሊም 'black, dark'

ṣalma ጸልመ, ṣalama ጸለመ (G) 'to grow dark, be black'

ṣamhayaya ጸምሀየየ, ṣamāhyaya ጸማህየየ (quinq.) 'to fade away, wither, decay'

ṣanʿa ጸነዐ, ṣanʾa ጸንአ (G) 'to be strong, be powerful'

ṣaqāwəʿ ጸቃውዕ 'honeycomb'

ṣawwəʿa ጸወዐ (D) 'to call, call upon, summon'

ṣeḥa ጼሐ (G) 'to make level, make even'

ṣədq ጽድቅ 'justice, righteousness, truth'

ṣəduq ጽዱቅ 'true, sincere, just'

ṣəduqāwi ጽዱቃዊ 'who likes truth'

ṣəḥuf ጽሑፍ 'written, inscribed'

ṣəmuʾ ጽሙእ 'thirsty, parched'

ṣənuʿ ጽኑዕ 'strong, firm, powerful'

ṣərḥ ጽርሕ 'chamber, upper chamber, inner chamber'

ṣəwwəʿā ጽውዓ 'call, invitation, summons'

ṣora ጾረ (G) 'to carry, bear'

taʾamāri ተአማሪ 'interpreter, augur, soothsayer'

taʾamlaka ተአምለከ (t-quadr.) 'to become God, be worshiped'

taʾammara ተአመረ (Dt) 'to show oneself, be signaled'

taʾangada ተአንገደ (t-quadr.) 'to travel about, become a stranger, lodge as a guest'

taʾantala ተአንተለ (t-quadr.), taʾantaltala ተአንተልተለ 'to be impatient, be irritated'

taʾarwaya ተአርወየ (t-quadr.) 'to become wild, become savage'

taʿad(a)wa ተዐደወ/ተዐድወ (Gt) 'to pass over, go beyond, transgress'

taʿaggala ተዐገለ (Dt) 'to oppress, force, deceive', + verb 'to do by force'

taʿaqaba ተዐቀበ (Gt) 'to be watched, watch oneself'

tabāʿi ተባዒ 'male, strong'

tabāʿtāy ተባዕታይ 'male, masculine'

tabaqqəlo ተበቅሎ 'punishment, vengeance'

tabāraka ተባረከ (Lt) 'to be blessed, praised; to bless one another'

tabəhla ተብህለ (Gt) 'to be spoken, said, be named'

tābot ታቦት 'ark of Noah, ark of the Covenant, altar'

tadallawa ተደለወ (Dt) 'to be prepared, get ready'

tadangala ተደንገለ (t-quadr.) 'to be a virgin'

tadawwaya ተደወየ (Dt) 'to feign illness'

tadlā ተድላ 'pleasure, delight, glory, dignity'

tafalṭa ተፈልጠ (Gt) 'to be separated, be divided, be distinct'

tafannawa ተፈነወ (Dt) 'to be sent, dismissed'

tafaqda ተፈቅደ (Gt) 'to be wanted, required, needed'

tafaqra ተፈቅረ (Gt) 'to be loved, cherished'

tafaśśəḥa ተፈሥሐ (Dt) 'to rejoice, be glad, be comforted'

tafṣām ተፍጻም 'completion, ending'

tafṣāmet ተፍጻሜት 'completion, fulfillment, end'

tafṣāmi ተፍጻሚ 'last'

tagābəʾa ተጋብአ (Lt) 'to gather together (intr.), take back, be collected'

tagabra ተገብረ (Gt) 'to be done, made, produced'

tagas(a)sa ተገሰሰ (Gt) 'to be touched, be palpable'

tagbār ተግባር 'work, occupation, labor'

tagəḥśa ተግሕሠ (Gt) 'to withdraw, retreat, turn away'

tagbərot ተግብሮት 'labor'

tagʷāḥnawa ተጓህነወ (t-quadr.) 'to be interpreted (mystery), revealed (mystery)'

tagʷāḥnawa ተግኣሕነወ (t-quadr.) 'to shout to one another'

tahawaka ተሀወከ (Gt) 'to be stirred up, be perturbed'

taḥaśya ተሐሥየ (Gt) 'to rejoice, be happy, exult'

taḥatāti ተሐታቲ 'investigator, examiner'

tāḥta ታሕተ (tāḥte- ታሕቴ- with pronominal suffixes) 'below, under'

tāḥtāy ታሕታይ 'lower, inferior'

tāḥtu ታሕቱ 'below, under' (adv.)

taḥālafa ተጋለፈ (Lt) 'to wander to and fro'

taḥaśśa ተኀሠ (Gt) 'to be sought; to dispute, demand'

takabta ተከብተ (Gt) 'to be hidden, concealed, kept secret'

takāḥəda ተካሕደ (Lt) 'to argue with, dispute'

takarya ተከርየ (Gt) 'to be dug'

takāyada ተካየደ (Lt) 'to make a treaty, make a covenant, to stipulate, promise'

takl ተክል 'plant, tree'

takʷannana ተኮነነ (Dt) 'to be judged, governed; be subject to power'

talawa ተለወ (G) 'to follow, come behind, succeed'

taləʔka ተልእከ (Gt) 'to be sent, serve, assist'

tamahar ተመህር 'instruction, teaching, study'

tamahara ተመህረ (Gt) 'to be taught, learn'

tamahāri ተመሃሪ 'disciple, student'

tamāḥdana ተማሕፀነ (t-quadr.) 'to receive in trust, seek protection, take refuge'

tamannana ተመነነ (Dt) 'to be despised, rejected'

tamargʷaza ተመርጎዘ (t-quadr.) 'to lean on, rely'

tamart ተመርት 'date, date palm'

tamathata ተመትሀተ (t-quadr.) 'to appear as a specter, appear in disguise'

tamaṭṭawa ተመጠወ (Dt) 'to receive, accept, take'

tamayṭa ተመይጠ (Gt) 'to turn, go back, turn back'

tamhār ተምህር 'teaching, study'

tamoʔa ተሞአ (Gt) 'to be conquered, defeated'

tamr ተምር 'date, date palm'

tamyān ተምያን 'fraud, deceit, falseness'

taməʿʕa ተምዕዐ, tamməʿa ተምዐ, tamaʿaʕa ተመዐዐ (Gt) 'to be angry, rage, be irritated'

tanabbaya ተነበየ (Dt) 'to act as a prophet, prophesy'

tanabbāyi ተነባዪ 'who prophesies, who acts as a prophet'

tanāgara ተናገረ (Lt) 'to speak to one another, converse'

tanassəḥa ተነስሐ (Dt) 'to repent'

tanaśʾa ተነሥአ (Dt) 'to be taken, lifted'

tanśəʾa ተንሥአ (quadr.) 'to rise up'

tanśəʾot ተንሥኦት 'raising up'

taqāraba ተቃረበ (Lt) 'to approach one another, adjoin'

taqāwama ተቃወመ (Lt) 'to oppose, rise (against)'

taqʷanādaya ተቄናደየ (t-quadr.) 'to be proud, be haughty'

tarāʾaya ተራአየ (Lt) 'to look at one another, look upon'

tarassaya ተረሰየ (Dt) 'to adorn oneself, clothe oneself'

tarfa ተርፈ, tarafa ተረፈ (G) 'to be left, be left behind, remain'

targʷama ተርጐመ (quadr.) 'to interpret, translate'

tasʿu/ā ተሥዑ/ተሥዓ see under təsʿu/ā ትሥዑ/ትሥዓ

tasaʾala ተሰአለ (Gt) 'to enquire, demand, ask'

tasālāqi ተሳላቂ 'one who jokes, derides, mocks'

tasallaṭa ተሰለጠ (Dt) 'to be finished, be made perfect, prosper'

tasanāʾawa ተሰናአወ (t-quadr.) 'to be at peace with, live in peace'

tasanāsala ተሰናስለ (t-quadr.) 'to be linked together, chained together'

tasəʾna ተስእነ (Gt) 'to be impossible'

tasəʾla ተስእለ (Gt) 'to be asked; to enquire, demand, ask'

tasfā ተስፋ 'hope, expectation, promise'

taśawwāʿi ተሠዋዒ 'sacrifice, offering'

taśāyaṭa ተሣየጠ (Lt) 'to sell, buy back'

taṣābəʾa ተጻብአ (Lt) 'to fight with one another, wage war'

taṣaddaqa ተጸደቀ (Dt) 'to appear righteous, be judged just'

taṣ/ḍəʿəno fars ተጽ/ፀዕኖ ፡ ፈርስ 'riding a horse'

tataḥata ተተሐተ (Gt) 'to be made low, humble oneself, be submissive'

taṭawāqaya ተጠዋቀየ (t-quadr.) 'to oppress one another'

tawālada ተዋለደ (Lt) 'to procreate, bear (children)'

tawalda ተወልደ (Gt) 'to be born'

tawdās ተውዳስ 'praising'

tawsāk ተውሳክ 'addition, increase'

tazakkara ተዘከረ (Dt) 'to remember, recall'

tazkār ተዝካር 'remembrance, reminder, record'

tərsit ትርሲት 'ornament, adornment, equipment'

təʾəlfit ትእልፊት 'ten thousand-fold, in the thousands'

təʾəmərt ትእምርት (pl. taʾammər ተአምር) 'sign, signal'

təʾəzāz ትእዛዝ 'commandment, command, edict, law'

təʾəbit ትዕቢት 'haughtiness, pride, conceit'

təfśəḥt ትፍሥሕት 'joy, gladness'

təguh ትጉህ (pl. təguhān ትጉሃን) 'watcher; watchful'

təḥtənnā ትሕትና 'modesty, humility, humbleness'

təgbərt ትግብርት 'production, produce, yield'

təḥut ትሑት 'lowered, low'

təkāt ትካት 'ancient times, antiquity'

təkāta ትካተ 'before, once, in the old time'

təmʾət ትምእት 'hundredfold'

təmāləm ትማልም 'yesterday'

təmhərt ትምህርት 'teaching, study'

tənabbu ትነቡ (besides tənabbəbu ትነብቡ) 'you (mp) are speaking'

tənbit ትንቢት 'prophecy, oracle, prediction'

tənśāʾe ትንሣኤ 'ascent, rising, resurrection'

tərbəʿt ትርብዕት 'fourfold, quadruple, four times'

təsʿu ትስዑ, tasʿu ተስዑ 'nine'

təsʿā ትስዓ 'ninety'

təsʿatu ትስዐቱ, tasʿatu ተስዐቱ 'nine'

təsbəʾt ትስብእት 'assumption of human nature, manhood, incarnation'

təśləst ትሥልስት 'Trinity, threefold'

təwlədd ትውልድ 'tribe, family, offspring, generation'

təzmədd ትዝምድ 'family, affinity, species, tribe'

tosḥa ቶስሐ (quadr.) 'to mix, mingle, confuse'

tusāʿe ቱሣዔ 'the union of nine'

ṭāʾṭəʾa **ጣእጥአ** (quadr.) 'to be properly arranged, be settled'

ṭaʿama **ጠዐመ** (G) 'to taste, be tasty'

ṭāʿm **ጣዕም** 'taste, flavor, delight, pleasantness'

ṭāʿot **ጣዖት** (pl. ṭāʿotāt **ጣዖታት**) 'idol, ungodliness'

ṭabbāb **ጠባብ** (f. of ṭabib **ጠቢብ**) 'wise'

ṭabḥa **ጠብሐ** (G) 'to slaughter, slay'

ṭabib **ጠቢብ** (f. ṭabbāb **ጠባብ**, pl. ṭabibān **ጠቢባን** and ṭabbabt **ጠበብት**) 'wise, wise
    man'

ṭāgəʿa **ጣግዐ** (L) 'to adhere tightly'

ṭall **ጠል** 'dew, moisture'

ṭanqaqa **ጠንቀቀ** (quadr.) 'to be exact, strict, be accurate'

ṭayyaqa **ጠየቀ** (D) 'to observe, examine, explore'

ṭəʿya **ጥዕየ** (G) 'to be healthy, prosper, heal'

ṭəʿinā **ጥዒና** 'health, prosperity'

ṭəʿuy **ጥዑይ** 'healthy, sound'

ṭəbab **ጥበብ** 'wisdom, knowledge, intelligence'

ṭəmqat **ጥምቀት** 'baptism'

ṭəmuq **ጥሙቅ** 'baptized'

ṭənt **ጥንት** 'beginning'

ṭəqqa **ጥቀ** 'exactly, precisely, surely'

ṭərāy **ጥራይ** 'raw, crude'

ṭəyyuq **ጥዩቅ** 'certain, sure, exact'

ṭəyyəqənnā **ጥይቅና** 'exactness, thoroughness'

wa- **ወ-** 'and, but'
    wa- ... -hi/-ni **ወ** ... **-ሂ/-ኒ**, (wa-) ... -hi/-ni (**ወ-**) ... **-ሂ/-ኒ** 'and also,
    further'
    wa-ʾəmma-ʾakko **ወእመአኮ**, wa-ʾəmmāʾəkko **ወእማእኮ** 'and if not, otherwise'
    wa-ʾəmma(-hi) **ወእመ(ሂ)** 'either ... or'

wāʿ(ə)y **ዋዕይ** 'heat, burning heat'

waʿāli **ወዓሊ** 'guard, servant, soldier'

wadaya **ወደየ** (G) 'to put, add, lay'

waddəʾa **ወድአ** (D) 'to finish, complete'

wadqa **ወድቀ**, wadaqa **ወደቀ** (G) 'to fall, collapse'

waḍ'a **ወፅአ** (G) 'to go out, go forth'

wagara **ወገረ** (G) 'to throw, stone, cast'

wahaba **ወሀበ** (G) 'to give, bestow, allow'

wāḥaya **ዋሐየ** (L) 'to walk about, visit, inspect'

wāḥəd **ዋሕድ** 'only, unique, one'

walada **ወለደ** (G) 'to give birth, beget'; tawalda **ተወልደ** 'to be born'

walādi **ወላዲ** 'procreator, parent'

walādit **ወላዲት** 'parent, procreator (f.)'

walatt **ወለት** 'daughter, girl'

wald **ወልድ** (pl. wəlud **ውሉድ**) 'son, child, boy'

waldənnā **ወልድና** 'filiation, sonship'

waltā **ወልታ** 'shield'

walwala **ወልወለ** (quadr.) 'to doubt, hesitate'

wangelāwi **ወንጌላዊ** 'evangelist, evangelical'

waqāri **ወቃሪ** (pl. waqart **ወቀርት**) 'excavator, one who digs, hews'

warada **ወረደ** (G) 'to descend, go down'

warawa **ወረወ** (G) 'to throw, throw away'

warḫ **ወርኅ** (pl. 'awrāḫ **አውራኅ**) 'moon, month'

warq **ወርቅ** 'gold'

wārəs **ዋርስ** 'heir'

wasada **ወሰደ** (G) 'to take, lead, lead away'

wasan **ወሰን** 'boundary, border'

wassaka **ወሰከ** (D) 'to add, augment, increase'

wassana **ወሰነ** (D) 'to delimit, determine, fix'

watra **ወትረ**, wətura **ውቱረ** 'continually, always'

waṭana **ወጠነ** (G) 'to begin, commence'

way **ወይ** 'woe!, alas!'

     way lita **ወይ፡ሊተ**, way-ləya **ወይልየ** 'woe to me!'

wayn **ወይን** 'vine, wine'

wə'ətomu **ውእቶሙ** 'they (mp)'

wə'əton **ውእቶን** 'they (fp)'

wə'ətu **ውእቱ** 'he'

wə'ya **ውዕየ** (G) 'to burn, burn up'

wə'yat **ውዕየት** 'burning, blaze'

wəʕuy **ው·ዑይ** (f. wəʕit **ው·ዒት**) 'hot, burning, burnt'

wəḥza **ው·ሕዘ** (G) 'to flow, flow out'

wəsta **ው·ስተ** 'in, into, to, at'

    wəsta māʔkala **ው·ስተ ፥ ማእከለ** 'in, within'

wətura **ው·ቱሬ**, watra **ወትሬ** 'continually, always'

yabbaba **የበበ** (D) 'to jubilate, shout with joy'

yabsa **የብሰ** (G) 'to be dry, be arid, withered'

yamān **የማን** 'right, right side, right hand'

yawwāh **የዋህ** 'gentle, mild, innocent'

yawwəhat **የው·ሀት** 'mildness, innocence, modesty'

yawwəhənnā **የው·ህና** 'gentleness, mildness'

yəʔəti **ይእቲ** 'she'

yəʔəze **ይእዜ** 'now, at present'

yəbe **ይቤ** 'he said' (√bhl)

yəbusa/ ʕəṣuba ləbb **ይቡሰ/ዕጹብ ፥ ልብ** 'hard of heart'

yəbusa kəsād **ይቡሰ ፥ ክሳድ** 'stiff-necked'

yogi **ዮጊ** 'perhaps, possibly'

yom **ዮም** 'today'

za– **ዘ–** (f. ʔənta **እንተ**, pl. ʔəlla **እለ**) relative pronoun

    za-ʔənbala **ዘእንበለ** 'without, except'

    za-ʔənbala ʔəmma **ዘእንበለ ፥ እም** 'unless'

    za-ʔi-yəmāssən **ዘኢይማስን** 'indestructible'

    za-ʔi-yətḫʷellaqʷ **ዘኢይትጐለቀ·** 'uncountable'

    za-ba-ʔənta **ዘበእንተ** 'about, concerning, regarding'

    za-kama **ዘከመ** 'as, just as'

    za-kama-zə **ዘከመዝ** 'like this'

    za-la-ʕālamənnā **ዘለዓለምና** 'everlasting, eternal'

    za-wəʔətu **ዘው·እቱ** 'that is to say, namely'

zakkara **ዘከረ** (D) 'to mention, remind'

zamad **ዘመድ** 'kin, family, tribe'

zammāri **ዘማሪ** 'musician, psalmist'

zanab **ዘነብ** 'tail'

zangʷagʷa **ዘንጐጐ** (quadr.) 'to mock, deride'

zarʾ ዘርእ 'seed, offspring'

zātti ዛቲ (acc. zātta ዛተ) 'this (f.)'

zāwaga ዛወገ (L) 'to be equal'

zawg ዘውግ 'pair, associate'

zazza ዘዘ distributive 'each'

zenā ዜና 'information, report, news, message'

zenawa ዜነወ (quadr.) 'to inform, tell'

zə– ዝ– 'this (m.)'

    zə-bəʾəsi ዝብእሲ 'this man'

    zə-wəʾətu bəhil ዝውእቱ፡ ብሂል 'this means'

zəkku ዝኩ (f. ʾəntəkku እንትኩ, pl. ʾəlləkku እልኩ) 'that'

zəkr ዝክር 'record, remembrance, mention'

zəlufa ዝሉፉ 'continually, forever, always'

zənām ዝናም (pl. zənāmāt ዝናማት) 'rain'

zəntu ዝንቱ 'this (m.)'

zəya ዝየ 'here, hither'

ziʾa– ዚአ– (+ pronominal suffix) possessive pronoun

ziya ዚየ 'here, hither'